NASHVILLE TO
NEW ORLEANS
Road Trip

MARGARET LITTMAN

CONTENTS

DISCOVER
the Nashville to New Orleans Road Trip

Connecting some of the most iconic cities in the American South, these paths trace the very root of the American experience. Travel from Nashville, where country music came into its own, and Memphis, birthplace of the blues, to New Orleans, home of that Dixieland jazz, and you'll better understand not only the nation's musical legacy, but also its creation and expansion.

Your road trip starts in Nashville, home to the Grand Ole Opry, a radio show that brought country music to the masses. It also boasts a rich civil rights legacy, and a reputation as a cosmopolitan city with world-class food and entertainment. Continue on to Memphis to lose yourself in barbecue and blues.

You'll end in boisterous New Orleans, where jazz is perhaps the loudest sound in a heady mix of blues, rock, soul, zydeco, and Cajun music. It's also a place where gardens bloom, streetcars run, and beignets make everything sweeter.

Connecting these cities is the Natchez Trace Parkway, a verdant landscape rich in history and lore. Along this route your pace will slow as the sounds of raucous music give way to the melodies of birds and the rustling of leaves and grass. Follow in the footsteps of Native Americans, Confederate soliders, and thousands of others who helped to mold this region into its current form.

This journey is an outdoor adventure, a concert on wheels, a history lesson, and a culinary quest. Start it with a biscuit and a country tune and end with a beignet and a sax riff.

PLANNING YOUR TRIP

Where to Go

This drive along the Natchez Trace Parkway originates in Nashville, crosses through Tennessee, cuts across a corner of Alabama, and then traverses much of Mississippi before ending in Natchez. From there, you're just a short drive from New Orleans.

Nashville

Nashville is the epicenter of **country music.** It's home to the **Grand Ole Opry,** the **Country Music Hall of Fame and Museum,** and hundreds of **recording studios.** It's the place where thousands of musicians and songwriters come to

make it, and the city's nightlife is all the richer for it. **Fine arts** and a contemporary **culinary scene** appeal to sophisticates, while **museums, historical sites,** and the grand **Tennessee State Capitol** recall the city's history.

The Trace: Tennessee

This is where your drive starts: at the northern terminus of the **Natchez Trace Parkway.** This northernmost stretch features **rolling hills, secluded hikes,** and significant **historic sites,** including the somber and reverential **Meriwether Lewis Monument and Gravesite.** Close to the parkway are quaint suburbs and towns, including **Franklin** and **Leiper's Fork,** where you can visit **Civil War sites** and spot country music celebrities.

The Trace: Alabama

The **shortest section** of the Natchez Trace Parkway covers just a tiny corner of Alabama but contains tons of history. Contemplate the somber **Wichahpi Commemorative Stone Wall,** an homage to the Trail of Tears. Close to the Trace, the **Quad Cities** region is home to **Muscle Shoals,** an important part of music history, and **Florence,** which is a surprising epicenter of fashion and design.

The Trace: Northern Mississippi

This part of the state is known as "the hills" of Mississippi. And along this winding stretch of the parkway, you'll find **scenic views** and opportunities for **camping, hiking,** and **bicycling.** This section ends in **Tupelo,** birthplace of the King of Rock 'n' Roll, Elvis Presley. The **Natchez Trace Parkway Headquarters and Visitor Center** is ground zero for information about the Natchez Trace.

Memphis and the Mississippi Blues Trail

This route starts in **Memphis,** Tennessee, and winds south for 140 miles into the Mississippi Delta. The **blues** were born in Memphis, and they still call Memphis home in **nightclubs** on **Beale Street** and **juke joints** around the city. But Memphis is more than music. It's an urban center with **fine dining, parks,** and **art museums.** Watch the resident ducks at **The Peabody Memphis** or fuel up with a plate of **barbecue.**

Drive the Mississippi Blues Trail to explore the **roots of American music.** Visit **small towns** that are home to big history, like **Tunica, Cleveland,** and **Indianola.**

The Trace: Central Mississippi

Through **farmland** and past **Indian mounds,** the Natchez Trace Parkway is a leisurely, easy drive in this section of the Magnolia State. Exit the parkway for two of the state's academic and tourism treasures: **Oxford** and **Starkville.** Plan leisurely stops to stroll these quintessential college towns.

The Trace: Southern Mississippi

The southernmost stretch of the parkway is bookended by two of the state's most significant cities—the capital city of **Jackson** and historic **Natchez,** the **southern terminus** of the Trace. This is an opportunity to explore **civil rights sites, Civil War battlefields,** and **antebellum homes** and gardens.

New Orleans

New Orleans is unlike any other city, steeped as it is in many unique cultures. Its reputation of being a party place is accurate, but it's also home to **beautiful architecture, museums, gardens,** and, of course, tempting Cajun and Creole food. Louisiana capital **Baton Rouge** has some of NOLA's spunk but also its own traditions, charms, and a mammoth campus.

When to Go

The Natchez Trace Parkway has its charms year-round. Visitors are steady throughout the year, with July and

October slightly more popular times to travel the road. **Spring** is the most desirable time to visit. Colorful wildflowers will be in bloom, making overlooks and hikes stunning, but greenery won't yet block vistas, as happens in summer. In spring the days will be long enough to get miles and stops in on the Trace before sunset, but summer's crowds won't yet be nabbing campground spaces. Spring weather is temperate, not the oppressive heat of summer.

Summer is the peak travel season for Nashville and Memphis, when crowds and temperatures are at their highest. It's also when some of the biggest music festivals and events are going on. In New Orleans, summer is the least crowded time to visit; hurricane season is June-September.

Fall is also popular; the parkway is one of the best places in the South to see the leaves change. Stark white cotton bolls in bloom are a breathtaking contrast to the rich yellows and golds on the trees. Fall is a good time to explore Nashville, Memphis, and New Orleans, as the temperatures are cooler and the crowds have dispersed.

Winter is generally low season for this region—except in New Orleans, when people flock to the city for Mardi Gras and temperate weather. The Trace is rarely troubled by inclement weather, as the region sees little snow.

Before You Go

Fly into **Nashville International Airport** and out of New Orleans's **Louis Armstrong New Orleans International Airport.** Memphis, Jackson, and Birmingham, Alabama, are other nearby cities that are good alternatives for those who want to do just a portion of the drive.

Pack light, particularly if you want to see the Natchez Trace by bicycle, motorcycle, or on horseback. Pack **hiking boots** and **sunscreen** for exploring the Trace's

Clockwise from top left: Music (and Elvis) are everywhere in Tupelo; Mardi Gras spirit lives year-round in New Orleans; the stage of the Grand Ole Opry in Nashville.

many scenic pleasures, and tents and sleeping bags if you plan to camp.

If you're planning to stop over in the cities on this route, make **advance reservations.** Nashville has a **hotel room shortage,** especially during the summer music festival season. Football games in the Mississippi college towns of Oxford and Starkville make fall a tough time to find a hotel room. New Orleans accommodations are in demand during Mardi Gras (February or March) and Jazz Fest (April or May). Natchez is almost exclusively a B&B town, and these small inns are often booked in advance during the town's Spring and Fall Pilgrimage.

Most B&Bs along the Trace accommodate bicycle travelers. Call ahead to confirm there are safe spaces to store your gear.

Driving Tips

The Natchez Trace Parkway is a scenic 444-mile paved road managed by the National Park Service. The entire parkway is well marked with brown **mile markers** on the east side of the road. Crossroads are also marked, and there are signs at intersections letting you know how many miles to the next major city. It is very difficult to get lost on the Trace if you pay attention. Some of the stops have maps posted in their parking areas as well.

There are virtually no commercial stops on the route. That means you must exit the parkway at major crossroads to get gas. Some of the stops on the parkway have restrooms and vending machines, and there are three official campgrounds on the Trace, but for the most part, you'll need to exit for restaurants and accommodations as well.

Many people travel the Trace on **bicycle.** If you are in a car, you must allow at least three feet for cyclists when passing. You are encouraged to pass in the opposite lane (when safe) when there are bicyclists present.

Cell phone reception is very spotty on much of the parkway, though generally reliable in the cities. Most hotels, even small B&Bs, have Wi-Fi, making it possible to connect on the road.

Drought in the summer of 2016 caused what the Park Service calls "severe cracking and movement of the parkway motor road surface" in Mississippi. In a car, you may not notice these conditions, but on motorcycle or bicycle you may encounter a high number of potholes.

It's rare for roads to be closed for inclement **weather.** Pay attention to alerts for snow, tornadoes (during extreme temperature changes), dense fog, and flash floods; check with park rangers (662/680-4025) to get updated weather forecasts. They will also know about any unexpected road closures due to construction. That information is also posted on the parkway website (www. nps.gov/natr). Note that the Trace is a two-lane road with frequent pullouts. If a bridge or road is closed due to an accident, patience will be required. If a road is blocked due to an accident, you have to wait for it to clear or backtrack and find a detour.

Preparing to Bike the Trace

If you're traveling the Trace by bicycle, as many do, you'll have to plan ahead, as 444 miles is a significant ride. People of all fitness levels, ages, and abilities complete this ride, which ESPN rates as one of the 10 best bike routes in the country. The lack of dangerous road traffic combined with beautiful scenery and mild weather makes it particularly appealing to newbies and experienced pedalers alike.

Before you begin, figure out approximately how many miles you plan to bike a day. If you plan to do the trip in a week, you'll need to average at least 75 miles per day, with limited detours. Make a **training plan** that gets you up to that mileage.

Wondering what to bring? Here's a start:

A bike. Obviously, you'll need to buy or rent a bicycle. The entirety of the parkway is paved, so a road or touring bike is your best bet (as opposed to a mountain bike).

Changes of clothes, particularly rain gear. Thunderstorms in the South can be soakers. So, while you want to pack light, you also want to have the clothes you need when Mother Nature shows you who's boss. Layering is key.

Clip-in shoes. If clip-ins and cleats are your thing, bring 'em. If not, that's fine, too, but in either case bring shoes (and hiking boots) to wear when not on your bike.

Locks. You'll want your gear to be safe when you hike, explore towns on side trips, and take breaks for food.

Maps. Much of the parkway has limited cell service. Have a paper map in case your GPS fails you.

Snacks. You may not need gas on a bike, but your body needs fuel. Have protein bars or other snacks in your pack.

Padded shorts. It's 444 miles on a bike seat. Enough said.

Reflective gear and lights. It isn't recommended that you bike on the Trace at night. Remember, there are limited roadway lights. But you'll still want to make sure you can be seen when the sun is down. A helmet, first-aid kit, and safety gear are also essential.

A good attitude. You never know what will happen on a long trek. Some cyclists say the repetitive nature of the landscape bores them silly. Others find it meditative. Traffic, storms, construction, wild turkeys: Who knows what you will encounter. Keep an open mind and keep pedaling.

Companions. Many tour companies offer guided or supported bike rides on the Trace (meaning a van carries your meals and gear while you ride). These are great options for those who don't want to be on two wheels alone on the road. See the Bike Tours and Shuttles section in the Essentials chapter (page 413) for more information.

HIT THE ROAD

The 12-Day Nashville to New Orleans Road Trip

With just under two weeks, you can wind your way from one epic music and food city to the next. The total drive is **620 miles;** 444 of these curve down the National Park Service's Natchez Trace Parkway. You'll hear everything from country to Creole; visit the birthplace of the King and a place where civil rights stood proud. You can easily reverse the route from south to north, ending in Tennessee.

The trip will take longer on two wheels or horseback, but the Natchez Trace is well-suited for such modes of transport. Check out the Essentials chapter (page 412) for more specifics on planning such a journey.

The parkway mileposts are numbered from south to north, so it's easy to **start your trip in New Orleans** and follow this guide in reverse to end your journey in Nashville. Either way, your trip is bookended by good food and music.

Days 1-2: Nashville
Spend your first two days in Nashville (see details and suggestions on page 25).

Day 3: Tennessee
NASHVILLE TO ALABAMA BORDER (120 MILES)

Up and at 'em! Fuel up both yourself and your car with biscuits from **Loveless Cafe** and gasoline from a nearby station. Your first stop on the Natchez Trace Parkway is a prime photo spot: the **Double Arch Bridge.**

If you're up for exiting the scenic parkway, you have several good options for food, drink, and entertainment in

Franklin, **Leiper's Fork,** and **Columbia,** which is where you'll find the **James K. Polk Home & Museum.** Other highlights include the **Franklin Theatre.** While in Franklin, take a tour at **Carnton,** a historic former plantation, where you can experience Civil War history from an intimate vantage point.

Along the Trace itself you should stop at the **Meriwether Lewis Monument and Gravesite,** which is a somber memorial to a man who helped the country expand. This is also where to camp for the night before crossing into Alabama.

Day 4: Alabama
ALABAMA BORDER TO MISSISSIPPI BORDER (30 MILES)

You'll be covering fewer miles on the Trace today but plenty of territory when it comes to Native American, music, and military history. Stop at the **Wichahpi Commemorative Stone Wall** and learn about the Trail of Tears.

Take a side trip to the Quad Cities region, where the namesake cities of Muscle Shoals, Florence, Sheffield, and Tuscumbia offer myriad opportunities. Muscle Shoals is home to important music sites like **3614 Jackson Highway** and **Fame Studios.** Shop for unique clothing items or souvenirs in Florence, then tuck in for the night.

Day 5: Northern Mississippi
MISSISSIPPI BORDER TO TUPELO (45 MILES)

Don't forget to get gas in the Quad Cities before heading back to the Trace. Next you'll head south on the Trace, bound for Tupelo, stopping at **Bear Creek Mound** and **Pharr Mounds** on the way.

Once you arrive in Tupelo, sample the blueberry doughnuts at **Connie's Fried Chicken,** and then head to the **Elvis Presley Birthplace,** where you'll honor the King's legacy and learn how he got to be who he was. Catch a show at the **Blue Canoe,** then head back to your hotel so

Best Views

The history and the beauty of the Trace come together at Tobacco Farm.

Scenic overlooks are some of the Natchez Trace Parkway's strengths. Here are some of the best spots to get memorable views.

- **Birdsong Hollow (milepost 438):** From atop the Double Arch Bridge at Birdsong Hollow, you'll see far and wide from 155 feet above the valley (page 98).

- **Tobacco Farm and Old Trace Drive (milepost 401.4):** Leave from this replica of an old tobacco farm and take a two-mile drive along the Old Trace, where you'll see meadows and fields peeking through the trees (page 123).

- **Lauderdale (milepost 328.7):** This spot on the shore of the Tennessee River is the best place for views of the John Coffee Memorial Bridge, the longest bridge on the parkway (page 140).

- **Old Town Overlook (milepost 263.9):** Choose from watching the thriving pond life, including turtles, or watching the cars and bikes wind their way down the parkway (page 170).

- **Black Belt Overlook (milepost 251.9):** The pastoral landscape of central Mississippi is evident in the limestone layers here (page 247).

- **Reservoir Overlook (milepost 105.6):** More of a park than a mere viewpoint, Reservoir Overlook allows you to take in the beauty of Ross Barnett Reservoir (page 267).

- **Emerald Mound (milepost 10.3):** Unlike at other Indian mounds, here you are encouraged to walk to the top of the flat-top relic, where you can view the surroundings from 360 degrees (page 283).

you can be rested and ready to go in the morning.

Days 6-7: Memphis
TUPELO TO MEMPHIS (110 MILES)
Spend these two days in Memphis (see details and suggestions on page 185). Head back to Tupelo on the evening of day seven, so that you'll be ready for the side trip to Oxford, Mississippi, the next morning.

Day 8: Central Mississippi
TUPELO TO RIDGELAND (275 MILES WITH OXFORD)
Before you leave Tupelo, stop by the

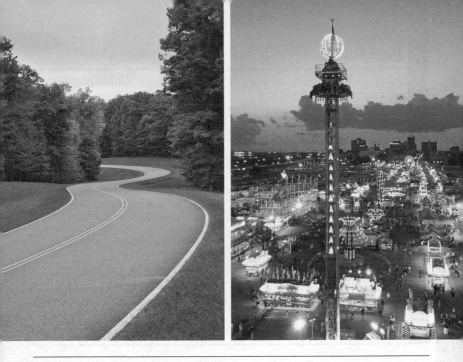

Clockwise from top left: Natchez Trace Parkway in early fall; Mississippi State Fair; Johnny Cash Museum.

Best Hikes

The Natchez Trace Parkway isn't just a great drive. It's also an access road to great walks, some short, some long. Here are a few of the best.

- **Garrison Creek (milepost 427.6):** As the northern terminus of the Highland Rim Trail, this is the place serious hikers go to escape the hubbub. Make it long and strenuous, or just do a quick section (page 113).

- **Wichahpi Commemorative Stone Wall (milepost 338):** Meditate and contemplate while walking along this mile-long unmortared wall, which honors those who walked the Trail of Tears (page 139).

- **Rock Spring (milepost 330.2):** Take a 20-minute hike to a bubbling brook, sheltered from the sun under a canopy of trees (page 140).

- **Bailey's Woods Trail (Oxford):** Though doing this 20-minute wooded walk means taking a side trip to Oxford, Mississippi, it's worth it for the chance to visit William Faulkner's home, which connects to the trail (page 241).

- **Cypress Swamp Loop Trail (milepost 122):** Less than a half mile, this boardwalk stroll spans a serene swamp of water tupelos and bald cypress (page 259).

- **Natchez Trace Multi-Use Trail (milepost 105-100):** A paved path winds next to the parkway and is great for walkers, strollers, hikers, and bikers (page 268).

Natchez Trace Parkway Headquarters and Visitor Center on the Trace itself. This is the best place on the 444-mile route to meet with rangers, ask questions, watch a film, and buy some souvenirs.

Gas up the car for the 45-minute drive to Oxford, home of Ole Miss. Wander the **University of Mississippi** campus, where you can tour the **University Museum** and several of the campus's historic civil rights sights. Visit **Rowan Oak,** William Faulkner's home, then get lunch in **The Square,** the center of all things Oxford.

You have about an hour on the road to hook back up with the parkway (remember to fuel up). Then continue south. Two of five Native American ceremonial mounds are visible at the **Owl Creek Mounds Archaeological Site,** just off the parkway. Stop here to see sites that were likely Indian temples and then head south to the six Indian burial mounds at **Bynum Mounds.**

Take a quick hike at **Cypress Swamp,** then make for **Ridgeland,** another 150 miles down the Trace, to spend the night.

Day 9
RIDGELAND TO NATCHEZ (110 MILES)

Ridgeland is just east of Jackson, Mississippi's capital city. You have many museums from which to choose on your days in Jackson. The perfectly preserved **Eudora Welty House and Garden** feels like the author has just run out to lunch and she'll be back in a few. The civil rights collection at the **Margaret Walker Center** on the Jackson State campus, and the **Smith Robertson Museum** show different perspectives on the state's complicated civil rights history.

From Jackson you'll head back on the Trace for the last piece of your parkway drive. Appreciate the leisurely pace as you drive, stopping to read historical signs. Allocate enough time at **Mount Locust Historic House,** an 1800s building and grounds with cemeteries, walking trails, and more. Drive on to **Emerald Mound,** because while you may have seen a lot of Indian mounds on this trip, this is one on which you can climb. Like Mount Locust, **Elizabeth Female Academy** is one of the

Best of Southern Cuisine

Honey-baked hams, biscuits, and pecan pies: A trip through the Deep South is tasty. Yes, you can find vegetables and kombucha, but when in the south... . Here's where to eat some regional specialties.

• **Loveless Cafe, Nashville:** They may not be the best biscuits in Nashville, but they are the most iconic, and they're at the northern terminus of the parkway (page 81).

• **FloBama Music Hall, Florence:** Whole smoked chicken, ribs, and live music. There's nothing more Southern than that (page 153).

• **Connie's Fried Chicken, Tupelo:** This is the place to stop for fried

chicken, biscuits, and blueberry doughnuts (page 176).

• **Ajax Diner, Oxford:** The turnip green dip, po'boys, and fried catfish are said to be favorites of football legend Eli Manning (page 244).

• **The Biscuit Shop, Starkville:** A good biscuit isn't hard to find in the South, but these are some of the best, with varieties you never imagined (page 253).

• **Carriage House Restaurant, Natchez:** Fried chicken and blue plate specials are served in the antebellum mansion Stanton Hall (page 290).

few remaining buildings (or portions thereof) on the parkway.

You've made it to the southern terminus! Natchez is known for its antebellum architecture. Don't miss the opportunity to stay in one of these sweet, restored homes. At **Devereaux Shields House** you'll get a wine reception at night, perfect for after you pull off the road. Check in, wander the manicured garden, and then head to **King's Tavern** for flatbread and beer for dinner. The restaurant, which may be haunted, is in the oldest building in the state.

Day 10
NATCHEZ TO BATON ROUGE (100 MILES)
From Natchez, take US 61 south and continue to Baton Rouge, capital of Louisiana. Tour both **Louisiana's Old**

State Capitol and the current **Louisiana State Capitol,** an art deco limestone stunner. Drive through **Spanish Town,** the city's oldest neighborhood, dating to 1805. Visit the **Old Louisiana Governor's Mansion,** which first resident Huey Long wanted to look like the White House.

Order boudin balls and fried green tomatoes at **Beausoleil Restaurant and Bar** for dinner. Continue the history vibe by spending the night at **Hilton Baton Rouge Capitol Center,** which is on the National Register of Historic Places.

Days 11-12
BATON ROUGE TO NEW ORLEANS (80 MILES)
Spend your last two days exploring lively New Orleans (see details and suggestions on page 301).

Nashville

Nashville is where America goes to make music. This city of more than 679,000 on the banks of the Cumberland River is where tomorrow's hits are written, performed, and recorded today.

Cumberland River

NASHVILLE

Fontanel Mansion ★
Carl Van Vechten Gallery ★ ★ Grand Ole Opry
The Parthenon
J. Percy Priest Lake
The Bluebird Café ★
Country Music Hall of Fame and Museum
Civil Rights Room at the Nashville Public Library

Nashville

© AVALON TRAVEL

GRAND OLE OPRY HOUSE

GRAND OLE OPRY HOUSE

Highlights

★ **Country Music Hall of Fame and Museum:** Learn about the genre's complex roots and then you'll be ready to explore the city's live music bounty (page 27).

★ **Civil Rights Room at the Nashville Public Library:** The public library houses the best exhibit about the historic Nashville sit-ins of 1960 and their role in the U.S. civil rights movement (page 33).

★ **Carl Van Vechten Gallery:** This museum on the Fisk University campus houses a remarkable collection of American art, a gift from Alfred Stieglitz (page 36).

★ **The Parthenon:** This life-size replica of the Greek Parthenon, complete with a statue of Athena, is a gathering place, a museum, and one of the reasons Nashville is called "the Athens of the South" (page 39).

★ **Fontanel Mansion:** Music and nature come together at Barbara Mandrell's former home, now a museum and music venue with acres of hiking trails (page 50).

★ **Grand Ole Opry:** Get an introduction to the depth and breadth of country music (page 52).

★ **The Bluebird Café:** The quintessential Nashville listening room hosts intimate music sessions with the people who really do write the songs (page 55).

There are songs in the air all around this city—in the honky-tonks lining lower Broadway, in the studios along Music Row, and in Music Valley, modern home of the Opry.

During the annual Country Music Association (CMA) Music Festival in June, the whole city is alive with the foot-tapping rhythm of country music. But locals like Jack White, Robert Plant, and the Kings of Leon have done their part to make Music City's sound more than just twang.

Nashville is also the city where performers and songwriters come to make it in the music business. Listening rooms and nightclubs all over the city are the beneficiaries of this abundance of hopeful talent, and their creativity and energy seep into almost everything in this city.

It is wrong to think that music, country or otherwise, is all there is to Nashville. After the Civil War and Reconstruction, Nashville became known as the Athens of the South because it was a center for education and the arts. Nashville offers visitors much more than a night at the Opry: Art buffs love the Frist Center for the Visual Arts, Carl Van Vechten Gallery, and Cheekwood art museum, not to mention neighborhood and downtown gallery districts. The Nashville Symphony Orchestra plays in the elegant, acclaimed, and renovated Schermerhorn Symphony Center downtown.

Downtown is dominated by tall office towers and stately government buildings, including the state capitol. Meat-and-three restaurants serve irresistible Southern-style meals, East Nashville welcomes award-winning chefs, while eateries along Nolensville Pike reflect the ethnic diversity of the city. This is a city that strikes many notes but sings in perfect harmony.

Planning Your Time

In just **two days** you can see a few of the city's attractions and catch a show at the Grand Ole Opry before taking off down the Trace. Musical pilgrims, history enthusiasts, and outdoors enthusiasts should plan to spend more time in Music City.

Downtown is a good home base for many visitors. Hotels are within walking distance of many attractions, restaurants, and nightclubs. They are also the most expensive accommodations in the city. Visitors who are primarily interested in seeing a show at the Grand Ole Opry or shopping at Opry Mills can shack up in Music Valley, where there is a wide cross-section of affordable hotel rooms, as well as the luxury of the Opryland Resort.

If you're planning to fly to town and rent a car, bike, or motorcycle for the Natchez Trace Parkway exploration, you might as well pick up your rental upon arrival. While some neighborhoods, like downtown and 12 South, are walkable, it's easier to explore the city with transportation, and you can opt for accommodations outside of the city center. There are affordable hotels in midtown and smaller bed-and-breakfasts in Hillsboro and East Nashville. These neighborhoods have their charms but are less tourist-centric than downtown and Music Valley. The city's lone hostel is in midtown and is a good choice for budget travelers.

Getting There
Car

Driving is the most popular way to get to Nashville. The city is 250 miles from Atlanta, 330 miles from St. Louis, 400 miles from Charlotte, 550 miles from New Orleans, and 670 miles from Washington DC.

No fewer than three major interstate highways converge in Nashville. I-40 runs east-west, connecting Nashville

Best Restaurants

★ **Arnold's Country Kitchen:**
Everyone stands in this cafeteria-style spot's lines for some of the best Southern food around (page 76).

★ **Capitol Grille:** This elegant restaurant has its own farm and herd of cattle—bringing farm-to-table to a new level (page 76).

★ **Chauhan Ale & Masala House:**
The menu of Indian street food with a Southern twist means sampling dishes you can't find anywhere else (page 77).

★ **Loveless Cafe:** With its iconic signage and famous biscuit recipe, this is a must for breakfast before heading out on the Natchez Trace (page 81).

★ **Prince's Hot Chicken Shack:**
Nashville-style hot chicken is in hot demand across the country. Eat it at the place that invented it (page 81).

★ **Bastion:** With just 24 seats and an open kitchen, this restaurant offers an interactive evening with some of the best chefs in the city (page 82).

★ **The Family Wash:** If you're looking for a place to get great food and listen to live music, there are few better picks than this institution (page 82).

★ **Butcher & Bee:** Low light and an open kitchen combine with an inventive small plates menu to give this restaurant its community feel (page 83).

with Knoxville and Memphis. I-65 runs north-south, connecting the city with Louisville, Kentucky, and Birmingham, Alabama. I-24 travels at a southeastern angle down to the city, connecting it with the cities of Clarkesville, Georgia, and St. Louis in the north, and Chattanooga and Atlanta in the south.

Air
Nashville International Airport (BNA, 1 Terminal Dr., 615/275-1675, www.fly-nashville.com) is eight miles east of the city center. To get downtown from the airport, head west on I-40; it's a short 15-minute drive. The flat one-way taxi fare from the airport to downtown or Music Valley is $25. The airport has been renovated Music City style. It has outposts of local restaurants and musicians playing live music (and selling CDs).

Airport Transportation
Many of the major hotels offer shuttles from the airport; there's a kiosk on the lower level of the terminal to help you find the right one.

Jarmon Transportation (615/275-0146, http://jarmontransportation.hudsonltd.net) offers regular shuttle service from the airport to downtown, West End, and Music Valley hotels. The shuttle departs from the airport every 15-20 minutes 4am-11pm; reservations are not required. Call ahead to book your hotel pickup. Fare is $20 one-way and $35 round-trip.

There is a designated ride-hailing area on the ground floor where you can find your Lyft or Uber driver.

Bus
Greyhound (800/231-2222, www.greyhound.com) serves Nashville, with bus service to the city from Memphis, Jackson, Chattanooga, and Knoxville, Tennessee, as well as Paducah and Bowling Green, Kentucky. The **Greyhound station** (709 5th Ave. S, 615/255-3556) is well marked and well staffed, with ample parking, and is several blocks west of downtown. Expect to pay about $50 for a one-way ticket from Memphis to Nashville if you buy directly

Best Accommodations

★ **SoBro Guest House:** Feel like a local in these converted apartments, with lots of hip amenities, in walking distance of downtown (page 84).

★ **Union Station:** This hotel, a renovated train station, will capture your imagination (page 84).

★ **Hermitage Hotel:** For more than a century this has been the most historic hotel in town (page 84).

★ **Thompson:** You'll be treated to refined, but not stuffy, service at this hip standout (page 87).

★ **Hutton Hotel:** Enjoy sleek luxury with a clean conscience at this ecofriendly hotel (page 88).

★ **Urban Cowboy Nashville:** Enjoy the campfire, and many other offbeat amenities, at this eight-room inn (page 89).

★ **Hotel Preston:** An airport hotel doesn't have to be generic; this one has tons of personality and a convenient location (page 91).

at the station, or about half that if you buy in advance online.

Getting Around
Driving
The easiest way to get around Nashville is by car. Although visitors staying downtown will be able to find plenty to do and places to eat within walking distance, many of the best attractions are located outside of the city center.

A dozen different major rental agencies have a presence at the airport, including **Alamo** (615/340-6546, www.alamo.com), **Avis** (615/361-1212, www.avis.com), and **Hertz** (615/361-3131, www.hertz.com). Most agencies also have outposts near downtown.

Parking
There is metered parking on most downtown streets, but some have prohibited-parking signs effective during morning and afternoon rush hours. Always read the fine print carefully.

There is plenty of off-street parking in lots and garages. Expect to pay about $22 a day for garage parking. **Park It! Downtown** (www.parkitdowntown.com) is a great resource for finding downtown parking deals, plus information about the

shuttle to Nissan Stadium during downtown events.

Public Transportation
Nashville's **Metropolitan Transit Authority** (MTA, www.nashvillemta.org) operates city buses. Pick up a map and schedule from either of the two downtown visitors centers or online.

Few tourists ride the buses because they can be difficult to understand if you're new to the city. One favorite is the **Music City Circuit,** a free bus that runs between downtown and the Gulch. These blue and green Circuit buses stop at 75 different spots on three routes. Another helpful route is the **Opry Mills Express,** which travels from downtown Nashville to Music Valley, home of the Grand Ole Opry, Opryland Hotel, and Opry Mills, the shopping mall. The Opry Mills Express departs the Bridgestone Arena 13 times a day on weekdays. Fare is $1.70 one-way ($0.85 for senior citizens). You can pick up a detailed route timetable from either of the two downtown visitors centers or online.

Commuter Rail
The **Music City Star Rail** (615/862-8833, www.musiccitystar.org) operates Monday

Two Days in Nashville

Day 1

Arrive in Nashville. Check into a downtown or South Nashville hotel, such as the **Thompson** or **Union Station**. Set out on foot to the **Tennessee State Capitol** and the **Civil Rights Room at the Nashville Public Library**.

Feast at **Chauhan Ale & Masala House** for lunch. Stroll **lower Broadway** and enjoy dancing at the honky-tonks on your first night in town. Grab dinner at **Pinewood Social**.

Day 2

Visit the **Country Music Hall of Fame** **and Museum** in the morning and grab an early lunch at **Arnold's Country Kitchen** to fuel up. In the afternoon, check out the **Ryman Auditorium** and **Johnny Cash Museum**.

In the evening, see a show at the **Grand Ole Opry**. Call **Jake's Bakes** to have warm cookies delivered to your hotel room before you tuck yourself in.

As you head west to the Natchez Trace Parkway the next morning, drive by **Centennial Park** and see **The Parthenon**.

---

to Friday, several times a day. Trains connect Donelson, Hermitage, Mount Juliet, and Lebanon to downtown Nashville (near Broadway and First Avenue). There is often additional service during special events, such as the Fourth of July celebration downtown.

One-way tickets can be purchased for $2-5 from vending machines at any of the stations. You can pre-purchase single-trip tickets, 10-trip packs, and monthly passes at a discount online. For a complete list of ticket outlets, contact the railway.

Taxis

Licensed taxicabs have an orange driver permit, usually displayed on the visor or dashboard. Several reliable cab companies are **Allied Cab Company** (615/333-3333, www.nashvillecab.com), **Checker Cab** (615/256-7000, www.nashvillecheckercab.com), **American Music City Taxi** (615/865-4100, www.musiccitytaxi.com), and **United Cab** (615/228-6969, www.unitedcabnashville.com). Taxi rates are $3 to start plus $2 per mile.

Ride-hailing companies, including **Lyft** and **Uber,** are popular in Nashville. Download their apps to find a local to drive you to your destination. **Joyride Nashville** (615/285-9835, http://joyrideus.com) offers rides around downtown in a golf cart for a pay-what-you-wish model (drivers work on tips alone). Many of the drivers are happy to provide recommendations and tours as well as transportation.

Orientation

Even locals are perplexed by Nashville's city planning, with street names that repeat and change, and few straight roads. The interstates are a little easier to navigate than side streets. I-65 and I-24 create a tight inner beltway that encircles the heart of the city. I-440 is an outer beltway that circles the southern half of the city, while I-40 runs east to west. Briley Parkway, shown on some maps as TN-155, is a highway that circles the north and east perimeters of the city.

City residents use the interstates not just for long journeys, but also for short crosstown jaunts. Most businesses give directions according to the closest interstate exit.

Non-interstate thoroughfares emanate from Nashville like spokes of a wheel. Many are named for the communities that they eventually run into. Murfreesboro Pike runs southeast from the city; Hillsboro Pike (Route 431) starts out as 21st Avenue South and takes you to Hillsboro Village and Green Hills.

Broadway becomes West End Avenue and takes you directly to Belle Meade and, eventually, the Loveless Cafe and the northern terminus of the Natchez Trace Parkway.

Nashville is built on a hill. Walking between Broadway and the state capitol is perfectly doable, but on a hot summer day, or with small children in tow, you may need to take breaks (or hop on one of the free Music City Circuit buses).

Broadway and Downtown

Downtown Nashville sits on the west bank of the Cumberland River, climbing gradually from Broadway to the Tennessee State Capitol. It's defined by landmarks including the AT&T Building, the tallest building in Tennessee, better known by many as the "Batman Building" for the two tall antennae that spring from the top.

Downtown is where you will find major attractions like the Country Music Hall of Fame, the Ryman Auditorium, and lower Broadway, a Bourbon Street-like strip of clubs and bars.

North of the state capitol and Bicentennial Mall is **Germantown,** a compact historic neighborhood now home to a few shops, galleries, restaurants, and studios.

Follow 12th Avenue as it heads south from downtown to find **The Gulch,** the city's hot spot for high-rise housing and urban condos.

Music Row

Perhaps the most famous neighborhood in all of Nashville, Music Row is where country music deals are done. The tree-lined streets of 16th and 17th Avenues, a few blocks southwest of downtown, shade dozens of different recording studios, record labels, and producers.

Midtown

Encompassing the neighborhoods of Elliston Place and Hillsboro Village, midtown is west of downtown. **Elliston**

Place is a block of nightclubs, restaurants, and two famous Nashville eateries: Elliston Place Soda Shop and Rotier's. The youthful energy of nearby Vanderbilt and Belmont Universities keeps **Hillsboro Village** one of the most consistently vibrant neighborhoods in Nashville.

East Nashville

The John Seigenthaler Pedestrian Bridge spans the Cumberland River, taking you from Riverfront Park to the heart of East Nashville. Now dominated by Nissan Stadium, home of the NFL's Tennessee Titans, the eastern reaches of Nashville are also home to some of the most charming residential neighborhoods.

While East Nashville is short on tourist attractions, visitors should consider the growing number of bed-and-breakfasts and private rentals (via companies like Airbnb) here. This area is close to downtown and boasts its own unique characters, including nightlife and restaurants.

Music Valley

A neighborhood created entirely for the tourist trade, Music Valley is the zone of hotels, restaurants, and retail that has popped up around the Opryland Hotel and the Grand Ole Opry House. Located inside a narrow loop of the Cumberland River, Music Valley lies northeast of downtown Nashville. It's a quick drive from the airport along Briley Parkway.

Belle Meade

Nashville's most posh neighborhood, Belle Meade, is actually a city with its own government. Named after an antebellum plantation, Belle Meade, the city, is home to Nashville's elite, and it famously possesses one of the most wealthy zip codes in America.

Around Belle Meade are other nice neighborhoods where Nashville's professionals and the upper class live. **West End Avenue,** the area's thoroughfare, is home to lots of nice restaurants. As you head westward, you pass Cheekwood, the Warner Parks, and eventually meet up with the Natchez Trace Parkway.

South Nashville

South of the city center are several distinct neighborhoods: **8th Avenue South,** close to downtown, is the antiques district. Along 12th Avenue below Wedgewood Avenue is **12 South.** An influx of young professional property owners has given rise to new restaurants, boutiques, and coffee shops.

Sights

Broadway

This is the tourism and entertainment hub of Nashville. Walk along Lower Broad, as the blocks from 5th Avenue to the river are called, and you will pass dozens of different bars (honky-tonks), restaurants, and shops catering to visitors. The vibe of lower Broadway has become more like Bourbon Street in recent years, particularly on weekend nights. Parking is not permitted on this stretch of Broadway and diagonal crosswalks funnel revelers through the intersections. Expect crowds.

★ Country Music Hall of Fame and Museum

The distinctive design of the **Country Music Hall of Fame and Museum** (222 5th Ave. S., 615/416-2001, www.countrymusichalloffame.org, 9am-5pm daily, adults $25, seniors $22.50, children 6-12 $15, free for children 5 and under) is the first thing you will notice about this monument to country music. Vertical windows at the front and back of the building resemble piano keys, the sweeping arch on the right side of the building portrays a 1950s Cadillac fin, and from above, the building resembles a bass clef. The Hall of Fame was first established in 1967, and its first inductees were Jimmie Rodgers, Hank Williams, and Fred Rose. The original hall was located on Music Row, but in

2002 it moved to this signature building two blocks off Broadway in downtown Nashville.

Country music fans are drawn by the carload to the Hall of Fame, where they can pay homage to country's greatest stars, as well as to the lesser-known men and women who influenced the music. Those who aren't fans when they walk in generally leave with an appreciation of the genre's varied roots. The hall's slogan is "Honor Thy Music."

The museum is arranged chronologically, beginning with country's roots in the Scotch-Irish ballads sung by the southern mountains' first settlers, and ending with displays on some of the genre's hottest stars of today. In between, exhibits detail themes, including the rise of bluegrass, honky-tonk, and the world-famous Nashville Sound, which introduced country music to the world.

There are a half dozen private listening booths where you can hear studio-quality recordings of seminal performances, as well as a special display of a few of the genre's most famous instruments. Here you can see Bill Monroe's mandolin, Maybelle Carter's Gibson, and Johnny Cash's Martin D-355.

If you are interested in learning something about country music while you're here, splurge on the audio guide ($5), which adds depth to the exhibits.

The Hall of Fame itself is set in a rotunda. Brass plaques honor the 100 inductees, and around the room are the words "Will the Circle Be Unbroken?" from the hymn made famous by the Carter Family.

The only way to visit Music Row's famous **RCA Studio B,** where Elvis once recorded, is to buy your ticket at the museum box office and hop on the Hall of Fame's guided tour bus. The tour takes about an hour, including the 10-minute drive to Music Row and back. The Studio B tour is an additional fee to your admission, but you can buy it as a package all at once. The Platinum Package (adults $40,

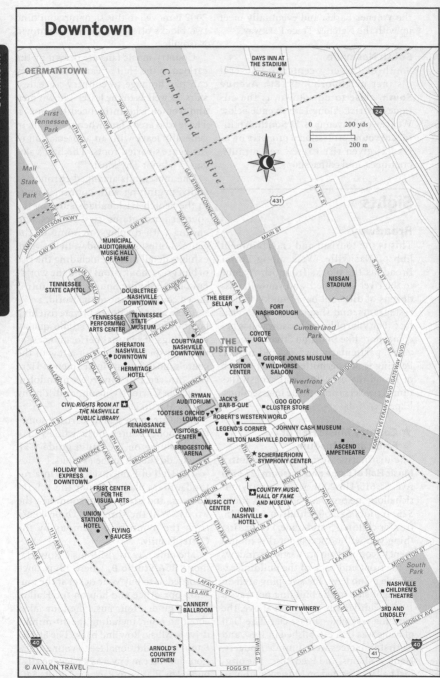

Downtown

GERMANTOWN

First Tennessee Park

Cumberland River

Mall State Park

DAYS INN AT THE STADIUM
OLDHAM ST

24

0   200 yds
0   200 m

JAMES ROBERTSON PKWY

GAY ST

MAIN ST

431

NISSAN STADIUM

MUNICIPAL AUDITORIUM/ MUSIC HALL OF FAME

TENNESSEE STATE CAPITOL

DOUBLETREE NASHVILLE DOWNTOWN

THE BEER SELLAR

FORT NASHBOROUGH

Cumberland Park

TENNESSEE PERFORMING ARTS CENTER

TENNESSEE STATE MUSEUM

COYOTE UGLY

SHERATON NASHVILLE DOWNTOWN

COURTYARD NASHVILLE DOWNTOWN

THE DISTRICT

VISITOR CENTER

GEORGE JONES MUSEUM
WILDHORSE SALOON

HERMITAGE HOTEL

Riverfront Park

CIVIL RIGHTS ROOM AT THE NASHVILLE PUBLIC LIBRARY

RYMAN AUDITORIUM

JACK'S BAR-B-QUE

GOO GOO CLUSTER STORE

TOOTSIES ORCHID LOUNGE

ROBERT'S WESTERN WORLD

RENAISSANCE NASHVILLE

VISITORS CENTER

LEGEND'S CORNER

JOHNNY CASH MUSEUM

BRIDGESTONE ARENA

HILTON NASHVILLE DOWNTOWN

SCHERMERHORN SYMPHONY CENTER

ASCEND AMPETHEATRE

HOLIDAY INN EXPRESS DOWNTOWN

FRIST CENTER FOR THE VISUAL ARTS

MUSIC CITY CENTER

COUNTRY MUSIC HALL OF FAME AND MUSEUM

OMNI NASHVILLE HOTEL

UNION STATION HOTEL

FLYING SAUCER

South Park

NASHVILLE CHILDREN'S THEATRE

CANNERY BALLROOM

CITY WINERY

3RD AND LINDSLEY

40

ARNOLD'S COUNTRY KITCHEN

41

40

FOGG ST

© AVALON TRAVEL

children $30) includes the audio tour, museum admission, and Studio B.

The Taylor Swift Education Center is an interactive space where kids and parents can learn to play instruments and think creatively about songwriting and music making during scheduled programs. The museum has several gift shops, one of which is chock-full of much of the music you hear in the museum. The iconic Hatch Show Print store, art gallery, and printing facility is now in the Hall of Fame complex as well.

Ryman Auditorium

Thanks to an $8.5 million renovation in the 1990s, and another $14 million in 2015, the historic **Ryman Auditorium** (116 5th Ave. N., 615/889-3060, www. ryman.com, 9am-4pm daily, adults $20, children $15) remains one of the best places in the United States—let alone Nashville—to hear live music. Built in 1892 by Capt. Thomas Ryman, the Union Gospel Tabernacle, as the Ryman was then called, was designed as a venue for the charismatic preaching of Rev. Samuel P. Jones, to whom Ryman owed his own conversion to Christianity.

Managed by keen businesswoman Lula C. Naff during the first half of the 20th century, the Ryman began to showcase music and performances. In 1943, Naff let the Ryman host a popular barn dance called the Grand Ole Opry. The legacy of this partnership gave the Ryman its place in history as the so-called Mother Church of Country Music.

The Opry remained at the Ryman for the next 31 years. After the Opry left in 1974, the Ryman fell into disrepair and was virtually condemned when Gaylord Entertainment, the same company that owns the Opry, decided to invest in the grand old tabernacle. Today, it is a popular concert venue, booking rock, country,

Top to bottom: RCA Studio B at the Country Music Hall of Fame Museum; Ryman Auditorium; Johnny Cash Museum.

and classical acts, plus comedy and more. Performers still marvel at the fabulous acoustics of the hall and like to show them off, playing a number or two without a mic. The Opry returns here during the Christmas season, and in the summer there's a weekly bluegrass series.

Seeing a show at the Ryman is by far the best way to experience this historic venue, but if you can't do that, pay the admission fee to see a short video and explore the auditorium on your own, which includes museum-style exhibits about the musicians who have performed here through the ages. You can sit a few minutes on the old wooden pews and even climb on stage to be photographed in front of the classic Opry backdrop. A guided tour that takes you backstage (adults $30, children $25) isn't just for die-hard fans. It gives lots of insight into how stars behaved when they were behind these famous walls. The guides tend to throw in an extra tall tale or two. Plus, you get to walk on the storied stage yourself. More than one marriage proposal has taken place at this point on the tour.

The 2015 renovation improved the visitor experience, with more exhibits in its tours, easier ticket booth areas, and the addition of Café Lula (www.cafelula. net, 9am-8pm daily, with extended hours during events) for snacks. None of the original 1892 architecture was changed during the expansion.

John Seigenthaler Pedestrian Bridge

Built in 1909, the Sparkman Street Bridge was slated for demolition in 1998 after inspectors called its condition "poor." But citing the success of the Walnut Street Bridge in revitalizing downtown Chattanooga, Tennessee, advocates succeeded in saving the bridge. The now-named **John Seigenthaler Pedestrian Bridge** reopened in 2003 as a footbridge and bike bridge.

Today, the John Seigenthaler Pedestrian Bridge connects East Nashville neighborhoods with downtown. It is frequently featured on ABC's *Nashville* because of its great views of the city, and many folks get their iconic Music City photos taken there (including this author). It is named after the civil rights crusader and journalist. At the base of the east side of the bridge is **Cumberland Park** (592 S. 1st St., 615/862-8508, www.nashville.gov/parks, dawn-11pm daily) and the East Bank Landing's kayak, canoe, and paddleboard launches.

Johnny Cash Museum

Opened in April 2013, the **Johnny Cash Museum** (119 3rd Ave. S., 615/256-1777, www.johnnycashmuseum.com, 9am-7pm daily, adults $19, seniors and military $18, children $15) looks like a small storefront with a tiny gift shop. But back behind the cash register is a wealth of information on all things Johnny Cash. The collection was amassed by one fan-turned-collector, and it features interactive listening booths, the jumpsuit the Man in Black wore when he flipped the bird in public, and other memorabilia from a varied and lauded career. Locals are crazy for the rebuilt stone wall that was taken from Cash's fire-destroyed suburban home. This is one of the city's most visited attractions.

George Jones Museum

Known as "the Possum," George Jones was a country music great who passed away in 2013 at the age of 81. He struggled with alcohol abuse: He famously drove a John Deere tractor to the liquor store once because his brother-in-law hid his car keys, and was known for being a no-show for performances. His wife devoted her time to helping him get better. Now she's devoting her time to preserving his musical legacy. The **George Jones Museum** (128 2nd Ave. N., 615/818-0128, http://georgejonesmuseum.com, 10am-10pm daily, adults $17, seniors and military $16, youth $13) is filled with artifacts from his life and career, from stage costumes to awards to, yes, a replica of that John Deere tractor. Some exhibits include a hologram of Jones, to give the experience of seeing the legend. A rooftop bar looks out at the Cumberland River.

Tennessee Sports Hall of Fame

Sports fans will enjoy the **Tennessee Sports Hall of Fame** (Bridgestone Arena, 501 Broadway, 615/242-4750, www.tshf. net, 10am-5pm Tues.-Sat., adults $3, children $2). Located in a state-of-the-art 7,500-square-foot exhibit space inside Bridgestone Arena, the hall chronicles the history of sports in Tennessee from the 1800s to today's heroes.

Customs House

Located at 701 Broadway, the old Nashville **Customs House** is a historic landmark and architectural beauty. Construction on the Customs House began in 1875, and President Rutherford B. Hayes visited Nashville to lay the cornerstone in 1877. The building is an impressive example of the Victorian Gothic style. It was designed by Treasury architect William Appleton Potter and was completed in 1916. Although it is called a customs house, the building served as the center of federal government operations in the city: Federal government offices, courts, and treasury offices were housed in the building.

Hume-Fogg

Located across Broadway from the Customs House is **Hume-Fogg** Magnet School. It sits on land formerly occupied by Hume School, Nashville's first public school. The four-story stone-clad 1912 building was designed by William Ittner of St. Louis in the Norman Gothic style with Tudor Gothic details. Today, it's a public magnet school with a reputation for high academic standards.

Frist Center for the Visual Arts

Nashville's foremost visual art space is the **Frist Center for the Visual Arts** (919

Broadway, 615/244-3340, http://fristcenter.org, 10am-5:30pm Mon.-Wed. and Sat., 10am-9pm Thurs.-Fri., 1pm-5:30pm Sun., adults $12, seniors and students $9, military $7). The Frist is located in a stately building that once housed the 1930s downtown post office (and there's still a working post office in the basement). High ceilings, art deco finishes, and unique hardwood tiles distinguish the museum. Look carefully in the hallways, and you can see the indentations in the walls from folks who leaned here while waiting for their turn in line at the post office.

With no permanent collection of its own, the Frist puts on about 12 major visiting exhibitions annually. At any given time, you will see 3-4 different exhibits, many of which are regional or national premieres. There are typically plenty of ongoing educational activities paired with the exhibitions. ArtQuest, a permanent part of the Frist, is an excellent hands-on arts activity room for children and their parents. The Frist's café serves better-than-expected salads and sandwiches, and has a nice patio for alfresco dining.

Downtown

Downtown is dominated by large office buildings and federal, state, and city government structures. From Commerce Street northward to the state capitol, you will find historic churches, museums, and hordes of office workers.

Tennessee State Capitol

Set on the top of a hill and built with the formality and grace of classic Greek architecture, the **Tennessee State Capitol** building (600 Charlotte Ave., 615/741-0830, tours 9am-3pm hourly Mon.-Fri., free) strikes a commanding pose overlooking downtown Nashville. Construction of the capitol began in 1845, two years after the state legislature finally agreed that Nashville would be the permanent capital city. Even with the unpaid labor of convicts and slaves, it took 14 years to finish the building.

The capitol is built of limestone, much of it from a quarry located near present-day Charlotte and 13th Avenues. In the 1950s, extensive renovations were carried out, and some of the original limestone was replaced. The interior marble came from Rogersville and Knoxville, and the gasoliers were ordered from Philadelphia. The capitol was designed by architect William Strickland, who considered it his crowning achievement and who is buried in a courtyard on the north end of the capitol.

Visitors are welcome at the capitol. Ask at the information desk for a printed guide that identifies each of the rooms and many of the portraits and sculptures both inside and outside the building. If the legislature is not in session, you can go inside both the House and Senate chambers, which look much as they did back in the 19th century. In the 2nd-floor lobby, you can see two bronze reliefs depicting the 19th and 14th amendments to the U.S. Constitution, both of which were ratified by the State of Tennessee in votes held at the capitol.

Guided tours of the capitol depart hourly 9am-3pm Monday-Friday. Ask at the information desk inside for more details.

Other important state buildings surround the capitol. The **Library and Archives** (403 7th Ave. N.) sits directly west of the capitol and next to the **Tennessee Supreme Court** (401 7th Ave. N.). The **Tennessee War Memorial** (301 6th Ave. N.) is a stone plaza on the south side of the capitol and a nice place to people-watch (and where, in 2000, Al Gore told supporters he would fight on in the presidential election against George W. Bush). This is where Occupy Nashville protesters gathered in 2011. A number of state office buildings are nearby, and state employees can be seen walking to and fro, particularly at lunchtime.

Frist Center for the Visual Arts

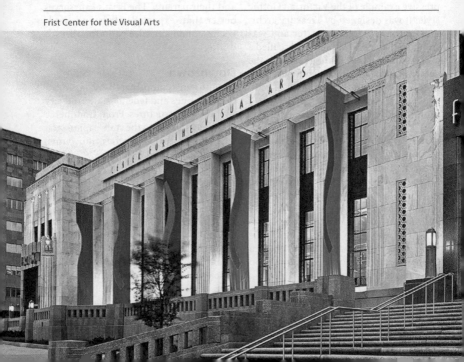

Tennessee State Museum

If you are used to the flashy multimedia exhibits found in many of today's top museums, the **Tennessee State Museum** (505 Deaderick St., 615/741-2692, www.tnmuseum.org, 10am-5pm Tues.-Sat., 1pm-5pm Sun., free) might seem like a musty throwback to the past. The displays are largely straightforward combinations of text and images, and they require visitors to read and examine on their own. There are but a few video presentations. But for patrons with enough patience to give the displays their due, the museum offers an excellent overview of Tennessee history from the Native Americans to the New South era of the 1880s.

Exhibits detail the state's political development, explore the Revolutionary and Civil Wars, and profile famous Tennesseans, including Andrew Jackson and Davy Crockett. They also cast a spotlight on the lifestyles and diversions of Tennesseans of various eras, from the early frontiersmen and frontierswomen

to a free African American family before emancipation. Special artifacts include the top hat worn by Andrew Jackson at his presidential inauguration, a musket that belonged to Daniel Boone, and the jawbone of a mastodon.

Plans are under way for a $160 million, 140,000-square foot update of the museum, which will be located near the Nashville Farmers Market and Bicentennial Mall; it is slated to open in 2018.

The **Military Branch Museum** (Legislative Plaza, 615/741-2692, 10am-5pm Tues.-Sat., free) is associated with the Tennessee State Museum and highlights America's overseas conflicts, beginning with the Spanish-American War in 1989 and ending with World War II. The exhibits examine the beginnings of the wars, major battles, and the outcomes. There is a special exhibit about Alvin C. York, the Tennessee native and World War I hero. The military museum is located in the War Memorial Building on the south side of the capitol.

★ Civil Rights Room at the Nashville Public Library

The **Nashville Public Library** (615 Church St., 615/862-5800, 9am-6pm Mon.-Fri., 9am-5pm Sat., 2pm-5pm Sun., free) houses a powerful exhibit (615/862-5782, www.library.nashville.org/civilrights/home.html) on the movement for civil rights that took place in Nashville in the 1950s and 1960s. Nashville was the first Southern city to desegregate public services, and it did so relatively peacefully, setting an example for activists throughout the South.

The story of the courageous men and women who made this change happen is told through photographs, videos, and displays in the **Civil Rights Room at the Nashville Public Library.** The library is a fitting location for the exhibit since the block below on Church Street was the epicenter of the Nashville sit-ins during 1960.

Inside the room, large-format photographs show school desegregation, sit-ins, and a silent march to the courthouse. A circular table at the center of the room is symbolic of the lunch counters where young students from Fisk, Meharry, American Baptist, and Tennessee A&I sat silently and peacefully at sit-ins. The table is engraved with the 10 rules of conduct set out for sit-in participants, including to be polite and courteous at all times, regardless of how you are treated. A timeline of the national and Nashville civil rights movements is presented above the table.

Inside a glass-enclosed viewing room you can choose from six documentary videos, including an hour-long 1960 NBC news documentary about the Nashville sit-ins. Many of the videos are 30 minutes or longer, so plan on spending several hours here if you are keenly interested in the topics.

The centerpiece of the Civil Rights Room is a glass inscription by Martin Luther King Jr., who visited the city in 1960 and said, during a speech at Fisk University: "I came to Nashville not to bring inspiration, but to gain inspiration from the great movement that has taken place in this community."

Nashville is planning a new and much-needed museum dedicated to its African American history and culture, which will be located at the corner of Jefferson and 8th Avenues, near the farmers market. Until this museum is built, the Nashville Public Library is the best place to learn about the city's racially segregated past and the movement that changed that.

The Civil Rights Room is on the 2nd floor of the library, adjacent to the room that houses its Nashville collection.

The Arcade

One of Nashville's most distinctive urban features is the covered arcade that runs between 4th and 5th Avenues and parallel to Union Street. The two-story arcade with a gabled glass roof was built in 1903 by developer Daniel Buntin, who was inspired by similar arcades he saw in Italy.

From the moment it opened, the **Arcade** (65 Arcade Alley, 615/248-6673, http://thenashvillearcade.com) was a bustling center for commerce. Famous for its peanut shop, the Arcade has also been the location of photo studios, jewelers, and a post office for many years. Today, restaurants (including Manny's House of Pizza) crowd the lower level, while art galleries, artists' studios, and professional offices line the 2nd floor. Don't miss the bustling activities here during the Art Crawl on the first Saturday of the month.

Downtown Presbyterian Church

William Strickland, the architect who designed the Tennessee State Capitol, also designed the **Downtown Presbyterian Church** (154 5th Ave. N., 615/254-7584, www.dpchurch.com), a place of worship now on the National Register of Historic Places. Built in 1848 to replace an earlier church destroyed by fire, the church is in the Egyptian revival style that was popular at the time. It is, however, one of only three surviving churches in the country to be built in this style.

Downtown Presbyterian, which added the word "Downtown" to its name in 1955, was used as a Union hospital during the Civil War, and it is where James K. Polk was inaugurated as Tennessee governor in 1839. Visitors are welcome to come for a self-guided tour 9am-3pm Monday-Friday; groups of five or more can call in advance.

Musicians Hall of Fame & Museum

Not to be confused with the Country Music Hall of Fame, the **Musicians Hall of Fame & Museum** (MHOF) (401 Gay St., 615/244-3263, www.musicianshalloffame.com, 10am-5pm Mon.-Sat., adults $24, seniors and military $20, youth $14) honors the people who pick and strum. Not necessarily the stars and not the songwriters, but the guitar players and drummers and others, regardless of genre

The Nashville Sit-Ins

Greensboro, North Carolina, is often named as the site of the first sit-ins of the American civil rights movement. But, in truth, activists in Nashville carried out the first "test" sit-ins in late 1959. In these test cases, protesters left the facilities after being refused service and talking to management about the injustice of segregation. In between these test sit-ins and the moment when Nashville activists would launch a full-scale sit-in campaign, students in Greensboro took that famous first step.

The Nashville sit-ins began on February 13, 1960, when a group of African American students from local colleges and universities sat at a downtown lunch counter and refused to move until they were served. The protesting students endured verbal and physical abuse, and were arrested.

Community members raised money for the students' bail, and black residents of the city began an economic boycott of downtown stores that practiced segregation. On April 19, the home of Z. Alexander Looby, a black lawyer who was representing the students, was bombed. Later the same day, students led a spontaneous, peaceful, and silent march through the streets of downtown Nashville to the courthouse. Diane Nash, a student leader, asked Nashville mayor Ben West if he thought it was morally right for a restaurant to refuse to serve someone based on the color of his or her skin. Mayor West said, "No."

The march was an important turning point for the city. The combined effect of the sit-ins, the boycott, and the march in 1960 caused Nashville to be the first major Southern city to experience widespread desegregation of its public facilities. The events also demonstrated to activists in other parts of the South that nonviolence was an effective tool of protest.

The story of the young people who led the Nashville sit-ins is told in the book *The Children* by David Halberstam. In 2001, Nashville resident Bill King was so moved by the story of the protests that he established an endowment to fundraise for a permanent civil rights collection at the Nashville Public Library. In 2003, the **Civil Rights Room at the Nashville Public Library** was opened. It houses books, oral histories, audiovisual records, microfilm, dissertations, and stunning photographs of the events of 1960. The words of one student organizer, John Lewis, who went on to become a congressman from Georgia, are displayed over the entryway: "If not us, then who; if not now, then when?"

or instrument, who make a song something to which we want to tap our toes. The MHOF was displaced when the city built the mammoth Music City Center. Located in Municipal Auditorium—once the city's leading concert venue—since 2013, the MHOF displays memorabilia and instruments from the unsung heroes of the industry. Inductees are nominated by current members of the American Federation of Musicians and others. An 8,500-square-foot Grammy Museum Gallery expansion is in the works.

One of the country's most cutting-edge contemporary art collections is inside a hotel. The **21c Museum** (223 3rd Ave. N., 615/610-6400, www.21cmuseumhotels.com, 24 hours daily, free) opened in Nashville in 2017 with a mission to make contemporary art part of everyday life. Exhibits rotate annually and tend to be thought-provoking works.

Bicentennial Capitol Mall State Park

Tennessee celebrated its 100th anniversary in 1896 with the construction of the beloved Centennial Park, so it must have seemed like a good idea to celebrate its 200th anniversary in much the same way. The **Bicentennial Capitol Mall State Park** occupies 19 acres on the north side of the capitol building. It offers excellent views of the capitol, which towers over the mall. The mall and the capitol are separated by a steep hill and more than 200 steps, which may look daunting but are worth the climb for the views and access to downtown.

The mall has dozens of features that celebrate Tennessee and Tennesseans, including a 200-foot granite map of Tennessee embedded in concrete; a River Wall with 31 fountains, each representing one of Tennessee's rivers; and a timeline with Tennessee events, inscriptions, and notable quotes from 1796 to 1996. A one-mile path that circles the mall's perimeter is popular with walkers and joggers, and a 2,000-seat amphitheater is used for special events. The park may be a civics lesson incarnate, but it is also a pleasant place to pass the time. Ninety-five carillon bells (for the state's 95 counties) play "The Tennessee Waltz" every hour on the hour.

To the west of the mall is the amazing **Nashville Farmers Market** (www.nashvillefarmersmarket.org, 8am-6pm daily), where you can buy fresh produce, flowers, gourmet breakfasts and lunches, and locally made crafts. Locals often picnic in the mall with goodies from the market. There's plenty of free parking here, but don't speed. Because this is a state park, tickets come from the state police, and they're pricier than metro Nashville tickets.

Fisk University

Founded in 1866 to educate newly freed slaves, **Fisk University** (1000 17th Ave. N., 615/329-8500, www.fisk.edu) has a long and proud history as one of the foremost U.S. black colleges. W. E. B. Du Bois attended Fisk, graduating in 1888, and Booker T. Washington married a Fisk alumna and sent his own children to Fisk. In more modern times, Knoxville native and poet Nikki Giovanni attended Fisk.

Fisk sits at the corner of Jefferson Street and Dr. D. B. Todd Jr. Boulevard, about 10 blocks west of downtown Nashville. The campus is a smattering of elegant red-brick buildings set on open green lawns, although a few more modern buildings, including the library, detract from the classical feel. One of the oldest Fisk buildings is **Jubilee Hall,** on the north end of the campus, which is said to be the first permanent building constructed for the education of African Americans in the country. It was built with money raised by the Fisk Jubilee Singers, who popularized black spirituals during a world tour 1871-1874. Another notable building is the **Fisk Little Theatre,** a white clapboard building that once served as a Union hospital during the Civil War.

The **Aaron Douglas Gallery** (Jackson St. and 17th Ave. N., 10am-5pm Mon.-Fri., free) houses Fisk's collection of African, African American, and folk art. It also hosts visiting exhibits and others by Fisk students and faculty. It is named after painter and illustrator Aaron Douglas, who also established Fisk's first formal art department. The gallery is located on the top floor of the Fisk library. **Cravath Hall** houses several Aaron Douglas murals that, while in need of restoration, are worth seeing. If a curator at the Van Vechten is available, you may be lucky enough to have them take you on a quick guided tour of the murals, as well as a small art gallery on the third floor of the library.

Fisk welcomes visitors, but there is no central information desk or printed guide. A map is posted just inside the library, and this is the best place to start your visit. Historical markers provide details of each of the main campus buildings. To see the famous painting of the Jubilee Singers, enter Jubilee Hall and bear right to the Appleton Room, where it hangs at the rear.

★ Carl Van Vechten Gallery

The **Carl Van Vechten Gallery** (Dr. D. B. Todd Jr. Blvd. and Jackson St., 615/329-8720, 10am-5pm Mon.-Fri., adults $10,

Fisk's Stieglitz Collection

When photographer **Alfred Stieglitz** died in 1946, his wife, **Georgia O'Keeffe,** herself one of the most important artists of her generation, was left with the responsibility of giving away his massive art collection. Stieglitz had collected more than 1,000 works by artists who included O'Keeffe, Arthur Dove, Marsden Hartley, Charles Demuth, and John Marin. He also owned several African sculptures.

Stieglitz's instructions regarding this art collection were vague. In his will he asked O'Keeffe to select the recipients "under such arrangements as will assure to the public, under reasonable regulations, access thereto to promote the study of art."

O'Keeffe selected several obvious recipients for parts of the collection: the Library of Congress, the National Gallery of Art in Washington, the Metropolitan Museum of Art, the Art Institute of Chicago, and the Philadelphia Museum of Art. Nashville's **Fisk University** was a surprise, and Carl Van Vechten, a writer, photographer, and friend of Stieglitz and O'Keeffe, is credited with making the suggestion. Van Vechten was keenly interested in African American art and was close friends with Fisk president Charles Johnson.

The Stieglitz Collection at Fisk consists of 101 remarkable works of art, including 2 by O'Keeffe, 19 Stieglitz photographs, prints by Cézanne and Renoir, and 5 pieces of African tribal art.

Cash-strapped Fisk sought to sell parts of the collection to raise funds. An agreement between the university and Walmart heiress Alice Walton's Crystal Bridges Museum in Bentonville, Arkansas, means that the collection spends every two years in Bentonville and then returns to Fisk for two years. The $1 million from the partnership allowed Fisk to remodel and hire curatorial staff, and also to highlight the school's impressive collections of works by African American artists while the Stieglitz is in Bentonville.

seniors $6, college students $5, children free) is named for the art collector who convinced artist Georgia O'Keeffe to donate to Fisk a large portion of the work and personal collection of her late husband, Alfred Stieglitz. The collection includes works by Stieglitz and O'Keeffe, as well as acclaimed European and American artists, including Pablo Picasso, Paul Cézanne, Pierre-Auguste Renoir, Diego Rivera, Arthur Dove, Gino Severini, and Charles Demuth. For seven years a legal battle waged in courts as the college sought to sell parts of the collection to raise funds. Fortunately, a compromise was struck. Crystal Bridges Museum of American Art (http://stieglitzcollection.crystalbridges.org) in Bentonville, Arkansas, entered into a partnership with Fisk, allowing both institutions to display the collection; rotating every two years.

The collection is one worth seeing,

and the new funds and partnership make that more possible, because the gallery now has a staff and regular hours. The school's works by African American artists are impressive as well, and make the gallery a worthwhile detour even when Stieglitz is not in residence. The gallery is closed when school is not in session; check the website for exact annual spring and fall break dates.

Meharry Medical College
Just across Dr. D. B. Todd Jr. Boulevard from Fisk is **Meharry Medical College** (1005 Dr. D. B. Todd Jr. Blvd., 615/327-6000, www.mmc.edu), the largest private, comprehensive, historically black institution educating medical professionals. It was founded in 1876 as the Medical Department of the Central Tennessee College of Nashville, under the auspices of the Freeman's Aid Society of the Methodist Episcopal Church.

The Jubilee Singers

In 1871, Fisk University needed money. Buildings at the school established in old Union army barracks in 1866 were decaying while more and more African Americans came to seek education.

So, in what might later be considered a very Nashville-style idea, the school choir withdrew all the money from the university's treasury and left on a world tour. The nine singers were Isaac Dickerson, Maggie Porter, Minnie Tate, Jennie Jackson, Benjamin Holmes, Thomas Rutling, Eliza Walker, Green Evans, and Ella Sheppard. Remembering a biblical reference to the Hebrew "year of the jubilee," Fisk treasurer and choir manager George White gave them their name, the Fisk Jubilee Singers.

The choir struggled at first, but before long audiences were singing their praises. They toured first the American South, then the North, and in 1873 sailed to England for a successful British tour. Their audiences included William Lloyd Garrison, Wendell Phillips, Ulysses S. Grant, William Gladstone, Mark Twain, Johann Strauss, and Queen Victoria. Songs like "Swing Low, Sweet Chariot" and "Nobody Knows the Trouble I've Seen" moved audiences to tears. The singers introduced the spiritual to mainstream white audiences and erased negative misconceptions about African Americans and African American education.

In 1874, the singers returned to Nashville. They had raised enough money to pay off Fisk's debts and build the university's first permanent structure, an imposing Victorian Gothic six-story building now called **Jubilee Hall.** It was the first permanent structure built solely for the education of African Americans in the United States.

Every October 6, the day in 1871 that the singers departed Fisk, the university recalls their struggle and their triumph with a free convocation featuring the modern-day Jubilee Singers. Jubilee Day, as it is called, also includes a pilgrimage to their gravesites to lay wreaths made from campus magnolia leaves.

Meharry was at one time responsible for graduating more than half of all African American doctors and nurses in the United States. Today it has an enrollment of almost 800 students.

Marathon Village

This "new" neighborhood is actually one that dates back to 1881. A former auto factory, **Marathon Village** (1305 Clinton St., www.marathonvillage.com) now houses sleek urban condos, restaurants, the Corsair Artisan Distillery, Bang Candy Company, and shops, including Antique Archaeology Nashville, owned by Mike Wolfe of *American Pickers* TV fame. It's also becoming a destination for entertainment, thanks to live music venue Marathon Music Works, one of the best places to see non-country concerts, and Third Coast Comedy Club, the city's first comedy club, featuring stand-up, improv, and sketch acts. Of course, the architecture brings in history buffs who love the buildings' bones.

Hadley Park

Founded in 1912, **Hadley Park** (1037 28th Ave. N., 615/862-8451, dawn-dusk daily) is believed to be the oldest public park developed for African Americans in the South and, most likely, the United States. The park got its start when Fisk University president George Gates requested that the city buy land and create a park for its black citizens. This was in the era of segregation, so other city parks were not open to blacks. The request was granted, and the park opened in July 1912. An old farmhouse was converted into a community center, and benches and a playground were installed. It is now home to a state-of-the-art gym and fitness center, computer labs, meeting rooms, and tennis courts.

Tennessee State University

Founded in 1912 as a normal (teacher's) school for blacks, **Tennessee State University** (3500 John A. Merritt Blvd., 615/963-5000, www.tnstate.edu) is now a comprehensive university with more than 9,000 students. In 1979, as a result of a court order to desegregate the state's universities, TSU merged with the Nashville campus of the University of Tennessee. Today, TSU's student body is 75 percent African American.

Music Row

Home to the business end of the country music industry, Music Row can be found along 16th and 17th Avenues south of where they cross Broadway. While there are few bona fide attractions here, it is worth a jaunt to see the headquarters of both major and independent music labels all in one place (this might be your best chance for a celebrity sighting).

Music Row's most famous, or infamous, landmark is *Musica,* the sculpture at the Music Row traffic circle. The sculpture, by local artist Alan LeQuire, caused a stir when it was unveiled in 2003 for the larger-than-life anatomically correct men and women it depicts. Regardless of your views on art and obscenity, it is fair to say that *Musica* speaks more to Nashville's identity as the Athens of the South than as Music City USA.

RCA Studio B

As a rule, the music studios in Music Row are open for business, not tours. The lone exception is historic **RCA Studio B** (1611 Roy Acuff Pl., 615/416-2001, http://studiob.org, $30-40). The RCA studio was the second recording studio in Nashville and the place where artists including the Everly Brothers, Roy Orbison, Dolly Parton, Elvis Presley, and Hank Snow recorded hits. Also called the RCA Victor Studio, this nondescript studio

operated from 1957 to 1977. Visitors on the one-hour tour, which departs from the Country Music Hall of Fame downtown, hear anecdotes about recording sessions at the studio and see rare footage of a 1960s Dottie West recording session.

Tours can only be purchased in conjunction with admission to the Country Music Hall of Fame. Tours depart hourly 10:30am-2:30pm daily.

The Upper Room Chapel and Museum

Three million Christians around the world know the Upper Room Daily Devotional Guide, a page-a-day pocket devotional available in 106 countries and 40 languages. Headquartered in Nashville, the Upper Room Ministry has established a bookstore, museum, and chapel to welcome visitors. **The Upper Room Chapel and Museum** (1908 Grand Ave., 615/340-7207, http://chapel.upperroom.org, 8am-4:30pm Mon.-Fri., free, $5 suggested donation) features a small museum of Christian-inspired art, including a wonderful collection of Nativity scenes from around the world made from materials ranging from needlepoint to camel bone. Visitors may also tour the chapel, with its 8- by 20-foot stained-glass window and 8- by 17-foot wood carving of Leonardo da Vinci's *Last Supper.* A 15-minute audio presentation discusses features of the carving and tells the history and mission of The Upper Room.

Midtown
★ The Parthenon

In 1893, funds began to be raised for a mighty exposition that would celebrate the 1896 centennial of the state of Tennessee. Though the exposition would start a year later, in 1897, it would exceed all expectations. The old West Side Race Track was converted to a little city with exhibition halls dedicated to transportation, agriculture, machinery, minerals, forestry, and African Americans, among other themes. There were Chinese, Cuban, and Egyptian villages; a midway; and an auditorium. The exposition attracted 1.7 million people between May and October. While the event turned only a modest profit for its organizers, it no doubt contributed in other ways to the local economy and to the stature of the state.

When the exposition closed in the fall of 1897, all the exhibition halls were torn down except for a life-size replica of the Greek Parthenon, which had housed an art exhibit during the centennial. The exposition grounds were made into a public park, aptly named Centennial Park, and Nashvillians continued to admire their Parthenon.

The Parthenon replica had been built out of wood and plaster, and it was designed only to last through the centennial. Remarkably, it survived well beyond that. But by the 1920s, the Parthenon was crumbling. City officials, responding to public outcry to save the Parthenon, agreed to restore it.

Today, the **Parthenon** (Centennial Park, 2500 West End Ave., 615/862-8431, www.nashville.gov/parthenon, 9am-4:30pm Tues.-Sat., Sun. only 12:30pm-4:30pm June-Aug., adults $6, seniors and children $4) remains one of Nashville's most iconic landmarks. It's most beautiful from the outside, particularly when lit dramatically at night.

As breathtaking as it is from the exterior, it's worth paying to go inside the Parthenon. The landmark has three gallery spaces; the largest is used to display works from its permanent collection of 63 pieces of American art. The other two galleries host interesting, changing exhibits. But upstairs is the remarkable 42-foot statue of Athena, by local sculptor Alan LeQuire. Athena is designed to replicate how the statue would have looked in ancient Greece, in all her golden glory.

Vanderbilt University

Named for philanthropist "Commodore" Cornelius Vanderbilt, who donated $1 million in 1873 to found a university that would "contribute to strengthening the ties which should exist between all sections of our common country," **Vanderbilt University** (211 Kirkland Hall, 615/322-7311, www.vanderbilt.edu) is now one of the region's most respected institutions of higher education.

A private research university, Vanderbilt has an enrollment of 6,800 undergraduates and 5,700 graduate students. The university comprises 10 schools, a medical center, public policy center, and The Freedom Forum First Amendment Center. Originally just 75 acres, the university had grown to 250 acres by 1960. When the George Peabody School for Teachers merged with Vanderbilt in 1979 another 53 acres were added.

Vanderbilt's campus life is vibrant, and there is a daily roll call of lectures, recitals, exhibits, and other special events for students, locals, and visitors alike. Check the website for an up-to-date listing of all campus events.

Prospective students and their parents can sign up for a campus tour. Vanderbilt also offers a self-guided tour of the campus's trees, which form the Vanderbilt Arboretum. Most trees on the tour are native to Nashville and Middle Tennessee. This is a nice activity for people who want to hone tree identification skills. Download the podcast, print a copy of the tour from the website, or contact the university for more information.

Vanderbilt University also has two excellent art galleries: the **Sarratt Gallery** (Sarratt Student Center, Vanderbilt Pl. near 24th Ave., 615/343-0491, 9am-9pm Mon.-Fri., 10am-10pm Sat.-Sun. Sept.-mid-May, 9am-4:30pm Mon.-Fri. mid-May-Aug., free), which has a more contemporary bent, and the **Vanderbilt University Fine Arts Gallery** (1220 21st Ave. S., 11am-4pm Mon.-Fri., 1pm-5pm Sat.-Sun. Sept.-early May, noon-4pm Tues.-Fri. 1pm-5pm Sat. early

May-mid-June, free), which includes works that demonstrate the development of both Eastern and Western art, plus six different traveling exhibits annually. The Fine Arts Gallery is near the intersection of West End and 23rd Avenues. Both galleries are closed or limit their hours during university holidays and semester breaks, so it's a good idea to call ahead.

There is designated visitor parking in several lots on the Vanderbilt campus. Look on the eastern edge of the sports facilities parking lot off Natchez Trace, in the Wesley Place parking lot off Scarritt Place, or in the Terrace Place parking lot between 20th and 21st Avenues, north of Broadway. Pay attention to these signs, as the university parking monitors do ticket those who park in prohibited areas.

Belmont University

The school for girls founded in the Belmont Mansion in 1890 evolved in 1913 to the Ward-Belmont School for Women and in 1951 to coed Belmont College. Since 1991, it has been **Belmont University** (1900 Belmont Blvd., 615/460-6000, www.belmont.edu), a higher-education institution with links to the Tennessee Baptist Convention. Today Belmont is a fast-growing university with highly respected music and music business programs. In 2011, the school opened the first new law school in the state in the last century. Belmont, which hosted one of the 2008 presidential debates, has a student enrollment of 6,400. Campus tours are available twice a day on weekdays.

Several Belmont facilities are of interest to the public, including the **Curb Event Center** (2002 Belmont Blvd., 615/460 8500), which hosts sporting events, concerts, and lectures.

Belmont Mansion

The elaborate "summer home" of Adelicia Acklen was constructed in 1853 and was named Belle Monte. **Belmont Mansion** (1900 Belmont Blvd., 615/460-5459, www.

belmontmansion.com, 10am-4pm Mon.-Sat., noon-4pm Sun., adults $12, seniors and military $11, children 6-12 $3), as it is known today, is a monument to the excesses of the Victorian age.

Adelicia was born to a wealthy Nashville family in 1817. When she was 22, Adelicia married Isaac Franklin, a wealthy bachelor 28 years her senior. When Franklin died seven years later, Adelicia inherited his substantial wealth. Adelicia remarried to Joseph Acklen, a young lawyer, and together they planned and built Belmont Mansion. The home was built in the Italian style, with touches of Egyptian revival style.

The home boasted 36 rooms and 16,000 square feet of space, including a grand gallery where the Acklens hosted elaborate balls and dinner parties. The property included a private art gallery, aviary, zoo, and conservatory, as well as a lake and acres of manicured gardens. After the Civil War, Adelicia traveled to Europe, where she purchased a number of paintings and sculptures that are now on display in her restored mansion.

Shortly before her death, Adelicia sold Belmont to two female educators, who ran a girls school from the property for 61 years. Later, it was purchased by the founders of Belmont College.

Visitors to the mansion are given a 45-minute guided tour of the property, which includes the downstairs sitting and entertaining rooms and three of the upstairs bedrooms. To get here, enter "1700 Acklen Avenue" in your GPS.

Belle Meade
Belle Meade Plantation

The mansion at the former **Belle Meade Plantation** (5025 Harding Pike, 615/356-0501, http://bellemeadeplantation.com, 9am-5pm daily, adults $20, seniors $18, students $12, youth $10) is the centerpiece of present-day Belle Meade Plantation and one of the finest old homes in the city. Its name means beautiful pasture, and indeed it was Belle Meade's pastures

Midtown and West End

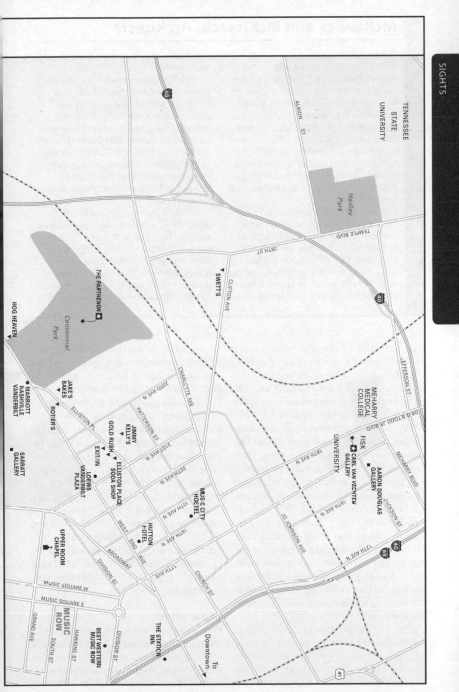

TENNESSEE
STATE
UNIVERSITY

ALBION ST

Hadley
Park

TEMPLE BLVD

28TH ST

CLIFTON AVE

SWETT'S ▲

40

JEFFERSON ST

THE PARTHENON ★

Centennial
Park

HOG HEAVEN ▲

JAKE'S
BAKES ▲

MARRIOTT
NASHVILLE
VANDERBILT ●

ROTIER'S ●

ELLISTON PL

CHARLOTTE AVE

23RD AVE N

GOLD RUSH ▲
EXIT/IN ▲

JIMMY
KELLY'S ▲

PATTERSON ST

21ST AVE N

MEHARRY
MEDICAL
COLLEGE

FISK ★
CARL VAN VECHTEN
GALLERY

DR D B TODD JR BLVD

UNIVERSITY

N 18TH AVE

AARON DOUGLAS
GALLERY

MEHARRY BLVD

JACKSON ST

SARRATT
GALLERY ■

LOEWS
VANDERBILT
PLAZA

ELLISTON PLACE
SODA SHOP

20TH AVE N

19TH AVE N

MUSIC CITY
HOSTEL ■

18TH AVE N

N 16TH AVE

JO JOHNSON AVE

N 15TH AVE

N 13TH AVE N

40
65

12TH AVE N

UPPER ROOM
CHAPEL ◄

WEST END AVE

HUTTON
HOTEL ■

17TH AVE N

BROADWAY

DIVISION ST

CHURCH ST

MUSIC SQUARE W

MUSIC SQUARE E

MUSIC
ROW

GRAND AVE

HAWKINS ST

BEST WESTERN
MUSIC ROW ■

DIVISION ST

THE STATION
INN ●

SOUTH ST

To
Downtown

41

McKissack and McKissack, Architects

The oldest African American architectural firm in Tennessee can trace its roots to **Moses McKissack** (1790-1865), a member of the West African Ashanti tribe. He was sold into slavery to William McKissack of North Carolina. Later, McKissack moved to Middle Tennessee. Moses became a master builder, and he passed his knowledge on to his son, Gabriel Moses McKissack, born in 1840. Gabriel Moses passed his knowledge of the building trade to his own son, Moses McKissack III, born in 1879.

Moses McKissack III was born in Pulaski, where he received a basic education in the town's segregated schools. In 1890 he was hired by a local white architect. Until 1905, McKissack designed and built homes throughout the area, including many in Mount Pleasant in Maury County. He developed a reputation as an excellent architect and tradesman.

In 1905, McKissack moved to Nashville, where he started his own construction company. Within a few years, he was working on major projects. He built a home for the dean of architecture and engineering at **Vanderbilt University** and the Carnegie Library at **Fisk University.** In 1922, Moses's brother, Calvin, joined him, and they opened McKissack and McKissack, Tennessee's first black architectural firm.

The McKissacks continued to distinguish themselves in the building industry, and they have also kept the business in the family. Since 1991 the company has been led by Cheryl McKissack, a fifth-generation McKissack. The firm employs more than 100 people and has corporate offices in Philadelphia and New York City.

that gave rise to the plantation's fame as the home of a superb stock of horses. Purchased as 250 acres in 1807 by Virginia farmer John Harding and his wife, Susannah, the estate grew to 5,400 acres at its peak in the 1880s and 1890s.

Belle Meade was never a cotton plantation, although small amounts of the cash crop were grown here, along with fruits, vegetables, and tobacco. Instead it was the horses, including the racehorse Iroquois, that made Belle Meade famous. The mansion was built in 1820 and expanded in 1853. Its grand rooms are furnished with period antiques, more than 60 percent of which are original to the house. The estate also includes outbuildings, including a smokehouse, dairy, and the original log cabin that Harding built for his family when they moved to Belle Meade in 1807.

The plantation also includes a slave cabin, which houses an exhibit on Belle Meade's enslaved population, which numbered more than 160 at its peak. Two of these slaves are described in detail.

Susanna Carter was the mansion's housekeeper for more than 30 years, and she remained with the family even after the end of slavery. On her deathbed, Selena Jackson, the mistress of Belle Meade for many years, called Susanna "one of the most faithful and trusted of my friends." The other African American who features prominently at the museum is Bob Green, whose skill and experience as a hostler earned him one of the highest salaries ever paid to a horse hand of the day.

Visitors to Belle Meade are given a one-hour guided tour of the mansion and then visit the outbuildings and grounds on their own. While the address on Harding Place is official, enter "110 Leake Avenue" into your GPS to get to the visitors entrance.

Cheekwood

Plan to spend a full morning or afternoon at **Cheekwood** (1200 Forrest Park Dr., 615/356-8000, http://cheekwood.org, 9:30am-5pm Tues.-Sun., adults $16, seniors $14, students and children $9-12) so you can experience the full scope of this magnificent art museum and botanical garden. Galleries in the Cheekwood mansion house the museum's American and European collections, including an excellent contemporary art collection. Cheekwood has the largest public collection of works by Nashville artist William Edmondson, the sculptor and stoneworker. Cheekwood usually displays items from its permanent collection as well as traveling exhibitions from other museums. Many exhibits have special ties with Nashville.

But the Cheekwood is far more than just an art museum. The mansion overlooks hundreds of acres of gardens and woods, and it is easy to forget that you are near a major American city when you're at the Cheekwood. Walk the mile-long **Carell Woodland Sculpture Trail** past works by 15 internationally acclaimed artists, or stroll past the water garden to the Japanese garden. There are dogwood gardens, an herb garden, a delightful boxwood garden, and much more. Wear comfortable shoes and pack a bottle of water so you can enjoy the grounds in comfort.

The Cheekwood owes its existence to the success of the coffee brand Maxwell House. During the 1920s, Leslie Cheek and his wife, Mabel Wood, invested in the new coffee brand being developed by their cousin, Joel Cheek. Maxwell House proved to be a success and earned the Cheeks a fortune, which they used to buy 100 acres of land in West Nashville. The family hired New York residential and landscape architect Bryant Fleming to create a 30,000-square-foot mansion and neighboring gardens. Cheekwood was completed in 1933.

Leslie Cheek lived in the mansion just two years before he died, and Mabel lived there for another decade before deeding it to her daughter and son-in-law, who later offered it as a site for a museum and garden. Cheekwood opened to the public in 1960.

Visitors pay admission at a guard gate at the entrance; parking is $5 per vehicle. Once inside, drive to parking lot B so you can explore the art museum and grounds. Parking lot A is for the museum shop and restaurant.

South Nashville
Fort Negley

Early in the Civil War, the Union army determined that taking and holding Nashville was a critical strategic link in their victory. So after Nashville fell in 1862, the Federals wasted no time fortifying the city against attacks. One of the city's forts was **Fort Negley,** built between August and December 1862 on St. Cloud Hill south of the city center.

Fort Negley owes its existence to the 2,768 men who were enrolled to build it. Most were blacks, some free and some slave, who were pressed into service by the Union army. These men felled trees, hauled earth, and cut and laid limestone for the fort. They slept in the open and enjoyed few, if any, comforts while they labored. Between 600 and 800 men died while building the fort, and only 310 received payment.

When it was completed, Fort Negley was the largest inland masonry fortification in North America. It was never challenged. Fort Negley was abandoned by the military after the war, but it remained the cornerstone of one of Nashville's oldest African American communities, now known as Cameron-Trimble. During the New Deal in the 1930s, the Works Progress Administration rebuilt large sections of the crumbling fort, and it became a public park.

In 2007, the city opened a visitors center to tell the story of the fort. **Fort Negley Park** (Fort Negley Dr., 615/862-8470, noon-4pm Tues.-Thurs., 9am-4pm Fri.-Sat. June-Aug., noon-4pm Tues.-Fri., 9am-4pm Sat. Sept.-May, free) includes a museum about the fort and Nashville's role in the Civil War. There is a short, paved loop trail around the base of the fort, plus raised boardwalks through the fortifications themselves. Historical markers tell the story of the fort's construction and detail its military features.

City Cemetery

Right next to Fort Negley Park, off Chestnut Street, is the old **City Cemetery** (1001 4th Ave. S., www.thenashvillecity-cemetery.org, 9am-5pm daily). Opened in 1822, City Cemetery was the final resting place of many of Nashville's most prominent early citizens, including founder James Robertson; William Driver, the U.S. Navy captain who named the flag "Old Glory"; Mabel Lewis Imes and Ella Sheppard, members of the original Fisk Jubilee Singers; and 14 Nashville mayors.

During the Civil War, the cemetery was contracted to bury more than 15,000 Union and Confederate dead, although they were later reinterred in different cemeteries.

Visitors are welcome 9am-5pm daily; if the gate is locked, call the phone number on the gate to be let in. Consult the information board in the Keeble Building for help with your self-guided tour. Guided tours and special events, such as living history tours, garden tours, and historical lectures, take place on the second Saturday of each month. The events are aimed at telling the history of Nashvillians who are buried at this historical cemetery.

Adventure Science Center

Children and their caretakers will enjoy the hands-on science education available at the **Adventure Science Center** (800 Fort Negley Blvd., 615/862-5160, www.adventuresci.com, 10am-5pm daily, adults $15, children $11). Interactive exhibits explore how the body works, the solar system, and other scientific areas. A multistory climbing tower in the building's center features a giant guitar and other instruments.

The center's **Sudekum Planetarium** (www.sudekumplanetarium.com,

additional $6) is the largest planetarium in Tennessee. The 164-seat planetarium offers a variety of space-themed shows. There are also star-viewing parties, gravity-suspending rides, and other exhibits about space flight, the moon, the solar system, and other things found in space.

Tennessee Central Railway Museum

Railroad enthusiasts should make a detour to the **Tennessee Central Railway**

The Battle of Nashville

During most of the Civil War, Nashville was occupied by Federal forces. After Fort Donelson, 90 miles northeast of Nashville, fell in mid-February 1862, Nashville was in Union hands. The Union turned Nashville into an important goods depot for the Northern cause and set strict rules for city residents during occupation.

As the war drew to a close in late 1864, Nashville was the site of what war historians now say was the last major battle of the Western Theater.

The Battle of Nashville came after a string of defeats for the Confederate army of Tennessee, commanded by John Bell Hood. After his bloody and humiliating losses at Spring Hill and Franklin a few miles south, Hood moved north and set up headquarters at **Travellers Rest,** the home of John Overton. His plan was to set up his troops in an arc around the southern side of the city. Union major general George H. Thomas did not plan to wait for Hood's attack, however. He devised to attack first and drive the Confederates away from Nashville.

A winter storm and frigid temperatures delayed the battle. For two weeks, from December 2 to 14, 1864, the two armies peered at one another across the no-man's-land between the two lines. Then, at dawn on December 15, 1864, the Union attack began. Union troops on foot and horse, including at least four U.S. Colored Infantry brigades made up of African American soldiers, attacked various Confederate posts around the city. By the close of the first day of fighting, Hood withdrew his troops two miles farther south from the city.

The dawn of the second day of battle augured more losses for the Confederates. Unable to hold their line against the Union assault, they fell back again. As darkness fell, Union major general Thomas wired Washington to announce his victory. Pursued by a Union cavalry commanded by Major General James Wilson, what remained of the Confederate army of Tennessee marched south, and on the day after Christmas they crossed the Tennessee River into Alabama. Four months later, the war was over.

The **Battle of Nashville Preservation Society, Inc.** (www.bonps.org) offers guided tours ($100-150) of the battlefield sites. Customers drive their own vehicle and the guide rides along; prices are per vehicle, not per person.

Museum (220 Willow St., 615/244-9001, http://tcry.org, 9am-4pm Mon.-Fri., 9am-3pm Sat., free). This institution is best known for its special railroad excursions, but it also collects railroad equipment and paraphernalia, which are on display at the museum. The museum is located in an otherwise industrial area between the interstate and the railroad tracks, one block north of Hermitage Avenue and east of Fairfield Avenue.

Nashville Zoo at Grassmere

See familiar and exotic animals at the **Nashville Zoo at Grassmere** (3777 Nolensville Pike, 615/833-1534, www.nashvillezoo.org, 9am-4pm daily Jan.-mid-Mar., 9am-6pm daily mid-Mar.-mid-Oct., 9am-4pm daily mid-Oct.-Dec., adults $16, seniors $14, children ages 3-12 $11, children under 3 free, parking $5). Many of the zoo's animals live in beautiful habitats like Lorikeet Landing, Gibbon Islands, and Bamboo Trail. The zoo's meerkat exhibit, featuring the famously quizzical and erect animals, is one of its most popular. The Wild Animal Carousel is an old-time carousel with 39 brightly painted wooden animals.

The zoo is located at Grassmere, the onetime home and farm of the Croft family. The historic Croft farmhouse has been preserved and is open for guided tours in October and December.

Travellers Rest Plantation and Museum

Travellers Rest Plantation and Museum (636 Farrell Pkwy., 615/832-8197, www.travellersrestplantation.org, 10am-4:30pm Mon.-Sat., adults $12, seniors $11, students 6-17 $10, children 5 and under free) was the home of John Overton, a Nashville lawyer who helped found Memphis, served on the first Tennessee Supreme Court, and was a trusted advisor to Andrew Jackson, the seventh U.S. president and the first from Tennessee.

Overton was born in Virginia and studied law in Kentucky before he decided to move to Middle Tennessee, what was then the western frontier of the United States. When workmen were digging the cellar for the original home in 1799, they uncovered Native American skeletons and artifacts—Overton had chosen a Mississippian-era Indian mound for the site of his home. But the archaeological finds did not stop Overton, who initially named his home Golgotha, or "hill of skulls." The name did not stick, however; tradition has it that Overton later renamed the home Travellers Rest because it was his place of rest between long trips as a circuit judge in Middle and East Tennessee.

Travellers Rest underwent two major expansions in its lifetime: one in 1808 and another 20 years later. The additions allowed Overton first to accommodate a growing number of young students who wished to study law with him; later his wife, Mary, and their children; and, finally, the elaborate parties that Overton hosted to further the political career of Andrew Jackson.

John Overton was many different things in his lifetime. Among them was slave owner. Records show that 30-80 slaves lived at Travellers Rest before emancipation. While Overton's plantation was not the primary source of his wealth, it no doubt contributed to his status and prominence. Sadly, when the

a white tiger at the Nashville Zoo at Grassmere

L&N Railroad purchased the Overton property in the 1940s, the company destroyed not only the Overton family burial ground and peach orchard, but also the slave cabins that remained at the rear of the house.

Visitors to Travellers Rest may choose to skip the mansion tour; admission to the grounds alone is just $5 for everyone over the age of 4. But to get the full story and flavor of the property, choose the 45-minute guided tour.

Tennessee Agricultural Museum

The **Tennessee Agricultural Museum** (Ellington Agricultural Center, 440 Hogan Rd., 615/837-5197, www.tnag-museum.org, 9am-4pm Mon.-Fri., free) celebrates the ingenuity and dedicated labors of farm life from the 17th to the 20th centuries. Operated by the Tennessee Department of Agriculture and set on the department's pleasant South Nashville campus, the museum depicts various facets of Tennessee farm life.

There are exhibits about clothes washing, blacksmithing, coopering, plowing, weaving, and more. Outside, there is a small kitchen garden with heirloom vegetables, and replicas of a log cabin, one-room schoolhouse, and outdoor kitchen. A short self-guided nature trail illustrates the ways that settlers used various types of native Tennessee trees.

Music Valley

A collection of tourist attractions separated from the rest of Nashville by the Cumberland River, **Music Valley** is most known for being the new home of the Grand Ole Opry. The area was one of those hit hardest by the 2010 flood, leading to some significant improvements and upgrades, along with some closures. This strip of motels, restaurants, and country music "museums" is tourist-centric. It is more campy than authentic, although it does offer some fun, affordable ways to explore Music City's kitsch.

If you're game, however, head straight for **Cooter's Place** (2613 McGavock Pike, 615/872-8358, www.cootersplace.com, 8:30am-9pm Sun.-Thurs., 8:30am-10pm Fri.-Sat., free), a gift shop and museum dedicated to the *Dukes of Hazzard* television show. The museum features a mind-boggling array of toys, ornaments, and model cars manufactured in the 1970s and 1980s to profit off the Dukes' popularity. You can also see one of the bright-orange Dodge Chargers that became the Dukes' icon. In the gift shop, buy a pair of "official" Daisy Dukes or any number of General Lee souvenirs. Cooter's Place is operated by Ben Jones, who played Cooter, the affable sidekick mechanic, in the original television series. In recent years, Jones has been one of the forces behind DukeFest, a wildly popular annual celebration of fast cars and the General Lee held at the Nashville Motor Speedway. Jones has been determined to keep the signature

Music Valley

BEST WESTERN NEAR OPRYLAND
COURTYARD BY MARRIOTT OPRYLAND
TEXAS TROUBADOUR THEATER
FIDDLER'S INN
NASHVILLE PALACE
GAYLORD OPRYLAND HOTEL
OPRY MILLS SHOPPING CENTER
GENERAL JACKSON SHOWBOAT

PENNINGTON BEND
COMFORT INN OPRYLAND AREA
MUSIC CITY CIR

GAYLORD SPRINGS GOLF COURSE

GRAY LINE TOURS
OPRY BACKSTAGE GRILL
COOTER'S
WILLIE NELSON AND FRIENDS MUSEUM

RIVERVIEW DR.
OPRYLAND DR.
OPRY
MILLS DR.
BRILEY PKWY.

Cumberland River

GRAND OLE OPRY

EXIT 12
EXIT 11

155
Pedestrian Bridge

EXIT 10

TWO RIVERS GOLF COURSE
TWO RIVERS PKWY.

Cornelia Fort Airpark

Shelby Bottoms Park

Stones River

McGAVOCK PIKE

0   0.5 mi
0   0.5 km

EXIT 8   70   24

© AVALON TRAVEL

Confederate flag as part of the art associated with the *Dukes of Hazzard,* despite controversy over the flag.

A few doors down from Cooter's Place, you will find **Willie Nelson and Friends Museum and General Store** (2613 McGavock Pike, 615/885-1515, http://willienelsongeneralstore.com, 8:30am-9pm daily, $8), which showcases a number of things that once belonged to Willie Nelson, including his golf bag, a replica of his tour bus, and the guitar he played during his first performance at the Grand Ole Opry. Many of the Willie Nelson items were purchased by museum operators Jeannie and Frank Oakley at an IRS auction.

Grand Ole Opry House
Since 1974, the Grand Ole Opry has been most often staged at the specially built **Grand Ole Opry House** (2804 Opryland Dr., 615/871-6779, www.opry.com) in Music Valley. This is the Opry's sixth regular home, and it was completely renovated after it was shuttered due to the 2010 flood. The Opry House may have been closed, but the Opry went on. The show still made the airwaves for every scheduled performance, playing at different venues around town while construction went on around the clock.

With the renovated Opry came an updated backstage tour. Daytime tour tickets go on sale two weeks in advance and are generally offered every 15 minutes; if you are buying tickets to a show, you can also purchase postconcert backstage tours. On this docent-led tour you'll get to see dressing rooms, learn lots of Opry history, and hear plenty of juicy stories about performers and their backstage behavior. One of the highlights of the guided tour is going on stage and having your photo taken under the lights. If you book a postshow tour, you'll see a performer or two. Tickets are $27 for adults, $22 for children; VIP tour $150 after a show; daytime tours are $22 adults, $17 children. The Opry performs at least two times a week, Friday and Saturday, with additional shows on Tuesday night most weeks.

Greater Nashville
★ Fontanel Mansion
The former estate of country music icon Barbara Mandrell, **Fontanel Mansion** (4125 Whites Creek Pike, 615/724-1600, www.fontanel.com, 9am-3pm daily, adults $24, seniors $22, children 7-15 $14, 6 and under free) has been a surprising draw for locals and tourists alike since it opened in 2010. These 136 acres include walking trails, a music venue, a restaurant with its own live music, an art gallery, and a gift shop. But the main attraction is the mansion, a 27,000-square-foot log cabin, which is the city's only country music mansion tour. Fans get to see how the

most famous of the Mandrell sisters once lived. Tours are sometimes given by Mandrell's daughter, who throws in lots of personal tidbits. Even those who don't love "I Was Country When Country Wasn't Cool" will appreciate the music history, artifacts such as Gretchen Wilson's "Redneck Woman" Jeep, the indoor shooting range, and the bucolic scenery.

Tours
NashTrash Tour

Nashville's most notorious tour guides are Sheri Lynn and Brenda Kay Jugg, sisters who ferry good-humored tourists around town in a big pink school bus. The **NashTrash Tour** (615/226-7300 or 800/342-2123, www.nashtrash.com, $33-36) is a raunchy, rollicking, rib-tickling tour of city attractions, some of which you won't even find in this guidebook. Be prepared to be the butt of some of the jokes yourself. Its "I Got Trashed" T-shirts have a double meaning. You'll snack on canned cheese, and there's a pit stop to buy beer. Not appropriate for children or adults who aren't comfortable laughing at themselves and others. As Sheri Lynn says, "If we haven't offended you, just give us some time." NashTrash Tours sell out early and often. If you think you want this perspective of the city, make your reservation now. Tours depart from the Nashville Farmers Market.

Gray Line Tours

Nashville's largest tour company, **Gray Line** (2416 Music Valley Dr., 615/883-5555 or 800/251-1864, http://graylinetn.com) offers more than 12 different sightseeing tours of the city. The three-hour Discover Nashville tour costs $49 per adult and includes entrance to the Ryman Auditorium and the Country Music Hall of Fame, and stops at other city landmarks.

The 3.5-hour Homes of the Stars tour takes you past the domiciles of country stars, including Jack White, Taylor Swift, Dolly Parton, and others for $49. There is also a hop-on, hop-off double-decker tour for $39 (children $20) and a 2.5-hour Nashville Walking Food tour ($49).

General Jackson Showboat

Gaylord Opryland's **General Jackson Showboat** (2812 Opryland Dr., 615/458-3900, http://generaljackson.com, tickets $45-135) offers campy, big-budget-style musical shows on the stage of a giant riverboat as it lumbers down the Cumberland River. Show dates and times vary by season, but typically there are midday lunch and evening dinner cruises. A smaller boat, the *Music City Queen,* offers tailgating cruises before Tennessee Titans NFL football games. Because of the meal and the live entertainment, these cruises aren't necessarily the best way to see the river, as you're focused on the stage rather than the scenery.

Nashville Pedal Tavern

Have 15 friends and a taste for beer? Then the **Nashville Pedal Tavern** (1516 Demonbreun St., 615/390-5038, www.nashvillepedaltavern.com, 11:30am-11pm daily, $380 Sun., $350 Mon.-Wed., $300 Thurs., $400 Fri.-Sat.) is for you. You board what is basically a giant group bicycle and pedal together to move forward through downtown or midtown, stopping at various pubs on the route. Members of your party pass out food and drink while you pedal. Each tour includes two or three pub stops; at each spot there's a special for Pedal Tavern customers. Expect to be photographed by people on the street as you ride by.

River Queen Voyages

Choose between several different kayak tours down the Cumberland River with **River Queen Voyages** (1900 Davidson St., 615/933-9778, http://rqvoyages.com, hours vary May-Oct., $29-79). The three-mile guided tour starts in Shelby

Bottoms Greenway, winding under railway bridges, and ending downtown with the skyline in sight. The four-mile, two-hour option takes you from Opryland to Shelby Bottoms.

Walk Eat Nashville

Former *Tennessean* editor Karen-Lee Ryan started her **Walk Eat Nashville** (locations disclosed upon reservation, 615/587-6138, www.walkeatnashville. com, 12:30pm-3:30pm Wed. 1:30pm-4:30pm Thurs., 11am-2pm Fri., 1:30-4:30pm Sat., $53-58) walking culinary tours as a way to show off her neighborhood of East Nashville. They were so popular, she soon expanded to midtown and downtown. The walking tours include food tastings at six restaurants and artisan food shops. Ryan and her informative guides narrate as you walk (and taste) and you get the benefit of her considerable knowledge of the city. You'll leave satisfied, but not full.

Tennessee Central Railway

The **Tennessee Central Railway Museum** (220 Willow St., 615/244-9001, www.tcry. org) offers an annual calendar of sightseeing and themed railway rides in central Tennessee, including kids' trips, Old West shoot-outs, and murder mysteries. Excursions include fall foliage tours, Christmas shopping expeditions, and trips to scenic small towns. All trips run on the Nashville and Eastern Railroad, which runs east, stopping in Lebanon, Watertown, Cookville, or Monterrey. Prices vary based on the trip but run $32-180 for adults.

These tours are not just train rides, but well-organized volunteer-led events. You might get "robbed" by a Wild West bandit (the cash goes to charity) or taken to a scenic winery. The volunteers know their railroad trivia, so feel free to ask questions. The cars vary depending on what is available, but one car doubles as a gift shop and another is a concession stand, although you are welcome to bring your own food on the train. Trips sell out early, so book your tickets well in advance.

Entertainment and Events

From live music to theater, Nashville offers visitors plenty of diversions. Even if you are not a fan of country music, you will find plenty to do in Music City.

Live Music Venues

No trip to Nashville is complete without listening to some live music. Music City overflows with musicians and opportunities to hear them. So whether you catch a show at the Opry, stake out a seat at The Bluebird Café, or enjoy a night at the symphony, be sure to make time for music during your visit.

Even before you arrive in the city, you can plan out your nights, thanks to the **Nashville Convention and Visitors Bureau** (www.nashvillecvb.com). Through a handy feature on the bureau's website you can check out upcoming concerts a month or more in advance. Many venues will let you buy tickets in advance over the phone or online. But don't panic if you can't plan ahead. Because there are so many shows, there is always something that hasn't sold out.

Published on Wednesday, the *Nashville Scene* provides detailed entertainment listings and recommendations. The *Nashville Tennessean,* the city's daily paper, publishes its entertainment insert on Friday. **Now Playing Nashville** (www. nowplayingnashville.com) is a great resource for both entertainment listings and discounted tickets. Now Playing Nashville has a kiosk in the Nashville airport.

★ Grand Ole Opry

If there's any one thing you really must do while in Nashville, it's go to see the **Grand Ole Opry** (2804 Opryland Dr.,

The Origins of the Grand Ole Opry

Nashville's most famous broadcast can trace its roots to October 1925, when Nashville-based National Life and Accident Insurance Company opened a radio station in town. Its call letters (then and now), WSM, stood for "We Shield Millions," the company's motto.

WSM hired George D. "Judge" Hay, a radio announcer who had worked in Memphis and Chicago, to manage the station. Hay—who, while in Chicago, had announced one of the nation's first live country radio shows—planned to create a similar program in Nashville.

On November 25, 1925, Hay invited a 78-year-old fiddler, Uncle Jimmy Thompson, to perform live on Saturday night over the radio airwaves. The response was electric, and WSM continued to broadcast live old-time music every Saturday night. In May 1927, Hay was segueing from the previous program of classical opera to the barn dance, and he came up with the famous name: "For the past hour, we have been listening to music taken largely from Grand Opera. From now on, we will present the Grand Ole Opry," he said. The name stuck.

During the first few years, most Opry performers were unknowns. But as the show gained popularity, some acts were able to make it professionally, including Uncle Dave Macon, the Vagabonds, and the Delmore Brothers. By 1939, the Opry gained a slot on the NBC radio network, allowing it to reach a national audience.

615/871-6779 or 800/733-6779, www. opry.com, $37-77). Really. Even if you think you don't like country music. For more than 90 years this weekly radio showcase of country music has drawn crowds to Nashville. Every show at the Opry is still broadcast live on WSM, a Nashville AM radio station. Shows are also streamed online, and some are televised on cable. But nothing beats the experience of being there.

The Opry runs Tuesday through Saturday nights, with two shows (7pm, 9:30pm) on Saturday. Shows start and end right on time.

Every Opry show is divided into 30-minute segments, each of which is hosted by a different member of the Opry. This elite country music fraternity includes dozens of stars that you've heard of and others you haven't. The host performs two songs—one at the beginning of his or her half-hour segment and one at the end. In between the host will introduce two or three other performers, each of whom will sing about two songs. In between segments, the announcers read radio commercials and stagehands change around the stage set.

It's a fast-paced show that keeps your toes tapping. Even when the biggest stars appear on the Opry stage, they rarely sing more than a few numbers. Fans are welcomed, and even encouraged, to walk to the front of the seating area to take photographs during the performances.

The Opry usually releases the full lineup for each show about a week in advance. Some fans wait until then to buy their tickets so they're sure to catch a big-name artist. The best advice is to buy tickets to any show at all. Each show is carefully balanced to include bluegrass, classic country, popular country, and, sometimes, gospel or rock. It's a true showcase that music and Americana fans will enjoy.

Most Opry shows take place in the Grand Ole Opry House, a 4,400-seat auditorium. A circle of the original stage from the Ryman Auditorium was cut out and placed in the center of the Opry House stage, and it's here that artists perform. During the Christmas season the Opry returns to its Ryman roots (and the Radio City Rockettes take the Opry House stage).

Tickets for the Opry House's guided

backstage tour (adults $27, children $22) go on sale two weeks in advance; times vary based on the time of year and day. The tours include a peek at the Green Room, Opry stars' mailboxes, and other behind-the-scenes treasures. If you book one of the evening tours, you're likely to see performers jamming in folding chairs after a show. Glitzy costumes, juicy stories, and a chance to walk on that stage are all part of the tour offerings. It's also possible to book combination packages that include the backstage tour, an Opry performance, and accommodations and meals at the Gaylord Opryland Resort.

Ascend Amphitheatre

This open-air concert venue offers the chance to rock out by the river in Metro Riverfront Park. Between folding seats, box seats, and the lawn, it can hold 6,800 concert-goers, all of whom get a view of the skyline and great sightlines of the stage. **Ascend Amphitheatre** (310 1st Ave. S., 615/999-9000, www.ascendamphitheater.com, hours and cost vary by event) is the place to see a big show, with big-name national acts on the schedule as well as the Nashville Symphony. Locals have been known to picnic nearby to listen to shows without being inside.

Texas Troubadour Theatre

Known as the Texas Troubadour, Ernest Tubb started a tradition when he set up a live radio show at the back of his Broadway record shop. The **Ernest Tubb's Midnite Jamboree** was broadcast after the Opry shut down across the street, and it lived up to its name. The Jamboree continues, now broadcast from the **Texas Troubadour Theatre** (Music Valley Village, 2416 Music Valley Dr., 615/889-2472, http://etrecordshop.com, no cover). Located across the street from the Gaylord Opryland Resort, the Jamboree gets started early in the evening, while the Opry is still on, but things really get swinging after midnight.

The Texas Troubadour Theatre is also home to the **Cowboy Church** (2416 Music Valley Dr., 615/859-1001, http://nashvillecowboychurch.org). Every Sunday at 10am, locals and tourists dressed in anything from shorts to Stetsons gather here for a lively praise-and-worship country gospel church service led by Dr. Harry Yates and Dr. Joanne Cash Yates. The church was founded in 1990 with just six souls; today it attracts hundreds to its weekly services. Country and gospel music legends make cameo performances now and again, but the real star is Jesus.

Ryman Auditorium

The most famous music venue in Nashville, the **Ryman Auditorium** (116 5th Ave. N., 615/889-3060, http://ryman.com, cover varies) continues to book some of the best acts in town, of just about every genre you can imagine. In 2015, a $14 million renovation gave the Ryman a café, better entrances and ticket areas, and a revamped backstage tour. The hall still boasts some of the best acoustics around, but the pew-style bench seats are just as uncomfortable as ever. Seeing the reverence performers have for this venue makes it hard to notice anything else. Musicians love to show off the acoustics here, often playing a song or two without a mic.

Country Music Hall of Fame

The **Country Music Hall of Fame** (222 5th Ave. S., 615/416-2100, http://countrymusichalloffame.org) hosts concerts, readings, and musical discussions regularly in an auditorium located inside the hall. These daytime events are often aimed at highlighting one type of country music or another, but sometimes you'll find big names playing. Entry is free with your paid admission to the hall, so it is a good idea to plan your trip to the hall on a day when there's a concert scheduled (separate admission to concerts is not typically available). Check the website for a listing of upcoming events.

Carl Black Chevy Woods Amphitheater

Opened in 2010, this 4,500-seat outdoor concert venue is nestled, as its name suggests, in the woods at Fontanel, a spot that used to be the home of country star Barbara Mandrell. The **Carl Black Chevy Woods Amphitheater** (4225 Whites Creek Pk., 615/727-0304, www.fontanel. com) has space for picnicking on the lawn during a concert and VIP boxes, as well as folding chairs for a more traditional concert experience. Fontanel often operates free shuttles to and from downtown, for those who don't want to drive to Whites Creek for a concert. This can be a bonus, as the driveway to the parking lot can get congested.

Marathon Music Works

The 14,500 square feet at **Marathon Music Works** (1402 Clinton St., 615/891-1781, www.marathonmusicworks.com, prices vary by event) are some of Nashville's most progressive when it comes to concert-going. Located in the historic Marathon Village, this venue has exposed brick, a swanky VIP loft area, multiple bars, and plenty of space for cutting the rug. Musical acts booked run the gamut from The Black Belles to the Yonder Mountain String Band.

★ The Bluebird Café

No other music venue is as quintessentially Nashville as **The Bluebird Café** (4104 Hillsboro Pike, 615/383-1461, http://bluebirdcafe.com, cover varies). It's intimate and homey. It books some of the best up-and-coming country and acoustic acts in the business, as well as the songwriters who penned the lyrics you are used to hearing other people sing. There is no talking during the acts and virtually none of the usual bar pickup scene. In short, The Bluebird is a place where music comes first and everything else is a distant second.

Opened in 1982 by Amy Kurland, The Bluebird is located in a nondescript shopping mall a few miles south of Hillsboro Village. While it started out as a casual restaurant with live music, over the years it evolved into a destination for music lovers who appreciate its no-nonsense take on live music, and who hope that they just might stumble onto the next big thing. The Bluebird is famous as an early venue for then-unknown Garth Brooks, but its stage has also hosted the likes of Emmylou Harris, Kathy Mattea, Gillian Welch, Trisha Yearwood, and Steve Earle.

The Bluebird is open every night of the week, and most evenings the entertainment starts at 6pm. Cover is usually under $15. There are just 20 tables and a few additional seats at the bar, so, depending on the show, you have to be on your toes to get a spot. Reservations are only taken online and are in high demand. Generally, reservations open about three weeks before the date. Some shows are first-come, first-seated only.

Once you've successfully nabbed a seat at The Bluebird, sit back and enjoy some fine live music (but really, no talking—you will be shushed). Lines have always been long, but since the show *Nashville* first aired, they're even longer.

Concert Series

Thursday nights in August and September transform downtown's Public Square Park for **Live on the Green** (www. liveonthegreen.com, free). The outdoor concert series tends to attract indie rock acts, and the crowd is young, hip, and socially aware. Food and arts and crafts vendors line the sidewalks under tents.

Also taking place on Thursday nights in the summer, **Bluegrass Nights at the Ryman** (116 5th Ave. N., 615/889-3060, http://ryman.com/bluegrass, 7:30pm Thurs. late June-late July, $29.50) is a concert series that features some of the best pickers in the country. Starting in June and ending in July, this Ryman Auditorium series is always popular.

Held in early summer and early fall,

Let's Go Honky-Tonkin'

It may be known locally as honkytonk, honky tonk, or honky-tonk, and it may be used as a noun (a bar that plays Western swing, where people dance), a verb (dancing to Western swing), or an adjective (a descriptor of the type of music), but one thing is for sure, in Nashville honky-tonk is what makes Music City sing.

These bars are across the city, but the main strip is found along lower Broadway in the heart of downtown. They play a specific strain of country and western swing music, with a live band. Small or large, these venues all have some empty space to cut the rug, because dancing is an essential part of Nashville honky-tonk.

The best places to go honky-tonking include: **Tootsie's Orchid Lounge, Nudie's Honky Tonk, Legends Corner,** and **Robert's Western World.** Most of these establishments are open to all ages during the day but convert to 21 and over after 6pm. They typically don't have a cover charge, although when the cowboy hat is passed for the band, don't forget to drop a few dollars in.

Musicians Corner (2500 West End Ave., http://musicianscornernashville.com, 11am-5pm Sat. summer-fall, free) is a concert series at an eponymous location inside Centennial Park. There's some permanent seating in the form of stone benches, but most people bring blankets and camp chairs and hang for the day. Food trucks and kids' activities are on-site, but the focus is the music.

Nightlife
Clubs
Most bars and clubs (except for honky-tonks) charge a cover when there is a performer, while songwriter nights and open mics are usually free.

Country
Nashville's most colorful country music establishments are the honky-tonks that line Broadway. These all-day, all-night bars and music clubs cater to visitors, who take advantage of the high energy, cheap beer, and talented musicians found here. Whether you're looking for a place to drown your sorrows or kick off a night on the town, Broadway's honky-tonks are a good place to go. They are always open and typically free, although you are encouraged to contribute when the hat is passed for the band.

Tootsie's Orchid Lounge (422 Broadway, 615/726-0463, www.tootsies.net, 10am-3am daily, no cover) is a painted purple and exudes classic country every day of the week beginning as early as 10am. Three doors down from Tootsie's is **Robert's Western World** (416 Broadway, 615/244-9552, www.robertswesternworld.com, 11am-2am daily, no cover), voted the city's best honky-tonk. Originally a store selling boots, cowboy hats, and other country music regalia, Robert's morphed into a bar and nightclub with a good gift shop. Another choice is **The Stage on Broadway** (412 Broadway, 615/726-0504, www.thestageonbroadway.com, 11am-3am daily, no cover), with a large dance floor and music every night.

Memorabilia of Nashville's past adorns the walls at **Legends Corner** (428 Broadway, 615/248-6334, http://legendscorner.com, 10am-3am daily, no cover), a popular and authentic club for live music and rollicking crowds.

Nudie's Honky Tonk (409 Broadway, www.nudieshonkytonk.com, 11am-3am daily) might be one of the newer honky-tonks on Lower Broad, but it has a serious connection to the past. Owned by the same folks who opened the Johnny Cash Museum, this bar celebrates all things Nudie Cohn. Nudie was the tailor who made suits for Johnny Cash and Elvis, among others. The bar is also a museum, with many of Nudie's famous works behind glass and one of his ostentatious cars, a $400,000 Cadillac El Dorado, hanging from the wall.

Mega country star Alan Jackson bought one of Lower Broad's long-time honky-tonks, The Wheel, and opened **AJ's Good Time Bar** (421 Broadway, 615/678-4808, www.ajsgoodtimebar.com, 1pm-3am Mon.-Wed., 11am-3am Thurs.-Sun.) in 2016. The honky-tonk, named after one of Jackson's popular songs, features a focus on country music.

The **Wildhorse Saloon** (120 2nd Ave. N., 615/902-8200, http://wildhorsesaloon. com, 4:30pm-close Mon., 11am-close Tues.-Sun., cover varies) is a boot-scoo-tin', beer-drinkin' place to see and be seen that's occupied almost exclusively by tourists. The huge dance floor is often packed with cowboys and cowgirls line dancing to the greatest country hits. Free dance lessons are offered every day (times vary by season). The Wildhorse books big-name acts many nights of the week, including country music, roots rock, and classic rock stars. From 10pm on, the Wildhorse is a 21-and-over club. The Wildhorse is owned by Gaylord, the same folks who own the Ryman, Opryland, and the Opry, and often offers deals for hotel guests. There is a shuttle back to the Opryland Hotel for folks staying there.

It doesn't look like much from the outside, but inside this cinder block box is the city's most popular venue for bluegrass and roots music, **The Station Inn** (402 12th Ave. S., 615/255-3307, www.stationinn.com, 7pm-midnight daily, cover varies). There is no cover for the Sunday-night bluegrass jam. Monday nights feature the Time Jumpers, a world-class Western swing jam band. Most Tuesday nights the hilarious parody act **The Doyle & Debbie Show** (www.doyleanddebbie. com, $20) takes the stage. This homey and casual club opens nightly at 7pm, with music starting about 9pm. This is a 21-and-over club, unless you come with a parent or guardian. There is no cover for the Sunday-night bluegrass jam.

The **Nashville Palace** (2611 McGavock Pike, 615/889-1540, http://nashville-palace.com, no cover) is a restaurant, nightclub, and dance floor across from the Opryland Hotel. Live music is on tap daily starting at 11am Monday through Saturday and noon Sunday.

Jazz and Blues
If you need to get that country twang out of your head, a good dose of the Memphis blues will do it. **B. B. King's Blues Club** (152 2nd Ave. N., 615/256-2727, http:// bbkings.com/nashville, 11am-midnight Sun.-Thurs., 11am-1am Fri.-Sat., cover varies) is a good place to start for a night of the blues. The club is a satellite of King's original Beale Street club in Memphis, and it books blues acts every night. The cover charge is usually under $10.

In Printer's Alley, the **Bourbon Street Blues and Boogie Bar** (220 Printer's Alley, 615/242-5867, www.bourbonstreetbluesandboogiebar.com, 11am-3am daily, cover varies) is a hole-in-the-wall nightclub that specializes in New Orleans-style jazz and blues.

While not a club per se, the **Nashville Jazz Workshop** (1319 Adams St., 615/242-5299, www.nashvillejazz.org, cover varies) has live performances in its Jazz Cave as well as at special events around town. Ticket prices are typically modest.

Eclectic
Clubs listed here may book a rock band one night and folk the next. Always check the free weekly *Nashville Scene* for the latest entertainment listings.

The **Exit/In** (2208 Elliston Pl., 615/321-3340, www.exitin.com, ticket prices vary) has been a favorite rock music venue for years, although it also books alternative country, blues, and reggae. Located on Elliston Place, the club is convenient to Vanderbilt and downtown.

Coffee shop by day, bar and live music

venue by night, **Café Coco** (210 Louise Ave., 615/321-2626, http://cafecoco.com, 24 hours daily, cover varies) in Elliston Place is the best of both worlds. Tuesday and Thursday are singer-songwriter nights. Jazz and rock bands play other nights.

The Basement (1604 8th Ave. S., 615/254-8006, http://thebasementnashville.com, cover varies) calls itself a cellar full of noise, but it's a good kind of noise. Indie rock is the most common art form here, but it books other types of acts, too. The Basement's "New Faces Nite" on Tuesday is a popular place to hear singer-songwriters. Admission is 21 and over, unless accompanied by a parent or guardian. The brick walls and subterranean feel give The Basement its cool atmosphere. It is nestled under **Grimey's New and Preloved Music,** one of the city's best record stores. Park behind the club and on side streets. In 2015 the team behind The Basement expanded into East Nashville with **The Basement East** (917 Woodland 8th Ave. S., 615/645-9174, http://thebasementnashville.com, cover varies). This venue quickly became one of the city's leading places to hear new and non-country music, and it's open seven days a week. Parking is at a premium in this area; park at the Fireman's Credit Union or East Nashville Self Storage.

Located in an old warehouse that has housed a flour mill, jam factory, and country music concert hall, **Cannery Ballroom** (1 Cannery Row, 615/251-3020, www.mercylounge.com, cover varies) and its derivative **Mercy Lounge** are two cool venues for live music. Cannery Ballroom is a large, somewhat cavernous space with lots of nice cherry-red touches, hardwood floors, and a shiny red bar. It can hold up to 1,000 people. The Mercy Lounge upstairs is a bit more intimate, with a capacity of up to 500 people. The Mercy Lounge hosts 8 Off 8th on Monday nights, an open-mic event, where eight different bands get to perform three songs. Both venues book rock, country,

soul, and all sorts of other acts. It is off 8th Avenue South.

A neighborhood bar and grill, **3rd and Lindsley** (818 3rd Ave. S., 615/259-9891, www.3rdandlindsley.com, cover varies) showcases rock, alternative, progressive, Americana, soul, and R&B music. Over the years it has developed a reputation for booking good blues acts. It serves a full lunch and dinner menu, the bar is well stocked, and the club offers a great atmosphere and sound quality. Most Monday nights host The Time Jumpers, a Western swing band including Vince Gill and many more talented musicians.

The **Douglas Corner Café** (2106-A 8th Ave. S., 615/298-1688, http://douglascorner.com, generally 6pm-midnight, cover varies) offers a Tuesday open-mic night and country and other acts the rest of the week. It is known as a place where singer-songwriters are discovered, and it is laid-back in both attitude and ambience. An intimate setting, full menu, and good acoustics make this a popular choice for music listening. Several live albums have been recorded here.

Yes, **The City Winery** (609 Lafayette St., 615/324-1010, www.citywinery.com/nashville, 5pm-11pm Mon.-Thurs., 5pm-midnight Fri., 10:30am-2pm and 5pm-midnight Sat., 10:30am-2pm and 5pm-11pm Sun., ticket prices vary) live music venue/restaurant/wine bar is a chain (it has locations in Chicago, New York, Atlanta, and Boston). But it's the brainchild of Michael Dorf, who created the iconic Knitting Factory club earlier in his career, which means that the musical lineup is impressive. Tickets typically include seating, so you can eat and drink and not crane your neck to see the act; dining begins two hours prior to showtime. This isn't a place where people generally get up and dance.

Bars

Barhopping is best enjoyed downtown, where there is the greatest concentration of nightclubs, restaurants, and bars.

Even on weeknights lower Broadway and its side streets are crowded with people. This is the official entertainment district of Nashville, and it is well patrolled by police. Outside of downtown, several other enclaves of nightlife cater more to residents than visitors.

Nashville won't issue a liquor license unless the establishment also serves food, so all of the bars in this section double as restaurants.

Downtown

A few blocks from downtown, near the Frist Center for the Visual Arts, you'll find one of the city's best beer bars. Behind the Union Station Hotel on the west side of downtown, the **Flying Saucer** (111 10th Ave. S., 615/259-3039, www. beerknurd.com, 11am-2am Mon. and Fri.-Sat., 11am-1am Tues.-Thurs., noon-midnight Sun., no cover) has one of the best selections of beer in town. Monday is pint night, when you can get $3.50 pints of just about any of the beers on the wall.

Midtown

Elliston Place is home to college hangouts (thanks to its location just blocks from Vanderbilt), several live music clubs, and a few neighborhood bars. **The Gold Rush** (2205 Elliston Pl., 615/321-1160, www. goldrushnashville.com, 11am-3am daily, no cover) is a time-worn but beloved late-night mellow hangout.

Cabana (1910 Belcourt Ave., 615/577-2262, www.cabananashville.com, 4pm-midnight Mon.-Sat., 4pm-10pm Sun., no cover) is a popular, if trendy, place to people-watch and unwind. It is a bar/restaurant/late-night hangout that attracts a youthful and well dressed crowd. Lounge at the bar or in the expansive backyard. Choose from dozens of beers, wines, and some excellent martinis. There is a $250 minimum for cabana seating on Friday

Top to bottom: The Station Inn; The City Winery; Patterson House.

and Saturday nights; advanced reservations are required.

There's no sign on the exterior, but that hasn't kept people across the country from discovering **Patterson House** (1711 Division St., 615/636-7724, http://thepattersonnashville.com, 5pm-1am Mon.-Wed., 5pm-3am Thurs.-Sat., no cover). Cocktails are mixed with care, and there's no standing room. You must have a seat in order to be served, both of which contribute to a civilized cocktail hour.

Near the Mall at Green Hills, **Greenhouse Bar** (2211 Bandywood Dr., 615/385-3357, www.thefoodcompanynashville.com/green-house-bar, 4pm-3am Fri.-Sun., no cover) offers specialty drinks, beers, and lots of hanging plants. To find it, look for the Green Hills Kroger and take a left. Its location means you'll find more locals than tourists.

Built in the steam room of an old laundry, **Old Glory** (1200 Villa Pl. #103, 615/679-0509, 4pm-1am Sun.-Thurs., noon-2am Fri.-Sat.) is one of the most striking bars in the city. It can be tricky to find the entrance (in the alley-like corridor of Edgehill Village, behind Taco Mamacita), but when you get there, you'll see it was worth the exploration. Order a carefully crafted seasonal cocktail plus a few smart appetizers, such as *harissa* carrots with leeks and goat cheese ($9).

East Nashville

Edgefield Sports Bar & Grille (921 Woodland St., 615/228-6422, 3pm-3am Mon., 11am-3am Tues.-Sat., 3pm-midnight Sun., no cover) is a no-frills watering hole that caters to East Nashville residents.

No. 308 (407 Gallatin Ave., 615/650-7344, http://bar308.com, 5pm-3am, no cover) is a sleek, mod, hipster hangout with hand-crafted drinks. Come during happy hour (5pm-7pm Sun.-Fri.), when these custom cocktails are more budget-friendly. A small taco bar menu pairs with the drinks.

Another Nashville mixology house that has received national attention, **Holland House Bar & Refuge** (935 W. Eastland Ave., 615/262-4190, www.hollandhousebarandrefuge.com, 4pm-10pm Mon.-Thurs., 4pm-midnight Fri.-Sat., no cover) specializes in handmade, old-fashioned cocktails. The bar stocks an impressive selection of whiskey and bourbon, and it hires bartenders who know how to use them.

You might think you're south of the border at the **Rosepepper Cantina** (1907 Eastland Ave., 615/227-4777, www.rosepepper.com, 11am-2pm and 4pm-9:30pm Mon.-Thurs., 11am-10:30pm, Fri.-Sat., 11am-9:30pm Sun., no cover), a Mexican restaurant and bar. Choose from 30 different variations of the margarita, and enjoy the house band on weekend nights.

12 South

Snag a seat on the crowded patio outside **Mafiaoza's Pizzeria and Neighborhood Pub** (2400 12th Ave. S., 615/269-4646, www.mafiaozas.com, 4pm-3am Tues.-Fri., 11am-3am Sat.-Sun., no cover), a popular neighborhood hangout known for its pizza, which you watch be slid into the giant ovens.

The extensive list of brews on tap has earned **12 South Taproom & Grill** (2318 12th Ave. S., 615/463-7552, http://12southtaproom.com, 11am-midnight daily) a loyal following. The above-average bar food includes several vegetarian-friendly options.

Gay and Lesbian Nightlife

You don't have to be gay to enjoy **Tribe** (1517-A Church St., 615/329-2912, http://tribenashville.com, 5pm-2am Sun.-Thurs., 5pm-3am Fri.-Sat., no cover), but it helps to be beautiful, or at least well dressed. The dance floor is one of the best in the city, and the atmosphere is hip. Martinis and other specialty drinks are the poison of choice at this standard-setting club, which stays open until the wee hours.

Right next door to Tribe is **Play** (1519 Church St., 615/322-9627, http://play-dancebar.com, 8pm-2:45am daily, cover varies), the city's highest-energy gay club, with drag shows and performances by adult-film stars.

Women outnumber men at the **Lipstick Lounge** (1400 Woodland St., 615/226-6343, www.thelipsticklounge.com, 5pm-1am Tues.-Fri., 10am-3am Sat.-Sun., cover varies), a cool yet homey club in East Nashville. Live music, pool, and great food attract a crowd nearly every night.

Comedy

If it's stand-up comedy you want, head to **Zanies** (2025 8th Ave. S., 615/269-0221, ticket prices vary), where you can hear stand-up comics every weekend and some weeknights. Doors open 30-90 minutes prior to show time. Opened in 2016, **Third Coast Comedy Club** (1310 Clinton St., 615/745-1009, www.third-coastcomedy.club, showtimes and prices vary) is a classic, dedicated comedy club with improv, sketches, and more.

There are many other spots to amuse you, including **The Doyle & Debbie Show** at **The Station Inn** (402 12th Ave. S., 615/255-3307, http://www.doyleand-debbie.com) and the **NashTrash Tour** (615/226-7300 or 800/342-2123, www.nashtrash.com, $33-36).

The Arts

Before Nashville was Music City, it was the Athens of the South, a city renowned for its cultural, academic, and artistic life. Universities, museums, and public arts facilities created an environment for artistic expression unparalleled by any other Southern city. It has an opera company of its own, not to mention an award-winning symphony (and symphony center), an innovative arts scene, and ample opportunities to sample contemporary and classic music, film, and theater.

Theater

Opened in 2013, **OZ Arts** (6172 Cockrill Bend Circ., 615/350-7200, www.ozartsnashville.org) is a 500-seat arts space in an off-the-beaten-track location, producing the city's most groundbreaking theater and dance. Many of the artists it brings to town are world-renowned disrupters. You won't see revivals of plays from your youth here.

The **Nashville Repertory Theatre** (505 Deaderick St., 615/782-4000, www.nashvillerep.org) is Tennessee's largest professional theater company. It stages five big-name shows plus the Ingram New Works project annually. The Rep performs in the Tennessee Performing Arts Center, located in the James K. Polk Cultural Center in downtown Nashville. This is the same building that houses the Tennessee State Museum, plus some Nashville Opera performances and the Nashville Ballet. Some of its productions have included *The Crucible, I Hate Hamlet,* and *Doubt.* The season runs October-May.

Artists' Cooperative Theatre (no phone, http://act1online.com), a.k.a. **ACT 1,** is an organization dedicated to bringing theatrical gems, both classic and modern, to Nashville audiences. Founded in 1989, ACT 1 has presented productions of more than 90 of the world's greatest plays. Each year the theater puts on four or five productions. ACT 1 performs at the Darkhorse Theater (4610 Charlotte Ave.).

New theatrical works are given the spotlight by the **Actors Bridge Ensemble** (Darkhorse Chapel, 4610 Charlotte Ave., 615/498-4077, http://actorsbridge.org), a theater company for new and seasoned actors. It brings provocative and new plays to Nashville, often performing at the Belmont Black Box Theater in midtown.

Circle Players (www.circleplayers.net) is the oldest nonprofit, all-volunteer arts association in Nashville. As it's a community theater, all actors, stagehands,

Famous Nashvillians

Nashville is used to celebrity, what with all the big-name music stars around. But it's not just musicians who call, or called, Nashville home:

- **"Jefferson Street Joe" Gilliam,** one of the first African American quarterbacks in the National Football League, played college ball at Tennessee State University. The former quarterback for the Pittsburgh Steelers died in 2000 in his hometown of Nashville, five days before his 50th birthday.

- **Madison Smartt Bell** was born and raised in Nashville. The novelist's works include *All Souls Rising, Ten Indians,* and *The Year of Silence.*

- **Oprah Winfrey** was raised in Nashville by her father, Vernon. In her second year at Tennessee State University she was hired as Nashville's first female and first African American news anchor at WTVF-TV.

- **Julian Bond,** civil rights activist, political activist, and the chairman of the NAACP, was born in Nashville and lived here until he was five years old.

- **Bobby Jones,** host of BET's *Bobby Jones Gospel,* was once a professor at Tennessee State University. The program is the longest-running show on cable television and is taped in Nashville.

- **Red Grooms** was born and raised in Nashville. Grooms is a prominent modern American artist whose pop art depicts frenetic scenes of urban life.

- **Carla Hall,** chef, TV's *Top Chef* fan favorite, and talk show host on *The Chew,* was born and raised in Nashville.

- **Reese Witherspoon** is an actress, producer, and entrepreneur who grew up in Nashville and considers it home. It's also the location of her first Draper James boutique.

- **Al Gore Jr.,** though born in Washington DC and raised in Carthage, Tennessee, is closely associated with Nashville. After the Vietnam War, he attended Vanderbilt University for one year and then spent five years as a reporter for the *Tennessean.* The former U.S. vice president has had a home in Nashville for many decades.

- Aussie actress **Nicole Kidman** may have moved to Nashville because of the career of her country-singing hubby, **Keith Urban,** but she has made it her own. She is frequently seen around town with her family.

directors, and other helpers are volunteers. The company stages four or five performances every year at theater locations around the city. Performances include classic theater, plus stage adaptations of popular cinema and literature.

Transplanted New Yorkers Theo Antoniadis and Veta Cicolello opened **Ovvio Arte** (425 S. Chestnut St., 615/838-5699, http://ovvioarte.com, hours vary) in 2008. This performance space and art gallery is a venue for the unexpected. It offers regular theater, dramatic readings, and art shows.

Children's Theater

Nashville Children's Theatre (25 Middleton St., 615/254-9103, www.nashvillechildrenstheatre.org) is the oldest children's theater company in the United States. During the school year, the company puts on plays for children from preschool to elementary-school age in its colorful theater. In the summer there are drama classes for youngsters, plus lots of activities that include Mom and Dad.

Don't miss the **Marionette Shows at the Nashville Public Library** (615 Church St., 615/862-5800). Using marionettes from the collection of former library puppeteer Tom Tichenor, plus others, the library's children's room staff put on excellent one-of-a-kind family entertainment. They also offer the Puppet Truck, run by Wishing Chair Productions, the library's puppet troupe.

Dinner Theater

Chaffin's Barn Dinner Theatre (8204 Hwy. 100, 615/646-9977, www.dinnertheatre.com, adults $43-56, children $21-29) was Nashville's first professional theater and continues to put on Broadway-style plays for dinner patrons. There's nothing cutting-edge about the shows or the meal, but they are family-friendly fun. The theater company changed owners in 2016 (for a $2 million price tag), and more productions are in the works.

Music

The **Nashville Symphony Orchestra** (1 Symphony Pl., 615/687-6400, www.nashvillesymphony.org) is housed in the remarkable Schermerhorn Symphony Center next to the Country Music Hall of Fame, one of the downtown buildings that was renovated as a result of 2010 flood damage. Nominated for four Grammy Awards and selling more recordings than any other American orchestra, the symphony is a source of pride for Music City. Costa Rican conductor Giancarlo Guerrero is the symphony's seventh music director.

The symphony puts on more than 200 performances each year, including classical, pops, and children's concerts. Its season spans September-May. Buying tickets online is a breeze, especially since you can easily choose where you want to sit. There is discounted parking for symphonygoers in the Pinnacle at Symphony Place, across the street from the Schermerhorn.

During the summer, the symphony plays its **Centennial Park Concert Series.** Head to the Centennial Park band shell to hear free big-band, ballroom, and classical concerts with other parkgoers. It is a classic Nashville experience.

The **Blair School of Music** (2400 Blakemore Ave., 615/322-7651) presents student, faculty, and visiting artist recitals frequently during the school year. Vanderbilt University's music school, Blair addresses music through academic, pedagogical, and performing activities.

Opera

Middle Tennessee's only opera company, the **Nashville Opera Association** (www.nashvilleopera.org) puts on an average of four main-stage performances per season (Oct.-Apr.) and does a six-week tour to area schools. They perform at the Tennessee Performing Arts Center (505 Deaderick St.) and the Noah Liff Opera Center (3622 Redmon St.).

Ballet

Founded in 1981 as a civic dance company, the **Nashville Ballet** (505 Deaderick St., www.nashvilleballet.com) became a professional dance company in 1986. Entertaining more than 40,000 patrons each year, the ballet performs both classical and contemporary pieces at the Tennessee Performing Arts Center (505 Deaderick St.).

Festivals and Events
January to March

There's only one day all year that the **Hermitage,** the home of Andrew Jackson (4580 Rachel's Ln., 615/889-2941, www.thehermitage.com, 9am-5pm daily) is free to the public, and that's to celebrate the former president's victory at the Battle of New Orleans. The free day is typically on a weekend closest to January 8.

More than 150 dealers set up in the Music City Center for the upscale **Antiques and Garden Show of Nashville** (201 Fifth Ave. S., 615/352-1282, http://antiquesandgardenshow.com, $20) in February. One of the largest such shows that combines indoor furniture and outdoor garden antiques, the event includes

The Hermitage

Andrew Jackson's plantation and home, 16 miles east of Nashville, is the area's best historical tourist attraction. The **Hermitage** (4580 Rachel's Ln., 615/889-2941, www.thehermitage.com, 9am-5pm daily, adults $20, seniors $17, students 13-18 $15, children 9-12 $10, active military and children 5 and under free) is where Jackson retired following his two terms as president of the United States, and it is where he and his beloved wife, Rachel, are buried.

Jackson bought the property in 1809; he and Rachel initially lived in a rustic log cabin, which has since been restored. Jackson ran a successful cotton plantation on the property, owning as many as 150 slaves. In 1819, he and Rachel started construction of what is now the mansion. They moved in two years later.

At the end of Jackson's second term in office in 1837, he retired to the Hermitage and lived here happily until his death in 1845. Following President Jackson's death, the Hermitage remained in family hands until 1853, when it was sold to the state of Tennessee to pay off the family's debts. It was restored and opened as a museum in 1889. Many of the furnishings are original, and even the wallpaper in several rooms dates back to the years when Jackson called it home.

The Hermitage tour and museum focus not only on Jackson and the construction and decoration of the mansion, but also on the African American slaves who worked at the Hermitage plantation, making no effort to gloss over some of Jackson's less-favorable legacies. Curators and archaeologists have studied the Hermitage to learn about the hundreds of men and women who made it profitable and successful for so many years. The tour of the grounds takes visitors to Alfred's Cabin, a slave cabin occupied until 1901 by former Hermitage slave Alfred Jackson. You also learn about the agriculture that took place on the plantation and can see cotton being cultivated during the summer. To learn even more about the Hermitage's slaves, take an add-on wagon tour, offered April-October ($10).

Even if you are not typically an audio-tour-type person, consider the one of the grounds, which includes a kids' version narrated by Jackson's pet parrot. Plan on spending at least three hours to make the most of your visit. Try to come when the weather is good.

workshops, demonstrations, and vintage finds to meet most budgets and tastes. Proceeds from the show benefit Cheekwood.

Many Nashville music events celebrate the performers. But the **Tin Pan South Songwriters Festival** (http://tinpansouth.com) honors the people who come up with the lyrics for all those great tunes. Typically held the last week of March, Tin Pan South, organized by the Nashville Songwriters Association International, schedules performances at venues across the city.

April to May
The **Country Music Television Music Awards** (www.cmt.com) was country music's first fan-voted awards show. Founded in 2002, the show lets fans participate in both the first and final rounds of voting. The show is broadcast live on television from Nashville, usually from the Bridgestone Arena.

Film lovers throughout the country look forward to the **Nashville Film Festival** (http://nashvillefilmfestival.org), held every April at Regal Hollywood Stadium 27 and RPX Nashville. The film festival was founded in 1969 as the Sinking Creek Film Celebration. These days, upwards of 20,000 people attend the weeklong event, which includes film screenings, industry panels, and lots of parties.

The **Rock 'n' Roll Nashville Marathon**

(www.runrocknroll.com) takes place every April. More than 15,000 professional and amateur runners take part, and tens of thousands more come out for the live music and cheer squads that line the racecourse. The postrace concert usually boasts nationally known country music artists.

Held in Centennial Park, the May **Tennessee Crafts Fair** (http://tennessee-crafts.org) showcases the work of more than 180 fine craftspeople. Some 45,000 people come to the three-day event every year, which also includes craft demonstrations, a food fair, and entertainment. The fair repeats in September.

For something a little different, plan to attend the **Iroquois Steeplechase** (www.iroquoissteeplechase.org) at Percy Warner Park. Taking place on the second Saturday of May, the race is the nation's oldest continuously run weight-for-age steeplechase in the country. Fans in sundresses or suspenders and hats enjoy watching some of the top horses in the country navigate the race course. You can pay for general admission to sit on the hillside overlooking the stadium. Pack a blanket, food, and drinks (and mud boots if it has rained recently), and you'll have an excellent day. Various tailgating tickets are available and are priced according to how good the view is from the parking spot. If you want to tailgate, you need to buy tickets well in advance.

June to August

What was once called Fan Fair and is now hosted by the Country Music Association and called the **CMA Music Festival** (www.cmaworld.com) is a four-day mega-music show in downtown Nashville. The stage at Riverfront Park along the Cumberland River is occupied by day with some of the top names in country music. At night the hordes move to Nissan Stadium to hear a different show every night. Four-day passes, which cost $200-400 per person, also give you access to the exhibit hall, where you can get autographs and meet up-and-coming country music artists, although there are plenty of free shows going on at the same time. This is one of Nashville's biggest events of the year, and you are wise to buy your tickets and book your hotel early. Get a room downtown so you don't need a car; parking and traffic can be a nightmare during the festival. Locals tend to steer clear of downtown during CMA Fest.

Early June sees Nashville's gay, lesbian, bisexual, and transgender community show its colors at the **Nashville Pride Festival** (www.nashvillepride.org), a two-day event at Public Square Park.

Independence Day (www.visitmusiccity.com/july4th) is celebrated in a big way with fireworks and a riverfront concert that's broadcast live on television. The event is free and attracts upwards of 100,000 people every year.

The **Music City Brewer's Festival** (www.musiccitybrewersfest.com) is a one-day event at the Music City Walk of Fame downtown. Come to taste local brews, learn about making your own beer, and enjoy good food and live music. Tickets are required, and the event usually sells out.

The temperature is almost always hot at the **Music City Hot Chicken Festival,** but so is the chicken. This east side event (http://hot-chicken.com/festival) is a feast of Nashville's signature spicy pan-fried dish.

The **Tomato Art Festival** (www.tomatoartfest.com) is a tongue-in-cheek celebration of tomatoes and the hip, artsy vibe of East Nashville. Events include a parade of tomatoes, the "Most Beautiful Tomato Pageant," biggest and smallest tomato contests, tomato toss, and Bloody Mary taste-off. The festival usually takes place on the second Saturday of August.

September to October

The Hermitage hosts **Fall Fest** (http://fallfestatthehermitage.com) every October, featuring art, music, and historically themed activities.

The **John Merritt Classic** (www.merrittclassic.com), held over Labor Day, starts with fashion shows and concerts, and culminates with a football contest between the Tennessee State University Tigers and another historically black collegiate football team. The annual showdown is named for legendary former TSU football coach John Ayers Merritt.

A multi-venue conference/music showcase, the **Americana Music Festival** (www.americanamusic.org), a.k.a. AmericanaFest, has become one of the city's most popular events. Professionals (musicians, songwriters, producers, and more) come for the connections and the workshops during the day. Locals join them at night for concerts—more than 215 at 14 different venues—that show off the genre. There's an awards show and an end-of-week big budget concert at Ascend Amphitheatre.

Jubilee Day at Fisk University (http://fisk.edu) is held on October 6, the anniversary of the day the Fisk Jubilee Singers set out in 1871 to raise funds for their school. The day includes a convocation and free concert, free admission at the Carl Van Vechten Gallery, and a pilgrimage to the singers' tombstones. This is one of the most powerful events in the city, and shouldn't be missed if you are in town on October 6.

November to December
The **Franklin American Mortgage Music City Bowl** (www.musiccitybowl.com) pits a Southeastern Conference team against a Big Ten rival. This nationally televised football game is held at Nissan Stadium and typically includes a night-before free concert downtown.

New Year's Eve near downtown Nashville at Bicentennial Mall, called **Music City Midnight** (www.visitmusiccity.com/newyearseve) includes—what else?—a music note drop. This is one of the biggest celebrations in the country, with big crowds and lots of free outdoor fun. It has been part of the national program *Dick Clark's New Year's Rockin' Eve*. Mega acts like Kings of Leon and Keith Urban play free concerts.

Shopping

You'll find many good reasons to shop in Nashville. Who can pass up Western wear in Music City? Fine boutiques cater to the well-heeled in tony West End. Downtown you'll find unique art and gifts. East Nashville is a mecca for those who crave handmade goods. Many of the museums have excellent gift shops.

Nashville's largest flea market takes place on the fourth Saturday of every month at the Tennessee State Fairgrounds. The **Tennessee State Fairgrounds Flea Market** (615/862-5016, www.thefairgrounds.com) is a bargain lover's dream, with thousands of sellers peddling clothes, crafts, and all sorts of vintage and used housewares, often at lower prices than you'd find in bigger cities. The fairgrounds are on 4th Avenue, south of downtown. Admission is free, but parking is $5.

Downtown
The Texas Troubadour, Ernest Tubb, founded his famous record store on Broadway in 1947. The **Ernest Tubb Record Shop** (417 Broadway, 615/255-7503, http://etrecordshop.com, 10am-10pm Sun.-Thurs., 10am-midnight Fri.-Sat.) remains a good source of classic and modern country music recordings, as well as DVDs, books, clothing, and souvenirs. At the back of the shop you can see the stage where Ernest Tubb's Midnite Jamboree was recorded and aired after the Grand Ole Opry on Saturday nights. The Jamboree still airs, but it's recorded at the Texas Troubadour Theatre in Music Valley.

After Ernest Tubb, the most famous place to shop in Nashville is **Hatch Show Print** (224 5th Ave. S., 615/256-2805,

Where to Stock Up for a Road Trip

If you're about to embark on the 444-mile trip down the Natchez Trace, you need to stock up. These are the best places in the area to find quality camping and hiking gear, waterproof supplies, water bottles, and everything else you need for hiking and other outdoor activities. The salespeople at these spots can offer tips about traveling on the Trace.

- **LifeView Outdoors** (2844 Logan St., 800/395-5433, http://lifeviewoutdoors. com, 9am-7am Mon., Wed., and Fri., 9am-5:30pm Tues. and Thurs., 10am-5pm Sat.)

- **Friedman's Army/Navy Surplus & Outdoors** (2101 21st Ave. S., 615/297-3343, 9am-6pm Mon.-Sat.)

- **Cumberland Transit** (2807 West End Ave., 615/321-4069, http://cumberlandtransit.com, 10am-6pm Mon.-Sat., noon-5pm Sun.)

- **Bass Pro Shops at Opry Mills** (323 Opry Mills Dr., 615/514-5200, http://basspro.com, 10am-9pm Mon.-Sat., 10am-7pm Sun.)

http://hatchshowprint.com, 9:30am-6pm Sun.-Wed., 9:30am-8pm Thurs.-Sat.). Hatch has been making colorful posters for more than a century, and its iconic letterpress style is now one of the trendiest looks in modern design. It continues to design and print handouts, posters, and T-shirts for local and national customers. Gaze at the cavernous warehouse operation and buy small or large samples of the shop's work, including reproductions of classic country music concert posters. This is a great place to find a special souvenir of your trip to Nashville or just see another part of Music City's history. Hatch posters are up all over town, including in the airport.

If you need clothes to fit the Nashville part, **Boot Country** (304 Broadway, 615/259-1691, 10am-10:30pm Mon.-Thurs., 10am-11pm Fri., 11am-7:30pm Sun.) specializes in all styles and sizes of cowboy boots and often offers a free pair of boots when you buy two pairs. It's popular with both tourists and locals for its deals. **Manuel Exclusive Clothier** (800 Broadway, 615/321-5444, http://manuelcouture.com, 10am-6pm Mon.-Fri.) is the Western wear designer to the stars. This is a clothing shop where cowboy shirts start at $750 and jackets at more than $2,000. This is where to go when you

want a custom outfit for your big stage debut.

Fire Finch (305 Church St., 615/385-5090, www.welovefirefinch.com, 10am-6pm Mon.-Sat., noon-5pm Sun.) is a sweet store known for trendy jewelry and accessories and a few home decor items.

As the neighborhood of Germantown has gentrified, boutiques have popped up left and right. **Abednego** (1210 4th Ave. N., 615/712-6028, 11am-6pm Tues.-Sat., noon-5pm Sun.) carries local- and American-made clothes and accessories. Owned by a local musician, Abednego stocks goods for men and women in a minimalist loft-like environment. Phillip Nappi, owner of **Peter Nappi** (1308 Adams St., 615/248-3310, www.peter-nappi.com/studio, 11am-6pm Mon.-Sat., 11am-3pm Sun.) has turned boot- and shoe-making into an art. The shop's studio is in Italy, where artisans create footwear in the old-world style in limited runs, with the highest quality vegetable-tanned leathers. There's a second location of this shop in 12 South.

New York transplants Ivy and Josh brought their interior design eyes to the South. The duo opened a Germantown atelier called **Wilder** (1212 4th Ave. N., 615/679-0008, www.wilderlife.com, 11am-6pm Mon.-Sat., noon-5pm Sun.)

to show off their transformational wares. Come browse the furnishing, textiles, lighting, mirrors, and more, all with a modern sensibility and many not found elsewhere in the area.

While downtown, check out the many art galleries. One of the most accessible and eclectic, **The Arts Company** (215 5th Ave. of the Arts, 615/254-2040, www. theartscompany.com, 11am-5pm Tues.-Sat.) offers outsider art, the works of local artists, and other contemporary works ranging from the avant-garde to the everyday. Perhaps the most cosmopolitan of all Nashville's galleries, **The Rymer Gallery** (233 5th Ave. of the Arts, 615/752-6030, www.therymergallery.com, 11am-5pm Tues.-Sat.) installs thought-provoking exhibits with works from artists of national renown. The Rymer is also home to Nashville's **Herb Williams** (www.herbwilliamsart.com), a gifted artist who creates sculpture from crayons. Williams's work has been on display in the White House and other prestigious addresses.

The upper level of **The Arcade** (http://thenashvillearcade.com), between 4th and 5th Avenues, houses several artist studios that open as galleries during downtown's monthly **Art Crawl,** which takes place the first Saturday of each month.

A boot is not just a boot—at least not in Nashville, where boots are a status symbol as much as footwear. And in a town that loves boots, people really love **Lucchese Boot Co.** (503 12th Ave. S., 615/242-1161, www.lucchese.com, 10am-7pm Mon.-Sat., noon-6pm Sun.). Pronounced "LU-kay-see," this brand has been around since 1883, but only since 2012 has it had its own retail shop in The Gulch.

Midtown

For new and used CDs, DVDs, and vinyl, go to **Grimey's New and Preloved Music** (1604 8th Ave. S., 615/254-4801, www. grimeys.com, 11am-8pm Mon.-Fri.,

10am-8pm Sat., 1pm-6pm Sun.). Here you'll find a wide selection of not just country, but rock, folk, blues, R&B, and other genres. The staff is knowledgeable and friendly.

If you want to *make* your own music, head to **Gruhn Guitars** (2120 8th Ave. S., 615/256-2033, http://guitars.com, 9:30am-6pm Mon.-Sat.), a guitar shop with one of the best reputations in the music world. Founded by guitar expert George Gruhn, the shop is considered by some to be the best vintage guitar shop in the world. Shiny guitars, banjos, mandolins, and fiddles look like candy hung up on the walls of the Broadway storefront, which serves both up-and-coming and established Nashville musicians.

Third Man Records (623 7th Ave. S., 615/891-4393, http://thirdmanrecords. com, 10am-6pm Mon.-Sat., 1pm-4pm Sun.) is a record label, recording studio, and record store all in one fairly small building. The idea behind the label is simple: All the music in the building has Jack White's stamp on it in some way. It's not a bad thing. Blue Series records are recorded by bands traveling through town, recording one or two songs, and are available on seven-inch vinyl. Green Series are nonmusical recordings, such as spoken word, poetry, or instructional discussions.

Owned by Grammy Award-winning songwriter Liz Rose and her daughter, **Castilleja** (1200 Villa Pl., Ste. 403, 615/730-5367, http://castillejanashville. com, 10am-6pm Mon.-Thurs., 10am-7pm Fri.-Sat., noon-4pm Sun.) brings a little taste of Texas to Tennessee. Expect to find home decor with a Lone Star twist, including blankets, leather goods, pillows, and lots of items made with turquoise and silver. The shop is nestled in the Edgehill Village complex.

Like old stuff? Check out the **Eighth Avenue Antique Mall** (2015 8th Ave. S., 615/279-9922, 10am-6pm Mon.-Sat., noon-5pm Sun.), which has lots of antiques dealers willing to part with their treasures.

At **Hey Rooster** (1711 21st Ave. S., www.heyrooster.com, 10am-6pm Mon.-Sat., 1pm-4pm Sun.), proprietor Courtney Webb stocks lovely handmade gifts from art to jewelry, plus prepared foods and ingredients, as well as a few books.

East Nashville

There are two collections of small boutiques in East Nashville, great for browsing for local goods. The bigger is the **Shoppes on Fatherland** (1006 Fatherland St., 615/227-8646, http://fatherland-district.com), which has art galleries, clothing shops, and even a place for fly-fishing gear. Also here is **Project 615** (www.project615.org, noon-6pm Sun.-Thurs., 11am-6pm Fri.-Sat.), which puts local landmarks like the Trace's Double Arch Bridge on t-shirts. The other collection of stores, **1108 Shops at Woodland,** includes the bookstore **East Side Story** (http://eastsidestorytn.com, 1pm-5pm Tues.-Fri., 11am-5pm Sat.), plus vintage clothing boutiques.

Two Son (918 Main St., 615/678-4953, http://twoson.co, 10am-7pm Tues.-Sat., 1pm-5pm Sun.) is an ultra hip, well-edited clothing and accessory shop. Come here for brands including Industry of All Nations and Norse Projects, and a serious minimalist vibe.

Joelle Herr has two decades of experience working in books. Her latest project is the 550-square-foot **Her Bookshop** (1035 W. Eastland Ave. #105, 615/485-5420, www.herbookshop.com, 11am-6pm Mon.-Fri., 11am-5pm Sat., noon-4pm Sun.), a carefully curated collection of paper between covers. The emphasis here is on "beautiful books," such as those that are illustrated, and fiction.

Music Valley

Shuttered for almost two years after the city's 2010 flood, the discount mall **Opry Mills** (433 Opry Mills Dr., 615/514-1000, http://simon.com; hours vary by store) in

Music Valley is the city's most maligned favorite destination. Locals love to hate it, in part because it replaced the old Opryland amusement park on this same site and, in part, because it is so popular—one of the area's leading tourist attractions—the lines for the parking lot back up along Briley Parkway. If you live near other national-brand outlet malls, you don't need to come here. But if good deals on name-brand merchandise appeal to you, or you are looking to kill time before a show at the Opry, Opry Mills is the mall for you. Brands include Old Navy, Disney, LEGO, Coach, Kate Spade, Ann Taylor, H&M, and Torrid. The mammoth Bass Pro Shops is a great place to get gear before heading out on the Trace. The famous wax museum **Madame Tussauds** (515 Opry Mills Dr., 212/512-9600, www.madametussauds.com/nashville, 10am-9pm daily, $19-43) opened an outpost in Opry Mills in 2017. As expected, it is chock-full of country music stars' likenesses and kitsch.

West End

Jamie (4317 Harding Pike, 615/292-4188, www.jamie-nashville.com, 10am-5:30pm Mon.-Fri., 10am-4:30pm Sat.) has long been the height of couture for Nashville women who want something without rhinestones. Go there for attentive service and killer shoes, but be prepared to pay for it.

Bargain-hunting fashionistas cannot skip **UAL** (2918 West End Ave., 615/340-9999, http://shopual.com, 9am-8pm Mon.-Fri., 10am-8pm Sat.-Sun.). Designer samples of clothes, handbags, shoes, and jewelry are shoved onto crowded racks in this shop near the Vanderbilt campus. UAL stocks both men's and women's clothing, but the women's selection is significantly larger. There's a second location in Hillsboro Village (1814 21st Ave. S., 615/540-0211, 10am-8pm Mon.-Fri., 9am-8pm Sat.-Sun.).

South Nashville

Find fine crystal, tableware, jewelry, and other upscale housewares at **AshBlue** (2170 Bandywood Dr., 615/383-4882, www.ashblue.com, 10am-6pm Mon.-Sat.). This sophisticated shop is perfect for bridal registries, housewarming gifts, or that special touch for your home or office.

Owned by famous singer-songwriter Holly Williams (granddaughter of Hank), **White's Mercantile** (2908 12th Ave. S., 615/750-5379, http://whitesmercantile.com, 10am-6pm Mon.-Sat., noon-5pm Sun.) is a modern general store stocked with high-end gifts, home decor, artsy trinkets, and kitchenware. Williams says she seeks inspiration for the shop when she's out on the road.

Celebrities like Gwyneth Paltrow love 12 South's **Imogene + Willie** (2601 12th Ave. S., 615/292-5005, http://imogeneandwillie.com, 10am-6pm Mon.-Fri., 11am-6pm Sat., 1pm-5pm Sun.). The shop carries clothes for men and women, but its specialty is custom-fit blue jeans at a price tag of $200 and up.

Nashville native Reese Witherspoon launched the flagship location of her shop/lifestyle brand **Draper James** (2608 12th Ave. S., 615/997-3601, www.draperjames.com, 10am-6pm Mon.-Wed., 10am-7pm Thurs.-Sat., 11am-5pm Sun.) in her hometown. Find pillows, cocktail napkins, and more—with a Southern twist.

Ceri Hoover (2905 12th Ave. S., #105, 615/200-0991, http://cerihoover.com, 11am-6pm Tues.-Fri., 10am-7pm Sat., 11am-5pm Sun.) designs luscious high-end leather handbags, shoes, and wallets. These accessories are head-turners, and on the arms of most of the city's most fashionable people.

A famous owner (novelist Ann Patchett) meant that the opening of **Parnassus Books** (3900 Hillsboro Pike, 615/953-2243, www.parnassusbooks.net, 10am-8pm Mon.-Sat., noon-5pm Sun.) in 2011 made national headlines. Located in

Jack White's Third Man Records

a strip mall across from the Mall at Green Hills, Parnassus specializes in a well-edited selection, personal service, and literary events for both kids and adults.

Near the old 100 Oaks Mall in South Nashville you'll find Nashville's largest and most popular antiques mall. **Gaslamp Antiques & Decorating Mall** (100 Powell Ave., 615/297-2224, www.gaslampantiques.com, 10am-6pm Mon.-Sat., noon-6pm Sun.) is squeezed behind a Staples and next to a Home Depot. It has more than 150 vendors and a great selection of all types of antiques.

Sports and Recreation

Parks
Centennial Park
Nashville's best city park, **Centennial Park** (2500 West End Ave., 615/862-8400, dawn-11pm daily) is best known as home of the Parthenon. It is also a pleasant place to relax. A small lake provides

a habitat for ducks and other water creatures; paved trails are popular for walking during nice weather. The park hosts numerous events during the year, including Shakespeare in the Park each August and September.

Radnor Lake State Natural Area
Just seven miles southwest of downtown Nashville, **Radnor Lake State Natural Area** (1160 Otter Creek Rd., 615/373-3467) provides an escape for visitors and residents of the city. Eighty-five-acre Radnor Lake was created in 1914 by the Louisville and Nashville Railroad Company, which impounded Otter Creek to do so. The lake was to provide water for the railroad's steam engines. By the 1940s, the railroad's use of the lake ended, and 20 years later the area was threatened by development. Local residents, including the Tennessee Ornithological Society, successfully rallied against development, and Radnor Lake State Natural Area was established in 1973.

There are six miles of hiking trails around the lake, and Otter Creek Road, which is closed to vehicular traffic, is open to bicycles and walkers. A nature museum at the visitors center describes some of the 240 species of birds and hundreds of species of plants and animals that live at Radnor. The visitors center is open 8:30am-4pm daily (closed noon-1pm; restrooms open at 7am).

Edwin and Percy Warner Parks
The largest city parks in Tennessee, **Edwin and Percy Warner Parks** (7311 TN-100, 615/352-6299, www.nashville.gov, dawn-11pm daily) are a 2,600-acre oasis of forest, fields, and quiet pathways located just nine miles southwest from downtown Nashville. Nashvillians come here to walk, jog, ride bikes and horses, and much more. The parks have scenic drives, picnic facilities, playgrounds, cross-country running trails, an equestrian center, bridle trails, a model-airplane field, and athletic fields. Percy

Warner Park is also home to the Harpeth Hills Golf Course, and Edwin Warner Park has a nature center that provides year-round environmental education. The nature center also hands out maps and other information about the park.

Warner Parks hosts the annual Iroquois Steeplechase in May. A 10-mile bridle path is open to horseback riding year-round. Visit the park's **Equestrian Center** (2500 Old Hickory Blvd.) for more information.

J. Percy Priest Lake

J. Percy Priest Lake (miles 6-7 of the Stones River, www.percypriestlake.org) was created in the mid-1960s when the U.S. Army Corps of Engineers (USACE) dammed Stones River east of Nashville. The lake is a favorite destination for fishing, boating, swimming, paddling, and picnicking.

J. Percy Priest Lake sprawls over 14,200 acres. Access is provided through more than a dozen different parks and access areas on all sides of the lake. Many of these areas bear the names of communities that were inundated when the lake was created.

The lake's main **visitors center,** operated by the USACE, is at the site of the dam that created the lake. The visitors center is on Bell Road at exit 219, off I-40 heading east from downtown Nashville. There you will find a lake overlook and one of four marinas on the lake.

The **Three Hickories Nature Trail** is an easy 1.6-mile hiking trail found in the Cook Recreation Area. To get there, take I-40 east from downtown Nashville, exit at 221B and go right at Old Hickory Boulevard, then left on Bell Road, and follow signs to the entrance of the recreation area. There's a $5 fee during April-September. **Anderson Road Fitness Trail** is a paved one-mile trail that travels through woodlands and along the lake. To get there, take I-40 east from downtown Nashville for five miles to exit 219. Go right on Stewarts Ferry Pike, continue

Nissan Stadium is home of the NFL's Tennessee Titans.

onto Bell Road for five miles, turn left on Spring Road, and follow signs to the entrance.

Boating, fishing, and water sports are among the most popular activities on J. Percy Priest Lake. Launch ramps are found in Long Hunter State Park and at several marinas around the lake. **Elm Hill Marina** (3361 Bell Rd., 615/889-5363, www.elmhillmarina.com, 8am-8pm daily) is the marina closest to downtown Nashville.

The USACE operates three day-use **swim areas** (6am-7pm daily Apr.-Oct.) that have sand beaches, bathrooms, and other amenities for a day in the water. These swim areas are located at Anderson Road, Cook Campground, and Seven Points Campground. There is a $5 vehicle fee at Anderson and Cook.

Greenways
Nashville has a remarkable network of connected green spaces, thanks to its **greenways** (www.nashville.gov/

greenways). The master plan is for this system to eventually connect the entire city. Today there are more than 190 miles of paved pathways and 80 miles of primitive trails used by bicyclists, runners, dog walkers, and more. The greenways run through the city's prettiest natural areas and, in places, along the Cumberland River. Some greenways include nature centers and other educational facilities. For the most part, the routes are clean and safe. Good maps are available for download from **Greenways for Nashville** (www.greenwaysfornashville.org).

Biking
Nashville has a fast-growing bike culture, and it's easy to pedal your way across the city to see its highlights. It's easy to connect to more than 90 miles of greenways and 130 miles of bike lanes and shared-use bike routes.

Nashville's only dedicated mountain bike trail is at **Hamilton Creek Park** (www.nashville.gov) on J. Percy Priest Lake, on the east side of the Nashville airport. This 10-mile bike trail consists of an eastern trail, better for beginning bikers, and a western trail, for advanced bikers. The two trails meet at a tunnel that crosses Bell Road.

The **Harpeth Bike Club** (www.harpeth-bikeclub.com) is Nashville's largest bike club. It organizes weekend and weekday group rides April-October, plus races and social events where you can meet other bike enthusiasts.

For the inside scoop on biking around Nashville and recommended routes in the surrounding countryside, check out **Nashville Cyclist** (www.nashvillecyclist.com), an online community of bikers.

Bike Shops
There are several good bike shops in Nashville. If you need bike gear, repairs, or advice before you head out on the Trace, check out **Cumberland Transit** (2807 West End Ave., 615/321-4069, http://cumberlandtransit.com,

10am-6pm Mon.-Sat., noon-5pm Sun.), or **Trace Bikes** (8400 TN-100, 615/646-2485, http://tracebikes.com, 10am-6pm Mon.-Fri., 10am-5pm Sat.), next to the Loveless Cafe near the Natchez Trace Parkway. East Nashville's **EastSide Cycles** (103 S. 11th St., 615/469-1079, www.eastside-cycles.com, 11am-7pm Mon.-Fri., 10am-6pm Sat.) has bike tools around back if you need to make some repairs outside business hours. The focus at **Halcyon Bike Shop** (2802 12th Ave. S., 615/730-9344, http://halcyonbike.com, 10am-6pm Tues.-Sat., 1pm-5pm Sun.) is restored and recycled bicycles. They have a great repair shop, fun accessories, and a passionate staff.

Paddling

Nashville's easy access to multiple rivers and lakes makes it a natural gateway for kayaking, canoeing, and stand-up paddleboarding. **Nashville Paddle Co.** (2901 Bell Rd., 615/682-1787, www.nashvillepaddle.com, dawn-dusk Thurs.-Mon. May-Sept., rentals start at $20/hour) offers lessons and rentals for stand-up paddleboarding, which is well suited for Middle Tennessee's flat water. (Full disclosure: The author of this book is one of the owners of Nashville Paddle Co.)

Spectator Sports
Football

You simply cannot miss 68,000-seat **Nissan Stadium,** home of the NFL's **Tennessee Titans** (1 Titans Way, 615/565-4000, www.titansonline.com). The stadium, which was finished in 1999 and renovated after the 2010 flood, towers on the east bank of the Cumberland River, directly opposite downtown.

The Titans moved to this stadium (then called LP Field) in 1999 and initially sold out almost every home game. But a spotty win-loss record in recent years has made tickets easier to come by. If you want to see a game on short notice, your best bet is the online NFL ticket exchange, where season ticket holders can sell their seats to games they don't want to attend.

The most distinctive brand of football played in Nashville is Australian Rules. The **Nashville Kangaroos** (http://nashvillekangaroos.org) were founded in 1997 and were one of the first Australian Rules football teams in the United States. The "Roos" play at Elmington Park (3531 West End Ave.) and sometimes practice with Vanderbilt's own Aussie rules squad. One of the missions of the club is to promote cultural understanding and exchange, so the social calendar can be just as grueling as the sports one. The Roos also sponsor a women's netball team.

Baseball

What an appropriate name for a minor-league baseball team. The **Nashville Sounds** (401 Junior Gilliam Way, 615/690-4487, www.nashvillesounds.com, tickets $9-33) are an affiliate of the Oakland Athletics, and they play about 30 home games a year June-October. In 2015 the team moved from the aging Greer Stadium to the spectacular **First Tennessee Park** between downtown and Germantown. The new stadium has a guitar-shaped scoreboard, plus a mini-golf course (yes, inside the stadium), better-than-average-stadium food and drink from **The Band Box** (http://thebandboxnashville.com), and great sightlines. There's an alcohol-free section, which appeals to families with small kids.

Ice Hockey

Nashville proved itself to be a hockey town when its beloved National Hockey League franchise, the **Predators** (501 Broadway, www.nhl.com/predators), went to the Stanley Cup playoffs in 2017. It was a sweet victory for fans who fought to keep the team in the city in the face of lackluster support from the community with a "Save the Predators"

Follow That Food Truck!

Like every big city with a hipster population worth its salt, Nashville has scores of food trucks driving to and fro, selling gourmet delicacies from their wheel-based restaurants. These snack-masters tend to show up at places with big lunch crowds, late-night after concerts, and large public events, so you may just run into them. Centennial Park is a popular stop for many of the trucks, but they do make it to many neighborhoods at some point during the week.

The website for **Nashville Food Truck Association** (http://foodtrucksnash.org) lists menus and upcoming planned stops for more than 60 trucks. If you prefer your meals alfresco, check out this list.

• One of Nashville's first food trucks, **The Grilled Cheeserie** (http://grilled-cheeserie.com) serves delicious grilled cheese sandwiches and tomato soup. It travels all over the city, particularly to

farmers markets in the summer. Track it via Twitter (@GrilldCheeserie). They even have a brick-and-mortar location (2003 Belcourt Ave., 615/203-0351).

• It's hard to miss the bright pink presence that is **Barbie Burgers.** To find its tasty burgers and sweet potato fries, follow Barbie Burgers on Twitter (@BarbieBurgers).

• **Califarmia** (http://califarmiatruck. com) is a farm-to-truck purveyor of Latin-infused California dishes. Follow the truck on Twitter (@CalifarmiaTruck).

• **Bao Down** (www.baodownnashville. com) uses local meats to fill its authentic Chinese steamed buns, for a Tennessee take on a traditional food. Follow the truck on Twitter (@baodownTN) for its current location.

---

campaign. The Predators play in the 20,000-seat Bridgestone Arena, located on Broadway in the heart of downtown. Home games include live country music performances and other activities for the fans. The regular season begins in October and ends in early April. Single-game tickets start at $35 and can cost as much as $400, although there are often special discounts.

College Sports

In addition to Nashville's smorgasbord of professional and semiprofessional sports teams, the city's colleges provide lots of good spectator sports. Vanderbilt plays football, men's and women's basketball, and baseball in the Southeastern Conference. Tennessee State University and Belmont University play Division 1-A basketball, and Lipscomb University is a member of the Atlantic Sun Division. Vanderbilt football games are an unusual sporting event, as students traditionally

dress in coats and ties or dresses and high heels.

Food

You can eat in a different restaurant each day in Nashville and never get bored. Southern cooking stars at meat-and-three diners and barbecue joints, fine-dining restaurants cater to the well-heeled, and international eateries reflect the city's surprising diversity.

More than a few high-profile chefs—including *Chopped*'s Maneet Chauhan, *Top Chef*'s Dale Levitski, and world-famous Jonathan Waxman—have opened local kitchens.

Downtown
The Arcade
One of two downtown food destinations, the **Arcade** is an old outdoor shopping mall that lies between 4th and 5th Avenues. The ground floor of the Arcade

is full of small, casual restaurants that cater to the downtown lunchtime crowd with quick, cheap eats. Upstairs are a few art galleries and artists' studios. Most restaurants at the Arcade have limited seating inside, or you can sit outside and watch the world go by.

The Greek Touch (13 Arcade, 615/259-9493, 10:30am-2:30pm Mon.-Fri.) has gyro, sausage, veggie, and divine chicken sandwiches, platters, and salads, all for under $6. There are also several sandwich shops and **Manny's House of Pizza** (15 Arcade, 615/242-7144, http://mannyshouseofpizza.com, 10am-6pm Mon.-Fri., 11am-5pm Sat., $3-6), which many consider the city's best slice.

Southern

Run, don't walk, to ★ **Arnold's Country Kitchen** (605 8th Ave. S., 615/256-4455, www.arnoldscountrykitchen.com, 10:30am-2:45pm Mon.-Fri., $7-10) for some of the best Southern cooking in town. Set in a red cinder-block building on the southern edge of downtown, Arnold's is a food-lover's dream. No haute or fusion cuisine here—this is real food. Start out by grabbing a tray at this cafeteria-style spot and select from chocolate pie, juicy sliced tomatoes, turnip greens, squash casserole, macaroni and cheese—and that's just the "vegetables." Choose a vegetable plate, or a meat-and-three for just about a buck more. Common meat dishes include ham, baked chicken, fried fish, and beef tips. All meals come with yeast rolls or corn bread. The full lunch, plus a drink, will run you less than $10. There's almost always a line out the door.

There's no shortage of fried chicken south of the Mason-Dixon. Even so, people often throng to one of the three locations of **Puckett's Grocery & Restaurant** (500 Church St., 615/770-2772, http://puckettsgro.com, 7am-10pm Sun.-Thurs., 7am-11pm Fri.-Sat.) for what folks say is among the area's best fried chicken. The downtown outpost of this regional mainstay has classic Southern food (don't skimp on the fried green beans) in a casual, often crowded environment. There's live music many nights and a full bar, but the real appeal is stick-to-your-ribs comfort food in a restaurant that will get you in and out in time to see a show at the Ryman.

Barbecue

If you are downtown and craving barbecue, **Jack's Bar-B-Que** (416 Broadway, 615/254-5715, 10:30am-8pm Mon.-Thurs., 10:30am-10pm Fri.-Sat., 11am-6pm Sun., $6-15) is your best option for a bite on Broadway. Choose from barbecue pork shoulder, brisket, turkey, ribs, or sausage, and pair it with classic Southern sides like green beans, macaroni and cheese, and fried apples. Jack's serves five types of barbecue sauce, including classic Tennessee, Texas, and Kansas City. Most diners opt for a plate of one meat, two vegetables, and bread, but if you're really hungry, go for the three-meat platter. Adding to the appeal of the decent, affordable food is the fact that Jack's service is fast and friendly. There's a second location (334 W. Trinity Ln., 615/228-9888, 10:30am-8pm Mon.-Thurs., 10:30am-9pm Fri.-Sat., 11am-7pm Sun.) near East Nashville and a third (1601 Charlotte Ave., 615/341-0517, 10:30am-8pm Mon.-Thurs., 10:30am-9pm Fri.-Sat., 11am-7pm Sun.) called **Jack's Cawthon's Bar-B-Que.** Summer hours may be extended.

Contemporary

Rub elbows with legislators, lobbyists, and other members of the jet set at the ★ **Capitol Grille** (23 6th Ave. N., 615/345-7116, www.capitolgrillenashville.com, 6:30am-2pm and 5pm-10pm daily, $10-50). Located on the ground floor of the elegant Hermitage Hotel and a stone's throw from the Tennessee State Capitol, this is the sort of restaurant where marriages are proposed and deals are done.

The menu is fine dining at its best: choice cuts of meat prepared with exacting care and local ingredients (grown at the nearby Farm at Glen Leven). The provenance of each dinner entrée (elk, pork, sea bass) is noted on the menu. Breakfast ($4-17) may be the most decadent of all, with cinnamon-swirl French toast, eggs Benedict, lobster and shirred eggs, and an array of fresh pastries and fruit. The Sunday brunch (11am-2pm) features the best of the grill's lunch and breakfast menus, and is consistently popular. Adjacent to the Capitol Grille is the old-school Oak Bar, a wood-paneled and intimate bar for pre- or postdinner drinks.

Little Octopus (505 12th Ave. S., 615/454-3946, http://littleoctopusnashville.com, 5pm-10pm Mon.-Sat., 10am-2pm and 5pm-10pm Sun., $9-42) offers its contemporary American food, with global influences, from a permanent location in The Gulch. Namesake octopus with smoked fingerling potatoes and fregola is super popular, as are the goat curry with gnocchi and the Sunday brunch.

Built in the old Trolley Barns that look out over downtown, **Pinewood Social** (33 Peabody St., 615/751-8111 www.pinewoodsocial.com, 7am-1am Mon.-Fri., 9am-1am Sat.-Sun., pool open 11am-11pm daily summer, $7-25) has something for everyone—literally. This breakfast, lunch, brunch, dinner, and late-night restaurant is designed to appeal, no matter whether you need a cup of coffee while you check your e-mail or if you want to bowl with friends at one of the six lanes here. There's even a small pool open in summer. The cocktails are delicious, as is the fried broccoli.

International

Maneet Chauhan is known for appearing on *Iron Chef America, The Next Iron Chef,* and *Chopped.* She opened ★ **Chauhan Ale & Masala House** (123 12th Ave. N., 615/242-8426, http://chauhannashville.com, 11am-2:30pm and

5pm-10pm Sun.-Thurs., 11am-2:30pm and 5pm-11pm Fri., 5pm-11pm Sat., $12-28). The eatery brought Indian street food and a fusion of dishes and tastes to a city that wasn't known for its Indian cuisine. The vibe is fun and friendly, the cocktails go down easy, and there is even an interpretation of a Nashville hot chicken dish.

Diners and Coffee Shops

Provence (601 Church St., 615/664-1150, www.provencebreads.com, 7am-4pm Mon.-Fri., 9am-3pm Sat.-Sun., $6-13), inside the Nashville Public Library, serves excellent European-style pastries, breads, and salads, as well as coffee. Provence's signature sandwiches include creamy chicken salad and turkey and brie. Save room for a decadent pastry or a cookie, which come in varieties like raspberry hazelnut and chocolate espresso. For breakfast, nothing beats a buttery croissant spread with jam. Provence also has locations in Hillsboro and in the Nashville Airport.

For homemade salads, wraps, and sandwiches, follow the crowds of downtown office workers to the **Frist Center Café** (919 Broadway, 616/244-3340, http://fristcenter.org, 10am-5:30pm Mon.-Wed. and Sat., 10am-9pm Thurs.-Fri., noon-5:30pm Sun., $5-8), at the rear of the Frist Center for the Visual Arts. Sandwiches are available whole or half, and you can add soup, salad, or fries for a well-rounded lunch.

Next door to the Johnny Cash Museum, **Sun Diner** (105 3rd Ave. S., 615/742-9099, http://sundinernashville.com, 24 hours daily, $15-20) is downtown's 24-hour diner, with a menu that pays homage to Sun Records. This is where to get a doughnut breakfast sandwich. Due to its prime location, prices are higher than at traditional diners.

Desserts

Nashville's legendary candy company **Goo Goo Cluster** (116 3rd Ave. S., 615/490-6685, http://googoo.com, 10am-8pm daily) has been selling sweets for more than a century. In this flagship red, white, and blue location, you'll find the company's full array of sweets, plus some varieties made only in this open kitchen. Watch the chef create something you'll love. Goo Goo-branded hats, T-shirts, Hatch Show Print posters, and other goodies are also for sale. Don't miss the historical exhibit about the brand.

Farmers Markets

The **Nashville Farmers Market** (900 Rosa L. Parks Blvd., 615/880-2001, www.nashvillefarmersmarket.org, daily, hours vary by merchant) has undergone a resurgence in recent years and, as a result, is one of the best places to grab an interesting meal in the city. The outdoor components of the market include a farm shed with fresh produce year-round. This is a growers' market, so produce is farmed locally. When you're hungry, head to the interior for the Market House food court, with choices ranging from Southern specialties to Caribbean cuisine. **Jamaicaway** (615/255-5920, 10:30am-6pm Sun.-Thurs. 10:30am-4:30 Fri., $9) serves oxtail, steamed fish, and Jamaican patties Sunday-Friday. Other options include Mexican food, wood-fired pizza, local beers, barbecue, and Greek dishes, as well as enough baked goods to give you a toothache. The monthly **night market** brings specialty food and drink, plus live music, dancing, and a magical ambience.

Midtown
Contemporary

To describe **The Catbird Seat** (1711 Division St., 615/810-8200, http://thecatbirdseatrestaurant.com, 5:30pm-9:15pm Wed.-Sat., $115) as a restaurant is a bit of a misnomer. It is a culinary performance that happens to include dinner. There are just 32 seats in this U-shaped space. Once you get a coveted reservation (available online only), you'll be treated to a seasonal meal made before your eyes. Reservations are accepted up to 30

days in advance. The multicourse tasting menu is $115 per person without drinks. The nonalcoholic pairings are as inventive as the wines.

Southern

One of Nashville's most beloved meat-and-threes is **Swett's** (2725 Clifton Ave., 615/329-4418, http://swettsrestaurant.com, 11am-8pm daily, $8-12), family owned and operated since 1954. People come from all over the city to eat at this Nashville institution, which combines soul food, Southern cooking, and barbecue with great results. The food is homemade and authentic, down to the mashed potatoes, the vinegary greens, and the yeast rolls. Start by grabbing dessert—the pies are excellent—and then move on to the good stuff at this cafeteria-style spot: Country-fried steak, pork chops, meatloaf, fried catfish, and ham are a few of the usual suspects. A standard plate comes with one meat, two sides, and a yeast roll or corn bread, but you can add more sides if you like. Draw your own iced tea—sweet or unsweet—and then find a seat if you can.

Barbecue

Near Centennial Park and Vanderbilt, **Hog Heaven** (115 27th Ave. N., 615/329-1234, www.hogheavenbbq.com, 10am-7pm Mon.-Sat., $5-10) is a nondescript yet well-known landmark for barbecue. Pulled-pork sandwiches and beef brisket are among the most popular at this mostly takeout eatery; locals like the white barbecue sauce.

Steakhouses

Jimmy Kelly's (217 Louise Ave., 615/329-4349, http://jimmykellys.com, 5pm-10pm Mon.-Thurs., 5pm-11pm Fri.-Sat., $18-42) is a family-run old-school steakhouse. Set in an old Victorian mansion a few blocks from Centennial Park and Vanderbilt, Jimmy Kelly's has been operated by the Kelly family since 1934—serving excellent steaks and other grilled foods. Dinner begins with irresistible corn cakes. Entrée choices include a half dozen different steaks, lamb, grilled chicken, and seafood, including the best blackened catfish in the city. Tables are set throughout what were once parlors, bedrooms, and porches in the old home, with low lighting and wood paneling. Jimmy Kelly's offers attentive, but not fussy, service.

Union Common (1929 Broadway, 615/329-4565, www.unioncommon. com, 5pm-10pm Sun.-Wed., 5pm-11pm Thurs.-Sat., $12-38) is a neighborhood steakhouse with big windows, a light airy feel, and delicious cocktails. While close to the Vanderbilt campus, this is a grown-up place to dine, not a college hangout.

International

The venerable **International Market & Restaurant** (2010 Belmont Blvd., 615/297-4453, www.internationalnashville.com, 11am-9:30pm daily, $5-10) near Belmont University and Hillsboro Village is a time-honored choice for a cheap lunch in Nashville. The cafeteria serves lots of vegetable, noodle, and rice dishes, many of them Thai in origin, at prices that seem not to have risen much since the restaurant was established in 1975. If you want to splurge, order a "from the kitchen" special of pad thai or another dish, which will be made from scratch just for you. Owner Patti Myint is the mother of *Top Chef* contestant and local restaurateur Arnold Myint.

For the best Italian food in Nashville, head west to the neighborhood of Sylvan Park, where you'll find **Caffe Nonna** (4427 Murphy Rd., 615/463-0133, www.caffe-nonna.com, 11am-2pm and 5pm-9pm Mon.-Thurs., 11am-2pm and 5pm-10pm Fri., 5pm-10pm Sat., $12-21). Inspired by Chef Daniel Maggipinto's own *nonna* (grandmother), the café serves rustic Italian fare. Appetizers include salads

Top to bottom: Chauhan Ale & Masala House; Bastion; Martin's Bar-B-Que Joint.

and bruschetta, and entrées include the divine Lasagne Nonna, made with butternut squash, ricotta cheese, spinach, and sage. The service at Caffe Nonna is friendly and attentive, and the atmosphere is cozy, but the space is small. Call ahead for a table.

Located just west of the Kroger grocery store, **K&S World Market** (5861 Charlotte Pike, 615/356-8771, 8:30am-8pm daily), the second in a chain whose original location is on Nolensville Pike, will keep any foodie happy for hours with its obscure and unusual food items. In the same shopping center you'll find Nashvillians' favorite Vietnamese restaurants, **Kien Giang** (5825 Charlotte Pike, 615/353-1250, 11am-9pm Tues.-Sun., $6-12) and **Miss Saigon** (5849 Charlotte Pike, 615/354-1351, http://misssaigontn.com, 10am-9pm Mon., Wed.-Sun., $7-12).

Drive a bit farther out to find **La Hispana Panaderia** (6208 Charlotte Pike, 615/352-3798, 6am-9pm daily), whose bread and pastries are as good as the finest European bakery but at a fraction of the cost.

One of Nashville's oldest Indian restaurants, **Shalimar** (3711 Hillsboro Rd., 615/269-8577, www.shalimarfinedining.com, 11am-2:30pm and 5pm-10pm Mon.-Sat., 5pm-10pm Sun., $15-17) offers fine food and efficient service. The Saturday lunch buffet brings in mall shoppers and ladies who lunch. At dinner, Shalimar takes on a slightly more elegant cast with vegetarian, chicken, lamb, and seafood entrées in popular preparations, including masala, biryani, tikka, *saag*, and korma. Shalimar is BYOB.

Diners and Coffee Shops

There's a lot of hype surrounding Nashville's favorite breakfast restaurant, the **Pancake Pantry** (1796 21st Ave. S., 615/383-9333, www.thepancakepantry.com, 6am-3pm Mon.-Fri., 6am-4pm Sat.-Sun., $6-14). Founded in 1961 and still family owned, the Pantry serves some of the most popular pancakes in the city.

Owners say that the secret is in the ingredients, which are fresh and homemade. Many of the flours come from Tennessee, and the syrup is made right at the restaurant. The menu offers no fewer than 21 varieties, and that doesn't include the waffles. Try the fluffy buckwheat cakes, savory cornmeal cakes, sweet blintzes, or the old standby buttermilk pancakes. Most of the other breakfast platters on offer come with a short stack of pancakes, too. The Pantry offers no-yolk omelets for the health conscious, and it's very kid friendly as well. On weekend mornings and many weekdays, the line for a seat at the Pantry goes out the door.

In today's retro-happy world, it isn't too hard to find an old-fashioned soda shop. But how many of them are the real thing? **Elliston Place Soda Shop** (2111 Elliston Pl., 615/327-1090, www.ellistonplacesodashop.com, 7am-8pm Mon.-Thurs., 7am-10pm Fri.-Sat., $5-11), near Centennial Park and Vanderbilt, is one of those rare holdovers from the past, and it's proud of it. The black-and-white tile floors, lunch counter, and Purity Milk advertisements may have been here for decades, but the food is consistently fresh and good. Choose between a sandwich or a plate lunch, but be sure to save room for a classic milkshake or slice of hot pie with ice cream on top.

Nashville's original coffee shop, **Bongo Java** (2007 Belmont Blvd., 615/385-5282, www.bongojava.com, 7am-11pm daily, $3-9) is just as popular as ever. Located near Belmont University, Bongo is regularly full of students chatting, texting, and surfing the Internet, thanks to free wireless Internet. Set in an old house with a huge front porch, Bongo feels homey and welcoming, and a bit more on the hippie side than other Nashville coffee shops. Expect the latest in coffee drinks, premium salads, and sandwiches. Breakfast, including Bongo French toast, is served all day.

Bongo Java's big brother, **Fido** (1812 21st Ave. S., 615/777-3436, www.

bongojava.com/fido-cafe, 7am-11pm daily, $5-13) is more than a coffee shop. It is a place to get work done, watch deals being made, and see and be seen. Take a seat along the front plate-glass windows to watch the pretty people as they stroll by Posh, one of Nashville's most upscale clothing boutiques. In addition to coffee, sandwiches, and salads, baked goods are on the menu.

Said to have the best burger in Nashville, **Rotier's** (2413 Elliston Pl., 615/327-9892, 10:30am-9:30pm Mon.-Tues., 10:30am-10pm Wed.-Fri., 9am-10pm Sat., www.rotiersrestaurant.com, $7-20) is also a respected meat-and-three diner. Choose from classic sandwiches or comfort-food dinners. The Saturday breakfast will fuel you all day long. Ask about the milkshake, a city favorite that appears nowhere on the menu. Don't miss the hash brown casserole.

Dessert takes center stage at **Bobbie's Dairy Dip** (5301 Charlotte Ave., 615/292-2112, http://bobbiesdairydipnashville.com, 11am-8:30pm Mon.-Thurs., 11am-9:30pm Fri.-Sat. spring-fall, $4-6), a walk-up ice cream joint. The cheeseburgers and chili dogs are the comfort food you've dreamed of, and you can finish off with soft-serve ice cream, dipped cones, sundaes, and banana splits. Bobbie's closes during the winter months and may stay open later in the summer; call ahead to confirm.

Desserts
Need to satisfy your sweet tooth? Call **Jake's Bakes** (2422 Elliston Pl., 615/645-5916, www.jakesbakesnashville.com, 10am-11:30pm Mon.-Fri., noon-11:30pm Sat.-Sun.) and within 30 minutes warm cookies will be delivered to your hotel room, conference center, meeting room, or college dorm room. You can add milk to your order, too.

West End
Southern
The ★ **Loveless Cafe** (8400 TN-100, 615/646-9700, 7am-9pm daily, $7-17) is an institution, and some may argue it's a state of mind. The Loveless got its start in 1951, when Lon and Annie Loveless started to serve good country cooking. Over the years the restaurant changed hands, but Annie's biscuit recipe remained the same, and it was the biscuits that kept Nashvillians coming back for more. The biscuits are fluffy and buttery, the ham salty, and the eggs, bacon, and sausage will hit the spot. The supper and lunch menu includes Southern standards like fried catfish and chicken, pit-cooked pork barbecue, pork chops, and meat loaf, as well as a few salads. Loveless is about 20 miles from downtown Nashville; plan on a 30-minute drive along TN-100. It's the last place you'll pass before getting on the Natchez Trace Parkway.

Music Valley
Southern
Nashville's most sublime food experience is not to be found in a fine restaurant or even at a standard meat-and-three cafeteria. The food that you'll still be dreaming about when you get home is found at ★ **Prince's Hot Chicken Shack** (123 Ewing Dr., 615/226-9442, http://princeshotchicken.com, 11:30am-10:30pm Tues.-Thurs., 11:30am-4am Fri., 2pm-4am Sat., $5-7). No hot chicken shop does this spicy, pan-fried dish quite as well as Prince's, where it comes in three varieties: mild, hot, and extra hot. Most will find the mild variety plenty spicy, so beware. When you walk into Prince's, head to the back, where you'll place your order at the window, pay, and be given a number. Then take a seat—if you can find one—while you wait for your food. You can order to go or eat in. Your food is made to order, and Prince's is very popular, so the wait often exceeds 30 minutes. Take heart, though—Prince's chicken is worth the wait. Prince's has a second location (5814 Nolensville Rd., 615/810-9388, 10am-10pm Mon.-Thurs., 11am-midnight Fri.-Sat.) in South Nashville.

Outside of the cuisine at the Gaylord Opryland Resort hotel, Music Valley isn't much known for its food. But the **Opry Backstage Grill** (2401 Music Valley Dr., 615/231-8854, www.marriott.com, 11am-10pm Sun.-Thurs., 11am-11pm Fri.-Sat., $8-26) tries to offer something that is at least unique to Nashville, albeit with the flair of a chain. This themed restaurant serves classic Southern dishes amid photos and art of classic Opry performers and occasionally hosts live concerts for ambience.

South Nashville
Barbecue
Tucked on Nolensville Pike, the land of international eateries, is one of the city's favorite barbecue houses. **Martin's Bar-B-Que Joint** (7215 Nolensville Pike, 615/776-1856, www.martinsbbqjoint. com, 11am-9pm daily, $4-15) has pulled pork, barbecue spareribs, smoked wings, and beef brisket, plus all the side dishes you could want: coleslaw, green beans, potato salad, and the best corn cakes this side of town. You can also order burgers and a mean catfish po'boy. Martin's is inside the Nolensville city limits, about a 30-minute drive south from downtown Nashville. Other locations include the mammoth downtown Nashville outpost (410 4th Ave. S., 615/288-0880, 11am-10pm), which has a backyard beer garden.

Contemporary
★ **Bastion** (434 Houston St., 615/490-8434, www.bastionnashville.com, 5:30pm-9:30pm Wed.-Sat., à la carte menu $9-15) is one of the best restaurants in town, helmed by James Beard award-nominated chef Josh Habiger. Bastion has just 24 seats—the idea being that you can have an up-close-and-personal experience with the staff as they work. Bastion offers an à la carte menu that they recommend combining into a five-course meal. Reservations, which include an advance ticket/deposit, are essential. The restaurant can't accommodate groups of more than six people.

International
Nolensville Pike is a mecca for international food. Among them is **Dunya Kabob** (2521 Nolensville Pike, 615/242-6664, 11am-9pm daily, $5-10), which offers Kurdish specialties of chicken, lamb, beef, and seafood kabobs and gyro sandwiches. Nashville has a large Kurdish immigrant population; this is the place to try the cuisine.

Not far from Nolensville, you'll find two more international favorites in the same shopping center on Trousdale Drive. **Back to Cuba** (4683 Trousdale Dr., 615/837-6711, 11am-9pm Tues.-Sat., $8-12) serves traditional Cuban favorites: Grilled sandwiches of pork, ham, cheese, and pickle are a popular choice at lunchtime. For dinner, try the roast pork or grilled shrimp, and don't skip the lacy fried plantains and spicy black beans.

For homemade, old-school Italian fare, go to **Mama Mia's** (4671 Trousdale Dr., 615/331-7207, 11am-2pm and 5pm-9pm Mon.-Thurs., 11am-2pm and 5pm-10pm Fri., 5pm-10pm Sat., $7-16), which offers lasagna, ravioli, chicken, veal, and seafood dishes. Bring your own wine.

East Nashville
Contemporary
Named for the former coin laundry in which it was located when it first opened, ★ **The Family Wash** (626A Main St., 615/645-9930, www.familywash.com, 8am-1am Mon.-Sat., 9am-3pm Sun., $6-14) is part live-music listening room, part bar, part restaurant, part neighborhood gathering place. It captures the offbeat energy that so well defines Nashville. Come to hear local musicians of all stripes and eat supper that is better than average bar food. Locals love the shepherd's pie. There's a small take-out coffee area for an early-morning caffeine fix.

There's something about a place that pays attention to the details, and

Holland House Bar and Refuge (935 W. Eastland Ave., 615/262-4190, www.hollandhousebarandrefuge.com, 4pm-10pm Mon.-Thurs., 4pm-midnight Fri., 10am-2pm and 4pm-midnight Sat., 10am-3pm Sun., $9-28) is one of those spots. This East Nashville hideaway is a refuge from louder restaurants and more frantically paced bars. The impressive cocktail and food menus change seasonally, and the bartender will craft your drink with precision (try the truffled popcorn while you wait). The food is made with local and seasonal ingredients ranging from duck to catfish. Locals like Monday night's happy hour and its burger special. Kids are welcome for Sunday brunch but not at other times. The folks at Holland House are the minds behind **The Pharmacy Burger Parlor & Beer Garden** (731 McFerrin Ave., 615/712-9527, http://thepharmacynashville.com, 11am-10pm Sun.-Thurs., 11am-11pm Fri.-Sat., $8-11) right next door. The Pharmacy makes sodas by hand and has a killer grassy backyard beer garden.

★ **Butcher & Bee** (902 Main St., 615/226-3322, http://butcherandbee.com, 11am-2pm and 5pm-10pm Mon.-Tues., 11am-2pm and 5pm-11pm Wed.-Thurs., 11am-2pm and 5pm-midnight Fri., 10am-2:30pm and 5pm-midnight Sat., 10am-2:30pm and 5pm-10pm Sun., $14-20) serves Israeli-influenced tapas—the whipped feta is joy in a bowl—in an ambience that is hip but not intimidating. At the end of the night your check will be delivered inside of a book.

On a small side street, **The Treehouse** (1011 Clearview Ave., 615/454-4201, http://treehousenashville.com, 6pm-1am Mon. Sat. $12 26) was named after the actual treehouse on the property when it was owned by fiddle player Buddy Spicher. Locals love to dine outside, where it does feel like you are eating in a treehouse, albeit one with good service and solid, seasonal dishes and great cocktails.

Diners and Coffee Shops
Not a deli in the traditional sense, **Mitchell Delicatessen** (1306 McGavock Pike, 615/262-9862, http://mitchelldeli.com, 7am-10pm Mon.-Sat., 8am-4pm Sun., $6-9) is the most creative sandwich shop in town. Order the roasted lamb and raita; a Vietnamese-style creation with pork, liver pâté, and veggies; or a BLT fit for a king. Breakfast is served until 11am, and there is a daily menu of soups and hot plate specials. Stop here for top-notch bread, cheese, and meats for your own sandwiches, too.

To call **Barista Parlor** (519B Gallatin Ave., 615/712-9766, www.baristaparlor.com, 7am-8pm Mon.-Fri., 8am-8pm Sat.-Sun., $8-16) a coffee shop is an understatement. It's more an art gallery where the coffee is the work of art. Housed in a renovated auto shop, this is a big, well-designed space with signage made by local artists, uniforms crafted by local designers, interesting furniture, and attentive servers. They take coffee seriously and are happy to answer your questions about their pour-over style and different blends. Be patient as your caffeine fix is prepared.

Accommodations

Nashville houses some 35,000 hotel rooms, with another 11,000 in the works. That's because a lot of people want to come to Music City. Accommodations range from historic downtown hotels to standard motels, many of which have Music City touches, from recorded wake-up calls from country stars to guitar-shaped swimming pools.

Downtown and The Gulch have the most appealing and convenient hotels. More budget-friendly options are found in midtown and Music Valley.

Downtown
Hotels in this neighborhood are as close as you can get to attractions including

the Country Music Hall of Fame and Broadway honky-tonks.

$150-200

Located across Broadway from the Frist Center for the Visual Arts, **Holiday Inn Express Nashville-Downtown** (902 Broadway, 615/244-0150, www.ihg.com, $145-170) offers a comfortable compromise between value and location. It has an on-site fitness room, free wireless Internet, a business center, and a guest laundry. Guest rooms have desks, coffeemakers, and two telephones. Suites ($270) have refrigerators and microwave ovens. All guests enjoy free continental breakfast. On-site parking is available for $28 a day. The Holiday Inn is about five blocks from lower Broadway.

An apartment building converted into a hotel, ★ **SoBro Guest House** (310 Peabody St., 615/965-4545, www.sobroguest.com, $150-189) is one of the area's best-kept secrets. Every room is a smartly decorated suite, with kitchens, record players with vinyl, games, free Wi-Fi, and a real downtown perk: free parking. It is walking distance to downtown, but still very quiet. You can ask for your grocery shopping to be done ahead of time for you: The fridge will be stocked when you arrive. There's no front desk; you check in with your mobile phone.

Over $200

One of Nashville's most notable downtown hotels is ★ **Union Station** (1001 Broadway, 615/726-1001, www.unionstationhotelnashville.com, $234-274), a 125-room hotel located in what was once the city's main train station. High ceilings, lofty interior balconies, magnificent iron work and molding, and an impressive marble-floored great hall that greets guests make this one of Nashville's great old buildings, which was renovated in 2016. Union Station is a refined hotel, with amenities like free turndown service, a fun fitness center, Wi-Fi, and room service. Because the hotel is in an old train station, rooms vary depending on what their former use was. Some have cathedral ceilings, stylish furnishings, and a subtle art deco touch; others are updated and modern, but small.

The all-suite **Hilton Nashville Downtown** (121 4th Ave. S., 615/620-1000, www.nashvillehilton.com, $279-349) is next door to the Country Music Hall of Fame, Broadway's honky-tonks, and the home of the Nashville Symphony. All of the hotel's 330 suites have two distinct rooms—a living room with sofa, cable television, microwave oven, refrigerator, and coffeemaker, and a bedroom with one or two beds. The rooms are appointed with modern, stylish furniture and amenities. An indoor pool, workout room, valet parking, and two restaurants round out the hotel's amenities.

The last of a dying breed of hotels, the ★ **Hermitage Hotel** (231 6th Ave., 615/244-3121, www.thehermitagehotel.com, $300-800) has been the first choice for travelers to downtown Nashville for more than 100 years. The 123-room hotel was commissioned by prominent Nashville citizens and opened for business in 1910, quickly becoming the favorite gathering place for the city's elite. Prominent figures including Al Capone, Gene Autry, seven U.S. presidents, and modern country stars have stayed at the Hermitage. Guests enjoy top-of-the-line amenities, including 24-hour room service, pet walking, and valet parking. Rooms are furnished in an opulent style befitting a luxury urban hotel and have refreshment centers, marble baths, and high-speed wireless Internet access. Many rooms have lovely views of the capitol building and city. Check for last-minute specials on its website, when rates will dip to $200. You can choose to have $2 from your room rate contributed to the Land Trust for Tennessee.

Courtyard by Marriott (179 4th Ave. N., 615/256-0900, www.marriott.com, $200-289) is a 181-room renovated hotel set in a century-old downtown high-rise.

It is right next to Printer's Alley and midway between the downtown business district and Broadway's entertainment attractions. Guest rooms are tastefully decorated, with web TV, wired Internet access, coffeemakers, ironing boards, cable TV, voice mail, and super-comfortable beds. There are two restaurants on-site, and guests can take advantage of valet parking for $22 a day.

Just steps from the Tennessee State Capitol and near dozens of downtown office buildings, the **Doubletree Hotel Nashville** (315 4th Ave. N., 615/244-8200, http://doubletree.hilton.com, $190-250) is a popular choice for business travelers. Rooms are spacious and bright, and even basic rooms have a comfortable desk and chair, coffeemaker, free Internet access, voicemail, and ironing boards. The hotel boasts a beautiful indoor swimming pool, business center, above-average fitness center, and on-site restaurant and coffee shop. Parking is valet only ($24 per day).

The **Sheraton Downtown Nashville** (623 Union St., 615/259-2000, www.sheratonnashvilledowntown.com, $200-270) is a city landmark. The 472-room hotel stands tall above neighboring buildings, providing most guest rooms with views of the city below. Located in the middle of Nashville's bustling downtown business district, near the capitol building, it is another good option for business travelers. The hotel is 100 percent smoke-free and has a fitness room, business center, indoor pool, and laundry and concierge services. Internet access and on-site parking are available for an additional fee.

The Omni Nashville Hotel (250 5th Ave. S., 615/782-5300, www.omnihotels.com, $219-308) is adjacent to the 1.2 million-square-foot Music City Convention Center. It has more than 80,000 square feet of meeting and event space, more than 800 guest rooms, plus easy access to the convention center, the Hall of

Top to bottom: SoBro Guest House; Union Station; the Thompson.

Fame, restaurants, and other attractions south of Broadway. Don't miss the cool displays of musicians' costumes in the hallway that connects Hatch Show Print to the hotel.

In 2017 Nashville became the next city to welcome a **21c Museum Hotel** (223 3rd Ave. N., 615/610-6400, www.21cmuseumhotels.com, $299-600), a 124-room hotel with a contemporary art museum inside. The public is welcome to tour the museum for free, while guests enjoy rooms ranging from a single king bed to suites with terraces. Perks include free Wi-Fi, free bottled water, a docking station for your phone, bathrobes, and original art in every room. The hotel also features a bar and restaurant with a menu by executive chef Levon Wallace.

Opened in late 2016, the 27-story **Westin Nashville** (807 Clark Pl., 615/248-2800, http://westinnashville.com, $225-390) is a big-city type of hotel, with a full-service spa, a rooftop pool and bar, and valet-only parking. The Decker & Dyer restaurant serves breakfast, lunch, dinner, and craft cocktails in a shared space in the lobby, so you can see-and-be-seen. An Oak Steakhouse, an outpost of the Charleston original, is scheduled to open downstairs. The 453-room hotel is pet-friendly.

For those who prefer more private accommodations, **The 404 Hotel** (404 12th Ave. S., 615/242-7404, http://the-404nashville.com, $280-449) is a good option. It has just five rooms and an on-site manager who provides "invisible service," making The 404 a luxury hotel for people who don't want to stay in a hotel. Rooms have sumptuous linens, work by local artists, fruit and pastries, and free Wi-Fi. It's walking distance to all of The Gulch's charms but is not a place for kids under 15 or pets. Adjacent to the hotel, in an old shipping container, is **404 Kitchen** (615/251-1404, 5pm-10pm Mon.-Thurs., 5pm-11pm Fri.-Sat., 5pm-9pm Sun.), an award-winning 56-seat restaurant.

Take in the view from the Westin Nashville's rooftop lounge.

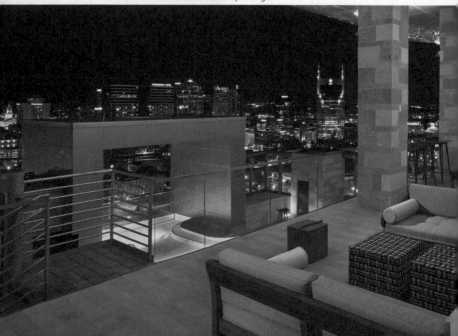

The ★ **Thompson** (401 11th Ave. S., 615/262-6000, www.thompsonhotels. com, $295-579) offers Nashville a lot of things that seem at odds with one another: It is in the heart of The Gulch, but still quiet enough to sleep. It's in a modern high rise, but feels like a small, boutique hotel. Enjoy pet-friendly rooms with hardwood floors, midcentury modern-style furnishings, honor bars with local spirits, bluetooth speakers, and rain showers. Chef John Besh heads up the two on-site restaurants. There's also a coffee shop on the first floor.

Midtown

Midtown hotels are near Music Row, Vanderbilt and Belmont Universities, and the entertainment, dining, and shopping attractions of Hillsboro Village.

Under $100

The **Music City Hostel** (1809 Patterson St., 615/497-1208, www.musiccityhostel.com, $25-110) is among doctors' offices and

commercial buildings in between downtown Nashville and Elliston Place. The low-slung '70s-style building looks like nothing much on the outside, but inside it is cheerful, welcoming, and a comfortable home base for budget travelers. Music City Hostel offers the usual dorm-style bunk-bed accommodations, as well as a handful of private apartments. You can also book a private bedroom with private bath plus shared kitchen and common room. Common areas include a large kitchen, dining room, reading room, cable TV room, computer with Internet access, and a coin laundry. The entire facility is smoke-free. Parking is free, and the hostel is within walking distance of restaurants, a bus stop, car rental agency, post office, and hospitals. It is a hike to get downtown on foot from here.

$100-150

Best Western Music Row (1407 Division St., 615/242-1631, www.nashvillebest-western.com, $110-170) is a no-nonsense motel with an outdoor pool, free continental breakfast, Internet access, and indoor corridors. Rooms have cable TV, AM/FM alarm clocks, and coffeemakers. Pets are allowed for $10 a day, and parking is free. The 75-room hotel is a few steps away from the Music Row traffic circle and nearby restaurants.

$150-200

A bed-and-breakfast choice in this part of the city is **1501 Linden Manor B&B** (1501 Linden Ave., 615/298-2701, www.nashville-bed-breakfast.com, $175-275). This cheerful yellow-brick home on a corner lot has three guest rooms, each with stylish furniture and hardwood floors; one room has a private whirlpool, and another has a fireplace.

The **12 South Inn** (918 Knox Ave., 615/260-8015, http://bedanbreakfast-nashville.com, $180-195) has suites, giving you lots of extra room, with private porches, private entrances, and, in the case of the king suite, a separate living room. Unlike some B&Bs that lack hotel-style amenities, the 12 South Inn has free wireless Internet, TV, refrigerators, and other perks, as well as the home-style digs that separate an inn from a traditional hotel. Discounted rates are available for extended stays.

Over $200

For luxurious accommodations near Vanderbilt, consider **Loews Vanderbilt Plaza** (2100 West End Ave., 615/320-1700, www.loewshotels.com, $195-310), a 340-room hotel on West End Avenue close to Centennial Park and Hillsboro Village. Loews boasts 24-hour room service; luxurious sheets, towels, and robes; natural soaps; and spacious bathrooms. Guests enjoy in-room tea kettles and top-of-the-line coffee, evening turndown service, and free high-speed Internet access. Many rooms have views of the Nashville skyline; premium rooms provide guests with access to the concierge lounge, continental breakfast, evening hors d'oeuvres, and a cash bar. All guests can enjoy a fine fitness room, spa, art gallery, and gift shop.

You can't get closer to Vanderbilt University than the **Marriott Nashville Vanderbilt** (2555 West End Ave., 615/321-1300, www.marriott.com, $150-300). Set on the northern end of the university campus, the Marriott has 301 guest rooms, six suites, and meeting space. It is across West End Avenue from Centennial Park, home of the Parthenon, and a few steps from Vanderbilt's football stadium. It has an indoor pool, full-service restaurant, concierge lounge, ATM, and business center.

Since its opening in 2009, the ★ **Hutton Hotel** (1808 West End Ave., 615/340-9333, www.huttonhotel.com, $229-400) has become Nashville's eco-friendly darling. This swanky hotel near the Vanderbilt campus also offers an easy commute to Music Row and downtown, but regular visitors stay here less for the great location and more for the ambience.

The lobby and guest rooms are stocked with well-edited art collections, the bathrooms include sleek granite showers, and the entire hotel has an emphasis on sustainability, with biodegradable cleaning products and bamboo flooring. The pet-friendly property has all the expected amenities, such as flat-screen TVs and Wi-Fi access. An added bonus is the likelihood of a celebrity sighting.

East Nashville

While it has more appeal for locals than it does for visitors, there are a few good reasons to stay in East Nashville. For football fans, this part of the city is close to the Tennessee Titans' stadium. Others will enjoy bed-and-breakfasts in Edgefield, the intimate live music venues, and a cool, laid-back, and diverse residential neighborhood. Good dining and funky shopping abound, and downtown is a short drive or walk across the Cumberland River.

Under $100

On the east bank of the Cumberland River, **Clarion Hotel at the Stadium** (211 N. 1st St., 615/254-1551, www.choicehotels.com, $75-129) is near Nissan Stadium, where the Tennessee Titans play. The hotel's 180 rooms have cable TV and Wi-Fi. Some have nice views of the Nashville skyline, but this is strictly a budget hotel. A shuttle to downtown runs every 30 minutes.

$150-200

The Big Bungalow (618 Fatherland St., 615/256-8375, www.thebigbungalow.com, $155-250), a Craftsman-style early-1900s town house, offers three guest rooms, each with its own private bath and television. Guests have shared access to a computer (no wireless Internet), microwave, and refrigerator. Common areas are comfortable and stylish, with tasteful decor and hardwood floors. Hostess Ellen Warshaw prepares breakfast for her guests and sometimes hosts in-the-round concerts in her living room. She is also a licensed masseuse and sometimes offers discounted massage rates with your room. This is a pet-free, nonsmoking facility; children over 10 are welcome. The bed-and-breakfast is about seven blocks from the John Seigenthaler Pedestrian Bridge, which takes you to the heart of downtown.

It almost sounds like a joke about the hipster-ness of the East Nashville neighborhood. The owners of Urban Cowboy Brooklyn went looking for a second location for their hip, sleek, well-designed inn and settled on Nashville. But the eight-room ★ **Urban Cowboy Nashville** (1603 Woodland St., 347/840-0525, www. urbancowboybnb.com, $195-295) is the real deal. Service is attentive but not overbearing. The location is in walking distance to many of East Nashville's charms. The B&B's **Public House** (4pm-11pm Sun.-Thurs., 4pm-midnight Fri.-Sat.) in the back stable house of the Queen Anne mansion is popular with East Nashville locals.

Music Valley

There are a dozen or more chain hotels in Music Valley, all close to restaurants and a short drive from the Grand Ole Opry and Opry Mills mall. Nashville's most famous hotel, Gaylord Opryland Resort, is luxurious and a destination on its own.

These hotels tend to provide more for your money than downtown digs, but it's a 15- to 20-minute drive to the city center.

Under $100
If you're looking for a clean, comfortable room, look no farther than the **Fiddler's Inn** (2410 Music Valley Dr., 615/885-1440, www.fiddlersinnopryland.com, $65-85). This 202-room no-frills hotel offers a solid Tennessee welcome to its guests, who come in droves to see the Opry and enjoy other Music Valley attractions. It's right next to a Cracker Barrel restaurant, and there's plenty of parking for cars and tour buses. Guests enjoy cable TV,

free coffee and pastries in the morning, an outdoor pool, and a gift shop stocked with kitschy Nashville souvenirs.

The all-suite **Best Western Suites Near Opryland** (201 Music City Cir., 615/902-9940, www.bestwestern.com, from $112) is a comfortable compromise between the luxury of the Opryland Hotel and the affordability of a motel. Each of the hotel's 100 suites has a couch, desk, high-speed Internet access, coffee- and tea maker, microwave, ironing board, and refrigerator. Rooms with whirlpool tubs are available for about $80 more per night. Guests enjoy an on-site fitness room, 24-hour business center, outdoor pool, free continental breakfast, and weekday newspaper. The Best Western is located along a strip of motels and restaurants about one mile from the Grand Ole Opry and other Opryland attractions.

Located about two miles from the Opryland, **Quality Inn Opryland Area** (2516 Music Valley Dr., 615/889-0086, www.qualityinnopryland.com, $69-90) offers 121 clean, comfortable guest rooms with cable TV, free HBO, wireless Internet, ironing board, hair dryer, free breakfast and free daily newspaper. Amenities include free outdoor parking, interior corridors, exercise room, business center, and an outdoor pool. Pets are permitted with an additional fee.

$150-200
Guests at the **Courtyard by Marriott Opryland** (125 Music City Cir., 615/882-9133, www.marriott.com, $129-200) enjoy refurbished rooms with soft beds, wireless Internet, coffeemakers, ironing boards, and refrigerators. The on-site restaurant serves breakfast, and business rooms come with a desk, dataport, voicemail, and speakerphone.

Over $200
Gaylord Opryland Resort
Said to be the largest hotel without a casino in the United States, the **Gaylord Opryland Resort** (2800 Opryland Dr.,

The *Nashville* of the Small Screen

It is perhaps the most meta of Music City's attractions: Since 2012 the hour-long drama *Nashville* has been filmed on location in the city. Many of the show's actors, who are also songwriters and singers, have relocated to Music City to launch their music careers.

As the show has become more popular (having started on ABC and currently playing on CMT), the lines between the real Nashville and the one on TV have blurred. Many of the actors have now appeared on the stage of the Grand Ole Opry both in character and as themselves. There are CDs and concert tours from the cast. The homes and sets of the characters have been featured on HGTV. Eric Close, who once played the mayor on TV, has led the city's annual Christmas parade several times, instead of the city's actual mayor!

Part of the reason the show is popular is that, for all its soap opera-ness, part of it feels authentic. Episodes are named using Hank Williams song titles, a hat tip to the man who made country music what it is. Backup musicians on the show are actual full-time, professional musicians who live and work in Nashville.

For fans, it is easy to tour the sites of the series as part of a tour of Nashville. The most comprehensive is from Gray Line: a 3.5-hour tour showing off characters' homes and venues that pop up in the show (http://graylinetn.com/abcs-nashville, $52). Grand Avenue offers a custom *Nashville* tour (www.grandavenueworldwide.com/tours/nashville-tour.html, $75). Many of the city's popular attractions, including The Bluebird Café and Ryman Auditorium, now have sections of their tours devoted to the TV show. Art imitates life.

615/889-1000, www.marriott.com, $199-450) is more than just a hotel. Completely renovated after the 2010 flood shuttered it for six months, the 2,881-room luxury resort and convention center is built around a nine-acre indoor garden. Glass atriums let in sunlight, and miles of footpaths invite you to explore the climate-controlled gardens. Highlights include a 40-foot waterfall and flatboats that float along a river.

Set among the gardens are dozens of restaurants and cafés, ranging from casual buffets to elegant steakhouses. Hundreds of room balconies overlook the gardens, providing some guests with views of the well-kept greenery, even in winter. If you stay, choose between a traditional view looking outside the hotel and an atrium view.

The property has a full-service salon, spa, and fitness center; multiple swimming pools (indoor and outdoor); on-site child care and "kids' resort"; and a car rental agency. You can walk to Opry Mills mall and the Grand Ole Opry from the

hotel or take the free shuttle. Guest rooms are luxurious and feature coffee- and tea makers; two telephones; wireless Internet access; pay-per-view movies, games, and music; daily national newspapers; and other usual amenities. Service is impeccable. Press the "consider it done" button on the phone in your room, and any of your needs will be met. Guests can buy onetime or daily passes on the downtown shuttle for about $20 a day, and the airport shuttle costs $30 round-trip. Self-parking is $24 a day; valet is $32 per day.

While room rates at Opryland can be steep, the hotel offers resort-style packages that add on other Gaylord-owned attractions and properties. These often include tickets to the Grand Ole Opry, a ride on the General Jackson Showboat, trips into Nashville to visit the Ryman Auditorium or the Wildhorse Saloon, and extras like spa visits and golf games at the hotel. Many of these packages are a good deal for travelers who want to pay one price for their whole vacation. Christmastime always brings interesting kid-friendly packages. In the works is a new $90 million Soundwaves water park, open only to hotel guests.

Airport
Under $100
The **Alexis Inn and Suites Nashville Airport** (600 Ermac Dr., 615/889-4466, www.alexisinn.com, rooms $80-100, suites $95-140) is a comfortable and convenient place to stay near the airport. Rooms have all the usual amenities, plus guests get free popcorn in the lobby, a free airport shuttle 7am-9pm daily, and free continental breakfast. All rooms have refrigerators, and most have microwaves. There is a business center on-site.

$100-150
Drury Inns and Suites (555 Donelson Pike, 615/902-0400, www.druryhotels.com, $79-195) offers guests an appealing array of extras, including a free hot breakfast, free evening beverages and snacks, a free airport shuttle, 60 minutes of free long-distance calls, and $7 daily park-and-fly parking. It has both an indoor and outdoor pool and a fitness center. Drury Inn is about two miles north of the airport and five miles south of Music Valley.

$150-200
★ **Hotel Preston** (733 Briley Pkwy., 615/361-5900, www.hotelpreston.com, $149-260) is a boutique hotel near the airport. Youthful energy, modern decor, and up-to-date rooms set this property apart from the crowd. Rooms are stocked with Tazo tea and Starbucks coffee, and there's a 24-hour fitness center. The "You-Want-It-You-Got-It" button in each room beckons the 24-hour room service, and whimsical extras, including a lava lamp, pet fish, and an art kit, are available by request when you check in. Two restaurants, including the Pink Slip bar and nightclub, which features a sculpture by local artist Herb Williams, is known to

both locals and hotel guests as a place with friendly barkeeps and good energy. Café Isabella serves a classic Italian menu and also provides room service to those staying in the hotel.

Information and Services

Visitors Centers
Nashville's main **visitors center** (615/259-4747, www.visitmusiccity.com/visitors, 8am-5pm Mon.-Sat., 10am-5pm Sun.) is at the corner of 5th Avenue and Broadway, inside the Bridgestone Arena. Here you can pick up brochures, get a free map, and find answers to just about any question. It is open late when there is an event at Bridgestone.

There is another visitors center a few blocks uptown (150 4th Ave. N., 615/259-4700, 8am-5pm Mon.-Fri.).

Emergency Services
Dial 911 for police, fire, or ambulance in an emergency. For help with a traffic accident, call the **Tennessee Highway Patrol** (615/741-3181).

Because health care is such a big industry in Nashville, there are a lot of hospitals. The **Monroe Carell Jr. Children's Hospital at Vanderbilt** (2200 Children's Way, 615/936-1000, www.childrenshospital.vanderbilt.org) is among the best in the country. **Saint Thomas Midtown Hospital** (2000 Church St., 615/284-5555, www.sthealth.com) and **Saint Thomas West** (4220 Hardin Pl., 615/222-2111, www.sthealth.com) are other major players.

Rite Aid, CVS, Walgreens, and the major grocery store chains have drugstores all over Nashville. Try the **CVS** at 426 21st Avenue South (615/321-2590, www.cvs.com) if you need 24-hour service. Many drugstores have urgent care clinics inside.

The Trace: Tennessee

You've stocked up in Nashville on gas, snacks, and downloads of honky-tonk music. You have a spare inner tube for the bike and a rain tarp for the tent. Now your epic Trace road trip begins.

DOUBLE ARCH BRIDGE

Double Arch Bridge

Carnton

Gordon House and Ferry Site

President James K. Polk Home & Museum

Mule Day

131 MI/ 211 KM

Meriwether Lewis Monument and Gravesite

CYPRESS CREEK

TENNESSEE
ALABAMA

The Trace: Tennessee

The hills roll and the road winds. The sun rises over wildflower meadows and peeks through lush green tree canopies. You've just left Nashville, but it already seems worlds away.

The Tennessee section of the Trace isn't the best known—Mississippi holds that honor. But it reliably immerses you into the scenic wonderland that is the Trace. As soon as you hop on at the northern terminus, just 17 miles southwest of downtown Music City, you're transported into a lush forest. No matter the time of year, you'll witness nature's bounty, be it colorful leaf changing in the fall (September and October) or riotous flower blooms in the spring (April and May). This may be the only stretch of the Trace where you can experience cold temperatures in the winter. You may even get relief from the southern summer heat and humidity under the shade of these trees.

The idea of a road trip like one down the Natchez Trace is that the journey is the destination. Unlike a drive to a national park, in this case, the drive is the national park. On your leisurely 131-mile drive you'll pass through green, green grasses, historic landmarks and Native American monuments, campgrounds, waterfalls, hiking trails, and the best bridge on the entire Trace. One of the Trace's most solemn monuments, the gravesite of Meriwether Lewis, is found on this stretch, as well as numerous opportunities for hikes and picnics.

Quick detours and side trips off of the Natchez Trace in Tennessee offer access to Civil War and presidential history, good food, and great live music (we're close to Music City, U.S.A., after all). You're likely to meet strangers who will

Highlights

★ **Double Arch Bridge:**
This arched bridge is the ultimate selfie stop (page 98).

★ **Carnton:** This mansion
served as a Confederate field
hospital during the Battle of
Franklin (page 100).

★ **President James K.
Polk Home & Museum:**
James Polk's ancestral home
gives insight into the 11th
president (page 115).

★ **Mule Day:** This four-day
festival celebrates the work
animals that were essential
to farmers and the area's
growth (page 117).

★ **Gordon House and
Ferry Site:** Once a refuge for
travelers, this is one of just
a few remaining structures
from the old Trace (page
120).

★ **Meriwether Lewis
Monument and Gravesite:**
The famous explorer's
gravesite is both somber and
scenic (page 127).

become friends, many with good yarns to tell and recommendations for great roadside barbecue.

Route Overview

This section of the Trace, southwest of Nashville through to the Alabama border, covers **131 miles.** There are more than 25 interesting overlooks, historical markers, and sites to see on this stretch of the Trace alone. This stretch could easily take **two days,** without leaving the Trace itself, and it's a great excuse to **camp overnight** at the Meriwether Lewis Monument and Gravesite Campground.

Side trips into Franklin, Leiper's Fork (a favorite of Nashville celebrities), and Columbia could add another two days to your itinerary. If you want to camp, hike more, and enjoy the great outdoors, you won't be bored if you add another day or two to your trip.

Driving Considerations

This northern section of the Natchez Trace could be waylaid by snow and ice in the winter. Even light snowfall here is rare enough that roads aren't often salted or plowed. Drive with caution if you happen to be on the Trace during or after a snowfall.

Fuel and Services

This section of the Trace is the least remote, running near suburban **Franklin** and **Leiper's Fork** as well as **Columbia,** all towns with a plethora of amenities, including places to sleep, eat, gas up, and play. The proximity to these towns also means that you're likely to be near a cell tower for some of your drive, although cell service should never be taken for granted anywhere on the Trace.

Many people like to have their last meal before hitting the road at the famous **Loveless Cafe** (see page 81) in Nashville, which is less than a mile from the terminus of the Natchez Trace. Grab some of their famous biscuits and then get gas at the adjacent Shell station on

TN-100 and McCrory Lane. Attached to the station is the delicious **Bar-B-Cutie** restaurant, if that's more your taste.

Just north of McGlamery Stand (milepost 352.9) is the town of **Collinwood,** a good place to stop and get gas. Once you're there, drive two blocks west to the **Wayne County Welcome Center** (219 E. Broadway, 931/724-4337, 9am-5pm daily) for parkway maps and information about attractions in the area.

Getting to the Starting Point

Start at the very beginning. Or, as the Trace mile markers say, at the very end: **Milepost 444** is just 17 miles southwest of downtown Nashville. Get here by turning south onto the Trace from TN-100. The entry onto the Trace is well-marked with National Park signage. The first sight, the Double Arch Bridge, is at milepost 438, just six miles from the starting point.

Car, Motorcycle, or Bicycle

If you're not bringing your own car, motorcycle, or bicycle for this epic road trip, you can rent one in Nashville, a major city with many options. Nashville International Airport (BNA) is on the opposite side of town from the Natchez Trace, about a 28-mile drive. If you are flying into town to start your road trip, the airport is as good a place as any to pick up a rental car. Most of the major car rental companies, including **Avis** (300 N. 1st St., 615/743-4740, www.avis.com), **Enterprise** (606 Lafayette St., 615/254-6181, or 1 Terminal Dr., 615/275-0011, http://enterprise.com), and **Budget** (1803 Church St., 615/366-0806, http://budget.com), have desks at the airport, and rates are often competitive. There are also car rental offices downtown and at many of the major hotels.

The siren song of the open road is loud on the Natchez Trace, and many choose to answer it from a motorcycle. If you don't have your own, rent from **EagleRider Nashville** (2233 NW Broad St., Murfreesboro, 800/342-1681,

Best Restaurants

★ **Merridee's Breadbasket:** Its founder may have grown up in Minnesota, but this restaurant has become synonymous with Southern cooking (page 108).

★ **Saffire:** This is Franklin's must-stop for fine dining before catching a show (page 109).

★ **Jack and Jameson's Smokehouse:** People might have started coming here because of celebrity owner Jonathan Jackson, but they stay for the barbecue (page 109).

★ **Red Pony Restaurant:** Innovative Southern food is served in a cosmopolitan setting (page 109).

★ **Puckett's Grocery & Restaurant:** Legendary Southern eats, great live music, and perfect people-watching pack 'em into Puckett's (page 112).

★ **Muletown Roasted Coffee:** Head here for a cup of locally roasted goodness (page 119).

http://eaglerider.com, 9am-5:30pm Mon.-Sat.), which, despite its name, is in Murfreesboro, about 50 miles from the northern Trace terminus. **Sloan's Motorcycle and ATV Supercenter** (2233 NW Broad St., Murfreesboro, 866/808-8179, 9am-6pm Mon.-Sat.) and **Harley-Davidson Cool Springs** (7128 S. Springs Dr., Franklin, 615/425-3494, http://hd-coolsprings.com, 9am-7pm Mon.-Sat., 11am-5pm Sun.) are other options.

If you prefer your two wheels nonmotorized, stop at **Trace Bikes** on TN-100 (8080-B TN-100, 615/646-2485, http://tracebikes.com, 10am-6pm Mon.-Fri., 10am-5pm Sat.) for rentals and helpful gear for touring this road on bike power. Trace Bikes is not open on Sunday.

Air

As Nashville has grown and become more of a tourist destination, **Nashville International Airport** (BNA, http://fly-nashville.com) has grown, too. In 2016, it saw more than 12 million travelers through its gates and announced significant expansion plans. The airport is easy to navigate and is the best bet for flying into Music City. BNA offers email updates that tell travelers when to expect congestion, so they can plan accordingly.

The four-runway airport is filled with local art, live music, and comfortable waiting areas for those picking up passengers. There's even a health clinic for routine medical care. Most of the major airlines serve BNA, including Delta, United, Southwest, Frontier, American, JetBlue, Alaska, and AirCanada.

Exchange currency at **SunTrust Bank** near A/B concourse or at the **Business Service Center** (Wright Travel, 615/275-2658) near C/D concourse.

Many of the major hotels offer shuttles from the airport; there's a kiosk on the lower level of the terminal to help you find the right one. BNA was the first airport in the United States to include "transportation network companies" such as Lyft and Uber in their plans. There is a designated ride sharing area on the ground floor where hotel shuttles wait.

Train and Bus

Amtrak does not have service to Nashville. **Greyhound** (709 5th Ave. S., www.greyhound.com) fully serves Music City, with daily routes that crisscross the state in nearly every direction. In 2012 the city opened a LEED-certified depot, about 20 miles from the terminus of the Natchez Trace. The environmentally friendly building has parking for

Best Accommodations

★ **The Cabin at Cedar Run Farm:** In this two-story log cabin, 1890s style meets modern amenities (page 111).

★ **The Inn at Bigby Creek:** This former home of a Columbia mayor makes for swanky lodging on 1.5 pretty acres (page 119).

★ **Meriwether Lewis Monument and Gravesite Campground:** It may sound creepy to set up your tent near a gravesite, but this solemn spot is full of history and great vistas (page 128).

★ **Fall Hollow B&B and Campground:** This is a perfect spot for groups that can't decide between camping and glamping (page 130).

passenger pickup, a restaurant, a vending area, and ample space for buses. Service goes to major cities in most directions, including Atlanta, Chattanooga, Memphis, and Louisville.

Budget-friendly **Megabus** (http://us.megabus.com) also leaves from the same station. Megabus boasts free Wi-Fi on board and, perhaps because of that, attracts a younger clientele.

★ Double Arch Bridge (MP 438)

Just six miles into the drive on the Natchez Trace, you come to milepost 438. Nothing like starting off a trip with one of the highlights. This bridge is a feat of engineering and design.

At its most utilitarian, the bridge allows the two-lane Natchez Trace to span TN-96, which takes you off the Trace and into charming Franklin. But this bridge is much more than merely practical and, as a result, is one of the most-photographed stops on the Trace. Built in 1994, it was the first bridge in the country built from segments of concrete (in the end there were 122 arch segments). The arches aren't symmetrical, and instead flow with the rolling hills of the countryside.

There are two places to stop and take it all in. The first is the northern pull-off just before the bridge on the right side of the road, called **Birdsong Hollow**

(milepost 438), about 155 feet above the valley. You can park in this small lot and walk just a few steps to see the bridge from above, and even walk along the bridge itself, but you can't stop your car on the bridge. In the thick of summer, some of the view may be obstructed by foliage. There are no amenities other than parking and epic views.

The best view of the bridge itself is from the second pull-off. From the parkway, cross the bridge and follow the sign for the exit to TN-96. Turn left off the Trace. The road swoops back toward the bridge and takes you to a **pull-off** with several parking spaces and a view that takes in the scope of the bridge. Afterward, return to the parkway from the way you came.

TN-96 to Franklin

For much of its life, Franklin was just another small town in Tennessee. The bloody Battle of Franklin that took place in the fields surrounding the town on November 30, 1864, was probably the single most important event to take place there. Like other towns in the region, it took many years for Franklin to fully recover from the impact of the Civil War.

Starting in the 1960s, Franklin underwent a metamorphosis. Construction of I-65 near the town spurred economic development. Today, Franklin is a

Fuel Up

The noncommercial aspect of the Natchez Trace can also be its downfall. No billboards! No businesses! No bright lights! No gas stations.

Don't let an empty tank stop your road trip. Here's a quick list of places to exit the parkway in Tennessee so that you can refuel at the closest gas station. (Some stops may take you to small towns, others will be just a single service station.) The National Park Service also posts a list of nearby supply stations at most Trace rest areas, although the list is not updated regularly.

- **Milepost 444:** Exit at TN-100, just east of the northern terminus.

- **Milepost 438:** Exit at TN-96; drive seven miles west.

- **Milepost 429:** Exit at TN-46; drive one mile east toward Leiper's Fork.

- **Milepost 391.1:** Exit at US 412; drive seven miles west.

- **Milepost 385.9:** Exit at TN-20; drive six miles west to Hohenwald, which has many options.

- **Milepost 369.9:** Exit at US 64; drive less than 0.75 mile west.

- **Milepost 354.9:** Exit at TN-13; drive less than 0.5 mile east to Collinwood.

- **Milepost 350.7:** Exit on TN-13.

well-heeled bedroom community for Nashville professionals and music industry bigwigs. The city, whose population runs around 69,000, is the 10th largest in Tennessee and one of the wealthiest in the state. What sets Franklin apart from other small towns in the state is the effort it has made to preserve and protect the historic downtown. Its location, only 20 miles from Nashville and just a quick, straight drive along TN-96 from the Double Arch Bridge, is also a major plus.

Franklin's attractions are all within a few miles of the city center.

Leaving the Trace

The drive to Franklin from the Double Arch Bridge is about 10 miles and takes about 15 minutes. Cross the bridge, then turn left at the first intersection. After 0.5 mile on this frontage road, make a right onto TN-96 East. Continue for just under 10 miles to reach Franklin.

This is a good place to stop for gas. There's a BP station at the southwest corner of TN-96 and Downs Boulevard. It can be hard to see from the road, but it's there.

Getting Around

Traffic can be heavy in and around Franklin. Because it's a bedroom community for commuters working in Nashville, the morning and afternoon rush hours are to be avoided.

Franklin offers a **trolley bus service** (http://tmagroup.org/franklin-transit, westbound 6am-5pm Mon.-Fri., 8am-5pm Sat., eastbound 7am-6pm Mon.-Fri., 9am-6pm Sat., adults $1, children $0.50) in town and to outlying areas. The trolleys run three different routes. Kids small enough to sit in your lap ride free. You can pick up a full schedule and route map from the visitors center or download it from the website for the TMA Group (http://tmagroup.org).

Sights
Franklin Theatre

The newest gem in historic downtown Franklin is the **Franklin Theatre** (419 Main St., 615/538-2076, www.

A Day on the Trace: Tennessee

For a great day on Tennessee's Trace, fuel up in suburban Franklin at **Puckett's Grocery and Restaurant.** Stroll these quaint downtown streets, window shopping and taking in the restored **Franklin Theatre**. While there, take a tour at **Carnton,** where you get an intimate look at Civil War history.

Now it's time to fuel up the car and enter the parkway at TN-96, right at the base of the breathtaking **Double Arch Bridge.** Not only is this a feat of engineering, but its scale and beauty help frame the scenery you are about to see on your drive.

Lace up the hiking boots for a walk along the **Highland Rim Trail** section of the Natchez Trace National Scenic Trail. This 24-mile path has many entrance points, so you can modify the hike for as short or long a distance as you like. **Burns Branch** is a good place for a quick less-than-two-mile walk to stretch your legs and take in the flora and fauna, but still leave time for more exploring down the parkway. Next head to the **Gordon House and Ferry Site,** one of only two remaining structures on the Trace. Think

about what this rest area would have meant to early settlers and take an easy walk to the ferry site on the Duck River and back to the parking lot.

History continues on your side trip to Columbia, where you can get gas, eat, and tour the **President James K. Polk Home & Museum,** residence of the 11th president of the United States. **Christy's 6th Street Restaurant** is great for a sit-down soul-food lunch. If you'd rather grab picnic supplies for dining on the Trace, stop at **Bypass Deli** before the 20-minute drive back to the parkway. Continue to admire the road's vistas and historical monuments before pulling into the parking lot at **Fall Hollow Waterfall** (milepost 391.9). Walk to the bottom (take a hiking pole) to gaze at nature and reflect on everything you've seen.

It's a quick six-mile drive to **Meriwether Lewis Monument and Gravesite,** the last stop of the day. Find a site at the campground for the night and then enjoy the trails and the monument.

Get up early the next day to finish this section of the route (about 50 miles) before crossing into Alabama.

---

franklintheatre.com, box office noon-5pm Mon., 11am-6pm Tues.-Sat.), a 1937 movie theater that had seen better days when it finally closed in 2007. In 2011, it reopened after an $8 million restoration, funded primarily by donations from locals through the efforts of the Heritage Foundation. The renovation is spot on, bringing the theater, including its striking outdoor marquee, back to its former glory. Lush carpeting, detailed wallpaper, comfortable seats—everything about the theater evokes moviegoing in a different era.

But the Franklin Theatre isn't stuck in the past. Many modern amenities make it a great place to have a night out, such as a concession stand that serves beer, wine, and spirits, with a menu that delineates Jack Daniel's from bourbon and whiskey.

The Franklin Theatre hosts live concerts as well as films, ranging from black-and-white classics to recent releases.

★ Carnton

When Robert Hicks's novel *The Widow of the South* became a best seller in 2005, the staff at the former plantation known as **Carnton** (1345 Carnton Ln., 615/794-0903, www.carnton.org, 9am-5pm Mon.-Sat., noon-5pm Sun., adults $15, seniors $12, children 6-12 $8, children under 5 free) noticed an uptick in the number of visitors. The novel is a fictionalized account of Carrie McGavock and how her home, Carnton, became a Confederate hospital during the Battle of Franklin in the Civil War.

The Carnton mansion was built in 1826 by Randal McGavock, a former

Franklin

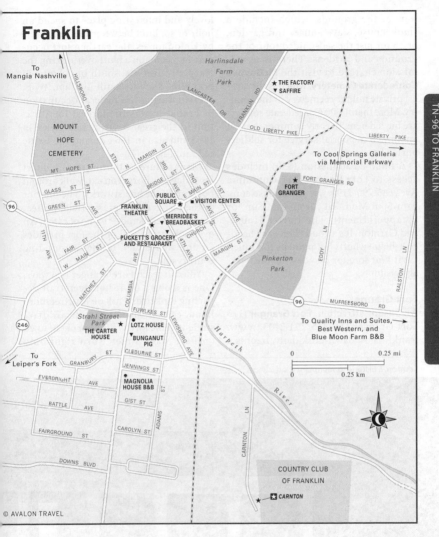

© AVALON TRAVEL

Nashville mayor and prominent lawyer and businessman. Randal had died by the time of the Civil War, and it was his son, John, and John's wife, Carrie, who witnessed the bloody Battle of Franklin on November 30, 1864. Located behind the Confederate line, Carnton became a hospital for hundreds of injured and dying Confederate soldiers. As late as six months after the battle, the McGavock home remained a refuge for recovering veterans.

In the years that followed the battle, the McGavocks raised money, donating much of it themselves, to construct a cemetery for the Confederate dead and donated two acres of land to the cause.

A visitors center provides space for the museum and gift shop. Visitors to Carnton can pay full price for a guided tour of the mansion and self-guided tour of the grounds, which include a smokehouse, slave house, and garden, or $5 for just the self-guided tour of the grounds and gardens. There is no admission charged to visit the **McGavock Confederate Cemetery,** which is the largest private military cemetery in the country. More than 1,500 Confederate soldiers are buried here. In early summer there is an annual memorial service for soldiers buried here.

A bundled admission ($30) includes access to **Lotz House** (1111 Columbia Ave., 615/790-7190, www.lotzhouse.com, 9am-5pm Mon.-Sat., 1pm-4pm Sun. or by appointment), The Carter House, and Carnton. It's a good choice for hardcore history buffs but perhaps too much Civil War lore for one day for the average visitor.

Fort Granger

An unsung attraction, **Fort Granger** (113 Fort Granger Dr., 615/794-2103, www. franklin.gov, dawn-dusk daily, free) is a lovely and interesting place to spend an hour or so. Built between 1862 and 1863 by Union forces, the earthen fort occupies 14.5 acres on a bluff overlooking the Harpeth River just south of downtown Franklin. The fort, built by Capt. W. E. Merrill during the Federal occupation of Franklin, was the largest fortification in the area. It saw action twice in 1863 and also in 1864 during the Battle of Franklin.

Many features of the fort remain intact for today's visitors. You can walk around portions of the breastworks. The interior of the fort is now a grassy field, perfect for a summer picnic or game of catch. An overlook at one end of the fort provides an unmatched view of the surrounding countryside.

You can reach Fort Granger two ways. One is along a short but steep trail departing Pinkerton Park on Murfreesboro Road, east of town. Or you can drive straight to the fort by heading out of town on East Main Street. Turn right onto

Carnton, a historic former plantation

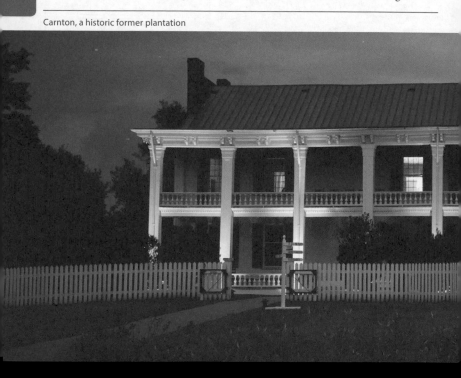

Liberty Pike, right onto Eddy Lane, and, finally, right again onto Fort Granger Drive.

The fort is maintained by the City of Franklin. While there is no office or visitors center at the fort, you may contact Franklin's parks department (615/794-2103) for more information.

The Carter House

Some of the fiercest fighting in the Battle of Franklin took place around the farm and house belonging to the Carter family on the outskirts of town. The family took refuge in the basement while Union and Confederate soldiers fought hand to hand right above them. Today, **The Carter House** (1140 Columbia Ave., 615/791-1861, www.boft.org/carter-house.htm, 9am-5pm Mon.-Sat., noon-5pm Sun., $15) is the best place to come for a detailed examination of the battle and the profound human toll that it exacted on both sides.

You will see hundreds of bullet holes, which help to illustrate the ferocity of the fight. Guides describe some of the worst moments of the battle and bring to life a few of the people who fought it. The house also holds a museum of Civil War uniforms and memorabilia, including photographs and short biographies of many of the men who were killed in Franklin. A video about the battle shows scenes from a reenactment.

If you can't get enough Civil War history, consider one of the packages that offer discounts on joint admission to nearby **Lotz House** (www.lotzhouse.com), The Carter House, and Carnton.

Tours

Pick a topic (Civil War history, ghosts, food, crime, etc.) and **Franklin on Foot** (114 E. Main St., 615/400-3808, www.franklinonfoot.com, adults $15-45) will lead you on a walking tour that meets your needs. Most tours occur daily, but book ahead to be sure. Want something faster? Try **Franklin Segway Tours** (615/905-6263, http://franklinsegway-tours.com, $60); tours leave from Handy Hardware (731 Columbia Ave.). The 90-minute experience includes 30 minutes of training and a 60-minute guided Segway tour.

Entertainment and Events
Live Music

As great as the Grand Ole Opry is (and it *is* great), sometimes the music seems a little, well, dated. Experience an Opry-style live radio show, but with more cutting-edge country, Americana, and bluegrass acts during **Music City Roots** (www.musiccityroots.com, tickets $10) on Wednesday nights at **The Factory** (230 Franklin Rd.). This two-hour-plus multiple-act show includes live interview segments with the artists, on-the-air commercials, and an audience that often gets up and dances. Stay till the very end for the jam, when all the night's performers cram on stage for one last song. The show is also broadcast on WMOT-FM, a radio station that focuses on Americana music.

Other venues that sometimes offer live music include restaurants **Saffire** (The Factory, 230 Franklin Rd., Bldg. 11, 615/599-4995), **Puckett's Grocery and Restaurant** (120 4th Ave. S., 625/794-5527), **The Bunganut Pig** (1143 Columbia Ave., 615/794-4777), and **Jack and Jameson's Smokehouse** (509 Hillsboro Rd., 615/465-6253), a restaurant co-owned by singer/actor Jonathan Jackson.

The **Franklin Theatre** (419 Main St., 615/538-2076, www.franklintheatre.com) has an impressive concert schedule, typically with affordable ticket prices.

Theater

Franklin's community theater troupe is **Pull-Tight Players** (112 2nd Ave. S., 615/791-5007 or 615/790-6782, www.pull-tight.com, adults $18, seniors $16, children $12). Performing in an intimate theater in downtown Franklin, the Pull-Tight Players put on about six productions each season, which runs September-June. Productions include many classic stage favorites.

Cinemas

The restored **Franklin Theatre** (419 Main St., 615/538-2076, www.franklintheatre.com, $5) shows classic black-and-white films as well as recent releases (although typically not first-run movies). Kid-friendly flicks are shown on the weekends.

Festivals and Events
Spring

One of the city's biggest festivals of the year is the **Main Street Festival** (615/591-8500, www.historicfranklin.com, Apr.) during the last full weekend of April. Local arts and crafts are the major draw of this showcase, which also includes food, music, theater, and children's activities. The event is hosted by the Heritage Foundation of Franklin & Williamson County.

The town's Rotary Club organizes the annual **Franklin Rodeo** (www.franklinrodeo.com, May), a weeklong event in May that includes a Rodeo Parade, Miss Tennessee Rodeo pageant, and a Professional Rodeo Cowboys Association (PRCA)-sanctioned rodeo with steer wrestling and bronco and bull riding. It takes place at the **Williamson County Ag Expo Park** (4215 Long Ln. #100, 615/595-1227), and proceeds go to local service projects.

Summer

During the first full weekend of June you can join the **Heritage Foundation on a Town and Country Tour of Homes** (www.historicfranklin.com, June). Tours go to private and historic homes that are closed to the public during the rest of the year.

Franklin celebrates Independence Day with **Franklin on the Fourth** (www.tneventinfo.com, July 4), a patriotic family concert on the public square. The fireworks finale takes place near Mack Hatcher/Hillsboro Road.

During the last weekend in July the city celebrates **Bluegrass Along the Harpeth** (615/390-3588, www.bluegrassalongtheharpeth.com, July, free), a music festival featuring bluegrass, old-time string bands, and buck dancing.

The **Williamson County Fair** (www.williamsoncountyfair.org, Aug.) starts on the first Friday in August and features agricultural exhibits, a midway, live entertainment, and competitions. It takes place at the **Williamson County Ag Expo Park** (4215 Long Ln. #100, 615/595-1227).

Fall

Re-enactors descend on Franklin for **Blue and Gray Days** (www.boft.org, Nov.), two days of living history, including a Civil War soldiers' camp. This celebration is staged at The Carter House (1140 Columbia Ave., 615/791-1861) and Carnton (1345 Eastern Flank Circle, 615/794-0903).

In just a few years the **Pilgrimage**

Music & Cultural Festival (http://pilgrimagefestival.com, Sept.) has become a major player on the concert festival circuit, which is really saying something in the land of Bonnaroo. The fest, which takes place in September at The Park at Harlinsdale Farm (239 Franklin Rd., 615/794-2103), attracts acts including Grace Potter, Hall & Oates, and Kacey Musgraves. Megastar and Tennessee native Justin Timberlake is one of the partners in the festival.

Winter
During the second full weekend of December, the city of Franklin is transformed into a bustling Victorian town at **Dickens of a Christmas** (http://historicfranklin.com, Dec.). There are costumed characters like Oliver Twist, carolers, artisans, strolling minstrels, and unique foods.

Shopping
Shopping is Franklin's greatest attraction (at least for those not interested in Civil War history). Trendy downtown shops, the unique environment of The Factory, and proximity to a major mall make this a destination for shoppers. It is also one of Tennessee's most popular antiques shopping destinations.

Antiques
Franklin declares itself the New Antiques Capital of Tennessee. Indeed, antiquing is one of the most popular pursuits of Franklin's visitors, and at least two dozen antiques shops serve to quench the thirst for something old. The town's antiques district is huddled around the corner of Margin Street and 2nd Avenue. Here you'll find no fewer than six major antiques stores. Other shops are found along Main Street in the downtown shopping district.

Top to bottom: downtown Franklin; shops and storefronts in downtown Franklin; The Carter House.

The best place to start antiquing is the **Franklin Antique Mall** (251 2nd Ave. S., 615/790-8593, www.franklinantiquemall. com), located in the town's old icehouse. The mall is a maze of rooms, each with different goods on offer. Possibilities include books, dishware, quilts, furniture, knickknacks, and housewares. You can also follow 5th Avenue about two blocks south of downtown to find **Country Charm Antique Mall** (301 Lewisburg Ave., 615/790-8998, www.countrycharm-malltn.com), whose three buildings house a vast array of furniture, quilts, glassware, china, and home decor.

Just outside the Franklin Antique Mall are at least five other antiques shops to roam through, including **J. J. Ashley's** (125 S. Margin St., 615/791-0011), which specializes in French and English country accessories, as well as European furniture. **Scarlett Scales Antiques** (212 S. Margin St., 615/791-4097, http://scarlettscales.com), located in a 1900s shotgun house, has American country

furnishings, accessories, and architectural elements arriving daily.

Downtown

Retail is alive and well in Franklin's downtown. West Main Street is the epicenter of the shopping district, although you will find stores scattered around other parts of downtown as well. Home decor, classy antiques, trendy clothes, and specialty items like candles, tea, and gardening supplies are just a few of the things you'll find in downtown Franklin.

Most shops are open by 10am, and many stay open until the evening to catch late-afternoon visitors. You can easily navigate the downtown shopping district on foot.

Bink's Outfitters (421 Main St., 615/599-8777, www.binksoutfitters.com, 10am-9pm Mon.-Sat., 11am-7pm Sun.) is the perfect place to stock up on outdoor clothing and equipment before biking or hiking the Trace.

Check out **Jondie** (412 Main St.,

Franklin's Main Street

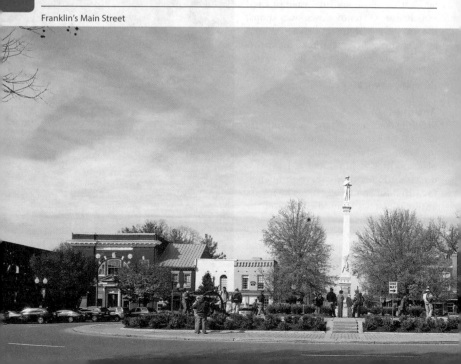

615/807-2386, www.jondie.com, 10am-6pm Mon.-Wed., 10am-7pm Thurs., 10am-8pm Fri.-Sat., 11am-6pm Sun.) for women's clothing and accessories, then pop into **Avec Moi** (418 Main St., 615/791-9121, www.avecmoifranklin.com, 10am-5:30pm Mon.-Thurs., 10am-9pm Fri., 10am-6pm Sat., noon-4pm Sun.) for both vintage and new jewelry.

The city's best bookstore is **Landmark Booksellers** (114 E. Main St., 615/791-6400, http://landmarkbooksellers.com, 10am-5pm daily), found about a block east of the town square. It has a wide selection of used and new books, including many regional and rare titles. It is friendly and welcoming, with fresh coffee for sale in the mornings.

Toys old and new are on sale at **Main Street Toy Co.** (412 Main St., 615/790-4869, 10am-6pm Mon.-Thurs., 10am-7pm Fri.-Sat., noon-5pm Sun.). For the best in paper, gift wrap, and stationery, go to **Rock Paper Scissors** (317 Main St., 615/791-0150, www.rockpaperscissor.

com, 10am-6pm Mon.-Fri., 10am-5pm Sat.). Head to **Tin Cottage** (123 S. Margin St., 615/472-1183, www.tincottage.com, 10am-5pm Mon.-Sat.) for local prepared foods and kitchen goodies, housewarming gifts, and the thank-you gift for the person holding down the fort at home while you travel.

The Factory

Franklin's most distinctive retail center is **The Factory** (230 Franklin Rd., 615/791-1777, www.factoryatfranklin.com). A 250,000-square-foot complex of 11 old industrial buildings, The Factory once housed stove factories and a textile mill. In the mid-1990s, Calvin Lehew bought the dilapidated eyesore and began the lengthy process of restoring the buildings and converting them to a space for galleries, retail shops, restaurants, and other businesses.

Today, The Factory is a vibrant commercial center for the city of Franklin. It houses a refreshing array of local independent retailers, including galleries, salons, candy shops, and a pet boutique. **The Little Cottage** (615/794-1405, www.thelittlecottagechildrensshop.com, 9:30am-5pm Mon.-Thurs., 9:30am-6pm Fri., 10am-6pm Sat., noon-5pm Sun.) sells children's fashions.

There are also several studios and learning centers, including **South Gate Studio & Fine Art** (615/559-3660, www.southgatestudio.com), which offers art classes. Additionally, The Factory has four restaurants and a fish market, and is home to the weekly Americana show *Music City Roots*.

Sports and Recreation

To add a little height (and adrenaline) to your Franklin area recreation, head to **SOAR Adventure Tower** (3794 Carothers Pkwy., 615/721-5103, www.soaradventure.com, 10am-9pm Tues.-Thurs., 10am-10pm Fri.-Sat., 10am-8pm Sun. June-July, adults $45, children 8-17 $40, children 3-7 $35), where you can climb obstacles in the sky. Or opt for the easy float of **Middle Tennessee Hot Air Adventures** (615/584-6236, www.tnballoon.com, shared flight $200/passenger, private two-passenger flight $750).

Parks

Franklin's **Parks Department** (615/794-2103, www.franklin.gov) is in charge of the city's network of parks, which make up over 700 acres of land.

Pinkerton Park (405 Murfreesboro Rd.), just southeast of town off Murfreesboro Road, is a pleasant city park. Walking trails, playgrounds, and picnic tables draw dozens of town residents, who come to exercise or simply relax. A short hiking trail takes you to Fort Granger, overlooking the city. You can also take the Sue Douglas Berry Memorial pedestrian bridge over the Harpeth River and walk the six blocks to the town square.

Jim Warren Park (705 Boyd Mill Ave.) is a large public park with baseball and softball fields, tennis courts, covered picnic areas, and 2.5 miles of walking trails. Take a stroll around a Civil War monument and 61-acre historic battle site at **Winstead Hill Park** (4023 Columbia Ave.). The park also has a short walking trail and restrooms. **Aspen Grove Park** (3200 Aspen Grove Dr.) offers 14 acres of fun, including a half-mile walking trail, a creek (Spencer Creek), playground, and picnic pavilion with grills.

The Park at Harlinsdale Farm

One of the most famous Tennessee Walking Horse breeding farms became a public park in 2007. **The Park at Harlinsdale Farm** (239 Franklin Rd.) was a famed Franklin landmark for many years, thanks to a very famous horse. Midnight Sun, a stallion, was a world champion Walking Horse in 1945 and 1946, and all subsequent champions can trace their ancestry to him.

In 2004, Franklin bought the 200-acre farm for $8 million, and three years later the first 60 acres opened as a public park. It is a pleasant place to walk or picnic, with a dog park, a pond for catch-and-release fishing, and a 5K turf track.

Golf

Located a few miles southeast of Franklin, **Forrest Crossing Golf Course** (750 Riverview Dr., 615/794-9400, www.forrestcrossing.com, greens fees $34 Mon.-Fri., $50 Sat.-Sun., $28 seniors) is an 18-hole par 72 golf course designed by Gary Roger Baird. Just shy of 7,000 yards, the course rating is 77.8, and the slope is 135.

There are more golf courses in Cool Springs, a few miles north of Franklin. **Vanderbilt Legends Club** (1500 Legends Club Ln., 615/791-8100, www.legendsclub.com, greens fees $75-85) is a top-of-the-line golf club. There are two 18-hole courses at the club, as well as a complete array of club services, including a putting green and chipping green. Greens fees include use of a cart. Lower rates are available after 3pm. No blue jeans, T-shirts, or athletic shorts are allowed.

The **Fairways on Spencer Creek** (285 Spencer Creek Rd., 615/794-8223, www.fairwaysonspencercreek.net, greens fees $16) is a nine-hole alternative. The course rating is 64.6, and the slope is 105.

Food

The best choice for baked goods, coffee, and light fare, including soups, salads, and sandwiches, is ★ **Merridee's Breadbasket** (110 4th Ave., 615/790-3755, www.merridees.com, 7am-5pm Mon.-Wed., 7am-9pm Thurs.-Sat., $3-11). Merridee grew up in Minnesota and learned baking from her mother, a Swede. When Merridee married Tom McCray and moved to Middle Tennessee in 1973, she kept up the baking traditions she had learned as a child. In 1984, she opened Merridee's Breadbasket in Franklin. Merridee McCray died in 1994, but her restaurant remains one of Franklin's most popular. Come in for omelets, scrambled eggs, or sweet bread and fruit in the morning. At lunch choose from the daily soup, casserole, or quiche, or order a cold or grilled sandwich. Merridee's also bakes fresh bread daily; take home a loaf of the always-popular Viking bread. Merridee's attracts a variety of people—students, businesspeople, and families out on the town. The creaky wood floors and comfortable seating make it a pleasant and relaxing place to refuel.

Puckett's Grocery & Restaurant (120 4th Ave. S., 625/794-5527, http://puckettsgro.com, 7am-3pm Mon., 7am-9pm Tues.-Sat., 7am-7pm Sun., $7-10), the Leiper's Fork institution, has a second location in Franklin (and a third in Nashville). The Franklin shop offers traditional breakfasts with eggs, bacon, country ham, and biscuits, and plate lunches during the day. In the evening, order up a handmade burger (the locals swear that they're the best in town), a Southern dinner of fried catfish, or a traditional steak, chicken, or fish entrée. For vegetarians, they offer a veggie burger or a vegetable plate, as well as salads. Do not skip the fried green beans. The food is well prepared and the service friendly, and there's almost always a crowd, regardless of whether or not there's live music on tap.

Always popular, award-winning ★ **Saffire** (The Factory, 230 Franklin Rd., Bldg. 11, 615/599-4995, www.saffirerestaurant.com, 11am-9pm Sun. and Tues.-Thurs., 11am-10pm Fri.-Sat., $12-35) uses primarily organic and biodynamic ingredients. The menu sparkles with upscale dishes, such as prime rib and ahi tuna. The fried chicken is dusted with panko, topped with country ham gravy, and served with luscious macaroni and cheese. Saffire has an extensive wine and cocktail list, including organic choices. Take $4 off signature cocktails during happy hour (5pm-6pm), and on Tuesday nights most bottles of wine go for half price. Set within an old warehouse, Saffire's dining room is spacious, with exposed brick and beams. The kitchen opens out onto the dining room, so you can watch the cooks work. With live music many nights, Saffire is a solid choice for excellent food in a pleasant and exciting environment.

Nashville (the TV show) is a Nashville (the city) favorite. So when Jonathan Jackson, an actor and singer on the show, paired with his old *General Hospital* pal Steve Burton to open a live music venue/barbecue joint, locals were supportive. Show up at ★ **Jack and Jameson's Smokehouse** (509 Hillsboro Rd., 615/465-6253, 11am-10pm Sun.-Fri., 11am-midnight Sat., $10-20) for better-than-average burgers, mac-and-cheese, and Southern favorites. Many drinks and dishes are served in Mason jars, but this isn't a hipster joint. There's a kids' menu and family-friendly vibe. Check out the beers on draft when you come for a live music show.

Since 2006, ★ **Red Pony Restaurant** (408 Main St., 615/595-7669, http://redponyrestaurant.com, 4pm-10pm Mon.-Thurs., 4pm-11pm Fri.-Sat., $25-48) has been a Franklin favorite. The chefs call the menu "sophisticated Southern," which translates to lots of bacon, okra, grits, and game meats served in innovative ways. Combine a traditional pork chop with a lighter cucumber and feta salad to enjoy a leisurely meal (without your cell phone, by request of the kitchen), but it won't be so heavy that you won't be able to get up and hike or bike the next morning. Thanks to details like printing names on daily menus, Red Pony is a perfect place to celebrate a birthday or anniversary.

Need a cup of joe before you hit the road? **Frothy Monkey** (125 5th Ave. S., 615/465-6279, www.frothymonkey.com, 6am-9pm Mon.-Thurs., 6am-10pm Fri., 7am-10pm Sat., 8am-9pm Sun., $6-17) is a locally beloved coffee shop chain with solid sandwiches and salads. Need other kinds of drinks? Try **Juice Bar Franklin** (232 5th Ave. N., 615/656-1144,

www.ilovejuicebar.com, 7am-6:30pm
Mon.-Fri., 8am-6:30pm Sat., 11am-5pm
Sun., $6-10) for the healthy stuff and
Mantra Artisan Ales (216 Noah Dr. #140,
615/628-8776, www.mantrabrewing.com,
3pm-9pm Mon.-Thurs., 3pm-10pm Fri.,
noon-10pm Sat., noon-6pm Sun.) for
adult beverages. Mantra is only a taproom and does not serve food.

Franklin Farmers Market

The **Franklin Farmers Market** (230
Franklin Rd., www.franklinfarmers-
market.com, 8am-noon Sat. May-Oct.,
9am-1pm Sat. Nov.-Dec., 9am-noon Sat.
Jan.-Apr.) takes place at the rear of The
Factory. This is one of the finest small-
town farmers markets in the state, featuring a wide variety of fruit and vegetable
growers and cheese, milk, and meat sellers, as well as craftspeople and live music.

Accommodations

Franklin has two types of accommodations: cozy bed-and-breakfast inns and
chain motels. The bed-and-breakfasts are
located in downtown Franklin and the
surrounding countryside. The chain motels are around exit 65 off I-65, about two
miles from the city center. The bed-and-
breakfast accommodations are far more
congruous with Franklin's charm than
the interstate motels. This is also a good
area to search for alternative accommodations, like those offered on **Airbnb**
(http://airbnb.com).

Under $100

A hotel room shortage in Nashville has
meant higher prices in all the surrounding areas. A few good bets for affordable
rooms include the **Comfort Inn Franklin**
(4202 Franklin Commons Ct., 800/916-
4339, http://comfortinn.reservations.
com, $95-110), which offers free Wi-Fi

Top to bottom: the water tower at The Factory
in Franklin; historical sign at Leiper's Fork;
Garrison Creek, a popular place to start a Trace
hike.

and complimentary breakfast, and allows pets.

$150-200

The **Magnolia House Bed and Breakfast** (1317 Columbia Ave., 615/794-8178, www.bbonline.com/tn/magnolia, $160) is less than a mile from downtown Franklin, near The Carter House. A large magnolia tree shades the early-20th-century Craftsman home. There are four carpeted guest rooms, each with a private bath. Three house queen-size beds; the fourth has two twin beds. Common areas include a polished sitting room, cozy den, and sunroom that looks out on the quiet residential neighborhood. Hosts Jimmy and Robbie Smithson welcome guests and prepare a homemade breakfast according to your preferences.

The log cabin that is now ★ **The Cabin at Cedar Run Farm** (5330 Old Harding Rd., 615/799-9391, http://cabinatcedarrunfarm.com, $175-250) may have been built in 1840, but this isn't roughing it. The two-story cabin has a full kitchen, Internet access, and a cute front porch perfect for sipping your morning coffee.

A hip, urban option is **Aloft/Cool Springs** (7109 S. Springs Dr., 615/435-8700, www.aloftnashvillecoolsprings.com, $149-184). The hotel boasts a saltwater pool, a better-than-average hotel bar, and a good location for business or recreation in Franklin.

Back to the Trace

Take TN-96 west for just under 10 miles. Turn left when you see the brown Natchez Trace Parkway sign just before the Double Arch Bridge. Follow this frontage road for about 0.5 mile, then turn left to get back on the Trace, headed south.

Leiper's Fork (MP 428)

Part bucolic small town, part rarified enclave, Leiper's Fork is a pleasant place to spend a few hours—or a lifetime. The town runs for several miles along Leiper's Fork, a tributary of the West Harpeth River. Beautiful old farmhouses line Old Hillsboro Road, which serves as the main thoroughfare through town.

One of the earliest settlers of the area was the Benton family, including Thomas Hart Benton, who would go on to become a U.S. senator from Missouri. For many years, Leiper's Fork was called Hillsboro after Hillsborough, North Carolina, where many of its early settlers came from. There is another Hillsboro in Coffee County, Tennessee, however, so when this Hillsboro petitioned for a post office in 1818, the U.S. Postal Service insisted that it change its name. Leiper's Fork was born.

Acclaimed furniture maker Dick Poyner was from the Leiper's Fork area. Poyner, a former slave, was famous for his sturdy ladder-back wooden chairs, one of which is on display at the Tennessee State Museum in Nashville.

Leiper's Fork is a pleasant community, with die-hard locals who are seriously proud of their town. Art galleries and antiques shops line the short main drag. Unusually good food can be found at local restaurants, and a laid-back let's-laugh-at-ourselves attitude prevails. A few bed-and-breakfasts in the area make it a viable place to rest before the next leg of your trip.

Many music powerhouses, from producers to performers, live here, including Justin Timberlake, who owns two businesses. But, please, if you see a celebrity, don't make a fuss. They choose to live in Leiper's Fork to be away from the crowds. When you do see them around town, expect them to be in boots and jeans, just like everyone else.

Leiper's Fork is less than two miles off the Trace. Take the exit at milepost 428 for TN-46, which will veer right onto an unnamed frontage road for 0.1 mile. At the intersection with TN-46, turn right and follow the highway. Turn left at the stop sign, then continue for about a mile on the highway to reach the Leiper's Fork Historic District.

Entertainment and Events

Friday night is songwriter night at **Puckett's Grocery & Restaurant** (4142 Old Hillsboro Rd., 615/794-1308, www.puckettsofleipersfork.com). For $30 you can enjoy dressed-up dinner—fresh seafood, poultry, and steak are usually among the options—at 7pm and an in-the-round performance from Nashville singer-songwriters starting at 8:30pm. Or pay $12 for the concert only. Reservations are essential for either, so call ahead. Check the website to find out who is performing.

Jailhouse Industrys operates the Leiper's Fork **Lawnchair Theatre** (615/477-6799) behind Leiper's Creek Gallery (4144 Old Hillsboro Rd.) from May to September. Bring your lawn chair or blanket and enjoy classic movies and kids' favorites on Friday and Saturday nights, plus concerts.

Shopping

This is the town to browse for one-of-a-kind gems. Leiper's Fork retailers are generally open 10am-5pm Wednesday-Saturday and 1pm-5pm Sunday.

The **Leiper's Creek Gallery** (4144 Old Hillsboro Rd., 615/599-5102, www.leiperscreekgallery.com) is the finest gallery in town. It shows a wide selection of paintings by local and regional artists and hosts arts events year-round.

Neena's Primitive Antiques (4158 Old Hillsboro Rd., 615/790-0345) specializes in primitive antiques, linens, home decor items, and leather goods.

The 3,000-square-foot **Serenite Maison** (4149 Old Hillsboro Rd., 615/599-2071, www.serenitemaison.com) houses a well-edited inventory thanks to the smart design sense of Alexandra Cirimelli. A California transplant, Cirimelli has appeared on an episode of *American Pickers* and is known for finding her well-heeled clients (including Holly Williams and several actors from *Nashville*) the perfect farm table or pie safe for their kitchen. Don't overlook the pickin' corner, where locals stop in to play the antique guitars, banjos, and mandolins that hang on the walls.

Food

★ **Puckett's Grocery & Restaurant** (4142 Old Hillsboro Rd., 615/794-1308, www.puckettsofleipersfork.com, 6am-7pm Mon.-Thurs., 6am-10:30pm Fri.-Sat., 6am-6pm Sun. Mar.-Nov., more limited hours Dec.-Feb., $6-25) is the heartbeat of Leiper's Fork. An old-time grocery with a small dining room attached, Puckett's serves breakfast, lunch, and dinner to the town faithful and visitors alike. The original country store opened in 1953. In 1998, Andy Marshall bought the store and expanded the restaurant offerings. Solid country breakfasts are the order of the day in the mornings, followed by plate lunches. The pulled pork is a favorite, as is the Puckett Burger. Dinner specials include catfish nights, family nights, and a Saturday-night seafood buffet. Friday night the grocery turns upscale with a supper club and live music. Reservations are essential for Friday night. Puckett's hours vary by season, so it's best to call ahead, especially for dinner. A second Puckett's Grocery location in Franklin offers a more varied menu.

Accommodations

Innkeepers Eric and Samantha have three different places to stay under the name **Pot N' Kettle Cottages** (615/864-3392, www.potnkettlecottages.com, $150-295). The cottages, all on the same street, are within walking distance of downtown Leiper's Fork and sleep 5-9 people. Amenities include bicycles to cruise around town and Wi-Fi. Discounts are available for groups that book more than one cottage at a time.

Garrison Creek (MP 427.6)

The history is as rich as the forest at this creek and trailhead. In the 18th century the woods gave way to a garrison (hence the name) to protect troops from Native American attacks. The long-gone fort was used again in the parkway's history, most recently as a base during road construction.

Today a paved lot at the site of the former fort includes plenty of parking spots, restrooms, and picnic tables nestled under the shady trees, and room for horse trailers (in the back of the lot). It makes a good place to stretch your legs and eat lunch.

Walk just a few minutes from the parking lot to see small Garrison Creek, which winds its way through the forest. Unlike other waterways along the Trace, this creek is too shallow for swimming. But it makes for pretty scenery and a place for dogs or horses to take a drink.

As the northern terminus of the Highland Rim Trail section of the Natchez Trace National Scenic Trail, **Garrison Creek Trailhead** is popular with day hikers, backpackers, and equestrians. You will need to cross the creek if you decide to hike here. There's not a bridge, but several logs and fallen trees make crossing possible.

This is also the starting point for November's 46-mile **Natchez Trace Trail Run** (www.hardwinadventures.com), an out-and-back double marathon trail run.

This is the last restroom stop until Gordon House and Ferry Site (milepost 407.7).

War of 1812 Monument (MP 426.3)

From a parking area on the left side of the road, a paved pathway leads to this stone monument memorializing soldiers who fought in the War of 1812 and are buried along the Old Trace. Then, the parkway was an important route for moving troops through Tennessee. General Andrew Jackson marched with his troops along this route, and many who fought (and were victorious) in the Battle of New Orleans used this path to get home.

The small marker has text detailing how the now-disappeared inns on the Natchez Trace functioned as hospitals for soldiers far from home.

Burns Branch (MP 425.4)

This picnic area and parking lot on the left side of the road offers a nice, shady respite. It is well-marked with official signage and the lot is paved.

The tree canopies here are perfect for offering shade in the heat of summer and for admiring color in the fall. There are picnic tables and a small creek for a contemplative rest stop. There are trash receptacles but no other amenities.

From Burns Branch it's possible to hike a section of the **Highland Rim Trail,** part of the greater Natchez Trace National Scenic Trail, going either north toward Garrison Creek or south as far as the Gordon House and Ferry Site. Good signage makes it clear which way to go, should you decide to hike. This rest stop offers hitching posts and has room for trailers in the parking lot, for those looking to traverse the trail on horseback.

Tennessee Valley Divide (MP 423.9)

This well-marked rest stop, which is on the left side of the road, may at first look like another of the parkway's magnificent scenic views. And it is, offering an open meadow and a wide, open expanse for taking in the big sky and the fresh air. But this spot also has both geographical and historical significance.

Rivers and streams on the south

Hiking the Highland Rim Trail

Today the Natchez Trace Parkway is an easily traveled roadway for drivers, bikers, cyclists, and equestrians. Two centuries ago, it was a more arduous trip. The **Natchez Trace National Scenic Trail** (www.nps.gov/natt) offers the chance to experience the undeveloped landscape of the area as travelers did so many years ago.

The Natchez Trace National Scenic Trail is composed of five different trails totaling more than 60 miles. Tighten your hiking boot laces: The Leiper's Fork District of the Natchez Trace National Scenic Trail runs for 24 miles, starting near milepost 427 and ending at milepost 408, where TN-50 crosses the parkway. This trail, part of the **Highland Rim Trail,** is one of several preserved sections of the Old Trace.

The most popular access point for the Highland Rim Trail is from **Garrison Creek** (milepost 427), the northernmost entrance. Heavy rains may make conditions muddy. Be sure that you aren't accidentally trespassing on private property: Stay on the marked trail at all times.

Garrison Creek to Burns Branch

Garrison Creek is one of the most popular places to hit the Highland Rim Trail section of the Natchez Trace National Scenic Trail, not only because it's the most scenic, but because it's so easy to access—it's also the northern terminus of the trail. The first part of the trail is an open meadow, with no shade to speak of, but it soon winds its way next to Garrison Creek.

Start here to complete the full 24-mile southbound trek—or do any number of shorter hikes. It's just 2.3 miles from Gar-

rison Creek to Burns Branch and 3.7 miles to the Tennessee Valley Divide. Most of this section is well shaded by trees, except for the access points next to the parking lots.

From Garrison Creek you can hike or ride south, where you can take in several sights and, if you are on foot, check out several small side trails, most of which are small dirt paths of the Old Trace and not accessible to horses. While here, stop quickly at the small stone **War of 1812 Memorial** (milepost 426.3), near a spot that was cleared for use as a postal road in the early 1800s.

Burns Branch to the Tennessee Valley Divide

Continue 2.3 miles to Burns Branch, where you'll work out your thighs and calves on rolling hills (rather than steep inclines). The dense forest provides shade from the hot summer sun, although serious trail runners prefer this path in winter, when some of the lush green overgrowth is gone and they can make their way without foliage or branches in the way. When you get to Burns Branch, you'll find a parking lot on the left side of the road and several picnic tables along this branch of the creek. Enjoy lunch in the shade and rest, or continue on toward the Tennessee Valley Divide, which offers similar scenery on a longer hike. Most walkers and hikers just do the section to Burns Branch, so if you continue on, you'll have few companions on your hike. Some locals do use this space for trail running, so pay attention and move aside if someone wants to pass you.

side of the divide flow to the Duck and Tennessee Rivers, while those to the north head to the Cumberland River (a 600-plus-mile river that wends its way through downtown Nashville). Historically, this divide was significant because it was the boundary between the Chickasaw Nation (to the south) and

the United States (to the north). In the mid-1800s the Chickasaw people, along with other Native American tribes, were forced from their homes along what was to become known as the Trail of Tears. Today the Chickasaw Nation is largely in Oklahoma.

From this spot it's possible to hike a

section of the **Highland Rim Trail,** part of the greater Natchez Trace National Scenic Trail, going either north toward Garrison Creek or south as far as the Gordon House and Ferry Site. This spot is a hiker-only access point.

Creekview Farm Retreat B&B (MP 416)

The three-bedroom **Creekview Farm Retreat B&B** (5177 Leipers Creek Rd., Santa Fe, 931/446-7993, $95-290) is on a working farm, just three miles from the parkway itself. But don't worry. You can admire the livestock from a screened-in porch; no one is going to make you do farm chores. In colder months, the fireplace is the perfect place to curl up and reflect on your travels and your trip. Guests are welcome to use the B&B's kitchen (breakfast is provided, of course). Children are welcome, but those traveling with pets will need to stay elsewhere.

To get here, exit the parkway at TN-7 (milepost 416) and head east for less than one mile to Leipers Creek Road. Turn south (right) and drive for less two miles to reach the B&B.

TN-7 to Columbia

Columbia is the seat of Maury County. Founded in 1809 and named for Christopher Columbus, Columbia was the commercial hub for Middle Tennessee's rich plantations. In 1850 it became the third-largest city in Tennessee, behind Nashville and Memphis. A decade later Maury County was the wealthiest county in the whole state. The city's prominence did not survive, however. The economic trauma of the Civil War was largely to blame.

No city in all of Tennessee is more closely associated with mules than Columbia. During the 19th and early 20th centuries, Columbia's mule market

opened on the first Monday of April, and people flocked here to buy and sell mules. Other towns, including Lynchburg and Paris, were known for large "First Monday" sales, but Columbia's was the largest. As a nod to its roots, the city is home to the Muletown Music Festival, with big-name acts, each October.

Leaving the Trace

Exit the parkway at TN-7 (milepost 416) and head east for 17 miles. TN 7 (also known as Water Valley Road) winds its way into downtown Columbia. Stay on it until you hit North Garden Street (Business 412), then turn right. Continue five blocks until you are in the center of the charming downtown district. The total drive time for this 20-mile drive should be less than 30 minutes.

★ President James K. Polk Home & Museum

The 11th president of the United States, James Knox Polk, was born in North Carolina but moved to Middle Tennessee with his family when he was 11 years old. Before moving to town, Polk's family lived for several years on a farm north of Columbia, from where Polk's father ran successful plantations, speculated in land, and was involved in local politics.

The home where Polk lived as a teenager and young man in Columbia is the only house remaining, besides the White House, where Polk ever lived. It is now known as the **President James K. Polk Home & Museum** (301-305 W. 7th St., 931/388-2354, www.jameskpolk.com, 9am-5pm Mon.-Sat., 1pm-5pm Sun. Apr.-Oct., 9am-4pm Mon.-Sat., 1pm-5pm Sun. Nov.-Mar., adults $10, seniors $8, youths 6-18 $5-7, children under 6 free) and is dedicated to Polk's life and presidency. Free parking is available along High Street or in the lot across 7th Street.

The home has furnishings that belonged to President Polk and his wife, Sarah, while they lived at the White House. Other pieces come from Polk

The Natchez Trace Wine Trail

The Natchez Trace Parkway isn't Napa Valley by any stretch of the imagination. But just off the Tennessee section of the Trace, there are four places to stop and explore nearby wineries.

Housed in a log cabin, **Grinder's Switch Winery** (2119 Hwy. 50 W. Loop, Centerville, 931/729-3690, http://gswinery.com, noon-5pm Sun.-Thurs., 10am-6pm Fri.-Sat.) has sweet and dry reds and whites. The bucolic green landscape is the appeal here, but there is an urban tasting room in Nashville's Marathon Village as well. Grinder's Switch is 20 miles west of the Trace where it intersects with TN-50.

Sweet wines, free tastings, and live music are the draw of **Keg Springs Winery** (361 Keg Springs Rd., Hampshire, 931/285-0589, http://kegsprings.com, 11am-6pm Wed.-Sun.). Keg Springs is just a short distance east of the parkway along Keg Springs Road, but you must travel south past Devil's Backbone State Natural Area and exit at US 412 East, then work your way north along Ridgetop Road and Catheys Creek Road to reach the winery.

Novelty fruit wines, dry reds, and a pastoral setting are the calling cards of **Amber Falls Winery & Cellars** (794 Ridgetop Rd., Hampshire, 931/285-0088, http://amberfallswinery.com, 10am-6pm Mon.-Fri., 10am-8pm Sat., 12:30pm-6pm Sun.). Amber Falls is near Keg Springs. Exit the Trace at US 412 East. After about two miles, turn north onto Ridgetop Road to reach the winery.

Old World techniques, with an emphasis on sustainable growing, is the philosophy at **Natchez Hills Vineyard** (109 Overhead Bridge Rd., Hampshire, 931/285-2500, http://natchezhills.com, by appointment Mon.-Thurs., noon-5pm Fri.-Sun.). Natchez Hills is just off US 412. From the Trace, turn onto US 412 East and continue for about six miles. When US 412 turns north, continue straight onto Overhead Bridge Road to reach the winery.

Place, the home that the couple planned and built in Nashville following the end of Polk's presidency in 1849. Sadly, Polk died of cholera just five months after leaving office and so had little opportunity to enjoy the home; Sarah Polk lived for another 42 years following her husband's death, and she spent them all at Polk Place.

The Polk home in Columbia was comfortable, but not luxurious, for its time. It was while living here that Polk began his career as a Tennessee lawyer and eventually won his first seat in the U.S. House of Representatives. He would go on to serve 14 years in the House, four of them as Speaker. He was governor of Tennessee from 1839 to 1841 and defeated Henry Clay, a Whig, to become president in 1845. Polk's presidency was defined by his drive to expand the Union westward, and it was during his term in office that the United States added California, Texas, and Oregon to the territory of the United States.

Historic Athenaeum

Once part of a famous finishing school for girls, the **Historic Athenaeum** (808 Athenaeum St., 931/381-4822, http://historicathenaeum.com, tours 10am-4pm Thurs.-Sat., by appointment Mon.-Wed., Feb.-Dec., $5), formerly called the Athenaeum Rectory, is also an unusual architectural gem. Designed and built by Maury County master builder Nathan Vaught, the rectory was the home of Rev. Franklin Gillette Smith and his family. Smith came to Columbia from Vermont in 1837 to run the Columbia Female Institute, an Episcopal girls' finishing school.

In 1851, Smith decided to open his own school for girls. He built the Columbia Athenaeum School next to the rectory, which remained his family home. Its name refers to Athena, the goddess of wisdom, and has come to mean "seat of learning."

For 52 years the Athenaeum educated young women in art, music, history, science, and business. The library housed more than 16,000 volumes, and the school sat on 22 wooded acres of land. Ladies took part in gymnastics, bowling, croquet, and tennis. At its peak, the Athenaeum boarded 125 students, plus day students from the surrounding area.

The Athenaeum remained open until 1904; after the deaths of Reverend Smith and his wife, it was operated by their son. From 1904 to 1914, the Athenaeum served as the community's high school, and in 1915 the school was torn down and the Columbia High School built in its place. The Athenaeum Rectory was preserved, however, and visitors can tour the Moorish-Gothic structure that housed the parlor and reception area for the school.

The building is operated by the Association for the Preservation of Tennessee Antiquities (www.theapta. org) and is open only for tours and special events. For a week every summer it offers the 1861 Athenaeum Girls' School, when 14- to 18-year-old girls dress up in period clothing and study topics like etiquette, penmanship, and archery. Every May, they offer a weekend course for women 19 and older.

Elm Springs

The **Sons of Confederate Veterans International Headquarters** (740 Mooresville Pike, 931/380-1844, http://elmsprings.scv.org, 9am-5pm Mon.-Fri., free) is located in this 1837 Greek Revival-style house known as **Elm Springs.** The antebellum-era home was originally built by two wealthy New Orleans cotton merchants as a gift for their sister. A daughter, Susan Todd, inherited the property. Todd married Abram M. Looney, a local attorney known for being outspoken

about politics and more. During the Civil War, Looney served the Confederacy as a captain, later promoted to colonel, in Company H, 1st Tennessee Infantry. It was one of the few homes in the area that wasn't burned during fighting of the Civil War.

The home changed owners several times over the decades. It has been restored and is now home to the Sons of Confederate Veterans International Headquarters, which offers tours and operates a gift shop.

★ Mule Day

Columbia's **Mule Day** (931/381-9557, www.muleday.com, Apr.) takes place over four days in mid-April and is perhaps the thing for which Columbia is best known. The festival's roots are in the First Monday mule market that took place in Columbia during the period when work animals were indispensable to Tennessee farmers. In many cases, mules were a farmer's most valuable asset—a good pair of mules could make a poor farmer rich.

Mules were more expensive than horses or oxen because they were more highly prized. They were said to be stronger, smarter, and more surefooted than other work animals. Their temperament can be stubborn, but some mules are easy and willing to work. For this reason, mule breeders were important, influential, and, often, quite wealthy.

Today's Mule Day is more festival than mule market, although the event still includes mule sales, mule and donkey seminars, and mule shows and competitions. The highlight is Saturday morning's Mule Day Parade, when thousands of people crowd to see school bands, mules, and colorful troops parade down the road. There is also live music, storytelling, dancing, gospel singing, and the crowning of the Mule Day Queen. Activities take place at various locations in Columbia, but the heart of Mule Day is the Maury County Park on Lion Parkway.

Sports and Recreation

One of the reasons travelers take a detour from the Trace in this area is to take advantage of the great water sports. The **River Rat's Canoe Rental** (4361 US 431, 931/381-2278, http://riverratcanoe.com, 9am-6pm Mon.-Fri., 8am-6pm Sat.-Sun. Apr.-Oct., $25-50) offers self-guided Class I trips via canoe or kayak, either five miles (starting at Milltown Dam coming back to River Rat's, about 3-4 hours) or nine miles (starting at River Rat's to Carpenter's Bridge, about 5-6 hours). Rentals include life jackets, paddles, and a ride to the river. Have your own kayak, paddleboard, or canoe? Ask about shuttle service only.

What does an equestrian need? Hiking, biking, birding, fishing, swimming, and campgrounds designed for campers traveling with horses. That's **Chickasaw State Park** (20 Cabin Ln., Henderson, 800/458-1752, http://tnstateparks.com, 7am-10pm daily, free). There are rowboats and pedal boats for rent on Lake Placid, and horses

are also available for rent to ride on the hour-long trail. Areas of interest also include the Brewer's Cabin (built in 1876), Sagamore Lodge (Arts and Crafts style building built in the 1930s), and the Aviary (which houses an owl and a red-tailed hawk). Want to stay longer? Check out one of the 13 cabins ($95-110), which sleep up to six people.

Food

Located on the courthouse square, **Square Market and Café** (35 Public Sq., 931/840-3636, www.squaremarketcafe. com, 9am-4pm Mon.-Thurs., 9am-9pm Fri., 10:30am-9pm Sat., $8-10) serves breakfast and lunch throughout the week and dinner on Friday and Saturday nights. The weekday menu features salads, sandwiches, and soups. The signature Polk's Roasted Pear Salad of greens, blue cheese, walnuts, and roasted-pear vinaigrette is a favorite for lunch. Heartier appetites can choose hot steamed sandwiches or the Tennessee Hot Brown, a hot

President James K. Polk Home & Museum

open-faced turkey sandwich topped with white sauce, cheddar cheese, and bacon. The café brews good coffee, and the desserts are homemade. Weekend dinner includes entrées like baked salmon with dill caper sauce, spinach-and-garlic ravioli, and Eastern Shore crab cakes. There is live music, too.

For country cooking, hearty breakfasts, and plate-lunch specials, head to **Bucky's Family Restaurant** (1102 Carmack Blvd., 931/381-2834, 6am-2pm daily, $6-8).

If you're headed to New Orleans, you might as well get inspired with some NOLA-inspired cuisine at **River Terrace** (1000 Riverside Dr., 931/223-5135, www.riverterracerestaurant.com, 4pm-8:30pm Mon.-Thurs., 4pm-9pm Fri.-Sat., $8-25). Start the meal off with some specialty martinis. Chef Randy Landry is a New Orleans native, so he knows his way around the kitchen.

Soul food and southern cuisine are the signature at **Christy's 6th Street**

JAMES KNOX POLK

Restaurant (109 E. 6th St., 931/388-7109, 11am-2:30pm Tues.-Fri., 10:30am-2:30pm Sun., $6-9). This is a lunch-only eatery, with a buffet on Sunday.

Get more than a cup of coffee at ★ **Muletown Roasted Coffee** (23 Public Sq., 931/901-0220, www.muletowncoffee.com, 7am-6pm Mon.-Thurs., 7am-8pm Fri.-Sat.), where you can hang out and learn all the Columbia goings-on. This hip coffee shop roasts its own beans and sells bags of coffee (including single origin options) for $12-20, along with espresso drinks, drip coffee, and pastries. There's also a second location, **Muletown West** (1390B Hampshire Pike, 931/901-0700, 6am-9pm Mon.-Sat.).

The **Bypass Deli** (1323 S. James Campbell Blvd., 931/381-9634, 8am-10pm Mon.-Sat., $4-6) serves affordable basics, such as burgers, BLTs, club sandwiches, tuna salad, grilled cheese, po'boys, salads, and deli sandwiches. This is a great takeout option for heading back to one of the Trace's pretty picnic spots.

Accommodations

Columbia has many decent chain hotel options. A host of motels are found around exit 46 on I-65, about 10 miles east of Columbia. They include **Comfort Inn** (1544 Bear Creek Pike, 931/388-2500, $86-117) and **Holiday Inn Express** (1558 Bear Creek Pike, 931/380-1227, $134-141).

Locally owned, the **Richland Inn** (2405 Pulaski Hwy., 931/381-4500, www.richlandinncolumbia.com, $85-100) is a 107-room inn with singles, doubles, and suites. There is a continental breakfast and a family restaurant next door.

Built in 1960, ★ **The Inn at Bigby Creek** (1306 Trotwood Ave., 931/982-6226, www.innatbigbycreek.com, $125) might be more modern than the word "inn" usually conjures up. But this house, the former home of a Columbia mayor, is a perfect getaway. There are three guest rooms, with amenities like free Wi-Fi, private bathrooms, high-end sheets, and a full breakfast. Stroll through the 1.5 acres before continuing your travels.

Back to the Trace

It should take you no more than 30 minutes to rejoin the parkway at milepost 416 from downtown Columbia. Take North Garden Street (Business 412) north, then turn left onto North James Campbell Boulevard. Continue on this road, which turns into TN-7 in about 0.5 mile, for a total of about 17 miles. Pass under the parkway, then turn right and follow the road to rejoin the parkway.

Water Valley Overlook (MP 411.8)

If you haven't used the wide-angle lens or panoramic setting on your camera or phone yet, this scenic overlook on the left side of the road is the place to give it a try. The parking lot is small, but you'll be looking at the expanse of rolling hills and Middle Tennessee foliage. Picnic tables provide a perfect place to rest and overlook the top of a ridge, with an impressive 180-degree view of the Water Valley. Unlike some other vantage points along the parkway, this view is rarely obscured by brush or other growth. This is one of the wide-open places on the parkway where you can imagine seeing what early settlers saw when they first came to the area. Today you may see some farms and houses in the distance but no other significant development, traffic, or billboards.

The overlook is marked with the signature parkway signage.

★ Gordon House and Ferry Site (MP 407.7)

As a modern-day stop along the parkway, the **Gordon House and Ferry Site,** the 200-year-old home of John Gordon and Dolly Cross Gordon, just south of

TN-50, may not look imposing. But centuries ago, this two-story brick building near the Duck River was essential. It was a trading post, a place to cross the Duck River, and a refuge after a long journey, and it signaled that Nashville was close by.

John Gordon was a postman, farmer, and a businessman, before leaving to serve his country in the War of 1812. One of the Captain of the Spies (the name for the leaders of Andrew Jackson's scouting units), he fought from the Battle of Talladega in 1813 through the Battle of Horseshoe Bend in 1814, and he was partially responsible for some of the country's worst legacies: forcing Native Americans from their homeland.

While he was at war, he supervised long distance the building of this Federal-style house, designed to be elegant but also safe in a frontier environment. The Gordon House and Ferry Site is not open to visitors (due to unsafe conditions), but exploring the grounds and the exterior is a worthy stop along the parkway, as this is one of only two buildings remaining from the Old Trace era. It is listed on the National Register of Historic Places, and was restored to 1818 style after it was acquired by the NPS in the 1970s.

Follow the short paved trail from the parking area, past the house, and imagine yourself as one of the early travelers along the Old Trace. From there, turn right. You'll find a bridge to cross the small Fattybread Branch creek (something those who walked these footsteps centuries ago would not have found) to the old ferry site on the banks of the wider, faster-moving Duck River. This ferry ran for nearly 100 years (long after the trading post was no longer necessary), making travel easier and helping trade in the area thrive until a bridge was built. This is a gently sloped walk, with equal parts shade and sun, and shows off the variety of the Water Valley landscape.

The site has restrooms and picnic

tables and, as the closest place to the southern terminus of the **Highland Rim Trail,** is a good place to stock up on water. Walk 0.3 mile north to the TN-50 parking lot, where you'll find hitching posts for horses, ample parking, and signage to take you the few hundred feet to the trailhead.

Baker Bluff Overlook (MP 405.1)

Pull into the Baker Bluff Overlook, on the left side of the road, to take in a view of the area farmland and the Duck River from above. Informative signage explains the conservation methods that local farmers use today to help preserve these pristine surroundings. This is one of only a few vantage points on the Tennessee section of the parkway where you are looking at farmland from above and don't have views obscured by trees, no matter the time of year.

This spot is popular with photographers wanting to get the perfect shot. The overlook view is to the east, so your best bet is to try to stop in the afternoon or before sunset so that the sun is at your back. This is a scenic and educational stop, as well as pit stop, as it has a restroom and several picnic tables. From here you can hike a steep descent to Jackson Falls.

Baker Bluff Trail

Distance: 0.75 mile one-way
Duration: 40-60 minutes
Difficulty: Moderate

After taking in the sights from the overlook, follow the signed Baker Bluff Trail down to Jackson Falls (which is also the next stop on the parkway). The first section of this trail from Baker Bluff is an ascent, a steep 0.1 mile uphill, before heading downhill toward the falls. This trail is short, less than a mile, but very steep. Depending on weather conditions and how sure-footed you are, it may take you 20-30 minutes each way. If you have a

hiking pole with you, this is a good place to use it.

Like many hikes along the Trace, this one is wooded, which is great for shade but means you may have to maneuver around branches on your way. While this trail takes you to Jackson Falls, and you may hear the water from here, there is not a vantage point of the water until you get to milepost 404.7, so many people choose to do the hike from the parking lot at Jackson Falls.

Jackson Falls (MP 404.7)

As is the case with many landmarks in Tennessee, these falls were named for President Andrew Jackson. No one knows if he actually ever took in their beauty, but regardless, you shouldn't miss them. Fortunately, this scenic stop is designed to accommodate everyone.

Following the signs for Jackson Falls, pull into the parking lot by turning right off the Trace. You'll loop underneath it to end up on the left side of the parkway. You'll see both the standard arrowhead-shaped parkway sign and a brown directional one pointing the way.

There are benches (plus restrooms) at the top of the falls, where you can take in some of the view without walking. But if you're up to it, walk at least halfway down the path, which is paved for the beginning. From here you can stop at a bench and look at the water crashing over the limestone rock. Or, continue farther (about 900 feet downhill, in total), to the base of the falls.

This is the last restroom stop until Meriwether Lewis Monument and Gravesite (milepost 385.9).

Jackson Falls Trail

Distance: 900 feet one-way
Duration: 30 minutes
Difficulty: Moderate

The trail down to a clear pool and a view of Jackson Falls is paved in concrete, which makes this steep 900-foot-long hike considerably easier to navigate. The trail is short, but steep, and could take 15 minutes to walk each way. When you get to the bottom, there's some serious payoff for your exertion: a clear pool and dramatic waterfalls cascading down a limestone outcropping. The water is clear and runs year-round. Even when other small creeks dry up in Tennessee's hot summers, this water keeps flowing—at least at a trickle. The small Jackson Branch used to flow directly into the Duck River, but floods, erosion, and other factors ate away at the bluffs, creating these falls.

At the bottom of the falls is a bench, as well as some flat rocks perfect for perching on to dip your toes in the pool. This is more a wading spot than a swimming hole—the pond isn't particularly big or deep.

Old Trace (MP 403.7)

All along the official Natchez Trace Parkway are places where the Old Trace, the original road that was most active from the 1790s to the early 1800s, intersects. At each of these spots, you can get out and stretch your legs for a quick out-and-back hike.

To see this section, pull into the parking lot on the right side of the road at the Old Trace sign. Here, follow signage for an easy 2,000-foot walk, which shouldn't take more than 10-15 minutes, along a ridge with a view of the Duck River. As you wend your way through the forest and look out at the farmland, think about how different this once was for soldiers and explorers than it is for modern travelers on the parkway.

As you drive south to the next landmark, there's a tiny **cemetery,** but it isn't marked and doesn't have a parking lot. Less than 0.5 mile from milepost 403.7,

Top to bottom: the 200-year-old Gordon House; former tobacco farm; Sheboss Place.

look for a bridge and pull over just before it. On the left side is the Cathey Family cemetery. The graves are very close to the end of the bridge, perhaps 30 steps away, although due to foliage, you may not see them as you drive by. Only a few of the tombstones are legible. Be respectful of the dead and their families if you choose to stop and take a look, and pay attention to traffic as you are pulling off and on the road.

Old Trace Walk

Distance: 2,000 feet one-way
Duration: 15 minutes
Difficulty: Easy

At milepost 403.7 is a 2,000-foot section of the Old Trace. This ridgeway walk gives you a glimpse of what passage along the route was like before there was a paved parkway. This small hike should take no more than 15 minutes at a leisurely pace. It offers shade from the hot summer sun, as much of the trail goes through the dense forest of the area. At certain vantage points you'll have views of the Duck River Valley below. This is an out-and-back path, not a loop, so when it dead-ends, turn around to return to the parking lot.

Tobacco Farm and Old Trace Drive (MP 401.4)

At this mile marker, pull off the parkway on the left and to see an old tobacco farm and to drive a dirt portion of the Old Trace.

First, you'll see a tobacco farm from the early 1900s, complete with old wooden barn and tobacco both growing in the ground and hanging to dry inside the barn.

Park in the lot and follow the signage for a very easy, flat walk through a field. This replica of the kind of tobacco farm that would have existed here before the Park Service took over shows you how

the land on and around the Trace has sustained its residents and neighbors for generations. This stop is a great one for those traveling with kids, as the signage explains exactly what they are witnessing.

If that's enough for you, you can simply exit the parking lot and continue south on the parkway. Or, you can drive on a one-way dirt road that is a section of the Old Trace for about two miles. This dirt road isn't suitable for RVs or other oversized vehicles, but it's easy (if dusty) for standard cars or motorcycles.

This very narrow loop road winds through the forest and brings you back to the parking lot where you started. Most preserved sections of the Old Trace are for hiking or horseback riding only. This is one of only a few portions of the Old Trace that allow cars. Along the short drive, you'll get several vantage points of the surrounding valley and its wildflowers, trees, and wildlife. Look for wild turkeys roaming here.

Sheboss Place (MP 400.2)

In the early 1800s this stop was a stand (frontier trading post) and inn where weary travelers could rest, eat, and get supplies. No structure exists today, but you can pull off the left side of the road to learn about the stand's history.

Legend has it that the stand was run by a widow named Cranfield and her Native American husband (the Chickasaw tribe permitted the establishment of such businesses as long as they were run by fellow Chickasaw members). Lore suggests the husband didn't speak English well; the name comes from what he would say to Trace travelers who came up to him: "She boss." There's no way to know if that's fact or fiction, but it is entertaining for those who stop here today.

This stop is great for a photo op and a history lesson; there are no other amenities.

Devil's Backbone State Natural Area (MP 394)

Technically, this park is adjacent to the Trace, not on it. Stop here to take a pretty, moderate-effort hike through the woods, without a lot of other people around. Devil's Backbone was named a Class 1 Scenic Recreation Area in 1997. It has a diversity of flora and fauna that can be seen during the hike.

Enter the parking lot at milepost 394 (on the right side of the road). There are no amenities for non-hikers here.

Devil's Backbone Hike

Distance: 3.2-mile loop
Duration: 1.5 hours
Difficulty: Moderate

This 3.2-mile hiking trail starts at the parking lot and gives hikers an experience out in the Highland Rim (not to be confused with the Highland Rim Trail), the ridge of a geographic basin. This hike winds beside a creek and loops back to the starting point. Despite the short distance, there are about 200 feet of elevation change, making for some steep areas, but it should be easy enough for the average hiker. A babbling brook crosses the trail and breaks up the forest scenery, primarily comprising oak, hickory, and tuliptree.

Folks often liken this hike to the one at Meriwether Lewis Monument and Gravesite (milepost 385.9), given the terrain, the difficulty, and the foliage. But Devil's Backbone is typically much less crowded than the Meriwether Lewis hike—great for those who want to commune with nature in solitude.

Because this area isn't used often, the trail can be overgrown. Few blazes mark the way, so pay attention in order to stay on the trail. Leashed dogs are popular companions to hikers on this trail.

Swan View Overlook (MP 392.5)

Pull in to this small, well-marked parking lot up the hill on the right side of the road and grab the camera. There aren't any restrooms or other amenities, but you want to stop for a good view of the water tower in nearby Hohenwald, to the west. Hohenwald is the highest elevation town between New Orleans and Chicago, and a quick photo shouldn't be missed, particularly during leaf-changing season. Unlike much of the Trace, which is dense with forest and leaves, here the views of the rolling hills, Swan Creek, and farmland are uninterrupted.

Fall Hollow Waterfall (MP 391.9)

After pulling into the parking lot at this stop, you only need to step about 10 feet away from your car to hear and see Fall Hollow. But venture beyond the parking lot to an easy, paved pathway. The path leads to a wooden bridge and platform about halfway down the falls with a simple bench where you can sit and take in the sights and sounds of the waterfall. In the late summer butterflies flitter around like a scene from a Disney movie. This is easily one of the prettiest places on the Tennessee section of the Trace and a great spot for a picnic. (Picnic tables are at the top, but it's better to stay here if you can nab a spot on the bench.)

For a bit longer and steeper hike, continue past the bench onto the unimproved dirt path to the bottom of the falls. You will see more dramatic water cascades at this spot. This is a good spot to use a trekking pole. The path to the bottom is undeveloped and steep, and may take an additional 10 minutes to walk.

◈ US 412 to Mount Pleasant

Just a quick drive from Fall Hollow takes you from the shaded forest of the Trace to the small, sweet town of Mount Pleasant. Once known as the Phosphate Capital of the World, Mount Pleasant is now a quiet town with an unusually large number of beautiful antebellum homes. Many of them were built with money earned from the phosphate industry. During the early boom years of the 1890s, the promise of quick money attracted hundreds of men to work in the mines. Law and order was haphazard until a Texas Ranger named Captain Russell arrived.

Leaving the Trace

It's about a 30-minute, 15-mile drive to Mount Pleasant from Fall Hollow. From Fall Hollow, continue south on the Trace for 0.5 mile, then take the left-turn exit for US 412. At the stop sign, turn right to join US 412 East. Follow US 412 for three miles. Turn right onto Big Swan Creek Road and continue for another three miles. Turn left onto Mount Joy Road and drive for almost eight miles, then turn left to head into town via Main Street.

Sights

You can learn about the phosphate industry at the **Mount Pleasant/Maury County Phosphate Museum** (Public Sq., 931/379-9511, 9:30am-4:30pm Mon.-Sat., free, donations accepted). In addition to information about phosphate, the three-story museum houses artifacts of local history, Civil War memorabilia, and local crafts.

Mount Pleasant has a nice variety of historic homes, but most are closed to the public. An exception is the **Breckenridge Hatter's Shop** (205 N. Main St., 931/379-3399, 10am-5pm Tues.-Sat.), believed to be the oldest building still standing in town. This original log cabin, covered with weatherboarding in the 1920s, is on the National Register of Historic Places. A former hatter named David Breckenridge lived and did business here; now it's an antiques shop. There's no charge for admission; just come in and browse. The **Price-Jackson House** (209 N. Main St.) was built in 1849 and served as an insurance office for many years.

A few blocks away from the town square, Pleasant Street is home to at least three elegant old homes. **Manor Hall** (300 Pleasant St.) once sat on a property of more than 1,200 acres. Martin Luther Stockard had it built in 1859 for his second wife, using money he inherited from his first wife and her brother. The **John Ruhm-Graham Home** (106 Pleasant St.) was built in 1910 for Mr. John Ruhm, one of the "captains of the phosphate industry." It has the only elevator in Mount Pleasant. The **Jenkins-Bradburn House** (104 Pleasant St.) is a three-story log house built in 1917.

Drive north on Main Street/TN-243 to find more stately homes. **Walnut Grove** (510 N. Main St.) was built in 1858 and includes a detached kitchen believed to be the oldest brick building in Mount Pleasant.

Rattle and Snap Plantation

Considered by some to be the finest antebellum home in Tennessee, **Rattle and Snap Plantation** (1522 N. Main St./TN-243, 931/379-1700, www.rattleandsnapplantation.com, by appointment only, adults $20, children 7-12 $8, children under 7 free) was built by George Washington Polk in 1845. Its extravagance was unmatched by any other home of the period: The 10 Corinthian columns that stand at the front of the mansion were made in Cincinnati, shipped by steamboat to Nashville, and brought over land by oxcart to Maury County. The marble mantels came from Italy, the gardens were designed by a German landscape architect, and a glorious Waterford chandelier hangs over the dining room table. The fine craftsmanship throughout the home is attributed to slaves who labored on the construction.

The story goes that Rattle and Snap was named after an eponymous popular game of the period involving dried beans that were rattled and rolled with a snap of the fingers. Polk claimed that he won the land on which the mansion sits in a rattle and snap game with the governor of North Carolina.

The house was spared during the Civil War, reportedly after the Union commander and field captain noticed that Polk was wearing a Masonic ring in his portrait. Polk's wealth did not survive the war, however, and in 1867 he sold the property to J. J. Granberry, who occupied the home for 50 years and renamed it Oakwood Hall. In 1919, it changed hands again, and for many years tenant farmers lived in the deteriorating mansion. Rattle and Snap owes its restoration to Amon Carter Evans, former publisher of the *Nashville Tennessean*.

Today, Rattle and Snap is open year-round for group tours (by appointment only). Please call at least three days in advance to book and pay for a tour reservation. Overnight guests are also welcome at its Carriage House, and special events are hosted here. Even without a tour, you can admire the property from the highway.

Accommodations

Sleep in the Carriage House at **Rattle and Snap Plantation** (1522 N. Main St./TN-243, 931/379-1700, www.rattle-andsnapplantation.com, $250 up to two guests, $25 each additional person), and you will enjoy your own private tour of one of the state's most famous antebellum homes. The Carriage House is a three-bedroom guesthouse at the rear of the mansion. It includes two queen-size bedrooms and a sleeping loft with two twin beds. It also has a kitchen, sitting room, and patio where guests can relax and prepare meals. No children are allowed, and smoking is not permitted. There is a two-night minimum stay.

the Meriwether Lewis Monument and Gravesite

Back to the Trace

To return to the Trace from central Mount Pleasant, hop on Main Street headed south. Turn right onto Mount Joy Road and drive west for eight miles. Turn right onto Big Swan Creek Road and follow it for about three miles. Make a left onto US 412 West. After three miles, turn left at the sign for Natchez Trace Parkway. This road will deposit you back on the Trace in 0.2 mile; turn left to continue southbound.

★ Meriwether Lewis Monument and Gravesite (MP 385.9)

Meriwether Lewis, the U.S. army captain and private secretary to President Thomas Jefferson, is best known as the leader, along with William Clark, of the Lewis and Clark Expedition to the Pacific Ocean from 1804 to 1806.

The **Meriwether Lewis Monument and Gravesite** (www.nps.gov/natr) sits along the Natchez Trace Parkway about seven miles east of Hohenwald. This is where Lewis died, under mysterious circumstances, while traveling the Trace bound for Washington DC in 1809.

According to accounts, Lewis, who was appointed governor of the Louisiana Territory following his successful expedition, was upset by accusations of financial mismanagement. He was traveling to Washington to clear his name, and on the night of October 11, 1809, he stayed at Grinder's Stand, a homestead whose owners boarded travelers along the Trace. In the morning, Lewis was found shot to death in his bed. His death was called a suicide, although a few months later a friend came to investigate the circumstances and pronounced that Lewis was murdered. Lewis was just 35 years old when he died.

While the circumstances of Lewis's death remain a mystery, his legacy lives on. Plan to spend time here exploring his story as well as the great outdoors. Several monuments to Lewis have been erected at and around his gravesite, with ample signage. Chief among them is the monument over the grave. This solemn stone column was erected by the state of Tennessee in 1848 to commemorate Lewis's life. If the top seems broken or unfinished, don't be surprised: The design represents a life cut short.

If you are at the site on a weekend, stop in the small log cabin (noon-4:15pm Fri.-Sat., free) near the site where the original Grinders' Stand stood. No one knows for sure what the inn where Lewis spent his last night looked like, but this replica mimics the style of the day. Inside are interpretive displays about his life.

The complex also offers flat, wheelchair-accessible pathways through central Tennessee landscape. These walkways allow you to commune with nature, despite the crowds. All of the paths are on a well-marked loop, taking you past the

Grinder's Stand site and the monument, across a section of the Old Trace and Little Swan Creek, and back to the parking lot. The interior driving road leads to smaller loops for picnic areas, restrooms, and the campground.

This site also houses a pioneer cemetery near the gravesite. In 1927 the National Park Service placed commemorative markers at each gravesite to represent the lives of early residents of the area, more than 100 in all.

The site is on the west side of the parkway. Exit to the right before TN-20 near milepost 386.

Accommodations

The ★ **Meriwether Lewis Monument and Gravesite Campground** (800/305-7417, free) has 32 campsites. There are no fees and reservations are not accepted; this is a first-come, first-served situation. There's a cross-section of wooded, secluded spots, and some with wide-open views of the landscape. All of the spots are fairly close to one another, but thanks to the foliage that grows so quickly in this climate, you won't feel like the folks in the site next to you can see into your tent.

☞ TN-20 to Hohenwald

The unassuming county seat of Lewis County, Hohenwald developed in the 1890s when a railroad was built through the rural county. Starting in 1895, immigrants from Switzerland moved to the area as part of a settlement scheme advanced by a Swiss American developer, J. G. Probst. The immigrants laid out and built New Switzerland immediately adjacent to the older town of Hohenwald. The two communities are now united.

Tucked into the rural landscape of central Tennessee near the small town of Hohenwald, more than 20 African and Asian elephants retired from circuses and zoos have found refuge at The Elephant Sanctuary, a 2,700-acre

Fall Hollow B&B and Campground

park that's not open to the public. At the **Elephant Discovery Center** (27 E. Main St., 931/796-6500, www.elephants.com, 11am-4pm Thurs.-Fri. or by appointment), you can watch videos of the elephants in the sanctuary, look at photo exhibits, and browse the gift shop, where proceeds from purchases benefit the sanctuary.

Leaving the Trace
Downtown Hohenwald is an easy 10-minute, six-mile drive northwest on TN-20 from the Meriwether Lewis Monument and Gravesite.

Natural Bridge
One of the area's most remarkable natural attractions, a **double-span natural bridge** (Tennessee Fitness Spa and Retreat, 299 Natural Bridge Rd., 931/722-5589, www. tfspa.com, 9am-5pm Sun., free) is hidden away at a privately owned and operated spa. A tributary of the Buffalo River has etched away at the bedrock for

thousands of years, eventually creating a natural bridge formation that is marvelous to look at.

The bridge invites exploration. You can walk along the side of the trickling stream and climb up to view the bridge from above. The sight of layer upon layer of rock, which has been carved out over many thousands of years, is remarkable. A few hundred yards from the natural bridge is a small cave, also open to visitors. Lights have been placed inside to make it easy to explore.

Natural Bridge is along State Route 99, between Hohenwald and Waynesboro. Tennessee Fitness Spa, the property owner, allows the public to visit Natural Bridge and the cave on Sundays only, 9am-5pm. Check in at the office first.

Entertainment and Events
Amber Falls Winery & Cellars (794 Ridgetop Rd., 931/285-0088, http://amberfallswinery.com, 10am-6pm Mon.-Sat., 12:30pm-6pm Sun.) has a tasting room and a live music series called Music on the Ridge.

The emphasis at **Keg Springs Winery** (361 Keg Spring Rd., 931/285-0589, www. kegspringswinery.net, 11am-6pm Wed.-Sun.) is fruit wines, including blackberry, peach, cherry, and strawberry.

There's a beautiful porch at **Natchez Hills Vineyard** (109 Overhead Bridge Rd., 931/285-2500, www.natchezhills. com, noon 5pm Wed.-Sun.). Enjoy an umbrella-shaded table while you sip your wine.

Food and Accommodations
Stop for lunch (sandwiches and more) or to pick up homemade Amish baked goods and snacks at **Yoders Homestead Market** (3555 Summertown Hwy., 931/796-1646, 8:30am-5:30pm Mon.-Sat.). There's a table where you can sit outside and admire the well-kept garden, as well as one inside. A small general store section includes games and books for kids and

Meriwether Lewis: The Man Behind the Legend

Being half of perhaps the most famous explorer team in U.S. history, Meriwether Lewis (1774-1809) is tied inexorably to his partner William Clark. But Lewis, who died along the Natchez Trace and whose gravesite with its memorial is on the parkway (milepost 385.9), is a legend in his own right.

Born in Virginia in 1774, Lewis grew up about 10 miles from Monticello, the home of Thomas Jefferson, who would be a mentor and friend to Lewis.

Lewis served in the Frontier Army, rising through the ranks. By 1801 President Jefferson appointed Lewis to be his personal secretary. In 1803, Congress had approved an expedition of the territory acquired in the Louisiana Purchase. Lewis's military training, his interest in plant life, his intellect, and his diplomatic and leadership skills made him a natural choice to lead this epic undertaking. William Clark, under whom Lewis had served in the army, was named co-commander of the expedition that would change the American West.

The team started in St. Louis, Missouri, in May 1804. With the help of Sacagawea, a Shoshone woman, the team traveled by boat, on foot, and on horseback. By November 1805 they had reached the Pacific coast, successfully completing the first transcontinental expedition. But the 8,000-mile trip was difficult physi-

cally and mentally. Lewis, Clark, and the rest of their group—now referred to as the Corps of Discovery—coped with everything from harsh weather conditions to hunger on the trek. At one point Lewis was accidentally shot in the thigh during a hunting trip. At another point he slipped and fell more than 20 feet in a cave, saving himself by using a knife to stop his fall.

On their return, the team was treated like celebrities and heroes. Lewis was named governor of the Louisiana Territory and set to work to publish the journals of their voyage, documenting the plants and animals they encountered, as well as the people and the geography.

Lewis died at age 35 of gunshot wounds along the Natchez Trace. Lewis likely suffered from depression, and the transition back to everyday life after the expedition was difficult. The journals, with their observations deemed crucial to the development of the American West, were being published at a slower pace than expected. Lewis was in debt, and may have suffered from malaria, a disease that, untreated, could cause hallucinations. He also suffered from alcoholism and had attempted suicide in the past.

Despite his untimely death, there's no question that America would not be the country it is without Lewis's service, his intellectual pursuits, and his vision.

homeopathic health supplies. Bring cash or checks; credit cards are not accepted.

Sometimes you're traveling with folks who want different things. Some people want to pitch a tent, while others want a real mattress. At ★ **Fall Hollow B&B and Campground** (1329 Columbia Hwy., 931/796-1480, http://fallhollow.com, primitive campsites $20, RV sites $40, rooms $80-100), both options are possible. The B&B has two motel-style rooms, plus two rooms in the main house; rates include breakfast. The campground has 21 RV hookup sites, plus tent camping and a bathhouse with heated showers.

Back to the Trace

From central Mount Pleasant, it's a quick drive back to the Trace. Hop on TN-20 heading east and drive for about six miles. Turn left onto Meriwether Lewis Park Road, then right onto Campground Road. Another right turn gets you back on the Trace headed south.

Metal Ford and Buffalo River (MP 381.8)

Named for the smooth stone bottom of the Buffalo River that flows here, Metal

Ford is a good place to rest. Pull into the parking lot on the right side of the parkway. The river bank is just steps away from the lot, as are a few picnic tables. There are no other amenities here.

Follow the easy, signed 0.15-mile loop trail through the woods and along the river bank. This is a nearly flat walk that should take about 10 minutes. In the early 1800s a steel mill stood at this site. There are few remnants from the facility, but signage both in the parking lot and along the trail helps you imagine how the area might have looked when it was active.

This was one place where settlers used to cross the Buffalo River. It can be fast moving, but is relatively shallow and about 25 feet wide in summer (though width and depth will vary based on rain levels). Because its banks are accessible, this spot is a popular swimming hole in hot summer months. Wear water shoes and beware slippery rocks.

Old Trace Drive (MP 375.8)

This pullout on the left side of the road leads you onto a section of the original Old Trace. Unlike some of the Old Trace sections that are only open to foot traffic, this 2.5-mile loop is open to vehicles, making it a great option for those who want to see the Old Trace but aren't interested in hiking.

Drive slowly (keep it to 20 mph or less) and watch for three distinct overlooks of the surrounding countryside. Because this is a narrow, one-way road and it's difficult for cars to pass each other, it isn't recommended that you stop or park on the drive. This old road is only suitable for cars, motorcycles, and bicycles. It isn't an option for those traveling by RV.

Laurel Hill Lake (MP 370)

If you have a rod and reel with you, you'll want to detour three miles east to **Laurel Hill Lake;** exit the parkway onto US 64/TN-15, near milepost 370, then turn left at Peter Cave Road and follow Brush Creek Road to the lake entrance. This state-managed lake is one of several in Tennessee specifically designed for anglers. You'll need a state fishing license ($6 per day), which you can buy at the **Laurel Hill Tackle Shop and Deli** (931/762-7200, 5:30am-8pm daily, closed Wed. Labor Day-Memorial Day and when the fishing is too tempting for the folks here to resist). From there, you can rent a kayak, launch your own boat, or sit on shore to cast your reel. You'll need to sign in to launch at the lake, regardless of whether or not someone is in the shop. Recreational boating is not permitted.

Accommodations
Nearby **Laurel Hill Trail & Camp** (39 Peter Cave Rd., Lawrenceburg, 931/762-7200, http://laurelhilltn.com, $10-25) offers a campground with 38 trailer hookups (water and electric) and restrooms. There are barns to keep horses in, as well as horse trails, making it a great place to stop if you're an equestrian Trace traveler.

Dogwood Mudhole
(MP 367.3)

This small depression in the landscape is so named for its native dogwood trees and its impassability after rain. Today you can pull into the parking lot on the right side of the road with ease, but such conditions could have caused a day's delay for those with wagons a century ago. There's not much to do or see at this stop, and there aren't any amenities, but it's a good reminder that today's annoyance was a significant obstacle for frontierspeople.

Glenrock Branch
(MP 364.5)

Nestled below a parking lot on the left side of the road is a natural amphitheater, a sweet area consisting of a small creek and a limestone bluff. Unlike at many other stops along the parkway, you can't see its wonders from the road. Park in the small lot, where you'll also find picnic tables and restrooms. At the top of the rocky area, look down and you can see the amphitheater and the short loop trail. The trail down to the amphitheater is steep but short (fewer than 50 steps), and the payoff is one of the prettiest picnic areas on the parkway.

Some of the signage on the parkway calls this "Lower Glenrock." There's also an easy 0.6-mile out-and-back trail to Upper Glenrock, another picnic area.

Sweetwater Branch (MP 363)

This creek was so named because the water was fresh (or "sweet") to the Trace pioneers who stopped to drink here. This pullout on the right side of the road offers only a few parking spots and trailhead access.

Sweetwater Branch Walk

Distance: 0.5-mile loop
Duration: 20 minutes
Difficulty: Moderate

Consider taking a quick stroll along Sweetwater Branch. It's a quiet, pretty area along the creek banks. This is the last hiking trail before you cross the Alabama-Tennessee state line. The walk includes some stairs and hilly terrain, so it isn't appropriate for wheelchairs.

Soak in the beauty at Sweetwater Branch.

McGlamery Stand (MP 352.9)

This stop on the right side of the road is the site of an old frontier trading post (also called a "stand") for Trace travelers, reportedly established in 1849 by Jon McGlamery. The closest village was named McGlamery Stand in his honor. The stand didn't make it through the Civil War, but today you can still see an old fire tower among the trees and admire the foliage from cute rocking chairs near the parking area. There aren't any other amenities at this site.

Sunken Trace (MP 350.5)

The name says it all. This section of the Old Trace was often too waterlogged and sunken to allow wagons and horses to traverse it. Here, three preserved pathways come together to the right side of the parking lot, evidence of how Trace travelers would alter their route depending on which area was most easily crossed. The pull-off for this stop is on the left side of the road.

Cypress Creek (MP 343.5)

Cypress Creek is a quick rest stop on the right side of the road. The creek is small and babbling, appropriate for wading and cooling off. This is your last stop before you cross the Tennessee state line and move into Alabama. A few picnic tables with grills sit under leafy, shady trees, and you can rest in the parking lot, but it has no other amenities. Don't confuse Cypress Creek with Cypress Swamp, which is at milepost 122 in Mississippi.

The Trace: Alabama

This section of road crosses over the Tennessee River and includes much of what is magical about the Trace: beautiful, serene scenery combined with important historical sites.

TENNESSEE
ALABAMA

WICHAHPI
COMMEMORATIVE
STONE WALL

★ Wichahpi
Commemorative
Stone Wall

33 MI/53 KM

MISSISSIPPI
ALABAMA

Tennessee River

Shopping in
Downtown Florence ★

FLORENCE ⊛

Fame Studios ★

Ivy Green ★

FREEDOM HILLS
OVERLOOK

The Trace: Alabama

The Trace runs through just a small corner of Alabama, only 33 miles of the parkway's total 444.

Among them are a monument to the Trail of Tears and the sites of several former inns that sheltered soldiers, Native Americans, and other travelers.

This section of the Trace, while short, was essential for General Andrew Jackson's soldiers to travel south during the Battle of New Orleans. Long before, Native Americans used this route as a thoroughfare for traversing the region.

The Trace's short hikes and overlooks and wooded oases offer a shady respite to what can be hot summer temperatures in Alabama. Wildflowers bloom in spring and early summer, leaves change to oranges and reds in fall. Winter is crisp and cool, but generally mild.

The essential side trip on US 72 takes you to the Shoals region, also called the Quad Cities—Tuscumbia, Muscle Shoals, Sheffield, and Florence. In addition to their Civil War history, they are thriving communities. Muscle Shoals continues to play an important role in the nation's music evolution and Florence has a strong designer and maker community.

Route Overview

There are just eight stops on this **33-mile** section of the Trace, but they are some of the Trace's most powerful and most scenic, including a somber reminder of

Highlights

★ **Wichahpi Commemorative Stone Wall:** This wall, built one stone at a time, is one man's moving tribute to the Trail of Tears (page 139).

★ **Ivy Green:** Reacquaint yourself with Helen Keller's inspirational story of perseverance at her birthplace (page 145).

★ **Fame Studios:** Visit one of the most influential music studios in the country, where many legendary performers have recorded (page 145).

★ **Shopping in Downtown Florence:** Explore the creative and eclectic boutiques in the funky town of Florence (page 149).

Best Restaurants

★ **City Restaurant:** The menu changes daily, but the southern goodness is constant at this local favorite (page 152).

★ **Odette:** This restaurant highlights farm-to-table cuisine with an update on Southern classics—plus delicious craft cocktails (page 152).

★ **Trowbridge's Ice Cream and Sandwich Bar:** This beloved old-fashioned soda fountain serves all your favorite childhood desserts (page 153).

★ **Ricatoni's Italian Grill:** Settle in for wood-fired pizza in a cozy location (page 154).

U.S. history. It's worth setting aside at least **one day and one night** to explore the area.

Just 14 miles southeast of the Trace, Alabama's Quad Cities offer an entertaining side trip and the region's best music, creative/maker cultures, and, of course, great food. Plan to spend at least one night in the area, using your campground or hotel as your home base to explore. All four cities have their charms, but Florence has the highest concentration of restaurants and hotels. Depending on how much time you want to spend at museums, shopping, and at restaurants, you easily could stretch this to two or three nights.

You'll likely have cell service for the entirety of your short drive in Alabama. If you are in need of bike, motorcycle, or car repair, this is one of the best areas to look for what you need before you head south into more remote areas.

Getting to the Starting Point
Car, Motorcycle, or Bicycle
As you drive or ride southbound on the Trace, you slip from Tennessee into Alabama as you ease past the state-line sign.

From **Memphis,** it's a 2.5-hour, 150-mile drive east along US 72 to milepost 320 on the Trace. To reach the Wichahpi Commemorative Stone Wall, the first stop of this section, you'll need to head north on the Trace for about 18 miles.

If you're coming from **Huntsville,**

it's possible to join the Trace as well as enjoy the Quad Cities by taking I-565 and US 72 ALT west. This 80-mile route takes you through the Quad Cities and then north to the Wichahpi Commemorative Stone Wall, the first stop on the Alabama section of the route. This drive takes about 1.5 hours. From Huntsville, take I-565 west for about seven miles, after which the interstate ends and becomes US 72 ALT. In another few miles, AL-20 joins with US 72 ALT and you'll cross the Tennessee River into Decatur, a small city with beautiful views of Wheeler Lake. Continue west for another 40 miles until you reach the US 43/US 72 East junction. Turn right onto US 72 East, following signs for Florence/Muscle Shoals. In less than a mile you'll be in the heart of Muscle Shoals. (See *US 72 to the Quad Cities,* on page 141, for ideas on how to spend some time in this area.) To get to the Trace from Florence, the city north of the river, hop on AL-20 West for about 14 miles. Follow signs for Natchez Trace Parkway by exiting on the right, then turning right at the stop sign to go north on the parkway. In 1.5 miles, turn right at the intersection with County Road 8 to reach the Wichahpi Commemorative Stone Wall.

Air
This isn't the easiest section of the Trace to access by air, but if that's your preference, the **Memphis International**

Best Accommodations

★ **Muscle Shoals Music House:** Sleep where stars like Bob Dylan once did in this scenic B&B (page 155).

★ **Marriott Shoals Hotel & Spa:** Great views and service make this the area's premiere place to stay (page 155).

★ **Residence Inn Marriott:** This is a surprisingly well-appointed chain hotel with spot-on service (page 155).

★ **Joe Wheeler State Park:** Reserve a cabin or campsite and relish the great outdoors (page 155).

Airport (MEM, www.flymemphis. com) is a good choice. MEM is served by Delta, Southwest, United, and other major airlines, with a number of nonstop routes. The three-concourse airport offers free Wi-Fi and many local dining options.

The **Huntsville International Airport** (HSV, www.flyhuntsville.com) is closer to this portion of the Trace, but it is a smaller airport, with mostly regional destinations served and higher prices. American, Delta, and United serve this northeastern Alabama city.

Train and Bus

Memphis Central Station (545 S. Main St., www.amtrak.com) is a stop on Amtrak's 900-mile City of New Orleans route, which runs from New Orleans to Chicago, and is your best bet for getting near this section of the Trace by train. Central Station is conveniently located downtown, where most major rental car companies have offices.

Greyhound serves the Bluff City via the **Memphis Bus Station** (3033 Airways, www.greyhound.com), which is adjacent to the Memphis International Airport and close to major car rental companies.

Budget-friendly **Megabus** (3921 American Way, http://us.megabus. com) serves Memphis from Atlanta, Birmingham, Chicago, Dallas, Little Rock, and St. Louis, from a station near the airport. Megabus boasts free Wi-Fi on board.

★ Wichahpi Commemorative Stone Wall (MP 338)

The first stop while heading south on the Trace after crossing the Alabama-Tennessee state line (milepost 341.8) is the somber, yet inspiring, **Wichahpi Commemorative Stone Wall** (256/764-3617, 8am-4pm daily, free), referred to by locals as "Tom's Wall."

Named for the late Tom Hendrix, the man who spent more than 30 years building what has become the largest unmortared wall in the country, the mile-long wall is a monument to Hendrix's great-great grandmother, Te-lah-nay, and her journey on the Trail of Tears. Each stone, hand-placed by Hendrix (or visitors) beginning in 1988, symbolizes a single step Te-lah-nay took. Today the wall includes stones from more than 120 different countries.

Once here, you can walk in solitude along the maze-like wall, reflecting on its significance and the way in which the United States has treated Native Americans. The land is largely flat and easy to traverse, with many places to stop and rest along the way. Some parts of the path may be difficult for wheelchairs to maneuver. Much of the wall winds its way under oak tree canopies, providing welcome shade in the hot Alabama summer. Some people believe certain stones have specific properties, such as one that is said to cure infertility.

The entrance to this magnificent site

Fuel Up

Here's a quick list of places to exit the parkway in Alabama so that you can refuel at the closest gas station. (Some stops may take you to small towns, others will be just a single service station.)

The National Park Service also posts a list of nearby supply stations at most Trace rest areas, although the list is not updated regularly.

• **Milepost 338:** Exit at Lauderdale County Road 8; drive four miles east, then turn right (southeast) on AL-157

to the Pure station/Cloverdale Quick Mart.

• **Milepost 336:** Exit at AL-20; drive less than 0.5 mile east to the Texaco station in Waterloo.

• **Milepost 320:** Exit at US 72; drive less than two miles east to Cherokee. The BP station on the south side of Lee Highway/US 72 is the most convenient. There's also an Exxon station to the west of the Trace on US 72—again, about two miles away.

is not technically on the Trace itself, but in recent years the National Park Service and Trace enthusiasts have embraced it and are helping to spread the word. If you are traveling with a large group (10 people or more), call to reserve a time for a tour.

Set aside at least 30 minutes to walk along the wall; double that if you want to sit and listen to stories told by Hendrix's family. Visitors are welcome to bring their own rocks to add to the wall. Please note that Hendrix's family considers this a sacred space; treat it respectfully.

Take the first left turn (east) after milepost 338 onto County Road 8 (CR-8). The entrance to the monument is 150 yards down on the right. Because it isn't an official Trace stop, this is one of the few places on the Trace where you won't see clear signage (though the signage for County Road 8 is clear). To get back on the Trace after you visit the wall, simply turn around on CR-8, drive 150 yards, and turn left to continue heading south on the parkway.

Rock Spring (MP 330.2)

The first true Alabama Trace stop is a pretty oasis and easy hike. On the left side of the road, follow a short road to a

loop parking lot. The parking lot is not visible from the parkway, so look for signage on the right.

From here you can access a simple half-mile **loop trail** to a bubbling spring. Allot about 20 minutes to walk in this shaded oasis. The terrain is easy, with some picturesque square stepping stones that enable you to cross Colbert Creek (this portion isn't wheelchair accessible). Birders and wildlife-watchers love this area because the spring provides a home to beavers, ruby-throated hummingbirds, salamanders, and other wildlife. This is a good place to take in wildflowers as well, particularly in the late summer and early fall, when delicate jewelweed is in bloom.

Other than a few parking spots, picnic tables, and the trail, there are no other amenities at this stop.

Lauderdale (MP 328.7)

This picnic area on the shore of the Tennessee River is the best spot for views of the John Coffee Memorial Bridge. The bridge, which is the longest on the parkway, was built in 1964. It's named for John Coffee, who fought with Andrew Jackson in the Battle of New Orleans. Coffee was married to an aunt of Rachel Donelson, Jackson's wife. From this vantage point

A Day on the Trace: Alabama

Any day is a great day to be in this tiny corner of Alabama. It starts off with much of what makes the Trace so special: local history, Native American spirituality, and scenic views at **Wichahpi Commemorative Stone Wall** (a.k.a. Tom's Wall). Start here by strolling the mile-long wall built by the late Tom Hendrix to honor his ancestors. Head back on the Trace for a few minutes to take in more views along a 20-minute hike at **Rock Spring.**

After that, it will be time to fuel up, which you can do by driving the 20-plus miles to the Quad Cities. On the way, stop at the **Key Underwood Coon Dog Cemetery** and honor the memorials people have left for their faithful companions. From there, grab lunch at one of downtown Florence's delicious eateries, such as **Odette,** topping off

your meal with an ice cream sundae from **Trowbridge's Ice Cream and Sandwich Bar.** Browse the city's creative shopping community with stops at **Billy Reid** and **Alabama Chanin.**

Even if you don't have time to tour either spot, drive by **3614 Jackson Highway** and **Fame Studios** in Muscle Shoals, important sights in music history. Pull into the **Hampton Inn Florence-Downtown,** then explore downtown Florence on foot, perhaps with a cocktail at **On the Rocks** and dinner at **Ricatoni's Italian Grill.** Catch live music at the **FloBama Music Hall** before turning in for the night.

The next morning, return to the Trace via US 72 (just under 30 miles) to finish this section of the route (about 12 miles) before crossing into Mississippi.

it's easy to imagine how difficult it was for settlers to traverse the river in the 1700s without the aid of such a bridge.

Signage here isn't as clear as the other markers along the Trace. This is the only road immediately to the north of the bridge, so it's very easy to spot. Entrance to the loop parking lot is on the left side of the road.

Colbert's Stand and Ferry Site (MP 327.3)

In its heyday, Colbert's Stand was an essential stop on the Old Trace. George Colbert and his brother Levi operated a ferry that took Trace travelers across the Tennessee River from 1800 to 1819. George also ran an inn on this site. Lore suggests that Colbert once charged Andrew Jackson $75,000 to ferry his Tennessee militiamen across the river, a princely sum in those days.

After crossing the Tennessee River, pull off the Trace into a well-marked

park on the right side of the road. There are restrooms at the Colbert's Ferry site, the only stop with such amenities in the Alabama section of the Trace (the next restrooms are at Tishomingo State Park at milepost 304.5).

From the parking lot, walk 50 yards up the path to see where the inn once stood. Here you'll find Native American themed exhibits, which were added in 2017, a joint effort of the Chickasaw Nation and the Natchez Trace Parkway Association. The exhibits provide information about the rich Native American history at this site.

🔷 US 72 to the Quad Cities

Tuscumbia, Muscle Shoals, Sheffield, and **Florence** are four cities sometimes called the Quad Cities, in a region referred to as The Shoals. These neighboring towns have long been rich in music history, creative communities, and natural beauty.

The Remembrance Wall One Man Built

One of the country's most compelling landmarks was started as a quiet family monument. Tom Hendrix had heard the stories about his great-great-grandmother, Te-lah-nay, a member of the Yuchi tribe, who was forced from her home, like many Native Americans during the Indian Removal Act of 1830. After her exile to Oklahoma, Te-lah-nay spent five years walking back home to Florence, Alabama, longing for the Tennessee River that she believed sung to her.

Motivated by an elder of the Yuchi tribe who said to him: "All things shall pass. Only the stones will remain," Hendrix started to build a wall to honor Te-lah-nay's journey home, with just his own hands (and, eventually, more than three trucks, 22 wheelbarrows, and some 3,500 pairs of gloves). No stonemasons or other professionals pitched in.

For years this site, a monument of irregular height and thickness, was simply called Tom's Wall (and most locals still refer to it as such). But lore goes that one day, a spiritual person named Charlie Two Moons walked the length of the wall and said to Hendrix: "The wall does not belong to you, Brother Tom. It belongs to all people. You are just the keeper. I will tell you that it is *wichahpi*, which means 'like the stars.' When they come, some will ask, 'Why does it bend, and why is it higher and wider in some places than in others?' Tell them it is like your great-great-grandmother's journey, and their journey through life: It is never straight."

Now it is officially called the **Wichahpi Commemorative Stone Wall,** after Charlie Two Moons's vision, and is registered in the Library of Congress. Hendrix wrote a self-published book, *If the Legends Fade* (www.ifthelegendsfade. com), about Te-lah-nay and other Native American women, filled with legends of the Tennessee River and other stories. Hendrix passed away in 2017. His children now maintain the site, with hopes of preserving it, and their family history, for generations.

U.S. history comes alive here, too, with many Civil War and Native American sites. World-class golf courses and water sports on the Tennessee River attract lovers of the outdoors.

Until recently, The Shoals had been something of an insider secret, thanks to its location, tucked away in northwest Alabama. In 2013, the documentary *Muscle Shoals* was released, and the secret was out. Now folks are flocking here to see the place where black and white musicians have long worked together in harmony.

Leaving the Trace

The cities can be reached a number of ways from the parkway, but the easiest and most direct is to take US 72 (near milepost 320) and head east about 20 miles. To get to downtown Tuscumbia, take US 72 for 19 miles, then turn left (north); the road continues as US 72.

Sixth Street marks Tuscumbia's downtown area.

US 72 continues north for several blocks into Muscle Shoals. As the highway travels north, you'll pass Sheffield on the west. Take either 2nd Street or Hatch Boulevard to get into downtown Sheffield. To reach Florence, stay on the highway as it crosses the river. Park near Pine and Court Streets to explore downtown Florence.

Stopping at the Rattlesnake Saloon

It's just a quick detour off US 72 on the way to the Quad Cities to the famous **Rattlesnake Saloon** (1292 Mt. Mills Rd., 256/370-7220, 11am-10pm Thurs.-Sat., 11am-3pm Sun. Apr.-Sept., 11am-10pm Thurs.-Sat. Feb.-Mar. and Oct.-Nov., $12). It's worth the extra miles—when else will you be able to eat in a Western-themed restaurant that also happens to be inside a cave? This is a standing-room-only,

Shiloh Military Park

True military history buffs will want to make the hour-long detour to **Shiloh Military Park** (1055 Pittsburg Landing Rd., Shiloh, 731/689-5696, www.nps.gov, sunrise-sunset daily, free). Run by the National Park Service, this 4,000-acre park in Shiloh, Tennessee, preserves the Shiloh and Corinth battlefields, two of the bloodiest sites from the Civil War.

At the time, the April 1862 Battle of Shiloh was the largest ever fought in the country. In just two days, more than 3,400 soldiers (on both Union and Confederate sides) were killed and 2,000 captured. Ultimately, the Union troops, led by Generals W. H. L. Wallace and Benjamin Prentiss, won the battle, outfoxing the surprise attack from the Confederate army under command of General P. G. T. Beauregard.

The nation was shocked by the brutality on both sides. It was this battle that brought home what was happening to many.

The exhibits at both the Shiloh Battlefield Visitor Center and the Corinth Civil War Interpretive Center are ADA compliant, and the driving road is accessible as well. The site includes the Shiloh National Cemetery, Shiloh Indian Mounds Site, and a bookstore.

Getting There

To get to Shiloh from the Trace, exit the Trace at AL-20 (milepost 336). Drive northwest across the Tennessee state line, where the road turns into TN-69, for a total of 31 miles. Turn left on TN-128 for 2.8 miles. Turn left again on TN-22 for 9 miles to Pittsburg Landing Road.

burgers-and-beer kind of place, where everyone is wearing cowboy boots. It's popular, so be prepared to wait. If you're coming in spring or fall, bring a jacket. All seating is outdoors and it can get cold.

Get to the restaurant from the Trace by taking US 72 east for about eight miles. Turn right (south) onto Mount Mills Road and continue for about seven miles. To continue on to the Quad Cities after you've eaten, continue south down Mount Mills Road for one mile, then turn left onto Bald Knob Road. After about a mile, turn left (north) onto AL-247. In about seven miles, turn right (east) to pick up US 72.

Sights
Tuscumbia

The lobby of the **Alabama Music Hall of Fame** (617 US 72 W., 256/381-4417, www.alamhof.org, 9am-5pm Tues.-Sat., $10 adults, $8 seniors and students, $7 children under 12) features bronze stars on the floor—its Walk of Fame—and a chandelier that projects a light show set to music. Exhibits include plaster casts of Lionel Richie and Sonny James, a wax figure of Nat King Cole, instruments played by members of Styx, and costumes and memorabilia from the many (and often surprising) pop culture and music icons who have a connection to the state of Alabama. A recording studio lets you record your own video or single from a catalog of songs, many of which have a connection to the area.

The **Tuscumbia Railroad Historic Depot** (204 W. 5th St., 256/389-1357, 9am-3pm Tues.-Fri., $2) honors the city's heritage as a pioneer railway town. The depot, built circa 1888, has been restored and turned into a museum. Exhibits include train memorabilia, a telegraph demo, and a train simulator.

Some believe that the design of **Belle Mont Mansion** (1569 Cook Ln., 256/381-5052, 10am-4pm Wed.-Sat., $6 adults, $5 students, seniors, and active military, children under 6 free) was influenced by President Thomas Jefferson's architectural style, due to its signature brick and wood work. Well-situated on a hill, the Palladian-style plantation house was built around 1827 and now proudly has a spot on the National Register of Historic Places. Call ahead for reservations for group tours.

The coonhound is a quintessential part of the Southern landscape. In 1937 a man named Key Underwood buried his faithful companion, Troop, at the site that would later become the **Key Underwood Coon Dog Cemetery** (Coondog Cemetery Rd., 256/412-5970, http://coondogcemetery.com, dawn-dusk daily). Today it's a one-of-a-kind site and a tourist stop, where only coon dogs can be buried, and where tombstones demonstrate loving devotion to pals named Smoky, Ralston, and, of course, Troop. More than 185 coonhounds are now buried here. Each Labor Day, the Friends of the Coondog Cemetery host a celebration, with music, dancing, and a liar's contest. The cemetery is off US 72, seven miles southwest of Tuscumbia. Turn right on Coondog Cemetery Road and follow signs.

Built in 1972, the **Tennessee Valley Museum of Art** (511 N. Water St., 256/383-0533, www.tvaa.net, 9am-5pm Mon.-Fri. 1pm-3pm Sun., $5 adults, $3 students and children, free Sun.) is the art museum of this corner of Alabama. The permanent exhibit houses the Martin Petroglyph and a set of boulders with Native American carvings from 600-1,000 years ago. Traveling exhibits feature photography, painting, and other fine art.

A historical white-brick building built in 1881, the **Colbert County Courthouse** (201 N. Main St., 256/386-8500, 8am-4pm Mon.-Fri., free) still houses county government offices. It was damaged by a fire in 1908, and the clock tower you see today was added during the renovations.

Top to bottom: Belle Mont Mansion; Colbert County Courthouse; a sculpture of the famous water pump at Ivy Green, where Helen Keller learned to sign.

★ **Ivy Green**

Built in 1820 by Helen Keller's grandparents, **Ivy Green** (300 N. Commons St., West Tuscumbia, 256/383-4066, www.helenkellerbirthplace.org, 8:30am-4pm Mon.-Sat., $6 adults, $5 seniors, $3 students) is the birthplace and historic home of the brilliant woman who would become a leader for education and rights for the blind and deaf. Tours are available for the home, which is listed on the National Register of Historic Places, as well as the grounds. The clapboard house has been left mostly how it was in Keller's time.

One of the highlights of the 640-acre property is the well pump where "Miracle Worker" Anne Sullivan taught the young Keller to spell out "water" with hand symbols, connecting those symbols to a concrete meaning. By the end of that day, Keller, who had been largely unable to communicate, knew 30 words. Six months later she knew the alphabet and 625 words.

While the building itself is interesting, it is the stories told here of Sullivan and Keller's friendship and hard work that are compelling for kids and adults alike. *The Miracle Worker* is performed here each summer as part of the annual Helen Keller Festival.

Ivy Green is in West Tuscumbia, two miles north of US 72.

Muscle Shoals

Muscle Shoals is one of the fastest-growing cities in Alabama and, of its Quad Cities brethren, the best known—thanks, in part, to the documentary that bears its name. Today most visitors come to the area to learn about its musical heritage and to make music themselves.

To reach downtown Muscle Shoals from the parkway, take US 72 for 25 miles (stay on US 72 as it turns north), then turn right on Avalon Avenue. It is less than three miles from Tuscumbia to Muscle Shoals.

A major regional landmark built in the 1920s, the **Wilson Lock and Dam** (704 S. Wilson Dam Rd., 256/764-5223, www.tva.gov, 7am-7pm Fri.-Sun.) made it possible for the Shoals to become a major transportation hub for the area. One of 10 locks on the 650-mile Tennessee River, it's the highest single lift lock east of the Rocky Mountains and provides both electricity and flood protection to the region. With a normal lift between 93 and 100 feet, Wilson Lock and Dam is a feat of engineering. When construction began in 1918, this dam, named for Woodrow Wilson, was the largest hydroelectric installation. Call ahead because the dam may be closed for cleaning or security reasons. The dam is 1.3 miles south of US 72, on the banks of the Tennessee River.

★ **Fame Studios**

What do Etta James, the Osmonds, Aretha Franklin, Cher, Alicia Keys, the Civil Wars, Otis Redding, and Jamey Johnson have in common? They're all part of the long list of performers who have recorded at **Fame Studios** (603 Avalon Ave., 256/381-0801, www.fame2.com, tours 9am-10am and 4pm-6pm Mon.-Fri., 10am-2pm Sat., $10). This legendary recording studio was founded in 1959. During its heyday in the 1960s, it was one of the few places in the country where blacks and whites could record together without incident, in part because its remote location kept it off the radar for those outside the music industry. But many musicians would travel to work here, and the famous Muscle Shoals sound was born.

You can take a guided tour of this still working studio, where you'll hear many stories about the musicians who have recorded here, as well as those who have simply paid homage. The walls are heavy with music memorabilia. Avalon Avenue is one block east of US 72.

The Muscle Shoals Sound

Fame Studios in Muscle Shoals

People in Muscle Shoals like to say that music is in the water here. The area was the birthplace of W. C. Handy, known as "The Father of the Blues." Sun Studio and Sun Records owner Sam Phillips, also known as "The Father of Rock and Roll," was born in Florence.

But perhaps it's Rick Hall who deserves the most credit for creating the Muscle Shoals sound, which is funk-meets-soul-meets-rock. Hall created an all-white house band, Muscle Shoals Rhythm Section, and helped them record at his Fame Studios in 1967. In 1969, the group moved on to form their own Muscle Shoals Sound Studio in nearby Sheffield. From there they got big, and became known as The Swampers, a moniker that stuck only after Lynyrd Skynyrd name-checked them in "Sweet Home Alabama": "Now Muscle Shoals has got the Swampers; And they've been known to pick a song or two."

W. C. Handy Birthplace, Museum, and Library

The name William Christopher Handy may not be immediately familiar. But when you immerse yourself in his life at the **W. C. Handy Birthplace, Museum, and Library** (620 W. College St., 256/760-6434, 10am-4pm Tues.-Sat., $2 adults, $0.50 students), you'll realize you were familiar with his music.

The modest cabin that was W. C. Handy's birthplace in 1873 now is the site of this museum, which houses memorabilia from the man who created St. Louis Blues, Beale Street Blues, and Memphis Blues. Handy is considered the "Father of the Blues." The African American composer had a significant impact not just on

blues, but on the music that eventually would become rock 'n' roll.

Tour guides are knowledgeable and impart more information than you might expect. Artifacts include Handy's piano and lots of sheet music. The museum also helps organize the W. C. Handy Music Festival each July and a birthday party for Handy each November. College Street is six blocks north of US 72.

Sheffield

Tiny Sheffield, Alabama, is the oft-forgot member of the Quad Cities, sometimes overshadowed by Muscle Shoals' music and Florence's creative scene. But Sheffield is crucial in a tour of the area, given its role in U.S. history and music. In 1815 General Andrew Jackson brought his troops here to cross the Tennessee River on the way to the Battle of New Orleans. Several sites important to the Muscle Shoals sound, such as the legendary 3614 Jackson Highway studio, are technically in Sheffield city limits.

Sheffield is slightly northwest of the other Shoals cities. To get there from the parkway, follow US 72 east for 20 miles (into Tuscumbia), then turn right on Hook Street, which will become Montgomery Avenue. Follow this for 10 miles.

3614 Jackson Highway

Perhaps once the best-known music studio in Muscle Shoals, **3614 Jackson Highway** (256/978-5151, www.msmusic-foundation.org, 10am-4pm Mon.-Sat.), also known as **Muscle Shoals Sound Studios,** is listed on the National Register of Historic places. It may look familiar: It's appeared on the cover of a Cher album named after the famous address. In addition to nabbing a requisite selfie in front of the famous door, you can also take a **tour** (hourly 10:30am-3:30pm Mon.-Sat., $12, free for kids under 6). See memorabilia of the famous people who recorded here and listen to stories of the music history made here. Tour reservations are not accepted; tours are offered on a first-come, first-served basis.

Florence

From early Native American explorers and Civil War soldiers to 19th-century musicians and contemporary artists, Florence has been attracting people for generations. Much of the quaint downtown district is on the National Register of Historic Places; most of the buildings were constructed between 1880 and

Top to bottom: Tennessee Valley Museum of Art; W. C. Handy Birthplace, Museum, and Library; George Carroll Lion Habitat.

1920. Allow time to stroll here, and for shopping, listening to music, eating, and drinking.

Florence is 29 miles east of the parkway on US 72. Park near Pine and Court Streets to explore downtown.

Drive by this strange-looking sight and you'll see columns left from **The Forks of Cypress cotton plantation** (Jackson Rd.). The Greek Revival house, built in 1830, was famous for its columns surrounding the entire home. It was the only building in the state that had such a colonnade around a two-story building. It was struck by lightning in 1966, but 24 columns stayed upright. Forks of Cypress is about a 10-minute drive from downtown Florence. Take Pine Street northwest for about 1.5 miles, where it will turn into Jackson Road. Stay on Jackson Road for 3 miles, crossing Cypress Creek. The ruins will be on your left.

In 1974 former University of North Alabama (UNA) president Robert M. Guillot brought a 35-pound lion cub to the campus. Named Leo, the lion spent the next 14 years helping lead the school to victory. The original Leo died in 1988, but the tradition didn't, and a long succession of lions came to campus. Today Leo III and Una (a female lion companion) live next to a waterfall in the 12,764-square foot **George Carroll Lion Habitat** (1 Harrison Plaza, 800/825-5862, www.una.edu/lioncam, free). Note that there is not an official address for the habitat, but the main address for UNA brings you to the main parking lot and fountain at the front of campus, which are adjacent to the habitat.

One of the Quad Cities' oldest buildings, **Pope's Tavern and Museum** (203 Hermitage Dr., 256/760-6439, 10am-4pm Tues.-Sat., $2 adults, $0.50 students) has been a stagecoach stop, tavern, an inn, a hospital, and army command center (for both the North and South). Today it is an affordable, engaging museum chock-full of artifacts,

Wichahpi Commemorative Stone Wall

particularly those from the Civil War era. Don't miss the vertically strung piano, one of only four ever made.

Frank Lloyd Wright Rosenbaum House

Architecture critic Peter Blake once called four of Frank Lloyd Wright's buildings among America's most beautiful. One of them was **Rosenbaum House** (601 Riverview Dr., 256/718-5050, http://wrightinalabama.com, 10am-4pm Tues.-Sat., 1pm-4pm Sun., $9 adults, $5 students and seniors), the only Frank Lloyd Wright building in the state of Alabama.

Rosenbaum House is an example of Wright's Usonian-style architecture, and perhaps one of its best examples. The L-shaped red brick house was designed to be affordable and functional and was owned by Mildred and Stanley Rosenbaum and family from 1940 to 1999. The house has a strong connection to the outdoors, where the large lot blends with the house through the tall glass windows. Tours last 45 minutes. Admission sales are in the gift shop across the street from the house.

Festivals and Events

The week-long **Helen Keller Festival** (www.helenkellerfestival.com, June) brings antique car shows, live music, amusement rides, and more to Tuscumbia's Spring Park (1 Spring Park Rd.). This festival is timed to coincide with the annual production of *The Miracle Worker,* produced at Ivy Green, Keller's birthplace.

The 10-day **W. C. Handy Music Festival** (www.wchandymusicfestival.org, July) celebrates the Father of the Blues. Since 1982 this festival has been played around Tuscumbia—in churches, bars, and parks.

The **Trail of Tears Commemorative Motorcycle Ride** (http://al-tn-trailoftears. net, Sept.) revs its engines from Bridgeport to Waterloo, Alabama, along the Trail of Tears on the third Saturday of September each year.

★ Shopping

Florence has long fostered a culture of creativity, with a particular strength in fashion. As a result, the shopping scene is especially eclectic. Designers Billy Reid and Natalie Chanin, who both have outposts in Florence, have attracted others to this corner of the state. Expect to find lots of one-of-a-kind items in the many boutiques.

Downtown Florence

Court Street is Florence's main drag, and it's where some of the top shops dress their windows. Stroll this historic area, especially between Tennessee and Tombigee Streets, to window shop or stock up on gifts, home decor, and women's clothing and jewelry.

Perhaps most responsible for the Southern preppie movement is **Billy Reid** (114 N. Court St., 256/767-4692, www.billyreid.com, 10am-5:30pm

Mon.-Sat.). This designer has stores in New York, New Orleans, Atlanta, Austin, Charleston, Dallas, Houston, Nashville, Chicago, and Washington DC. But the multi-story headquarters is in an old Florence bookstore, selling designs for both women and men. The brand combines Southern aesthetics with New York fashion and helped put Florence on the map. Even if you're not in the market for pricy threads, stopping in the well-merchandised and -decorated store is worthwhile.

Dixie Garage (110 E. Mobile St., 256/627-6545, www.dixiegarage.com, 11am-7pm Tues.-Sat.) sells men's clothing, accessories, grooming goods, and home decor. **Firenze** (114 W. Mobile St., 256/760-1963, www.firenzeinteriors.com, 10am-5pm Tues.-Fri., 10am-3pm Sat.) is where to stop for home decor, antique furniture, jewelry, and art. Locals know this is where to go for baby gifts and bridal registries. **Printers & Stationers Inc.** (113 Court St., 256/764-8061, http://

printersandstationers.com, 8am-5pm Mon.-Fri., 11am-4pm Sat.) was founded in 1933. Come here for stationery, invitations, and thank-you notes for your house sitters.

Check out **Alabama Outdoors** (119 N. Court St., 256/764-1809, http://alabamaoutdoors.com, 10am-7pm Mon.-Sat., noon-5pm Sun.) to buy clothing suitable for the state's great weather and open spaces. This statewide chain offers clothing and gear for outdoor adventuring of all sorts, from climbing to skiing to hiking.

My Favorite Things (126 N. Court St., 256/483-0064, 11am-5pm Mon.-Tues. and Thurs.-Sat., 11am-4pm Wed.) carries women's clothing, jewelry, and Capri Blu, the line of candles that Anthropologie has made famous. A few blocks southwest is **The Eclectic** (411 E. Tennessee St., 256/718-7999, www.theeclectic.biz, 11am-7pm Mon.-Sat.), where you can stock up on global gifts and clothing with a nouveau hippie vibe. Think: caftans,

Rosenbaum House is an example of Frank Lloyd Wright's Usonian style.

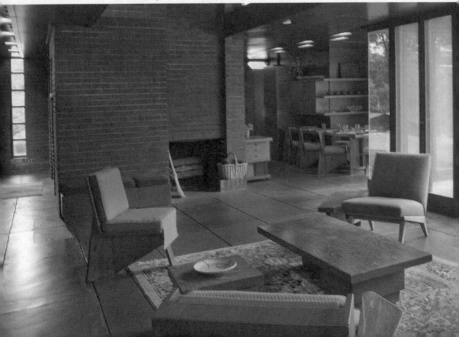

tunics, crystals, dream-catchers, incense, and silver and stone jewelry.

North Florence

Locals consider Wood and Royal Avenues to be North Florence, even though the area is just a quick walk (about a mile) north of historic downtown. Situated above the University of North Alabama campus, the area is dotted with antiques shops and has more of a residential vibe than downtown.

Alabama Chanin (462 Lane Dr., 256/760-1090, http://alabamachanin. com, 10am-5pm Mon.-Fri., 10am-3pm Sat.), the company started by Florence native Natalie Chanin, is another brand that has defined the town. Alabama Chanin sells clothing and other goods made from organic cotton grown and sewn in the United States (and, in many cases, in the state). For those who are so motivated, the company also offers workshops to learn the signature design technique.

Marigail Mathis (1631 Darby Dr., 256/764-9444, 10am-5pm Mon.-Sat.) sells contemporary women's clothing, including brands such as Eileen Fisher, BB Dakota, and Lilla P NYC. **Relique** (1136 N. Wood Ave., 256/767-4810, 11am-4pm Tues.-Sat.) is a great place to search for one-of-a-kind jewelry, such as vintage pieces and those with an industrial look or made from repurposed objects. A wood-sided house is home to **Frolic** (1326 N. Pine St., 256/710-1937, www. frolicclothing.net, 11am-5pm Tues.-Wed., 10am-5pm Thurs.-Fri., 10am-4pm Sat.), where fashion-forward yet affordable women's clothing rules the racks. Most items are in the $25-50 range.

Sports and Recreation

A namesake spring runs through **Spring Park** (1 Spring Park Rd., Tuscumbia, 9am-9pm daily), which boasts a playground, picnic pavilions, and a stage that is well-used for live music and other shows year-round. Don't miss the water show and lighted waterfall. You can even trout fish here (in season and with a license, of course).

The **Cypress Lakes Golf & Tennis Club** (1311 E. 6th St., Muscle Shoals, 256/381-1232, www.cypresslakesgolfandtennis. com, 7:30am-7pm daily, greens fees $18-42) is open to the public. Of the 18 holes, 15 have a water challenge. There are five sets of tees, so the course accommodates golfers of all skill levels. Tennis courts and a swimming pool are also open in warm weather.

Alabama's **Robert Trent Jones Golf Trail** (www.rtjgolf.com) is not just a golf course (or a collection of golf courses): It is the largest golf course construction project ever attempted. Today the trail includes 26 golf courses at 11 different sites across Alabama, including two 18-hole courses in Muscle Shoals: **Fighting Joe** and **Schoolmaster** (990 SunBelt Pkwy., Muscle Shoals, 256/446-5111, greens fees $65 and up).

In Sheffield, the preserved

wood-and-metal **Old Railroad Bridge** (2100 Ashe Blvd., Sheffield, 256/383-0783, http://oldrailroadbridge.com, dawn-dusk daily, free), built in 1840, was once the main way to cross the Tennessee River. This bridge no longer fully spans the river. Walk 0.75 mile out to get great views of the river or connect to nearby walking trails for a longer (yet still easy) hike.

Pretty **Wilson Park** (E. Tombigee St. and Wood Ave., Florence) is in the center of Florence's downtown, across the street from the stately Florence-Lauderdale public library. You can get to the fountain in the center of the park by following one of four pathways, one from each corner of the park. The fountain is a great backdrop for photos. The park houses a **sculpture of W. C. Handy,** Father of the Blues. Numerous events, including the juried Arts Alive show, Music in the Park, Haunted Ghost Tour, and the Alabama Renaissance Faire, take place here.

If seeing so many equestrians along the Trace has you wanting to ride horseback, head to **Seven Springs Lodge** (1292 Mt. Mills Rd., Tuscumbia, 256/370-7218, $5 per day). The lodge offers 20,000 acres of woodland for horseback riding, as well as camping ($10-20), fishing, and stables for those with their own horses. Guided horseback rides are offered the second week of each month.

Just five miles off of US 72, **Hawk Pride Mountain Offroad** (3834 Hawk Pride Mountain Rd., Tuscumbia, 256/349-4150, www.hawkpridemountainoffroad.com, drivers $15-35, passengers $10-20, children under 10 free) is a 1,000-acre park with ATV trails, rock crawling trails, and other outdoor activities. Want to stay and play? Camping, cabins, and RV sites are available, too.

Food
Tuscumbia
A soda fountain housed in an 1833 building, **The Palace Ice Cream and Sandwich Shop** (100 S. Main St., 256/386-8210, 11am-5pm Mon.-Sat., $8-15) is one of those time-travel kind of stops. A bicycle hangs from the ceiling, the waitresses call you "sweetie," and the milkshakes are delicious. The Palace offers a full lunch menu, with burgers, sandwiches, and more, but most people just come for the ice cream.

Old-school Southern cooking sticks to your ribs at local favorite ★ **City Restaurant** (108 W. 5th St., 256/383-9809, 7am-3pm Mon.-Fri., $7-12). The menu changes daily but is chock-full of classics, such as meatloaf, fried chicken, and pot pie. The downtown location means you'll see lots of local government officials here during lunch.

Muscle Shoals
Locals love **New Orleans Transfer** (1682 S. Wilson Dam Rd., 256/386-0656, 11am-2pm Mon.-Thurs., 11am-8pm Fri.-Sat., $8-18), particularly for weekday lunches. Po'boys are available in modest half sizes as well as gut-busting whole portions. Other Cajun specialties include gumbo and fried oysters.

A regional chain, **Champy's Chicken** (120 2nd St., 256/389-9985, http://champyschicken.com, 10:30am-10pm Sun.-Thurs., 11am-midnight Fri.-Sat., $12-18) serves fried chicken, beans, coleslaw and other traditional sides, and plenty of beer. Live music makes it a popular hangout as well as a place to eat. The decor is eclectic.

Florence
People love to eat in Florence as much as they like to shop. Start your culinary tour at ★ **Odette** (120 N. Court St., 256/349-5219, www.odettealabama.com, 11am-2pm and 5pm-10pm Mon.-Fri., 11am-3pm and 5pm-10pm Sat.), where you'll find a menu stocked with farm-to-table American cuisine using lots of southern influences and ingredients. Pair everything with a drink from the craft cocktail menu ($7-24). On your way out, stop in the gift shop, which has

handmade goods from local artisans—dishware, glasses, and bowls, both decorative and functional.

On the Rocks (110 N. Court St., 256/760-2212, http://florenceontherocks.com, 11am-2am Mon.-Sat., 4pm-2am Sun., $7-13) is a friendly neighborhood pub with live music. The crew supports a lot of local causes, so the neighborhood shows up. Expect traditional bar food and burgers.

If you're looking for something healthy, but with a twist, **Dish Gourmet Café** (118 W. Mobile St., 256/766-2414, http://dishgourmetcafeandcatering.com, 11am-3pm Mon.-Thurs., 11am-3pm and 5:30pm-9:30pm Fri., $8-10) is your place. The menu includes salads, sandwiches, quinoa bowls, wraps, and, because this is the South, a pimento cheese burger.

FloBama Music Hall (311 N. Court St., 256/764-2225, 11am-2am Mon.-Sat., 11am-10pm Sun., $7-10) is both a full-service restaurant and a live music venue with a stage and projection screens. Enjoy Southern barbecue, including ribs, whole smoked chickens, their signature hickory-smoked wings, and sandwiches.

Perhaps Florence's best-known and best-loved eatery, ★ **Trowbridge's Ice Cream and Sandwich Bar** (316 N. Court St., 256/764-1503, 9am-5:30pm Mon.-Sat., $2-5) is an old-fashioned ice cream parlor and sandwich shop, just like Grandma used to love. Grab a stool at the fountain and enjoy pimento cheese sandwiches, ham salad, chicken salad, and more, or go straight for dessert. The options are all your childhood favorites: malts, milkshakes, ice cream sodas, and sundaes.

Yumm Thai Sushi and Beyond (117 N. Court St., 256/349-2074, 11am-2pm and 5pm-9pm Mon.-Thurs., 11am-2pm and 5pm-10pm Fri.-Sat., $10-16) delivers what its name promises: rice and noodle

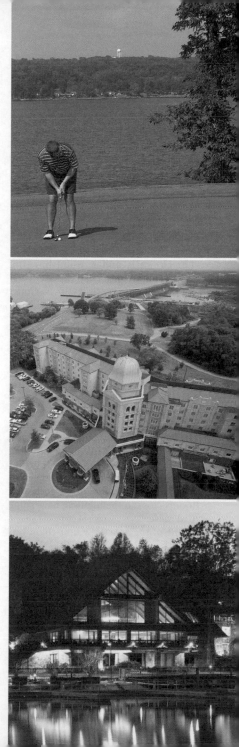

Top to bottom: Robert Trent Jones Golf Trail; Marriott Shoals Hotel & Spa; lodge at Joe Wheeler State Park.

dishes, curries, traditional sushi, and contemporary maki. When the weather is nice, choose the cute sidewalk seating out front and take in the downtown sights.

Craft cocktails, funky hot dog combinations, nachos, flatbreads, and late-night hours make **Wildwood Tavern** (180 Mobile St., 256/349-2139, www.keepflorencefunky.com, 11am-2am Mon.-Sat., 4pm-2am Sun. $6-12) a go-to for locals and visitors alike. The drink menu ($7) includes spiked lemonades, craft cocktails with boutique ingredients such as shrubs, and funky drinks made with Fruity Pebbles-infused simple syrup.

Brick walls and a wood-burning oven combine for a cozy experience at ★ **Ricatoni's Italian Grill** (107 N. Court St., 256/718-1002, www.ricatonis.com, 11am-10pm daily, $16-32). This two-story downtown eatery serves Italian classics such as pizza, pasta, and chicken marsala.

Accommodations
Tuscumbia
A clean and serviceable chain hotel, **Comfort Inn & Suites Tuscumbia— Muscle Shoals** (5101 US 43 S., Tuscumbia, 256/248-0850, www.choicehotels.com, $73-91) offers decent amenities, including free Wi-Fi, a free (if uninspired) breakfast buffet, an outdoor pool, and access to a fitness center. Pets are not allowed. Rooms close to the highway have some road noise.

One of the area's few non-chain hotels, the **ColdWater Inn** (712 US-72, Tuscumbia, 256/383-6844, www.coldwater-inn.com, $89-99) has one big advantage: It is right across the street from the Alabama Music Hall of Fame. Amenities in the 74-room hotel include free Wi-Fi, pillow-top beds, free continental breakfast, and access to a fitness center and an outdoor pool. You can't miss the large columns out front.

You may not feel like you're in Florida while at the **Key West Inn** (1800 US 72, Tuscumbia, 256/383-0700, http://staykeywesthotels.com, $74-117). But

with in-room refrigerators and microwaves, free Wi-Fi, a hot tub, and a free continental breakfast, you will feel perfectly comfortable. The hotel has just 43 rooms, so the staff has time to attend to your requests. The US 72 location makes it a quick drive to and from the parkway.

Every campsite at **Heritage Acres RV Park** (1770 Neil Morris Rd., Tuscumbia, 256/383-7368, www.heritageacresrvpark.com, $29-32) has water, sewer, and electrical hookups, plus 48 TV channels. This is a great place to do laundry and check email if you are traveling by RV. The park is open year-round and offers free Wi-Fi.

Colbert County Rose Trail Campground (9395 Riverton Rose Rd., Cherokee, 256/360-2764, $14-18) is in nearby Cherokee (not to be confused with Cherokee County, which is farther away) on Pickwick Lake. This is a scenic place to park the RV, with access to electricity, water, sewage, bathhouse, and boat ramps. During the late night in the winter, water access may be shut off to keep water lines from freezing, but it is turned back on in the morning.

Muscle Shoals
A serviceable hotel with free Wi-Fi and a basic breakfast, the **Days Inn** (2701 Woodward Ave., Muscle Shoals, 256/383-3000, www.wyndhamhotels.com, $63-83) is right off of US 72 and close to Wilson Dam.

Park your RV and camp at **Colbert County Alloys Park and Campground** (180 Alloys Park Lake, Muscle Shoals, 256/577-9619, www.colbertcounty.org, $18) on Wilson Lake. Electricity, water, sewage, bathhouse, and boat ramps are open year-round.

Sheffield
The pet-friendly **Radisson Hotel Sheffield** (4900 Hatch Blvd., 256/381-4710, www.radisson.com, $67) offers free continental breakfast, free Wi-Fi, and an outdoor pool. Ask for a room with a microwave and refrigerator.

You don't have to be famous (or talented) to stay at ★ **Muscle Shoals Music House** (117 Lakewood Dr., 256/436-9990, $109-119). This two-room B&B on the banks of the Tennessee River claims to be where Bob Dylan and others stayed when they came to record at Muscle Shoals Sound Studio. Room rate includes breakfast. Free Wi-Fi is offered. A two-night stay is required.

Florence

The area's most luxurious hotel is the ★ **Marriott Shoals Hotel & Spa** (10 Hightower Pl., 256/246-3600, www.marriott.com, $124-154). The 360-degree views from the top of the hotel are unparalleled. Rooms include free mini-fridges and are pet friendly (additional $75 fee). The hotel has both indoor and outdoor pools, a fitness center, a spa, and two on-site restaurants.

The ★ **Residence Inn Marriott** (1000 Sweetwater Ave., 256/764-9966, www.marriott.com, $89-139) is a surprising find. The all-suites hotel features rooms with kitchens, a nice pool with outdoor seating, and an outdoor barbecue area. The hotel has green hotel certification, nice sculptures in the hallways, and decent views. The free breakfast has plenty of gluten-free and non-pork options.

If you want to be in the heart of the action, **Hampton Inn Florence-Downtown** (505 S. Court St., 256/767-8282, http://hamptoninn3.hilton.com, $105-123) is the place to stay. It's walking distance to shops and restaurants. You'll get a free hot breakfast, free Wi-Fi, and access to a lobby with fireplace, business center, indoor pool, and fitness center.

A basic motel, **Baymont Inn** (115 Ana Dr., 256/764-5326, www.wyndhamhotels.com, $69-79) is conveniently located off of US 72. It offers free Wi-Fi and breakfast, an outdoor pool, and a fitness center, and is pet-friendly.

If you want the great outdoors, combined with great fishing, plan to rest at ★ **Joe Wheeler State Park** (4403 McLean Dr., 256/247-1184, www.alapark.com, $77-222 rooms and cabins, $25-29 campsites). This 2,550-acre park on Wheeler Lake includes a lodge with restaurant and convention center, an 18-hole golf course and clubhouse, marina, and campsites (both modern sites with amenities and primitive ones).

Information and Services
Visitor Information

The 7,500-square-foot **Florence/Lauderdale Visitor's Center** (200 Jim Spain Dr., 256/740-4141 or 888/356-8687, 9am-5pm Mon.-Fri., 10am-4pm Sat.) has a design inspired by Frank Lloyd Wright and a wealth of information on all the sights and sounds of the Quad Cities. Take a break on benches made from local wood and take your time perusing all the information inside on the region, much of which is stored on interactive iPad displays. There's a Frank Lloyd Wright model and a well-stocked gift shop. The staff is particularly friendly and helpful. The center is on the edge of McFarland Park.

Medical and Emergency Services

If you need medical attention in Muscle Shoals, head to **Shoals Hospital** (201 W. Avalon Ave., Muscle Shoals, 256/386-1600, www.shoalshospital.com), which has a full emergency room. In Sheffield, **Helen Keller Hospital** (1300 S. Montgomery Ave., 256/386-4196, www.helenkeller.com) is a full-service hospital with an emergency room.

The **Muscle Shoals Police Department** (1000 Avalon Ave., Muscle Shoals, 256/383-6746, www.mspolice.org) is centrally located. The **Sheffield Police Department** (600 N. Montgomery Ave., Sheffield, 256/383-1771) is downtown.

Repair Services

For those traveling the Trace by hog, **Natchez Trace Harley-Davidson** (595 US-72 Alt., Tuscumbia, 256/383-5814, 9am-6pm Mon.-Sat., 1pm-5pm Sun.) is

Alabama Fishing

Northwest Alabama is an angler's paradise. Once you get a fishing license, check out these nearby places to cast your rod and reel:

- **Joe Wheeler State Park** (4401 McLean Dr., Rogersville, 256/247-6971, $3 parking fee) is a favorite of bass fishers, but it's also a good place to find catfish, crappie, bream, and stripe. The park is about an hour's drive east of the Natchez Trace. Take US 72 east for 38 miles to AL-101/Wheeler Dam. Drive north for 12 miles, where you'll reconnect with US 72. Turn right, drive east for four miles, and then turn right on McLean Drive.

- **Wilson Lake** (www.wilsonlake.info) is a reservoir on the Tennessee River, which is home to smallmouth and spotted bass, plus sunfish, catfish, and more. Wilson Lake is 22 miles east of the parkway on US 72.

- **Pickwick Lake** (www.tennesseelakeinfo.com) is chock-full of crappie, bass, and catfish. It is northwest of the parkway near Waterloo. Exit near milepost 333 at County Road 14 and continue east for 10 miles to the lake entrance.

the place to stop for parts, gear, and more. **T&M Cycles and ATVs** (3922 Cloverdale Rd., Florence, 256/768-3011) can also get you rolling again.

The **Spinning Spoke Cycle Hub** (221N S. Seminary St., Florence, 256/349-5302, www.spinningspoke.com, 10am-6pm Mon.-Fri., 9am-5pm Sat.) is a Trek bike dealer but will service all manner of cycles. Expedited service may be available if you need to get back on the Trace ASAP.

Back to the Trace

Retrace your steps on US 72, heading west for about 20 miles from Tuscumbia to get back to the parkway. You'll rejoin the Trace near milepost 320, where you can continue your drive south.

Buzzard Roost Spring (MP 320.3)

Once called Buzzard Sleep, Buzzard Roost was a shelter for travelers run by Levi Colbert, a Chickasaw chief and brother of George Colbert. Together the two brothers ran Colbert's Ferry, which took early settlers across the Tennessee River. Like his brother's stand, Levi's was well regarded as a place where weary travelers could rest and eat. The spring here was a water source for the Colbert house.

The site of Levi's stand and that of his brother seem very close to one another, just seven miles apart on the parkway. But in the days of the Old Trace, it may have taken as long as two hours to reach one stand from the other on horseback.

The physical building no longer exists. Informational signs, including some with buttons playing recorded messages, give you a sense of what life was like for travelers who stopped here. The short trail to the spring itself includes many rock steps. While the walk isn't particularly strenuous or long, it does have elevation changes and is not wheelchair accessible. It's worth the walk down, as the water in the spring is impossibly clear and the stairs shaded, making the area a refuge on a hot Alabama day. Some visitors claim to have witnessed ghosts or paranormal activity at this stop, as well as at Colbert's Ferry.

Buzzard Roost isn't visible from the road, but clear signage makes its entrance, on the right side of the parkway, hard to miss. There are no other amenities at this stop.

Freedom Hills Overlook (MP 317)

This quick stop features the **highest point** on the Trace in the state of Alabama. If you stop in spring, summer, or fall, when leaves are still on the trees, it's unlikely that you'll be able to see the type of view expected at an overlook. In winter, you may have more of a chance, but much of the overlook is gone, as trees have blocked the view over the years. It remains a pretty oasis, particularly for fall foliage. To get the full experience, take the 0.25-mile paved path up and back. A few benches at the top allow you to recover from the initial steep ascent.

Access to this overlook is well-marked on the right side of the parkway and the parking area is visible from the road. There are no other amenities.

The Trace: Northern Mississippi

Wind your way through sun-dappled curves and meadows blooming with wildflowers. On this short drive through the hills of northern Mississippi, you'll come across countless opportunities to camp, hike, bike, fish, and swim.

The Trace: Northern Mississippi

Y ou don't have to have a particularly active imagination to picture the significance this section of land had on the country.

Beyond the forty-three miles of the paved Natchez Trace Parkway, there are also opportunities to walk in the deep grooves of the sunken Old Trace, the original trail worn by thousands of footsteps of travelers, settlers, and Native Americans. On your way you'll visit several Civil War battlefields and a gravesite of 13 unknown Confederate soldiers.

The entirety of this stretch of the road trip, from milepost 304.5 south to 261.8,

takes place in Mississippi: Seek shelter under shady dogwoods and oaks during the hot summer sun or choose to explore the other three seasons of the year, when the forecast will be more temperate.

The main stop in this corner of Mississippi is just a short drive off the parkway. Tupelo is known for its contribution to the American music scene—it's the birthplace of Elvis Presley.

Route Overview

The northern Mississippi section of the Natchez Trace Parkway starts at the Alabama-Mississippi border and continues south just past the city of Tupelo. It's **43 miles,** just about 10 percent of the entire length of the Trace. But this section, nestled in the hills of the Magnolia State, is chock-full of sights to see, including three significant archaeological

Highlights

★ **Bear Creek Mound:** This site was likely once a temple or chief's house circa AD 1100-1300 (page 164).

★ **Tishomingo State Park:** Fish, camp, and explore at this lakeside oasis (page 166).

★ **Pharr Mounds:** This site of eight Native American burial mounds is among the most significant in the state (page 167).

★ **Confederate Gravesites:** This resting place of 13 unknown soldiers buried along the Old Trace is a solemn reminder of the costs of war (page 169).

★ **Chickasaw Village Site:** Imagine how life was for Native Americans on the Trace at this expansive former village (page 170).

★ **Elvis Presley Birthplace:** It's a popular stop, not just for fans of the King of Rock 'n' Roll, but for anyone who appreciates music history (page 171).

Best Restaurants

★ **Connie's Fried Chicken:** Come for the chicken and biscuits—then come back for the blueberry doughnuts (page 176).

★ **Johnnie's Drive-In:** Elvis ate here, and so should you (page 176).

★ **Blue Canoe:** Enjoy local beer, local bands, and local dishes made from local ingredients. Bring a Sharpie to sign the walls (page 176).

★ **Kermit's Outlaw Kitchen:** In a region of (delicious) fried foods, Kermit's offers farm-fresh alternatives, including vegetarian dishes (page 176).

sites, scenic hikes, several powerful war monuments, the headquarters for the parkway operations, and a trip to Tupelo, the city that gave us the King of Rock 'n' Roll.

One day is sufficient to see this portion of the Trace. Spend at least one night in Tupelo, the charming city just five miles off the Trace. Plan to use Tupelo as your command center to explore the region's music (including many things Elvis), delicious food, and one-of-a-kind shopping. If you're a true U.S. history buff, you might add an extra half day to your schedule to spend adequate time at the historic battlefields. They are packed with information and you don't want to feel rushed.

Driving Considerations

On this part of the parkway, you may encounter that urban affliction: traffic. The parkway's proximity to Tupelo means it does usher more cars through, particularly during rush hour. The section near Pharr Mounds, one of the most popular sights on the Trace (milepost 286.7) also sees some traffic delays on weekend days.

Fuel and Services

This section of the Trace is short—43 miles—and close to a major city, so the risk of running out of gas is low. Take advantage of a side trip to **Tupelo** to stock up on essentials for yourself and the car, bicycle, or motorcycle. You'll likely have cell service for most of your drive in northern Mississippi, with the best reception as you get closer to Tupelo.

The **Natchez Trace Parkway Headquarters and Visitor Center** (milepost 266; 2680 Natchez Trace Pkwy., Tupelo, 800/305-7417, www.nps.gov, 8am-5pm daily) is on this stretch and is the place to stop for any and all parkway-related services. Allot enough time here to talk to rangers about the Trace.

Tune your radio to 1610AM for recorded information about some of the sights and stops along the way.

For motorcycle repairs or parts, give **Tupelo Performance Cycles** (3402 Main St., 662/840-4488, www.tupeloperformancecycles.com, 8am-5pm Mon.-Fri.) a call. For bicycle help in Tupelo, there are several options very close to the parkway. Check in with **Trails and Treads** (549B Coley Rd., 662/690-6620, 10am-6pm Mon.-Sat.), about 3.5 miles from the Trace. **Bicycle Pacelines** (2120 W. Jackson St., 662/844-8660, www.bicyclepacelines.net, 11am-6pm Mon.-Fri., 10am-4pm Sat.) is just 100 yards from milepost 260.8.

Getting to the Starting Point
Car, Motorcycle, or Bicycle

As you drive or ride southbound on the Trace, you'll ease over the border from Alabama into Mississippi, north of Tishomingo State Park and the town of Tishomingo. Save for a small brown sign marking the state line, you won't notice a difference in the parkway.

Best Accommodations

★ **Bear Creek Saloon Guesthouse:** Close to the parkway, this is a great option for those bicycling the Trace (page 165).

★ **Tishomingo State Park:** Camp here with gear or reserve a historic Civilian Conservation Corps cabin (page 166).

★ **Piney Grove Campground:** Whether you have an RV or a tent, this is the place to stay on the Tenn-Tom Waterway (page 167).

★ **Moon Lake Farm B&B:** Enjoy the great outdoors with views and horseback rides, followed by a cozy night's sleep inside (page 177).

From **Memphis,** it's about 130 miles (just over two hours) to reach Tishomingo State Park, the first major stop on this section of the route. Take US 72 east for about 115 miles. This route goes through Corinth, Mississippi, a town rich in Civil War history. You can stop in the charming downtown for lunch or continue to the Trace. Exit US 72 at MS-25 (following signs for Iuka/Fulton), and continue south on MS-25 for about 13 miles. Follow signs for Tishomingo State Park and turn left onto County Road 90 to get to the park.

To get to the beginning of this section of the drive from **Huntsville,** Alabama, it's a 60-mile drive west along US 72. You'll join the Trace where US 72 intersects with the Trace, at milepost 320. Take the Trace for about 13 miles south to reach the Mississippi border.

Stopping in Corinth

If you're starting from Memphis, you'll drive through the town of Corinth, Mississippi. This charming town of 15,000 is one of the state's historic treasures. Once the crossroads of the Mobile and Ohio and Memphis and Charleston Railroads, Corinth was a major transport hub during the Civil War. Union and Confederate troops battled for control of Corinth, with the Union Army emerging the victor in October 1862.

Stops worth making if you're in the area include the **Veranda-Curlee House** (705 Jackson St., 662/287-8300, 9am-2pm Mon., 9:30am-4pm Thurs.-Sat., 1pm-4pm Sun., $15), an 1857 house that served as headquarters for both Confederate and Union generals during the war. The 15,000-square-foot **Corinth Civil War Interpretive Center** (501 W. Linden St., www.nps.gov/shil, 8am-5pm daily, free) is a significant draw, as are the tree-lined downtown streets with antiques stores, restaurants, and **Borroums Drug Store** (604 E. Waldron St., 662/286-3361, www.borroumsdrugstore.com, 11am-5pm Mon.-Fri., 11am-3pm Sat.), the oldest drugstore in continuous operation in Mississippi.

Borroums is also a classic soda fountain and lunch counter. This is the place to hear Corinth locals' tall tales along with your lunch. Other favorites include **Pizza Grocery** (800 Cruise St., 662/287-3200, www.pizzagrocery.com, 11am-2pm and 5pm-8pm Mon.-Thurs., 11am-2pm and 5pm-9pm Fri.-Sat., $9-17), which has a delightful outdoor patio, and **Abe's Grill** (803 US 72 W., 662/286-6124, www.abesgrill.com, 5am-3pm Mon.-Fri., $2-7), a classic, no frills diner.

Air

This isn't the easiest section of the Trace to access by air, but if that's your preference, the **Memphis International Airport** (MEM, www.flymemphis.com) is a good choice. MEM is served by Delta, Southwest, United, and other major airlines, with a number of non-stop routes. The three-concourse

Fuel Up

Thanks to the proximity to Tupelo on this section of the route, you're unlikely to be far from a gas station. Here's a quick list of places to exit the parkway in northern Mississippi so that you can refuel at the closest gas station. (Some stops may take you to small towns, others will be just a single service station.)

The National Park Service also posts a list of nearby supply stations at most parkway rest areas, although the list is not updated regularly.

* **Milepost 302.8:** Exit at MS-25 and drive three miles north to reach a 24-hour gas station and convenience store.

* **Milepost 282.2:** Exit at MS-371 (signs for Baldwyn). Go west (left) in 0.2 mile to follow MS-371, then turn right in 0.3 mile to get onto MS-370. Drive west on MS-370 for 12 miles to US 45 in Baldwyn. A Texaco, a Shell, a Chevron, and several other gas stations are on the highway north and south of 370.

* **Milepost 266:** Exit at MS-145 and drive 1.5 miles south to Tupelo.

* **Milepost 263:** Exit at McCullough Boulevard and drive 0.3 mile west. Alternatively, drive 0.6 mile east to Tupelo.

airport offers free Wi-Fi and many local dining options.

The **Huntsville International Airport** (HSV, www.flyhuntsville.com) is closer to this portion of the Trace, but it is a smaller airport, with mostly regional destinations served and higher prices. American, Delta, and United serve this northeast Alabama city.

Train and Bus

Train travel to the Trace is a tough proposition; riding the rails isn't the most efficient way to get around this area. **Amtrak** operates out of Memphis's **Central Station** (545 S. Main St., www.amtrak.com), a stop on the 900-mile City of New Orleans route, which runs from New Orleans to Chicago. Central Station is conveniently located downtown, where most major rental car companies have offices.

Greyhound serves the Bluff City via the **Memphis Bus Station** (3033 Airways, www.greyhound.com). The station is adjacent to the Memphis International Airport and close to major car rental companies. The Greyhound routes to Memphis are through Birmingham, Dallas, Jackson, Nashville, or St. Louis.

Budget-friendly **Megabus** (3921 American Way, http://us.megabus.com) serves Memphis from Atlanta, Birmingham, Chicago, Dallas, Little Rock, and St. Louis, from a station near the airport. Megabus boasts free Wi-Fi on board.

★ Bear Creek Mound (MP 308.8)

Immediately after crossing the state line into Mississippi you'll see the entrance to Bear Creek Mound and Village Site on the right side of the road. From there you'll be able to see a square, flat-topped mound that has existed since around AD 1100-1300, part of what is referred to as the Mississippian period in geology.

It may look like just a grassy knoll now, but the mound, likely built in stages, was intended for either ceremonial use or as a residence for an elite member of a tribe, like a chief. Archaeological excavations by the National Park Service suggest that the mound was the site of a temple or a chief's home, which would have been made of mud plaster and wooden posts. This is different from a burial mound,

A Day on the Trace: Northern Mississippi

Rise and shine bright and early! This is going to be a jam-packed day and you don't want to miss a thing. Today's destination is Tupelo, which is about 43 miles along the Trace from the Alabama-Mississippi border. On the way there, stop at the archaeological wonders at **Bear Creek Mound** and **Pharr Mounds.** Take a hike at the **Chickasaw Village Site,** which is just outside of Tupelo proper.

Your first stop in Tupelo must be **Connie's Fried Chicken** for one of their famous blueberry cake doughnuts. Make your way to the **Elvis Presley Birthplace,** where you'll learn about the King of Rock 'n' Roll and his connections to the area.

Next it's time for some late afternoon shopping downtown, including a stop at **Tupelo Hardware Company,** where Elvis got his first guitar. Have a healthy, farm-to-fork dinner at **Kermit's Outlaw Kitchen,** then get back in the car and head over to **Blue Canoe** for local beer and live music before you call it a night. Spend the night at one of Gloster Street's several reliable chains, like the **Holiday Inn Hotel & Suites Tupelo North,** which has a lovely atrium with a lively bar.

which you'll see at Pharr Mounds (milepost 286.7).

Over the years, Bear Creek's mound height had been reduced by plowing. After the 1965 excavation by the NPS, it was restored to its estimated original dimensions: approximately 8 feet high and 85 feet wide.

This mound was likely within a village, possibly dating back as far as 8000 BC. Nearby Bear Creek made for an environment rich in wildlife, and thus a fertile area for hunting and gathering.

Native American sites are protected by the Antiquities Law of Mississippi and the federal Archaeological Resources Protection Act. Treat these areas with respect for the many generations who came before.

There are no amenities here, but it is an essential stop, a place to understand and appreciate the long history of the Trace.

Cave Spring (MP 308.4)

Cave Spring is an oasis along the parkway. This rock cavern was carved by underground water slowly eroding the surrounding limestone. The cave itself is not safe to enter; instead, you can take

an easy walk on a paved loop path next to the cave entrance.

As you walk along the outside of the cave, you'll see the limestone and other sediments that have piled up over time, creating a layer cake of rock that's more than one story high. The namesake spring may resemble a small pond, so it can be hard to imagine how this water was responsible for carving away at stone. In the summer, this is a shaded, cool place, and in the autumn, migrating butterflies are in abundance.

It takes just a few minutes to walk the path and see the cave. There are stairs on each end, so the lower portion is not wheelchair accessible. However, you can take in the cave spring area from an observation point above.

The water is not safe to drink and there are no other amenities. To get to Cave Spring from the parkway, take the well-marked loop road on the right, which leads to the parking lot.

Accommodations

Less than three miles from Cave Spring and just 0.75 mile off the parkway is ★ **Bear Creek Saloon Guesthouse** (1338 MS-30, Tishomingo, 334/332-3474, www.bearcreekinnsms.com, $90 s, $15 for each additional guest). This unhosted guesthouse was once a family retreat and now sleeps 1-3 people (with a queen bed and twin bed). It also has a kitchen and laundry facilities. Because of its proximity to the Trace, it's perfect for those traveling by bicycle. Children are welcome, but pets are not allowed. The owners have provided a fire pit as well as information on food delivery.

★ Tishomingo State Park (MP 304)

Named for Chief Tishomingo, once leader of the Chickasaw Nation, **Tishomingo State Park** (105 County Road 90, 662/438-6914, www.mdwfp.com, $4 for up to six people) is more than 1,500 acres, a great place to recreate near the Trace. Limestone outcroppings provide the backdrop for lots of outdoor recreation options, including canoeing on 45-acre Bear Lake, fishing on well-stocked Bear and Haynes Lakes, swimming ($6 fee), picnicking, disc golf, volleyball, rock climbing, and hiking on the park's 13 miles of trails. One of the most popular paths is the **Bear Creek Outcropping Trail,** which starts at a 200-foot swinging bridge and continues for 3.5 miles. Rock climbing is allowed in the park, but you must bring your own gear and obtain a permit when you pay the park entrance fee.

To get to the park, turn right to exit the Trace at milepost 304. Drive for 0.5 mile, then turn right onto County Road 90; the park's gatehouse, where you pay the entrance fee, is just several hundred feet along this road.

Accommodations

The park offers ★ **campsites** for tents and RVs (62 sites, $13-20) and historic Civilian Conservation Corps **cabins** ($65-75), many of which are ringed by wildflowers and ferns in the spring. The cabins have fireplaces and screened porches. There is also an accessible cottage (linens not included). To make a reservation, call (662/438-6914) or book online (http://mississippistateparks.reserveamerica.com).

Eight miles south of the park in the tiny railroad town of Belmont is the **Belmont Hotel** (121 Main St., 662/454-7948). This 10-room hotel looks straight out of a movie set. Sit on the porch or in the renovated red lobby and talk to the innkeepers about the lore surrounding this 1924 building. A stay here is the only reason to come to Belmont; the town doesn't have much else to recommend it.

Jourdan Creek (MP 295)

This small picnic area on the left side of the road has views of a small, winding sunken creek. It's a short, but steep, walk from the parking area to the picnic table. There are no other amenities, but if you need a break, this is a good, uncrowded place to stop before you get to the more popular Pharr Mounds. The pullout is U-shaped, making it easy for RVs and trailers to get back on the parkway.

Tennessee-Tombigbee Waterway (MP 293.2)

This 234-mile-long canal linking the Tennessee River with the Tombigbee River opened in 1985, but the Tenn-Tom Waterway had been discussed for centuries leading up to its construction. In fact, Louis XIV once considered such a proposal. Congress mulled it over as early as 1810. Finally, in 1946 the U.S. Army Corps of Engineers approved a plan for a canal to connect the two bodies of the water and in 1971 building began.

Admire the feats of engineering that went into the canal at this stop on the Trace, where you'll cross the waterway via the **Jamie L. Whitten Bridge,** which is named after the Mississippi congressman who helped make the canal a reality.

This stop on the right side of the road has a small loop parking area with access to picnic areas and pretty, if not secluded, views of the waterway and bridge. It's particularly lovely at sunset, when the sky's colors hit the water.

Accommodations

Just before milepost 293.2, you can exit the Trace at John Rankin Highway to explore the Tennessee-Tombigbee landscape. There are eight different **campgrounds** managed by the Army Corps on the Tenn-Tom Waterway, five of which are in Mississippi. ★ **Piney Grove Campground** (662/728-1134, starting at $22), the closest to the parkway, has 114 RV sites, with a swimming beach, laundry, electricity, and other amenities. To get there, exit John Rankin Highway (County Road 3501) and take it north to County Road 3550, about 13 miles. Entrance to the campground will be on the left. Retrace your steps to return to the parkway.

★ Pharr Mounds

(MP 286.7)

One of the best-known and most significant stops on the Natchez Trace is **Pharr Mounds**, a complex of eight burial mounds that comprise the largest archaeological site in northern Mississippi, and one of the largest in the region.

Built between AD 1 and 200, in what's referred to as the Middle Woodland period, these mounds range in height from 2 to 18 feet, in an area of about 90 acres (about 100 football fields). In 1966, the National Park Service excavated four of the mounds and found fire pits, human remains, and ceremonial artifacts. Some of these artifacts included copper objects, decorated ceramics, lead ore like galena and mica, and a greenstone pipe. Copper, galena, mica, and greenstone aren't originally from Mississippi, so they must have been brought from long distances. This indicates that the local people participated in a trade network.

From the parking lot you can see three of the mounds—giant camelback shapes covered in grass. It's easy to spot the largest mounds, but the smaller ones may be all but invisible. The Park Service allows some of the area surrounding the mounds to be harvested for hay, so depending on the time of year, you may see some hay bales. The juxtaposition of the bales against the larger, green mounds can make for a striking visual. While observing, stay on the pathways, which are about 400 yards from the mounds. Remember to treat the area with the respect it deserves.

There are restrooms but no other amenities. These are the last restrooms until the Natchez Trace Parkway Headquarters and Visitor Center (page 169). The parking area for Pharr Mounds is on the left side of the parkway. The mounds are visible from the road.

Browns Bottom (MP 286.3)

Browns Bottom is a small, unsigned stop, just south of Pharr Mounds, on the same side of the road. Pull over here to take advantage of the picnic table among the pretty foliage. You can even unpack your fishing gear and cast away on a small pond.

Three-day Mississippi fishing licenses (601/432-2400, http://mdwfp.com/license/fishing) are $15 for nonresidents and $3 for those who live in the state.

Donivan Slough

(MP 283.3)

A slough is a swamp that might appear stagnant but, in fact, has moving water. That's what you'll find at this small stop on the right side of the parkway. A wooded boardwalk trail circles the swamp. The slough is home to bald cypress, tulip poplar, sycamore, and water oak trees that thrive in this moist environment. You'll see cypress "knees" (the roots of the cypress trees popping up through the water), and in the spring, wildflowers dot the land.

There's a picnic table near the parking lot, which is a good spot for a rest. There are no other amenities. The parking lot is directly off the parkway.

Donivan Slough Trail

Distance: 0.4-mile loop
Duration: 15 minutes
Difficulty: Easy

The trail is an easy 15-minute (less than 0.5 mile) loop on a boardwalk, accessible from the parking lot. It's shaded from the hot summer sun and a few degrees cooler, too. During the heat of the summer, if there has been drought, the water levels may be very low, but the foliage is worth taking in, regardless. After hard rains, water levels will be high, but thanks to the boardwalk you'll stay dry. Signage is posted along the trail, with brief information about the various flora.

Accessing the path requires descending about 15 steps (with a handrail) to access the trail; there is no wheelchair ramp. If you are walking near sunset in the summer, you may want to use bug spray or wear long sleeves.

Twentymile Bottom Overlook (MP 278.4)

This is an overlook along the parkway where you can take in the scope and depth of the landscape of the Old Trace from above. Drive up the hill on the right side of the parkway. From the hill, you can look out at the now-developed farmland and imagine what a hard route the area below (the "bottom") was for early settlers, Native Americans, soldiers, and others.

This parking lot is an out-and-back, not a loop, so those in large RVs or with

Pharr Mounds dates back to between AD 1 and 200.

horse trailers may want to avoid this stop. (It is clearly marked with a "no circular drive" sign.) Neither the overlook nor the parking area is visible from the road.

Dogwood Valley

(MP 275.2)

This easy 15-minute walk along a portion of the Old Trace is located, unsurprisingly, in a valley of dogwood trees. Dogwoods are a beloved tree in the south, and are known for their white or pink four-petal flowers. Some of the dogwoods in this valley are more than 100 years old and no longer flower. There's lots of signage along the way to teach you about this favorite tree. The walk is in the sunken part of the Old Trace and is not suitable for those in wheelchairs.

★ Confederate Gravesites and Old Trace (MP 269)

When you pull off the right side of the road to the small parking lot here, it doesn't look like much. But when you walk to the top of the hill (along a largely paved, if slightly steep, path), you get to one of the most moving sites on the entirety of the Trace. Here at the **Confederate Gravesites** are 13 headstones of unknown Confederate soldiers, arranged in a single line, shaded from the hot Mississippi sun under a canopy of trees. Each stone has an American flag next to it and, as is typical at military cemeteries, coins on top. Coins are often left on each headstone by visitors paying their respects; some believe the denomination of the coin has meaning. Sometimes you'll see flowers that visitors have left as well. If you walk off the pathway you can get a vantage point of the headstones from a sunken section of the **Old Trace.** The headstones were replaced by the Park Service after the originals were lost to time and later marble replacements were stolen.

No one knows how these Civil War soldiers died. Some suspect they perished in the Battle of Brices Cross Roads, while others think they may have died on the Trace on the way back home from the war. This site is a solemn, powerful reminder of the costs of war.

There are no amenities at this stop.

Natchez Trace Parkway Headquarters and Visitor Center (MP 266)

The one stop everyone traveling a section of the Trace should make is at the **Natchez Trace Parkway Headquarters and Visitor Center** (2680 Natchez Trace

Pkwy., Tupelo, 800/305-7417, www.nps. gov, 8am-5pm daily). This is the hub for all things Trace-related. Park rangers run a well-stocked gift shop and small museum, which includes a short orientation video narrated by country star Amy Grant. Any questions you have—from the history of the Trace to where to eat lunch—can be answered by the knowledgeable staff. This is also the place to send postcards, buy souvenirs for friends and family at home, or to get your National Parks Passport stamped. The gift shop has very basic concessions (just soda and candy)—there aren't any good meal options. Plenty of free maps are available, not just for the Tupelo area, but for the entirety of the parkway.

Ranger-led tours and other activities take place, including the popular Read with a Ranger program (monthly, free). You'll find ample parking for cars, trailers, and RVs, and plenty of picnic tables, restrooms, and other amenities. There are several short nature walks off of (and visible from) the parking lot, perfect for walking the dog or stretching your legs. You can jump on a longer hiking trail (part of the Natchez Trace Scenic National Trail) that connects you to Old Town Overlook (2.5 miles each way) and the Chickasaw Village Site (4 miles each way). These are relatively moderate hikes with elevation changes and are not wheelchair-accessible.

Old Town Overlook
(MP 263.9)

Old Town Overlook is named for a Chickasaw village whose name has been lost to history. At this spot, early Trace pioneers had a lovely view of that village, which they dubbed "Old Town." Today you can pull over on the right side of the road and see a thriving pond with turtles and other wildlife at this scenic spot. Rest and take in the views of both nature and the parkway itself. Unlike some other overlooks on the parkway, this one is in a meadow, so there isn't a lot of overgrowth blocking the vista.

It's possible to hike 2 miles south from here to the Chickasaw Village Site or 2.5 miles north to the Natchez Trace Parkway Headquarters and Visitor Center. This stretch is part of the Natchez Trace Scenic National Trail. Look for signage to direct you along the trails. These are easy, out-and-back hikes.

The driveway to the overlook is on the right when you enter the pullout; the pond is to the left.

★ Chickasaw Village Site (MP 261.8)

If you want to imagine what life along the Trace was like for the Native Americans who lived and traveled here, be sure to devote plenty of time to the **Chickasaw Village Site.**

Archaeologists believe that the Chickasaw people had a fort and several summer dwellings here in the 1700s, in what's now a wildflower-strewn meadow. A modern covered shelter has artist renderings of how the fort would have looked. Occasionally there are ranger-led activities at this site. Check the National Park Service website (www.nps.gov) or at the Natchez Trace Parkway Headquarters and Visitor Center for details.

There are several options for hikes. The first is an easy, sundappled 15-minute loop walk with signage pointing out the various plants that the Chickasaw used in their daily life for food and medicine. The 0.3-mile loop is slightly hilly but relatively easy. Stay to the right and you'll end up back behind the information shelter where you started. Because this trail is so close to Tupelo, it's very well maintained, and you won't encounter as much overgrowth as on some other Trace trails.

If you are up for a longer hike, you can take the trail to the right of the shelter (in the left corner if you are in the parking lot) two miles to Old Town Overlook or four miles to the parkway visitors center.

This is one of the larger stops along the Trace. The long driveway on the right has a gate, which is closed after dusk. Neither the parking area nor the site itself is visible from the road. There are no picnic tables or other amenities.

Tupelo

With a population of more than 35,000, Tupelo isn't close to being the state's biggest city (Jackson, Gulfport, Hattiesburg, and several others are larger). But thanks to some famous locals, including Elvis Presley himself, Tupelo is somewhere you can have big, unexpected fun.

Nestled in a region called the Hills of Mississippi, Tupelo is home to rich American music history, as well as a modern live music scene. There are plenty of museums to explore art and Civil War history, and more than enough places to eat and drink before you rejoin the Natchez Trace Parkway.

Tupelo was the first city to gain electricity under President Franklin Roosevelt's Tennessee Valley Authority initiatives. Don't miss the lighted neon TVA arrow sign on your way to downtown at the intersection of Main and Gloster. This landmark has been part of city history since 1945.

Several exits from the parkway lead to the city of Tupelo. The most direct way is to exit the parkway at US 45. Take US 45 for five miles, exiting at Front Street. Once you reach the intersection of Front Street and Main Street, you'll be in downtown Tupelo.

Sights
Brices Cross Roads
National Battlefield
The mammoth **Brices Cross Roads National Battlefield** (US 45 and MS-370, Baldwyn, 662/365-9699, www.nps.gov/

brcr, 9am-5pm Tues.-Sat., free) marks an important moment in American history. In June 1864 the scrappy Confederate army, led by Major General Nathan Bedford Forrest, defeated the larger Union army. Some counts suggest that as many as five times more Union troops died here than Confederate soldiers. This battle, also referred to as the Battle of Guntown or Tishomingo Creek, allowed the soldiers to secure supply lines between Nashville and Chattanooga, Tennessee.

History buffs should plan to spend at least 90 minutes at this collection of sites about 20 miles north of Tupelo proper.

The best-known site is a one-acre section of the battlefield, which includes an imposing concrete monument topped by an eagle. The **monument,** at the corner of the park near MS-370, honors those who lost their lives in the battle. It's surrounded by cannons and foliage. Pay your respects at the 96 Confederate graves at **Bethany A. R. P. Church Cemetery,** visit the church that became a field hospital after the battle, and walk along interpretive trails. These sites are close together, so it's an easy walk to see it all.

Nearby, in the town of Baldwyn, is the **Final Stands Interpretive Center** (607 Grisham St., Baldwyn, 662/365-3969, www.finalstands.com, 9am-5pm Tues.-Sat., adults $5, free for children under 7). This center has a 4,000-square-foot building with artifacts, museum-style exhibits, a bookstore, and two short films, for those who want to immerse themselves in the battle.

To get to Brices Cross Roads from Tupelo, take US 45 north for nearly 10 miles, exiting at MS-348. Go west for less than a mile, then turn right (north) onto County Road 833. Go five miles and continue straight when CR 833 becomes MS-370. The entrance will be on your right.

★ Elvis Presley Birthplace
If there is one thing for which Tupelo is

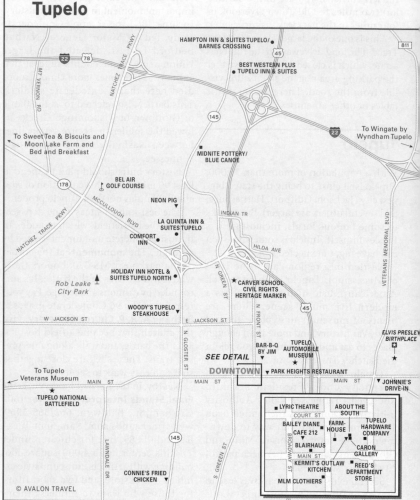

© AVALON TRAVEL

known, it is the **Elvis Presley Birthplace** (306 Elvis Presley Dr., 662/841-1215, http://elvispresleybirthplace.com, 9am-5pm Mon.-Sat., 1pm-5pm Sun., adults $17, seniors and students $14, children ages 7-12 $7, free for children under 7), which includes the house Elvis was born in, a museum, his childhood chapel, a gift shop, and much more.

Elvis Aaron Presley was born on January 8, 1935, in this two-room house that's been restored to its original condition. The family didn't live in the house long—hard financial times befell them. Elvis's talent was evident at a young age. When he was 11, his mother bought him a guitar at Tupelo Hardware Company. His pastor taught him to play, and the gospel music he learned in Tupelo influenced his entire career.

You can stop by the birthplace and see the exterior of the small home, as well as the chapel and one of the family's cars, without taking the **Grand Tour** (adults $17, seniors $14, children $8). But it's worth the cost to hear about how the blues and gospel influenced Elvis and how he created his signature sound, leading him to be the best-selling solo artist in history. With the tour, you'll also be able to go inside the museum, which is full of artifacts that celebrate his life and music.

It's also possible to take just the **house tour** (adults $8, children $5). The Elvis Presley Birthplace is a physically compact site, and it's accessible for fans of all ages.

Tupelo National Battlefield Site

For two days in July 1864, 20,000 Confederate and Union soldiers fought at the **Tupelo National Battlefield** (2083 Main St., www.nps.gov/tupe, dawn-dusk daily, free). Today the battlefield resembles a small city park. It houses a small statue with an eagle atop it next to two cannons and an American flag. It can be tricky to find parking right at the battlefield site, but there is plenty of street parking on surrounding blocks. The site is listed on the National Register of Historic Places.

Tupelo Automobile Museum

Founded in 2002, the **Tupelo Automobile Museum** (1 Otis Blvd., 662/842-4242, www.tupeloautomuseum.com, 9am-4:30pm Mon.-Sat., noon-4:30pm Sun., adults $10, seniors and military $9, children 5-12 $5, free for children 4 and under) was 28 years in the making. Nearly three decades of collecting were required to amass more than 150 cars. Check out lots of fun vehicles, including a 1981 DeLorean similar to the one in *Back to the Future*. And because all roads in Tupelo lead back to Elvis, the museum has a 1976 Lincoln Mark IV in its collection, a gift from the King.

Top to bottom: Tupelo Automobile Museum; Tupelo Veterans Museum; Johnnie's Drive-In.

Carver School Civil Rights Heritage Marker

Built in 1939, Carver Elementary School was an important part of the Tupelo civil rights movement, as a school for African American students as well as a meeting place for the black community. The **Carver School Civil Rights Heritage Marker** (910 N. Green St.), standing in front of what is still an elementary school today, acknowledges this history.

Oren Dunn City Museum

Housed in a converted dairy barn inside Ballard Park, the **Oren Dunn City Museum** (689 Rutherford Rd., 662/841-6438, www.tupeloms.gov, 9am-5pm Mon.-Fri., free) tells the story of Tupelo, Mississippi Hill Country, and Chickasaw cultural history. This is a great place to take the kids for an hour or two, thanks to its playgrounds, picnic areas, and a lakeside walking trail. The museum hosts the annual Dudie Burger Festival and the Dogtrot Rockabilly Festival.

Tupelo Veterans Museum

The **Tupelo Veterans Museum** (689 Rutherford Rd., 662/844-1515, www.tupeloveteransmuseum.com, 9am-4pm Tues.-Fri., 10am-3pm Sat., free) houses an impressive collection of military artifacts, but its beautiful and solemn grounds near Ballard Park are what make this a must-stop. Inside check out Civil War memorabilia and a document signed by Abraham Lincoln, plus uniforms and equipment from the Korean, Vietnam, and Gulf Wars. Outside see planes, flags, and memorials in a beautiful setting.

Entertainment and Events

An art deco-style building near downtown, the historic **Lyric Theatre** (201 N. Broadway St., 662/844-1935, www.tct.ms) is home to many of Tupelo's performing arts productions by the Tupelo Community Theatre. TCT also operates **TCT Off Broadway** (213 E. Franklin St.), an 80-seat cabaret space. Ticket prices and show times vary by performance.

Elvis Presley Birthplace

Folks in Mississippi love a festival. The Dudie Burger, named for the Dudie Diner, was a Tupelo mainstay, a burger made with meat, flour, and water. The diner is now part of the Oren Dunn City Museum, which brings the burger back for one day a year at the **Dudie Burger Festival** (662/841-6438) each May. May also brings people to downtown Tupelo for the two-day **GumTree Festival** (http://gumtreefestival.com), which includes a juried visual arts exhibition and singer/songwriter contest.

The **Tupelo Elvis Festival** (http://tupeloelvisfestival.com) honors hometown King Elvis Presley with live music for four days in early June.

Shopping

Shopping in downtown Tupelo is a browser's dream, with lots of small boutiques with one-of-a-kind wares. **About the South** (120 W. Main St., 662/844-2689, 10am-5pm Mon.-Fri., 10am-5pm Sat.) is a cute gift store with an emphasis on items made in the South. Come here for jewelry, housewares, and gourmet eats. Find linens, furniture, antiques, and art at **FarmHouse** (126 W. Main St., 662/269-2934, www.farmhousetupelo.com, 10am-5pm Mon.-Fri., 11am-4pm Sat.).

Even if you are not a shopper, you must stop at the historic **Tupelo Hardware Company** (114 W. Main St., 662/842-4637, www.tupelohardware.com, 7am-5:30pm Mon.-Fri., 7am-noon Sat.). Open since 1926, this is a traditional hardware store, but it is where Elvis Presley's mother, Gladys, bought him his first guitar. He wanted a .22 caliber rifle for his birthday, but she didn't want him to have a gun, so she bought the guitar instead and history was born. The store has a plaque out front.

Caron Gallery (128 Main St., 662/205-0351, http://thecarongallery.com, 10am-5pm Mon.-Fri., 10am-4pm Sat.) represents more than 50 artists from the state of Mississippi. Interior design firm **Blair Haus** (208 W. Main St., 662/269-2513, www.blairhaus.com, 10am-5pm Tues.-Fri., 11am-4pm Sun.) has a small storefront space that sells furniture, linens, and artwork.

The emphasis at **Bailey Diane** (109 Spring St., 662/321-2435, 10am-4pm Mon., 10am-5pm Tues.-Fri., 10am-3pm Sat.) is on women's clothing, most at affordable price points under $50. **MHM Clothiers** (108 S. Spring St., 662/842-4165, www.mlmclothiers.com, 9:30am-6pm Mon.-Fri., 10am-5pm Sat.) claims to be the oldest men's clothing store in Mississippi.

First opened in 1905 as a dry goods general store, **Reed's Department Store** (131 Main St., 662/842-6453, www.reedsms.com, 9:30am-5:30pm Mon.-Sat.) is now a favorite Southern department store with clothing for men, women, and children.

Not downtown, but worth the drive is **Midnite Pottery** (2004 N. Gloster St., 662/842-8058, 10am-5pm Mon.-Sat.), a pottery studio with a creative local take on ceramics. Come for dishes, platters, candles, and jewelry.

Food

★ **Connie's Fried Chicken** (821 S. Gloster St., 662/842-7260, 7am-8:30pm Mon.-Sat., 7am-2pm Sun., $8) is often referred to as the "Café Du Monde of Tupelo," a reference to New Orleans's famous beignets. Connie's is a chicken shack, sure, but one that also sells delicious blueberry doughnuts, a Tupelo favorite. The doughnuts are light and sweet, and are also featured as an ingredient in other local desserts. The fried chicken is tasty, too, and the biscuits are flaky, but the reason to come to Connie's is the doughnuts. Go ahead, get a dozen to go.

When in Tupelo, you must eat somewhere Elvis ate. And that somewhere should be ★ **Johnnie's Drive-In** (908 E. Main St., 662/842-6748, 7am-9pm Mon.-Sat.). The King loved the dough burgers—hamburgers with flour added to stretch the meat farther in lean times. Fried green beans, fried chicken, eggs, and biscuits round out the no frills menu. If it isn't crowded, you may be able to sit in Elvis's favorite booth, but they also have car service if you don't want to go inside.

Woody's Tupelo Steakhouse (619 N. Gloster St., 662/840-0460, www.woodyssteak.com, 4:30pm-9pm Tues.-Thurs., 4:30pm-9:30pm Fri.-Sat., $10-30) isn't your run-of-the-mill northern steakhouse, thanks to its wild game menu options, like quail and alligator. Locals like the burgers, po'boys, and catfish, and the karaoke lounge on Thursday nights.

Since 1982 **Park Heights Restaurant** (335 E. Main St., 662/842-5665, www.parkheightsrestaurant.com, $18-30) has been a downtown mainstay, with global, contemporary twists on southern classics. Park Heights is a good choice for quality seafood.

Locals are passionate about ★ **Blue Canoe** (2006 N. Gloster St., 662/269-2642, www.bluecanoebar.com, 3pm-midnight Mon.-Thurs., 3pm-1am Fri., 2pm-1am Sat., $8-13), a bar and restaurant with live music and a better-than-bar-food menu. There are two things you shouldn't skip: the fries with "crack dip" (an addictive sausage and cheese sauce) and the bread pudding, made with blueberry doughnuts from Connie's Fried Chicken. This is a great place to try local beers on tap or watch a football game.

The farm-to-table menu at ★ **Kermit's Outlaw Kitchen** (124 Main St., 662/620-6622, www.kermitsoutlawkitchen.com, 11am-3pm Mon.-Wed., 11am-3pm and 5pm-10pm Thurs.-Sat., $13-28) changes weekly, but it always features fresh, local, and delicious ingredients. Don't miss the Vegetable Art Project, a vegetarian entrée made with local seasonal veggies. Owned by the same folks, **Neon Pig Café** (1203 N. Gloster St., 662/269-2533, www.tupelo.eat-neonpig.com, 11am-9pm Mon.-Sat., 11am-4pm Sun., $7-12) is a two-room homage to all things pork. Order tacos, sandwiches, or burgers for take out or to eat in, or avail yourself of the butcher shop. This is a popular spot; lines can be long at night.

A casual coffee shop, **Cafe 212** (212 Main St., 662/844-6323, www.cafe212t-upelo.com, 7:30am-6pm Mon.-Thurs., 7:30am-3pm Fri., $5-7) serves coffee all day and lunch 11am-2pm. In addition to salads, grilled sandwiches, and cold sandwiches, there's a Blue Suede Grill inspired by Elvis: a grilled sandwich with bananas, peanut butter, and honey.

When in the South you don't want to miss the opportunity for a good pimento cheese sandwich. Order one at **Sweet Tea & Biscuits Café** (2025 McCullough Blvd., 662/322-7322, www.sweetteaandb.com, 11am-2pm Tues.-Sat., $8-9.50). The BLT made with fried green tomatoes is another South-inspired favorite.

If you can't resist the siren call of barbecue, **Bar-B-Q by Jim** (203 Commerce St., 662/840-8800, 10:30am-6pm Mon.-Wed., 10:30am-7:30pm Thurs.-Sat., $7-18) is a traditional mainstay. The smoked chicken salad is modern twist on a classic.

Accommodations

Tupelo has many chain hotels, totaling more than 1,900 rooms, many of which are affordable and well-located. There are also several options from **Airbnb** (www.airbnb).

The ★ **Moon Lake Farm B&B** (3130 Endville Rd., 662/420-1423, www.moonlakefarm.com, $129-149) has three guest rooms, all with their own entrances and decks offering great views of the property. You can fish on-site and go horseback riding.

Hampton Inn & Suites Tupelo/Barnes Crossing (1116 Carter Cove, 662/821-0317, www.hamptoninn.com, $109) is close to the mall. Choose from standard rooms or suites with kitchens. Take advantage of the outdoor pool, free hot breakfast, free Wi-Fi, and fitness center. East of the mall is the **Wingate by Wyndham** (186 Stone Creek Blvd., 662/680-8887, www.wyndhamhotels.com, $84), with a fitness center, whirlpool, business center, and free Wi-Fi and breakfast buffet. Also nearby is the **Holiday Inn Express & Suites Tupelo** (1612 McClure Cove, 662/620-8184, www.holidayinn.com/tupelo, $70-100), with a free breakfast buffet and indoor pool. **Fairfield Inn & Suites Tupelo** (3070 Tom Watson Dr., 662/680-6798, www.marriott.com, $99-104) includes evening welcome receptions with free beer and wine. **Best Western Plus Tupelo Inn & Suites** (3158 N. Gloster St., 662/847-0300, www.bestwestern.com, $93-99) offers a picnic area with grills.

Several hotels dot Gloster Street: **Holiday Inn Hotel & Suites Tupelo North** (923 N. Gloster, 662/269-0096, www.holidayinn.com/tupelo, $107), which has an indoor pool, a restaurant and bar on-site, and free Wi-Fi. Rooms at **LaQuinta Inn & Suites Tupelo** (1013 Gloster St., 662/847-8000, www.laquintatupeloms.com, $73-89) are pet friendly and have both a microwave and fridge in each room. Nearby is the affordable **Comfort Inn** (1532 McCullough Blvd., 662/269-1508, www.choicehotels.com, $68-85), with an outdoor pool and fitness center.

Information and Services

You can't miss the **Natchez Trace Parkway Headquarters and Visitor Center** (2680 Natchez Trace Pkwy., 800/305-7417, 8am-5pm daily) as you drive by. The headquarters has an interpretive center, a gift shop with some snacks, bathrooms, ample parking, picnic areas, and access to hiking trails. This is a great place to get questions answered from knowledgeable rangers. For information about the city's attractions, stop by the **Tupelo Convention & Visitors Bureau** (399 Main St., 662/841-6521, www.tupelo.net, 8am-5pm Mon.-Fri.).

Memphis and the Mississippi Blues Trail

Memphis may owe its existence to the mighty Mississippi, but it is music that defined this Southern metropolis. This region is a melting pot of cultural, musical, and culinary influences from across the entire Mississippi River Delta.

MEMPHIS

Beale Street
National Civil Rights Museum
The Peabody Memphis
Stax Museum of American Soul Music

Graceland

TN

Tunica

ARKANSAS

MISSISSIPPI

Friars Point

Clarksdale

Rosedale

Grammy Museum Mississippi

Cleveland

Indianola

Leland

Memphis

To Chucalissa and
T.O. Fuller State Park

To Tunica, MS

GRACELAND

MEMPHIS
INTERNATIONAL
AIRPORT

ELVIS PRESLEY BLVD

AIRWAYS BLVD

3RD ST

SOUTH PKWY

SOUTH
MEMPHIS

LAMAR AVE

78

240

55

61

14

Meeman Shelby State Park
and Reelfoot Lake

Lake
McKellar

Harbor
Canal

Robinson
Crusoe
Island

Mississippi River

Mud
Island

AR   TN

THE PEABODY
MEMPHIS

NATIONAL CIVIL
RIGHTS MUSEUM

EH CRUMP BLVD

POPLAR

DANNY

BEALE STREET

STAX MUSEUM OF
AMERICAN SOUL MUSIC

ELMWOOD
CEMETERY

SEE "DOWNTOWN
MEMPHIS"
MAP

To

3   51

40

SEE "MIDTOWN" MAP

MIDTOWN

UNION AVE

NORTH PKWY

JACKSON AVE

Overton Park

BROAD AVE

WALNUT

POPLAR AVE

GROVE

Audubon Park

EAST
MEMPHIS

Wolf River

14

To
Brownsville

40

1   79

RD

SHELBY
FARMS

240

LICHTERMAN
NATURE CENTER

NONCONNAH PKWY

385

Germantown

Lichterton

To
Shiloh

Wolfchase Galleria,
To Davies Manor Plantation,
Jackson, and Nashville

40

0   0

2 km

2 mi

© AVALON TRAVEL

Highlights

★ **Beale Street:** The street that gave birth to the Memphis blues celebrates its legacy every single night of the week (page 185).

★ **National Civil Rights Museum:** For years the Lorraine Motel represented merely the tragic assassination of Martin Luther King Jr. Today, it tells the story of the African American struggle for civil rights (page 188).

★ **The Peabody Memphis:** Even the ducks in the fountain get the red carpet treatment at this landmark hotel. The lobby is a must-visit (page 190).

★ **Stax Museum of American Soul Music:** Irresistible soul music is what made Stax famous in the 1960s. Exhibits bring to life the work of Otis Redding, the Staple Singers, Isaac Hayes, and more (page 196).

★ **Graceland:** The Elvis phenomenon is alive and well. Presley's south Memphis mansion is a testament not only to the King's music, but also his fans (page 196).

★ **Grammy Museum Mississippi:** The role of the Delta and the blues in American music is beautifully laid out to see and hear in this museum (page 228).

Memphis music started with the spirituals and work songs of poor Mississippi Delta cotton farmers who came to Memphis and created a new sound: the Memphis blues.

The blues then spawned its own off-spring: soul, R&B, country, and, of course, rock 'n' roll as sung by a poor truck driver from Tupelo named Elvis Presley. On any given night you can find joints where the music flows as freely as the booze.

The Mississippi Blues Trail is a path of markers, museums, houses, and other sights important to the evolution of American music. Drive a short section of this massive area by heading south from Memphis to towns like Friars Point, Tunica, and Indianola.

Planning Your Time

You can knock out Memphis's main attractions in a weekend. If you have more time to soak up the city's special mojo—the music, food, and laid-back attitude—by all means do; you won't be bored. But Memphis makes for a great starting spot for sections of the Mississippi Blues Trail and Natchez Trace. It's a great place in which to fly into if you want to explore the college-town charms of Oxford, Mississippi, or see the maker and music culture of Muscle Shoals, Alabama, and then continue south of the parkway.

The city center is home to the best bars, restaurants, sports venues, live-music clubs, and, of course, Beale Street. Downtown is also the liveliest, and one of the safest, parts of Memphis after the sun sets. While a lot of Memphis's attractions are downtown, others are located in the eastern and southern stretches of the city. A free shuttle is available to Graceland and Sun Studio from downtown, but for other attractions like the Stax Museum of American Soul Music and the Memphis Brooks Museum of Art, you will need a car or taxi. Take note that two of the city's best barbecue joints (a Memphis must), as well as its most famous juke joints (largely African American bars where dancing and drinking are done with enthusiasm), are not within walking distance of downtown.

Getting There

Car

Memphis is located at the intersection of two major interstate highways: I-40, which runs east-west across the United States, and I-55, which runs north-south from St. Louis to New Orleans.

From **Tupelo,** it's a 110-mile, two-hour drive along I-22 to Memphis.

To get to Memphis directly from **Nashville,** it's a 215-mile, 3.5-hour drive along I-40.

Air

Memphis International Airport (MEM, 901/922-8000, www.flybymemphis.com) is 13 miles south of downtown Memphis. The airport's main international travel insurance and business services center (901/922-8090) is in ticket lobby B and is open daily. Here you can exchange foreign currency, buy travel insurance, send faxes, make photocopies, and buy money orders and travelers checks. A smaller kiosk near the international arrivals and departures area at gate B-36 is open daily and offers foreign currency exchange and travel insurance. There is wireless Internet service in the airport, but it is not free.

To get to midtown Memphis, take I-240 north. To reach downtown, take I-55 north and exit on Riverside Drive. The drive takes 20-30 minutes.

Airport Shuttle

TennCo Express (901/645-3726, www.tenncoexpress.com) provides a shuttle

Best Restaurants

★ **Gus's World Famous Fried Chicken:** People come from miles around for this crispy, juicy chicken (page 213).

★ **Arcade:** Memphis's oldest restaurant is still in business for a reason (page 214).

★ **Central BBQ:** Please both those who like their barbecue dry rubbed and those who prefer sauce (page 216).

★ **The Beauty Shop:** The setting may be kitschy, but the kitchen serves seriously good food in Memphis (page 217).

★ **Airport Grocery:** What's not to like? Good blues and better barbecue are the draw at this Cleveland spot (page 229).

service from the airport to many downtown hotels. Tickets are $20 one-way and $30 round-trip. Look for the shuttle parked in the third lane near column number 14 outside the airport terminal. Shuttles depart every half hour 7:30am-9:30pm. For a hotel pickup, call at least a day in advance.

Train
Amtrak (800/872-7245, www.amtrak.com) runs the City of New Orleans train daily between Chicago and New Orleans, stopping in Memphis on the way. The southbound train arrives daily at Memphis's **Central Station** (545 S. Main St., 901/526-0052) at 6:27am, leaving about half an hour later. The northbound train arrives at 10pm every day. It is an 11-hour ride overnight between Memphis and Chicago, and about 8 hours between Memphis and New Orleans. Ticket and baggage service is available at Central Station 5:45am-11:15pm daily.

Bus
Greyhound (800/231-2222, www.greyhound.com) runs daily bus service to Memphis from around the country. Direct service is available to Memphis from a number of surrounding cities, including Jackson and Nashville,

Tennessee; Tupelo and Jackson, Mississippi; Little Rock and Jonesboro, Arkansas; and St. Louis, Missouri. The Greyhound station (3033 Airways Blvd., 901/395-8770) is open 24 hours a day.

Budget-friendly **Megabus** (http://us.megabus.com) also serves Memphis from six cities (Atlanta, Birmingham, Chicago, Dallas, Little Rock, and St. Louis), although from a different area near the airport (3921 American Way). Megabus boasts free Wi-Fi on board.

Getting Around
Car
Driving is the most popular and efficient to get around Memphis. Downtown parking is plentiful if you are prepared to pay; an all-day pass in one of the many downtown parking garages costs about $12. Traffic congestion peaks at rush hours and is worst in the eastern parts of the city and along the interstates.

Public Transportation
Buses
The **Memphis Area Transit Authority** (901/274-6282, www.matatransit.com) operates dozens of buses that travel through the greater Memphis area. For information on routes, call or stop by the North End Terminal on North Main Street for help planning your trip. The

Best Accommodations

★ **Talbot Heirs Guesthouse:** Enjoy a modern oasis in the heart of downtown Memphis (page 221).

★ **The Peabody Memphis:** This historic hotel is also the city's most famous, at least in part due to its resident ducks (page 222).

★ **The Guest House at Graceland:** A resort with all things Elvis lets you live like the King (page 224).

★ **Riverside Hotel:** Sleep where Ike Turner and Duke Ellington slept in this historic Clarksdale hotel (page 228).

★ **The Thompson House:** Experience serious Southern charm in this Queen Anne B&B on Leland's Deer Creek (page 231).

bus system is not used frequently by tourists. A daily pass is available for $3.50; weekly passes are $16.

Trolleys
Public trolleys (www.matatransit.com) run for about two miles along Main Street from the Pinch District in the north to Central Station in the south, and circle up on a parallel route along Riverfront Drive. Another trolley line runs about two miles east on Madison Avenue, connecting the city's medical center with downtown. The Main Street Trolleys run every 10-15 minutes at most times; however, the Madison Avenue trolleys run every 20 minutes until 6pm on weekdays only.

Fares are $1 per ride. You can buy an all-day pass for $3.50, a three-day pass for $9, or a monthly pass for $25. All passes must be purchased at the North End Terminal at the northern end of the Main Street route.

Sun Studio Free Shuttle Bus
Sun Studio runs a free **shuttle** (901/521-0664, http://memphisrocknsoul.org) between Sun Studio, the Memphis Rock 'n' Soul Museum at Beale Street, and Graceland. The first run stops at the Graceland Heartbreak Hotel at 9:55am, Graceland at 10am, Sun Studio at

10:15am, and the Memphis Rock 'n' Soul Museum at 10:30am. Runs continue throughout the day on an hourly schedule. The last run picks up at Heartbreak Hotel at 5:55pm, Graceland Plaza at 6pm, and Sun Studio at 6:15pm.

The shuttle is a 12-passenger black van painted with the Sun Studio logo. The ride is free, but consider tipping your driver. The published schedule is a loose approximation, so it's a good idea to get to the pickup point early in case the van is running ahead.

Motorcycle and Bicycle
If you are considering seeing the Natchez Trace Parkway on two wheels, Memphis is a good place to find them. **Bumpus Harley Davidson** (2160 Whitten Rd., 901/372-1121, http://bumpushdmemphis.com, 9am-6pm Mon.-Fri., 9am-4pm Sat., 11am-3pm Sun.) rents seven different Harley models and has storage for your car and extra belongings while you are on the road.

For bicycles, or parts and repairs for your existing bikes, try **Peddler Bike Shop** (3548 Walker Ave., 901/327-4833, http://peddlerbikeshop.com, 9am-6pm Mon.-Fri., 9am-5pm Sat., 1pm-5pm Sun.), which has three other locations in the greater Memphis area. The shop also offers bike rentals. **Bike Plus** (9445 Poplar

Two Days in Memphis

Day 1

Arrive in Memphis and check into a downtown hotel, such as the **Peabody** or **Big Cypress Lodge.** Head straight to **Graceland** to immerse yourself in the world of the King. Eat lunch at **The Little Tea Shop** downtown, and then head over to **Mud Island** for the afternoon.

Go treasure-hunting at **A. Schwab,** then grab some **Gus's World Famous Fried Chicken** for dinner.

Day 2

Stroll Beale Street in the morning, stopping at the **W. C. Handy Home and Museum.** Eat lunch along South Main, then go to the **National Civil Rights Museum,** followed by a trip to the **Stax Museum of American Soul Music** and the **Blues Hall of Fame Museum** that afternoon.

Head to dinner at the **Soul Fish,** then hang out for a drink or two at **Young Avenue Deli.**

Ave., 901/755-7233, http://bikesplus.net, 10am-6pm Mon.-Fri., 10am-5pm Sat.) is a full-service shop with two locations, each with repairs and rentals.

Taxis

Memphis has a number of taxi companies, and you will usually find available cabs along Beale Street and waiting at the airport. Otherwise, you will need to call for a taxi. Some of the largest companies are **Yellow Cab** (901/577-7777, www.yellowcabofmemphis.com), **City Wide Cab** (901/722-8294, www.citywidetaxi.net), **Arrow Transportation Company** (901/332-7769), and **Metro Cab** (901/322-2222, http://ridememphis.com). Expect to pay $25-35 for a trip from the airport to downtown; most fares around town are under $10. Taxis accept credit cards.

App-based ride-sharing services like **Uber** and **Lyft** ($15-20 from the airport to downtown) operate in Memphis and have agreements with the local government to allow them to make stops at the airport and other destinations.

Sights

Downtown

Downtown refers to the area south of Union Avenue in the city center. It is the heart of Memphis's tourist district.

★ Beale Street

If you want to delve into the history and character of Memphis music, your starting point should be **Beale Street,** home of the blues.

Beale Street has two distinct personalities. During the day it's a laid-back place for families or adults to stroll, buy souvenirs, and eat. You can also stop at one of several museums and attractions located on the street. At night, Beale Street is a strip of nightclubs and restaurants, a great place to people-watch, and the best place in the state, if not the country, to catch live blues seven nights a week.

Within **Elvis Presley Plaza** is a statue of Memphis's most famous native son, Elvis Presley, depicted during his early career.

W. C. Handy Home and Museum

The story of Beale Street cannot be told without mentioning William Christopher Handy, whose Memphis home sits at the corner of Beale Street and 4th Avenue. The building was originally located at 659 Jeanette Street, but it was moved to Beale Street in 1985. Now the **W. C. Handy Home and Museum** (352 Beale St., 901/527-3427, www.wchandymemphis.org, 10am-5pm Tues.-Sat. summer, 11am-4pm Tues.-Sat. winter, adults $6, children $4) is dedicated to telling the story of Handy's life. It was Handy who famously wrote, in his "Beale Street Blues": "If Beale Street could talk, married men

Downtown Memphis

would have to take their beds and walk, except one or two who never drink booze, and the blind man on the corner singing 'Beale Street Blues.' I'd rather be there than anyplace I know."

The Handy museum houses photographs of Handy's family, one of his band uniforms, and memorabilia of the recording company that he founded. You can also hear samples of Handy's music.

Orpheum Theatre

Near the corner of Beale and Main Streets is the **Orpheum Theatre** (203 S. Main St., 901/525-3000, www.orpheummemphis.com). This site has been used for entertainment since 1890, when the Grand Opera House opened there with a production of *Les Huguenots*. Later, the opera house presented vaudeville shows and theater. Fire destroyed it in 1923, but in 1928 it reopened as the Orpheum, a

W. C. Handy

W. C. Handy was born in a log cabin in Florence, Alabama, in 1873. The son and grandson of African Methodist Episcopal ministers, Handy was exposed to music as a child in his father's church. Handy was also drawn to the music of the black laborers of the area, and when he moved to Memphis in the early 20th century, he recognized the wealth of the blues music he heard in bars, on street corners, and in back alleys around Beale Street.

Handy was a trained musician, so he was able to set down on paper the music that had, up until then, been passed from one musician to another.

In 1909, Handy composed Memphis mayor Ed Crump's campaign song, "Mr. Crump," which he later published as the "Memphis Blues." But he is most famous for his composition "St. Louis Blues," published in 1914. Handy also created the "Yellow Dog Blues," "Joe Turner Blues," and "Beale Street Blues." Known as the Father of the Blues, Handy passed away in 1958.

movie theater and performing arts venue for the likes of Duke Ellington, Cab Calloway, Bob Hope, and Mae West. The Orpheum remains one of the city's premier venues for the performing arts, with Broadway productions, mainstream musical artists, and movies.

First Baptist Beale Street Church

Stately and old, the **First Baptist Beale Street Church** (379 Beale St.) was built between 1868 and 1885 and is home to one of the oldest African American congregations in Memphis. In the 1860s, the congregation started to meet under brush arbors at the present location, and the first temporary structure was erected in 1865. The cornerstone was laid for the present building in 1871. The First Baptist Beale Street Church was an important force in Memphis's African American history. It was here that black Memphians published their first newspapers, the *Memphis Watchman* and the *Memphis Free Speech and Headlight*.

Church Park

Today, **Church Park** (4th St. and MLK Ave.) is a humble city park. But in 1899, when Robert Church built Church Park and Auditorium at the eastern end of the Beale Street commercial district, the park was something truly special. Church is said to have been the first black

millionaire in the South. He was troubled that there were no public parks expressly for Memphis's African American residents, so in 1899 he opened Church Park and Auditorium on six acres of land along Beale Street. The park was beautifully landscaped and manicured, with bright flowers, tropical trees, and peacocks. The auditorium was a venue for black performers and speakers. Church Park remains a venue for community events, particularly the annual Africa in April event every spring.

Gallina Building

The facade of what was once the **Gallina Building** is held up by six steel girders. From the 1860s until 1914, this facade kept watch on the business empire of Squire Charles Gallina, who operated a saloon, restaurant, and 20-room hotel, as well as a gambling room. Housed within the building today is the Irish pub **Silky O'Sullivan's** (183 Beale St., 901/522-9596, www.silkyosullivans.com, 4pm-midnight Mon., 11am-midnight Tues.-Thurs. and Sun., 11am-3am Fri.-Sat.).

Memphis Rock 'n' Soul Museum

Music fans should plan to spend several hours at the **Memphis Rock 'n' Soul Museum** (191 Beale St., 901/205-2533, www.memphisrocknsoul.org, 10am-7pm daily, adults $12, children 5-17

$9), located right next to FedEx Forum, off Beale Street. An affiliate of the Smithsonian Institution, this museum tells the story of Memphis music from the Delta blues to *Shaft*. Start with a short video documentary, and then follow the exhibits with your personal audio guide, which includes recordings of dozens of Memphis-influenced artists, from B. B. King to Elvis. Exhibits are dedicated to Memphis radio stations; the influence of the Victrola, Sam Phillips, and Sun Studio; and, of course, all things Elvis, among others. It takes several hours to study all the exhibits in detail and to listen to all (or even most) of the music, so plan accordingly.

A free shuttle runs between the Rock 'n' Soul Museum, Graceland, and Sun Studio. Look for the black van with the Sun label's distinctive yellow sun on the side.

Gibson Guitar Factory

Across the street from the Rock 'n' Soul Museum is the **Gibson Guitar Factory** (145 Lt. George Lee Ave., 901/544-7998, ext. 4075, www.gibson.com, tours every hour on the hour 11:15am-4pm Mon.-Sat., noon-4pm Sun., ages 5 and up $10, under 5 not admitted, parking $5), one of three in the United States. The Memphis plant specializes in the semi-hollow-bodied guitar, and a wide range of models are for sale in Gibson's retail shop. On the hour-long tour of the factory floor you can see guitars being made, from the shaping of the top and sides to the painting and buffing of the finished product. Tours sell out, so reservations are recommended, particularly during the busier summer months. Most factory workers leave by 3pm and have the weekends off, so plan ahead if you want to see the factory floor in full swing.

★ National Civil Rights Museum

If you do nothing else while you are in Memphis, or, frankly, the state of Tennessee, visit the **National Civil Rights Museum** (450 Mulberry St., 901/521-9699, www.civilrightsmuseum.org, 9am-5pm Mon., Wed.-Sat., 1pm-5pm Sun., adults $15, students and seniors $14, children 4-17 $12, children 3 or younger free). Built on the Lorraine Motel site, where Dr. Martin Luther King Jr. was assassinated on April 4, 1968, the museum makes a thorough examination of the American civil rights movement, from slavery to the present day. Exhibits display original letters, audio recordings, photos, and newspaper clippings from events including the Montgomery bus boycott, *Brown v. Board of Education*, Freedom Summer, and the march from Selma to Montgomery. Original and re-created artifacts, such as the bus where Rosa Parks made her stand in 1955 and the cell where Dr. King wrote his famous *Letter from a Birmingham Jail*, help to illustrate the story of civil rights.

When Dr. King visited Memphis in March and then again in April 1968, the Lorraine Motel was one of a handful of downtown hotels that welcomed African Americans. The room (and balcony and parking lot) where he spent his final hours has been carefully re-created, and a narration by those who were with King tells the shocking story of his death. Across Mulberry Street, in the building that was once the boardinghouse from where James Earl Ray is believed to have fired his sniper shot, exhibits probe various theories about the assassination, as well as the worldwide legacy of the civil rights movement.

This is a large museum, and it is overflowing with information, so visitors who want to give the displays their due attention should plan on spending 3-4 hours here. A good way to visit would be to tour the Lorraine Motel exhibits first, take a break for lunch, and then go across the street for the second half of the museum when you are refreshed.

Spending half a day here is a powerful experience, and one that raises many thoughts about civil rights. Expect interesting conversations with your travel companions after coming here. The gift shop offers books and videos for more information on the topic.

Admission is free on Monday after 3pm to Tennessee residents. In June, July, and August the museum stays open until 6pm.

Belz Museum of Asian and Judaic Art

The **Belz Museum of Asian and Judaic Art** (119 S. Main St., 901/523-2787, www.belzmuseum.org, 10am-5:30pm Tues.-Fri., noon-5pm Sat.-Sun., adults $6, seniors $5, students $4, children under 4 free), formerly Peabody Place Museum, houses one of the largest collections of artwork from the Q'ing dynasty. Forged from the private collection of Memphis developers Jack and Marilyn Belz, owners of the Peabody and the now shuttered Peabody Place mall, the museum features some 1,000 objects, including an array of jade, tapestries, paintings, furniture, carvings, and other artifacts. The museum is also home to the largest U.S. collection of work by Israeli artist Daniel Kafri.

The Belz Museum's new Holocaust Memorial Gallery includes portraits and testimonials from Jewish survivors of the Holocaust in the *Living On* exhibit.

Blues Hall of Fame Museum

The **Blues Hall of Fame Museum** (421 Main St., 901/527-2583, www.blues.org, 10am-5pm Mon.-Sat., 1pm-5pm Sun., adults $10, students $8, children under 12 free with an adult) has existed as an entity—a project of the Blues Foundation—since 1980. But the physical building that you can tour and experience didn't open until 2015. The $2.9 million building is across the street from the National Civil Rights Museum at the Lorraine Hotel. It celebrates the music for which Memphis is famous and honors the musicians who make it.

More than 350 people have been inducted into the Blues Hall of Fame Museum; of the 130 performers, 120 of them are African American. At the museum, you can learn about all of the inductees and listen to their contributions to the genre.

Uptown

Uptown refers to locations along Union Avenue and points north in the center city district. Here downtown workers are more common than tourists, and tall office buildings rise above the city blocks.

Cotton Museum

The **Cotton Museum** at the Memphis Cotton Exchange (65 Union Ave., 901/531-7826, www.memphiscottonmuseum.org, 10am-5pm Mon.-Sat., noon-5pm Sun., adults $10, seniors $9, students $9, military $8, children 6-12 $7, children under 6 free) is in the broad rectangular room that once was the nerve center of the Mid-South's cotton trade. The Cotton Exchange was established in 1873, and it was here that buyers and sellers of the South's most important cash crop met, and where fortunes were made and lost. Located just steps away from the Mississippi River, the Exchange was the trading floor of Cotton Row, the area of town that was defined by the cotton industry.

The Cotton Museum is home to exhibits about cotton's history, its uses, and the culture that its cultivation gave rise to in Memphis and the Mississippi Delta. There are several videos you can watch, as well as a live Internet feed of today's cotton exchange—now conducted entirely electronically. The nicest thing about the museum, however, is seeing the chalkboard where the prices of cotton around the world were written by hand. There is also a replica of the Western Union office, where buyers and sellers sent telegrams using an intricate system of abbreviations known only to the cotton trade. The museum expanded in 2010, adding more hands-on exhibits and an educational wing.

★ The Peabody Memphis

The Peabody Memphis (149 Union Ave., 901/529-4000, www.peabodymemphis. com) is the city's most famous hotel. Founded in 1869, the Peabody was one of the first grand hotels of the South, a place as well known for its elegant balls and big-band concerts as for the colorful characters who sipped cocktails at its famous lounge. Named in memory of the philanthropist George Peabody, the original hotel was at the corner of Main and Monroe. It closed in 1923, and a new Peabody opened two years later in its present location on Union Avenue. It remained the place to see and be seen for generations of Memphians and Delta residents. It was historian and journalist David Cohn who famously wrote in 1935 that "the Mississippi Delta begins in the lobby of the Peabody Hotel in Memphis."

Even if you don't stay here, you must stop by the elegant hotel lobby to see the twice-daily march of the **Peabody ducks** (a trip to Memphis is incomplete without this experience). The ducks live on the roof of the hotel and make the journey—by elevator—to the lobby fountain every morning at 11am. At 5pm they march out of the fountain, back onto the elevator, and up to their accommodations on the roof.

The hotel employs a duck master who takes care of the ducks and supervises their daily trip downstairs. Watching the ducks is free, frenzied, and undeniably fun. It is also one of the most popular activities among visitors to Memphis, so be sure to get there plenty early (at least a half hour) and secure a good vantage point along the red carpet (or on the balcony upstairs) to watch the ducks march.

Mud Island

In Memphis, it is sometimes easy to forget that you are just steps away from the great Mississippi River. A trip to **Mud Island** will cure this misperception once and for all. A narrow band of land in the river, Mud Island is home to the **Mud Island River Park and Mississippi River Museum** (125 N. Front St., 901/576-7241, www.mudisland.com, 10am-5pm Tues.-Sun. Apr.-Oct., adults $10, seniors $9, children $7), which has exhibits about early uses of the river, steam- and paddleboats, floods, and much more. Last admission is one hour prior to closing. Admission to the park is free. You can pay $4 round-trip to ride the monorail to Mud Island (included in museum admission), or you can walk across the monorail bridge for free (offering a great photo/ selfie opportunity). The monorail station is on Front Street at Adams Avenue.

The park's **Mississippi River Museum** begins with a refresher course on European exploration of this region—de Soto, La Salle, and Marquette and Joliet— followed by information about early settlement. The highlight is being able to explore a replica of an 1870s steamboat. In the Riverfolk Gallery there are wax depictions of Mark Twain, riverboat gambler George Devol, and steamship entertainers. The museum also remembers the numerous river disasters that have taken place along the Mississippi.

Admission to the museum includes the **River Walk** at the Mud Island River Park, a five-block scale model of the entire Mississippi River—from Minnesota to the Gulf of Mexico. Walk along the model to see scale representations of cities along the river's path and read placards about the river's history. On a hot day, wear your bathing suit so you can swim in the wading pool at the end of the model of the river inside the park.

Mud Island River Park is also home to an outdoor amphitheater, which in summer hosts big-name concerts, a snack bar, outdoor tables, and restrooms. You can rent canoes, kayaks, and paddleboats to use in the still waters around the Mud Island harbor. Bike rental is also available. Mud Island is the site of the city's dragon boat races, which benefit the work of the Tennessee Clean Water Network. These fundraising events, also held in

Chattanooga, Oak Ridge, Knoxville, and Nashville, feature teams from local businesses and community organizations paddling 46-foot-long boats festooned with dragon heads.

Slavehaven Underground Railroad Museum

The legend of the Burkle Estate, a modest white clapboard house on North 2nd Street, has given rise to the **Slavehaven Underground Railroad Museum** (826 N. 2nd St., 901/527-3427, www.slavehaven-memphis.com, 10am-5pm Mon.-Sat. summer, 10am-4pm Mon.-Sat. winter, adults $10, seniors $9, youth $8). The museum tells the story of slavery and the legendary Underground Railroad, which helped thousands of slaves escape to freedom in the North (and, after the 1850 Fugitive Slave Act, to Canada). Jacob Burkle, a German immigrant and owner of the Memphis stockyard, is said to have built the Burkle Estate around 1850. Escaping slaves would have hidden in a root cellar beneath the house before making the 1,500-foot trip to the banks of the Mississippi, where they made a further journey north.

Skeptics say that there is no evidence of this story and even point to documents that show Burkle may not have purchased the property until 1871, well after the end of slavery. Advocates for the Underground Railroad story say that it was the nature of the railroad to be secret, so there is nothing unusual about a lack of concrete evidence.

Visitors today need not be too concerned with the details of the debate; the Slavehaven museum does a good job of highlighting the brutality of the slave trade and slavery and the ingenuity and bravery it took for slaves to escape. Perhaps the most interesting display is of the quilts that demonstrate the way that slaves used quilting patterns to send messages to one another. Other exhibits show advertisements for Memphis slave auctions and images from the early 20th century that depict damaging racial stereotypes.

The museum is operated by Heritage Tours of Memphis, and staff is available to conduct guided tours of the property.

Fire Museum of Memphis

The **Fire Museum of Memphis** (118 Adams Ave., 901/320-5650, www.firemuseum.com, 9am-6pm Mon.-Sat., 1pm-6pm Sun. summer, 9am-4:30pm Mon.-Sat. winter, adults $10, seniors and military $8, children $8, family pack for four $30) is a good place to take children. It has a huge display of fire-engine toys, lots of firefighting paraphernalia, and a "fire room" that presents important lessons on fire safety. You can also see old-fashioned fire engines, and youngsters will enjoy playing in the kid-friendly fire truck. The museum is located in the old Fire Station No. 1 in downtown Memphis.

St. Jude Children's Research Hospital

The sprawling complex of **St. Jude Children's Research Hospital** on uptown's northern fringe has been saving lives and bringing hope to children and their families since 1962. St. Jude was founded by entertainer Danny Thomas in fulfillment of his promise to God to give back to those in need. Over the years and thanks to the success of its fundraising arm—the American Lebanese Syrian Associated Charities—St. Jude has expanded many times over and now leads the world in research and treatment of catastrophic childhood diseases, especially pediatric cancers. Programs with country music stars only expand the reach of St. Jude's and its work. The hospital never turns anyone away due to inability to pay, and it never makes families without insurance pay for their treatment.

Call (or e-mail hospitaltours@stjude. org) in advance to tour a small museum about Danny Thomas and St. Jude in the **Danny Thomas ALSAC Pavilion** (332

The Birth of Mud Island

Mud Island rose from the Mississippi River as a result of two seemingly small events. In 1876, the river shifted slightly about 20 miles south of Memphis, causing the currents that flowed past the city to alter course. And then, in 1910, a U.S. Navy gunboat, the USS *Amphitrite,* anchored at the mouth of the Wolf River for almost two years, causing a further change in silt patterns. When the ship left in 1912, the sandbar continued to grow, and Mud Island was born.

Residents initially disliked the island, since it was ugly and proved to be a danger to river navigation. Beginning in the 1930s, poor Memphians squatted on Mud Island in ramshackle homes built of scrap metal and wood. Between 200 and 500 people lived on the island during this time.

In 1959, a downtown airport was built on the island, but the airport was closed in 1970 when the DeSoto Bridge was built. In 1974, plans were developed for what is the present-day Mud Island River Park, which includes a full-scale replica of a riverboat, a monorail to the island, and the signature 2,000-foot flowing replica of the Mississippi River.

N. Lauderdale St., 901/578-2042, www. stjudepavilion.org, 8am-4pm Sun.-Fri., 10am-4pm Sat., except when there are special events, free), a golden dome on the hospital grounds. Just outside are the graves of Danny Thomas and his wife, Rose Marie. Hospital tours are available Monday-Friday at 10am and 1pm.

The Pyramid

The Memphis **Pyramid** is the most physically dominating feature of the northern city skyline. Memphis's affiliation with all things Egypt began with its name and continued in 1897, when a large-scale replica of a pyramid was built to represent Memphis at the Tennessee Centennial Exhibition in Nashville. Pyramids were popular symbols on Memphis paraphernalia for many years.

The first serious proposal for a life-size pyramid to be built in Memphis was written in the 1970s, but the idea did not take off until the 1980s, when the city and county governments agreed to fund it. Denver developer Sidney Shlenker promoted the plan and promised restaurants, tourist attractions, and lots of revenue for the city. The 321-foot pyramid was built and opened in 1991, minus the money-making engines that Shlenker promised.

For years the $63 million "Great American Pyramid" sat empty. In spring 2015 this changed. **Bass Pro Shops at the Pyramid** (1 Bass Pro Dr., 901/291-8200, www.basspro.com/pyramid, 8am-10pm Mon.-Sat., 8am-7pm Sun.) opened what it modestly calls "one of the most dynamic, immersive retail stores in the world." This outdoor gear store includes a cypress swamp, 10 aquariums holding 600,000 gallons of water, a **Big Cypress Lodge** 105-room hotel (800/225-6343, www.big-cypress.com) with treehouse cabins, a spa, Ducks Unlimited National Waterfowling Heritage Center, Uncle Buck's Fishbowl and Grill nautical-themed restaurant, a giant 28-story free-standing elevator, and more. Obviously, this isn't an average store. There are regular **fish feedings** (10am and 5pm daily).

Midtown

You'll need a car to explore the attractions in midtown, which sprawls along Union, Poplar, and Madison Avenues as they head eastward from the city center.

Sun Studio

It is well worth your time to drop by the famous **Sun Studio** (706 Union Ave., 800/441-6249, www.sunstudio.com, 10am-6pm daily, adults, $12, kids 5-11

Midtown

free, under 5 not admitted), where Elvis Presley recorded his first hit, "That's All Right," and where dozens of blues, rock, and country musicians recorded during the 1950s. Founded by radioman and audio engineer Sam Phillips and his wife, Becky, the studio recorded weddings, funerals, events, and, of course, music. Phillips was interested in the blues, and his first recordings were of yet-unknown artists such as Rufus Thomas and Howlin' Wolf. In 1953, Elvis Presley came into the studio on his lunch break to record a $3 record of himself singing "My Happiness" for his mother. Phillips was not impressed with the performance, and it was not for another year—and thanks to the prodding of Phillips's assistant, Marion Keisker—that Phillips called Presley in to record some more. When Phillips heard Elvis's version of the blues tune "That's All Right," he knew he had a hit. And he did.

But the story of Elvis's discovery is just one of many that took place in the modest homemade Sun Studio, and this attraction is not just for Elvis fans. The one-hour tour of the studio leaves every hour on the half hour, and while you are waiting you can order a real fountain drink from the snack bar or browse the shop's collection of recordings and paraphernalia. The studio is still in business; you can record here for $75 an hour at night, and dozens of top-notch performers have, including Grace Potter, Beck, and Matchbox Twenty.

Tours start every half hour during business hours and take approximately 90 minutes. Children under the age of five are not permitted on the tours. There are free shuttles from Graceland and the Rock 'n' Soul Museum to Sun Studio.

Victorian Village

Set on a tree-lined block of Adams Avenue near Orleans Street is Victorian Village, where a half dozen elegant Victorian-era homes escaped the "urban

Stax Museum of American Soul Music offers insight into the Memphis sound.

renewal" fate of other historical Memphis homes.

Visitors can tour the **Woodruff-Fontaine House** (680 Adams Ave., 901/526-1469, www.woodruff-fontaine. com, noon-4pm Wed.-Sun., $12 adults, $10 seniors, $8 children), one of the street's most magnificent buildings. Built in 1870 for the Woodruff family and sold to the Fontaines in the 1880s, the house was occupied through 1930, when it became part of the James Lee Art Academy, a precursor to the Memphis Academy of Art. When the academy moved in 1959, the building became city property and stood vacant. Beginning in 1961, city residents raised funds to restore and refurnish the house with period furniture and accessories, and it opened as a museum in 1964. This was during the period of urban renewal that saw to the demolition of many of Memphis's other old homes, and some of the house's furnishings were taken from homes that were later demolished. Tours include all three floors and

the basement; there is no elevator to access the different levels. This is a good stop if you are interested in antiques.

The **Magevney House** (198 Adams Ave., 901/526-1484, free admission first Saturday of each month 1pm-4pm) and the **Mallory-Neely House** (652 Adams Ave., 901/523-1484, www.memphismuseums.org, 10am-4pm Fri.-Sat., adults $7, seniors $5, children 3-12 $5, children under 3 free) are two other historical homes in the district. The Magevney House is the oldest middle-class residence still standing in Memphis. It was built in 1836 by an Irish immigrant to the city, Eugene Magevney. The Mallory-Neely House is of the same vintage and is notable for the fact that it was not refurnished in more than 100 years and so remains remarkably true to the era in which it was built.

Memphis Brooks Museum of Art

Memphis's foremost art museum is in Overton Park in midtown, a short drive from downtown. **Memphis Brooks Museum of Art** (1934 Poplar Ave., 901/544-6200, www.brooksmuseum. org, 10am-8pm Wed., 10am-4pm Thurs.-Fri., 10am-5pm Sat., 11am-5pm Sun., adults $7, seniors $6, students and youth 7 and older $3, children 6 and under free) is the largest fine-art museum in Tennessee, and its permanent collection includes 8,000 works of art. This includes ancient African and Asian art, as well as 14th century-present European art and 18th century-present American art. There are 29 galleries at the Brooks, and special exhibitions have focused on the work of Annie Leibovitz, men's fashion in Africa, the silver work of Paul de Lamerie, Activist Photographers of the Civil Rights Movement, and American Folk Art. It also has also a museum shop and restaurant, as well as an auditorium often used to screen films.

Memphis Zoo

The **Memphis Zoo** (2000 Prentiss Pl.,

901/333-6500, www.memphiszoo.org, 9am-5pm daily Mar.-Oct., 9am-4pm daily Nov.-Feb., adults $15, seniors $14, children $10) has been expanding and is now the proud steward of two giant pandas, Le Le and Ya Ya; large cats; penguins; lions; tropical birds; and 3,500 other animal species. More hippos have been born here than at any other zoo. Its butterfly exhibit, open May-October, is a popular feature, and camel rides are available in the spring. The zoo is on the grounds of Overton Park. Parking is an additional $5 and a point of some contention in the city. (Parking on the grass during zoo events upsets those who use the magnificent Overton Park for other events and purposes. Be mindful when you visit until a solution is developed.)

Tennessee residents with ID can get in free on Tuesdays after 2pm, except in March; $3 fee for access to China/panda exhibit.

South Memphis
★ Stax Museum of American Soul Music
Perhaps there is no place in Memphis that better tells the story of the city's legendary soul music than the **Stax Museum of American Soul Music** (926 E. McLemore Ave., 901/942-7685, http://staxmuseum.com, 10am-5pm Tues.-Sat., 1pm-5pm Sun.-Mon. Apr.-Oct., 10am-5pm Tues.-Sat., 1pm-5pm Sun. Nov.-Mar., adults $13, seniors, students, and military $12, children 9-12 $10, children 8 or under free). The museum tour starts with a short toe-tapping video that sets the scene for the musical magic that took place here during the 1960s.

Exhibits include the sanctuary of an old clapboard Delta church, which illustrates the connection between soul and gospel music. You can also see Booker T. Jones's original organ, Otis Redding's favorite suede jacket, and Isaac Hayes's 1972 peacock-blue gold-trimmed Cadillac Eldorado, Superfly.

The museum also winds you through the studio's control room and into the studio itself, slanted floors and all. If you want to try your hand at singing, there is a karaoke machine, as well as a dance floor in case you can't help but move to the music. The Stax Museum is a must-see for music enthusiasts but also an educational journey for those who don't know the story behind some of America's most famous songs. It sits next door to the Stax Music Academy, a present-day music school that reaches out to neighborhood youth.

★ Graceland
The mansion that was once the home of Elvis Presley, **Graceland** (3717 Elvis Presley Blvd., 901/332-3322 or 800/238-2000, www.graceland.com or www.elvis.com, 9am-5pm Mon.-Sat., 9am-4pm Sun. Mar.-Oct., 9am-4pm daily Nov., 9am-4pm Wed.-Mon. Dec., 10am-4pm Wed.-Mon. Jan.-Feb.), opened to the public in 1982, and since then has been one of the main reasons people flock to Memphis. In 2017 the estate made the trek all the more worthwhile, opening a $45 million, 200,000 square-foot, state-of-the-art entertainment complex, now named **Elvis Presley's Memphis.** In addition to the Graceland mansion, it includes **Presley Motors Automobile Museum** and **Graceland Soundstage,** a live music venue.

Guests can choose from six different types of experiences. The mansion-only tour is about two hours (adults $39, seniors and students 13-18 $35, children 7-12 $17, children 6 and under free; online advance purchase only). The Elvis Experience adds on access to a new entertainment complex, which includes self-guided tours of Presley Motors Automobile Museum, Elvis: The Entertainer Career Museum, and the Elvis Discovery Exhibits (3.5-4 hours; adults $58, seniors and students $52, children $27). The Elvis Experience + Airplanes tour adds a self-guided tour of Elvis's Custom Jets exhibit (adults $63, seniors and students $57, children $32). Various VIP options include perks such as skipping the line at the mansion, a VIP tour, and a personal show-and-tell session in the Graceland archives ($94-150 per person). There is plenty of parking. Reservations are recommended.

The expansion also includes two themed restaurants named for Elvis's parents, Gladys and Vernon. You can get Elvis's favorite—grilled peanut butter and banana sandwiches—at **Gladys's** and barbecue at **Vernon's**. There's also **The Guest House at Graceland,** a new 450-room resort hotel. The whole expansion is designed, of course, to give visitors more excuses to come immerse themselves in all things Elvis. But it also aims to revitalize the surrounding Whitehaven community.

The mansion tour is conducted by audio guide. It includes the ground floor of the mansion (the upstairs remains closed to the public) and several outbuildings that now house exhibits about Elvis's life and career. High points include watching the press conference Elvis gave after leaving the army, witnessing firsthand his audacious taste in decor, and visiting the meditation garden where Elvis, his parents, and his grandmother are buried. There is also a plaque in memory of Elvis's lost twin, Jesse Garon. The audio tour plays many of Elvis's songs, family stories remembered by Elvis's daughter Lisa Marie Presley, and several clips of Elvis speaking. In 2015, Graceland opened two new exhibits: *Elvis: That's the Way It Is* is a documentary chronicling the legend's first Las Vegas performance, and *I Shot Elvis* features photos from the early years of his career and encourages museum guests to take a photo with a larger-than-life image of the King.

The exhibits gloss over some of the challenges Elvis faced in his life—his addiction to prescription drugs, his womanizing and failed marriage, and his unsettling affinity for firearms among them. But they showcase Elvis's generosity, his dedication to family, and his fun-loving character. The portrait that emerges is sympathetic and remarkably human for a man who is so often portrayed as larger than life.

The automobile museum features 33 vehicles, including Elvis's pink Cadillac, motorcycles, and a red MG from *Blue Hawaii,* as well as some of his favorite motorized toys, including a go-kart and dune buggy. His private planes include the *Lisa Marie,* which Elvis customized with gold-plated seat belts, suede chairs, and gold-flecked sinks. Other special Graceland exhibits include *Sincerely Elvis,* which chronicles Elvis's life in 1956, and *Elvis After Dark,* which describes some of Elvis's late-night passions, like roller skating.

The Graceland mansion was declared a National Historic Site in 2006. It attracts more than 650,000 visitors annually.

Elmwood Cemetery

Elmwood Cemetery (824 S. Dudley St., 901/774-3212, www.elmwoodcemetery. org, 8am-4:30pm daily), an 80-acre cemetery southwest of the city center, is the resting place of 70,000 Memphians—ordinary citizens and some of the city's most prominent leaders. It was founded in 1852 by 50 gentlemen who wanted the cemetery to be a park for the living as well as a resting place for the dead. They invested in tree planting and winding carriage paths so that the cemetery today is a pleasant, peaceful place to spend a few hours.

The cemetery is the resting place of Memphians like Annie Cook, a well-known madam who died during the yellow fever epidemic of 1878; Marion Scudder Griffen, a pioneering female lawyer and suffragette; and musician Sister Thea Bowman. Thousands of anonymous victims of the yellow fever epidemic were buried here, as were both Confederate and Union casualties of the Civil War. Prominent citizens, including Robert

Church Sr., Edward Hull Crump, and Shelby Foote, are also buried at Elmwood.

Visitors to the cemetery may simply drive or walk through on their own. But it is best to rent the one-hour audio guide ($10), which takes you on a driving tour and highlights 60 stops in the cemetery. Thanks to a well-written and well-presented narration, the tour comes closer than any other single Memphis attraction to bringing Memphis's diverse history and people to life.

The cemetery offers occasional lectures and docent-guided tours for $15 on select Saturday mornings. Call ahead or check the website to find out if any are scheduled during your visit. To find Elmwood, drive east along E. H. Crump Boulevard, turning south (right) onto Dudley, which dead-ends at the single-lane bridge that marks the entrance to the cemetery.

Docent-led walking tours of the 1,500 trees in the Carlisle S. Page Arboretum are also available for $10 per person.

Church of the Full Gospel Tabernacle

A native of Arkansas and longtime resident of Michigan, Al Green first made his name as one of history's greatest soul singers, with hits like "Let's Stay Together," "Take Me to the River," and "Love and Happiness." Following a religious conversion in 1979, he dedicated his considerable talents to God and founded the **Church of the Full Gospel Tabernacle** (787 Hale Rd.) in Memphis, where his Sunday sermons dripped with soulful gospel.

For almost 11 years, the Reverend Al Green left secular music, dedicating himself to God's music. He began his return to secular music in 1988, and in 1995 Green released the first of three new secular albums on Blue Note Records.

According to his official biography, *Take Me to the River,* Reverend Green faced some criticism when he returned to the secular scene. "I've got people in the church saying, 'That's a secular song,' and

Graceland shows you how the King lived.

I'm saying, 'Yeah, but you've got Monday, Tuesday, Wednesday, Thursday, Friday, and Saturday to be anything other than spiritual. You've got to live those days, too!'" Reverend Green writes. In the book he says he has not neglected his duty to God: "The music is the message, the message is the music. So that's my little ministry that the Big Man upstairs gave to me—a little ministry called love and happiness."

Despite his rebirth as a secular soul performer, Al Green, now a bishop, still makes time for his church. He preaches regularly, but not every Sunday, and continues to sing the praises of God. The Sunday service at his Memphis church begins at 11:30am. Visitors are welcome, and you can come—within reason—as you are. Please show respect, though, by being quiet when it's called for and throwing a few bucks in the offering plate when it comes around. And don't forget that the church is a place of worship and not a tourist attraction. If you're not in town on Sunday, you can catch the weekly choir rehearsal on Thursday at 7pm.

National Ornamental Metal Museum

An unusual delight, the **National Ornamental Metal Museum** (374 Metal Museum Dr., 901/774-6380, www.metalmuseum.org, 10am-5pm Tues.-Sat., noon-5pm Sun., adults $6, seniors $5, students and children $4) is dedicated to preserving and displaying fine metalwork. Its permanent collection numbers more than 3,000 objects and ranges from contemporary American sculpture to works up to 500 years old. The museum hosts special exhibits several times a year, showcasing various aspects of metalwork. There is also a working metalwork studio, and the museum grounds on the bluff overlooking the Mississippi are an attraction in themselves. This is reputed to be the site where Spanish explorer Hernando de Soto and his men camped when they passed through the area in 1542. Demonstrations may be available on weekend afternoons; call the museum in advance to confirm.

C. H. Nash Museum at Chucalissa

Platform and ridge mounds along the Mississippi River are the main attraction at **Chucalissa Archaeological Site** (1987 Indian Village Dr., 901/785-3160, www.memphis.edu/chucalissa, 9am-5pm Tues.-Sat., 1pm-5pm Sun., adults $6, seniors and children 4-11 $4). The mounds were once part of a Choctaw Indian community that existed AD 1000-1550. The village was empty when Europeans arrived, and the word *chucalissa* means "abandoned house."

The largest mound would have been where the chief and his family lived. The present-day museum, operated by the University of Memphis, consists of an exhibit about the Native Americans of the area and a self-guided tour around the mounds and courtyard area,

Soulsville

A lucky convergence of people, talents, and social forces led to one of Memphis's—and America's—most distinctive musical stories. **Stax Records** was founded in 1960 by Jim Stewart, an aspiring country fiddler, and his sister, Estelle Axton. The first two letters of the brother and sister's surnames came together to form Stax, a name now synonymous with the raw Memphis sound of performers like Rufus and Carla Thomas, Otis Redding, Sam and Dave, Isaac Hayes, Eddie Floyd, the Mar-Keys, the Staple Singers, and Booker T. & the MGs.

Stewart chose a closed movie theater in a working-class south Memphis neighborhood for his recording studio. He was on a tight budget, so he didn't bother to fix the sloped theater floor or angled walls, and the room's reverberating acoustics came to define the Memphis sound.

Motown was known as "Hitsville" for its smooth and palatable sound, so the artists at Stax began to call their neighborhood "Soulsville," a name that still refers to the area of south Memphis where Stax is located. The soul music that Stax recorded was raw and inventive, influenced by country, blues, gospel, and jazz.

The label's first hit was with WDIA-AM disc jockey Rufus Thomas and his daughter, Carla Thomas, who came in one day and recorded "Cause I Love You." The song became an overnight sensation.

Stax tapped into the talent of the neighborhood, and particularly the African American Booker T. Washington High School, which graduated such greats as the members of the Soul Children and the Mad Lads. As the Stax reputation developed, artists came from out of town to record, including a 21-year-old Otis Redding, who drove up from Georgia in

hopes of making a record and made a career instead.

Stax also operated **Satellite Records,** right next door to the studio, and here Estelle Axton was able to quickly test-market new recordings on the neighborhood youngsters who came in for the latest music. Wayne Jackson, a member of the studio's house band, the Memphis Horns, recalls that Estelle and Jim would invite hundreds of young people from the neighborhood into the studio to listen to their newest recording. Based on the group's response, they would choose the single.

Stax was unique for its time as an integrated organization, where the love of music trumped racial differences. As the civil rights movement evolved, Stax artists turned to serious social themes in their music. In 1972, Stax artists organized **WattStax,** an outdoor black music festival in Los Angeles.

Between 1960 and 1975, when the Stax magic ran out, the studio produced 800 singles and 300 albums, including 243 Top 100 and 14 number-one R&B hits. Isaac Hayes's theme from the movie *Shaft* was the fastest-selling album in Stax history, and one of three Stax songs that went to number one on the pop charts. Other big Stax hits were Otis Redding's "(Sittin' on) The Dock of the Bay," the Staples Singers' "Respect Yourself," and Sam and Dave's "Soul Man."

Sadly, Stax was destroyed financially by a bad distribution deal with CBS Records in 1975, and the studio was closed. Its rare master tapes were sold at auction, and the studio where soul was born was demolished.

Thankfully, the story of Stax was not forgotten. In 2001, ground was broken for a new Stax story, one that grew into the present-day music academy and the **Stax Museum of American Soul Music.**

where games and meetings would have been held. There is also a 0.5-mile nature trail along the bluff overlooking the river.

East Memphis

East Memphis is home to old suburbs, gracious homes, and some excellent parks and other attractions.

The Dixon Gallery and Gardens

The Dixon Gallery and Gardens (4339 Park Ave., 901/761-5250, www.dixon. org, 10am-5pm Tues.-Sat., 1pm-5pm Sun., adults $7, seniors and college students $5, children 7-17 $3, children 6 and under free), an art museum housed inside a stately Georgian-style home, has an impressive permanent collection of more than 2,000 paintings, many of them French impressionist and post-impressionist style, including works by Monet, Renoir, Degas, and Cézanne. It also mounts a half dozen special exhibits each year; previous ones have showcased the art of Lester Julian Merriweather, Rodin, and Brian Russell.

The Dixon is an easy place to spend several hours, immersed first in art and then in walking the paths that explore the house's 17 acres of beautifully tended gardens. There is a cutting garden, woodland garden, and formal gardens, among others.

Admission to the Dixon is free 10am-noon Saturday and pay what you wish on Tuesday. It's also open late (8pm) the third Thursday of each month.

Memphis Botanic Garden

The 100-acre **Memphis Botanic Garden** (750 Cherry Rd., 901/636-4100, www. memphisbotanicgarden.com, 9am-6pm daily summer, 9am-4:30pm daily winter, adults $10, seniors $8, children 2-12 $5, children under 2 free) is home to more than 140 different species of trees and more than two dozen specialty gardens, including a Sculpture Garden, Azalea Trail, and Iris Garden. Trails meander through the gardens, but for the greatest fun buy a handful of fish food and feed the fish and ducks that inhabit the pond at the Japanese Garden. The garden puts on a number of events, including blockbuster concerts, workshops, plant sales, wine tastings, and programs for children. **Fratelli's Café at the Garden** (901/766-9900, 11am-2pm Mon.-Sat.) is a good option for lunch on-site.

Pink Palace

A good destination for families, the **Pink Palace** (3050 Central Ave., 901/636-2362, www.memphismuseums.org, 9am-5pm Mon.-Sat., noon-5pm Sun.) is a group of attractions rolled into one. The **Pink Palace Museum** (adults $12.75, seniors $12.25, children $7.25, free after 1pm Tues.) is a museum about Memphis, with exhibits about the natural history of the Mid-South region and the city's development. There is a full-scale replica of the first Piggly Wiggly supermarket, plus an exhibit about how health care became such a large part of the Memphis economy. The museum is housed within the Pink Palace Mansion, the Memphis home of Piggly Wiggly founder Clarence Saunders.

The Pink Palace is also home to the **Sharpe Planetarium,** which includes a newly upgraded 3-D movie theater and a theater-in-the-round called the AutoZone Dome, with daily screenings. Special package tickets are available for all the Pink Palace attractions.

Art Museum of the University of Memphis

The **Art Museum of the University of Memphis** (142 CFA Building, 901/678-2224, www.memphis.edu/amum, 9am-5pm Mon.-Sat., free) houses excellent but small exhibits of ancient Egyptian and African art and artifacts, along with a noteworthy print gallery. There are frequent special exhibitions. The museum is closed during university holidays and in between temporary exhibits. Parking is free on weekends; otherwise it's $2 per hour in the parking garage.

Children's Museum of Memphis

You will know the **Children's Museum of Memphis** (2525 Central Ave., 901/458-2678, www.cmom.com, 9am-5pm daily, $15) by the large alphabet blocks outside spelling its acronym, CMOM. Bring children here for constructive and educational play: They can sit in a flight simulator and real airplane cockpit, climb through the arteries of a model heart, climb a skyscraper, and more. The museum has 26 permanent exhibits and several traveling exhibits. Beat the Memphis summer heat at the museum's **H2Oh! Splash** park, which has 40 water sprayers in which children can frolic.

Lichterman Nature Center

Lichterman Nature Center (5992 Quince Rd., 901/636-2211, www.memphismuseums.org/lichterman-overview, 10am-3pm Tues.-Thurs., 10am-4pm Fri.-Sat., adults $7, seniors $6, children ages 3-12 $5, children under 3 free) is dedicated to generating interest and enthusiasm for the Mid-South's nature. The park encompasses some 65 acres, and visitors will enjoy seeing native trees and flowers, including dogwood, lotus, and pine. It has a museum about the local environment, picnic facilities, and pleasant trails. Environmental education is the center's mission, and this certified arboretum is a popular destination for families and school groups.

Tours
History Tours
Heritage Tours of Memphis (901/527-3427, adults $35, youth 12-17 $27, children 4-11 $25) is the city's only tour company dedicated to presenting Memphis's African American history. Operated by Memphians Elaine Turner and Joan Nelson, Heritage Tours offers black heritage, musical heritage, civil rights, and Beale Street walking tours.

The company can also arrange out-of-town tours to area attractions, such as the **Alex Haley Museum and Interpretive Center** in Henning, Tennessee (adults $35, youth $30). Most local tours last about three hours.

The black heritage tour starts at the W. C. Handy Home and Museum and includes a stop at the Slavehaven Underground Railroad Museum plus narration that tells the story of black Memphians such as Ida B. Wells, Robert Church, and Tom Lee, and the events leading up to the assassination of Dr. Martin Luther King Jr. You will drive past the Mason Temple Church of God in Christ at 930 Mason Street, where Dr. King gave his famous "mountaintop" speech the night before his death.

River Tours
The **Memphis Queen Riverboat Tours** (901/527-2628, www.memphisriverboats.net, adults $20, seniors, college students, military, ages 13-17 $17, ages 4-12 $10, ages 2-3 $5, ages 2 and under free) leave daily at 2:30pm (boarding at 1:30pm) from the Port of Memphis, at the foot of Monroe Avenue on the riverfront. The afternoon tour lasts 90 minutes and takes you a few miles south of the city before turning around. Commentary tells some of the most famous tales of the river, but the biggest attraction of the tour is simply being on Old Man River. The views of the Memphis skyline from the water are impressive. Concessions are available on board. From May through August, an additional 5pm tour (boards 4:30pm) is offered Saturday and Sunday. The riverboats also offer dinner cruises at 7:30pm with live music for about $45 per person. See website to check dates and times.

Music Tours
Music-themed tours are the specialty at **Backbeat Tours** (143 Beale St. 901/527-9415, www.backbeattours.com, $15-51). You will travel on a reconditioned 1959 transit bus and be serenaded by live

musicians. Tours include the Memphis Mojo Tour (adults $28, students $26, children 7-12 $15), which takes you to Memphis music landmarks like Sun Studio and the Stax Museum, and the Hound Dog tour, which follows in Elvis Presley's Memphis footsteps. Backbeat can also take you to Graceland and offers two walking tours of Memphis—a Memphis Ghost Tour (adults $20, children $13), which explores the bloody and creepy side of history—and a Memphis historical walking tour (adults $20, children $10). Tickets must be reserved in advance.

Entertainment and Events

Memphis's vibrant, diverse personality is reflected in its entertainment scene. Blues, rap, R&B, and gospel are just some of the types of music you can hear on any given weekend. Alternative and indie rock find a receptive audience in Memphis, as do opera, Broadway productions, and the symphony. There's always a good excuse to go out.

Live Music

Memphis may be the birthplace of the blues, but there's a lot more to the music scene than that. It's true that you can catch live blues at a Beale Street nightclub or in a city juke joint. But you can also find hard-edge rock, jazz, and acoustic music most nights of the week. The best resource for up-to-date entertainment listings is the free weekly *Memphis Flyer* (www.memphisflyer.com), which comes out on Wednesday morning and includes a detailed listing of club dates and concerts.

Keep in mind that big-name artists often perform at casinos in Tunica, just over the state line in Mississippi. Many of these shows are advertised in Memphis media outlets, or check out the upcoming events on the **Tunica Convention and Visitors Bureau** website, www.tunica-travel.com.

Blues

One of the first things you should do when you get to Memphis is to find out if the **Center for Southern Folklore** (119 S. Main St., 901/525-3655, www.southernfolklore.com, 11am-6pm Mon.-Fri., 2pm-11pm Sat., 2pm-8pm Sun.) has concerts or activities planned during your stay. The center has been documenting and preserving traditional Memphis and Delta blues music since the 1970s. The free self-guided tour of all things traditional-Southern leads you through Heritage Hall. This is also the location of concerts, lectures, and screenings of documentaries; the center offers group tours and educational programs, and hosts the annual Memphis Music and Heritage Festival over Labor Day weekend. It often has live blues on Friday afternoon and offers a variety of special shows. This is one of the best places to hear authentic blues. The folklore store sells folk art, books, CDs, and traditional Southern food, and often hosts live music on Friday and Saturday nights. A sign stating "Be Nice or Leave" sets the tone as soon as you step into this colorful and eclectic shop, one of the best gift shops in the city. The center is a nonprofit organization and well worth supporting. You'll find live music in the Folklore Store most Friday and Saturday nights starting around 8pm.

Beale Street is the starting place for checking out Memphis's blues music scene. While some people lament that Beale has become a sad tourist shell of its former self, it can still be a worthwhile place to spend your evening. Indeed, no other part of Memphis has as much music and entertainment encompassing such a small area. On a typical night, Beale Street is packed with a diverse crowd strolling from one bar to the next. Beer seems to run a close second to music as the street's prime attraction, with many bars selling directly onto the

Juke Joints

In Memphis, there are only two reasons to go to a juke joint full of blues: because you feel good or because you feel bad. Beale Street is a reliable source seven nights a week, and your visit to Memphis wouldn't be complete without checking out its scene. But if you want to sneak away from the tourist crowd and catch some homegrown talent, check out a real Memphis juke joint. Live music is typical on Friday and Saturday nights and sometimes Sunday, but it gets scarce during the week. Generally music starts late (11pm) and finishes early (3am). Don't be surprised if the person you've engaged in conversation sitting next to you gets called to the stage sometime during the evening and delivers a beautiful song. Some say the term "juke" is derived from the Gullah word *joog*, meaning rowdy or disorderly. Certainly, a juke joint is somewhere you're likely to experience laughter, dancing, and drinking, not necessarily in that order. If you are looking for a staid music listening experience, this is not for you.

There are many juke joints in the Mississippi Delta and we've highlighted some of those in the Mississippi Blues Trail section. When in doubt, just ask a local and they'll give you directions where the party's started, often in a garage or shed. Remember that it's in the nature of things for these clubs to come and go. The following listings were current as of this writing, but they are always subject to change.

- **Wild Bill's** (1580 Vollintine Ave., 901/207-3975): A legendary club in Memphis. The patriarch himself passed away in the summer of 2007, but what he established will still carry on. This is the quintessential juke joint: small, intimate, an open kitchen serving chicken wings, and ice-cold beer served in 40-ounce bottles. Home to Ms. Nikki and the Memphis Soul Survivors.

- **CC Blues Club** (1427 Thomas St., 901/526-5566): More upscale. More mirrors. But it has a great dance floor, and don't you dare come underdressed. Security guards patrol the parking lot.

- **Blues Hall** (182 Beale St., 901/528-0150, www.eatdrinkboogie.com, 6pm-midnight Mon.-Thurs., 4pm-1am Fri.-Sat., 3pm-midnight Sun.): New Orleans has Preservation Hall; Memphis has Handy's Blues Hall. Everyone bad-raps Beale Street and its jangly tourism scene, but if you catch it on a good night, when Dr. Feelgood warms up his harmonica and you look around the room at the memorabilia on the walls, you could be in a joint at the end of a country road in Mississippi. Blues Hall is connected to Rum Boogie Café.

street through concession windows. The "Big Ass Beer" cups used by many establishments say it all.

Nearly all Beale Street bars have live music, but one of the most popular is **B. B. King's Blues Club** (143 Beale St., 901/524-5464, www.bbkings.com/memphis, 11am-midnight Sun.-Thurs., 11am-2am Fri.-Sat., cover $3-5 weekends). Local acts and some nationally known performers take the stage. B. B. King's draws a mostly tourist crowd, and it is a chain, but with the blues on full throttle, you probably won't care too much.

Also on Beale Street, **Blues City Café** (138 Beale St., 901/526-3637, www.bluescitycafe.com, 11am-3am Sun.-Thurs., 11am-5am Fri.-Sat., cover $3-5) books blues, plus a variety of other acts including doo-wop, zydeco, R&B, funk, and "high-impact rockabilly." The café-restaurant is one of the most popular on Beale Street, and its nightclub, **Rum Boogie Café** (182 Beale St., 901/526-0150, http://rumboogie.com, 11am-2am daily, cover $3-5), has an award-winning house band, Vince Johnson and the Boogie Blues Band, that performs most evenings.

Jazz

If you want a break from the blues, **King's Palace Café** (162 Beale St., 901/521-1851, http://kingspalacecafe.com, 11am-10pm Mon.-Thurs., 11am-1am Fri.-Sat., 11am-10pm Sun.) specializes in jazz. Lots of wood paneling and red paint make the bar and Cajun restaurant warm and welcoming. This is an unpretentious place to have a meal or listen to live music. There is a $1 per person entertainment charge when you sit at a table.

Rock

Alfred's On Beale (197 Beale St., 901/525-3711, www.alfredsonbeale.com, 11am-3am Sun.-Thurs., 11am-5am Fri.-Sat., cover varies) has rock acts five nights a week. On Sunday evening, the 17-piece Memphis Jazz Orchestra takes the stage. The dance floor at Alfred's is one of the best on Beale Street.

One of Beale Street's most historic concert venues, **The New Daisy** (330 Beale St., 901/525-8981, http://newdaisy.com, box office noon-4pm, cover $10 and up, ticket costs vary) books rock 'n' roll, independent, and a few R&B acts. There are shows most nights of the week; call ahead or check the entertainment listings for a schedule. The Daisy is an all-ages club, and many shows attract a young audience.

Off Beale Street, the **Hi-Tone Cafe** (412 N. Cleveland St., 901/490-0335, 5pm-3am daily, www.hitonememphis.com, cover and ticket prices vary, $2 charge for under 21) is probably the best place to see live music in town. The Hi-Tone books all kinds of acts, from high-energy rockers to soulful acoustic acts. They are really committed to bringing good live music to Memphis. The cover charge for local shows is a few bucks, but tickets for bigger-name acts can run $20 and more. The bar serves respectable burgers and finger foods, excellent martinis, and lots of beer.

Nightlife

Who knew your designated driver would be a kangaroo? It's a reality with **Ride the Roo** (www.ridetheroo.com, 5pm-2am Fri.-Sat., $2 per ride, $5 for all-night pass), a sleek black mini-bus with a martini-wielding kangaroo on top, which makes 12 stops along nightlife-heavy areas in Overton Square and Cooper Young.

Downtown

You can head to Beale Street for a night out, regardless of whether or not you sing the blues.

The best place to grab a beer downtown is the **Beale Street Tap Room** (168 Beale St., 901/521-1851, 4pm-1am Tues.-Sat., noon-midnight Sun.-Mon.). With more than 30 beers on tap, this is a great choice for beer lovers. The service is friendly and low-key, and regulars have their own mug.

Off Beale Street, **The Peabody Memphis** (149 Union Ave., 901/529-4000, www.peabodymemphis.com, 10am-midnight Sun.-Thurs., 10am-2am Fri.-Sat.) may be the best place to enjoy a relaxing drink. The lobby bar offers good service, comfortable seats, and a rarified atmosphere.

In the South Main district, **Earnestine and Hazel's** (531 S. Main St., 901/523-9754, http://earnestineandhazelsjukejoint.com, 5pm-3am Mon.-Fri., 11am-3am Sat.-Sun.) is one of Memphis's most celebrated pit stops for cold drinks and a night out. Once a brothel, Ernestine and Hazel's now has one of the best jukeboxes in town. Take a seat upstairs in one of the old brothel rooms and watch South Main Street below. Rumor is the joint is haunted, but folks come here for the jukebox, not the spirits.

If beer's your thing, check out the growler station at **Joe's Wine & Liquor** (1681 Poplar Ave., 901/725-4252, http://joeswinesandliquor.com, 8am-11pm Mon.-Sat.). Behind this iconic signage you'll find 30 beer taps.

Midtown

The **Young Avenue Deli** (2119 Young

Ave., 901/278-0034, www.youngavenue-deli.com, 11am-3am daily, kitchen closes at 2am) is a friendly neighborhood bar that books occasional live acts. Located in the hip Cooper-Young neighborhood, Young Avenue Deli has hundreds of beers on tap or in bottles. The bar attracts a diverse crowd, from young hipsters to older neighborhood denizens.

A favorite place for music, pool, and a night out in midtown is the **Blue Monkey** (2012 Madison Ave., 901/272-2583, http://bluemonkeymemphis.com, 11am-3am daily). Grab a pizza and a beer, shoot some pool, and then rock out to the live band. There's a second location downtown (513 S. Front St., 901/527-6665).

Murphy's (1589 Madison Ave., 901/726-4193, www.murphysmemphis.com, 11am-3am daily) is a neighborhood bar with a nice patio. Perfect for a business date or after-work pit stop, **The Grove Grill** (4550 Poplar Ave., 901/818-9951, www.thegrovegrill.com, 11am-2:30pm and 3pm-9pm Sun.-Thurs., 11am-2:30pm and 3pm-10pm Fri.-Sat.) is popular with office workers.

Two of Memphis's best sports bars are found in the eastern reaches of the city. **Brookhaven Pub & Grill** (695 W. Brookhaven Cir., 901/680-8118, www.brookhavenpubandgrill.com, 11am-3am daily) has big-screen plasma televisions, great beer on tap, and lots of fans. Tuesday night is Team Trivia night.

There's more to do than just watch the game at **Rec Room** (3000 Broad Ave., 901/209-1137, http://recroommemphis.com, 4pm-midnight Mon.-Thurs., 4pm-2am Fri., 11am-2am Sat., 11am-midnight Sun.). In addition to oversized screens for sports-watching, you can also get your game on with vintage video games, board games, and tabletop games such as foosball and Ping-Pong. Though Rec Room doesn't have a menu of its own, food trucks regularly pull up to the patio to tend to customers' cravings. Kids are welcome before 6pm if escorted by an adult; after 6pm, it's 18 and up. There's no cover

for adults, a $5 wristband charge for those under 18, and video game/TV rooms cost $10-25 per hour to rent, depending on the day of the week.

A modern reboot of a historic music venue, **Lafayette's Music Room** (2119 Madison Ave., 901/207-5097, http://lafayettes.com/memphis, 11am-10pm Mon., 11am-10:30pm Tues.-Wed., 11am-midnight Thurs., 11am-2am Fri.-Sat., 11am-midnight Sun., $15-24) features live music every night, a two-story patio, and Southern-inspired fare.

Gay and Lesbian Nightlife
Many Memphis gay and lesbian clubs don't get going until late night, after other clubs have closed.

Dru's Bar (1474 Madison Ave., 901/275-8082, www.drusplace.com, 1pm-midnight Sun.-Thurs., 1pm-2am Fri.-Sat.) is a welcoming bar that has weekly Drag Time and Beer Bust. The beer is cold and the liquor is BYO.

Club Spectrum Memphis (600 Marshall Ave., 901/292-2292, 9pm-4am Fri.-Sat.) is a gay-, lesbian-, and everyone-welcome dance club. This is a weekend-only spot to get your groove on.

The Pumping Station (1382 Poplar Ave., 901/272-7600, http://thepumpingstationmemphis.com, 4pm-3am Mon.-Fri., 3pm-3am Sat.-Sun.) is one of the city's favorite gay bars, with a full bar, craft beers on tap, and an outdoor beer garden (called The Backdoor Lounge, which is the only place you can smoke). It is housed in a building that once allowed a Jewish couple, evicted from another location, to open a liquor store, and is proud of its inclusive historical roots.

The Arts
Memphis has a growing arts scene. **ArtsMemphis** (901/578-2787, www.artsmemphis.org) provides funding for more than 20 local arts groups and is a reliable source of information about upcoming events.

Major arts venues include the **Cannon**

Center for the Performing Arts (255 N. Main St., 901/576-1200, www.thecannon-center.com) and the **Orpheum Theatre** (203 S. Main St., 901/525-3000, www.orpheum-memphis.com). They regularly book major artists and Broadway performances.

Theater

For theater, check out **Playhouse on the Square** (66 S. Cooper St., 901/726-4656, http://playhouseonthesquare.org). This dynamic Memphis institution serves as home to several of the city's acting companies and puts on 15-20 different performances every year. It also offers theater classes, school performances, and pay-what-you-can shows.

Theatre Memphis (630 Perkins Ext., 901/682-8323, www.theatrememphis.org) is a community theater company that has been in existence since the 1920s. It stages about 12 shows annually at its theater in midtown.

Music

The **Memphis Symphony Orchestra** (585 S. Mendenhall Rd., 901/537-2525, www.memphissymphony.org) performs a varied calendar of works year-round in its home at the Cannon Center for the Performing Arts (255 N. Main St.). The symphony was founded in 1952 and today has more than 850 musicians, staff, and volunteers.

Opera

Opera Memphis (6745 Wolf River Blvd., 901/257-3100, www.operamemphis.org) performs traditional opera at venues around town, including the historic Playhouse on the Square (66 S. Cooper St.) and the Germantown Performing Arts Centre (1801 Exeter Rd., Germantown). For the 30 days of September the company performs "pop-up" operas at different locations around the city.

Dance

Ballet Memphis (901/737-7322, www.balletmemphis.org) performs classical dance at the Playhouse on the Square (66 S. Cooper St.), the Orpheum (203 S. Main St.), and other venues throughout the city. The **New Ballet Ensemble** (901/726-9225, www.newballet.org) puts on performances around the city with "dancers in do-rags as well as tights," in the words of the *Commercial Appeal*.

Festivals and Events

Spring

Memphians celebrate their African heritage over a long weekend in mid-April. **Africa in April** (901/947-2133, www.africainapril.org) honors a specific country in Africa each year. Activities include cooking, storytelling, music, and a parade. The festival takes place at Church Park on the east end of Beale Street.

In early May, the Memphis-based Blues Foundation hosts the annual **Blues Music Awards** (www.blues.org), the Grammys of the blues world. Per the foundation, a nominee announcement, as well as ticket information for the event, is released each year in mid-December on their website.

Memphis in May (www.memphisinmay.org), the city's largest annual event, is really three major festivals rolled into one. The **Beale Street Music Festival,** which takes place at Tom Lee Park on the river, kicks things off with a celebration of Memphis music. Expect a lot of wow-worthy performers, plus many more up-and-coming talents. The festival has grown over the years, and it is now a three-day event with four stages of music going simultaneously. In addition to music, the festival offers excellent people-watching, lots of barbecue, cold beer, and festivity. You can buy daily tickets or a three-day pass for the whole weekend.

In mid-May, attention turns to the **World Championship Barbecue Cooking Contest,** a celebration of pork, pigs, and barbecue that takes place in Tom Lee Park. In addition to the barbecue judging, it offers entertainment, hog-calling contests, and other piggy antics. If you're not part of a competing team, you can buy barbecue from vendors who set up in the park.

A sunset symphony caps off the month-long festivities. Book your hotel rooms early for **Memphis in May,** since many hotels, particularly those in downtown, sell out.

Summer

Carnival Memphis (901/458-2500, http://carnivalmemphis.org) is a Mardi Gras-style celebration, not a fairgrounds-esque event. It features a parade, fireworks, a ball, and more. This celebration raises funds for local children's charities. Like carnivals elsewhere in the South, Carnival Memphis consists of several events, including the Crown & Sceptre Ball, Princess Ball, and a luncheon for businesses. Public ticket prices are released annually on the website.

The annual candlelight vigil at Graceland on August 15, the anniversary of Elvis's death, has grown into a whole week of Elvis-centric activities throughout Memphis. More than 30,000 people visit Graceland during **Elvis Week** (www.graceland.com/elvisweek), and during the vigil his most adoring fans walk solemnly up the Graceland drive to pay their respects at his grave. Special concerts, tribute shows, and movies are shown during the week as the city celebrates its most famous son even more than usual.

Fall

Organized by the Center for Southern Folklore, the **Memphis Music and Heritage Festival** (901/525-3655, www.southernfolklore.com), held over Labor Day weekend, sticks close to the roots of Memphis music. Performers include gospel singers, bona fide bluesmen and women, rockabilly superstars, and much more. Performances take place in the center's shop and concert hall on Main Street, making them more intimate than other blockbuster music festivals.

Since 2004 **Gonerfest** (www.

goner-records.com/gonerfest) has been the showcase for artists on the Goner Records label. Held in September, the fest features shows at venues downtown as well as opening and closing shows at Goner's gazebo. Tickets are sold at the door for single concerts, but if you are hardcore there's also a "Golden Ticket" that will get you into each and every show for $75.

End-of-summer fairs are a tradition for Southern and rural communities all over the United States. The 10-day **Mid-South Fair** (901/274-8800, http://midsouthfair.org) in September is a bonanza of attractions: livestock shows, rodeos, agricultural judging, concerts, beauty pageants, exhibitions, carnival rides, funnel cakes, and cotton candy. The fair is held in northern Mississippi, about 30 miles south of Memphis.

In mid-September, the Cooper-Young neighborhood throws its annual jamboree at the **Cooper-Young Festival** (http://cooperyoungfestival.com). This street carnival includes an arts and crafts fair, live music, and food.

The annual **Southern Heritage Classic** (http://southernheritageclassic.com) is one of the South's big football games. But the matchup of two historically black college rivals, Jackson State University and Tennessee State University, is more than just a game—it is a serious citywide festival.

Forty-six-foot-long boats with dragon heads and tails race at Mud Island River Park each September during the **Duncan-Williams St. Jude Dragon Boat Races** (www.stjude.org/dragonboat). Proceeds benefit the work of St. Jude Children's Research Hospital.

Winter

The colder weather welcomes a number of sporting events, including the **St. Jude Marathon and Half Marathon** (800/565-5112, www.stjudemarathon.org) in December, which is a qualifying race for the Boston Marathon. The **AutoZone**

Levitt Shell

Looking for a midtown local? **Levitt Shell at Overton Park** (1928 Poplar Ave., 901/272-2722, www.levittshell. org) is a good bet. Locals gravitate here because Levitt Shell hosts more than 50 free concerts a year. Past lineups have included The Soul Rebels, Cherry Poppin' Daddies, Steep Canyon Rangers, and Lera Lynn. Want to do Levitt like a local? Bring your own lawn chairs or blanket and chill out on the lawn. Concessions are sold and you can also bring your own food and drinks, including booze for those of age. There are also a few ticketed concerts every year, which are not free and to which outside food and drink are not permitted.

The space has history: It was built by the city in 1936 as part of the Works Progress Administration (WPA), designed by architect Max Furbringer. There were dozens of WPA band shells built, and Levitt is one of the few that remain in use. But more important to Memphians: On July 30, 1954, Elvis Presley had his first paid gig on this stage, opening for Slim Whitman.

Like many historic buildings, Levitt Shell (originally called Overton Park Shell and Shell Theater) sat vacant for many years. A neighborhood grassroots organization brought it back, raising funds for its renovation. The new Levitt Shell concert series launched in 2011.

Parking is generally free, and concerts are held rain or shine, but check ahead if you are concerned about more inclement weather. MATA bus routes 50 Poplar and 53 Summer make stops near Overton Park, while 50 Poplar stops closer to the shell.

Liberty Bowl (901/795-7700, www.libertybowl.org) typically welcomes two of the National Collegiate Athletic Association's (NCAA) best football teams to town on New Year's Eve.

Taking place over the weekend closest to Elvis Presley's January 8 birthday, the **Elvis Birthday Celebration** (www.graceland.com) draws Elvis fans with special performances, dance parties, and a ceremony at Graceland proclaiming Elvis Presley Day.

Shopping

Downtown

A half dozen shops along Beale Street sell gifts and souvenirs of the city. **A. Schwab** (163 Beale St., 901/523-9782, http://a-schwab.com, noon-6pm Mon.-Wed., noon-6pm Thurs., noon-8pm Fri.-Sat., 11am-5pm Sun.) has served Memphis residents for more than 140 years, although it focuses now on odd, out-of-date, and hard-to-find items rather than traditional general-store necessities. Stop in for a souvenir or to visit the A. Schwab "museum," a collection of old-fashioned household tools and implements. The shop may stay open later in the summer depending on crowds.

Another good place for gift shopping is the **Center for Southern Folklore** (123 S. Main St., 901/525-3655, www.southernfolklore.com, 11am-6pm Mon.-Fri., 2pm-6pm Sat.-Sun.), which has books, art, and music focusing on the region.

All of the city's museums have good gift shops, including the **National Civil Rights Museum** (450 Mulberry St., 901/521-9699, www.civilrights-museum.org, 9am-5pm Mon. and Wed.-Sat., 1pm-5pm Sun.), **Stax Museum of American Soul Music** (926 E. McLemore Ave., 901/942-7685, http://staxmuseum.com, 10am-5pm Tues.-Sat., 1pm-5pm Sun.), and **Sun Studio** (706 Union Ave., 800/441-6249, www.sunstudio.com, 10am-6pm daily), where everything is emblazoned with the distinctive yellow Sun label.

Memphis Music (149 Beale St., 901/526-5047, http://memphismusicstore.com,

10am-midnight Mon.-Sat., noon-10pm Sun.) has the best selection of CDs and DVDs for music fans.

Head to the South Main arts district to visit art galleries like **Robinson Gallery/Archives** (400 Front St., 901/576-0708, http://robinsongallery.com, 11am-5pm Mon.-Fri.), a photography gallery that houses the work of *Vogue* photographer Jack Robinson Jr.

Midtown

Shangri-La Records (1916 Madison Ave., 901/274-1916, www.shangri.com, noon-7pm Mon.-Fri., 11am-6pm Sat.), one of the city's best record stores, specializes in Memphis music. **Goner Records** (2152 Young Ave., 901/722-0095, www.goner-records.com, noon-7pm Mon.-Sat., 1pm-5pm Sun.) is both a record store and a record label.

The area between Cooper and East Parkway has the city's greatest concentration of antiques stores. **Flashback** (2304 Central Ave., 901/272-2304, www.flash-backmemphis.com, 10:30am-5:30pm Mon.-Sat., 1pm-5pm Sun.) sells both vintage furniture and clothes, including a whole lot of Levi's jeans.

In a city of characters, the most colorful shopping experience is found at **The Memphis Flea Market—The Big One** (940 Early Maxwell Blvd. at Tiger Ln., 901/276-3532, www.memphisfleamar-ket.com, adults $3, free for children), which takes place the third weekend of most months (exceptions are the fourth weekend of February and an extra market the first weekend of December) at the Memphis Fairgrounds. Between 800 and 1,000 vendors turn up each month with housewares, clothing, computers, jewelry, antiques, yard art, and so much more. Between 20,000 and 25,000 people come to shop. Parking is free.

South Memphis

In a city where vintage never went out of style, you can expect excellent thrift stores. The biggest and best is **AmVets**

Thrift Center (2526 Elvis Presley Blvd., 901/775-5010, 9am-8pm Mon.-Sat., 10am-6pm Sun.).

Sports and Recreation

With a professional basketball team, excellent downtown baseball club, and lots of city parks, Memphis is a great city in which to watch sports and get active yourself.

Parks

Downtown

Named for the legendary blues composer W. C. Handy, **Handy Park** (200 Beale St.), located between 3rd Street and Rufus Thomas Boulevard, seems a tad out of place among Beale's nightclubs and restaurants. A statue of the park's namesake guards its gates. The park hosts occasional outdoor concerts and festivals.

Uptown

Tom Lee Park (spanning Riverside Dr.), a long, 30-acre, narrow grassy park that overlooks the Mississippi, is a popular venue for summertime festivals and events, including the Memphis in May **World Championship Barbecue Cooking Contest**. It is also used year-round for walking and jogging and by people who simply want to look out at the giant river. The park is named for Tom Lee, an African American man who saved the lives of 32 people when the steamboat they were on sank in the river in 1925.

Located on the northern side of downtown Memphis, **Court Square** (62 N. Main St.), three blocks from the waterfront along Court Avenue, is a pleasant city park surrounded by historic buildings. Court Square is one of four parks included when the city was first planned in 1819. There are benches and trees, and it is a wireless Internet hot spot.

Memphis Park, located on Front Street between Court and Jefferson Streets, commemorates Civil War soldiers who died in the Battle of Memphis. There is a statue of Jefferson Davis in the center of the park. This is where many Memphians gathered to watch the Battle of Memphis in 1862, and it remains a good place to view the river below.

Midtown

Located in midtown Memphis, **Overton Park** (1914 Poplar Ave.) is one of the best all-around parks the city has to offer. This 342-acre park has a nine-hole golf course, nature trails through the woods, bike trails, an outdoor amphitheater called the Levitt Shell, and lots of green, open spaces. The park shares space with the Memphis Zoo and the Memphis Brooks Museum of Art, making the area a popular destination for city residents and visitors. Patience may be required when looking for a parking spot during an event at Overton.

The Madison Avenue trolley passes **Health Sciences Park,** along Madison Avenue between North Manassas and North Dunlap Streets, an ample city park once dedicated to the memory of the controversial Nathan Bedford Forrest. Forrest, a slave trader, Confederate, and the first grand wizard of the Ku Klux Klan, has an uncomfortable position of prominence in Memphis and the whole of western Tennessee. Both he and his wife are buried in the park. The name of the park was changed in 2013, but court cases continue as some constituents would like to see it changed back. Many locals just refer to this as "the park near the UT med school."

South Memphis

Southwest of the city center, about a 15-minute drive from the airport, is **T. O. Fuller State Park** (1500 Mitchell Rd., 901/543-7581, http://tnstateparks.com). The visitors center is open weekdays 8am-sunset. Amenities at the 1,138-acre park include sheltered picnic areas, tennis courts, a golf course, a swimming pool ($5 per person ages 4 and up), basketball

courts, a softball field, six miles of hiking trails, and camping facilities. T. O. Fuller State Park was the first state park east of the Mississippi River open to African Americans, and the second in the nation. An interpretive center opened in summer 2016 and features exhibits about the park's history, wildlife, and energy efficiency.

East Memphis

Located near the University of Memphis and Oak Court Mall, **Audubon Park** (4161 Park Ave.) has a golf course, tennis courts, walking trails, and other sports facilities. The Memphis Botanic Garden is located here.

Memphians celebrate the fact that their largest city park, **Shelby Farms** (6908 Great View Dr. N., 901/222-7275, www.shelbyfarmspark.org), is five times the size of New York's Central Park. But most of its 4,500 acres is pleasantly undeveloped. More than 500,000 people come here annually to go zip-lining, mountain biking, horseback riding, in-line skating, walking, or running along the many trails. You can also fish, raft, canoe, or sail on the park's six lakes. The park has a wheelchair-accessible trail, areas for picnicking, and a shooting range. Other features include a visitors center, retreat center, event pavilion, boat kiosk, and wetland walk. Shelby Farms is on the eastern side of the city, just outside the I-40/I-240 loop that circles Memphis. It is easily accessible from exits 12 and 14 off I-40, and exit 13 off I-240. Or follow Walnut Grove Road from midtown.

Biking

Most cyclists in the city bike as a form of recreation, rather than transportation. The City of Memphis has established six **bike routes** that circle the city and various neighborhoods. These routes are marked and have designated parking and restroom facilities at the start. They are not bike paths—you share the road with cars—and normal safety measures are necessary.

The **Memphis Hightailers Bicycle Club** (www.memphishightailers.com) organizes frequent rides for various levels, with distances ranging 20-100 miles. Regularly scheduled Urban Bicycle Food Ministry rides are listed for people to help distribute food while riding 10-12 miles.

Several parks near Memphis are bike friendly. **Meeman-Shelby Forest State Park** (910 Riddick Rd., 901/876-5215, 7am-10pm daily), north of the city, has five miles of paved bike paths, and cyclists use the main park roads for more extensive riding.

It is also noteworthy that the **Mississippi River Trail,** a bicycle route that runs 3,000 miles from the headwaters of the Mississippi River in Minnesota to the Gulf of Mexico, runs through Memphis and on to Mississippi. For maps and details, go to www.lmrcc.org/outdoor-recreation/bicycling.

Spectator Sports
Basketball
The NBA's **Memphis Grizzlies** play at the massive FedEx Forum, one of the largest arenas in the NBA. Ticket prices range from under $20 to several hundred dollars. For ticket information, contact the **FedEx Forum box office** (191 Beale St., 901/205-2640, www.fedexforum.com, 10am-5:30pm Mon.-Fri.) or purchase through Ticketmaster. The NBA season runs October-April.

You can also watch the **University of Memphis Tigers** basketball team play November-April at FedEx Forum. Tickets are available from the FedEx Forum box office, or contact University of Memphis Athletics (www.gotigersgo.com) for more information.

Baseball
From April to October, the **Memphis Redbirds** (901/721-6000, www.memphisredbirds.com, $6-26) play AAA ball

at the striking **AutoZone Park** in downtown Memphis. The stadium is bounded by Union Avenue, Madison Avenue, and 3rd Street, and is convenient to dozens of downtown hotels and restaurants. The Redbirds are an affiliate of the St. Louis Cardinals. Cheap tickets ($6) buy you a seat on the grassy berm, or you can pay a little more for seats in the stadium or boxes.

Racing
The **Memphis International Raceway** (5500 Victory Ln., 901/969-7223, www.racemir.com) is a short drive from downtown Memphis in Millington, northeast of the city center. The park includes a 0.75-mile NASCAR oval, a 0.25-mile drag racing strip, and a 1.77-mile road course. It hosts more than 200 race events every year, including a stop in the annual Busch Series races. Millington is about a 30-minute drive north of Memphis. From the west, take I-40 east toward Nashville. From the east, take I-40 west toward Memphis.

Food

Eating may be the best thing about visiting Memphis. The city's culinary specialties start—but don't end—with barbecue. Plate-lunch diners around the city offer delectable corn bread, fried chicken, greens, fried green tomatoes, peach cobbler, and dozens of other Southern specialties on a daily basis. And to make it even better, such down-home restaurants are easy on your wallet. For those seeking a departure from home-style fare, Memphis has dozens of fine restaurants, some old established eateries and others newcomers that are as trendy as those in any major American city.

Not sure where to start? Try a **Tastin' 'Round Town** food tour (901/310-9789, http://tastinroundtown.com). Choose from barbecue for $65 or Taste of Memphis for $50. These walking tours are multi-restaurant experiences that let you sample some of the city's best. Some tour times require a minimum of two tickets to purchase.

Memphis also has a decent food truck scene. Find one of the 24 trucks out and about (www.memphisfoodtruckers.org).

The closest gourmet grocery is in Harbor Town, the residential community on Mud Island, where **Miss Cordelia's** (737 Harbor Bend Rd., 901/526-4772, www.misscordelias.com, 7am-10pm daily) sells fresh produce, bakery goods, and staples. A deli in the back serves soups, salads, sandwiches, and a wide variety of prepared foods.

The **Memphis Farmers Market** (901/575-0580, www.memphisfarmersmarket.com, Sat. 7am-1pm Apr.-Oct., rain or shine, free) takes place in the pavilion opposite Central Station in the South Main part of town.

Downtown
Barbecue
Barbecue is serious business in Memphis, unlike anywhere else in the state. On the northern fringe of downtown Memphis is one of the city's most famous and well-loved barbecue joints: **Cozy Corner** (735 N. Parkway, 901/527-9158, www.cozycornerbbq.com, 11am-9pm Tues.-Sat., $7-20). Cozy Corner is tucked into a storefront in an otherwise abandoned strip mall; you'll smell it before you see it. Step inside to order barbecue pork, sausage, or bologna sandwiches. Or get a two-bone, four-bone, or six-bone rib dinner plate, which comes with your choice of baked beans, coleslaw, or barbecue spaghetti, plus slices of Wonder bread to sop up the juices. One of Cozy Corner's specialties is its barbecued Cornish hens—a preparation that is surprising but delicious. Sweet tea goes perfectly with the tangy and spicy barbecue.

Although aficionados will remind you that the ribs served at **Rendezvous** (52 S. 2nd St., 901/523-2746, http://hogsfly.com, 4:30pm-10:30pm Tues.-Thurs., 11am-11pm Fri., 11:30am-11pm Sat., $8-21) are not technically barbecue, they are one of the biggest barbecue stories in town. Covered in a dry rub of spices and broiled until the meat falls off the bones, these ribs will knock your socks off. If you prefer, you can choose Charlie Vergos's dry-rub chicken or boneless pork loin. Orders come with baked beans and coleslaw, but beer is really the essential accompaniment to any Vergos meal. The door to Rendezvous is tucked in an alley off Monroe Avenue. The smoky interior, decorated with antiques and yellowing business cards, is low-key, noisy, and lots of fun.

Southern
Tucked inside an unassuming storefront across from the valet entrance to the Peabody is **Flying Fish** (105 S. 2nd St., 901/522-8228, www.flyingfishinthe.net, 11am-10pm daily, $8-20), your first stop for authentic fried catfish in Memphis. If catfish isn't your thing, try the grilled or boiled shrimp, fish tacos, frog legs, or oysters. The baskets of fried seafood come with fries and hush puppies, and the grilled plates come with veggies, rice, and beans. The tangy coleslaw is a must. The atmosphere is laid-back; place your order at the window and come and get it when the coaster they give you starts to vibrate. The checkered tables are well stocked with hot sauce and saltines.

It would be a grave mistake to visit Memphis and not stop at ★ **Gus's World Famous Fried Chicken** (310 Front St., 901/527-4877, http://gusfriedchicken.com, 11am-9pm Sun.-Thurs., 11am-10pm Fri.-Sat., $6-12) for some of their delicious fried bird. The downtown location is a franchise of the original Gus's, which is a half-hour drive northeast out of town along US 70, in Mason. It is no exaggeration to say that Gus's cooks up some of the best fried chicken out there: It is spicy, juicy, and hot. It's served casually wrapped in brown paper. Sides include coleslaw, baked beans, and fried pickles.

The restaurant also serves grilled-cheese sandwiches. The service in this hole-in-the-wall establishment is slow but friendly, so come in with a smile on.

The ★ **Arcade** (540 S. Main St., 901/526-5757, http://arcaderestaurant.com, 7am-3pm Sun.-Thurs., 7am-11pm Fri.-Sat., $5-10) is said to be Memphis's oldest restaurant. Founded in 1919 and still operated by the same family (with lots of the same decor), this restaurant feels like a throwback to an earlier time. The menu is diverse, with pizzas, sandwiches, and plate-lunch specials during the week, and breakfast served anytime. The chicken spaghetti is a stick-to-your-ribs favorite.

Contemporary

The Majestic Grille (145 S. Main St., 901/522-8555, http://majesticgrille.com, 11am-10pm Mon.-Thurs., 11am-11pm Fri., 11am-2:30pm and 4pm-11pm Sat., 11am-2:30pm and 4pm-9pm Sun., $18-40) serves a remarkably affordable yet upscale menu at brunch, lunch, and dinner. It is in what was once the Majestic Theater, and the restaurant's white tablecloths and apron-clad waiters lend an aura of refinement. But with main courses starting at just $8-9, this can be a bargain. Flatbread pizzas feature asparagus, spicy shrimp, and smoked sausage, and sandwiches include burgers and clubs. Specialties include pasta, barbecue ribs, grilled salmon, and steaks. Don't pass on dessert, served in individual shot glasses, such as chocolate mousse, key lime pie, and carrot cake, among others.

If you're staying downtown, **Eighty3 food & drink** (83 Madison Ave., 901/333-1224, http://eighty3memphis.com, 6:30am-10:30am, 11:30am-2pm, and 5pm-10pm Mon.-Thurs., 11:30am-2pm and 5pm-11pm Fri., 6:30am-2pm and 5pm-11pm Sat., 6:30am-2pm and 5pm-10pm Sun., $15-38) is a reliable find-everything stop. You can feast on steaks and chops, with a "natural/organic/sustainable" slant. Or you can head here for

bar snacks while watching your favorite sports team, streetside seating for people-watching, or even grab-and-go breakfasts perfect for taking to explore the city. Check out their happy hour (5pm-7pm Mon.-Thurs.).

It is impossible to pigeonhole **Automatic Slim's Tonga Club** (83 S. 2nd St., 901/525-7948, http://automaticslims-memphis.com, 11am-11pm Mon.-Thurs., 11am-1am Fri., 9am-1am Sat., 9am-11pm Sun., $10-23), except to say that this Memphis institution consistently offers fresh, spirited, and original fare. Named after a character from an old blues tune, Automatic Slim's uses strong flavors to create its eclectic menu; Caribbean and Southwestern influences are the most apparent. A meal here isn't complete without a famous Tonga Martini or one of the delectable desserts: Pecan tart and chocolate cake are good choices. Automatic Slim's is a welcome departure from barbecue and Southern food. Its atmosphere is relaxed, and there's often a crowd at the bar, especially on weekends, when there's live music.

Chez Philippe (149 Union Ave., 901/529-4188, 6pm-10pm Wed.-Sat., $95-135), located in the Peabody, offers French-Asian fusion cuisine. The Asian influences are noticeable in the ingredients, but the preparation of most dishes at Chez Philippe remains traditional French. Entrées include grouper, bass, pork chop, and venison. Chez Philippe offers a prix fixe menu: Four-course meals are $95 and seven courses are $135.

International

Lively, funky **Oshi Burger Bar** (94 S. Main St., 901/341-2091, http://oshiburger.com, 11am-10pm Sun.-Thurs., 11am-midnight Fri.-Sat., $7-10) specializes in burgers and hot dogs with an Asian twist: think toppings such as kimchi slaw or nori flakes and sides such as tempura onion rings. Milkshakes with additions like Pop Rocks, sake, bacon dust, or bourbon are a fun treat.

Piggly Wiggly

Memphian Clarence Saunders opened the first **Piggly Wiggly** at 79 Jefferson Street in 1916, thus giving birth to the modern American supermarket. Until then, shoppers went to small storefront shops where they would ask the counter clerk for what they needed: a pound of flour, a half-dozen pickles, a block of cheese. The clerk went to the bulk storage area at the rear of the store and measured out what the customer needed.

Saunders's big idea was self-service. At the Piggly Wiggly, customers entered the store, carried a basket, and were able to pick out prepackaged and priced contain- ers of food that they paid for at the pay- ment station on their way out.

Suffice to say, the Piggly Wiggly idea took off, and by 1923 there were 1,268 Piggly Wiggly franchises around the country. Saunders used some of his prof- its to build a massive mansion east of the city out of pink Georgia limestone, but he was never to live in the Pink Palace, which he lost as a result of a complex stock transaction.

Today, Saunders's **Pink Palace** is home to the **Pink Palace Museum,** which includes, among other things, a replica of the original Piggly Wiggly supermarket.

Cafés and Diners

For the best burgers on Beale Street, go to **Dyer's Burgers** (205 Beale St., 901/527- 3937, www.dyersonbeale.com, 11am-1am Sun.-Thurs., 11am-5am Fri.-Sat., $7-17). The legend says the secret is that Dyer's has been using the same grease (strained daily) since it opened in 1912. Only in Tennessee could century-old grease be a selling point. True or not, the burg- ers here are especially juicy. Dyer's also serves wings, hot dogs, milkshakes, and a full array of fried sides.

For coffee, pastries, and fruit smoothi- es, **Bluff City Coffee** (505 S. Main St., 901/405-4399, www.bluffcitycoffee.com, 6:30am-6pm Mon.-Sat., 8am-6pm Sun.) is your best bet in this part of the city. Located in the South Main district of gal- leries and condos, the shop is decorated with large prints of vintage Memphis photographs, and it is also a wireless Internet hot spot.

Uptown
Southern

The Little Tea Shop (69 Monroe Ave., 901/525-6000, 11am-2pm Mon.-Fri., $5-9) serves traditional plate lunches through the week. Choose from daily specials like fried catfish, chicken pot- pie, and meat loaf with your choice of vegetable and side dishes by ticking off boxes on the menu. Every meal (except sandwiches) comes with fresh, hot corn bread that might as well be the star of the show. This is stick-to-your-ribs Southern cooking at its best, so come hungry. If you have room, try the peach cobbler or pecan ball for dessert. The staff's wel- coming yet efficient style makes this per- fect for a quick lunch.

The **Blue Plate Café** (113 Court Sq. S., 901/523-2050, 8am-2pm daily, $4-10) serves hearty breakfasts, plate lunches, and traditional home-style cooking. Its newsprint menu imparts wisdom ("Rule of Life No. 1: Wake up. Show up. Pay at- tention.") and declares that every day should begin with a great breakfast. It's not hard to comply at the Blue Plate. Eggs come with homemade biscuits and gravy, plus your choice of grits, hash browns, or pancakes. For lunch, try a meat-and- three or vegetable plate, slow-cooked white-bean soup, or a grilled peanut but- ter and banana sandwich. Locals swear by the fried green tomatoes. There is an- other location in an old house in mid- town (5469 Poplar Ave., 901/761-9696, 6am-2pm Mon.-Sat., 7am-2pm Sun.).

Alcenia's (317 N. Main St., 901/523- 0200, www.alcenias.com, 11am-5pm Tues.-Fri., 9am-3pm Sat., $9-12), located in the Pinch District, is among Memphis's best Southern-style restaurants. Known for its plate lunches, fried chicken, and pastries, Alcenia's has a style unlike any other Memphis eatery, witnessed in its offbeat decor of '60s-style beads, folk art, and wedding lace. Proprietor B. J. Chester-Tamayo is all love, and she pours her devotion into some of the city's best soul food. Try the spicy cabbage and deep-fried chicken, or the salmon croquette, and save room for Alcenia's famous bread pudding for dessert. Chicken and waffles is the Saturday morning specialty.

Midtown
Barbecue
★ **Central BBQ** (2249 Central Ave., 901/272-9377, http://cbqmemphis.com, 11am-9pm daily, $5-25) appeals to both those who love dry rub and those who want their sauces. Can't decide between the pulled pork, the brisket, and other local favorites? Easy solution: Get the combo platter. Central has several locations around town; they are, of course, centrally located, friendly, and clean.

Southern
Just follow the crowds to the **Cupboard Restaurant** (1400 Union Ave., 901/276-8015, http://thecupboardrestaurant.com, 7am-8pm daily, $6-12), one of Memphians' favorite stops for plate lunches. The Cupboard moved from its downtown location to an old Shoney's about a mile outside of town to accommodate the throngs who stop here for authentic home-style cooking. The Cupboard gets only the freshest vegetables for its dishes. The meat specials change daily but include things like fried chicken, chicken and dumplings, hamburger steak with onions, and beef tips with noodles. The corn bread "coins" are exceptionally buttery. For dessert, try the lemon icebox pie.

The Women's Exchange Tea Room (88 Racine St., 901/327-5681, www.

womans-exchange.com, 10am-4pm Mon.-Fri., 10am-2pm Sat., $8-15) feels like a throwback to an earlier era. Located one block east of the Poplar Street viaduct, the Women's Exchange has been serving lunch since 1936, and the menu has not changed much over the years. The special changes daily and always includes a choice of two entrées or a four-vegetable plate. Classics like chicken salad, salmon loaf, beef tenderloin, and seafood gumbo are favorites, and all lunches come with a drink and dessert. The dining room looks out onto a green garden, and the atmosphere is homey—not stuffy. The Exchange also sells gifts, housewares, and other knickknacks.

In the Cooper-Young neighborhood, **Soul Fish** (862 S. Cooper St., 901/725-0722, http://soulfishcafe.com, 11am-10pm Mon.-Sat., 11am-9pm Sun., $9-16) offers traditional plate lunches, vegetable plates, and several varieties of catfish. You can get the fish breaded and fried or blackened with a potent spice mix. Soul Fish is owned in part by Tiger Bryant, owner of the venerable Young Avenue Deli, and it has the hallmarks of a well-conceived eatery. The atmosphere is open and cheerful, with a few touches of subtle sophistication. In this case, the main attraction is good food at a good price—a combination that can be hard to find elsewhere in Cooper-Young. Soul Fish also has locations in east Memphis and Germantown.

Contemporary
Memphis restaurateur Karen Blockman Carrier's **Mollie Fontaine Lounge** (679 Adams Ave., 901/524-1886, http://molliefontainelounge.com, 5pm-late Wed.-Sat., $8-11) is an old-fashioned club where guests order upscale cocktails, relax with live music, and eat tasty Mediterranean-and Middle Eastern-inspired tapas. The restaurant has an upmarket but cozy atmosphere, with equal measures of funky and fine. The live piano jazz is the perfect

backdrop for the restaurant's artistic small plates.

Surprisingly good for a bookstore café, **The Booksellers Bistro** (387 Perkins Ext., 901/374-0881, http://thebooksellersatlaurelwood.com, 8am-9pm Mon.-Thurs., 8am-10pm Fri.-Sat., 9am-8pm Sun., $10-17) offers salads, soups, and sandwiches, as well as daily meat and fish specials. The soup-and-sandwich combo is filling and good. Breakfast may well be the best meal on offer, however. The morning menu features specials designed by celebrity chefs, including omelets, baked goods, and crepes.

One of Memphis's most distinctive restaurant settings is an old beauty shop in the Cooper-Young neighborhood. ★ **The Beauty Shop** (966 S. Cooper St., 901/272-7111, http://thebeautyshoprestaurant.com, 11am-2pm Mon.-Sat. and 5pm-10pm Mon.-Thurs., 5pm-11pm Fri.-Sat., 10am-3pm Sun., $23-27) takes advantage of the vintage beauty parlor decor to create a great talking point for patrons and food writers alike. The domed hair dryers remain, and the restaurant has put the shampooing sinks to work as beer coolers. At lunch, the Beauty Shop offers a casual menu of sandwiches and salads. For dinner, the imaginative cuisine of Memphis restaurateur Karen Blockman Carrier, who also owns Mollie Fontaine Lounge and Automatic Slim's Tonga Club, takes over.

If you enjoy your beer as much as or more than your meal, then head straight for **Boscos Squared** (2120 Madison Ave., 901/432-2222, www.boscosbeer.com, 11am-2am Mon.-Thurs., 11am-3am Fri.-Sat., 10:30am-2am Sun., $11-24). Boscos is a brewpub with fresh seafood, steak, and pizza. Its beer menu is among the best in the city, and many of the brews are made on the premises.

Bounty on Broad (2519 Broad Ave., 901/410 8131, http://bountyonbroad.com, 5pm-9:30pm Tues.-Thurs., 5pm-10pm Fri. 11am-2pm and 5-10pm Sat., 11am-2pm. Sun., $12-32) serves family-style dishes with a farm-to-table slant. Cash is not accepted, just credit cards.

One of chef Kelly English's restaurants, the French Creole **Restaurant Iris** (2146 Monroe Ave., 901/590-2828, http://restaurantiris.com, 5pm-10pm Mon.-Sat., last seating 9:30pm, $30-39) is one of Memphis's favorites. Located in a former home in Overton Square, the restaurant's dishes change frequently. A typical dinner menu might include surf and turf with New York strip steak stuffed with blue cheese and fried oysters and shrimp and grits with andouille sausage.

As the name suggests, **The Farmer** (3092 Poplar Ave., 901/324-2221, http://thefarmermemphis.com, 11am-2:30pm Sun.-Mon., 11am-2:30pm and 5:30pm-9pm Tues.-Sat., $16-27) offers farm-to-table dishes with southern flair. The menu changes regularly, depending on what's in season. On a nice night, reserve a spot on the little shrub-lined patio with umbrellas.

A modern restaurant in a former gas station, **Fuel Café** (1761 Madison Ave., 901/725 9025, http://fuelcafememphis.com, 11am-9pm Tues.-Sat., $7-21) specializes in grass-fed meats but also offers lots of vegan and vegetarian options, like the vegetarian Salisbury steak TV dinner, made with organic ingredients. Can't make it in? Try their food truck, which you can find on Twitter (@ FuelFoodTruck).

International

The **India Palace** (1720 Poplar Ave., 901/278-1199, 11am-2:30pm and 5pm-9:30pm Mon.-Thurs., 11am-2:30pm and 5pm-10pm Fri., 11am-3pm and 5pm-10pm Sat.-Sun., $9-17) is a regular winner in readers' choice polls for Indian food in Memphis. The lunchtime buffet is filling and economical, and the dinner menu features vegetarian, chicken, and seafood dishes. The dinner platters are generous and tasty.

Pho Binh (1615 Madison Ave., 901/276-0006, 11am-9pm Mon.-Fri., noon-9pm

Sat., $4-9) is one of the most popular Vietnamese restaurants in town. You can't beat the value of the lunch buffet, but you can order from the dizzying array of Chinese and Vietnamese dishes, including spring rolls, vermicelli noodle bowls, rice, and meat dishes. There are lots of vegetarian options.

The atmosphere at **Bhan Thai** (1324 Peabody Ave., 901/272-1538, www.bhan-thairestaurant.com, 5pm-9:30pm Sun.-Mon., 11am-2:30pm and 5pm-9:30pm Tues.-Thurs., 5pm-10:30pm Fri.-Sat., $14-25) in midtown is almost as appealing as its excellent Thai food. Set in an elegant 1912 home, Bhan Thai makes the most of the house's space, and seating is spread throughout several colorful rooms and on the back patio. Choose from dishes like red snapper, masaman curry, and roasted duck curry. The Bhan Thai salad is popular, with creamy peanut dressing and crisp vegetables.

It's the regulars who are happy at the **Happy Mexican Restaurant and Cantina** (385 S. 2nd St., 901/529-9991, www.happymexican.com, 11am-10pm Sun.-Thurs., 11am-11pm Fri.-Sat., $7-15). Serving generous portions of homemade Mexican food for lunch and dinner, Happy Mexican is destined to become a downtown favorite. The service is efficient and friendly, and the decor is cheerful but not over the top. It's just a few blocks south of the National Civil Rights Museum. There are two other locations in the greater Memphis area.

Ecco on Overton Park (1585 Overton Park, 901/410-8200, www.eccoonovertonpark.com, 11am-2pm and 5:30pm-9pm Tues.-Thurs., 11am-2pm and 5:30pm-9:30pm Fri., 10am-2pm and 5:30pm-9:30pm Sat., $12-28) channels all the comforts of a European café, with dishes such as cioppino pasta puttanesca and coq au vin. Drink as the Italians do with an Aperol spritz or sip a bit of Spain with a bottle of rosé from Rioja.

Robata Ramen & Yakitori Bar (2116 Madison Ave., 901/410-8290, http://robatamemphis.com, 11am-2pm and 5pm-midnight Mon.-Fri., 11pm-midnight Sat., 11am-9pm Sun., $7-15) is equal parts fun and affordable, with an array of yakitori (bite-size meats and veggies that are skewered, then grilled) sold by the piece and a create-your-own ramen menu.

Raw Girls Memphis (http://raw-girls-memphis.myshopify.com) runs two food trucks that dole out cold-pressed juices, snacks, soups, salads, and sandwiches. The eats are as clean as it gets—free of gluten, dairy, and refined sugar, a boon for those navigating food allergies or sensitivities—featuring organic, locally grown produce to boot. Look for the trucks parked in midtown (242 S. Cooper St., 10am-6pm Wed.-Sun., $7-9) and East Memphis (5502 Poplar Ave., 10am-6pm Wed.-Sun.).

Cafés and Diners
Few restaurants have a larger or more loyal following in midtown than **Young Avenue Deli** (2119 Young Ave., 901/278-0034, www.youngavenuedeli.com, 11am-3am daily, $4-8), which serves a dozen different specialty sandwiches, grill fare, including burgers and chicken sandwiches, plus salads and sides. The Bren—smoked turkey, mushrooms, onions, and cream cheese in a steamed pita—is a deli favorite. The food is certainly good, but it's the atmosphere at this homey yet hip institution that really pulls in the crowds. There is live music most weekends, and the bar serves a kaleidoscope of domestic and imported beer, including lots of hard-to-find microbrews. The deli serves lunch and dinner daily.

For a good cup of coffee in the Cooper-Young neighborhood, head to **Java Cabana** (2170 Young Ave., 901/272-7210, www.javacabanacoffeehouse.com, 9am-10pm Tues.-Thurs., 10am-11pm Fri.-Sat., noon-9pm Sun., $4-7). Java Cabana serves fair-trade coffee and light breakfast fare, including pancakes and omelets, all day. For lunch or later, you can order simple sandwiches or munchies like apple slices and peanut butter or potato chips.

Coffee shop and general store **City & State** (2625 Broad Ave., 901/249-2406, http://cityandstate.us, 7am-6pm Mon.-Fri., 8am-6pm Sat., 8am-2pm Sun.) peddles tea, coffee, pastries, and sandwiches alongside locally made goods for retail sale, right in the heart of the Broad Avenue Arts District. They take credit cards only.

Restaurant Iris chef Kelly English also runs a more casual restaurant, **The Second Line** (2144 Monroe Ave., 901/590-2829, www.secondlinememphis.com, 11am-10pm Sun.-Thurs., 11am-11pm Fri., 11am-11pm Sat., $15-18), right next door. The kitchen rolls out New Orleans-inspired classics such as fried oyster po'boys and barbecue shrimp alongside global wild cards, like roasted beet and feta shawarma or roasted pork enchiladas.

South Memphis
Barbecue
Jim Neely's **Interstate Bar-B-Que** (2265 S. 3rd St., 901/775-2304, http://interstate-barbecue.com, 11am-11pm Mon.-Thurs., 11am-midnight Fri.-Sat., 11am-7pm Sun., $5-23) was once ranked the second-best barbecue in the nation, but the proprietors have not let it go to their heads; this is still a down-to-earth, no-frills eatery. Large appetites can order a whole slab of pork or beef ribs, but most people will be satisfied with a chopped pork sandwich, which comes topped with coleslaw and smothered with barbecue sauce. Families can get the fixings for 6, 8, or 10 sandwiches sent out family style. For an adventure, try the barbecue spaghetti or barbecue bologna sandwich. If you're in a hurry, Interstate has a drive-up window, too, and if you are really smitten, you can order pork, sauce, and seasoning in bulk to be frozen and shipped to your home.

Southern
Gay Hawk Restaurant (685 S. Danny Thomas Blvd., 901/947-1464, 11am-3pm Mon.-Fri., 11am-5pm Sun., $6-10) serves country-style food that sticks to your ribs and warms your soul. Chef Lewis Bobo declares that his specialty is "home-cooked food," and it really is as simple as that. The best thing about Gay Hawk is the luncheon buffet, which lets newcomers to Southern cooking survey the choices and try a little bit of everything. The Sunday lunch buffet practically sags with specialties like fried chicken, grilled fish, macaroni and cheese, greens, and much, much more. Save room for peach cobbler.

East Memphis
Contemporary
To many minds, Memphis dining gets no better than **Erling Jensen, The Restaurant** (1044 S. Yates Rd., 901/763-3700, www.ejensen.com, 5pm-10pm daily, $33-48). Danish-born Erling Jensen is the mastermind of this fine-dining restaurant that has consistently earned marks as Memphians' favorite restaurant. Understated decor and friendly service are the backdrop to Jensen's dishes, which are works of art. The menu changes with the seasons and is based upon availability, but usually it includes about six different seafood dishes and as many meat and game choices. Black Angus beef, elk loin, and buffalo tenderloin are some of the favorites. Meals at Jensen's restaurant should begin with an appetizer, salad, or soup—or all three. The jumbo lump crab cakes with smoked red-pepper sauce are excellent. Reservations are a good idea at Erling Jensen, and so are jackets for men. Expect to spend upwards of $80 per person for a four-course meal; $60 for two courses. Add more for wine.

Memphis's premier steak house is **Folk's Folly** (551 S. Mendenhall Rd., 901/762-8200, www.folksfolly.com, 5:30pm-10pm Mon.-Sat., 5:30pm-9pm Sun., $30-70), just east of Audubon Park.

Brews in Bluff City

Memphians love their beer. There's never been a shortage of places to pop a cold one. Now the number of places that make beer in the city is increasing. Check out a few of these local microbreweries.

* The **Memphis Made Brewing Co.** (768 S. Cooper St., 901/207-5343, http://memphismadebrewing.com, 4pm-10pm Fri., 1pm-10pm Sat., 1pm-7pm Sun.) has some serious beer cred. Head brewer/co-founder Drew Barton was former head brewer at French Broad Brewery in North Carolina. Co-founder Andy Ashby also helped launch the Cooper-Young Beerfest. The brewery puts out three year-round brews plus a handful of seasonals. Try them in the taproom. There's no food on the menu, but local food trucks often stop by.

Wiseacre Brewing Co.

* Take a tour of **High Cotton Brewing Co.** (598 Monroe Ave., 901/543-4444, http://highcottonbrewing.com, 4pm-8pm Thurs.-Fri., 2pm-10pm Sat., 1pm-6pm Sun.) on Saturday at 3pm. The cost is $12 and includes a pint glass and samples. Or come by for a drink and live music throughout the week.

* Tours and brews that have been given nods from national magazines like *Men's Journal* are available at **Wiseacre Brewing Co.** (2783 Broad Ave., 901/888-7000, http://wiseacre-brew.com, 4pm-8pm Mon.-Thurs., 1pm-10pm Fri.-Sat.). The brewery was founded by brothers Kellan and Davin Bartosch, after the name their grandmother used to call them.

Diners flock here for prime aged steaks and seafood favorites. For small appetites, try the 8-ounce filet mignon for $36; large appetites can gorge on the 28-ounce porterhouse for $69. Seafood includes lobster, crab legs, and wild salmon. The atmosphere is classic steak house: The lighting is low, and there's a piano bar on the property.

Some say **Acre Restaurant** (690 S. Perkins Rd., 901/818-2273, www.acre-memphis.com, 11am-1pm and 5pm-9pm Mon., 11am-1pm and 5pm-10pm Tues.-Fri., 5pm-10pm Sat., $22-35) is Memphis's best. Certainly, it has one of the best wine lists in town. The menu combines Southern and Asian traditions with locally grown and raised ingredients in a modern setting.

International
Andrew Michael Italian Kitchen (712 W. Brookhaven Circle, 901/347-3569, http://andrewmichaelitaliankitchen.com, 5pm-10pm Tues.-Sat., $12-30) is home to chefs Andrew Ticer and Michael Hudman—who were honored as finalists in the Best Chef: Southeast category for the 2015 James Beard Foundation Awards. They learned the nuances of Italian cooking from their grandmothers as well as travels throughout Italy. Ticer and Hudman also own Porcellino's Craft Butcher across the street.

Cafés and Diners
Porcellino's Craft Butcher (711 W. Brookhaven Circle, 901/762-6656, http://porcellinoscraftbutcher.com, 7am-9pm

Tues.-Sat., $10-28) is first and foremost a butcher shop selling cuts from local farms. It also doubles as a coffee shop in the morning and a sandwich shop come lunchtime, serving meaty options such as banh mi with twice-cooked pork belly or saucy meatballs on sourdough baguette. When the sun sets, the space morphs into a cocktail bar serving small plates and heartier entrees centered around fresh cuts from the butcher case.

Accommodations

There are thousands of cookie-cutter hotel rooms in Memphis, but travelers would be wise to look past major chains. If you can afford it, choose to stay in downtown Memphis. With the city at your doorstep, you'll have a better experience both day and night. Downtown is also where you'll find the most distinctive accommodations, including fine luxury hotels, charming inns, and an antebellum guest home.

Budget travelers have their pick of major chain hotels; the farther from the city center, the cheaper the room. Beware of very good deals, however, since you may find yourself in sketchy neighborhoods. There is a campground with tent and RV sites within a 15-minute drive of downtown at T. O. Fuller State Park.

Downtown
$150-200
The ★ **Talbot Heirs Guesthouse** (99 S. 2nd St., 901/527-9772, www.talbotheirs. com, $130-275), in the heart of downtown, offers a winning balance of comfort and sophistication. Each of the inn's eight rooms has its own unique decor—from cheerful red walls to black-and-white chic. All rooms are thoughtfully outfitted with a full kitchen and modern bathroom, television, radio and CD player, sitting area, desk, and high-speed Internet. Little extras, like the refrigerator stocked for breakfast, go a long way,

as does the cheerful yet efficient welcome provided by proprietors Tom and Sandy Franck. Book early since the Talbot Heirs is often full, especially during peak summer months.

Over $200
In 2007, Memphis welcomed the **Westin Memphis Beale Street** (170 George W. Lee Ave., 901/334-5900, www.westin-memphisbealestreet.com, $185-369), across the street from FedEx Forum and one block from Beale Street. The hotel's 203 guest rooms are plush and modern, each with a work desk, high-speed Internet, MP3-player docking station, and super-comfortable beds. The location can be noisy when Beale Street is in full swing. Expect to pay $19 a day for parking ($27 for valet).

The **Hampton Inn & Suites** (175 Peabody Pl., 901/260-4000, www.bealestreetsuites.hamptoninn.com, $165-320) is less than a block from Beale Street. The Hampton Inn has 144 standard rooms with high-speed Internet and standard hotel accommodations. The 30 suites ($250) have kitchenettes and separate living quarters. The entire hotel is nonsmoking. Add $19 per day for parking.

Uptown
$100-150
The most affordable downtown accommodations are in chain hotels. One of the best choices is the **Sleep Inn at Court Square** (40 N. Front St., 901/522-9700, www.choicehotels.com, $107-299), with 124 simple but clean and well-maintained rooms. Guests have access to a small fitness room, free parking, and a free continental breakfast. For those with a bigger appetite, the excellent Blue Plate Café is just across the square. It's a five-block walk to Beale Street from Court Square, but the trolley runs right past the front door of the hotel. Parking will run you $12 each day.

Even closer to the action is the 71-room **Comfort Inn Downtown** (100 N.

Front St., 901/526-0583, www.comfortinndowntownmemphis.com, $137-184). This hotel is within easy walking distance of all the city-center attractions. Rooms aren't anything special, but the staff is often quite friendly; guests get free breakfast, Internet access, and indoor parking; and there's an outdoor pool. Ask for a room facing west, and you'll have a nice view of the Mississippi River. Parking is $10 a day.

$150-200

Near AutoZone Park and a lot of restaurants is **Doubletree Downtown Memphis** (185 Union Ave., 901/528-1800, www.doubletree.hilton.com, $134-299). A 272-room hotel set in the restored Tennessee Hotel, the Doubletree maintains a touch of the old grandeur of the 1929 hotel from which it was crafted. Rooms are large, and it has an outdoor swimming pool and a fitness room. Valet parking is $25 or more per night.

If you want to be in the middle of things but can't afford to stay at the swanky Peabody, consider the **Holiday Inn Memphis-Downtown** (160 Union Ave., 901/525-5491, www.hisdowntownmemphis.com, $119-199). Located across the street from the Peabody and near AutoZone Park, this Holiday Inn routinely gets good reviews from travelers.

Over $200

★ **The Peabody Memphis** (149 Union Ave., 901/529-4000, www.peabodymemphis.com, $300-410) is the city's signature hotel. Founded in 1869, the Peabody was the grand hotel of the South, and the hotel has preserved some of its traditional Southern charm. Tuxedoed bellhops greet you at the door, and all guests receive a complimentary shoeshine. Rooms are nicely appointed with plantation-style furniture, free wireless Internet, and in-room safes, as well as all the amenities typical of an upper-tier hotel. Several fine restaurants are on the ground floor, including the lobby bar, which is the gathering place for the twice-daily red carpet march of the famous Peabody ducks.

A 28-room boutique hotel on Mud Island, the **River Inn of Harbor Town** (50 Harbor Town Sq., 901/260-3333, www.riverinnmemphis.com, $257-645) offers great river views and a unique location that is just minutes from downtown. Set in the mixed residential and commercial New Urban community of Harbor Town, the River Inn provides guests with super amenities like a fitness center, reading rooms, free wireless Internet, free parking, modern decor and furniture, two restaurants, a 1.5-mile walking trail, and spa. Even the most modest rooms have luxurious extras like 32-inch flat-screen televisions, port and chocolate truffle turndown service, and full gourmet breakfast at Paulette's, one of three restaurants on the property. The River Inn offers the best of both worlds—a relaxing and quiet getaway that is uniquely convenient to the center of Memphis.

The decor at the **Madison Hotel** (79 Madison Ave., 901/333-1200, www.madisonhotelmemphis.com, $340-400) is modern, with a touch of art deco. Guests enjoy perks from valet parking to room service to live music and a hip, welcoming vibe. The daily continental breakfast and afternoon happy hour are opportunities to enjoy the view from the top floor and rooftop deck of the old bank building that now houses the hotel. The 110 rooms are small but well appointed, with wet bars, Internet access, and luxurious bathrooms.

It is hard to describe the **Big Cypress Lodge** (1 Bass Pro Dr., 800/225-6343, http://big-cypress.com, $305-329) without making it sound a little crazy. First of all, this 103-room hotel is inside a giant pyramid that houses a Bass Pro Shop retail store. Opulent rooms are designed to look like treehouses and duck-hunting cabins. Rooms overlook the cypress swamp filled with alligators and fish and the retail shopping of the Bass Pro Shop.

But for all its quirkiness, this hotel, which opened in 2015, is a luxury resort, with all the associated amenities, including a spa and a bowling alley. Expect to pay a $20 resort fee plus $20 per day for parking.

Midtown

Midtown hotels are cheaper than those in downtown. By car or trolley line, they are convenient to city-center attractions as well as those in midtown itself.

Under $100

There are a few budget hotels within trolley distance of downtown. The **Quality Inn** (42 S. Camilla St., 901/526-1050, http://choicehotels.com, from $73) is about two blocks from the Madison Avenue trolley and has an unremarkable but free breakfast. The **Motel 6** (210 S. Pauline St., 901/528-0650, www.motel6. com, $50-72) is about three blocks from the trolley. These choices are certainly not ritzy, but they're acceptable and welcome a large number of budget travelers.

$100-150

The **Best Western Gen X Inn** (1177 Madison Ave., 901/692-9136, www.best-western.com, $92-200) straddles downtown and midtown Memphis. It's about two miles from the city center along the Madison Avenue trolley line, so Gen Xers can get downtown on the trolley in about 15 minutes, with a little luck. The hotel, which has free parking and breakfast, is also accessible to the city's expansive medical center and the attractions around Overton Park. These rooms are standard hotel style, enhanced with bright colors, flat-panel plasma TVs, and a general aura of youthfulness. The whole hotel is nonsmoking, and guests enjoy a good continental breakfast and a special partnership with the downtown YMCA for gym use. This is a good choice for travelers who want to be near downtown but are on a budget, particularly those with a car. No pets are permitted.

$150-200

The **Holiday Inn-University of Memphis** (3700 Central Ave., 901/678-8200, www. holidayinn.com/memphis, $115-165) is part of the university's hospitality school. All rooms are suites, with a wet bar and microwave, sitting room, and spacious bathrooms. The lobby contains an exhibit on Kemmons Wilson, the Memphis-born founder of Holiday Inn, who is credited with inventing the modern hotel industry. It is about six miles from downtown Memphis.

Over $200

The five rooms available in **The James Lee House** (690 Adams Ave., http://james-leehouse.com, 901/359-6750, $245-450) may be in one of the most opulent homes you've had the pleasure to stay in. The building may have been built in the 19th century, but the inn's amenities, such as wireless Internet and private gated parking, are 21st century.

South Memphis

There are two reasons to stay in south Memphis: the airport and Graceland. But even if you are keenly interested in either of these places, you should think twice about staying in this part of town. You will need a car, as some of these neighborhoods are seedy and south Memphis is not within walking distance of anything of interest.

Under $100

If you need to be close to the airport, the **Holiday Inn Memphis Airport Hotel & Conference Center** (2240 Democrat Rd., 901/332-1130, www.ihg.com, $68-160), which caters to business travelers, gets points for location, if not much else. There is a guest laundry, free airport shuttle, room service, a business center, and a decent fitness room.

The **Days Inn at Graceland** (3839 Elvis Presley Blvd., 901/346-5500, www.wyn-dhamhotels.com, from $72) is one of the most well-worn properties in the venerable Days Inn chain. The hotel has amped up the Elvis kitsch; you can tune into free nonstop Elvis movies or swim in a guitar-shaped pool. There is a free continental breakfast. Book early for Elvis Week.

The **Magnuson Grand Memphis Hotel** (1471 E. Brooks Rd., 901/332-3500, www. magnusonhotels.com, $34-125) is a tidy, safe oasis in an otherwise unappealing part of town. Before its remodel, being close to Graceland and the airport were the only draws of this budget hotel. It remains affordable, but now it has the added perk of being clean, with updated rooms and bathrooms, plus a restaurant and bar. Amenities include a decent outdoor pool, a small fitness room, and a upgraded lobby. Book early for Elvis Week.

$150-200
Opened in 2016, ★ **The Guest House at Graceland** (3600 Elvis Presley Blvd., 901/443-3000, http://guesthousegraceland.com, from $199) is a 430-room Elvis themed resort, not a mere hotel. The property has 20 themed suites, the designs of which were supervised by Priscilla Presley herself, and which evoke the feel of Graceland itself. In addition, the luxury hotel has two full-service restaurants (Delta's Kitchen, EP's Bar & Grill) and a grab-and-go café (Shake Rattle & Go) plus an outdoor pool and a 464-seat theater for performances and films. The decor is sleek and contemporary, but you still get plenty of Elvis kitsch. Pets weighing less than 35 pounds are welcome with an additional $35 daily fee.

Camping
You can pitch your tent or park your RV just a 15-minute drive from downtown Memphis at **T. O. Fuller State Park** (1500 Mitchell Rd., 901/543-7581, http://tn-stateparks.itinio.com, $20-24). The park has 45 tent and RV sites, each with a picnic table, fire ring, grill, lantern hanger, and electrical and water hookups.

The Guest House at Graceland

On the north side of Memphis, **Meeman-Shelby Forest State Park** (910 Riddick Rd., Millington, 901/876-5215, http://tnstateparks.com, $24-105) is a half-hour drive from downtown. Stay in one of six lakeside cabins, which you can reserve up to one year in advance; book at least one month in advance to avoid being shut out. The two-bedroom cabins can sleep up to six people. Rates are $90-105 per night, depending on the season and day of the week. There are also 49 tent/RV sites ($24) with electrical and water hookups, picnic tables, grills, and fire rings. The bathhouse has hot showers.

Information and Services
Visitors Centers
The city's visitors center is the **Tennessee Welcome Center** (119 Riverside Dr., 901/543-6757, www.tnvacation.com/welcome-centers, 7am-11pm daily), located on the Tennessee side of the I-40 bridge. The center has lots of brochures and free maps and staff who can answer

your questions. The center assists more than 350,000 travelers annually.

Emergency Services
Dial 911 in an emergency for fire, ambulance, or police. The downtown police department is the **South Main Station** (545 S. Main St., 901/636-4099). Police patrol downtown by car, on bike, and on foot.

Hospitals
Memphis is chockablock with hospitals. Midtown Memphis is also referred to as Medical Center for the number of hospitals and medical facilities there. Here you will find the **Regional One Health** (877 Jefferson Ave., 901/545-7100, www.regionalonehealth.org), a 325-bed teaching hospital affiliated with the University of Tennessee; and the **Methodist University Hospital** (1265 Union Ave., 901/516-7000, www.methodisthealth.org), the 617-bed flagship hospital for Methodist Healthcare.

In east Memphis, **Baptist Memorial Hospital** (6019 Walnut Grove Rd., 901/226-5000, www.baptistonline.org/memphis) is the cornerstone of the huge Baptist Memorial Health Care System, with 771 beds.

Mississippi Blues Trail

There are nearly 200 sites included as part of the **Mississippi Blues Trail** (http://msbluestrail.org). Visiting all of them is a considerable undertaking, but diehard blues fans will want to make the pilgrimage. The must-see stops covered in this guide delve into the history and influence of blues greats like Muddy Waters and B. B. King. However, there are many more, some mere markers or plaques about artists from the town or what happened on that spot—even blues fans might want to skip some. If you're only casually acquainted with the blues, it's likely that this side trip isn't for you. But embarking on this trip may convert you!

This section covers **140 miles** of the Blues Trail, heading as far south as Leland, Mississippi. Driving from Memphis through to Leland will take just over three hours, not including time for sightseeing and meals, so you'll want to devote at least one day to driving this route. Consider an overnight stay in Leland before you turn back to Memphis. It's also possible to drive east along US 82 after visiting Indianola (the penultimate stop of this section of the Blues Trail) to cut back over to the Trace. This 100-mile, 1.5-hour drive will get you back onto the parkway at about milepost 204.

On this drive you'll visit Tunica, Friar's Point, Clarksdale, Indianola, and Leland. Make sure your car has good speakers and your phone is charged up, because you'll be in the mood to listen to a lot of music.

Tunica
Getting There
Tunica is 30 miles southwest of downtown Memphis. It's a 40-minute drive down US 61 to get there.

Gateway to the Blues Museum
Tunica is best known as a gateway to casinos, just over the state line from Memphis. But the **Gateway to the Blues Museum** (13625 US 61 N., 888/488-6422, www.tunicatravel.com, 8:30am-5pm Mon.-Fri., 10am-5pm Sat., 1pm-5pm Sun., adults $10, children 12 and under $5) shows Tunica is more than a place for slot machines. This 3,500-square-foot museum has six different galleries, where you can learn about the history of the blues and how the geography contributed to the genre. There's even an exhibition where you can record your own blues song (which will be emailed to you).

Housed in an old railroad station, the museum is connected to the **Tunica Visitors Center,** where you can get free information about the area and browse the gift shop.

Friars Point

Music is in the water here in tiny Friars Point. Country legend Conway Twitty (born Harold Lloyd Jenkins) was born here, and Robert Nighthawk, considered one of the foremost blues guitarists, lived here off and on for years, even working the town into song lyrics. Nighthawk's Blues Trail marker is right outside historic **Hirsberg Drug Store,** where many legendary musicians, including Robert Johnson, have played.

Getting There

Friars Point is about a 45-minute drive south of Tunica along US 61. After about 25 miles on US 61, turn right onto Friars Point Road. Continue for about 8 miles, turn right onto Sheriff Ridge Avenue, then turn left onto Washington Street after two blocks. Make a right onto 2nd Street to get to North Delta Museum.

North Delta Museum

Friars Point is home to the **North Delta Museum** (784 2nd St., 662/383-2233, 9am-2pm Mon.-Fri., adults $4, children under 7 $2), a small local heritage museum with lots of blues-related artifacts. The museum has been closed for renovation but is scheduled to reopen in 2017.

Clarksdale

At the intersection of Old US 49 and Old US 61, Clarksdale is often referred to as The Crossroads. Legend goes that bluesman Robert Johnson sold his soul to the devil at this crossroads in exchange for his musical talent. Today the intersection (Desoto Ave. and N. State St./MS-161) is marked by a crossroads sign with giant guitars. This Mississippi Delta town was also important to civil rights history. In 1958 Martin Luther King Jr. visited the town for the first major meeting of what would become the Southern Christian Leadership Conference (SCLC).

Getting There

Clarksdale is about a 20-minute drive from Friars Point. Take Friars Point Road south for about 13 miles to get into the heart of Clarksdale.

On your way into Clarksdale from Friars Point, you can take a short detour and drive by the former site of **Muddy Waters's Cabin at Stovall Farms** (4146 Oakhurst Stovall Rd., 662/624-2153), where the legend was born. The sign is just past the entrance to the farm. From Friars Point, take Friars Point Road south for about three miles to MS-1 South. After about two miles, turn left onto Old River Road, which will soon turn into Oakhurst Stovall Road. Follow this for two miles to reach the cabin. Continue on Oakhurst Stovall Road for four miles to reach Clarksdale.

Delta Blues Museum

Created in 1979 and made a stand-alone museum in 1999, the **Delta Blues Museum** (1 Blues Alley Ln., 662/627-6820, www.deltabluesmuseum.org, 9am-5pm daily Mar.-Oct., 10am-5pm Mon.-Sat. Nov.-Feb., adults $10, children 6-12 $8, children under 6 free) is the state's oldest music museum. It's housed in an old train depot, originally built in 1918 for the Yazoo and Mississippi railroad lines, and has both permanent and changing exhibitions. Muddy Waters's cabin has been relocated here from its original site a few miles northwest.

Next door is the **Ground Zero Blues Club** (387 Delta Ave., 662/621-9009, www.groundzerobluesclub.com, 11am-2pm Mon.-Tues., 11am-11pm Wed.-Thurs., 11am-2am Fri.-Sat.), a restaurant and bar with live music in a juke joint atmosphere. It is partly owned by actor and Mississippi Delta advocate Morgan Freeman, and the menu includes barbecue, catfish, and tamales, a favorite dish in this region.

Rock & Blues Museum

Music memorabilia from 1920 to 1970 is on display at the **Rock & Blues Museum**

The Blues Highway

You may have come to the area for the Natchez Trace Parkway, but there's another famous roadway around these parts. US 61 is often called the Blues Highway, and some say it rivals Route 66 as the most famous road in American music history.

Tons of songs reference the route, Dozens of blues artists have recorded songs about Highway 61; Bob Dylan even named an album after it in 1965. But the first one was Roosevelt Sykes's "Highway 61 Blues," recorded back in 1932.

As is the case with Natchez Trace Parkway and the Old Trace, there's an original Old Highway 61 and the newer one that is part of the U.S. highway system. The old route (west of the new road) was winding and, in the state of Mississippi, largely unpaved. It was one long road from New Orleans to Grand Portage, Minnesota, near the Canadian border.

Honestly, much of this route today ain't much to look at. It's not particularly scenic. Like many highways, it goes through patches of desolation and clusters of commercial developments. But it is the fastest way to see many of the sights along the Blues Trail and to get a feel for the towns of the Mississippi Delta.

(113 E. 2nd St., 901/605-8662, www.blues-2rock.com, 10am-5pm Sat.-Sun., $5). This small museum is a good place to see (and hear) how blues music connects to other genres.

Festivals and Events

If you really want to get your feet tapping, consider coming to Clarksdale for the **Sunflower River Blues & Gospel Festival** (www.sunflowerfest.org) in August or the **Juke Joint Festival** (www.jukejoint-festival.com) in April. Hotel rooms are at a premium then, so plan ahead.

Accommodations

If you want to stay overnight in Clarksdale, do so at the historic ★ **Riverside Hotel** (615 Sunflower Ave., 662/624-9163, $70-110), where both Duke Ellington and Ike Turner lived. The rooms aren't fancy, but they're clean and there's Wi-Fi. If you want to stay somewhere more traditional, there are several chain hotels in town.

Cleveland

Thanks to Delta State University and a quaint, thriving downtown, Cleveland has sweet boutiques in which to shop and plenty of restaurants and bars, plus a handful of chain hotels.

Getting There

Cleveland is about 40 minutes south of Clarksdale. To get there, take US 278 West/US 61 South for about 33 miles to get into town.

★ Grammy Museum Mississippi

Opened in 2016, the **Grammy Museum Mississippi** (800 W. Sunflower Rd., 662/441-0100, www.grammymuseumms. org, 10am-5:30pm Mon.-Sat., noon-5:30pm Sun., adults $12, seniors and students $10, children $6) is the institution's first outside Los Angeles. This says a lot about how seriously the music establishment takes preserving the blues and educating people about the role the Mississippi Delta had in American music. In September 2016 it became the 192nd marker on the Mississippi Blues Trail.

This is a spectacular 28,000-square-foot facility. The building itself is designed to honor the architecture of the region, with a large front porch where people can hang out and listen to music, and building materials reflective of the types of materials used in the area, albeit on a much grander scale. The museum was purposefully located next to the campus of Delta State University, so that it can be an educational force was well as a tourism draw. The **Delta Center** for **Culture and Learning** (http://delta-centerdsu.com) is also nearby on campus and hosts educational programming.

The Grammy Museum has more than 12 different interactive exhibits, many designed for you to share with your fellow tourists. Plan to stay for several hours to listen to all the music, including in a 140-seat theater that often has concerts. The museum does an excellent job of linking the blues to other genres. There are exhibits where you can try to make your own music and poignant displays of artifacts from musicians from the region. It has a decent gift shop as well.

The Grammy Museum, by a function of its backers, is more professional than most of the other small, labor of love museums that dot US 61. To be sure, there's a homegrown quality in those other venues that is lost here. But the professionalism doesn't give way to slickness; the character of the Delta and its music has been preserved. The museum has the feel of an important American institution, albeit in an out-of-the-way place.

Food

Pull in to ★ **Airport Grocery** (3606 US 61, 662/843-4817, www.airportgrocery.net, 11am-10pm Mon.-Sat., 5pm-9pm Sun., $7). You'll find a friendly staff serving po'boys, barbecue, and burgers, plus fried and charcoal-grilled fish entrées, inside what was once a grocery store. Live blues music is played many nights.

Closer to downtown, **Hey Joe's** (118 E. Sunflower Rd., 662/843-5425, www.eatheyjoes.com, 11am-9pm Mon.-Sat., $7-9) serves gourmet burgers, wings, salads, and chili dogs in a casual but hipster environment. Don't miss the signature dessert: the Moon Man, a deep-fried moon pie. This is a casual, kid-friendly spot for lunch, or a place to grab a beer and hear live music at night. If neither of

Top to bottom: Grammy Museum Mississippi; sign at Airport Grocery; Jim Henson Boyhood Home Museum.

these appeal, stroll down Cotton Row and Sharpe Avenue, where you'll find several charming options.

Information and Services

Bolivar Medical Center (901 MS-8 E., 662/846-0061, www.bolivarmedical. com) is centrally located near downtown Cleveland.

Indianola
Getting There

Indianola is about 30 miles south of Cleveland. Take US 278/US 61 south for nearly 10 miles, then turn left onto MS-448 and follow it for 15 miles.

B. B. King Museum and Delta Interpretive Center

The impressive **B. B. King Museum and Delta Interpretive Center** (400 2nd St., 662/887-9539, http://bbkingmuseum. org, noon-5pm Sun.-Mon., 10am-5pm Tues.-Sat. Apr.-Oct., noon-5pm Sun., 10am-5pm Tues.-Sat. Nov.-Mar., adults $15, seniors $12, students and children 5-7 $10, children 5 or younger free) chronicles the legend's rise to fame. The galleries, located in an old cotton gin, cover the music of the Delta in the 1920s, Memphis in the 1950s, and beyond. There are high-tech recordings and videos, lots of artifacts, and a gift shop. The museum opened in 2008; when King died in 2015 he was buried here and a garden was planted in his honor. King was born in tiny Itta Bena, about 25 miles east of Indianola.

Leland

The Delta town of Leland is home to several quirky stops. US 61 runs right downtown; several of the city's sights are designed to highlight Leland's past: part hard-drinking music hub and part genteel Southern getaway. In the works is the **Leland Blues Project Murals** (www.highway61blues.com).

B. B. King Museum and Delta Interpretive Center

Getting There

Leland is 15 miles west of Indianola on US 82, a 20-minute drive.

Highway 61 Blues Museum

The old Montgomery Hotel in the heart of downtown is home to the **Highway 61 Blues Museum** (307 N. Broad St., 662/686-7646, www.highway61blues.com, 10am-5pm Mon.-Sat., $7). This is a labor of love, jam-packed with blues artifacts and info compiled by local enthusiasts. This particular museum has more visual art, including paintings and photography by Delta artists, than most music museums. If you call ahead, they'll do their best to have some musicians show up to play while you peruse, an experience no blues fan should miss. As is the case at many homespun museums, you should allow plenty of time to have conversations with the enthusiastic staff.

Jim Henson Boyhood Home Museum

When in Leland you must swing by the **Jim Henson Boyhood Home Museum** (415 SE Deer Creek Dr., 662/686-7383, www.birthplaceofthefrog.org, 10am-5pm Mon.-Thurs. late May-early Sept., 10am-4pm Mon.-Sat. early Sept.-late May, free, donations encouraged). Henson was born in the Delta, and his family donated many artifacts to this odd roadside museum chock-full of Muppets and memorabilia, such as a large Kermit the Frog sitting on a lily pad, straight out of *The Muppet Movie*. "The Rainbow Connection" plays on a loop. The gift shop is well-stocked, but tiny.

Mississippi Wildlife Heritage Museum

Opened in 2017, the **Mississippi Wildlife Heritage Museum** (302 N. Broad St., 662/686-7789, www.mswildlifeheritagemuseum.com, 10am-5pm Mon.-Fri., adults $10, seniors $7, free for kids 16 and under) displays artifacts relating to the region's agricultural past inside a renovated hardware store downtown.

Food and Accommodations

For dinner, head to downtown **Vince's** (207 Main St., 662/686-2112, 5:30pm-9pm Wed.-Thurs. and Sat.-Sun., 5:30pm-10pm Fri., $12-18), an Italian eatery with higher-end dishes, such as seared tuna with asparagus risotto, lamb chops, and barbecue oysters. Vince's is a local favorite for music.

If you want to explore longer, book a night at ★ **The Thompson House** (111. N. Deer Creek Dr. W., 662/820-7829, www.thompsonhousebb.com, $125-185), a 1902 Queen Anne home converted into a B&B and event center.

The Trace: Central Mississippi

Central Mississippi along the Natchez Trace is full of dense, intimate scenery, outdoor recreation opportunities, and rich history.

Holly Springs National Forest

University of Mississippi

Rowan Oak

BLACK BELT OVERLOOK

Owl Creek Mounds

Tombigbee

Bynum Mounds

Holly Springs National Forest

139 MI/ 224 KM

Tombigbee National Forest

Cypress Swamp Loop Trail

CYPRESS SWAMP LOOP TRAIL

Bienville National Forest

The Trace: Central Mississippi

© AVALON TRAVEL

Highlights

★ **University of Mississippi:** Explore the charms of Ole Miss (page 239).

★ **Rowan Oak:** Visit the family home that served as William Faulkner's creative inspiration (page 241).

★ **Owl Creek Mounds:** These unusually shaped Native American mounds are a sight to see (page 247).

★ **Bynum Mounds:** These six burial mounds are some of the Trace's most significant archaeological sites (page 249).

★ **Cypress Swamp Loop Trail:** This easy boardwalk trail meanders through water tupelos and bald cypress, offering four seasons of beauty (page 259).

Best Restaurants

★ **Canoodle by Oxford Canteen:** Oxford's best Asian eatery serves patrons through a window down a small alley (page 244).

★ **Bottletree Bakery:** At this popular diner-turned-bakery, order a delicious pastry for breakfast to start your morning right (page 244).

★ **City Grocery:** John Currence's restaurant put Oxford dining on the map (page 244).

★ **The Biscuit Shop:** Indulge in delicious biscuits of unusual varieties—but hurry, they sell out fast (page 253).

The parkway winds its way through the northern section of Tombigbee National Forest, so all you can see for miles is green.

Central Mississippi is also one of the places to clearly see the marks of former users of the Trace. Before Native Americans were forcibly removed from their land via the Trail of Tears, this region was the epicenter of the Chickasaw and Choctaw Nations; the former sites of their villages and lives are marked along this section. At times in its history the Trace has been called both the "Chickasaw Trail" and the "Path to Choctaw Nation." Several burial mounds further explore what life was like when the Chickasaw lived here.

There are opportunities to get out and experience these wilds, including one of the three campgrounds on the parkway, and fishing and water recreation options on Davis Lake.

Route Overview

This section of the drive covers the Natchez Trace Parkway from mileposts 261 to 122, with a number of opportunities to get off the parkway and explore.

Starting at Black Belt Overlook and ending at Cypress Swamp, the Central Mississippi section of the Trace covers a **139-mile** stretch of parkway, all within the state of Mississippi. This is a doable section for **one day,** allotting plenty of time for nature walks and hikes and to explore Owl Creek Mounds and French Camp at a leisurely pace.

Side trips are possible to Mississippi's leading college towns, both of which have their own charms. The drive to **Oxford** is 45 miles (40 minutes) each way, although it would be hard to take advantage of all Oxford has to offer without spending at least one night; two is better. The side trip to **Starkville** is about 20 miles (30 minutes) each way and could be done as a day trip, without an overnight stay.

Driving Considerations

This section of the parkway is well-maintained, and there are ample pullouts to allow for safe sightseeing. The speed limit is 50 mph.

Dense fog is occasionally an issue on fall and winter mornings. Drought in the summer of 2016 caused what the Park Service called "severe cracking and movement of the parkway motor road surface" in Mississippi. In some places the cracking has made the surface uneven. Cyclists and motorcyclists should use extra caution until the roads are fully patched up.

Fuel and Services

This section of the drive, both on the Trace and on the side trips to **Oxford** and **Starkville,** is composed of rural roads connecting metropolitan areas. While you are in the cities and smaller towns,

Best Accommodations

★ **The Z Bed & Breakfast:** This welcoming inn is a home-away-from-home in Oxford (page 246).

★ **Davis Lake Campground:** Commune with nature under the stars here (page 248).

★ **Hotel Chester:** Starkville's premier hotel has loads of history (page 253).

★ **Jeff Busby Campground:** It's one of just three places you can camp overnight on the parkway itself (page 254).

★ **French Camp B&B:** Learn about the Trace of yore at this hideaway (page 255).

you'll have access to gas, restaurants, bike repair, and other basic services. When you're on the scenic rural stretches, you likely won't have cell service. Depending on your carrier, you may not have cell service outside of Starkville and Oxford.

Tune your radio to 1610AM for recorded information about some of the specific sights and stops along the way.

Getting to the Starting Point
Car, Motorcycle, or Bicycle

As you leave Tupelo, you'll slide back onto the parkway and ride southbound on the Trace. This portion of the route starts about 10 miles outside of Tupelo.

From **Memphis,** it's about 120 miles (two hours) to reach Black Belt Overlook, the first major stop on this section of the route, via the most direct route, I-22. However, it's also possible to visit **Oxford** on your way to the parkway by taking I-55 south from Memphis, then US 278/MS-6 east. This 140-mile route will take about 2.5 hours, not including any time you choose to spend in Oxford.

To get to the beginning of this section of the drive from **Birmingham,** Alabama, it's a 150-mile, two-hour drive west along I-22. This route will take you directly into Tupelo. From there, head south on the Trace.

Budget Car Rental (2763 W. Jackson St., 662/840-3710, 8am-5pm Mon.-Fri., 8am-noon Sat., noon-5pm Sun.) is near the Tupelo Regional Airport. **Enterprise**

Car Rental (551 Daybrite Dr., 662/842-2237, 7:30am-6pm Mon.-Fri., 8am-1pm Sat.) is south of downtown Tupelo.

Air

This isn't the easiest section of the Trace to access by air, but if that's your preference, the **Memphis International Airport** (MEM, www.flymemphis.com) is a good choice. MEM is served by Delta, Southwest, United, and other major airlines, with a number of non-stop routes. The three-concourse airport offers free Wi-Fi and many local dining options.

Birmingham-Shuttlesworth International Airport (BHM, 5900 Messer Airport Hwy., www.flybirmingham.com) is served by Delta, Southwest, United, and American Airlines. The easy-to-navigate airport has free Wi-Fi.

Contour Airlines (http://contourairlines.com) offers small craft service to **Tupelo Regional Airport** (2763 W. Jackson St., 662/841-6570, www.flytupelo.com) from Nashville five times a day.

Train

Train travel to the Trace is a tough proposition; riding the rails isn't the most efficient way to get around this area. **Amtrak** operates out of **Memphis Central Station** (545 S. Main St., www.amtrak.com), a stop on the 900-mile City of New Orleans route, which runs from New Orleans to

Fuel Up

Nothing puts a damper on a road trip like noticing you are nearly out of gas when you are miles from a filling station. Here's a quick list of places to exit the parkway between Tupelo and Kosciusko so that you can refuel at the closest gas station. (Some stops may take you to small towns, others will be just a single service station.)

The National Park Service also posts a list of nearby supply stations at most Trace rest areas, although the list is not updated regularly.

- **Milepost 260:** Exit at MS-6/Main Street, the last exit before you leave Tupelo. Drive east one mile to a Marathon station or west one mile to an Exxon.

- **Milepost: 255.7:** Exit at Palmetto Road and drive 0.7 mile east to Palmetto Quick Stop in Verona.

- **Milepost 239:** Exit at MS-32 and drive east nine miles to a cluster of five or six gas stations. This route often has heavy truck traffic.

- **Milepost 219.6:** Exit at MS-46 and drive one mile west to Mantee.

- **Milepost 204.2:** Exit at US 82. Drive east one mile to the Shell station in Mathiston or two miles west to Fox Run Quick Stop.

- **Milepost 195.3:** Exit at MS-9 and drive six miles north to Ackerman.

- **Milepost 159.8:** Exit at MS-19, near the Kosciusko Information Center. Drive one block north to Parkway Pure.

- **Milepost 135.5:** Exit at MS-16 and drive 1.5 miles west to Canton.

Chicago. Central Station is conveniently located downtown, where most major rental car companies have offices.

Birmingham also has Amtrak service from New Orleans and Atlanta, operating out of a small station (19th St. N., www.amtrak.com).

Bus

Greyhound serves the Bluff City via the **Memphis Bus Station** (3033 Airways Blvd., www.greyhound.com). The station is adjacent to the Memphis International Airport and close to major car rental companies. The Greyhound routes to Memphis are through Birmingham, Dallas, Jackson, Nashville, and St. Louis.

The Greyhound bus from Memphis, Atlanta, and Birmingham stops in **Tupelo** at a supermarket (1074 N. Eason Blvd., 662/842-4557, 10am-5pm daily).

Budget-friendly **Megabus** (3921 American Way, http://us.megabus.com) serves both Memphis and Birmingham and boasts free Wi-Fi on board.

US 278 to Oxford

The city of Oxford is unlike anywhere else in the state of Mississippi. Founded in May 1837, it was built on land that had once belonged to the Chickasaw Nation. It was named after Oxford, England, aspiring to be a university town. By 1841 the Mississippi legislature indeed voted to make Oxford the home of the University of Mississippi, the state's first, and the city's fate as an intellectual hub was sealed. Today, Ole Miss, as it is called, is a major public university.

Life hasn't always been easy in Oxford. In 1864 the city was nearly destroyed when Union troops set fire to the town. It was rebuilt, and in 1962 conflict came again, when James Meredith entered the University of Mississippi as its first African American student, amid protests of more than 2,000 people.

Like many college towns, today Oxford is known for its rich intellectual and

A Day on the Trace: Central Mississippi

If you've only got one day in this region, start early so you'll be hungry by the time you arrive in Oxford. After the 40-minute drive to Oxford from the Trace, drive up to **Big Bad Breakfast** to caffeinate and feast on a large Southern breakfast, then head over to **Rowan Oak** for a tour of William Faulkner's home.

Leave the car parked and wander through Wood Trail to the **University of Mississippi** campus. Take in a few important sights, such as the **Lyceum,** where civil rights history was made. Walk back to the car and head to **The Square** for a quick lunch from **Canoodle by Oxford Canteen.** Then you'll have time to browse the many shops there. Don't miss **Square Books,** which is a lively space. Swing by **Bottletree Bakery** for some pastries for the car ride, and then drive the 40 minutes back to the parkway. You will have driven about 110 miles total in the first part of your day.

Check out some important parkway sights along the way, including **Owl Creek Mounds** and **Bynum Mounds.**

Stretch your legs at **Cypress Swamp** and then continue into southern Mississippi (see page 261) and head to Ridgeland, near milepost 100, to spend the night. If that 150 miles on the Trace is too much driving after Oxford, pick a B&B in **Kosciusko** (near milepost 160) to crash in for the night.

cultural life, having been home to authors ranging from William Faulkner to John Grisham, plus a tradition of art and music.

Few sights are far from one another in this small town. Unless you are visiting during the height of summer heat and humidity, Oxford is a walkable town.

Leaving the Trace

As you are driving south on the Trace, after leaving Tupelo exit the parkway at MS-6/Main Street/US 278 near **milepost 260**. Drive west for 45 miles (40 minutes); about 9 miles in, the road will jog to the right and then the left. Turn right (north) onto South Lamar Boulevard. You'll reach downtown Oxford in about 1.5 miles.

Sights

★ University of Mississippi (Ole Miss)

First things first: No one calls the **University of Mississippi** (123 University Circle, 662/915-7211, http://olemiss.edu) by its proper name. It's "Ole Miss." Founded in 1848, the school today has more than 23,000 students. The city itself has a population of nearly 21,000, so

it is easy to see how the school dominates this area.

Wandering through campus reveals a picture-perfect backdrop. The **Lyceum** building is the center of the Ole Miss campus. The bullet holes above the doorway are a sign of the violence that broke out in 1962 when James Meredith tried to integrate the then-white-only school. Behind the building is a civil rights monument with Meredith's figure.

Ventress Hall, built in 1889, was the first major building erected on campus after the Civil War. It is said that author William Faulkner helped paint and renovate this building as a young man. **The Grove** is the open space where tailgating becomes a pastime before football games. This is also where graduation is held.

The **University Museum** (University Ave. and 5th St., 662/915-7073, http://museum.olemiss.edu, 10am-6pm Tues.-Sat., free) has an impressive collection and exhibition space. While the museum is free, there is an additional fee for special exhibits (adults $5, seniors $4, children $3). Guided tours are available by request. Past exhibitions have included Greek and Roman antiquities and the work of photographer William

Eggleston. It's possible to get here via the Bailey's Woods Trail from Rowan Oak. The museum operates Rowan Oak and the Walton-Young Historic House, which is closed for renovations.

The **J. D. Williams Library** (1 Library Loop, 662/915-7092, generally 7am-2am Mon.-Thurs., 7am-7pm Fri., 10am-6pm Sat., 1pm-2am Sun.) has an impressive archive, including William Faulkner collections, Civil War and civil rights materials, and comprehensive blues music materials. It's an excellent place to pass a few hours.

Confederate soldiers who died after the battle of Shiloh in 1862 are buried at **Confederate Cemetery** (Hill Dr. and Manning Way). At one time the cemetery had individual markers, but lore suggests a groundskeeper removed them to mow and forgot where they belonged. The cemetery is on campus, south of the Tad Smith Coliseum in a walled-in lawn area.

On weekdays, you'll need a visitor parking pass ($3 daily) to park on campus. Order one ahead of time online (662/915-7235, www.olemiss.edu/parking/visitors) or purchase one on-site at the Lyceum Circle welcome booth. There are a few metered spots on campus that don't require a permit (exact change only).

Oh, and if you hear anyone say, "Hotty Toddy," just say "Hotty Toddy" right back. It's the Ole Miss greeting, school cheer, and football game chant.

The Square

Nothing else fully encapsulates Oxford's charms as does **The Square** (Jackson Ave. and Courthouse Sq., http://visitoxfordms.com), its historic town square and center of the city. Three different bookstores (technically outposts of the same store) bring author readings, live music, and discussions to the area. Live music venues, bars, and restaurants attract faculty and students from Ole Miss, as well as other locals and tourists. There are plenty of shops, too, of the higher-end

The L. Q. C. Lamar House is a National Historic Landmark.

and university-focused sort. You could easily spend a weekend within walking distance of The Square.

L. Q. C. Lamar House

A National Historic Landmark, the **L. Q. C. Lamar House Museum** (616 N. 14th St., 662/513-6071, www.lqclamarhouse.com, 1pm-4pm Fri.-Sun., free) is dedicated to preserving the legacy of Lucius Quintus Cincinnatus Lamar II. Lamar was a senator and U.S. Secretary of the Interior (under President Grover Cleveland) and was included in President John F. Kennedy's Pulitzer Prize-winning book, *Profiles in Courage,* for his work trying to reunite the North and the South after the Civil War.

Housed in Lamar's former home, the museum is a labor of love. It is chock-full of information—more than the average history buff can read. The building itself has been restored, and docents can explain some of the decisions that were made in the restoration process.

★ Rowan Oak (William Faulkner House)

Even those who don't think of themselves as fans of the great Southern writer William Faulkner (1897-1962) will be charmed by **Rowan Oak** (916 Old Taylor Rd., 662/234-3284, www.rowanoak.com, grounds dawn-dusk daily, house 10am-4pm Tues.-Sat., 1pm-4pm Sun. Aug.-May, 10am-6pm Mon.-Sat., 1pm-6pm Sun. June-July; grounds free, house $5), his former family home. The Greek Revival-style house, sitting on 29 acres, offers insight about the Nobel and Pulitzer Prize winner, as well as his creative process. Rowan Oak feels like Faulkner is just out for a walk, with his outline for *A Fable* scrawled on the walls to help him focus and numbers scribbled next to the phone in the 1844 building. Faulkner restored much of the home himself.

The grounds are said to be the inspiration for Yoknapatawpha County, the fictional setting for all but three of Faulkner's works. The grounds connect to the University of Mississippi campus through the **Bailey's Woods Trail** (www.museum.olemiss.edu/baileys-woods-trail). It takes about 20 minutes to walk the length of this National Recreational Trail, which comes out at the University Museum. The trail is about two-thirds of a mile long and is well-maintained. Four footbridges span steep areas in the woods.

If you want more than a self-guided look around, call ahead to schedule a tour. Note that the entrance to the home is easy to miss when rounding the bend on Old Taylor Road. From town, drive slowly after passing 10th Street, then turn right.

North of University Avenue and up a few blocks is **Saint Peter's Cemetery** (Jefferson Ave. and N. 16th St.), where you can see William Faulkner's tombstone. The large monument is close to the sidewalk and often covered with whiskey bottles that fans leave for their favorite author.

Cedar Oak

Many structures were lost to fire by the Union troops during the Civil War. **Cedar Oak** (601 Murray St., 662/801-1427, www.cedaroaks.org, 11am-4pm Fri., free) survived, not because the armies spared it, but because Molly Turner Orr, the sister of William Turner, the man who built the house, organized a group of people to fight the fire. In the mid-1900s Cedar Oak was moved 2.2 miles away from its original location.

Tours of the Greek Revival structures are scheduled only on Fridays, although you may be able to make an appointment for another day by calling in advance.

Burns-Belfry Museum

Burns Methodist Episcopal Church was a church organized by freed African Americans. This beautiful 1910 brick building is now home to the **Burns-Belfry Museum** (710 Jackson Ave. E., 662/281-9963, www.burns-belfry.com, noon-3pm Wed.-Fri., 1pm-4pm Sun.,

free), a multicultural center that invites discussions of civil rights, slavery, and more. The museum exhibits are professional and thought-provoking. While the museum is free, donations are accepted to fund expansion and educational programs.

Entertainment and Events
Performing Arts

Originally built in the 1800s as a livery stable for William Faulkner's family, **The Lyric** (1006 Van Buren Ave., 662/234-5333, www.thelyricoxford.com, box office noon-5pm Wed.-Fri.) is the place to see concerts, film festivals, and other live events in Oxford.

People come to **Proud Larry's** (211 S. Lamar Blvd., 662/236-0050, www.proudlarrys.com, 11am-midnight Mon.-Wed. and Sat., 11am-1am Thurs.-Fri., 11am-2pm Sun.) for the impressive line up of live music acts. It also doubles as a restaurant.

The **Thacker Mountain Radio Hour**

Oxford's Double Decker Festival is named for the red buses that it imported from England.

(http://thackermountain.com, 6pm Thurs., fall and spring, free) is a lively, smart live radio show with author readings and music, broadcast from **Off Square Books** (129 Courthouse Sq.). Arrive early if you want a good seat. The show is rebroadcast every Saturday at 7pm on Mississippi Public Radio. It's produced only in the fall and spring.

Festivals and Events
Held over a week in late July at Ole Miss, the **Faulkner and Oknapatawpha Conference** (www.outreach.olemiss.edu/events/faulkner) discusses the work of Oxford's favorite son. A celebration of all things related to the written word, the **Oxford Conference for the Book** (http://oxfordconferenceforthebook.com) is held for three days in March each year at Ole Miss.

The **Double Decker Festival** (Historic Courthouse Sq., 662/232-2477, http://doubledeckerfestival.com) started as a modest event on a double-decker bus

imported from England. Now it's a two-day fest of music, arts, and food each April.

Shopping
Oxford's historic courthouse square, a.k.a. **The Square** (Jackson Ave. and Courthouse Sq.), is the hub of downtown and the place to start shopping.

Square Books (160 Courthouse Sq., 662/236-2262, www.squarebooks.com, 9am-9pm Mon.-Sat., 9am-6pm Sun.) actually has three locations on The Square. Aside from the main outpost, there's **Square Books Jr.** (111 Courthouse Sq., 662/236-2207, 9am-7pm Mon.-Sat., noon-5pm Sun.), just for kids, and **Off Square Books** (129 Courthouse Sq., 662/236-2828, 9am-8pm Mon.-Sat., noon-5pm Sun.), the company's "lifestyle and leisure" location. Off Square is also home of the Thursday night **Thacker Mountain Radio Hour** (http://thackermountain.com).

Amy Head Cosmetics (301 S. Lamar Blvd., 662/513-0711, www.amyheadcosmetics.com, 10am-5:30pm Mon.-Fri., 11am-5pm Sat.) sells a boutique makeup line.

Belles and Beaus (1005 Van Buren Ave., 662/236-6880, www.bellesandbeausoxford.com, 9:30am-6pm Mon.-Sat.) is the place for kids' clothing. Both **Lulu's Shoes and Accessories** (265 N. Lamar Ste. V, 662/234-4111, www.lulusoxford.com, 10am-6pm Mon.-Sat., 10am-2pm Sun.) and **Material Girl** (403 S. Lamar Blvd., 662/513-0888, www.shopmaterialgirls.com, 10am-6pm Mon.-Thurs., 10am-7pm Fri.-Sat., 1pm-4pm Sun.) are go-tos for women's clothing, jewelry, shoes, and accessories. **My Favorite Shoes** (138 Courthouse Sq., 662/234-0059, 10am-5:30pm Mon.-Thurs., 10am-6pm Fri.-Sat., 11am-3pm Sun.) and **Nella's Clothing** (103 Courthouse Sq., 662/281-8711, 10am-5:30pm Mon.-Sat.) are more good options for women.

Looking for something one of a kind? **Mississippi Madness** (141 Courthouse

Sq., 662/234-5280, 10am-5:30pm Mon.-Sat.) has gifts and home decor from Mississippi artists. The motto of **Neilson's** (119 Courthouse Sq., 662/234-1161, http://neilsonsdepartmentstore.com, 9am-5:30pm Mon.-Sat.) is "Where trends meet tradition." This Southern department store was established in 1839, so they know about tradition.

The End of All Music Record Store (1423 N. Lamar Blvd., 662/281-1909, http://theendofallmusic.com, noon-6pm Mon., 10am-6pm Tues.-Sat., noon-5pm Sun.) is a few miles from The Square, but it's worth the drive if you are an indie record shop fan. They stock country, rock, jazz, and anything else you want.

Food
The Square

★ **Canoodle by Oxford Canteen** (1006 Van Buren Ave., 662/234-5345, www.eatcanoodle.com, 11am-8pm Tues.-Sat., $7-9) may be the smallest restaurant you've ever been to. Delicious Asian noodle dishes (think: pho and ramen) are handed to you through a window in an alley next to The Lyric. There are bar stools and tables set up in the alley as well.

Chef John Currence is the man responsible, in large part, for Oxford's culinary renaissance. ★ **City Grocery** (152 Courthouse Sq., 662/232-0808, http://citygroceryonline.com, 11:30am-2:30pm and 6pm-10pm Mon.-Thurs., 11:30am-2:30pm and 6pm-10:30pm Fri.-Sat., 11am-2:30pm Sun., $10-30) was his first Oxford restaurant, one that combines fine dining with traditional Southern ingredients in an old livery stable. There's a casual bar menu upstairs and a more traditional fine dining experience downstairs. City Grocery is so much a part of the city fabric that some locals have standing reservations and their own table. Another John Currence restaurant, **Bouré** (110 Courthouse Sq., 662/234-1968, http://citygroceryonline.com, 11am-10pm Mon.-Thurs.,

11am-10:30pm Fri.-Sat., $11-32) serves Creole-inspired dishes from the second floor of The Square.

Expect a wait at ★ **Bottletree Bakery** (923 Van Buren Ave., 662/236-5000, 7am-2:30pm Tues.-Fri., 8am-2:30pm Sat., 8am-2pm Sun., $6-8), a funky diner-turned-bakery with freshly made pastries and sandwiches.

Football legend Eli Manning reportedly counts **Ajax Diner** (118 Courthouse Sq., 662/232-8880, www.ajaxdiner.net, 11:30am-11pm, $8-15) as a favorite. Both the lunch and dinner menus highlight soul food, such as turnip green dip, po'boys, and fried catfish.

Brunch fans should make reservations at **McEwen's Oxford** (1110 Van Buren Ave., 662/234-7003, http://mcewensoxford.com, 11am-2pm and 5pm-9pm Tues.-Thurs., 11am-2pm and 5pm-10pm Fri., 5pm-10pm Sat., 10:30am-2pm Sun., $23-35). This is also the place to go for fancy cocktails.

A sleek, modern pizza parlor, **Saint Leo** (1101 Jackson Ave. E., 662/380-5141, 11am-midnight Mon. and Wed., 11am-1am Thurs.-Fri., 11am-midnight Sat., 11am-9pm Sun., $13-20) is a sophisticated favorite of locals looking for alternatives to Southern food. They make some of their cheeses (ricotta and mozzarella) and cure some of their meats (pork belly) in-house.

North Lamar

The food served at chef John Currence's morning spot, **Big Bad Breakfast** (719 N. Lamar Blvd., 662/236-2666, http://citygroceryonline.com, 7am-1:30pm Mon.-Fri., 8am-3pm Sat.-Sun., $7-13) features ingredients such as house-cured Tabasco and brown sugar bacon. Also from John Currence's City Grocery group, **Snackbar** (721 N. Lamar Blvd., 662/236-6363, http://citygroceryonline.com, 5:30pm-10pm Mon.-Thurs., 5:30pm-10:30pm Fri.-Sat., $12-27) is a trendy eatery with a raw bar, charcuterie, and small plates.

Neon Pig (711 N. Lamar Blvd.,

662/638-3257, http://oxford.eatneonpig.com, 11am-9pm Mon.-Sat., 11am-4pm Sun., $7-10) is a butcher and seafood shop with an attached café serving sandwiches, salads, wraps, tacos, and burgers. A lot of their meats are cured in-house—and the restaurant smells like it. There's another location in Tupelo.

Tired of grits and fried chicken? **Jinsei Sushi** (713 Lamar Blvd., 662/234-0109, www.jinseisushi.com, 5pm-10pm daily, $15-20) is a sleek sushi bar with traditional sashimi and *nigiri*, plus contemporary maki and hot dishes, including a wagyu steak that you sear yourself on a hot rock.

Accommodations

If you want a hotel room the weekend of a big football game or other event at Ole Miss, book as far ahead as possible.

Inn at Ole Miss Hotel & Conference Center (120 Alumni Dr., 662/234-2331, www.theinnatolemiss.com, $109-135) has 146 rooms, with standards in the original Alumni House building and deluxe rooms in an addition. Deluxe rooms are a little bigger and have sleeper sofas. The hotel offers all the standard amenities, such free Wi-Fi and a fitness center (with an outdoor pool), plus a shuttle to downtown Oxford. Rates include breakfast.

A cute and quirky boutique hotel located on The Square, **Graduate Oxford** (400 N. Lamar Blvd., 662/234-3031, http://graduateoxford.com, $149-174) is a favorite of locals as well as visitors, thanks to the rooftop bar The Coop and the lobby lounge decorated with vintage books. Pets are welcome in this funky hotel.

There are several decent chain hotels in Oxford. **Courtyard by Marriott** (305 Jackson Ave. E., 662/638-6014, www.marriott.com, $160-180) has the standard amenities, plus a Green Roof Lounge that serves dinner and cocktails. **The**

Top to bottom: menu highlights from City Grocery; Big Bad Breakfast; and Ravine.

Hampton Inn Oxford/Convention Center (103 Ed Perry Blvd., 662/234-5565, www.hamptoninn.com, $143-169) is a non-smoking hotel with a fitness center, pool, and free Wi-Fi. **Holiday Inn Express & Suites Oxford** (112 Heritage Dr., 662/236-2500, www.holidayinn.com/oxford, $99-115) touts a business center, free breakfast bar, fitness center, and free Wi-Fi. You'll feel more at home at **Marriott TownePlace Suites** (105 Ed Perry Blvd., 662/238-3522, www.marriott.com, $123-129), where rooms have pullout sofa beds and a fully equipped kitchen.

Walking distance to downtown, ★ **The Z Bed & Breakfast** (1405 Pierce Ave., 713/927-1295, http://thez-oxford.com, $99-135) is a quirky, homey B&B with three rooms, each tastefully and uniquely decorated. Prices include full homemade breakfast plus wine and cookies nightly. There are two bikes available for your use, plus the backyard has a fire pit and grill. The owners have two other properties in town, The Z Shanty and The White House, which are appropriate for larger parties and family reunions.

The 5 Twelve (512 Van Buren Ave., 662/234-8043, www.the5twelve.com, $140-250) may be a B&B in a Greek Revival building, but these five rooms are contemporary, with bold design choices such as Marimekko-printed duvet covers.

Blue Creek Cabin (535 MS-30, East Oxford, 662/238-2897, www.bluecreekcabin.com, $138 s/d, $69 for each additional guest) is a good option for those not traveling with young kids (no children under the age of 10 are allowed) who want something a little different. This is a two-bedroom 1800s log cabin with shared bathroom and kitchenette.

Popular for weddings, the seven-room **Castle Hill** (120 Castle Hill Dr., 662/234-3735, http://castlehilloxford.com/inn, $99-225) has a ballroom, pool, dining rooms, and a courtyard.

A Victorian-style home converted into a B&B, with a horse pasture to boot, **Oak Hill Stables** (670 County Rd. 101, 662/234-8488, www.oakhillstablesbedandbreakfast.com, $100-200) isn't your average hotel. There are also guest rooms available in a converted barn.

Ravine (53 County Rd. 321, 662/234-4555, www.oxfordravine.com/inn, $135-195) is also a log cabin-style B&B with rooms with kitchenettes. Amenities include Wi-Fi, breakfast, and a pool. There's a 70-seat restaurant on the premises.

The Barn Loft at Willowdale Farm (28 County Rd. 225, 662/801-8600, http://thefarmatwillowdale.com, $78-158) is good if you want more than just a bedroom. Rent out the loft, the upper level of a barn that's been fashioned into a living space with a porch, living room, kitchen, washer and dryer, two bedrooms, a sleeper sofa, and a bathroom.

Information and Services

Your first stop in town should be the charming **Visit Oxford Visitor's Center** (1013 Jackson Ave. E., 662/232-2477, http://visitoxfordms.com, 8am-5pm Mon.-Fri., 10am-4pm Sat., 1pm-4pm Sun.). The office is filled with maps, information, and Southern hospitality.

Get bicycles serviced and find parts at **Oxford Bicycle Company** (407 Jackson Ave. E., 662/236-6507, 10am-6pm Mon.-Fri., 10am-4pm Sat.).

Baptist Memorial Hospital (2301 S. Lamar, 662/232-8100, www.baptistonline.org) is a full-service hospital.

Back to the Trace

To return to the parkway from downtown Oxford, take Lamar Boulevard south to US 278. Turn left and continue for 38 miles east. Exit to the right to continue on US 278 (following signs for US 278/MS-6/Main Street). Drive the last nine miles to the parkway, where you'll pass under the Trace, then turn right to rejoin the Trace near **milepost 260.** Turn left (follow signs for Jackson) to continue south.

The Louisiana Purchase

For 10,000 years the Natchez Trace has been a route inland from the Mississippi River. Native Americans and other hearty pioneers, even wildlife, would use it as access to food and water.

President Thomas Jefferson negotiated treaties with both the Chickasaw and Choctaw Nations for use of this land, hoping to connect the frontier to the settled eastern sections of the United States. When the Louisiana Purchase, which covered 828,000 square miles, was signed in 1803, there was even more motivation to have reliable access to the new land.

In 1806, motivated by their $11 million investment, Congress authorized construction to build roads on what had been the centuries-old Natchez Trace. For most of its history, travel on the Trace went northward. Settlers with their goods would travel by boat south on the Mississippi River and then return north via the Trace by foot or on horseback, which is why the milepost markers begin in Natchez and end in Nashville. Construction began in 1934. In 1938, the route was designated the Natchez Trace National Parkway.

If you don't mind missing a few miles of the parkway, you can shave off about five minutes of driving time without missing any sights. About 38 miles east of Oxford, at the US 278/MS-76 junction, continue on MS-76 instead of exiting. Continue for almost eight miles. You'll pass underneath the parkway, exit to the right (south), then turn left to rejoin the parkway near **milepost 257,** heading south.

Black Belt Overlook

(MP 251.9)

This scenic overlook on the right side of the road offers a wide open view of the pastoral landscape of central Mississippi. In another era, this land was under the sea, as archaeologists can tell from the shells and other marine organisms deposited to form the limestone. Over time, that limestone morphed into fertile soil of various colors. The area got its name from the rich black soil. Much of the region's "Black Belt" was once used for growing cotton.

Make a quick stop to take a few photos. The area has a U-shaped pull-in that can be seen from the road. There aren't any amenities.

Chickasaw Council House (MP 251.1)

This stop might not look like much as you turn left into the small pullout. In the 1820s, however, it was an important site: the capital of the Chickasaw Nation. In the council house that once stood here, tribal elders met to sign treaties and set laws and policies. Each summer more than 2,000 Chickasaw people came to receive an annual payment for lands they had sold to the federal government. The Pontotoc Creek Treaty of 1832, which ceded the last of the Chickasaw land east of the Mississippi River to the U.S. government, was signed here.

There are no physical remains of the council house at this site.

★ Owl Creek Mounds (MP 243.1)

Near milepost 243.1 is a worthwhile detour off of the parkway, in the Tombigbee National Forest. The **Owl Creek Mounds Archaeological Site** (dawn-dusk daily, free) consists of two Native American ceremonial mounds built AD 1100-1200. It's possible to see two mounds, one of which has a somewhat unusual crescent shape. However, archaeologists believe that there once were five mounds in this area. The taller mound likely housed a temple or chief's home. Research suggests that these mounds were used for a short time—less than a century.

There are paved pathways around the mounds, so you can explore from all sides. Clear, easy-to-read signage makes this an educational stop. Because they are not on the parkway, these mounds are not part of the National Park system, but instead are protected by the U.S. Forest Service. These were sacred spaces and should be treated with respect.

To get here, exit the Trace to the right just past the Hernando de Soto site, following signs for Owl Creek Mounds Archaeological Site and Davis Lake. Turn right on Davis Road and drive for three miles, past the Chickasaw OHV Trail. The mounds will be on your right. To return to the parkway, retrace your steps for three miles, turn left to rejoin the Trace, then turn right to continue south on the parkway.

Davis Lake Recreation Area

Instead of returning to the parkway from Owl Creek, another option is to continue on Davis Road for one mile (a total of four west of the parkway) to reach **Davis Lake Recreation Area** (877/444-6777), a 200-acre lake that's inside the **Tombigbee National Forest** (601/285-3264). This is a place to swim, fish, and hike, with a few miles of easy walking trails.

The **Chickasaw OHV Trail** (Apr.-Oct., $10 per ATV), which you'll pass on your way from the Trace, offers 12 miles of motorized trails for all-terrain vehicles. Eighteen miles of horseback riding trails and lots of bird-watching round out the fun. Leashed pets are allowed in the area and campgrounds but not on the beach.

★ **Davis Lake Campground** (662/285-3264, www.recreation.gov, starting at $20/night) has more than 20 campsites, 14 of which are on the lake itself. Some of the campsites have electricity, and

there are showers and other amenities. Davis Lake is one of two campgrounds in Tombigbee National Forest. The other, Choctaw Lake, is south of Starkville and farther from the parkway.

Follow Davis Road to reach the park entrance and ranger station. To return to the parkway, drive east on David Road for four miles. Turn left to exit Davis Road, then right to continue south on the Trace.

Chickasaw Agency
(MP 241.4)

Between 1802 and 1825, when this section of the Trace was the heart of Chickasaw Nation, the federal government sent representatives to the Chickasaws (one of whom was James Robertson, the founder of Nashville). The agency functioned similarly to a modern-day embassy. The agents' presence helped broker peaceful relations between the Chickasaws and white settlers. Their responsibilities also included removing trespassers and recovering stolen horses. During the winter, they were largely alone in the wilderness. During the summer thousands of Kaintucks, those hardy boatmen traveling north, would stop at the agency for sleep or nourishment.

Today this is just a historical marker on the Trace. The pullout is on the right side of the road, with a U-shaped parking area. The marker is visible from the road and there are no other amenities.

Witch Dance (MP 233.2)

This stop's alluring name comes from lore that says that witches once gathered here to dance and the grass withered beneath their feet wherever they touched the ground. There is a hidden spot here where grass stubbornly refuses to grow. (Hint: Look for it behind the sign and under the trees.)

This stop is popular with those

traveling the Trace with horses or on bicycle. It's a staging area for the Witch Dance Horse Trail in Tombigbee National Forest, with hitching posts and camping only for those traveling with horses or on bicycle. Signage marks the designated camping areas. The horseback riding trails are 9 and 15 miles long.

Amenities include restrooms, water fountains (most outdoor water is turned off in winter, but indoor faucets still flow), and several picnic areas. The next restroom stop headed south is not until the Jeff Busby Campground (milepost 193.1).

There are two ways to access Witch Dance. On the right side of the road before you get to the driveway there is a small pull-in parking area with a few steps up to the building with the restrooms. You can see this from the road. If all you need is a bathroom break, this works well. If you have a trailer, want to picnic, and would like to see where the witches once danced, pass the building and turn right into the marked driveway. It winds around and puts you on the opposite side of the bathrooms (this is also the accessible side for those in wheelchairs). There's plenty of parking and access to the trails.

★ Bynum Mounds
(MP 232.4)

This is one of the most significant sites on the parkway. Bynum Mounds' six burial mounds were built between 100 BC and AD 100 (known as the Middle Woodland period). Just two of the mounds, the two largest, have been restored to their original appearance and are available for public viewing. Detailed signage and displays give you an in-depth archaeological experience.

The southernmost of the two restored mounds, called Mound A, contained the remains of a woman, with copper spools at each wrist, placed between two burned

oak logs at the mound's base. In addition, cremated remains of two other adults and a child were found.

The largest mound, Mound B, covered a log-lined crematory pit. Here the Park Service found greenstone axe heads, copper spools, and other objects that didn't come from Mississippi. These finds demonstrate the long-distance trade networks used by the people living at the time.

These are sacred spaces and should be treated with respect. Stay on the well-marked paved pathways to circle the mounds and read the signage. Stop at the simple shelter off of the parking lot that has illustrated signage about what life would have been like on the Trace in the Middle Woodland period.

The Bynum Mounds site is not visible from the parkway, giving this stop an intimate feeling, even though it is quite large. Exit the parkway on the left side of the road and follow the driveway to the parking lot. There are no amenities.

Line Creek (MP 213.1)

A sole picnic table on the shaded banks of a small creek is what remains at what was once a significant spot on the Trace. This small creek was recognized by the Chickasaw and Choctaw people as the boundary between the two nations. It remained until the tribes were forced west on the Trail of Tears. Over the years Line Creek's meandering path has changed slightly, but this marker is very close to the original spot. Nearby was a stand, run by Noah Wall and his Choctaw wife, that offered food and shelter for travelers.

The U-shaped pullout and parking area is on the west side of the parkway. There are no other amenities.

⬧ US 82 to Starkville

A restored, vibrant downtown and the campus of Mississippi State University make sweet Starkville worth visiting. It's also known for its rabid fans of State's football team, the Bulldogs. If you're planning to visit in the fall, check football schedules in advance, book hotel rooms early, and don't forget the cowbell.

Native Americans lived in this area and worked the land for hundreds— even thousands—of years. Artifacts suggest people lived here more than 2,000 years ago. White settlers moved in after the Trail of Tears forced the Choctaw and Chickasaw people west in the 1830s. Once known as Boardtown, because of the clapboards made in a mill here, in 1835 the name of the town was changed to Starkville.

Leaving the Trace

From Line Creek, drive south on the Trace to **milepost 204.5.** Exit on the left, following signs for US 82/Mathiston. From the exit road, turn right and take US 82 east for 12 miles. Turn right to get on MS-182 and drive southeast for nine miles. Turn right on Jackson Street to reach Starkville's downtown, near the Hotel Chester. This drive should take less than 30 minutes.

Sights
Mississippi State University

Mississippi State University (75 B.S. Hood Dr., 662/325-2323, www.msstate. edu), referred to simply as "State," is the reason most people come to Starkville. The school, once Mississippi A&M, has more than 20,000 students—in a town with a population of 24,000. All over town you'll see signs proclaiming "Hail State," and most signage will be in the school color of maroon.

There are several free student-led campus tours (662/325-5198, www.visit. msstate.edu/publictours), including a children's tour, an art tour, a historical tour, and more. Tours vary by time of year but are generally on Saturday at 11am and 1pm. Call to reserve your spot.

If you are with a big group, book at least two weeks in advance. For guided art tours, call 662/325-2973.

In addition to **Davis Wade Stadium,** where the Bulldogs play, there's lots to see. The Welcome Center lobby is home to the Cullis & Gladys Wade Clock Museum, which boasts more than 400 American-made clocks dating back to the 1700s.

The school hosts many concerts and theater performances as well as academic lectures by State and visiting faculty, as well as the student-run Magnolia Film Festival each February. Everything comes to a halt for football here, so check game schedules before visiting.

Overstreet School

Constructed in 1897, **Overstreet School** (307 S. Jackson St.) was the first elementary school in Starkville and became the cornerstone for what is now the charming residential Overstreet Historic District. The building was renovated in 1949 and is a beautiful example of art moderne, a type of architecture that focuses on clean horizontal lines. The building's striking Indian motif honors the original residents of the area.

Architecture fans should take some time to explore the 180 homes in this area, just south of downtown. The Overstreet Historic District was added to the National Register of Historic Places in 1992 and includes examples of Craftsman, Victorian, art deco, and art moderne buildings.

Starkville City Jail

Johnny Cash was held overnight in 1965 in the **Starkville City Jail** (111 Dr. D. L. Conner Dr., 662/323-2421, www.sheriff.oktibbeha.ms.us/division/jail). It was this event that inspired Cash's song "Starkville City Jail." The building isn't much to look at, but its history makes it worth a drive-by (while listening to the song, of course).

The Cotton District

The Cotton District (104½ Maxwell St., http://cottondistrict.com) is considered one of the first New Urbanism developments in the world. The movement supports walkable mixed-use neighborhoods, with restaurants, bars, and places to live. Starkville's Cotton District was founded by developer Dan Camp in the 1960s, revitalizing a community that was in disrepair after the local cotton mill closed. Buildings inspired by Greek Revival, Classical, and Victorian architecture offer people an opportunity to live, work, and study in a walkable community. The **Cotton District Arts Festival** (www.cdafestival.com) is held here each April.

Oktibbeha County Heritage Museum

The historical Gulf Mobile and Ohio Railroad depot has been brought back to life as the **Oktibbeha County Heritage Museum** (206 Fellowship St., 662/323-0211, http://oktibbehaheritagemuseum.com, 1pm-4pm Tues.-Thurs. and by appointment, free), a surprisingly comprehensive museum to Starkville's history. You'll find artifacts about the region's growth, an old medical office, music, taxidermy, and displays about locals who have made it big, such as Portland Trailblazers basketball player Travis Outlaw. The museum is run by volunteers, so don't panic if it opens a few minutes late. It's also possible to call and schedule a private tour. Don't miss the outdoor garden, which emphasizes water conservation.

Entertainment

Starkville Community Theatre performs at **Playhouse on Main** (108 E. Main St., 662/323-6855, www.sct-online.org, tickets $10-15) in the heart of downtown.

Top to bottom: downtown Starkville; Mississippi State University; The Biscuit Shop.

There are typically four productions annually with a nine-show run for each.

The Greater Starkville Development Partnership's office is the home to the **GSDP Art Gallery** (200 E. Main St., 662/323-3322, http://starkville.org, 8am-5pm Mon.-Fri.). This isn't a full art gallery, but it is centrally located downtown and is worth browsing while you're strolling. Local artists are well represented.

Shopping

Downtown Starkville is chock-full of shops with handmade goods and jewelry, clothing, and art appealing to a college student crowd (and their parents).

Swanky B (209 E. Main St., 662/546-0897, www.swankyb.com, 10am-6pm Mon.-Fri., 10am-4pm Sat.) has women's clothing with a young, trendy vibe. **L.A. Green Boutique** (117 E. Main St., 662/324-6280, http://shoplagreen.com, 10am-6pm Mon.-Sat.) has women's and men's shoes, clothing, some home decor, and works of local artists.

Last Man Standing (103 N. Lafayette St., 662/341-1592, www.shoplastmanstanding.com, 10:30am-6pm Mon.-Sat.) makes sure Starkville men are well appointed with clothing, shoes, belts, watches, bags, wallets, and grooming gear. **Doodlebugs** (123 E. Main St., 662/268-8100, www.doodlebugs-asouthernstyle.com, 10am-5:30pm Tues.-Fri., 10am-4pm Sat.) is the local favorite for baby and kids' clothing.

Stop at **Thyme** (403 E. Lampkin St., 662/323-5979, 10am-5:30pm Mon.-Fri., 10am-4pm Sat.) if you need to help a grad student outfit a new condo with cookware or need a hostess gift.

Since 1905, **Reed's** (302 University Dr., 662/323-2684, http://reedsms.com, 9:30am-6pm Mon.-Sat.) has catered to Mississippi shoppers looking for outdoor gear and clothing. They also sell plenty of cowbells.

Farmers and artisans sell their goodies at the **Starkville Community Market** (200 E. Main St., 662/323-3322, http://visit. starkville.org, 4pm-6pm Tues., 7:30am-10:30am Sat. May-Aug.), which is also a great local hangout.

Food

You won't go hungry in Starkville, a town that's proud of its agricultural roots and Southern culture.

Two Brothers Smoked Meats (103-C Rue du Grand Fromage, 662/617-8095, http://twobrotherssmokedmeats.com, 2pm-10pm Tues.-Wed., 11am-10pm Thurs.-Sat., noon-9pm Sun., $7-13) makes burgers, tacos, and sandwiches with all manner of smoked meats: pulled pork, smoked duck, and smoked pork tenderloin. The nachos are made with pork rinds.

Harveys (406 MS-12 E., 662/323-1669, http://eatwithharveys.com, 11am-9:30pm Mon.-Thurs., 11am-10pm Fri.-Sat., 11am-9pm Sun., $9-19) is a Mississippi tradition, and this outpost is popular with students when Mom and Dad come to town. The menu is filled with fried appetizers (fried broccoli and mushrooms among them), plus salads, steaks, chops, and seafood.

Does one member of your party prefer Chicago-style pizza while another is all about New York-style pie? No worries, **Dave's Dark Horse Tavern** (410 Dr. Martin Luther King Jr. Dr. E., 662/324-3316, http://davesdarkhorse.com, 3:30pm-midnight Mon.-Thurs., 11am-1am Fri.-Sat., 11am-10pm Sun., $6-15) serves both. Locals like the cracker crust pizza. The menu includes a few gluten-free and vegan items, too.

There's nothing wrong with a restaurant that has a different mac and cheese every week. People also like **The Camphouse** (409 University Dr., 662/769-5665, 11am-9:30pm Mon.-Wed., 11am-11pm Thurs.-Sat.) for its outdoor patio.

Restaurant Tyler (100 E. Main St., 662/324-1014, http://eatlocalstarkville.com, 11am-2pm Mon., 11am-9pm Tues.-Thurs., 11am-10pm Fri., 5pm-10pm Sat., 10am-2pm Sun., $8-38) serves elevated

More Cowbell!

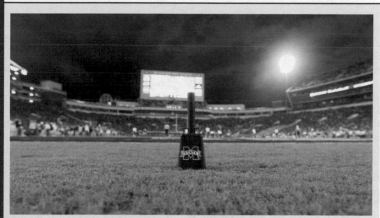

Cowbells are a much-loved football game tradition at Mississippi State University.

When shopping in Starkville you'll see—in every store, bar, and even gas station—cowbells. Cowbells have been rung at State football games since at least 1940, when the football team had an undefeated season. People debate which styles are best and which best help cheer the Bulldogs to victory, but a popular choice is a long-handled, bicycle-grip bell made of thin and tightly welded shells. Many cowbells are handed down in families, from one alumnus to the next. Monogrammed versions are given as gifts to new students and to women being courted by potential suitors.

Technically, the bells were outlawed by the Southeastern Conference (SEC), the football governing body, in 1974, but State fans kept sneaking them in and ringing them, making a game at Davis Wade Stadium one of the loudest you'll ever witness. In 2010 the SEC reversed the ruling, acknowledging that the cowbell was an integral part of the school's tradition. However, students and alumni alike must "ring responsibly."

If you plan on experiencing Starkville like a local, there are just two phrases you need to know: "Hail State" and "More cowbell!"

Southern classics with modern variations, such as jambalaya pasta and sweet potato gnocchi. The beautiful bar, called The Guest Room, boasts an excellent bourbon selection and knowledgeable bartenders. The Restaurant Tyler and Guest Room team gets more casual at **Bin 612** (612 University Dr., 662/324-6126, http://eatlocalstarkville.com, 11am-midnight Mon.-Thurs., 11am-1am Fri.-Sat., 11am-10pm Sun., $9-17) with a menu of burgers, panini, pizza, and wine.

It's worth getting up early to try the buttermilk biscuits made from scratch at

★ **The Biscuit Shop** (104 S. Washington St., 662/324-3118, www.thebiscuitlady. com, 6:30am-2pm Tues.-Sat., $1.50-2.50) before they sell out. They're known for their wacky flavors, like sausage-cheddar, s'mores, and peppermint-chocolate chip.

Accommodations

★ **Hotel Chester** (101 N. Jackson St., 662/323-5005, www.historichotelchester. com, $115-150) is downtown's signature boutique hotel. In a restored 1925 building, Hotel Chester is a funny combination of styles and history, with modern (if small) rooms, a glass elevator, and a lobby and exterior that are old world. There are several restaurants on-site, including The Beer Garden, whose claims to fame are a menu courtesy of Gordon Ramsay and a serene patio, perfect on spring and fall nights. The included breakfast is made-to-order.

Sharp Bed & Breakfast (1791 Watt Hill Rd., 662/615-4311, www.starkvillebedandbreakfast.com, $85-150) offers three bedrooms, a picnic pavilion, sweet rocking chairs on the porch, and a pet-friendly alternative for visitors.

There are several serviceable chain hotels in Starkville, which book up during football season. **The Holiday Inn Express & Suites** (110 MS-12, 662/324-0076, www.ihg.com, $95-100) and the **Days Inn & Suites** (119 MS-12, 662/324-5555, $58-70) both have Wi-Fi, a free breakfast bar, and an outdoor pool. The **Hilton Garden Inn** (975 MS-12, 662/615-9664, http://hiltongardeninn3.hilton.com, $101-124) is good for business travelers, with Wi-Fi, a fitness center, business center, indoor pool, restaurant, and bar, plus a 24-hour pantry.

Information and Services

The **Greater Starkville Development Partnership** (200 E. Main St., 662/323-3322, http://starkville.org, 8am-5pm Mon.-Fri.) is the place to start for visitor information, maps, and more.

Boardtown Bikes (200 S. Montgomery St., Ste. C, 662/324-1200, www.boardtownbikes.com, 10am-6pm Mon.-Sat.) sells road, mountain, and fitness bikes and can help with repairs and gear as you continue your ride on the Trace.

OCH Regional Medical Center (400 Hospital Rd., 662/323-4320, www.och.org) has a 24-hour emergency room.

Back to the Trace

To return to the Trace, take MS-182 northwest for nine miles to MS-82. Turn left, then take MS-82 west for 12 miles. Just before you pass underneath the Trace, exit to the right, then turn left to rejoin the Trace near **milepost 204.5** and continue south.

Jeff Busby Park (MP 193.1)

This park is named in honor of U.S. congressman Thomas Jefferson Busby, a Mississippian who, in 1934, introduced a bill authorizing a survey of the Old Natchez Trace. Just four years later, the road was incorporated into the National Park System. The park is nestled on Little Mountain, one of the higher elevation points in Mississippi (603 feet), which affords scenic views thanks to the Summit Overlook, which can be reached on foot or by car. On a clear day from the overlook, you can see for about 20 miles. The park also contains one of the three free campgrounds on the parkway.

It's possible to drive to the scenic Summit Overlook, or you can see it by hiking Little Mountain Trail. Starting from the campground, you'll hike out to Summit Overlook, atop Little Mountain. It's an uphill walk on the way back for a total of 1.6 miles out and back.

For those who don't want to do the Little Mountain Trail, the park also features a 0.5-mile loop trail that heads into a shady hollow, which is particularly welcome during hot Mississippi summers. Allow yourself up to 20 minutes to complete the gently rolling loop. Neither of the trails is wheelchair-friendly.

The entrance to the park is on the left side of the parkway. This is your last stop for restrooms until the Kosciusko Welcome Center (milepost 160).

Camping

The ★ **Jeff Busby Campground** (no reservations, free) has 18 first-come, first-served sites, with some primitive tent sites as well as RV sites. Most of the campsites are pull-throughs. There is also ample overflow parking.

Claim your spot by pitching your rent or parking your RV. There are picnic tables and a grill at each site. The campground has bathrooms but no showers or dumping stations.

French Camp Historic District (MP 180.7)

French Camp Historic District (1 Fine Pl., 662/547-6482, www.frenchcamp.org/historic) is one of the few tourist stops along the parkway. This area, named for Frenchman Louis LeFleur, who opened an inn (called a "stand") here in 1812, is today home to **French Camp Academy,** a Christian boarding school, as well as a collection of businesses run by the academy and its students. French Camp has a distinct vibe: part national park, part Disneyland, and part Sunday school.

In the historic district, you can tour several restored buildings, including the Drane House, and visit the Children of God Pottery Studio, a working studio where you can buy pottery and also talk to the academy students who are working and learning here. The pottery studio is located in what was the village's old post office.

French Camp isn't to everyone's taste, and that will dictate how long you spend exploring. If you like what you see, you could spend the better part of a day exploring, eating, shopping, praying, and talking to students and teachers. Due to the religious nature of the institution, the businesses are closed on Sunday and no alcohol or tobacco is permitted.

Explore several gift shops, stop into the **Council House Café** (10:30am-7pm Mon.-Sat., $6-8), then walk over to the pottery studio and historical compound. Don't skip the bread! It is made by hand and served in the café and the B&B and is for sale in the gift shop.

The academy also runs the ★ **French Camp B&B** (662/547-6835, $65-140), with an option of three different cabins and cottages, including a historic log cabin. Wi-Fi is available in the main house.

There's no alcohol or tobacco permitted. The included breakfast is served at the Council House Café. Pets are permitted for a $15 fee.

The academy's **Rainwater Observatory & Planetarium** (6810 MS-413, 662/547-6377, www.rainwaterobservatory.org, free) hosts monthly star-watching events for the public.

As you head south on the Trace, you'll pass two entrances to French Camp. The first is a U-shaped pullout on the east side of the Trace. You can park here and cross a footbridge to the French Camp Village. The second entrance is accessible by turning left (east) from the parkway on MS-413 and then immediately into the parking lot on your left.

Cole Creek (MP 175.6)

Stop here for an easy walk through a shaded cypress swamp. The turnout for Cole Creek is just past Bethel Mission on the east side of the parkway. The U-shaped parking area is visible from the road, but the hike and creek are not.

Cole Creek Trail

Distance: 0.4-mile loop
Duration: 10-15 minutes
Difficulty: Easy

This trail through a cypress swamp is flat with a few concrete steps on each side of the entrance. In some places you'll walk above the swamp on a wooden boardwalk, seeing cypress trees, tupelo, and other water-loving trees in their natural habitat. Cole Creek runs through the swamp. The walk shouldn't take more than 10-15 minutes.

Hurricane Creek (MP 164.3)

This stop offers a pretty little nature trail that makes for a perfect walk through the woods. The U-shaped pullout is on the right side of the parkway. The creek is not visible from the road, but the parking is. There are no other amenities.

Hurricane Creek Trail

Distance: 0.3-mile loop
Duration: 10 minutes
Difficulty: Easy

This loop trail is less than one-third of a mile, with a well-cleared path of dirt and pebbles. The terrain is stable and sure-footed, but you're walking into a creek bed, so there's a decline to get there and an incline to get back. You'll be shaded from the sun by southern pines, American beech, and other trees. This walk will take you less than 10 minutes unless you linger to read the signage about the foliage.

Kosciusko Information Center (MP 160)

The **Kosciusko Information Center** (Natchez Trace Pkwy., milepost 160, 662/289-2981, 9am-4pm daily) is a small resource offering maps and information about the Trace, as well as the history of the adjacent town of Kosciusko. There are restrooms and ample parking. The exit for the center is on the west side of the parkway at milepost 160, and is visible from the road.

Back in the days of the Old Trace, this was a campsite for travelers. It is named for a Revolutionary War hero, General Tadeusz Kościuszko.

Kosciusko

Sleepy Kosciusko (population 7,400) is known for a few things. It's named for Tadeusz Kościuszko, the Polish war hero who helped the United States during the American Revolution. (Note that the town name doesn't use the "z" in its spelling.) It is also the birthplace of several Americans of significance, including media mega-personality Oprah Winfrey and James Meredith, the civil rights activist who helped integrate the University of Mississippi. The town is also part of the Mississippi Blues Trail.

Many Trace travelers stop here because of its proximity to the parkway. Several B&Bs are easily accessible for cyclists, and restaurants are within walking and biking distance. There are gas stations and even a Walmart (on Veterans Memorial Dr.).

The downtown square is quaint, an actual four-sided square around the courthouse. There are some sweets shops and mom-and-pop restaurants in town, but nothing fancy.

Sights

In downtown Kosciusko, **Redbud Springs Park** (across from 120 S. Natchez St.) was created in 1976 for the United States' bicentennial. There's a statue of the city's namesake, General Tadeusz Kościuszko, and pretty foliage. The town was originally named Redbud Springs.

A Blues Trail marker at **Charlie Musselwhite Blues Trail** (Washington St. between Jackson and Madison) notes the birthplace of the famous harmonica player, who was born in 1944. Musselwhite's great uncle owned the shop that once stood on this spot. Musselwhite became known in the Memphis and Chicago blues scenes, winning Grammy and W. C. Handy awards.

Certainly media mogul Oprah Winfrey is Kosciusko's most famous daughter. But the **Oprah Winfrey First Home Site** (1 mile east of downtown at MS-12E and Oprah Winfrey Rd.) isn't much to see. A sign commemorates her birth in 1954, but the wood frame house in which she lived is long gone. Only the most diehard fans will appreciate this site, which is not particularly well cared for. If you really want to honor Oprah while in town, check out **The Oprah Winfrey Boys & Girls Club of Kosciusko/Attala County** (500 Knox Rd.,

662/289-4252), which opened in 2001. Her philanthropy helps area kids get breakfasts and lunches, tutoring, medical care, and more.

The 1899 Gothic-style church now houses the **Mary Ricks Thornton Cultural Center** (Washington St. and Huntington St.). The center doesn't have resources (or regular hours) for tourists, but architecture fans should plan to stop by and admire the exterior, including the stained-glass windows.

Festivals and Events

The city of Kosciusko is proud of its connection to the Trace, and no time is this more obvious than in April when it hosts the **National Natchez Trace Festival** (www.kosytrace.com/events/ntf). Held in downtown Kosciusko since 1969, the day's festivities include food vendors, arts and crafts booths, a Miss Natchez Trace Pageant, and live music.

Since 1909 the annual **Central Mississippi Fair** has been a highlight of August. Held at the Attala County Coliseum (550 MS-12, admission $6) over four days, it features all the standard fair fun: carnival rides, livestock showings, and more food on a stick than you can eat.

Shopping

Stroll around the historic downtown Court Square and browse some of the small boutiques, including **Claude Julian's** (141 N. Madison St., 662/289-4821, 9am-5:30pm Mon.-Sat.), which has contemporary men's and women's clothing; **Dakota Rose Boutique** (103 W. Jefferson St., 662/792-4095, 10am-5pm Mon.-Fri., 10am-3pm Sat.), which sells women's clothing with a young, trendy vibe; the family-owned **Patterson Jewelers** (122 N. Jackson St., 662/289-3731, http://pattersonjewelers.net, 9am-5pm Mon.-Fri.), which has been in business since 1950; and **Coghlan Jewelers** (201 W. Jefferson St., 662/289-4811, 10am-5pm Mon.-Fri.).

Food

You're likely to see the folks staying at your B&B eating at **Rib Alley** (201 N. Madison St., 662/289-9800, 8am-8pm daily, $4-12), thanks to its location downtown and close relationship with the innkeepers. It's nothing fancy, but stop for ribs, sandwiches, or soups if you want to eat somewhere on the square. Sarah, the owner, is also the cook, waitress, and dishwasher, so service can be slow when she has a lot of tables.

Outfielders Sports Bar (108 N. Jackson St., 662/792-4114, 11am-10pm Sun.-Thurs., 11am-midnight Fri.-Sat., $3-13) is, as you'd expect, a sports bar with wings, burgers, and sandwiches, including Philly cheesesteaks.

Located just off the Trace, **Old Trace Grill** (719 Veterans Memorial Dr., 662/289-2652, 10:30am-9pm Tues.-Sat., $7-10) serves fried chicken, barbecue, burgers, sandwiches, and ice cream. Lines are out the door in the summer. It has a drive-thru and takeout as well as eat-in dining.

Locals like the rib tip and brisket at **Frenchies Fine Foods & BBQ** (230 MS-12, 662/289-9940, http://frenchiesfinefoods.publishpath.com, 11am-9pm Wed.-Sat., $9 and up).

The parking lot at **Rodeo Family Mexican Restaurant** (1050 Veterans Memorial Dr., 662/289-9802, 11am-10pm daily, $8-13) is almost always full, as locals like this affordable Mexican eatery. There are plenty of lunch specials in the $5-9 range if you are looking to fuel up before rejoining the parkway.

Kosciusko restaurants close early. If you're looking for something open later, try **Bel Piatto Italian Restaurant** (1050 Veterans Memorial Dr., 662/289-9999, 7am-10pm daily, $9-18). It's not just Italian; there are American and even Tex-Mex items on the menu, too.

Accommodations

The folks who own the **Maple Terrace Inn** (300 N. Huntington St., 662/289-4131, www.mapleterraceinn.com, $135) offer several places to stay in Kosciusko, with a total of 35 guest rooms. Maple Terrace is in a 1912 building just blocks from Court Square, with antique furniture and architectural detailing. There's a secure garage for locking up bicycles overnight. Some lore suggests the Maple Terrace Inn is haunted. If you believe that sort of thing, listen closely, particularly on nights when you're the only guest in the house. **Martha's Cottage** (401 N. Huntington St., $250) is more private, with two guest rooms, a porch swing, piano, and indoor bicycle storage. The innkeepers also own the **Presidents Inn** (100 E. Washington St., $135). Their **Hammond-Routt House** (109 S. Natchez St., $135) is located on the Old Trace itself. Finally, the **Niles-Bailey House** (305 N. Huntington St., $135) is a Queen Anne Victorian mansion with a wrap-around porch. Prices for all include breakfast, which is served either in the residence or at a restaurant on the square; Wi-Fi; and other modern amenities. These are unattended bed-and-breakfasts: Fill out your menu when you check in and someone comes to cook breakfast in the morning, but otherwise, there's no one on-site, although there is a phone number for emergencies.

Information and Services
If you need medical help, **Trace Medical Clinic** (530 Veterans Memorial Dr., 662/289-9155) offers basic services during the week. The nearest full-service hospital is in Jackson, nearly 100 miles south.

Holly Hill (MP 154.3)

A small picnic area on the west side of the road, Holly Hill is one of the few areas that have grills as well as picnic tables, so if your plan is to roast some marshmallows or flip a burger, plan to be here at mealtime. One of the tables is wheelchair accessible. The view is of an open meadow, ringed by trees. There are restrooms as well, although this is just six miles from the Kosciusko Information Center. The next restrooms are at River Bend (milepost 122.6)

Red Dog Road (MP 140)

This road, built circa 1834, is historically important. Named for Choctaw chief Ofahoma, also called Red Dog, the road runs to Canton, Mississippi. Chief Ofahoma signed the Treaty of Dancing Rabbit Creek here on September 27, 1830, by which the Choctaws agreed to vacate their land and head west to Oklahoma.

The pullout is on the west side of the road, with a U-shaped parking area and informational signage.

Robinson Road (MP 135.5)

This is a historically significant road that's listed on the National Register of Historic Places. Robinson Road was built in 1821 through Choctaw country. It was this road that connected the towns of Jackson and Columbus, Mississippi. In 1822 this became the designated mail route north, taking some of the traffic off of the historic Trace.

The pullout is on the east side of the road, with a U-shaped parking area and informational signage.

Upper Choctaw Boundary (MP 128.4)

Signage here points to what was the Upper Choctaw Boundary, the border dividing the Choctaw nation from areas allocated for white settlers. The boundary was agreed to by the Choctaws and the American Commission under Andrew Jackson in the 1820 treaty of Doaks Stand. This was a reluctant agreement on the part of the Choctaw, as it forced them to give up about one-third of their land, some 5.5 million acres.

Near the parking lot, an easy 10-minute, flat loop trail will take you on a tour of southern pines in this area, with signage about different trees along the way.

River Bend (MP 122.6)

A significantly larger stop than many on the parkway, River Bend gives you access to the Pearl River. In 1698, the French explorer Pierre LeMoyne Sieur d'Iberville made his way into the mouth of this river and found pearls. Some 100 miles south, near Hattiesburg, Mississippi, the Pearl River has served as part of the border between Mississippi and Louisiana since 1812.

It's unlikely that you'll find any pearls here, but you can find a different kind of gem. There are beautiful views of lily-pad-filled waters, with wide grassy expanses for picnicking and playing, and grills and picnic tables on both sides of the parking lot.

The entrance is on the east side of the parkway. There are restrooms and covered picnic areas. The next restroom stop going south is at the Mississippi Craft Center (milepost 104.5).

Cypress Swamp (MP 122)

The Trace is full of astonishing natural beauty, but even with a lot of tough competition, this walk easily is one of the most scenic.

★ Cypress Swamp Loop Trail

Distance: 0.4-mile loop
Duration: 20 minutes
Difficulty: Easy

The **Cypress Swamp Loop Trail** takes you on a walk of just under half a mile. It starts on a bridge that leads to a boardwalk, which spans a swamp of water tupelos and bald cypress. Because this trail is away from the parking lot and the road, it is unusually quiet and serene. If you're lucky, you may see some wildlife, such as herons or alligators.

The boardwalk leads to a dirt trail, shaded in the woods, that loops around and comes back to the parking area. This is a very easy trail, about a 20-minute walk, assuming a leisurely pace to take in the unusual views. There are a few steps on the bridge to get down to the swamp level, so it is not wheelchair accessible.

The entrance is on the east side of the parkway. The parking area is visible from the road, but the swamp is not.

To access the Natchez Trace National Scenic Trail from this stop, cross the parkway (to the west side) and look for the green hiking sign. From here it is 14.1 miles south to the West Florida Boundary or 8.9 miles north to the Yockanookany Trailhead.

The Trace: Southern Mississippi

On this route through the Deep South, you'll encounter an awe-inspiring landscape and a smile-inducing culture. Learning the area's history will make you equal parts sad, angry, and proud.

BOYD MOUNDS
Mississippi Craft Center ★
Mississippi Agriculture and Forestry Museum ★
Eudora Welty House and Garden ★ ⓧ
JACKSON

Vicksburg National Military Park ★

122 MI/ 196 KM

Mississippi River

LOUISIANA
MISSISSIPPI

Mount Locust Historic House ★

Emerald Mound ★

NATCHEZ

Homochitto National Forest

The Trace: Southern Mississippi

(Map labels:)
Yazoo City
Canton
RESERVOIR OVERLOOK
BOYD MOUNDS
RIDGELAND
CHOCTAW AGENCY
BRASHEARS STAND AND OLD TRACT SITE
MISSISSIPPI CRAFT CENTER
MISSISSIPPI AGRICULTURE AND FORESTRY MUSEUM
EUDORA WELTY HOUSE AND GARDEN
JACKSON
Bolton
DEAN STAND SITE
Vicksburg
Utica
VICKSBURG NATIONAL MILITARY PARK
LOWER CHOCTAW BOUNDARY
ROCKY SPRINGS
OWENS CREEK WATERFALL
GRINDSTONE FORD
MAGNUM MOUND
SUNKEN TRACE
Port Gibson
Mississippi River
LOUISIANA
MISSISSIPPI
MUD ISLAND CREEK
BULLEN CREEK
COLES CREEK REST AREA
Church Hill
MOUNT LOCUST HISTORIC HOUSE
LOESS BLUFF
TURPIN CREEK
EMERALD MOUND
Natchez State Park
Roxie
OLD TRACE EXHIBIT SHELTER
HISTORIC JEFFERSON COLLEGE
ELIZABETH FEMALE ACADEMY
Natchez
Homochitto National Forest
To Baton Rouge
© AVALON TRAVEL

0 — 15 mi
0 — 15 km

This drive includes sites of some of the Civil War's bloodiest battles. It cuts through Jackson, the state capital and home to many important civil rights era sites.

It also skirts several large Indian mounds, sacred sites of Native American tribes who once lived in this area but were pushed west.

But despite its history, this part of Mississippi shines, too, through its friendly, welcoming residents; its reverence for history, particularly its architecture; its lush green landscapes and rolling hills along the banks of the mighty Mississippi; its love of music and art; and, of course, its delicious food. Pack your bags and come think, share, and explore.

Route Overview

Starting north of the Jackson metropolitan area and ending at the southern terminus of the Natchez Trace Parkway, this section of the drive covers **122 miles** of the National Park thoroughfare, plus side trips to some of Mississippi's most historic cities, including Port Gibson, Vicksburg, Jackson, and Natchez.

The amount of time you devote to this region depends on your personal interests. If Civil War battlefields and antebellum homes are your sweet spot, you'll want to devote at least **four days** in the area, being sure to focus on Vicksburg and Natchez. If the American civil rights movement is a passion, allot the same number of days, but weight your time around and near Jackson. If it's the allure of the great outdoors that motivates you, plan to spend **1-2 days** exploring Native American mounds and villages.

Highlights

★ **Mississippi Craft Center:** Browse the works of local artists and see them practice their craft at this oasis along the Trace (page 268).

★ **Mississippi Agriculture and Forestry Museum:** You can spend hours learning and exploring on these 39 acres (page 270).

★ **Eudora Welty House and Garden:** This landmark author's home is so well preserved it feels like Welty will be back at any moment (page 270).

★ **Vicksburg National Military Park:** 1,325 markers commemorate Civil War history at this mammoth site (page 278).

★ **Mount Locust Historic House:** Tour one of the few remaining historic structures on the parkway (page 282).

★ **Emerald Mound:** You can actually climb to the top of this particularly large Indian mound (page 283).

Best Restaurants

★ **Parlor Market:** Nosh on seasonal southern cuisine at this compelling spot (page 274).

★ **Brent's Drugs:** Indulge in a shake or a malt at this old-fashioned soda fountain (page 275).

★ **King's Tavern:** Wine and dine in the oldest restaurant in the state (page 289).

★ **Restaurant 1818:** Experience fine dining and even finer service (page 290).

Driving Considerations

This section of the parkway is well maintained and there are ample pullouts to permit safe sightseeing. The speed limit is 50 mph, and there is likely to be bicycle traffic. You may encounter traffic on the Trace around Jackson, but likely very little south of the city until Natchez. Keep your eyes peeled for wild turkeys and deer on the road.

Southern Mississippi is considered to have a "subtropical" climate. That means highs in the 60s in the winter and above 100°F in the summer. Snow or ice on the Trace in this region is rare. Call 800/305-7417 for up-to-date road conditions.

Because of soft soil and extended drought conditions in the area, there are uneven road surfaces throughout Mississippi. Those in cars are unlikely to be significantly impacted by these potholes, but bicyclists and motorcyclists should use caution.

Fuel and Services

This section of parkway is less rural than others, and you likely will have a cell signal when on the Trace near **Ridgeland, Jackson, Clinton,** and **Natchez.** Service is spottier in the rural areas, particularly en route to **Vicksburg** (though you should be able to connect again once you arrive in Vicksburg itself, depending on your mobile carrier).

Getting to the Starting Point
Car, Motorcycle, or Bicycle

If you've been following the Natchez Trace south, continue driving south from Cypress Swamp for about 15 miles to Boyd Mounds, the first stop of this leg.

It's about 20 miles from the **Jackson** airport to Boyd Mounds. Take MS-475 north to MS-25, then continue west to I-55. From here, it's about six miles until you hit the Trace. Turn right onto the parkway and then continue for about five miles until you reach Boyd Mounds. This drive will take around 40 minutes.

Rental car agencies in central Jackson include **Enterprise Rent-A-Car** (1010 S. State St., 601/948-0062, www.enterprise.com) and **Budget** (4450 US 80 W., 601/923-9504, www.budget.com).

Air

The **Jackson-Medgar Wiley Evers International Airport** (100 International Dr., www.iflyjackson.com) is served by American, Delta, United, and Southern Airways Express, with daily flights from select cities, including Atlanta, Charlotte, Chicago, Dallas, Memphis, Nashville, and Washington DC. The airport has ATMs and free Wi-Fi, but no currency exchange.

The airport is about a 15-minute drive from downtown, but you'll want a rental car if you plan to explore the city. Nine rental car companies have counters in Terminal 1, including **Avis** (601/939-5853, www.avis.com), **Hertz** (601/939-7600, www.hertz.com), and **Budget** (601/932-2126, www.budget.com).

Train and Bus

Amtrak operates out of Jackson's **Union Station** (300 W. Capitol St., 601/355-6350,

Best Accommodations

★ **Fairview Inn:** Step back in time at this 1908 hotel (page 276).

★ **Old Capitol Inn:** This swanky hotel has a rooftop bar that locals love (page 277).

★ **Devereaux Shields House:** Hospitality is the watchword at this B&B (page 292).

★ **Monmouth Historic Inn and Gardens:** Escape at this old-world southern resort (page 292).

www.amtrak.com), a stop on the 900-mile City of New Orleans route, which runs from New Orleans to Chicago. Union Station is centrally located in downtown Jackson.

Greyhound (601/353-6342, www.greyhound.com) serves Jackson out of Union Station. The Greyhound routes to Jackson are through Birmingham and Memphis.

⚑ MS-43 to Canton

Much of the sweet town of Canton is on the National Register of Historic Places. Those who love all things old will be charmed by the courthouse square, which is a historical shopping district and home to the twice-annual Canton Flea Market, a draw for bargain hunters.

Leaving the Trace

To get to Canton, exit the parkway at MS-43, near **milepost 115.** (The Ross Barnett Reservoir will be to your east.) Take MS-43 north for 6.6 miles. Turn left onto Peace Street. Drive 1.7 miles and turn left onto MS-16 to reach downtown Canton. The drive should take 15 minutes.

Shopping

Thanks to its many cute shops filled to the brim with vintage, antique, and specialty gift items, Canton is called the Antique and Gift Square of Mississippi.

Held in the town square twice a year, the popular **Canton Flea Market** (601/859-8055, http://cantonmsfleamarket.com,

8am-5pm second Thurs. of May and Oct.) hosts more than 1,000 vendors and artists, making it one of the largest of its kind in the South. The charming iron fence around the courthouse makes a great backdrop for artwork.

Canton Square Antiques (155 W. Peace St., 601/859-2209, 8am-5pm Mon.-Sat.) stocks vintage fine jewelry, furniture, and artwork. **La Di Da** (3334 N. Liberty St., 601/859-8106, http://shopladida.com, 10am-5pm Mon.-Tues. and Thurs.-Fri., 10am-2pm Wed. and Sat.) is a sweet gift boutique owned by two sisters. Come here for ceramics and other small home decor.

You can tell from the old cabinetry that **Unique Antiques** (171 W. Peace St., 601/667-3480, 10am-5pm Mon.-Sat.) is the real deal, located in the old Mosby Drugstore space. The space may be old, but the store is new, opened in 2016. They specialize in collectibles and antiques, including some primitive folk art styles.

The Emporium of Canton (3344 N. Liberty St., 601/667-3670, www.emporiumofcanton.com, 10am-5pm Mon.-Sat.) stocks the work of more than 40 Mississippi artisans and makers, including items like housewares, furniture, and jewelry.

Channel your inner Joanna Gaines to get the *Fixer Upper* look at **Farmhouse** (141 W. Peace St., 601/391-3129, http://farmhouseinterior.com, 10am-6pm Tues.-Fri., 10am-4pm Sat.). Opened in 2016, this shop carries farmhouse-chic furniture, home decor, and some gourmet food.

Fuel Up

On this section of the Trace, between major cities Jackson and Natchez, you're never particularly far from a gas station. You will easily find gas in the side trip destinations in this chapter, including Port Gibson and Vicksburg. Here's a quick list of places to exit the parkway in southern Mississippi so that you can refuel at the closest gas station. (Some stops may take you to small towns, others will be just a single service station.)

The National Park Service posts a list of supply stations at most of the Trace rest areas, although the list is not updated regularly.

• **Milepost 103.4:** Exit at Old Canton Road and head south. Drive 0.3 mile to the Chevron at the intersection with Rice Road.

• **Milepost 101:** Exit at I-55 North, then take exit 105B toward Ridgeland. Gas stations near this interchange include a Chevron on Old Agency Road.

• **Milepost 89:** Exit at Pinehaven Drive and turn south. Drive 0.4 mile to the Exxon or Quick Stop at the Northside Drive intersection in Clinton.

• **Milepost 79.0:** Exit at MS-467 and head southeast. Drive 2.5 miles to the Shell in Raymond.

• **Milepost 41.3:** Exit at MS-18 and drive west. There's a Citgo 1.3 miles from the parkway, or turn south onto US 61 to head into Port Gibson. There's a Shell on US 61 in the center of town.

Food

Canton Junction Sports Pub (399 Neponset St., 781/828-7878, www.junctionsportshub.com, 3pm-midnight Mon., 3pm-1am Wed., noon-1am Thurs.-Sat., noon-midnight Sun., $7-16) has the standard fare like pizza, burgers, wings, and salads, plus a better-than-average craft beer list.

If you are in Canton during the week, have lunch at **Culinary Cowboy** (116 Commercial Pkwy., 601/859-9953, 10:30am-2pm Mon.-Fri., $5-11). Don't skip the breads and pies baked in house.

It's a no-frills spot, but **Ms. Bar-B-Que** (3421 N. Liberty St., 601/859-9186, 10:30am-5pm Mon.-Thurs., 10:30am-7pm Fri.-Sat., $3-8) serves good meat, including made-to-order hamburgers, ribs, pulled pork, and fried chicken.

Have you ever had oysters on the half chip? That would be a fried oyster on a tortilla chip with pico de gallo and chipotle cream. You can try it at **Two Rivers** (1537 W. Peace St., 601/859-9999, http://tworiversrestaurant.letseat.at, 4:30pm-9pm Mon.-Thurs., 4:30pm-10pm Fri.-Sat.,

$10-30), which is the nicest restaurant in town.

Back to the Trace

Return to the parkway by taking Peace Street, the main thoroughfare, 1.7 miles east to MS-43. Turn right and drive 6.6 miles south on MS-43. Turn right to exit MS-43, then rejoin the parkway near **milepost 115** by turning left to continue heading south. The total drive should take 15 minutes.

Boyd Mounds (MP 106.9)

When you first spy this area, it may appear to be one large mound, but it's really three separate mounds within the larger, 100-foot-long mound. Archaeologists date pottery found in these mounds from AD 700. Remains of more than 40 burials were also found here.

The road leading to the mound is on the left (east) side of the parkway. The mound isn't visible from the parkway. The site is open sunrise to sunset only.

A Day on the Trace: Southern Mississippi

Gas up and get going! You'll start your day in the state capital, where history and progress meet. Have a traditional pork breakfast at **Big Apple Inn,** then visit the hands-on **Mississippi Agriculture and Forestry Museum.** Before leaving town, stop by the **Eudora Welty House and Garden** to learn about the life and works of one of Mississippi's favorite daughters.

Jump on I-20 West near milepost 86 and you'll reach Vicksburg in about 30 minutes. Explore **Vicksburg National Military Park,** then take in the river views during lunch at **10 South Rooftop Bar & Grill.**

Drive east to rejoin the parkway from I-20. As you approach the last 15 miles of the Trace, stop at **Mount Locust Historic House** and then **Emerald Mound,** one of the few archaeological sites on the Trace on which you may climb.

Take a photo as you reach the **southern terminus** of the Natchez Trace Parkway, and then ease into **Natchez,** where dinner should be at **King's Tavern,** the oldest restaurant in Mississippi—and one that can make a fine cocktail to toast your milestone. Spend the night at **Devereaux Shields House,** set in a Queen Anne Victorian.

Reservoir Overlook

(MP 105.6)

This stop is both a pretty overlook and a place to play. Overlooking **Ross Barnett Reservoir** (which is accessible from the nearby town of Ridgeland), this is a popular place for locals to spend an afternoon with a blanket, some sunscreen, and a book.

Depending on the time of year, water lilies, wildflowers, and lush trees provide contrast to the wide watery openness of the reservoir. Sunrises and sunsets reflecting off the reservoir can be stunning. It's not unusual to catch a wedding or engagement photo shoot here.

The **Natchez Trace Multi-Use Trail,** which runs parallel to the Trace for about 10 miles, has its northern terminus in the overlook's parking lot.

The parkway hugs the reservoir for 15 miles. The driveway is on the left (east) side of the road; the reservoir and parking lot are visible from the road.

Choctaw Agency

(MP 100.7)

This stop commemorates the Choctaw Agency. The agency was located here between 1807 and 1820, and functioned like an embassy in which the U.S. government and the Choctaw Nation would negotiate with each other. The U.S. government set up agencies within the borders of many Native American nations. Federal agents working out of this location would act as intermediaries between the two governments. The agents lived among the Choctaw and represented their interests while implementing U.S. policy.

All that's left of the agency today is a sign marking the site and explaining its significance. There's an access point for the **Natchez Trace Multi-Use Trail** in the parking lot; signs point the way. You can take the trail from here back to the Reservoir Overlook or continue onward. However, you'll have to turn around in about five miles, as there's no parking or other access to the trail beyond this stop.

Natchez Trace Multi-Use Trail

Yet another unexpected gem along the Natchez Trace Parkway is the **Natchez Trace Multi-Use Trail.** Designed for cyclists, pedestrians, and others not in motorized vehicles, this paved recreational trail parallels the parkway, offering a safe way to enjoy the scenery without being in traffic. The trail starts at **Reservoir Overlook** (milepost 105.6) and runs along the parkway for almost 10 miles. The southernmost access point on the trail is at the **Chocktaw Agency** (milepost 100.7). (You can continue walking or cycling south, but there is no parking or access to the trail beyond this.) There are plans to eventually extend the trail to the Clinton Visitor Center at milepost 89.

The trail also traverses the city of Ridgeland, where you can access shopping and local parks. Download a full map at www.visitridgeland.com.

Remember to look both ways when crossing the trail, as bikers and those on inline skates may be traveling at a speedy clip.

Ridgeland

Ridgeland is essentially a suburb of Jackson, but thanks to its location on Ross Barnett Reservoir and its commitment to outdoor recreation, it seems worlds away.

Sights
Parkway Information Cabin
Staffed by park rangers, the **Parkway Information Cabin** (milepost 102.4 Natchez Trace Pkwy., 800/305-7417, 9am-4pm Fri.-Sat.) is a good stop to get questions answered from people who know the Trace. Various ranger-led programs (free) cover everything from wildlife to Indian mounds. Some programs are specifically designed for kids, but all are family-friendly.

The cabin has a small gift shop, information about nearby Ridgeland, and picnic tables.

★ Mississippi Craft Center
Run by the Craftsmen's Guild of Mississippi, the **Mississippi Craft Center** (950 Rice Rd., 601/856-7546, http://craftsmensguildofms.org, 9am-5pm Mon.-Sat., noon-5pm Sun., free) is a surprising cornucopia of art right off of the parkway. This large building houses classes, local events, artisan demos, and fine art exhibitions. Browse the large gallery store for quilts, wood-carvings, ceramics, baskets, sculpture, jewelry, and metalworking made by local and regional craftspeople.

The building also has some outdoor sculpture, a sizable deck, and places to sit both inside and outside. There's no café, but there are a few vending machines and restrooms.

You can access the building two different ways. Near milepost 104.5 there's a turnoff on the left side of the road. There isn't yet a sign here for the center (it's marked as another stop of the Old Trace, though a new sign is in the works). You can park here and walk across a small bridge to the back of the building. To get to the main entrance, continue another mile south to Old Canton Road. Exit to the right to leave the Trace, then turn right onto Old Canton. Continue 0.2 mile to Rice Road. Turn left and drive one mile. The center will be on your left.

Sports and Recreation
Ross Barnett Reservoir (115 Madison Landing Circle, 601/856-6574, www.therez.ms.gov, $5 Sat.-Sun. and holidays Apr.-Sept.) is the reason locals and visitors gravitate to Ridgeland. The 33,000-acre reservoir and surrounding area (another 17,000 acres) provide the water supply for Jackson residents, but

recreation is the watchword here. There are 16 parks, multiple hiking and biking trails, two golf courses, five marinas, and 22 boat launches. The reservoir also has five campgrounds. There are a number of entrances to the reservoir. MS-43 crosses both the parkway and the reservoir itself, and is a well-trafficked place to enter.

Food

It doesn't seem like it'd be enough to sustain a whole restaurant, but **Tom's Fried Pies** (827 US 49, 769/257-7351, www.tomsfriedpies.com, 10am-7pm Tues.-Sat. $3-6) has savory and sweet fried half-moon-shaped pies, with varieties ranging from Tex-Mex to spinach and mushroom. The fruit pies include berry flavors as well as peach, apple, apricot, and cherry.

Anjou (361 Township Ave., 601/707-0587, http://anjourestaurant.net, 11am-9pm Mon.-Thurs., 11am-10pm Fri.-Sat., 10:30am-9pm Sun., $16-32) is a traditional white-tablecloth French bistro, with dishes such as beef tartare and steak frites.

Find authentic Mexican dishes at **Green Ghost Tacos** (1290 E. County Line Rd., 601/957-7436, www.greenghosttacos.com, 11am-9pm Sun.-Thurs., 11am-10pm Fri.-Sat., $3-12). This family-run restaurant offers tacos, tortas, burritos, and enchiladas, There's also a location in Jackson's Fondren neighborhood, as well as a food truck.

Accommodations

Ridgeland is a good, safe place to stop and crash for the night.

Embassy Suites Jackson/North Ridgeland (200 Township Ave., 601/607-7112, http://embassysuites3.hilton.com, $134-160) has two-room suites with wet bars, refrigerators, microwaves, and free breakfast cooked to order. The on-site restaurant, Flying Spoons, offers basic sandwiches and salads. The **Homewood Suites by Hilton** (853 Centre St., 601/899-8611, www.jackson.homewoodsuites.com, $119-128) has a similar setup.

Cozy up in the "lodge atmosphere" at **Cabot Lodge** (120 Dyess Rd., 601/957-0757, http://cabotlodgejacksonnorth.com, $80-114), a family-friendly hotel offering a free hot breakfast and evening cocktail hour.

Town Place Suites by Marriott (310 Southlake Ave., 601/898-9880, http://townplacesuites.marriott.com, $123-151) has a picnic and barbecue grill area and free continental breakfast. **SpringHill Suites by Marriott** (121 S. Town Ave., 601/898-3747, www.marriott.com, $139-159) is in The Township at Colony Park, within walking distance to restaurants and shopping.

Thanks to sofa sleepers in the rooms, **Hyatt Place** (1016 Highland Colony Pkwy., 601/898-8815, http://jacksonridgeland.place.hyatt.com, $142-164) is great for families. The lobby has a self-check-in kiosk, coffee, and a wine café.

Ross Barnett Reservoir (115 Madison Landing Circle, 601/829-2751, www.therez.ms.gov, RVs $13-30, tents $12-17) has five campgrounds (Timberlake, Goshen Springs, Coal Bluff, Leake County, and Low Head Dam), some of which offer pools, Wi-Fi, and laundry. If you don't need amenities and just want to be one with the land, primitive upriver camping is allowed on Pearl River north of MS-43 and south of Lease County Water Park. A permit (free) is required and is good for up to 10 days. To get your permit, call Goshen Springs Campground (601/992-9703) or the Reservoir Control Tower (601/992-9703).

Jackson

The Natchez Trace Parkway runs right through Jackson, Mississippi's energetic, complicated, and historic capital. Named after President Andrew Jackson, the city is known for its blues music, art museums, and complex civil rights history. It is the Magnolia State's biggest city.

Sights

A complex coined the **2 Mississippi Museums** (www.mdah.ms.gov/2MM) was developed as part of a celebration of Mississippi's bicentennial. An updated **Museum of Mississippi History** and a new **Mississippi Civil Rights Museum** fully document the history of the state and its civil rights struggles. These twin museums opened in December 2017.

Learn about Mississippi's famous athletes, including Cool Papa Bell, Boo Ferriss, Dizzy Dean, Walter Payton, Archie Manning, Jerry Rice, Brett Favre, Bailey Howell, Davey Whitney, and Van Chancellor at the **Mississippi Sports Hall of Fame** (1152 Lakeland Dr., 601/982-8264, http://msfame.com, 10am-4pm Mon.-Sat., adults $5, seniors $3.50, students 6-17 $3.50, free for children 5 and under).

Housed in the renovated Goodyear Building, the **City of Jackson Fire Museum** (355 W. Woodrow Wilson Ave., 601/960-2433, 8am-5pm Mon.-Fri., free) is stocked with historical fire-related gear, including a 1936 Seagrave, 1917 America LaFrance, 1904 horse-drawn steamer, helmets, and uniforms.

★ Mississippi Agriculture and Forestry Museum

Oft referred to as the Mississippi Ag Museum, the mammoth **Mississippi Agriculture and Forestry Museum** (1150 Lakeland Dr., 601/432-4500, www.msagmuseum.org, 9am-5pm Mon.-Sat., adults $5, seniors, students, and children $4, free for children under 3) is a hands-on experience. On 39 acres, the museum houses working printing presses, impressive model trains, arrowhead collections, a blacksmith shop, antique cars, and even a replica of an 1820s Mississippi town, complete with a general store that functions as the museum's gift shop. The staff is exceedingly knowledgeable and devoted to their mission of making Mississippi's agrarian roots interesting. Families of all ages could easily spend many hours here.

★ Eudora Welty House and Garden

A National Historic Landmark and listed on the National Register of Historic Places, the **Eudora Welty House and Garden** (1119 Pinehurst St., 601/353-7762, http://eudorawelty.org, tours 9am, 11am, 1pm, and 3pm Tues.-Sat. and by appointment, adults $5, students $3, free for children under 6) offers an in-depth look into the life and work of one of Mississippi's favorite daughters. The prolific Pulitzer Prize-winning author was deeply connected to her native Mississippi. Everything about Welty's home (in which she grew up and lived until her death)—the exterior, interior, and furnishings—is as it was in 1986 when she donated it to the State of Mississippi. Look at her paintings, photographs, and thousands of books. Stroll in her garden and see what inspired her. The gift shop has many of Welty's books for sale (as well as some of her photographs); you'll likely be motivated to read them after your visit. Admission is free on the 13th of the month if it falls on a day when the museum is open.

Smith Robertson Museum

Housed in the building that was formerly Smith Robertson School, the first public school built in Jackson for African American children, **Smith Robertson Museum and Cultural Center** (528 Bloom St., 601/960-1457, www.jacksonms.gov, 9am-5pm Mon.-Fri., 10am-1pm Sat., adults $5.50, seniors $4, students $3, children 4-17 $2, free for children 3 and under) honors that legacy. The museum's exhibits focus on the experiences of African Americans in the Deep South. Exhibits cover slavery, including a powerful slave ship display that details passage from Africa; historically black colleges and universities; Mississippi African

American folk art; and the history of the building.

Medgar Evers Home Museum

Medgar Evers was the first field secretary for the NAACP in Jackson. He was assassinated in his own driveway in June 1963 during Jackson's difficult and violent fight for civil rights. The **Medgar Evers Home Museum** (2332 Margaret Walker Alexander Dr., 601/977-7839, tours by appointment only, free) was named a National Historic Landmark in January 2017. Both inside and outside the home are panels detailing Evers's life, death, and work. Neighbor and local author Eudora Welty was moved by Evers's death, and during a sleepless night that followed his assassination, she wrote one of her most powerful stories, "Where Is the Voice Coming From?" from the point of view of Evers's killer.

Margaret Walker Center

The **Margaret Walker Center** (1400 J. R. Lynch St., 601/979-3935, 8am-5pm Mon.-Sat., free) is a multi-story archive and museum about African American history and culture. Originally founded in 1968 by Margaret Walker as the Institute for the Study of the History, Life, and Culture of Black People, the center honors Walker's legacy and continues her work. The art exhibitions on display change, but they tend to be thought-provoking and powerful. The museum is inside Ayer Hall on the Jackson State University campus. Free on-campus visitor parking is easy to find.

Farish Street Historic District

Farish Street Historic District (between Fortification St. and Amite St.) was the center of commerce and social activity for African Americans in Jackson after World War II. At that time the area

---

Top to bottom: Mississippi Agriculture and Forestry Museum; Eudora Welty House and Garden; Medgar Evers Home Museum.

Self-Guided Tours of Jackson

• Download a free brochure and take yourself on the self-guided **Belhaven Neighborhood Driving Tour** (www.greaterbelhaven.com). It features 18 sites, all tied to different quotes or moments in the movie *The Help*, written by Jackson native Kathryn Stockett. Fans will enjoy going by 805 Riverside Drive, headquarters of the Junior League of Jackson, and the homes of characters Hilly Hollbrook and Elizabeth Leefolt on Myrtle and Devine Streets.

• The self-guided **Historic Downtown Walking Tour** (www.visitjackson.com) provides precise walking directions for some of Jackson's prettiest sights. The downloadable brochure starts at the Old Capitol Museum

(1839-1902) and includes the Old U.S. Post Office (circa 1875), Central Fire Station (circa 1904), City Hall, and others.

• Another downloadable, self-guided option, the **Civil Rights Movement Driving Tour** (www.visitjackson.com/Visitor-Guides) includes a whopping 81 sites related to the civil rights movement in Jackson. The scope of the tour includes churches, public buildings, residences, and businesses in four different neighborhoods. The tour begins at the Smith Robertson Museum. Sites are marked by blue signs with a number in yellow that corresponds to the map. The stops on this tour are generally safe during daylight hours, but use common sense when visiting less populated areas.

---

thrived, as black-owned businesses attracted customers who were not welcome elsewhere in town. As the city became desegregated, the district fell into disrepair. There have been efforts to rehab and revitalize the area since the late 1970s, but it is still very much a work in progress. It's important to come here and read the signage to truly understand Jackson. But do so during daylight hours and pay attention to your surroundings. This area is not recommended at night.

International Museum of Muslim Cultures

The **International Museum of Muslim Cultures** (201 E. Pascagoula St. #102, 601/960-0440, www.muslimmuseum.org, 10am-5pm Mon.-Fri., by appointment only Sat.-Sun., adults $13, seniors $12, children $7) is a fascinating and comprehensive look at Islamic culture via artifacts and other exhibitions. Many of the displays are hands-on and include music and other elements to keep kids' attention.

Mississippi Museum of Art

An impressive world-class art museum in the heart of downtown, the **Mississippi Museum of Art** (380 N. Lamar St., 601/960-1515, http://msmuseumart.org, 10am-5pm Tues.-Sat., noon-5pm Sun., free; admission varies for special exhibits) has a permanent collection focused on Mississippi artists, in a building that will make you think you're in one of the world's art capitals. The brick and glass lobby is sleek and modern, yet welcoming, and flows into a 1.2-acre public garden with fountains and plants, where locals hang out for lunch. Extending the museum's collection to the outdoors, the sculptures in this outdoor patio area are vibrant.

The museum has a lovely café and a better-than-average gift shop.

Entertainment and Events

More than 120 concerts are performed annually by the **Mississippi Symphony Orchestra** (601/960-1565, http://msorchestra.com). Most shows take place at **Thalia Mara Hall** (255 E. Pascagoula St.), but there are popular special performances, such as the Pepsi Pops concert at Old Trace Park on the Ross Barnett Reservoir in nearby Ridgeland.

Held annually in August, the **Jackson Rhythm & Blues Festival** (http://jacksonrhythmandbluesfestival.com) is a two-day musical extravaganza inside the Jackson Convention Complex.

Think of this as the Olympics of ballet. The **USA International Ballet Competition** (www.usaibc.com) takes place every four years (2018 and 2022) for two weeks in June at Thalia Mara Hall, when the ballet world looks to Jackson. In addition to the competition itself, there are performances and also classes for students.

Held annually in October at the Mississippi State Fairgrounds, the 10-day **Mississippi State Fair** (1207 Mississippi St., 601/961-4000, www.msfair.net) is a big deal. Look for musical acts such as Boyz II Men and Travis Tritt, rides, contests (including a mother-daughter look-alike competition and a hula hoop contest), and lots of fair food. It's a nice bonus that the fairgrounds are in walking distance of downtown.

Shopping

In recent years the revitalized **Fondren District** (bounded by Northside Dr., I-55, Woodrow Wilson Ave., and the ICR railroad, www.finditinfondren.com) has become Jackson's hip arts district, home to many boutiques, galleries, and restaurants. If you're a browser and want one-of-a-kind items, this is where you should start.

Blithe and Vine (2943 Old Canton Rd., 601/427-3322, http://blithcandvine.com, 10am-5:30pm Mon.-Fri., 10am-5pm Sat.) features women's clothing, with an emphasis on upscale brands. Upscale brands like Trina Turk are also on the racks at

Top to bottom: Mississippi Museum of Art; a dancer at the USA International Ballet Competition; Two Sisters Kitchen.

Treehouse (3008 N. State St., 601/982-3433, 10am-5:30pm Mon.-Sat.). You'll know you're in the right place when you see the little white house with hot pink doors and shutters.

The Orange Peel (422 Mitchell Ave., 601/364-9977, noon-6pm Mon., 10am-6pm Tues.-Fri., 10am-5pm Sat.) is a vintage consignment shop selling clothing and jewelry.

Old House Depot (639 Monroe St., 601/592-6200, www.oldhousedepot.com, 9am-5pm Mon.-Sat. or by appointment) is the only Jackson store on the Mississippi Antique Trail. The focus here is on architectural salvage: building parts that have been rescued from a demolition site. Look for stained-glass panels, doors, doorknobs, and other hardware.

Highland Village Shopping Center (4500 I-55 N., 601/982-5861, www.highlandvillagems.com, 10am-6pm Mon.-Sat., noon-5pm Sun.) is the area's upscale shopping center, with pretty stonework, elevated walkways, fountains, and seasonal landscaping. The center has nearly 50 stores, including Kate Spade, Lululemon, and Whole Foods.

Food

Jackson has an interesting food scene: part sophisticated foodie, part old-school Southern. Pronounced like "Kate," **CAET** (3100 N. State St., 601/321-9169, www.caetwinebar.com, 4pm-11pm Tues.-Thurs., 4pm-midnight Fri.-Sat., $12-35) is a wine bar and small plates eatery in the Fondren District. Choose from more than 30 wines by the glass, and eat dishes such as lamb porterhouse, fried lobster tail, and cauliflower saganaki.

★ **Parlor Market** (115 W. Capitol St., 601/360-0090, http://parlormarket.com, 11am-2pm and 4:30pm-10pm Mon.-Fri., 5:30pm-10pm Sat., $10-30) is one of Jackson's most compelling restaurants. A cozy yet modern decor complements what the chef calls "seasonal Southern."

Brent's Drugs

Think: duck carbonara, General Tso's pork cheeks, and duck breast in a sweet tea brine.

Everyone who is anyone has lunch at **Two Sisters Kitchen** (707 N. Congress St., 11am-2pm Mon.-Fri., 11am-3pm Sun., $15), a cafeteria-style soul food place with a big patio and an even bigger following. It's cash only.

A daily happy hour with $1 select oysters and drink specials packs 'em in at **Saltine Oyster Bar** (622 Duling Ave., 601/982-2899, www.saltinerestaurant. com, 11am-10pm Mon.-Thurs., 11am-11pm Fri.-Sat., 11am-9pm Sun., $12-24). But thanks to a decent craft cocktail program, this contemporary oyster bar is good anytime.

Located in a new building in historic Bellhaven, **Manship Woodfired Kitchen** (1200 N. State St., 601/398-4562, http:// themanshipjackson.com, 7am-10am and 11am-9pm Mon., 7am-10am and 11am-10pm Tues.-Fri., 9am-10pm Sat., $7-22) serves wood-fired pizzas and other Italian-inspired dishes from the dining room, patio, or large bar.

Opened in 1946, ★ **Brent's Drugs** (655 Dueling Ave., 601/ 366-3427, www. brentsdrugs.com, 10am-5pm Mon.-Wed., 7am-5pm Thurs., 7am-8pm Fri., 8am-5pm Sat., 10am-3pm Sun., $3-6) was once the traditional pharmacy/soda fountain that every neighborhood used to have. Today, the soda fountain/restaurant has taken over the whole space, but the old-time feel remains. Come here for burgers, salads, penny candy, shakes, and malts, and to pose in a location from the movie *The Help.*

Since 1935 **Mayflower Café** (123 W. Capitol St., 601/355-4122, www.may-flowercafems.com, 11am-10pm Mon.-Fri., 4pm-10pm Sat., $15-35) has been a Jackson mainstay. It's the oldest restaurant in town, and was said to be Eudora Welty's favorite. Come here for seafood, steaks, and serious old-time ambience, plus an amazing neon sign.

Soul Wired Café (4147 Northview Dr., Ste. B, 601/790-0864, www.soulwired-cafe.com, 10am-3pm and 5pm-10pm Tues.-Fri., 10am-midnight Sat., $3-7) is a community-centric café with local art on the walls and live music and poetry readings on Thursdays and Saturdays. This is a good place for vegan and vegetarian options in a meat-centric city, thanks to the salad bar and extensive sandwich offerings.

Barbecue
The Pig & Pint (3139 N. State St., 601/326-6070, http://pigandpint.com, 11am-9pm Mon.-Sat., 11am-4pm Sun., $7-14) offers barbecue and craft beer. What more could you want? Barbecued meats are served in fun dishes (nachos, tacos, disco fries, and even salads). The signature is a sweet Mississippi-style barbecue sauce.

Breakfast and lunch are served at **Chimneyville Smokehouse** (970 High St., 601/354-4665, http://chimneyville. com, 6am-2pm Mon.-Fri., $10-16). Come

Jackson's Legal Still

Southerners are proud of **Cathead Distillery** (422 S. Farish St., 601/667-3038, http://catheadvodka.com, tours hourly 3pm-6pm Thurs.-Fri. or other times by appointment), which claims to be the state's first legal still (there are plenty of illegal moonshiners in these parts). The name comes from a phrase in the blues music community, "That cat can play," meaning someone was respected by their peers. Take a tour or find a local restaurant to mix you a cocktail.

hungry for the big country breakfasts. Ribs are St. Louis-style.

E&L Bar-b-que (1111 Bailey Ave., 601/355-5035, 10am-11pm Wed.-Sun. $7-20) is a local favorite with chicken wings, smoked turkey legs, hot links, and the Jackson specialty, the pig ear sandwich.

Named an "American classic" by the James Beard Foundation, **Bully's** (3118 Livingston Rd., 601/362-0484, 11am-6pm daily, $6-9) has a menu of traditional soul food dishes like ham hocks, smothered oxtails, chitterlings, smothered liver and onions, turkey necks, fried pork chops, fried okra, fried green tomatoes, and banana pudding.

For more than 70 years Jacksonians have been coming to the **Big Apple Inn** (509 N. Farish St., 601/354-9371, 7am-9:30pm Tues.-Sat., $5-10) for pig ear sandwiches and hot smoked sausage sandwiches (known as "smokes"). This is strictly no-frills, and an acquired taste, but definitely a classic.

Accommodations

Jackson has many hotels to accommodate state legislators and others visiting on official state business, as well as fans of Jackson State University's Baby Tigers. If you're coming to town when the legislature is in session or a football game is scheduled, room availability might be low. If you find yourself stuck, try suburban Ridgeland (to the north) or Clinton (to the south).

A well-located option in the heart of downtown, **Jackson Marriott** (299 E. Amrite St., 601/969-5100, www.marriott.com, $119-209) offers a choice between a buffet breakfast and continental breakfast. Bistro Restaurant is the in-house dining option; features include an outdoor pool and a good visitors center.

Once the historic King Edward Hotel, the **Hilton Garden Inn Jackson Downtown** (235 W. Capitol St., 601/353-5464, http://hiltongardeninn3.hilton.com, $126-256) has 186 rooms with old-world charm and modern amenities. The pretty lobby is appealing and the bar can be hopping at night. It also has a fitness room, lounge, and indoor pool.

Hilton Jackson Hotel & Convention Center (1001 E. County Line Rd., 601/957-2800, www.hiltonjackson.com, $129-236) is popular for convention-goers, with its location, a fitness center, outdoor pool, and the popular Fitzgeralds Lobby Bar.

Several options near the Mississippi Coliseum include the **Best Western Executive Inn** (725 Larson St., 601/969-6555, http://book.bestwestern.com, $89-114), which has Wi-Fi in public areas; the **Comfort Inn** (614 Monroe St., 601/352-8282, http://choicehotels.com, $92-102), which has Wi-Fi and an outdoor pool; and the **Hampton Inn** (320 Greymont St., 601/352-1700, http://hamptoninn.hilton.com, $119-136).

Head to the ★ **Fairview Inn** (734 Fairview St., 601/948-3429, http://fairviewinn.com, $199-339) for a Southern experience. This former 1908 Colonial Revival mansion on the Register of Historic Places is Jackson's only small luxury hotel. Amenities include a library, bar, restaurant, spa, and lovely gardens in which to stroll. The rooms are large, some with parlors and fireplaces and giant soaking tubs. Service is attentive, but more like a B&B than a traditional hotel.

Locals love to hang at the rooftop bar of the ★ **Old Capitol Inn** (226 N. State St., 601/359-9000, http://oldcapitolinn. com, $99-175), which is housed in a pretty brick building that was once a YWCA. In addition to the rooftop garden, the hotel has a ballroom and Jacuzzi suites. The fitness center is next door.

Information and Services

Visit Jackson (111 E. Capitol St., 800/354-7695, http://visitjackson.com) is a good place to stop in and find brochures and other basic information on the city.

Need bike parts or repairs? You'll have to go to the suburbs, but **The Bike Rack** (2282 Lakeland Dr., Flowood, 601/936-2100, 10am-6pm Mon.-Sat.); **Indian Cycle Fitness and Outdoor** (677 S. Pear Orchard Dr., Ridgeland, 601/956-8383, http://indiancyclefitness.com, 10am-6pm Mon.-Sat.); and **The Bike Crossing** 115 W. Jackson St., Ridgeland, 601/856-0049, http://thebikecrossing.com, 10am-6pm Mon.-Fri., 9am-5pm Sat.) are solid options.

Clinton Visitor Center (MP 89)

The **Clinton Visitor Center** (1300 Pinehaven Dr., 601/924-2221, www. clintonms.org, 9am-5pm Mon.-Sat., 1pm-5pm Sun.) is an impressive oasis on the parkway. Built in 2004, it has nice restrooms, a large parking area, a brick patio, a free "little library" book exchange space, plus a small museum with exhibitions on the Trace and a gift shop. There are a few snacks in the gift shop, and the knowledgeable staff will help you figure out where to go and what to see in historic Clinton (they'll even make reservations for you or let you use the Wi-Fi to make your own). Pets are not permitted inside the building, but

there are plenty of places to walk the dog on the grounds.

⬥ I-20 to Vicksburg

Vicksburg, on the banks of the Mississippi and Yazoo Rivers, is best known for its bloody battle during the Civil War. It was during the 47-day Siege of Vicksburg that the Union troops gained control of the Mississippi River, an event that many cite as the turning point in the Union's ability to win the war.

Today, Vicksburg is a city of more than 26,000, an attraction for those interested in military history and river culture.

The **Vicksburg Convention and Visitors Bureau** (52 Old Hwy. 27, 601/636-0177, http://visitvicksburg, 8am-5pm Mon.-Sat., 10am-4pm Sun.) operates a visitors center with a wealth of information about the region. There are **Mississippi Welcome Center** (4210 Washington St., 601/638-4269, www. visitmississippi.org, 8am-5pm daily) locations all over the state, of course, but this one is especially helpful because of Vicksburg's historical significance.

Leaving the Trace

Near **milepost 86,** turn left to exit the Natchez Trace Parkway, following signs for I-20 West. Drive west on I-20 for 29 miles (about 20 minutes). Take exit 4B to Vicksburg. Follow Clay Street to get into central Vicksburg.

Sights

Check out 21 exhibits about life on the river at the **Lower Mississippi River Museum & Riverfront Interpretive Site** (910 Washington St., 601/638-9900, www. lmrm.org, 9am-4pm Wed.-Sat., free). Highlights include exhibits about the steamboat and the river as a highway, a 1,515-gallon aquarium featuring local fish species, and the Mississippi Flood River Model.

A $2.4 million renovation of the

old railroad depot into **The Old Depot Museum** (1010 Levee St., 601/638-6500, www.vicksburgbattlefieldmuseum.net, 9am-5pm Mon.-Sat. Apr.-Sept., 10am-4pm Mon.-Sat. Oct.-Mar., adults $5.50, seniors and military $5, children ages 3-6 $1.10, free for children younger than 3) resulted in a museum focused on transportation. Check out railroad memorabilia and models of military ships and riverboats, and exhibits from the old Vicksburg Battlefield Museum.

The site of the first Coca-Cola bottling in 1894, the **Biedenham Coca-Cola Museum** (1107 Washington St., 601/638-6514, www.biedenharncocacolamuseum.com, 9am-5pm Mon.-Sat., 1:30pm-4:30pm Sun., adults and children over 12 $3.50, children 6-12 $2.50, free for children under 6) features vintage Coca-Cola ads and memorabilia, plus a gift shop.

Housed in the Old Warren County Court House, the **Old Court House Museum** (1008 Cherry St., 601/636-0741, http://oldcourthouse.org, 8:30am-4:30pm Mon.-Sat., 1:30pm-4:30pm Sun., adults $5, seniors $4.50, students $3) was built in 1858. The museum features Civil War artifacts of all kinds, including flags, furniture, and antebellum-era clothing.

Focused on the history and culture of African Americans in Vicksburg and America, the **Jacqueline House Museum** (1325 Main St., 601/636-0941, http://jacquelinehouse.weebly.com, 10am-5pm Sat. and by appointment) displays artifacts dating all the way back to the slave trade.

Choose between two different tours at **McRaven House** (1445 Harrison St., 601/501-1336, www.mcraventourhome.com, 10am-5pm Mon.-Thurs., 10am-5pm and 7pm-9pm Fri.-Sat., 1pm-5pm and 7pm-9pm Sun.). The History Tour (10am-4pm daily, adults $15, students $10, free for children under 6) details Civil War history and includes a look at the garden, which was used as a field hospital for Confederate soldiers. The Haunted Tour (7pm and 8:30pm daily,

adults and students $25, free for under 6) covers the deaths and hauntings at McRaven House.

★ **Vicksburg National Military Park**
Vicksburg National Military Park (3201 Clay St., 601/636-0583, www.nps.gov/vick, 8am-5pm daily, $15 per vehicle, $7 per motorcycle, $5 per pedestrian) should be the first stop for Civil War buffs in Vicksburg. This park includes 1,325 historical monuments and markers, 20 miles of reconstructed trenches, a 16-mile tour road, a 12.5-mile walking trail, two different antebellum homes, 144 cannons, a restored gunboat, and more. If you have the time and want to see everything in detail, allot 1.5-2 hours here. Vehicle and motorcycle admissions are good for seven days.

Pick up a map at the visitors center to take the self-guided driving tour. Some of the 15 sites on the driving tour include Fort Hill, an anchor of the Confederates' northern lines; Vicksburg National Military Cemetery, where 17,000 soldiers are buried (13,000 of whom are unknown); and Battery Selfridge, a naval cannon battery manned by the U.S. Navy.

While it's not possible to actually "get in the trenches," as the saying goes, you can get pretty close at Vicksburg. There are 20 miles of reconstructed trenches depicting those used during the Civil War. Get out of your car and look at them up close and imagine what it was like for soldiers on this battlefield. Don't miss the Confederate Trenches Exhibit in the visitors center, which shows what a trench looked like during that time, with model soldiers and supplies.

If you time your visit right, you can also tour the two antebellum homes in the park. The **Shirley House,** built in the 1830s, is the park's only wartime structure that's still intact; it served as headquarters for the 45th Illinois Infantry. Confederate soldiers were ordered to burn the houses, but reportedly, the soldier assigned to set fire to this house was shot before he could do so. The Shirley House is open for interior tours on weekends from Memorial Day through Labor Day. **Pemberton's Headquarters** (also called the Willis-Cowan House) is open to visitors 9am-4pm Monday in June and July. Confederate general John C. Pemberton used the house as his headquarters during the Siege of Vicksburg.

The **USS *Cairo* Gunboat and Museum** (3201 Clay St., 601/636-0583, www.nps. gov/vick) is part of the park complex. The large, ironclad gunboat, which was sunk in 1862, is a sight worth seeing. In 1964, the gunboat was pulled from the river in three pieces, after which it was restored and reassembled at Vicksburg. Check out the 13 mounted cannons, reconstructed wood beams, a few original floorboards, and artifacts such as sailors' supplies. The Cairo is one of four surviving Civil War-era ironclads.

A free **cell phone tour** (601/262-2100) complements the self-guided tour. If you'd like a guided tour, arrange a licensed guide from Vicksburg Convention and Visitors Bureau (601/636-0583, $40 per car per hour, $60 per van, $80 per bus, $20 for each additional hour).

Food

Enjoy views of the city from 10 stories up at **10 South Rooftop Bar & Grill** (1301 Washington St., 601/501-4600, www.10southrooftop.com, 11am-2pm and 5pm-10pm Tues.-Sun., $12-28). The restaurant has a casual vibe and classic American menu. For dessert try the chocolate-covered bacon and moon pie bread pudding.

Monsour's at the Biscuit Company (1100 Washington St., 601/638-1571, 11am-2am Mon.-Sat., 11am-9pm Sun., $11-30) is housed in the historic National Biscuit Company building. The lively bar

Top to bottom: The Old Depot Museum; 10 South Rooftop Bar & Grill; Mount Locust Historic House.

hosts karaoke plus live music. The menu is full of Southern-inspired dishes.

From the same chef-owner as 10 South, **Roca Restaurant & Bar** (127 Country Club Dr., 601/638-0800, http://rocarestaurant. com, 5pm-9pm Tues.-Thurs., 5pm-10pm Fri.-Sat., $12-27) serves pizzas, pastas, salads, and other American classic entrées.

Walnut Hills Restaurant (1214 Adams St., 601/638-4910, 11am-9pm Mon.-Sat., 11am-2pm Sun., http://walnuthillsms. com, $11-30) touts its "Southern plantation cuisine." The menu includes po'boys, fried chicken, fried catfish, shrimp and grits, and boiled shrimp.

Accommodations

After Civil War history, the thing Vicksburg is best known for is riverboat casinos. There are several from which to choose, if that's your thing. Each is listed here as a hotel, but you may visit and gamble without staying overnight.

The Ameristar (4116 Washington St., 601/638-1000, www.ameristar.com/vicksburg, 24 hours daily, $89-179) riverboat casino and hotel has 149 rooms, free Wi-Fi, an outdoor pool, and a shuttle between the hotel and casino (which are adjacent, but not connected). There are several on-site restaurants, including Bourbon's, a steakhouse with a river view.

Formerly Diamond Jacks, **WaterView Casino and Hotel** (3990 Washington St., 601/636-5700, www.waterviewcasino. com, $100-317) has Las Vegas-style table games as well as an event center and several restaurants. Both smoking and non-smoking rooms are available.

Another 24-hour casino, **Lady Luck Vicksburg** (1380 Warrenton Rd., 601/501-4368, http://vicksburg.isleofcapricasinos. com, $91-109) offers both slots and Las Vegas-style table games, as well as several restaurants. The hotel features upgraded king suites, some with whirlpools, and an indoor pool.

Courtyard Vicksburg (1 Underwood Dr., 601/636-8788, www.courtyard-vicksburg.com, $110-116) has the only Starbucks in Vicksburg. It offers a fitness center, heated indoor saltwater pool, and a manager's welcome reception during the week with beer, wine, and snacks.

Comfort Suites (100 Berryman Rd., 601/638-2290, www.choicehotels.com, $91-115) is an all-suites hotel with free Wi-Fi, an indoor heated pool, and free hot breakfast.

Anchuca reportedly means "happy home" in Choctaw. So, chances are, you'll be happy if you stay at **Anchuca Historic Mansion and Inn** (1010 1st East St., 888/686-0111, www.anchuca.com, $135-350). Some of the eight rooms in this Greek Revival mansion and neighboring carriage house have gas-burning fireplaces. There's an on-site restaurant and bar as well as an outdoor pool. Tours of the home are offered daily 9:30am-4pm.

There are 33 different rooms in five different buildings at **Cedar Grove Mansion, Inn & Restaurant** (2200 Oak St., 601/636-1000, www.cedargroveinn. com, $160-215). People love the sherry and chocolate turn-down service.

One of the oldest homes in Vicksburg, circa 1826, **The McNutt House** (815 1st East St., 601/529-2695, http://themc-nutthouse.com, $50-125) is walking distance to downtown Vicksburg. All six rooms have kitchens or kitchenettes, and the vibe is more like efficiency-style apartments than a fancy B&B.

Back to the Trace

Return to the Natchez Trace Parkway by taking I-20 east for 29 miles (about 30 minutes). Take exit 34 and follow signs for the Trace. Turn left at the stop sign to continue south on the Trace near **milepost 86.**

Mangum Mound and Grindstone Ford (MP 45.7)

This is one of the very few places on the parkway where the signage can be

Rodney, A Southern Ghost Town

one of two churches that remains in Rodney

In the 1800s, Rodney was so important to this region that it was the state capital. At its peak in the 1860s, there were as many as 4,000 people living in Rodney, and it was the busiest river port between New Orleans and St. Louis. The town sustained multiple banks, newspapers, churches, stores, and even Mississippi's first opera house.

But the town suffered from epidemics of yellow fever, fires from Civil War battles, and a slow economy, a result of being bypassed by the railroads. To add insult to injury, a sandbar formed in the Mississippi River, shifting the river two miles west of town, permanently crippling the city's economy.

Visitors to Rodney today can see remains from two 19th-century churches, plus a former store and a few other buildings. But this isn't quite an Old West ghost town—there are see more plants and wildlife than dusty tumbleweeds.

Getting There

Rodney is 10.4 miles west of the parkway off of MS-552. But these are winding, rural roads, so it may take more than 30 minutes to get there. About 10 miles south of Port Gibson, take MS-552 west for two miles. At Fellowship Road, turn left and after 0.6 mile, turn left again on Firetower Road. Take that for a mile and then veer to the right onto Rodney Road and continue for 6.5 miles. Retrace your steps to rejoin the Parkway. There are no services or amenities on this route.

confusing or inconsistent. Official maps and signage at the site itself call this Mangum Mound. However, the official Trace sign just says "Indian Mound." Follow this sign to the turnoff on the right side of the road for several options.

Veer to the left when the road splits to get to Mangum Mound, an Indian burial ground from the late prehistoric period, between AD 1350 and AD 1500. There is no informational signage here, so just

look at the hill and pay respects to the 84 people who are buried inside.

If you head right when the road splits, you'll follow a half-mile loop to Grindstone Ford. From here you can park in the parking lot and take a relatively easy 0.4-mile walk through a section of the Old Trace. The path isn't difficult and should take about 10 minutes to walk. It is not paved and there are elevation changes.

There are no amenities at either end of this stop. Your vehicle must have a clearance of 11 feet 6 inches to access this site.

⬆ MS-18 to Port Gibson

When Union general Ulysses S. Grant led troops here in May 1863 as part of the Vicksburg campaign, a battle was waged and more than 200 soldiers from both sides perished. But unlike so many cities in the Civil War, Port Gibson wasn't scorched, as Grant felt the city "was too beautiful to burn."

Today the beautiful buildings are still in place. Explore the historic buildings, as well as plantations and military sites.

Leaving the Trace

To get to Port Gibson, exit the parkway (near **milepost 41**) to the right, following signs for Port Gibson. When you come to MS-18, turn right and drive west for about a mile. Turn left at the intersection with US 61 and drive south. US 61 bisects Port Gibson.

Sights

More than 40 houses that date back to 1800 are part of the **Port Gibson Historic District** (www.portgibsononthemississippi.com). The district runs along US 61, which becomes Church Street once you get to Port Gibson, in between Orange Street to the north and Greenwood Street to the south. Don't miss Engelson House, which has the oldest formal gardens in the state. City Hall has a display of historical photos from early Port Gibson. There are three cemeteries in town; Confederate general Earl Van Dorn is buried in Wintergreen Cemetery.

Grand Gulf Military Park (12006 Grand-Gulf Rd., 601/437-5911, www.grandgulfpark.state.ms.us, adults $4, seniors $3, students $1) is eight miles northwest of Port Gibson and includes Fort Wade, Fort Cobun, and Grand Gulf Cemetery. You can spend as much time as you like, as there's also a campground (RV sites $25, tent sites $15), an observation tower, picnic tables, walking trails, and a small museum.

Accommodations

Opened in 2011, **Isabella B&B** (1009 Church St., 601/437-5097, www.isabellabedandbreakfast.com, $125 s/d, $25 for additional guests) is a B&B in a remodeled yellow Queen Anne home built in 1880. It features Wi-Fi, a full Southern breakfast, private bathrooms, and front porch with porch swing.

Back to the Trace

To return to the parkway, take US 61 south out of Port Gibson for about two miles. Exit the highway to the right, following signs for the Trace, then turn left to continue south (near **milepost 37**).

★ Mount Locust Historic House

(MP 15.5)

Since it was built in 1780, **Mount Locust** (no phone, 8:30am-5pm daily, free) has been an important place on the Trace. The site has a rich and complicated history. John Blommart originally built it as his homestead, but he quickly lost it after being jailed for leading a failed rebellion against the Spanish. It was purchased by William and Polly Ferguson in 1784. After William died, Polly eventually began running the farm as a rest stop and inn for the Kaintuck boatmen who used the Trace to return north after boating their goods down the Mississippi. By the mid-1820s, when development slowed the commercial traffic on the Trace, Polly turned Mount Locust into a vacation refuge for those from the town of Natchez.

Slavery was part of life at Mount Locust. The 1820 census lists 26 enslaved people at Mount Locust; a few decades later that number climbed to 51.

The National Park Service began restoring Mount Locust in 1954, and returned it to its 1820 state. Get a map from the ranger station and take a self-guided tour through the furnished home, former kitchen site, cemeteries, and more. The slave quarters are no longer standing and the slave cemetery did not have headstones. You can visit these sites, but you won't see physical structures. The pathway to the home is paved. Informative detailed signage is included throughout the site.

Mount Locust is visible from the parkway. The restrooms here are the last ones on the parkway, unless you exit at Natchez State Park. There are picnic areas as well. Mount Locust is a particularly good stop for kids and history buffs. Plan to stay 45 minutes to an hour.

Loess Bluff (MP 12.4)

It might not look like much, but this stop is a significant geological site. A silty type of topsoil called loess (pronounced like the name "Lois") is thought to have been deposited here by glaciers during the Ice Age. In the areas where the Trace passed over loess, it turned into sunken areas, which is why so many places on the Old Trace are below street level.

This stop on the left-hand side of the parkway offers a view of a steep bluff of loess, visible from the road. There are no amenities.

★ Emerald Mound
(MP 10.3)

Emerald Mound is, at 80 acres, the second largest ceremonial mound in the United States. Built between AD 1250 and 1600 by the Natchez people, this is the largest mound along the parkway.

Unlike at other mounds, you are encouraged to walk to the top of the flat-top mound, which is about 70 feet high.

There's a short but steep paved path to the base of the mound. This is wheelchair accessible (if you are experienced with braking). You can walk around the site at this level. Alternatively, take the steep wooden staircase to the top, where you'll have a 360-degree view of the mounds, the scenery, and area wildlife, including cardinals and other birds.

To get to Emerald Mound, turn right to exit at MS-553. When the highway curves to the right, stay straight and follow signs for Emerald Mound. This is a paved, but rough, road. The U-shaped parking lot is on the right after nearly one mile.

Natchez State Park (MP 10.3)

Natchez State Park (230 Wickliff Rd., 601/442-2658, day-use $4 per car) is a quick detour (5-10 minutes each way) off of the parkway. Here you'll find restrooms, showers, campsites ($20-35) and cabins (no pets permitted, $35-110), picnic areas, a boat launch, disc golf course, and a playground for kids. The park has more than 13 miles of hiking trails. Hunting and fishing are permitted with state licenses.

To get to Natchez State Park, turn left at MS-553. This is the same exit as Emerald Mound, but on the south side of the Trace. After about half a mile, the highway goes under US 61 and turns into State Park Road. Turn left on Wickliff Road and continue less than 0.4 mile to the park entrance.

Elizabeth Female Academy (MP 5.1)

Founded in 1818 by the Methodist church, this was the site of the first institution of higher learning for women in Mississippi. It is one of the few places on the parkway where you can see the ruins of the building itself, rather than just a marker. The site, which is on the National Register of Historic Landmarks, is open sunrise to sunset.

Check out the brick remains of the building, which was burned in a fire in 1870, long after it closed in 1845. The pathway to the ruins (0.3 mile) is wheelchair accessible and goes along the side road (Old US 84) to Washington, Mississippi. This is an out-and-back trail.

Exit the parkway on the right side and follow a long drive to the parking area, which is not visible from the road. There are no other amenities, but you're just five miles from the city of Natchez. This is your last stop on the parkway heading south.

Natchez

The Natchez Trace wouldn't exist without the sweet city of Natchez. French settlers built a fort on the banks of the Mississippi River in 1716; archaeological excavations suggest that people have been living on this land since the 8th century AD. It's been controlled by the French, the Spanish, and the British, and influences of all three still can be seen in the culture.

People from all over the world flock to Natchez to tour its antebellum homes, stay in restored B&Bs, and enjoy loads of Southern charm. As the southern terminus of the parkway, it's a great place to celebrate the end of your 444-mile trek and transition into Cajun culture before heading on to New Orleans.

Leaving the Trace

The southern terminus of the parkway is just north of Liberty Road in Natchez, about 2.5 miles east of downtown. To get to downtown Natchez, exit to the right and take Liberty Road west, which will

Top to bottom: Emerald Mound; Museum of African-American History and Culture; Grand Village of the Natchez Indians State Historic Site.

turn into John A. Quitman Boulevard, then Main Street. Consider turning into the small pullout on the left just before exiting to get a photo or two at the southern terminus and parkway signs.

Sights

A network comprises 5.6 miles of walkways and streets running through downtown Natchez and along the boardwalk near the Mississippi River bluff. Color-coded signs help direct you on thematic walks, and all along there are informational signs with details about local history, archaeology, and the environment. Pick up a map at the Natchez Visitor Center.

The William Johnson House (210 State St., 601/445-5345, www.nps.gov/natc, 9am-4:30pm Thurs.-Sun., free) is a brick building where freed-slave-turned-barber William Johnson and his family once lived. Downstairs is a museum that includes excerpts from Johnson's diaries. Upstairs the family home is preserved. It offers a fascinating look at slavery and African American history in the South.

Richard Wright, the author of *Uncle Tom's Children* and *Native Son,* grew up in Natchez. You can view the exterior of **Richard Wright's Childhood Home** (20 E. Woodlawn St.). See exhibitions about African American life in Natchez during the Civil War and the civil rights era at the **Museum of African-American History and Culture** (301 Main St., 601/445-0728, 10am-4:30pm Mon.-Fri., by appointment Sat.-Sun., free, $7 donation encouraged).

The 128-acre **Grand Village of the Natchez Indians State Historic Site** (400 Jefferson Davis Blvd., 601/446-6502, www.nps.gov, 9am-5pm Mon.-Sat., 1:30pm-5pm Sun., free) offers a look at the political and religious capital of the Natchez chiefdom of the late 17th century and early 18th century. Start in the small, dated museum with a seven-minute film to get an overview of the area. Check out the artifacts inside and then go outside and explore the three Natchez Indian

mounds. These are thought to have been used as a ceremonial plaza and residential areas, rather than burial mounds.

On the banks of the mighty Mississippi, the **Natchez National Cemetery** (41 Cemetery Rd., 601/445-4981, 8am-sunset daily) contains the headstones of many of Natchez's famous—and infamous—names, including two buffalo soldiers, members of the African American 24th U.S. Infantry regiments. The cemetery was established in 1866.

More than 500 photographs of Natchez throughout history are on display at the **Stratton Chapel Gallery** (405 State St., 601/442-4741, 9am-4pm daily, free, donations accepted). Come see the ups and downs of this river town through the lens of photographers throughout time. The exhibition is on the second floor of the First Presbyterian Church; enter through the side door.

Natchez Visitor Center

The mammoth **Natchez Visitor Center** (640 S. Canal St., 800/647-6724, http://visitnatchez.org, 8am-5pm daily) should be your first stop when you get to town. With a view of the Mississippi, this is not the average visitors center. The building houses a National Park Service office, museum exhibits about the city, a gift shop, a small movie theater with a 20-minute film ($2) about Natchez, and an outpost of **Natchez Pilgrimage Tours** (601/446-6631, http://natchezpilgrimage.com), where you can get tickets to one of the city's antebellum home tours. You can also grab all the maps and brochures you need and even a free cup of coffee.

Antebellum Homes

You could spend days in Natchez doing nothing but touring preserved and restored plantations and other historical homes (and sleeping in them, as some are B&Bs). If this is your thing, consider coming to town for **Fall and Spring Pilgrimage** (601/446-6631, http://

natchezpilgrimage.com), multi-week home and garden tour programs and dinners, combined with lectures, plays, and guides dressed in period costumes. Pilgrimage was the brainchild of local women in the 1930s who thought to open the city's antebellum homes for tours to help reverse Natchez's economic decline. Some were concerned that the tours glorified the city's past and ignored the African American experience. Today, discussions of slavery and race are incorporated into tours. During Pilgrimage, many private homes not open the rest of the year are on tour.

If you're not up for something that intense, pick just a few of the tours of year-round homes in this section. Prices listed are for individual tours. Lower price packages for multiple tours are available through **Natchez Pilgrimage Tours** (601/446-6631, http://natchezpilgrimage.com).

Managed by the National Park Service, **Melrose** (1 Melrose Montebello Pkwy., 601/446-5790, www.nps.gov/natc, 8:30am-5pm daily, adults $10, seniors and children ages 6-17 $5, free for children under 6) is the site of a former cotton plantation, with an 1849 Greek Revival-style home, gardens, outbuildings, and slave quarters. This is one of the many homes in the area where you can see a punkah, a larger, carved element that when pulled by a cord (usually by a slave) would keep flies away from food on the dining table. While the gift shop at Melrose accepts credit cards for purchases, the tour portion is cash or check only.

Owned and operated by the Mississippi State Society Daughters of the American Revolution (MSSDAR), **Rosalie Mansion and Bicentennial Gardens** (100 Orleans St., 601/446-5676, http://rosaliemansion.com, 9am-5pm daily Mar.-Oct., 10am-4pm daily Nov.-Feb., $15) was built in 1823. Over its history families who lived here helped found the Natchez Children's Home and housed orphans. In addition

Frogmore Cotton Plantation

to the mansion, there are several gardens on-site to tour: Janet Terreson Sims Memorial Rose Garden, Patricia Walton Shelby Bicentennial Garden, and Walter Reed Page Smith Garden. If you're interested in genealogical research, MSSDAR's library here is open to the public. Rosalie Mansion is popular for weddings and other events. Like most of the larger plantations, it has a decent gift shop (601/445-4555).

Stanton Hall (401 High St., 601/442-6282, www.stantonhall.com, tours every 30 min. 9am-4:30pm daily, $18) is a massive Greek Revival mansion that takes up a whole city block. Built by cotton merchant Frederick Stanton in 1859, Stanton Hall was occupied by Union soldiers during the Civil War and also housed Stanton College for Young Ladies. Now owned by the Pilgrimage Garden Club, Stanton Hall also has the **Carriage House Restaurant** (601/445-5151, 11am-2pm Wed.-Sun.), which serves Southern

cuisine, blue plate specials, and a Sunday buffet brunch.

Owned by the Pilgrimage Garden Club, **Longwood** (140 Lower Woodville Dr., 601/442-5193, tours every 30 min. 9am-4:30pm daily, $18) has a curious and sad story. What would have been the largest octagonal house in the world was begun in 1860 for Haller Nutt, a wealthy cotton planter. But Nutt's fortunes changed, and although he was a Union sympathizer, many of his fields were burned during the Civil War. The house was never completed and has been preserved as such, so you can see both the finished and unfinished sections. Stroll around the gardens and see the family cemetery.

Technically in Ferriday, Louisiana, **Frogmore Cotton Plantation & Gins** (11656 US 84, 318/757-2453, http://frogmoreplantation.com, 9am-3pm Mon.-Fri., 10am-3pm Sat. spring and fall, 9am-1pm Mon.-Fri. summer, hours vary winter, $5-25, kids under 5 free) is about 20 miles west of Natchez but worth the drive. Tours of this 1,800-acre working cotton plantation educate guests on the history of cotton production. The three different tours include Cotton...Then & Now (adults $15, students $5), which covers 1700 through today; Plantation Civil War (adults $12, students $5), which covers plantation life from 1861 to 1865; and Modern Cotton Farming & Ginning ($5), which gives an insight into the modern cotton-harvesting process, including the plantation's computerized cotton gin, which processes 900 bales of cotton per day. The price for all three tours is $10 for students and $25 for adults.

Entertainment and Events

The **Magnolia Bluffs Casino** (7 Roth Hill Rd., 601/235-0045, www.magnoliabluffscasinos.com) is all modern, with 450 slot machines and a venue for live music concerts, plus a buffet restaurant, a bistro, a steakhouse, several bars, and a full-service hotel.

The last weekend in February, the **Natchez Literary and Cinema Celebration** (www.colin.edu/nlcc) brings authors and others to lead readings and discussions and to sign books, all around a different annual theme. Most events are free, but some higher-profile events may be ticketed.

Held annually in March at the Grand Village of the Natchez Indians, **Natchez Pow-Wow** (400 Jefferson Davis Blvd., www.natchezpowwow.com, adults $5, children $3) includes dancing, music, and booths selling food and Native American crafts.

A three-day event held in July, the **Natchez Food & Wine Festival** (www.natchezfoodandwinefest.com, $15-125) offers multiple ticketed events, including lunches, dinners, chef events, and brewery and distillery tours.

The **Great Mississippi River Balloon Race** (100 Orleans St., 800/455-2510, www.natchezballoonrace.com) is one of Natchez's most beloved annual events,

held at the grounds of Rosalie Mansion each October. Pilots launch their balloons twice daily (weather dependent) and sail over the Mississippi. Tethered balloon rides are offered to the public.

Shopping

The shopping in Natchez is heavily skewed toward antiques. Most of the antebellum homes have gift shops with books, postcards, and other goods.

As You Like It Silver Shop (410 N. Commerce St., 601/442-0933, 11am-5pm daily) is located inside the carriage house on the Stanton Hall property. Hours can vary as it's a one-woman show. **Franklin Street Antique Mall** (512 Franklin St., 601/304-9367, www.fsantiquemall.com, 10am-5pm Mon.-Sat.) sells furniture and housewares, including crystal, china, and silver, plus estate jewelry and coins. There's also a general store with Amish cheeses, bacon, and sweets. **Mrs. Holder's Antiques** (636 Franklin St., 601/442-0675, www.mrsholdersantiques.com,

Great Mississippi River Balloon Race

11am-5pm Tues.-Sat.) is a full-service antiques store, with furniture, housewares, and linens.

Women's fashions, jewelry, and accessories can be found at a number of places, such as **A Gallerie** (400 Main St., 601/304-2115, 10am-5pm Mon.-Sat.). The shop also stocks some housewares and gifts. Opened in 2016 in an old bank, **Pique by Mush** (411 Franklin St., 601/653-0912, www.piquebymush.com, 1pm-7pm Tues. and Thurs., 10am-7pm Wed. and Fri., 9am-6pm Sat.) stocks professional clothing for women and offers personal styling services. **Soiree Boutique** (505 Main St., 601/442-5566, 10am-5pm Mon.-Fri., 11am-4pm Sat.) sells modern, on-trend clothing and accessories for women.

Turning Pages Bookstore (20 Franklin St., 601/442-2299, http://turningpages-books.com, 10:30am-5:30pm Mon.-Sat., 1pm-5pm Sun.) looks small but has a well-edited selection of books in a variety of genres. It has a particularly in-depth selection of garden and history books.

If you prefer your shopping of the edible variety, try **D'Evereux Foods** (312 Main St., 601/304-5522, www.devereux-foods.com, 10am-5pm Mon.-Sat.) for jams, jellies, and hot sauces made using family recipes under the D'Evereux label. **Darby's** (410 Main St., 601/446-9737, http://darbysfudge.com, 9am-6pm Mon.-Sat.) is the locally famous fudge shop, selling hand-crafted fudge as well as hot sauce. **Old South Trading Post** (600 S. Canal St., 601/446 5354, http://natchezshop.com, 8:30am-6pm Mon.-Sat., 8:30am-3pm Sun.) stocks some local jams and jellies, but this is also the place to find souvenirs, T-shirts, and other gifts to take home.

Food

Under-the-Hill Saloon (25 Silver St., 601/446-8023, daily 10am-3am or at bartender's discretion) has been around since the 1800s, still playing live music (and now offering karaoke) and serving beers. The courtyard is a nice place to hang out in temperate weather. If you want a full meal, try **The Camp** (21 Silver St., 601/897-0466, www.thecamprestaurant.com, 11am-9pm Sun.-Thurs., 11am-10pm Fri.-Sat., $12-18). This is a family-friendly sports bar with lots of local craft beer labels on tap and made-from-scratch sliders, burgers, sandwiches, fried catfish, ribs, and tacos. The backyard beer garden is serene; the porch seating has a river view.

Housed in the oldest building in Mississippi is ★ **King's Tavern** (613 Jefferson St., 601/446-5003, www.kingstavernnatchez.com, 11:30am-9pm Sun. and Thurs., 11:30am-10pm Fri.-Sat., $15-28), the oldest restaurant in Mississippi. While the building may have been constructed in 1789, the menu is anything but dated. Chef Regina Charboneau and her husband serve inspired flatbreads, sandwiches, and salads, many made with herbs and vegetables grown in their small plot. The cocktail bar serves small-batch spirits, including those from their adjacent **Charboneau Distillery** (619 Jefferson St., 601/861-4203, www.charboneaudistillery.com, tours hourly 5pm-8pm Fri., noon-6pm Sat.).

Mississippi is known for its blues music and its biscuits, so of course you want to combine them at **Biscuits and Blues** (315 Main St., 601/446-9922, www.biscuitsandblues.com, 5:30pm-11pm Tues.-Thurs., 5:30pm-11:30pm Fri., 5pm-11pm Sat., 5pm-10:30pm Sun., $12-28). Call ahead to confirm it's open; this Southern fare restaurant is only open on days when live music performances are scheduled.

If you're loving that antebellum experience, have lunch at **Carriage House Restaurant** (401 High St., 601/445-5151, www.stantonhall.com, 11am-2pm Wed.-Sun., $15), the restaurant at Stanton Hall. The menu offers Southern cuisine, like fried chicken, blue plate specials, and a Sunday buffet brunch.

Nestled in the former carriage house and stables at the Dunleith Historic Inn, **The Castle** (84 Homochito St., 601/446-8500, www.dunleith.com, 7:30am-10am, 11am-2pm, and 6pm-9pm Sun.-Thurs., 7:30am-10am, 11am-2pm, and 6pm-10pm Fri.-Sat., $12-30) was designed to look like a red brick castle. The menu is traditional Southern (crab cakes and bread pudding). Reservations are recommended. Business casual dress is requested but not required.

A favorite among the innkeepers and locals in Natchez, **Cotton Alley Café** (208 Main St., 601/442-7452, http://cottonalleycafe.com, 11am-2pm and 5:30pm-9pm Mon.-Sat., $16-32) serves Southern- and Italian-inspired fare, like pastas, burgers, sandwiches, and seafood, plus delicious desserts, in a cozy downtown environment. The bar is a good place to eat if you're traveling alone. The kitchen will make vegetarian dishes on request.

As you'd expect from its name, **Fat Mama's Tamales** (303 S. Canal St., 601/442-4548, http://fatmamastamales.com, 11am-9pm Mon.-Thurs.,

11am-10pm Fri.-Sat., noon-7pm Sun., $5-10) specializes in tamales sold by the half dozen and dozen, chili, taco salads, and taco soup. The frozen Knock-You-Naked margaritas are local favorites.

Fried and boiled food of all kinds—shrimp, crab, oysters, catfish, alligator, and frog legs: You name it, **Jughead's Fish Fry and More** (217 John R. Junkin Dr., 601/445-8999, 10am-10pm daily, $8-20) has it.

Mammy's Cupboard (555 US 61, 601/445-8957, 11am-2pm Tues.-Sat., $9-11) is a building shaped like a giant Aunt Jemima dress. The restaurant is "under" her skirt. It's definitely a relic from another era: While some may see a kitschy photo-op, others may be disturbed by its casual racism. Menu offerings include sandwiches on homemade sourdough, homemade pie, and other daily specials.

★ **Restaurant 1818** (36 Melrose Ave., 601/442-5852, www.monmouthhistoricinn.com, 6pm-8:30pm Tues.-Sun., $12-42) is the city's most elegant restaurant, housed in two parlors of the Monmouth Inn. You'll experience first-class service of contemporary American cuisine (think duck breast with green onion risotto, wilted spinach, blueberries, and crispy mushrooms). Hours are extended to seven days a week during Pilgrimage. Reservations required.

It doesn't look like much, but **The Donut Shop** (501 John R. Junkin Dr., 601/442-2317, http://thedonutshopnatchez.com, 6am-6pm Tues.-Sat., 6am-2pm Sun., $1-7) shouldn't be skipped. The food menu includes salad, sandwiches, gyros, and dinner platters such as country-fried steak. The doughnuts, with creative varieties that change daily, such as chocolate peanut butter chip and Froot Loop, are the reason the parking lot is packed all day.

Another blink-and-you'll-miss it Natchez staple, **The Malt Shop** (4 Homochitto St., 601/445-4843, 10am-9:30pm Mon.-Thurs., 10am-10pm Fri.-Sat., 11am-9pm Sun., $4-7) has been offering burgers and shakes since the 1960s. There's no indoor seating.

Accommodations

Natchez is primarily a B&B and historic inn kind of town, but there are some traditional hotels. For the B&Bs in this section, breakfast is included unless otherwise noted.

Hotel Vue (10 John R. Junkin Dr., 601/442-9976, www.hotelvuenatchez. com, $89-169) is one of the city's more contemporary spaces, with an outdoor pool, exercise room, and great views of the Mississippi River. Pilot House is the in-house restaurant and bar.

A free shuttle runs between the **Magnolia Bluff Casino-Hotel** (645 S. Canal St., 601/861-4600, www.magnoliabluffscasinos.com, $99-229) and the casino proper, as they are not in the same building. Breakfast is included in the room price. Magnolia Bluff also has Wi-Fi, a fitness center, and an outdoor pool.

It's hard to miss the **Natchez Grand Hotel and Suites** (111 N. Broadway St., 601/446-9994, www.natchezgrandhotel. com, $135-184), a large red brick building in downtown Natchez that was designed to look like the cotton baling factories of old. Rooms are either city view or river view. The hotel is adjacent to the Natchez Convention Center, and is walking distance to everything downtown, but it doesn't have a lot of common spaces in which you can hang out. You must upgrade to the business center package to get Wi-Fi. Cross the street to check out the stone marker that marks the start of the original Natchez Trace.

Doug Mauro and Don McGlynn bought and renovated the 1835 Federal-style **Oak Hill Inn** (409 S. Rankin St., 601/446-2500, http://historicoakhill. com, $135-160) and made it into an inn after retiring from New Jersey. The gourmet breakfast is served on china in the dining room. Tours are included in the room rate.

Just south of Emerald Mounds, **Brandon Hall Plantation** (73 Natchez Trace Pkwy., 601/304-1040, www.brandonhallplantation.com, $130-175) is as close as you can get to the parkway. The Greek Revival mansion is surrounded by a park with gardens, walking paths through the woods, and a stocked pond. They serve a full Southern breakfast. Some rooms have private baths.

Sixth-generation Conner descendants still own the **Linden Antebellum Bed & Breakfast** (1 Conner Circle, 601/445-5472, www.lindenbandb.com, $160-170), and their matriarch lives here and operates the inn. The Federal-style home is located on seven acres of land, but its real claim to fame is that its front door was the inspiration for Tara from *Gone with the Wind.* There are big galleries (balconies) along the front and back of the home and the side buildings. There aren't any common areas where you can sit and read; everything must be done in your room. Rooms have private baths and antique furniture. A home tour is included with the room rate.

The three-room **1888 Wensel House** (206 Washington St., 601/445-8577, http://1888wenselhouse.com, $115-125) is a sweet Victorian home converted into a B&B within walking distance of the heart of downtown Natchez. Your stay includes fruit and wine in the parlor and Wi-Fi.

Built in 1836, **The Burn Bed & Breakfast** (712 N. Union St., 601/442-1344, http://theburnbnb.com, $148-180) is a three-story building with a lot of history. It was used as a hospital during the Civil War and is the setting of the 1994 novel *Pilgrimage: A Tale of Old Natchez.* In addition to plenty of modern amenities, such as private baths, Wi-Fi, and an outdoor pool, there's also bicycle storage for those who have cycled the Trace. Children under 12 are not welcome; neither are pets. A home and garden tour is included with the room rate.

Owners Ron and Eleanor chose

Natchez as their retirement destination and running a B&B as their second career, and their passion for both is clear at every turn at ★ **Devereaux Shields House** (709 N. Union St., 601/304-5378, www.dshieldsusa.com, $135-188). The main house is a restored 1893 Queen Anne Victorian; down the street are four more rooms in Aunt Clara's Cottage, which is pet-friendly. Both have gardens in back and private baths, plus amenities such as white noise machines, Wi-Fi, cable, and fluffy robes. Welcome receptions with wine and cheese occur every afternoon. The common areas are as luxurious as the private rooms, and the owners are enthusiastic about helping guests see the best of Natchez.

On a property dotted with magnolia trees, **Magnolia Cottage Bed and Breakfast** (35 Homochito St., 601/807-5280, http://magnoliacottagebandb.com, $150) is a lodging option for adults only. You have the option of having your Southern breakfast brought to your room instead of served in the dining room.

★ **Monmouth Historic Inn and Gardens** (1358 John A. Quitman Blvd., 601/442-5852, www.monmouthhistoricinn.com, $160-300) feels more like a resort than a B&B. There are 15 suites and 15 rooms between the historic main house and the smaller outbuildings, each with period furnishings and modern amenities. TVs and Wi-Fi are present, but hidden, so as not to detract from the old-world charm. The bathrooms are modern and luxurious. Some rooms have spa tubs or fireplaces. Fine-dining can be found at Restaurant 1818, while a full Southern breakfast is served in a garden building and evening hors d'oeuvres are in the bar. Tours of the home and grounds are offered at 10am and 2pm daily (free for hotel guests).

Information and Services

The **Natchez Visitor Center** (640 S. Canal St., 800/647-6724, http://visitnatchez.

Linden Antebellum Bed & Breakfast

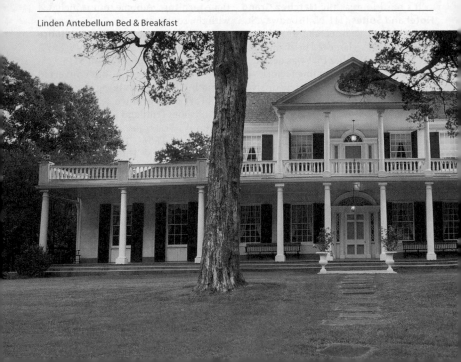

org, 8am-5pm daily) is a large and comprehensive facility and can direct visitors to almost everything they need.

Stan's Rock 'N' Roll Bike Shop (55 Seargent Prentiss Dr., Ste. 9, 601/445-9762, Mon.-Fri., 10am-noon Sun.) is just two miles from the southern terminus of the parkway, and it stocks bike parts as well as skateboards, guitars, and other toys. For motorcycle repair, try **House of Cycles** (730 US 61 N., 601/446-6211, www.houseofcycles.com, 8:30am-5:30pm Tues.-Fri., 8:30am-4pm Sat.).

Merit Health Natchez (54 Seargent Prentiss Dr., 601/443-2100, www.merithealthnatchez.com) is the hospital closest to the southern terminus of the parkway.

New Orleans

New Orleans is a city that's hard to forget. Nestled between the brackish Lake Pontchartrain and the serpentine Mississippi River, it has been home to pirates and soldiers, plantation owners and voodoo queens.

Lake Pontchartrain

Jackson Square
New Orleans Historic Voodoo Museum
The Historic New Orleans Collection
The New Orleans School of Cooking
City Park
Mardi Gras
New Orleans Jazz & Heritage Festival

NEW ORLEANS

The National WWII Museum
Ogden Museum of Southern Art

Blaine Kern's Mardi Gras World

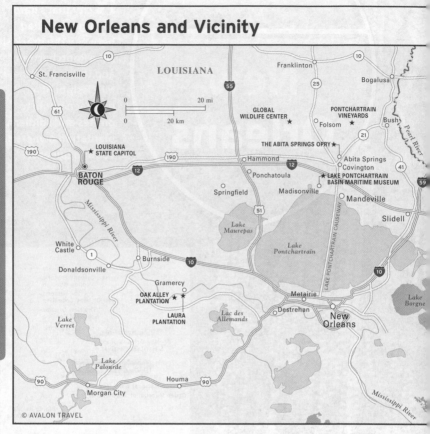

New Orleans and Vicinity

Although the city is famed for its raucous Mardi Gras, there's more to New Orleans. It's family-friendly, a mecca for art, and has countless historic sites.

Families come for kid-friendly places like the Audubon Aquarium of the Americas, Blaine Kern's Mardi Gras World, and the Audubon Zoo. Art lovers flock to the New Orleans Museum of Art, and outdoor enthusiasts appreciate oases like City Park. But it's history buffs who are particularly enamored with the Big Easy. Besides engrossing

exhibits at The National WWII Museum, the Crescent City—and especially the French Quarter—boasts an array of historic structures.

There's also history beyond the Quarter, from the distinctive homes of the Garden District to the crumbling cemeteries in the Tremé and Mid-City neighborhoods. In a city defined by water, many natives enjoy simply wandering through Woldenberg Riverfront Park alongside the Mississippi River.

While the destruction of Hurricane Katrina is still evident in places like Mid-City, the Ninth Ward, and New Orleans East, New Orleans has experienced a rebirth since 2005. This fast-growing city is now brimming with refurbished

Highlights

★ **Jackson Square:** The heart and soul of the French Quarter, this scenic spot is the perfect place to get your bearings before exploring the Big Easy (page 305).

★ **New Orleans Historic Voodoo Museum:** Dive into the city's colorful past, with tales of voodoo priestesses and zombies, ritual art, and a stroll through St. Louis Cemetery No. 1 (page 317).

★ **The Historic New Orleans Collection:** This complex encompasses several notable structures, from a Creole cottage to the Greek Revival-style Merieult House, each filled with art and antiquities (page 319).

★ **The New Orleans School of Cooking:** Want to make gumbo or shrimp Creole like a native? This is the place to learn (page 320).

★ **The National WWII Museum:** You'll be impressed by the wealth of exhibits at this museum (page 323).

★ **Ogden Museum of Southern Art:** Enjoy an impressive collection of Southern art and live music after hours on Thursday nights (page 327).

★ **Blaine Kern's Mardi Gras World:** Stroll amid kaleidoscopic parade floats in progress, observe artists at work, and get a behind-the-scenes look at Mardi Gras in the making (page 327).

★ **City Park:** This 1,300-acre swath of greenery boasts picturesque bridges, moss-covered oak trees, and the New Orleans Botanical Garden (page 330).

★ **Mardi Gras:** Few festivals exemplify the joyous spirit of New Orleans more than this (page 347).

★ **New Orleans Jazz & Heritage Festival:** Established in 1970, this musical extravaganza has grown to be nearly as popular as Mardi Gras (page 350).

attractions, brand-new establishments, and re-energized residents.

Planning Your Time

While you can get a taste of New Orleans in a long weekend, try to allow yourself at least **one week** to fully experience the city.

Although New Orleans is a year-round destination, **summer** is the least crowded time to visit, except during major events like the **Essence Festival** and **Southern Decadence.** Temperatures are fairly high June-September, with an average high of about 91°F, when hurricane season is at its peak. While **fall** is more comfortable, **winter** and **spring** constitute the high season here. Annual events, such as **Mardi Gras,** the **French Quarter Festival,** and the **New Orleans Jazz & Heritage Festival,** lure the bulk of out-of-towners during these months.

The date for Mardi Gras shifts every season (it is always 47 days before Easter). Lodging rates are inflated in high season, as well as during major events and holiday weekends, and advance reservations may be necessary.

Getting There
Car
From Natchez

The drive south from Natchez, Mississippi, the southern terminus of the Natchez Trace Parkway, to New Orleans, is about three hours on US 61 if you don't make any stops. But these 174 miles are a lot more fun if you take your time and stop in Baton Rouge. From Natchez, take US 61 south for about 80 miles. Take the exit for I-110 South, then follow the interstate for about eight miles. Take exit 1G to reach downtown Baton Rouge. Continue to Baton Rouge by taking I-10 east for about 85 miles.

From Baton Rouge

From downtown Baton Rouge, follow I-10 east for roughly 85 miles. From I-10, take exit 234B to Poydras Street; at this point you'll be just a few blocks south of the French Quarter. Without any stops, the drive should take about two hours.

From Jackson

If you want to skip to scenic route (and the southern terminus of the Natchez Trace Parkway), the drive from Jackson, Mississippi along I-55 is 187 miles of largely interstate driving. It takes just three hours and crosses Lake Pontchartrain. On this route you could easily add a 25-minute detour east on I-12 to see Abita Springs (page 399) and head south over the Lake Pontchartrain Causeway (toll required) and I-10 to reach New Orleans (45 miles, roughly one hour).

Air
Louis Armstrong New Orleans International Airport (900 Airline Dr., Kenner, 504/303-7500, www.flymsy.com), 15 miles west of downtown New Orleans via I-10, is a massive facility that accommodates the entire Gulf South with service on several airlines. It's easy to find direct flights from most major U.S. cities: Dallas, Houston, Atlanta, Orlando, Miami, Charlotte, Nashville, Newark, New York, Chicago, Minneapolis, Denver, Las Vegas, Reno, and San Francisco. British Airways flies direct from London four times per week. A new terminal, which will include 30 gates, 2,000 parking spaces, and a new access road, is slated to open in October 2018.

Commercial air service is also available to Baton Rouge and Lafayette. Situated roughly eight miles north of downtown Baton Rouge via I-110, **Baton Rouge Metropolitan Airport** (9430 Jackie Cochran Dr., 225/355-0333, www.flybtr.com) is served by American Airlines and Delta, with frequent direct flights to and from Atlanta, Dallas, Houston, and Memphis. **Lafayette Regional Airport** (200 Terminal Dr., 337/266-4400, www.lftairport.com) is three miles southeast

Best Restaurants

★ **Galatoire's Restaurant:** This quintessential old-school New Orleans spot serves superb Creole fare from time-tested recipes (page 368).

★ **Commander's Palace:** Book a table at this legendary restaurant in the Garden District (page 384).

★ **Jacques-Imo's Cafe:** This funky favorite is known for innovative Creole and Cajun food, huge portions, sassy service—and long waits (page 384).

★ **Angelo Brocato:** This quaint spot has doled out delicious homemade ice cream and Italian pastries for more than a century (page 385).

★ **Ralph's on the Park:** Part of the fun of brunch here is the creative and beautifully presented nouvelle Creole cuisine, but the other benefit is strolling adjacent City Park afterward (page 385).

★ **Drago's Seafood Restaurant:** Its delicious charbroiled oysters and other fresh Cajun and Creole seafood dishes have earned a cult following (page 385).

of downtown Lafayette via US-90. It is served by American Eagle, the Delta Connection, and United Express, with direct flights to and from Atlanta, Dallas, Houston, and Memphis. If you choose to fly into one of these regional airports, you'll have to rent a car to reach New Orleans. Avis, Budget, Hertz, National, and Enterprise serve both locales.

Airport Transportation

Depending on traffic, the 15-mile trip from the airport to the French Quarter can take 25-35 minutes by car. A **taxi** from the airport to the Central Business District (CBD) usually costs $33 for one or two passengers and $14 per person for three or more passengers. Pickup occurs on the airport's lower level, just outside the baggage claim area. Credit cards are typically accepted.

Using a **ride-sharing service** like **Lyft** or **Uber** costs about $33, plus a $4 airport surcharge. There's a designated meeting place on the ground level for these services.

If you'd prefer to travel in style, consider **Airport Limousine** (504/305-2450 or 866/739-5466, www.airportlimousineneworleans.com), the airport's official limo service, which has handy kiosks in the baggage claim area. The number of passengers will determine the type of vehicle selected: sedans for up to three passengers, SUVs for up to five, and limos for six or more. For one-way trips to the French Quarter and CBD, rates start at $58 for one or two passengers; a nominal fuel charge is applied to all rides.

To save a little money, opt for the **Airport Shuttle** (504/522-3500 or 866/596-2699, www.airportshuttleneworleans.com; one-way adults $24, round-trip adults $44, children under 6 free), which offers shared-ride service to hotels in the French Quarter, the CBD, and Uptown. From the upper level of the airport outside Door 7, you can also hop aboard the **E2 Airport Bus** (504/818-1077 or 504/364-3450, www.jeffersontransit.org; $2 pp). On weekdays, the bus takes about 35 minutes to reach the CBD; on weekends, it only travels to Mid-City and you'll have to rely on an RTA bus route to reach destinations in uptown or downtown New Orleans.

The **Tiger Airport Shuttle** (225/333-8167, www.tigerairportshuttle.com; rates vary) provides transportation to and from Baton Rouge.

Best Accommodations

★ **Royal Sonesta New Orleans:** Enjoy the revelry from this prime location on Bourbon Street (page 388).

★ **Hotel Monteleone:** This handsome hotel has long been a favored address among American writers (page 389).

★ **Omni Royal Orleans:** This place stands out not only for its stately historical architecture but also for its friendly and knowledgeable service (page 390).

★ **ACE Hotel:** A hipster haven with a rooftop pool, this art deco building is a buzzy center of activity, music, and coffee (page 394).

★ **International House New Orleans:** Whimsically and creatively decorated, this hotel draws a hip crowd (page 395).

★ **The Green House Inn:** This inn delights visitors with its funky, tropical decor, flower-named rooms, and clothing-optional pool (page 396).

★ **Terrell House Bed and Breakfast:** This B&B provides luxurious accommodations in a grand, Italianate-style mansion built in the mid-1800s (page 396).

Train

Amtrak (800/872-7245, www.amtrak.com) operates three rail routes across southern Louisiana, all of which include stops at the **New Orleans Union Passenger Terminal** (1001 Loyola Ave.; 5am-10pm daily).

These rail routes serve New Orleans:

- **City of New Orleans** runs daily from Chicago to New Orleans, with major stops in Memphis, Jackson, and Hammond (19 hours).

- **Crescent** runs daily between New York City and New Orleans, with major stops in Philadelphia, Baltimore, Washington DC, Charlotte, Atlanta, Birmingham, and Slidell (30 hours).

- **Sunset Limited,** an east-west train, runs from Los Angeles to New Orleans three times weekly, with major stops in Tucson, El Paso, San Antonio, Houston, Lake Charles, and Lafayette (48 hours).

Bus

Greyhound (800/231-2222, www.greyhound.com) is the definitive bus provider for New Orleans, with frequent and flexible service throughout the country. Buses depart daily from the **New Orleans Greyhound Station** (1001 Loyola Ave., 504/525-6075, 5:15am-9:30pm daily) with multiple stops throughout Louisiana to many neighboring states. Travel times can be significantly longer than by train (although not always), but fares are generally much cheaper.

Starting from New Orleans

Because the Natchez Trace is well-marked from south to north, it's easy to begin your road trip here. Head northwest via US 61 to Baton Rouge (79 miles; roughly two hours), then onward to Natchez (another 92 miles; roughly two hours). I-10 may be a faster alternative route between New Orleans and Baton Rouge—but it may also be slower, depending on traffic conditions leaving the Big Easy.

Getting Around
Public Transportation

New Orleans is served by an extensive network of buses and streetcars, operated by the **New Orleans Regional Transit**

Two Days in New Orleans

Day 1

Start your day in the French Quarter with some warm café au lait and sugar-covered beignets at the world-famous **Café Du Monde,** part of the historic **French Market,** a collection of eateries, gift stores, and praline shops.

After breakfast, stroll through picturesque **Jackson Square** and tour the stunning structures that surround this well-landscaped park and promenade. Besides the majestic **St. Louis Cathedral,** you'll see curious historical exhibits inside the **Cabildo** and the **Presbytère** and glimpse period Creole furnishings inside the **1850 House,** part of the lovely **Pontalba Apartments.**

Stroll past the quaint boutiques and verdant balconies of Chartres Street, stop by the **Beauregard-Keyes House and Garden Museum,** then cross the street for a self-guided tour of the **Old Ursuline Convent.** Afterward, walk over to Royal Street for a guided stroll through the **Gallier Historic House Museum.** A few blocks away, you'll spot the **Old U.S. Mint,** a magnificent, red-brick edifice that now houses a state-of-the-art concert space and an engaging museum about the city's musical heritage.

At night, don your finest attire for a quintessential French Creole dinner at **Galatoire's Restaurant** on Bourbon Street. Afterward, walk to the world-famous **Preservation Hall** for a short jazz concert. End your evening at the candlelit **Lafitte's Blacksmith Shop Bar** for a late-night drink.

Day 2

Board the **St. Charles streetcar** and head to the **Garden District,** where you can visit **Lafayette Cemetery No. 1** and stroll amid historic homes. Take time to explore the antiques shops, art galleries, and varied boutiques along funky **Magazine Street.**

In the afternoon, head through the CBD to **The National WWII Museum,** where you can watch an immersive documentary and experience exhibits pertaining to the Allied victory in World War II.

Splurge on a modern Creole dinner at the classic **Commander's Palace** restaurant. Afterward, catch some live rock, funk, jazz, and blues music at well-loved Uptown joints like **Tipitina's,** or venture to **Rock 'n' Bowl** for a concert and a round of bowling.

Authority (RTA, 504/248-3900, www.norta.com). The standard fare is $1.25 per person ($0.40 senior, free under 3) plus $0.25 per transfer; express buses cost $1.50 per person. You must pay with exact change by depositing coins or inserting $1 bills into the fare box at the front of the bus or streetcar. Food, beverages, smoking, and stereos are not permitted on buses or streetcars.

The handy **Jazzy Pass,** a magnetized card presented upon boarding the bus or streetcar, allows unlimited rides during the active period; it's available in 1-day ($3), 3-day ($9), or 31-day ($55) increments. The 1-day pass can be purchased on the bus or streetcar, though only cash is accepted. Other passes are available

from various hotels, banks, and retailers, such as Walgreens.

Bus

Bus service is available throughout the city, and all RTA buses can accommodate people with disabilities. The one-way fare is $1.25 (plus $0.25 per transfer), and passengers must pay with either exact change (coins or $1 bills) or the Jazzy Pass.

Tourists often utilize the **Magazine line** (11), which runs from Canal Street in the CBD through the Garden District and Uptown, along a six-mile stretch of galleries, shops, and restaurants, before ending at Audubon Park. Another important route is the **Jackson-Esplanade line** (91), which runs from Rousseau Street in the

Garden District, through the CBD, along the north edge of the French Quarter, up Esplanade Avenue, and past City Park, ending at the Greenwood Cemetery. For a complete map of all bus lines, plus individual maps and schedules, visit the RTA website (www.norta.com).

Streetcar

The RTA also operates New Orleans's iconic streetcars. The one-way fare is $1.25 per person (plus $0.25 per transfer), and passengers must pay with either exact change (coins or $1 bills) or the Jazzy Pass.

The famous **St. Charles streetcar** line, which operates 24 hours daily, runs along St. Charles and South Carrollton Avenues, from Canal Street to Claiborne Avenue; a one-way trip lasts about 45 minutes. Some passengers with disabilities may have trouble boarding, as they are not wheelchair-accessible. The St. Charles line has been in operation since 1835, when it began as the main railroad line connecting the city of New Orleans with the resort community of Carrollton, now part of the city; the olive-green cars date to the 1920s, when they were built by the Perley Thomas Company. Today, the line is a wonderful, scenic, and atmospheric way to travel between the CBD and Uptown. A one-way ride lasts about 40 minutes.

The **Canal Street streetcar** line extends from Canal Street to Mid-City before splitting into two branches. The Cemeteries branch (daily 5am-3am) runs from the foot of Canal Street, not far from the ferry terminal for Algiers Point, all the way up to the historical cemeteries along City Park Avenue. The City Park/Museum branch (daily 7am-2am) takes North Carrollton Avenue to Esplanade Avenue, right beside City Park and the New Orleans Museum of Art. A one-way trip along either branch lasts about 30 minutes.

The **Riverfront streetcar** line (daily 7am-10:30pm) uses newer streetcars and runs a short but scenic 1.8-mile route along the Mississippi River, from the French Quarter to the CBD. These modern red streetcars were built by New Orleans metal- and woodworkers; a one-way ride lasts about 15 minutes.

Ferry

The **Algiers Point/Canal Street ferry** (504/309-9789, www.nolaferries.com or www.friendsoftheferry.org; Mon.-Thurs. 6am-11:45pm Fri., 6am-9:45pm, Sat. 10:30am-11:45pm, Sun. 10:35am-9:45pm; $2 pp, $1 senior, free 2 and under) provides ferry service across the Mississippi River, from the foot of Canal Street in the CBD to Algiers Point. The five-minute service no longer transports vehicles; the boat departs every 30 minutes on either shore. The **Lower Algiers/Chalmette ferry** (6am-8:45pm daily; $2 per pedestrian or vehicle, $1 senior pedestrian or vehicle passenger, free 2 and under) offers hourly service between Lower Algiers and the East Bank community of Chalmette; the trip usually lasts 15-20 minutes.

Taxi and Pedicab

Taxis are *highly* recommended over public transportation at night, especially when traveling solo. This is the sort of city where it's easy to lose track of time, particularly if you're bar-hopping, so it's always a smart idea to have the name and number of a couple of cab companies with you at all times. Taxi rates within the city typically start at $3.50 per ride, plus $2 per mile thereafter; there's also a charge of $1 for each additional passenger. You will often find taxis waiting at major intersections near Bourbon Street and other nighttime hot spots in the Quarter. Be sure to use taxis operated by licensed and established cab companies, such as **Checker Yellow Cabs** (504/943-2411), **New Orleans Carriage Cab** (504/207-7777, www.neworleanscarriagecab.com), and **United Cabs** (504/522-9771 or 504/524-9606, www.unitedcabs.com). Taxi rates are often higher during peak times, such as Mardi Gras and Jazz Fest; expect to pay $5 per person at least.

Operated by knowledgeable guides and equipped with safety belts, headlights, and flashing taillights, ecofriendly pedicabs can accommodate up to three or four passengers. Currently, there are two pedicab companies in the city: **Bike Taxi Unlimited** (504/891-3441, http://neworleansbiketaxi.com), which serves the French Quarter, the CBD, the Arts/Warehouse District, and Uptown; and **NOLA Pedicabs** (504/274-1300, www.nolapedicabs.com), which mainly serves the Quarter, the CBD, and the Arts District. Standard fares are $5 per passenger for the first six blocks, after which each passenger will be charged $1 per city block. During special events, such as Mardi Gras, expect to pay $50 per half hour and $100 hourly.

Ride-hailing companies, including **Lyft** (www.lyft.com) and **Uber** (www.uber.com), are popular in New Orleans. Download their apps to find a local to drive you to your destination.

Driving

Many streets are one-way and riddled with potholes, street parking is scarce, and garage and hotel parking is expensive. On the other hand, the main neighborhoods are easily walkable, taxis are easy to find, and public transportation is decent, especially from the French Quarter to Uptown and Mid-City, so having a car isn't necessary. Given the city's compact size, many travelers rely on motorcycles and bikes, which are often much easier to park on the street.

Parking

Given New Orleans's high crime rate, parking here is a gamble: When parking on the street or in an unattended lot, keep as few of your belongings in your car as possible. For a bit more security, you can pay $15-50 nightly to park your car at a hotel or commercial lot. Relying

on hourly rates can be considerably more expensive, though many downtown businesses and stores offer free or discounted parking with minimum purchase and validated parking tickets. Even with secured parking areas, refrain from leaving valuables in plain sight.

Beyond the security concerns, finding street parking in the French Quarter, the CBD, and other tourist areas can be extremely difficult. Most blocks of the Quarter are restricted for residents with permits. Many hotel properties in the Quarter have no dedicated parking facilities. You'll find parking meters throughout the French Quarter and CBD—both coin-operated meters as well as ones that accept dollar bills and credit cards. The meters are typically enforced Monday-Saturday 8am-7pm. If you're staying beyond the downtown area, it might be better to park in the Uptown or Mid-City neighborhoods and use public transportation to visit the French Quarter and CBD.

Avoid parking vehicles longer than 22 feet overnight in the CBD. For general questions about parking in New Orleans, consult the city's **Parking Division** (504/658-8200).

Orientation

New Orleanians rarely refer to compass directions when discussing how to navigate the city. The city is bound on one side by the irregular Mississippi River, which forms the western, southern, or eastern border; main roads tend to run parallel or perpendicular to the river. Since the river's direction changes, this means that New Orleans's street grid also changes its axis in different places. As a result, most residents employ the terms "lakeside" (meaning north toward Lake Pontchartrain) and "riverside" (meaning south toward the Mississippi) when referring to streets perpendicular to the river. The terms "upriver" or "uptown" refer to westerly directions; the terms "downriver" or "downtown" are used for easterly directions. For example, Canal Street, which tourists generally consider a north-south thoroughfare, actually runs in a southeasterly direction toward the river. If you're still confused, be sure to have a city map with you at all times, as this is one place where it is absolutely indispensable—whether you're walking, driving, taking public transportation, or even using cabs. Residents refer to neighborhood names almost as much as specific streets.

The undisputed heart of New Orleans, the **French Quarter** beckons with its wealth of seafood restaurants, history museums, and varied street performers. Peruse the art galleries and antiques shops along Royal Street, stroll beside the Mississippi River, enjoy live music on Bourbon Street, or take a carriage ride through the fabled avenues. Iconic images like the St. Louis Cathedral, flickering gas lamps, and wrought-iron balconies make the Vieux Carré the city's most photographed neighborhood.

Northeast of the French Quarter, the residential **Faubourg Marigny** and **Bywater** neighborhoods lure their share of visitors. Sandwiched between Esplanade Avenue, the Mississippi River, and the Industrial Canal, this vast area is especially popular among local music lovers, who flock nightly to the moody jazz clubs and low-key eateries on Frenchmen Street.

Southwest of the French Quarter lies the **Central Business District (CBD).** Here, you'll encounter some of the city's finest hotels, plus diversions like the prominent Harrah's New Orleans casino. The adjacent **Arts District,** also known as the Warehouse District, contains numerous art galleries, the Contemporary Arts Center, The National WWII Museum, and Lee Circle.

The eclectic **Uptown** area is filled with as many rundown apartment buildings as well-landscaped estates. Shop for fashionable jewelry, clothing, and home furnishings along Magazine Street, ride

the streetcars on oak-shaded St. Charles Avenue, and explore popular bars and eateries in the Riverbend neighborhood. Uptown is also home to the famous Audubon Zoo, part of verdant Audubon Park.

Technically part of the expansive Uptown area, the **Garden District** comprises several mansions and art museums. Most of the attractions, restaurants, inns, and stores worth noting lie along or within several blocks of St. Charles Avenue, between the Pontchartrain Expressway and Louisiana Avenue. Browse antiques shops and vintage clothing boutiques on funky Magazine Street, savor classic local cuisine at the award-winning Commander's Palace, and explore landmarks like Lafayette Cemetery No. 1.

Two areas flooded by Hurricane Katrina, the **Tremé** and **Mid-City** have slowly rebounded since that devastating storm. Northwest of Rampart Street, the Tremé has nurtured many local musicians over the years and now entices tourists with places like Louis Armstrong Park and St. Louis Cemetery No. 1, site of Marie Laveau's celebrated tomb. Farther north, Mid-City features several popular attractions, including City Park, the New Orleans Museum of Art, and the Fair Grounds Race Course, home to the annual New Orleans Jazz & Heritage Festival.

Sights

Despite the round-the-clock presence of bicycles and cars, the French Quarter is a pedestrian-friendly neighborhood. Marked by traditional European architecture, lush Caribbean-style courtyards, high-end art galleries, Bohemian shops, traditional jazz clubs, and rowdy karaoke bars, this eclectic historical district appeals to tourists and residents alike. Walking amid the old-fashioned gas lamps constitutes a sight in itself—albeit a tantalizing, multisensory one. While strolling along the cracked, ankle-spraining sidewalks, enjoy the varied street musicians, the clip-clop of passing carriages, and an air often scented with the mingled perfume of sweet olive trees, chicory-laced coffee, boiled seafood, and, yes, mule manure.

Stay aware of your surroundings, particularly when walking at night. Crime rates in New Orleans are high.

French Quarter

★ Jackson Square

Jackson Square (Decatur St. and Chartres St. between St. Peter St. and St. Ann St., 504/658-3200, www.experienceneworleans.com; 8am-7pm daily summer, 8am-6pm daily winter; free) was named in honor of the seventh U.S. president, Andrew Jackson, who led the United States to victory during the Battle of New Orleans. A 14-foot-tall bronze statue of Jackson serves as the square's centerpiece and ranks among the city's favorite photo ops.

Filled with trees, benches, and grassy areas, Jackson Square is a wonderful place to sit and read a newspaper, eat a muffuletta from one of the nearby cafés, and absorb the oldest section of New Orleans. (No dogs or bikes are permitted.) More often than not, you'll spy mimes, musicians, and other entertainers along the promenades that fringe Jackson Square, sometimes even after the park has closed at night. Horse-drawn carriages usually line the gated park alongside Decatur Street, awaiting tourists for guided excursions through the Quarter.

This picturesque green space is surrounded by several historical buildings, including the gorgeous **St. Louis Cathedral,** as well as the **Cabildo** and the **Presbytère.** Along the northeastern and southwestern sides of the square lie the lower and upper **Pontalba Apartments,** the oldest apartment buildings in the country. Here, you'll find the historic **1850 House** and, on the lower levels, several eateries and worthwhile shops.

1850 House and Pontalba Apartments

The Pontalba Apartments were commissioned by Baroness Micaela Almonester de Pontalba in 1849 (the lower building, on St. Ann St.) and 1851 (the upper building, on St. Peter St.). She had inherited the land from her father, Don Andres Almonester, the man who had financed the Cabildo, the Presbytère, and St. Louis Cathedral after the devastating fire of 1788.

Each row of buildings contained 16 separate houses on the upper levels and a series of shops on the lower levels. After the Civil War, Jackson Square and its environs began to deteriorate and the Pontalba Apartments functioned as rather unfashionable tenements. In 1921, William Ratcliffe Irby bought the lower Pontalba building and willed the property to the Louisiana State Museum. The grand old townhouses were subdivided into smaller apartments.

The only Pontalba Apartment open to the public, the **1850 House** (523 St. Ann St., 504/524-9118, www.louisianastatemuseum.org; 10am-4:30pm Tues.-Sun.; adults $3, seniors, military, and students $2, free under 13) was restored in 1955. Most of the interior furnishings were donated to the museum but are authentic to the exact period. Today, the 1850 House is a small but popular museum, which also has an excellent book and gift shop. The actual apartment occupies the two floors above the shop. Visitors can stand at edges of the doorways and peer into the rooms, gaining a sense of an 1850s row house owned by a family of somewhat considerable means. Plaques on the third floor detail the lives of the home's inhabitants from 1850 to 1861.

Presbytère

Built in 1797 as a home for the priests of the St. Louis Cathedral, and standing just on the downriver side of it, the two-story **Presbytère** (751 Chartres St., 504/568-6968 or 800/568-6968, www.louisi-anastatemuseum.org; 10am-4:30pm Tues.-Sun.; adults $6, seniors, military, and students $5, free under 13) on Jackson Square bears a structural resemblance to the Cabildo. It was never used for its intended purpose, as its financier, Don Andres Almonester (a Spaniard of considerable means who also funded the Cabildo and St. Louis Cathedral), died before it was completed. The new U.S. government eventually completed it and used it to house the Louisiana state courts during the 19th century.

In 1911, it became part of the Louisiana State Museum, and today, it houses a colorful permanent exhibit on the history of Mardi Gras traditions both in the city and the state called Mardi Gras: It's Carnival Time in Indiana. Videos, audiotapes, and a wide array of artifacts detail how Louisianians have celebrated Carnival through the years and how this

event has grown to become one of the most popular festivals in the world. You'll also encounter Living with Hurricanes: Katrina and Beyond, a heartbreaking yet inspiring exhibit that utilizes photographs, eyewitness accounts, artifacts, and multimedia displays to explore the history and science of hurricanes. In particular, you'll learn more about the loss and destruction caused by Hurricanes Katrina and Rita in 2005, as well as the service, solidarity, and resilience demonstrated by residents and others in their aftermath.

St. Louis Cathedral

The lakeside end of Jackson Square is dominated by the **St. Louis Cathedral** (615 Père Antoine Alley, 504/525-9585, www.stlouiscathedral.org; 8:30am-4pm daily; self-guided tour pamphlet for $1 donation), one of the most magnificent cathedrals in the United States. The current building was constructed in 1794 in the Spanish style, with two round

Jackson Square

spires rising from the facade, and then virtually rebuilt and remodeled in 1849. Simpler churches have stood on this site since the 1720s, not long after the arrival of the French explorer Jean Baptiste Le Moyne, Sieur de Bienville, who established New Orleans as a permanent settlement in 1718. During the 1849 remodel, huge steeples were added to the two symmetrical round towers, and the building has received additional restorations over the years. The cathedral was designated a minor basilica in 1964 by Pope Paul VI. Mass is held every day, and the gift shop (10am-3pm daily) offers an assortment of religious and spiritual items. Visitors are welcome to take a guided tour of the property; as an alternative, simply wander inside and explore the gorgeous architecture, including kaleidoscopic stained-glass windows, on your own. Keep in mind that this is an actual church, so be respectful of those who have come for prayer and quiet reflection. If you're in town during December,

attend one of the free jazz concerts on offer here.

Cabildo

On the upriver side of the St. Louis Cathedral stands the **Cabildo** (701 Chartres St., 504/568-6968 or 800/568-6968, www.louisianastatemuseum.org; 10am-4:30pm Tues.-Sun.; adults $6, seniors, students, and military $5, free under 13), the building in which the formal transfer of Louisiana to the United States took place after the Louisiana Purchase. The Spanish first constructed the Cabildo as their seat of government in the 1770s, but it and its replacement were destroyed during both major city fires in the late 18th century. The current structure, made of brick and stucco and built in the Spanish style with Moorish influences, was erected in 1794, serving again as home to the Spanish administrative body, after which it became the Maison de Ville (Town Hall) during the brief time the French reclaimed New Orleans. It served as the Louisiana Supreme Court headquarters for much of the 19th and early 20th centuries, and it was actually the site where the landmark *Plessy v. Ferguson* decision (which legalized segregation) originated in 1892. Many prominent visitors have been officially received in the Cabildo, from the Marquis de Lafayette to Mark Twain. The building looks more French than Spanish today, because the original flat tile roof was replaced with a Second Empire mansard roof in the late 1840s.

Part of the Louisiana State Museum since 1908, the Cabildo contains a fascinating exhibit tracing the history of Louisiana through the past two centuries, beginning with the region's Native Americans and ending with Reconstruction. Each section uses maps, photographs, drawings, historical documents, and narrative signs to describe the period and theme. The museum is closed on state holidays.

NEW ORLEANS

French Quarter

STORYVILLE

Germaine Cazenave Wells
Mardi Gras Museum

New Orleans
Musical Legends
Park

The Hermann-Grima
Historic House Museum

BOURBON STREET

Waldhorn
& Adler

The Historic
New Orleans
Collection

ROYAL ST

EXCHANGE PL

EXCHANGE PL

CHARTRES ST

The Cabildo

The New Orleans
School of Cooking

DORSIERE ST

DECATUR ST

CLINTON ST

Audubon
Butterfly Garden
and Insectarium

N PETERS ST

Toulouse

N PETERS ST

Jean Lafitte
National Historical
Park and Preserve

N FRONT BLVD

Bienville

Woldenberg
Riverfront Park

BADINE ST W

BADINE ST E

Audubon Aquarium
of the Americas

Canal Street

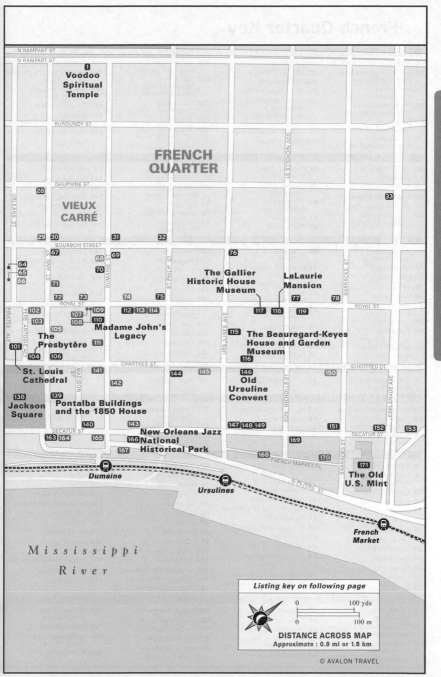

French Quarter Key

1 Voodoo Spiritual Temple

N RAMPART ST

BURGUNDY ST

FRENCH QUARTER

DAUPHINE ST

28

VIEUX CARRÉ

33

ORLEANS ST

29 **30**   **31**   **32**

GOV NICHOLLS ST

BOURBON STREET

67   **68** **69**   **76**

64
65   **70**   The Gallier   LaLaurie
66   **71**   Historic House   Mansion
72 **73**   **74** **75**   Museum   **77** **78**

ST ANN ST

DUMAINE ST

ST PHILIP ST

BARRACKS ST

ROYAL ST

ROYAL ST

102   **109**   **112** **113** **114**   **117** **118** **119**
103   **107** **108** **110**   **115**   The Beauregard-Keyes
105   Madame John's   House and Garden
101   The   Legacy   **116**   Museum
104 **106**   Presbytère **111**

URSULINES AVE

PERE ANTOINE ALY

PIRATES ALY

CHARTRES ST   CHARTRES ST

141   **144** **145**   **146**   **150**
St. Louis   **142**   Old   ESPLANADE AVE
Cathedral   Ursuline
138   **139**   Convent
Jackson   Pontalba Buildings
Square   and the 1850 House   **147** **148** **149**   **151** **152** **153**
140   **143**

MADISON ST

GOV NICHOLLS ST

S PETERS ST

BARRACKS ST

DECATUR ST   DECATUR ST

163 **164**   **165**   **166** New Orleans Jazz   **169**
167 National   **168** FRENCH MARKET PL   **170**   **171**
Historical Park   The Old
U.S. Mint

🚋 Dumaine

🚋 Ursulines

N PETERS ST

🚋 French Market

Mississippi

River

Listing key on following page

0   100 yds
0   100 m

DISTANCE ACROSS MAP
Approximate : 0.9 mi or 1.5 km

© AVALON TRAVEL

French Quarter Key

SIGHTS

1 Voodoo Spiritual Temple
12 Germaine Cazenave Wells Mardi Gras Museum
16 New Orleans Musical Legends Park
24 The Hermann-Grima Historic House Museum
57 The Historic New Orleans Collection
70 New Orleans Historic Voodoo Museum

99 The Cabildo
101 St. Louis Cathedral
104 The Presbytère
110 Madame John's Legacy
116 The Beauregard-Keyes House and Garden Museum
117 The Gallier Historic House Museum
118 Lalaurie Mansion

128 The New Orleans School of Cooking
130 Jean Lafitte National Historical Park and Preserve
132 New Orleans Pharmacy Museum
138 Jackson Square
139 Pontalba Buildings and the 1850 House

146 Old Ursuline Convent
154 Audubon Butterfly Garden and Insectarium
166 New Orleans Jazz National Historical Park
171 The Old U.S. Mint
172 Audubon Aquarium of the Americas
173 Woldenberg Riverfront Park

NIGHTLIFE

18 The Bombay Club
27 Cats Meow
28 Good Friends Bar
30 Bourbon Pub & Parade
31 The Cafe Lafitte in Exile
32 Lafitte's Blacksmith Shop Bar

37 21st Amendment at La Louisiane
40 Jean Lafitte's Old Absinthe House
42 Irvin Mayfield's Jazz Playhouse
52 Hermes Bar
53 The Dungeon

60 Preservation Hall
61 Pat O'Brien's
64 Orleans Grapevine Wine Bar & Bistro
67 Oz
78 Golden Lantern Bar
80 The Carousel Bar & Lounge

90 One Eyed Jacks
122 House of Blues
131 Napoleon House
147 Molly's at the Market
152 Balcony Music Club
153 Igor's Check Point Charlie
169 Palm Court Jazz Cafe

SHOPS

29 Marie Laveau's House of Voodoo
44 Royal Antiques
45 Keil's Antiques
46 Vintage 329
48 Moss Antiques
51 James H. Cohen & Sons, Inc.
54 Fleur de Paris
58 Trashy Diva Clothing Boutique
62 Reverand Zombie's House of Voodoo

65 Arcadian Books & Art Prints
71 Boutique du Vampyre
72 Bourbon French Parfums
84 Bevolo Gas & Electric Lights
85 Bottom of the Cup Tea Room
89 Roux Royale
91 M.S. Rau Antiques
96 Forever New Orleans
98 Faulkner House Books

103 Maskarade
109 Papier Plume
111 Voodoo Authentica
113 Idea Factory
114 Fifi Mahony's
120 Crescent City Books
129 Cigar Factory New Orleans
135 New Orleans Silversmiths
136 Lucullus
141 Queork
142 Java House Imports

143 Central Grocery
155 RHINOContemporary Crafts Co.
156 The Shops at Canal Place
157 Dollz & Dames
160 Southern Candymakers
161 Peaches Records
165 Aunt Sally's Creole Pralines
165 Evans Creole Candy Factory
168 French Market
170 Artist's Market & Bead Shop

SPORTS AND ACTIVITIES

2 The American Bicycle Rental Company

100 Friends of the Cabildo

162 Royal Carriages

ARTS AND CULTURE

50 Martin-Lawrence Galleries
73 Craig Tracy's Fine-Art Bodypainting Gallery
82 A Gallery for Fine Photography

83 Michalopoulos Gallery
88 Kako Gallery
92 Jamie Hayes Gallery
94 Le Petit Théâtre du Vieux Carré

102 Rodrigue Studio New Orleans
107 Tanner Original Art
108 Tanner Open Studio
121 Callan Fine Art

167 Dutch Alley Artist's Co-op

RESTAURANTS

5 Big Killer Poboys
9 Ralph Brennan's Red Fish Grill
10 Galatoire's Restaurant
11 GW Fins
13 Arnaud's
14 French 75
15 Remoulade's
17 Cafe Beignet
20 Déjà Vu Bar & Grill
21 Killer Poboys
22 Bayona
23 Kingfish
33 Port of Call

34 Dickie Brennan's Bourbon House Seafood
35 Felix's Restaurant & Oyster Bar
36 Acme Oyster House
38 Dickie Brennan's Steakhouse
39 Mr. B's Bistro
41 Restaurant R'evolution
47 Oceana Grill
49 Brennan's
54 Antoine's Restaurant
55 Antoine's Annex
59 The Court of Two Sisters
63 The Old Coffeepot Restaurant

69 Clover Grill
75 CC's Coffee House
76 Quartermaster
77 Verti Marte
79 Palace Café
86 Rib Room
93 Tableau
95 Gumbo Shop
97 La Divina Gelateria
106 Muriel's Jackson Square
112 Café Amelie
115 Croissant d'Or Patisserie
119 Mona Lisa Restaurant
123 Sekisui Samurai Sushi

124 SoBou
126 K-Paul's Louisiana Kitchen
127 NOLA
133 Johnny's Po-Boys
134 Crescent City Brewhouse
137 Café Maspero
140 Tujague's
144 Irene's Cuisine
148 Coop's Place
149 Trinity
151 En Vie Espresso Bar & Cafe
158 Felipe's Taqueria
163 Café du Monde

HOTELS

3 The Ritz-Carlton New Orleans
4 Courtyard New Orleans Downtown/Iberville
6 Chateau Le Moyne – French Quarter
7 Dauphine Orleans Hotel

8 Audubon Cottages
19 Prince Conti Hotel
25 The Olivier House Hotel
26 Four Points by Sheraton French Quarter
43 Royal Sonesta New Orleans

66 Bourbon Orleans Hotel
68 Biscuit Palace Guest House
74 The Cornstalk Hotel
81 Hotel Monteleone
87 Omni Royal Orleans
105 Place d'Armes Hotel

125 W New Orleans – French Quarter
145 Hôtel Provincial
150 Le Richelieu in the French Quarter
159 Bienville House Hotel

Big Easy Bargains

Admission fees in New Orleans can add up quickly, but money-saving tricks do exist, particularly in the form of combination packages. If you're planning to visit the **Audubon Zoo, Audubon Butterfly Garden and Insectarium, Audubon Aquarium of the Americas,** and **Entergy IMAX Theatre,** go for the **Audubon Experience Package** (www.auduboninstitute.org; adults $45, seniors $38, children 2-12 $35), which can save you up to $30 per person. The package (valid for 30 consecutive days) includes one visit to each facility. The ultimate combination ticket is the **New Orleans Power Pass** (www.visiticket.com; 1-day pass adults $90, children $65; 2-day pass adults $130, children $99; 3-day pass adults $170, children $130), which provides access to nearly 30 tours, attractions, and other diversions throughout the Crescent City and beyond, from **Blaine Kern's Mardi Gras World** to the **Oak Alley Plantation.**

Not far from the aquarium and the insectarium, pedestrians can enjoy an inexpensive trip across the Mississippi River via the **Algiers Point/Canal Street Ferry** (http://nolaferries.com; adults $2, seniors $1, free 2 and under), which transports you between the foot of Canal Street and historic Algiers Point. A cheap ride on the **St. Charles streetcar** (www.norta.com; adults $1.25, seniors $0.40, free 2 and under) will show you some of the gorgeous mansions, not to mention two historic universities, that line this verdant Uptown thoroughfare.

In the French Quarter, the **Louisiana State Museum** (www.louisianastatemuseum.org) operates several historical properties, including the **Old U.S. Mint** (free) and **Madame John's Legacy** (free), as well as the **Cabildo,** the **Presbytère,** and the **1850 House**—all of which surround Jackson Square, charge nominal $2-6 admission fees, and offer free entry to children under 13.

At **The National WWII Museum** (www.nationalww2museum.org) in the city's Arts District, admission isn't cheap (adults $26, seniors $22.50, students and military $16.50), but given the museum's size and comprehensive nature, you might wish to return the following day, which you can happily do for an additional $6 per person.

Naturally, New Orleans has plenty of free attractions as well. It costs nothing to visit the various local units of **Jean Lafitte National Historical Park and Preserve** (www.nps.gov/jela), which includes the **French Quarter Visitor Center** on Decatur Street and the **Chalmette Battlefield and National Cemetery** east of the city. The city's two largest urban parks—Uptown's **Audubon Park** and Mid-City's **City Park**—are also free to explore. Within City Park, the **New Orleans Museum of Art** (1 Collins Diboll Dr., 504/658-4100, http://noma.org; 10am-6pm Tues.-Thurs., 10am-9pm Fri., 10am-5pm Sat., 11am-5pm Sun.; adults $12, seniors and military $10, students $8, children 7-12 $6) offers free admission for Louisiana residents every Wednesday, and the adjacent **Sydney and Walda Besthoff Sculpture Garden** (10am-6pm Mon.-Fri., 10am-5pm Sat.-Sun.) is always free to the public.

Remember, too, that New Orleans itself is a bargain-friendly sight. It's absolutely free to stroll the streets of the **French Quarter,** absorbing all the architecture, hidden gardens, and sheer vibrancy of the city's oldest neighborhood. Although some of the historical sites charge entrance fees, other attractions—such as **Jackson Square,** the **St. Louis Cathedral,** the **French Market,** the **New Orleans Musical Legends Park,** and the art-filled windows along **Royal Street**—cost nothing. An enjoyable walk along the riverfront, from the **Moonwalk** to **Woldenberg Riverfront Park** is also delightfully free. Naturally, it's also free to explore the city's public plazas and historical churches, not to mention some of its legendary cemeteries.

An Architectural Driving Tour

For a fun cursory education of local architecture, take the following drive through this relatively compact city.

French Quarter

Jackson Square (700 block of Decatur St.) is a lovely park surrounded by the **Cabildo,** the **Presbytère,** and the **St. Louis Cathedral,** Spanish-style structures built in the 1790s. Along the southwestern and northeastern edges of the park lie the lower and upper **Pontalba Apartments,** commissioned in the mid-1850s and considered the oldest apartment buildings in America.

At the corner of Governor Nicholls and Royal stand the supposedly haunted **LaLaurie Mansion** (1140 Royal St.), an imposing gray structure built in the 1830s, and the 1857 Victorian **Gallier Historic House Museum** (1132 Royal St.), the former home of New Orleans architect James Gallier Jr.

Head to Chartres Street to the expansive **Old Ursuline Convent** (1100 Chartres St.), constructed in 1745 and the oldest existing building in the Mississippi River Valley. Across the street is the **Beauregard-Keyes House** (1113 Chartres St.), one of the few raised cottages in the French Quarter. This 1826 mansion was the home of Confederate general P. G. T. Beauregard. Novelist Frances Parkinson Keyes lived here from 1944 to 1969.

Central Business and Arts Districts

Follow Magazine Street to the 1891 **Confederate Memorial Hall** (929 Camp St.). Designed by architect Thomas O. Sully, this Romanesque structure is the state's oldest continuously operating museum.

Garden District

On Constance Street is the regal **St. Mary's Assumption Church** (2030 Constance St.). Constructed between 1858 and 1866, St. Mary's is a massive, German Baroque Revival-style structure with an intricate facade and arched stained-glass windows.

End at St. Charles Avenue, home to the Victorian-inspired **House of Broel** (2220 St. Charles Ave.) and Italianate-style **Van Benthuysen-Elms Mansion** (3029 St. Charles Ave.), both erected in the mid- to late 19th century.

New Orleans Jazz National Historical Park

Head to the visitor center in French Market District at the **New Orleans Jazz National Historical Park** (916 N. Peters St., 504/589-4841 or 877/520-0677, www. nps.gov/jazz; 10am-4:30pm Tues.-Sat.; free) to participate in weekly ranger-led programs, from lectures to musical demonstrations, that explore the origin, development, and evolution of jazz. You can pick up brochures featuring an 11-stop tour of historic jazz sites in the Crescent City as well as the **Jazz Walk of Fame** in Algiers Point, a line of old-fashioned lampposts that highlight several jazz greats, from Louis Armstrong to Louis Prima. Self-guided audio tours are also available through the website or by phoning 504/613-4062.

Moreover, the park oversees jazz-related exhibits at the **Old U.S. Mint** as well as special events at **Perseverance Hall,** a historic building in **Louis Armstrong Park** (701 N. Rampart St., 504/658-3200) that was once the oldest Masonic Lodge in Louisiana and later a multiuse event venue where African American jazz musicians would perform for black and white audiences.

Old U.S. Mint

Fashioned with a granite facade and made of stucco and Mississippi River mud brick, the **Old U.S. Mint** (400 Esplanade Ave., 504/568-6993 or 800/568-6868, www.louisianastatemuseum.org; 10am-4:30pm Tues.-Sun.; free) was constructed in 1835 at the behest of U.S. president Andrew Jackson. This is the only building in the country to have functioned as both a U.S. and a Confederate mint. It also housed Confederate troops for a time during the Civil War. With the Union occupation, the mint was shut down until Reconstruction, at which time it resumed service.

In 1909, the mint was decommissioned, and in 1981, it was added to the state museum system. Today, it's home to the **Louisiana Historical Center,** an archive open to the public and containing priceless collections of colonial-era maps and manuscripts. The site is also home to **Music at the Mint** (www.musicatthemint.org), which features a variety of music-related artifacts, such as posters, sheet music, and memorabilia, from Sidney Bechet's soprano sax to Fats Domino's piano. The Mint also houses historical musical recordings, showcases live performances, and presents on-site interviews of performing musicians. There's also a large tribute to Louis Armstrong, as well as three colorful murals depicting New Orleans's fabled Storyville red-light district, one of the city's cultivators of jazz. A small display is dedicated to the building's architect, William Strickland, who trained under famous Greek Revival architect Benjamin Latrobe and who also designed the Tennessee State Capitol, as well as the mints in Charlotte and Philadelphia.

Old Ursuline Convent
King Louis XV of France established the **Old Ursuline Convent** (1112 Chartres St., 504/503-0361, www.stlouiscathedral.org; 10am-4pm Mon.-Fri., 9am-3pm Sat.; adults $8, seniors $7, students $6, free under 8) in 1745 to house the Ursuline nuns who first came to New Orleans in the late 1720s, making them the first nuns to establish a permanent foothold in what is today the United States. This

convent was their second home, completed in 1753 and now believed to be the oldest extant building in the Mississippi River Valley; they moved to Dauphine Street in 1824, and then to their present Uptown home, at 2635 State Street, in 1912. In those early decades, the convent housed everyone from French orphans and wounded British soldiers to exiled Acadians and the city's destitute masses. During the early 1800s, the nuns conducted a school for the education of daughters of wealthy Louisiana plantation owners. Today, the Ursuline Academy still functions at its State Street locale as the country's oldest continuously operated school for women.

The convent on Chartres Street is part of a large ecclesiastic complex called the Archbishop Antoine Blanc Memorial, owned by the Catholic Archdiocese of New Orleans. The entire complex—which includes the adjacent gardens, the attached **St. Mary's Church,** and several related outbuildings—is named for the first archbishop of New Orleans, Antoine Blanc. Today, the complex and the St. Louis Cathedral in Jackson Square form the Catholic Cultural Heritage Center of the Archdiocese of New Orleans.

The **Old Ursuline Convent Museum,** which encompasses the exhibits on the first floor of the main convent building, is open for self-guided tours. Simply purchase a ticket in the gift shop (1112 Chartres St.), and then, at your own pace, explore the convent exhibits, the rear garden, and the adjacent church. The last admission is at 3:15pm on weekdays, 2:15pm on Saturdays.

Beauregard-Keyes House and Garden Museum
Opposite the Old Ursuline Convent stands the **Beauregard-Keyes House and Garden Museum** (1113 Chartres St., 504/523-7257, www.bkhouse.org; 10am-3pm Mon.-Sat.; adults $10, seniors and students $9, children 6-12 $4, free under 6 and military), one of relatively few

Faubourg Marigny

FAUBOURG MARIGNY

FRENCH QUARTER

Mississippi River

© AVALON TRAVEL

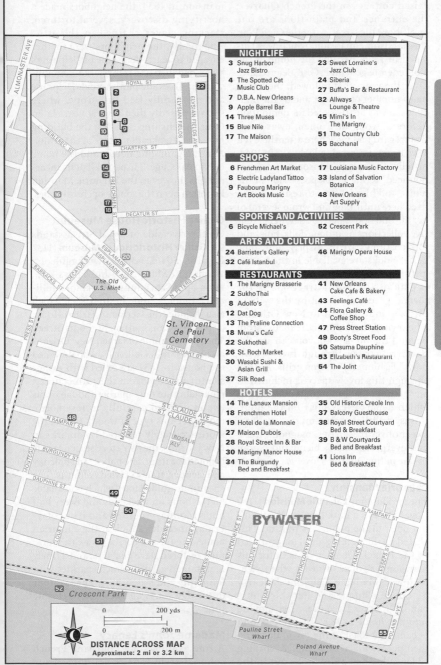

NIGHTLIFE

3 Snug Harbor
Jazz Bistro
4 The Spotted Cat
Music Club
7 D.B.A. New Orleans
9 Apple Barrel Bar
14 Three Muses
15 Blue Nile
17 The Maison

23 Sweet Lorraine's
Jazz Club
24 Siberia
27 Buffa's Bar & Restaurant
32 Allways
Lounge & Theatre
45 Mimi's In
The Marigny
51 The Country Club
55 Bacchanal

SHOPS

6 Frenchmen Art Market
8 Electric Ladyland Tattoo
9 Faubourg Marigny
Art Books Music

17 Louisiana Music Factory
33 Island of Salvation
Botanica
48 New Orleans
Art Supply

SPORTS AND ACTIVITIES

6 Bicycle Michael's
52 Crescent Park

ARTS AND CULTURE

24 Barrister's Gallery
32 Café Istanbul

46 Marigny Opera House

RESTAURANTS

1 The Marigny Brasserie
2 Sukho Thai
8 Adolfo's
12 Dat Dog
13 The Praline Connection
18 Mona's Café
22 Sukhothai
26 St. Roch Market
30 Wasabi Sushi &
Asian Grill
37 Silk Road

41 New Orleans
Cake Cafe & Bakery
43 Feelings Café
44 Flora Gallery &
Coffee Shop
47 Press Street Station
49 Booty's Street Food
50 Satsuma Dauphine
53 Elizabeth's Restaurant
54 The Joint

HOTELS

14 The Lanaux Mansion
18 Frenchmen Hotel
19 Hotel de la Monnaie
27 Maison Dubois
28 Royal Street Inn & Bar
30 Marigny Manor House
34 The Burgundy
Bed and Breakfast

35 Old Historic Creole Inn
37 Balcony Guesthouse
38 Royal Street Courtyard
Bed & Breakfast
39 B & W Courtyards
Bed and Breakfast
41 Lions Inn
Bed & Breakfast

St. Vincent
de Paul
Cemetery

The Old
U.S. Mint

BYWATER

Crescent Park

0   200 yds

0   200 m

DISTANCE ACROSS MAP
Approximate: 2 mi or 3.2 km

Pauline Street
Wharf

Poland Avenue
Wharf

raised cottages in the French Quarter; the entrance and main floor are one level above the street. After the Civil War, the handsome mansion, which was finished in 1826, became the home of the Confederate general P. G. T. Beauregard. Over the years that followed, the house had a number of owners, and by the mid-1920s, it was nearly slated for demolition before a group of women, aware that Beauregard had lived here after the Civil War, began a campaign to save it. In 1944, novelist Frances Parkinson Keyes (pronounced "KIZE") took possession of the house and hired a firm to restore it. She lived here until 1969 and wrote several of her 50-odd books here. Today, her extensive collections of antique dolls, fans, and folk costumes are on display, and some of her books are available in the on-site gift shop.

One of the lead attractions is the formal garden, laid out by the wife of Switzerland's consul to New Orleans, who owned the house in the 1830s. From beyond the outer wall, you can see the parterre garden through brick "windows" fashioned with iron grills. A stroll through this lovely space is included in any of the guided, 45-minute house tours, which depart every hour on the hour. Roses, daylilies, crape myrtle, azaleas, sweet olive trees, irises, magnolia trees, and evergreen shrubs blend and bloom in one of the Quarter's loveliest gardens.

LaLaurie Mansion

The curious gray **LaLaurie Mansion** (1140 Royal St.) has a dark history. While it's not open to the public, it's routinely included on the walking ghost tours offered in the French Quarter. This notorious mansion was once owned by the twice-widowed Madame Delphine Macarty de Lopez Blanque and her third husband, Dr. Louis LaLaurie. After moving into this home in 1832, the couple soon became the toast of the town, dazzling their peers with lavish parties. According to legend, when a fire broke out in the

mansion in 1834, the neighbors made a horrifying discovery: several tortured, starving slaves chained in the attic. Apparently, the neighbors were further enraged to learn that some of Delphine's slaves had died under mysterious circumstances. To evade punishment, Delphine and her family fled to Europe, where she supposedly died several years later. Over the ensuing decades, the building has served as headquarters of the Union Army, a gambling house, and the home of Nicolas Cage. Through all of its incarnations, however, the LaLaurie Mansion has often been the source of ghostly tales.

Gallier Historic House Museum

On the riverside of Royal Street stands the **Gallier Historic House Museum** (1132 Royal St., 504/525-5661, www.hgghh.org; 10am-3pm Mon.-Tues. and Thurs.-Fri., noon-3pm Sat.; adults $15, seniors, military, students, and children $12), which also includes the Hermann-Grima House (separate admission) on St. Louis Street. The former home of famed New Orleans architect James Gallier Jr., who designed the house in 1857, it's filled with exquisite furnishings from the 19th century, plus elaborate faux marble and faux bois (wood painted carefully to resemble a more precious type of wood). One of the more accurately restored landmarks in New Orleans, the two-story stucco facade is noted for its ornate balustrade balcony and slender, finely crafted columns. The 45-minute guided tour, which is available on the hour on weekends and every half hour Monday-Tuesday and Thursday-Friday, includes a look at the Victorian home, the on-site carriageway, the carefully restored slave quarters, and a finely maintained garden, which sparkles with fountains and slate walks. The last tour of the day starts an hour before closing time.

Madame John's Legacy

A fine example of a Louisiana French colonial-style (or Creole) home from

Romeo Spikes and Haint Blue Paint

As the city's oldest neighborhood, the Vieux Carré (French Quarter) boasts the lion's share of photogenic architectural styles, including the upper-level galleries, wrought-iron railings, and hidden courtyards ironically influenced by the city's Spanish era. You'll also spot structures anachronistically known as **slave quarters**—smaller, often two-story houses situated behind street-facing mansions. You may also notice protective spikes, broken glass pieces, and other deterrents atop gates and fences. Particularly ominous are the **Romeo spikes** at the top of ground-floor gallery polls; relics of 19th-century New Orleans, these cast-iron protrusions were installed to prevent male suitors from making nighttime visits to young women. Throughout the city, you'll encounter curiosities like **haint blue** paint on the underside of porch ceilings, meant to repel evil spirits, or **shotgun houses,** one-level structures in which all rooms are positioned consecutively and interconnected by doors in lieu of a hallway.

the late 18th century, **Madame John's Legacy** (632 Dumaine St., 504/568-6968 or 800/568-6968, www.louisianastatemuseum.org; 10am-4:30pm Tues.-Sun.; free) was built to replace a home lost in the Great Fire of 1788. It survived the next, smaller fire of 1794 and is today one of just a few remaining pre-1800s buildings in the Quarter. The complex, which fronts Dumaine Street, comprises three buildings: a main house, a two-story *garçonniere,* and a kitchen with a cook's living quarters. Designated a National Historic Landmark and now part of the Louisiana State Museum, the home currently houses The Palm, the Pine, and the Cypress: Newcomb Pottery of New Orleans, an exhibit that features more than 50 glazed ceramics pieces, plus archival photographs that document the history of this much-loved local pottery. The museum is closed on state holidays.

★ New Orleans Historic Voodoo Museum

Established in 1972, the small, somewhat cramped **New Orleans Historic Voodoo Museum** (724 Dumaine St., 504/680-0128, www.voodoomuseum.com; 10am-6pm daily; adults $7, seniors and students $5.50, children under 12 $3.50) offers a decent, respectful overview of a practice still shrouded in mystery yet taken seriously by its practitioners. Displays include masks, ritual art, and artifacts from Africa and Haiti, where the city's distinctive brand of voodoo practice originated. The exhibits, though ominous, aren't gory in nature, so kids often find them appealing. The focus is on Marie Laveau, the anointed voodoo priestess who lived in New Orleans from the 1790s until her death in 1881. Though you can arrange private consultations and healing seminars with museum staff, the true highlight is the historian-led walking tour (adults $19, children under 12 $12; call more than 24 hours in advance to schedule), which includes a stroll through St. Louis Cemetery No. 1 (supposed site of Marie Laveau's tomb), an encounter with a contemporary voodoo priestess, and plenty of engrossing stories about voodoo, zombies, jazz funerals, Mardi Gras Indians, and other curious aspects of the city's colorful history.

Voodoo Spiritual Temple

Operated by Priestess Miriam, the **Voodoo Spiritual Temple** (1428 N. Rampart St., 504/943-9795, www.voodoospiritualtemple.org; 10:30am-6pm Mon.-Sat., noon-2pm Sun.; free, donations accepted), a center of voodoo worship and healing, offers voodoo consultations, rituals, and workshops. An on-site gift shop sells handcrafted voodoo dolls, gris-gris and mojo bags, aroma

Marie Laveau: Voodoo Queen

Voodoo experienced its heyday in New Orleans in the 19th century, but while most voodoo paraphernalia available in the French Quarter today is bought by tourists, there's no question that some people still take the practice seriously. Unfortunately, misconceptions about voodoo abound and are often encouraged by its depiction in popular culture. Voodoo is based on the worship of spirits, called Loa, and a belief system that emphasizes spirituality, compassion, and treating others well. Although there's nothing inherently negative about voodoo, its practice does allow its followers to perform rites intended to bring calamity upon their enemies. These traditions, such as burning black candles or piercing miniature effigies with pins, are the most familiar among outsiders.

The origins of voodoo as a religious practice are unclear. Voodoo rituals are based on a variety of African religious traditions, which were brought to the United States by West African slaves. In 18th-century New Orleans, where slaves were kept by French and Spanish residents, voodoo began to incorporate some of the beliefs and rituals of Catholicism as well.

Marie Laveau (circa 1794-1881) is the historical figure most connected with southern Louisiana's rich voodoo tradition. A beautiful woman of French, African, and Native American extraction, she was New Orleans's high priestess of voodoo from roughly 1830 onward. She had numerous children, and at least one daughter continued to practice for many years after her mother's death, fueling rumors that the original Marie Laveau lived into the early 20th century. Her supposed grave in **St. Louis Cemetery No. 1,** on Basin Street, is still a site of pilgrimage for voodoo practitioners.

Laveau combined the understanding ear of a psychologist with the showmanship of a preacher to become one of the city's most vaunted spiritual figures. As a young woman, she practiced as a hair stylist in New Orleans, a position that afforded her the opportunity to work inside some of the city's most prominent homes. As she soaked up the gossip of the day, she also dispensed both practical and spiritual advice to her clients, no doubt sprinkling her words with healthy doses of voodoo mysticism and lore. Word of Laveau's talents as a voodoo priestess spread rapidly, and soon she was staging ceremonies in the small yard of her St. Ann Street home. Her most notorious ceremony, held annually in a swamp cabin along Bayou St. John on June 23 (St. John's Eve, the night before the Feast Day of St. John the Baptist), became the stuff of legend.

Laveau was the most famous priestess to captivate New Orleans's residents, but she wasn't the last. Throughout the centuries, a number of women and even some men have carried on the tradition of the voodoo priestess. According to legend, believers can invoke her powers by marking her tomb with three X's (a gris-gris, or charm), scratching the ground three times with their feet, knocking three times on the grave, and leaving a small offering before making a wish. In addition, many people in New Orleans continue to celebrate St. John's Eve and believe that, on this night, the spirit of the Voodoo Queen makes herself known.

oils, and books and CDs related to voodoo. The hours of the temple are flexible, so don't be surprised to find the front door locked at random times.

Hermann-Grima Historic House Museum

Just off rowdy Bourbon Street, you'll encounter one of the Quarter's best house-museums: the **Hermann-Grima Historic House Museum** (820 St. Louis St., 504/525-5661, www.hgghh.org; 10am-3pm Mon.-Tues. and Thurs.-Fri., noon-3pm Sat., by appt. Wed; adults $15, seniors, military, students, and children $12), a steep-roofed Federal-style mansion built in 1831 and resembling the sort of home you'd more often see in Savannah or other old cities of British origin. One unusual feature is the Quarter's only horse stable, adjacent to the charming courtyard garden. The house, which is run by the same folks who operate the Gallier House on Royal Street, offers informative, on-the-hour tours that reveal the customary lifestyle enjoyed by prosperous Creole families between 1830 and 1860. The last tour of the day starts an hour before closing time.

For an even greater understanding of dining and entertaining traditions in 19th-century New Orleans, opt for an **open-hearth demonstration** (most Thursdays Oct.-May) in the restored, open-hearth kitchen (the only functional one left in the French Quarter, a holdover from the home's antebellum days). These demonstrations enable you to watch the museum's culinary experts as they prepare seasonal dishes by utilizing traditional techniques of 19th-century New Orleans. Afterward, stop by **The Exchange Shop** (in the former carriage house), which offers books as well as jewelry, ceramics, textiles, photographs, and paintings from female artists based in Louisiana and along the Gulf Coast.

New Orleans Musical Legends Park

While strolling down Bourbon, note the small **New Orleans Musical Legends Park** (311 Bourbon St., 504/888-7608, www. neworleansmusicallegends.com; 8am-10pm Sun.-Thurs., 8am-midnight Fri.-Sat.; free), which was established in 1999 and now contains several bronze statues honoring some of the city's most legendary performers, including jazz clarinetist Pete Fountain, trumpet greats Al Hirt and Louis Prima, and singers Allen Toussaint and Irma Thomas. Additional statues, busts, and plaques will be added through the years as notable jazz musicians are inducted. Besides the statues, the park includes a lovely fountain, several tables and chairs, and a few food

stalls, selling surprisingly tasty fare, from gumbo to beignets. So, grab some food, find a seat, and listen to live jazz music (10am-close daily), courtesy of Steamboat Willie and other musicians. Leashed dogs are welcome in the park.

Germaine Cazenave Wells Mardi Gras Museum

Those curious about the glamour of Carnival should head to the **Germaine Cazenave Wells Mardi Gras Museum** (813 Bienville St., 504/523-5433, www.arnaudsrestaurant.com; 6pm-close Mon.-Sat., 10am-2:30pm and 6pm-close Sun.; free) at the fabled restaurant Arnaud's. The museum, named for the daughter of restaurant founder Count Arnaud, opened in 1983 as a tribute to Ms. Wells—the former queen of more than 22 Mardi Gras balls (1937-1968). On hand are several of Wells's elaborate ball costumes, intricate masks, lavish jewelry, and vintage photographs.

★ The Historic New Orleans Collection

Amid the art galleries of Royal Street lies one of the city's most underrated attractions, **The Historic New Orleans Collection** (THNOC, 533 Royal St., 504/523-4662, www.hnoc.org; 9:30am-4:30pm Tues.-Sat., 10:30am-4:30pm Sun.; free, docent-lead tours $5 pp). Established in 1966 by avid collectors General L. Kemper Williams and his wife, Leila, this complex includes the Greek Revival-style **Merieult House.** Built in 1792, the house now contains the **Williams Gallery,** featuring rotating history exhibits, and the **Louisiana History Galleries,** 13 chambers that each explore a specific period of the state's history (from the French colonial years to the 20th century) by using authentic maps, books, furniture, and artwork.

From the courtyard, you'll notice a few other buildings, such as the Spanish colonial-style **Counting House** and the three-story **Maisonette,** which now contain administrative offices. One exception is the **Williams Residence,** an 1880s Italianate townhouse that the museum founders occupied until 1963. Docent-led tours (10am, 11am, 2pm, and 3pm Tues.-Sat., 11am, 2pm, and 3pm Sun.) last 45 minutes and enable you to view this room-by-room survey of how an upscale early-20th-century home would have been furnished, including several antiques, various watercolors, and vintage maps of New Orleans. You can also join a guided architectural tour of the buildings and courtyards that compose the Royal Street complex.

This impressive complex of interconnected buildings also includes three structures on Toulouse Street: a former banking house, a Creole cottage, and the two-story **Louis Adam House,** where Tennessee Williams once boarded. While here, you should also make time for the impressive museum shop in the Merieult House, where you'll find everything from local novels and history books to vintage maps and iconic jewelry. In addition, THNOC oversees the **Williams Research Center** (410 Chartres St., 504/598-7171; 9:30am-4:30pm Tues.-Sat.; free), a Beaux Arts-style brick structure containing an extensive library of roughly 35,000 documents and manuscripts, plus more than 300,000 photographs, drawings, prints, and paintings about the history of New Orleans.

New Orleans Pharmacy Museum

The **New Orleans Pharmacy Museum** (514 Chartres St., 504/565-8027, www.pharmacymuseum.org; 10am-4pm Tues.-Sat.; adults $5, seniors and students $4, free under 6) occupies a genuine apothecary shop from the 1820s. Original shop owner Louis J. Dufilho Jr. was the first licensed pharmacist in the nation, having earned his certification in 1816. Displays show what a period pharmacy looked like, including rows of 1850s-style hand-carved mahogany cabinets filled with everything from established drugs to gris-gris voodoo potions; exhibits tell the story of Louisiana's development in medicine and health care. Interesting features include an assortment of blood-letting equipment, a medicinal herb garden in the courtyard, and an 1855 Italian marble soda fountain. Guided tours are offered Tuesday-Friday at 1pm.

★ The New Orleans School of Cooking

While most people visit New Orleans to taste its one-of-a-kind food, it's also possible to learn how to create such wonderful cuisine. Since 1980, **The New Orleans School of Cooking** (524 St. Louis St., 504/525-2665 or 800/237-4841, www.neworleansschoolofcooking.com; 9am-6pm Mon.-Sat., 9am-4pm Sun.), situated in a renovated, 19th-century molasses warehouse, has invited local Cajun and Creole chefs to teach residents and visitors alike the basics of Louisiana-style cooking, sharing history and tall tales along the way. The popular **demonstration lunch classes** (10am-12:30pm and 2pm-4pm Mon.-Sat., 10am-12:30pm Sun.; $28-33) include generous samplings of the demonstrated menu items, plus recipes, coffee, iced tea, and Abita beer. Three-hour, hands-on **cooking classes** (6pm-9pm Tues. and Fri., 10am-1pm and 6pm-9pm Sun.; $139 pp) are also available, provided you are 18 or older. Besides beverages and the prepared meal, you'll receive a souvenir apron and related recipes. Depending on the class, dishes may include gumbo, barbecue shrimp and grits, bananas foster crepes, and pralines. Non-chefs can peruse the on-site **Louisiana General Store,** which offers a plethora of Cajun and Creole products, from cookbooks and cookware to spices and gift baskets.

Jean Lafitte National Historical Park and Preserve

A couple of blocks upriver from Jackson Square is the main office of **Jean Lafitte National Historical Park and Preserve** (419 Decatur St., 504/589-2636 or 504/589-3882, www.nps.gov/jela; 9am-4:30pm Tues.-Sat.; free, donations accepted), established in 1978 to preserve natural and historical resources and properties throughout the Mississippi River Valley. The park actually has six distinct units: this one, the **French Quarter Visitor Center;** two others in metro New Orleans (**Chalmette Battlefield and National Cemetery,** just east of the city, as well as **Barataria Preserve** on the west bank); and three in Cajun Country (in Thibodaux, Lafayette, and Eunice) that deal in Cajun culture. Although the visitor center presents a film and several exhibits on various historical and cultural aspects of New Orleans, Louisiana, and the Mississippi River Delta, its best feature is its one-hour ranger-led walking tour along the riverfront, given at 9:30am-10:30am Tuesday-Saturday. These free tours are limited to 25 people and can fill up quickly; availability is first come, first served. The center is closed on federal holidays as well as Mardi Gras Day.

On a small grassy island along Decatur Street, across from the park's visitor center, note the dignified statue of the man who first plotted New Orleans at the site of the present-day French Quarter, Jean Baptiste Le Moyne, Sieur de Bienville, brother of the explorer Pierre Le Moyne, Sieur d'Iberville. Jean Baptiste's decision in 1699 to establish a fortification on this miserable swampy spot raised the skepticism of many, but, of course, New Orleans has become one of the world's most charming (yet swampiest and, at times, hottest) cities.

Woldenberg Riverfront Park
Named for philanthropist Malcolm Woldenberg (1896-1982), lovely **Woldenberg Riverfront Park** (1 Canal St., Mississippi River between Canal St. and St. Peter St.; 24 hours daily; free) is a 16-acre green space and redbrick promenade that extends along the riverfront from the aquarium to Jackson Brewery.

It's along this stretch that the site of New Orleans was established in 1718. Crape myrtle and magnolia trees shade the numerous park benches, affording romantic views of the Mississippi River. One of the original quays, **Toulouse Street Wharf,** is home to the palatial excursion riverboat, the **Steamboat** *Natchez.* Fringing the park is the **Moonwalk,** a wooden boardwalk that stretches along the riverfront, between St. Philip and St. Peter Streets. Musicians, tourists, and homeless individuals are all drawn to this scenic spot; it's often a little sketchy at night.

Within the park (which serves as one of the main sites for the French Quarter Festival and other annual events) are several significant sculptures. The stunning, 20-foot-tall *Monument to the Immigrant* statue, by noted New Orleans artist Franco Alessandrini, commemorates New Orleans's role as one of the nation's most prolific immigrant ports throughout the 19th century. It's fashioned from white Carrara marble. Other sculptures include Robert Schoen's bizarre *Old Man River,* an 18-foot tribute to the Mississippi River, and John Scott's *Ocean Song,* a series of eight slender, 10-foot-tall, stainless-steel pyramids, topped by a grid of rings. One favorite is the mesmerizing *New Orleans Holocaust Memorial* (www.holocaustmemorial.us), created by Israeli artist Yaacov Agam, dedicated in 2003, and featuring nine colorful panels, which meld to form different images depending on where you're standing.

Audubon Aquarium of the Americas
Established in 1990 by the Audubon Nature Institute—the same folks who operate the Audubon Zoo—the **Audubon Aquarium of the Americas** (1 Canal St., 504/565-3033 or 800/774-7394, www.auduboninstitute.org; 10am-5pm Tues.-Sun.; adults $30, seniors $25, children 2-12 $22, free under 2) is one of the most popular tourist destinations in downtown New Orleans. At the southern end

Bayou St. John

Bayou St. John may not draw in the tourists like the French Quarter, but it's an opportunity for a unique view of the city. Stretching from Lake Pontchartrain south along the edge of City Park on to Orleans Avenue, this waterway is what remains of the swamp that was drained to create the city of New Orleans. That doesn't sound appealing, but, in fact, the neighborhoods that back up to the canal, especially along Moss Street between Esplanade Avenue and Lafitte Avenue, are some of the city's most charming and livable.

Explore the bayou on foot or by kayak or paddleboard. **NOLA Paddleboards** (7840 Lakeshore Dr., 504/717-8847, open by appointment only, www.nolapaddle-boards.com, $30) will meet you on the bayou for a pleasant, boat-free paddle in the heart of the city. Lessons and rentals are available. **Kayak-Ti-Yak** (985/778-5034, http://kayakitiyat.com, $45) offers two-hour guided tours by boat.

Also on the bayou is the **Pitot House** (1440 Moss St., 504/482-0312, 10am-3pm Wed.-Sat., http://lousianalandmarks.org, $7-10), the only Creole colonial country house that is open to the public in the entire city. While in the neighborhood, stop at **Parkway Bakery & Tavern** (538 Hagan Ave., 504/482-3047, http://park-waypoorboys.com, 11am-10pm Wed.-Mon., $7-17). Don't be intimidated by the lines: They move fast and the po'boys are well worth the wait.

of 16-acre Woldenberg Riverfront Park, alongside the Mississippi River, this contemporary glass-and-brick building houses several intriguing exhibits, most notably the 400,000-gallon Gulf of Mexico habitat, which features sharks, stingrays, and other saltwater creatures amid the barnacled pilings of an offshore oil rig replica. Kids especially favor this family-friendly attraction, where they can touch cownose rays, climb above an Amazonian rainforest, and, via an underwater glass tunnel, stroll through the moray eels and tropical fish of a Caribbean coral reef.

Visitors to this exceptional, two-story aquarium will observe a wide array of aquatic and amphibious creatures. There are two gift shops on the premises. Adjacent to the aquarium is the **Entergy Giant Screen Theatre** (504/581-4629; 10am-5pm Tues.-Sun.; admission included with aquarium ticket), which typically showcases vibrant 3-D nature documentaries. Typically, the last ticket is sold an hour before closing. Discounted self-parking is available whether you have your ticket validated at the aquarium or the IMAX theater, and it's possible to save money by purchasing a combo ticket for both attractions (adults $29, seniors and children 2-12 $23, free under 2). The aquarium is closed most Mondays in fall, winter, and spring.

Audubon Butterfly Garden and Insectarium

Part of the stately U.S. Custom House, a 30,000-square-foot intimidating gray structure that occupies an entire block, is home to the **Audubon Butterfly Garden and Insectarium** (423 Canal St., 504/524-2847 or 800/774-7394, www.audubonin-stitute.org; 10am-5pm Tues.-Sun.; adults $23, seniors $20, children 2-12 $18, free under 2), which contains the largest freestanding collection of insects in the United States—about 900,000 species in all. Visitors have the opportunity to touch all kinds of creatures, although many others (like the despised cockroaches) are presented through clever displays from a safe distance. Even the museum's Tiny Termite Café has an insect-themed appearance—and the glass-topped tables are actually terrariums, so you might find yourself eating directly over a live tarantula. The museum's bug-cooking demonstration "café," Bug Appétit, illustrates how people around the world routinely snack on insects as an excellent source of protein. Less harrowing for squeamish visitors is the massive butterfly room set within a Japanese-style garden. The Audubon Butterfly Garden and Insectarium is closed most Mondays in fall, winter, and spring.

Central Business and Arts Districts
Gallier Hall

Gallier Hall (545 St. Charles Ave., 504/658-3627, www.nola.gov/gallier-hall, open for special events and by appointment), a hulking, white, Greek Revival-style building, was named for its architect, James Gallier Sr., who designed and erected the structure between 1845 and 1853. Boasting massive Ionic columns, the stunning, three-story marble structure served as the New Orleans City Hall from the mid-19th through mid-20th centuries. Today, it's used as a special-events facility and reception hall; it's also the spot where the city mayor greets the royal courts of Mardi Gras krewes like Zulu and Rex. Several important people have been laid in state here, including Confederate president Jefferson Davis, Confederate general P. G. T. Beauregard, and R&B musician Ernie K-Doe. Guided tours are available by appointment.

St. Patrick's Church

Not far from Lafayette Square and Gallier Hall, **St. Patrick's Church** (724 Camp St., 504/525-4413, www.oldstpatricks.org; hours vary daily; free, donations accepted) was the first place of worship built in the city's American Sector. The sector was so named because it's where 19th-century Americans built their homes and businesses in order to distinguish their lifestyles from those of the Creoles residing in the French Quarter, New Orleans's original settlement. Blessed by Bishop Antoine Blanc in 1838 and completed by 1840, St. Patrick's Church is one of the few structures left in a district once filled with magnificent mansions and high-end mercantile stores. When the parish was first established in 1833, the area was known as the Faubourg St. Mary; the church itself developed from a need for the Americans, many of whom were Irish, to worship in a structure as noteworthy as the French Quarter's St. Louis Cathedral.

In the early 1850s, it was this stunning church where Bishop Antoine Blanc received the pallium as the first archbishop of New Orleans. Though severely damaged by a hurricane in 1915, the church has since been renovated several times. Today, this National Historic Landmark is celebrated not only for its historic significance but also for its lavishly ornate interior, high vaulted ceilings, majestic paintings, and fine stained-glass windows.

Lee Circle

Lee Circle (St. Charles Ave. and Howard Ave.; 24 hours daily; free) is the hub for a small arts and museum district that has evolved on the streets just downriver from here since the mid-1990s. This is the one regal traffic circle in downtown New Orleans, and it imparts a slightly formal, urban air—a hint of Paris or London. Depending on which direction you're coming from, it serves as a gateway to the Garden District or the CBD.

★ The National WWII Museum

One of the nation's most exalted historians, the late Stephen Ambrose, founded **The National WWII Museum** (945 Magazine St., 504/528-1944, www.nationalww2museum.org; 9am-5pm daily; adults $26, seniors $22.50, military, students, and children 5-17 $16.50, free under 5) in the early 1990s. Ambrose, a professor at the University of New Orleans, lived in New Orleans until his death in 2002. He is best known for such riveting World War II histories as *Band of*

Central Business and Arts Districts

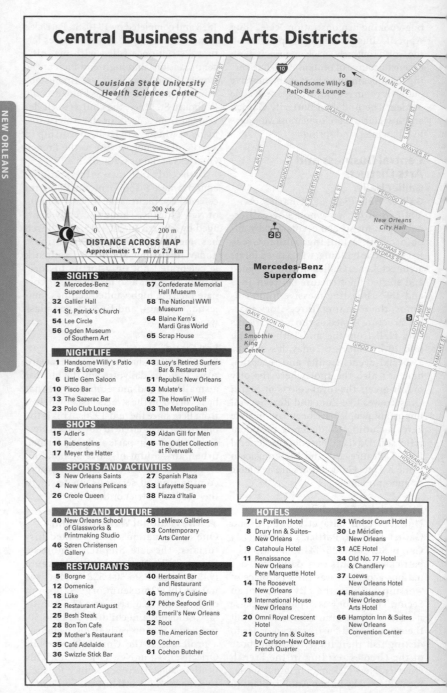

Louisiana State University Health Sciences Center

To Handsome Willy's ⬛1 Patio Bar & Lounge

Mercedes-Benz Superdome

New Orleans City Hall

0   200 yds
0   200 m
DISTANCE ACROSS MAP
Approximate: 1.7 mi or 2.7 km

Smoothie King Center

SIGHTS
- **2** Mercedes-Benz Superdome
- **32** Gallier Hall
- **41** St. Patrick's Church
- **54** Lee Circle
- **56** Ogden Museum of Southern Art
- **57** Confederate Memorial Hall Museum
- **58** The National WWII Museum
- **64** Blaine Kern's Mardi Gras World
- **65** Scrap House

NIGHTLIFE
- **1** Handsome Willy's Patio Bar & Lounge
- **6** Little Gem Saloon
- **10** Pisco Bar
- **13** The Sazerac Bar
- **23** Polo Club Lounge
- **43** Lucy's Retired Surfers Bar & Restaurant
- **51** Republic New Orleans
- **53** Mulate's
- **62** The Howlin' Wolf
- **63** The Metropolitan

SHOPS
- **15** Adler's
- **16** Rubensteins
- **17** Meyer the Hatter
- **39** Aidan Gill for Men
- **45** The Outlet Collection at Riverwalk

SPORTS AND ACTIVITIES
- **3** New Orleans Saints
- **4** New Orleans Pelicans
- **26** Creole Queen
- **27** Spanish Plaza
- **33** Lafayette Square
- **38** Piazza d'Italia

ARTS AND CULTURE
- **40** New Orleans School of Glassworks & Printmaking Studio
- **46** Søren Christensen Gallery
- **49** LeMieux Galleries
- **53** Contemporary Arts Center

RESTAURANTS
- **5** Borgne
- **12** Domenica
- **18** Lüke
- **22** Restaurant August
- **25** Besh Steak
- **28** BonTon Cafe
- **29** Mother's Restaurant
- **35** Café Adelaide
- **36** Swizzle Stick Bar
- **40** Herbsaint Bar and Restaurant
- **46** Tommy's Cuisine
- **47** Pêche Seafood Grill
- **49** Emeril's New Orleans
- **52** Root
- **59** The American Sector
- **60** Cochon
- **61** Cochon Butcher

HOTELS
- **7** Le Pavillon Hotel
- **8** Drury Inn & Suites–New Orleans
- **9** Catahoula Hotel
- **11** Renaissance New Orleans Pere Marquette Hotel
- **14** The Roosevelt New Orleans
- **19** International House New Orleans
- **20** Omni Royal Crescent Hotel
- **21** Country Inn & Suites by Carlson–New Orleans French Quarter
- **24** Windsor Court Hotel
- **30** Le Méridien New Orleans
- **31** ACE Hotel
- **34** Old No. 77 Hotel & Chandlery
- **37** Loews New Orleans Hotel
- **44** Renaissance New Orleans Arts Hotel
- **66** Hampton Inn & Suites New Orleans Convention Center

Storyville

French Quarter

Woldenberg Riverfront Park

14
13
12
11
15
16
17
10 9
6
7
18
19
20
21
22
23
24
25
26
27
28
29
30
Harrah's New Orleans
World Trade Center

Gallier Hall 32
33 *Lafayette Square*
Central Business District
31
35
36
37
Harrah's
38
40
39
41 **St. Patrick's Church**
42
43
44
45
46
47
Arts District
48 49 50
51
52
53
Lee Circle 54
55
56 **Ogden Museum of Southern Art**
57 **Confederate Memorial Hall Museum**
Ernest N. Morial Convention Center
58
59 **The National WWII Museum**
60
61
62
63
Scrap House 65
64 To Blaine Kern's Mardi Gras World
66

© AVALON TRAVEL

Brothers, The Wild Blue, D-Day, Citizen Soldiers, and *The Victors.*

The museum opened to the public on June 6, 2000, the 56th anniversary of the amphibious World War II invasion. This is the only museum in the United States dedicated to this event, which involved more than a million Americans. The Andrew Higgins factory, which now houses the museum, built ships during World War II, including some of the vehicles that transported infantrymen to Normandy.

A museum visit can be an all-day (or multiday) affair; after all, it might take that long to absorb the enormous collection of exhibits documenting the Allied victory in World War II, not to mention exploring Final Mission: The USS *Tang* Submarine Experience (9:35am-4:35pm Sun.-Thurs., 9:35am-5:35pm Fri.-Sat., $5 pp), which allows visitors to relive the last epic battle of the most successful submarine in World War II, or watching the immersive 4-D, Tom Hanks-narrated documentary *Beyond All Boundaries* (10am-4pm Sun.-Thurs., 10am-5pm Fri.-Sat., $5 pp) in the 250-seat **Solomon Victory Theater.** If you have time, have a meal at the on-site restaurant, **The American Sector** (11am-8pm Sun.-Wed., 11am-9pm Thurs.-Sat.), or an old-fashioned dinner theater experience in the **Stage Door Canteen** (hours vary depending on performance).

Confederate Memorial Hall Museum

The **Confederate Memorial Hall Museum** (929 Camp St., 504/523-4522, http://confederatemuseum.com; 10am-4pm Tues.-Sat.; adults $8, children 7-14 $5, free under 7) commemorates the military history and heritage of the American South. Alternatively known as Louisiana's Civil War Museum at Confederate Memorial

---

Top to bottom: Audubon Aquarium of the Americas; Blaine Kern's Mardi Gras World; Audubon Zoo.

Hall, it holds the country's second-largest collection of Confederate memorabilia, including uniforms, battle flags, and more than 500 tintypes, daguerreotypes, and other vintage photographic images, plus the personal items of General Robert E. Lee and General P. G. T. Beauregard. Designed by Thomas O. Sully, one of the city's most distinguished architects, and opened in 1891, this Romanesque structure is the state's oldest continuously operating museum.

★ **Ogden Museum of Southern Art**

Not far from Lee Circle and adjacent to the Confederate Memorial Hall Museum, you'll find it hard to miss the **Ogden Museum of Southern Art** (925 Camp St., 504/539-9650, http://ogdenmuseum. org; 10am-5pm Sun.-Wed. and Fri.-Sat., 10am-8pm Thurs., adults $13.50, seniors, students, military $11, children 5-17 $6.75, free under 5), which contains one of the country's largest collections of artwork related to the American South. This impressive complex comprises the contemporary, five-story Stephen Goldring Hall, the restored Howard Memorial Library, and the Clementine Hunter Education Wing, named for the famous Louisiana folk artist who grew up on a cotton plantation in Cloutierville and produced about 4,000 works during her storied career. The artwork includes all mediums and spans the 18th to 21st centuries, representing artists from 15 Southern states as well as Washington DC. The last admission to the museum is at 4:45pm each day, except for Thursday evenings, when the museum reopens for Ogden After Hours, presenting live music 6pm-8pm. Louisiana residents are entitled to free admission to the museum every Thursday, and docent-led tours are available at 2pm on the first and third Saturdays of each month.

Scrap House

As you drive past the enormous Ernest N. Morial Convention Center, keep an eye out for the colorful sculpture that's simply known as *Scrap House* (Convention Center Blvd. and John Churchill Chase St., www.sallyheller.com; 24 hours daily; free). Completed by artist Sally Heller in 2008 and fashioned from ordinary materials and recycled elements (wood, wallpaper, oil drums, and solar lights), this outdoor installation resembles a denuded tree that's cradling a ramshackle house. Not surprisingly, this powerful yet whimsical piece is meant to serve as a monument to Mother Nature's unpredictable powers, inspired as Heller was by the remnants of houses and other cultural debris left in the wake of Hurricane Katrina in 2005.

★ **Blaine Kern's Mardi Gras World**

The top reason to venture to the Port of New Orleans is **Blaine Kern's Mardi Gras World** (1380 Port of New Orleans Pl., 504/361-7821, www.mardigrasworld. com; 9am-5:30pm daily; adults $20, seniors and students $16, children 2-11 $13, free under 2). It's been the public face of world-renowned Kern Studios, which has been the largest builder of Carnival sculptures and parade floats in the country since 1947. Formerly situated in Algiers, Mardi Gras World is now across the river on the East Bank, between the Central Business District (CBD) and the Garden District, where visitors can take a joyful, informative guided tour of the facility. The one-hour tour includes a stroll amid kaleidoscopic floats, the observation of working artists and artisans, and a video about the history of the city's Mardi Gras celebration. Though Mardi Gras takes place over a short period each year, this place hums with activity every day. The first tour begins at 9:30am and the last tour begins at 4:30pm, and a complimentary shuttle (504/507-9315) is available for visitors in the CBD and French Quarter.

Mercedes-Benz Superdome

The massive, 52-acre **Mercedes-Benz**

Mister Mardi Gras

For many years, families have flocked to **Blaine Kern's Mardi Gras World** (www.mardigrasworld.com). This vibrant attraction offers visitors a behind-the-scenes glimpse at the magic of Mardi Gras, one of the city's oldest traditions. Here, you'll see a variety of colorful floats and get the chance to watch the artists and artisans of **Kern Studios** (www.kernstudios.com) hard at work.

As the names indicate, the heart and soul behind Blaine Kern's Mardi Gras World (also known simply as Mardi Gras World) and Kern Studios is Blaine Kern Sr. himself—the man known as Mister Mardi Gras. Born in 1927, Blaine grew up on the west bank of the Mississippi River. His early interest in the arts was inspired by his proximity to New Orleans as well as the vocation of his father, Roy, a sign painter who survived the Depression by painting names on the bows of freighters. When Blaine's mother was hospitalized, he offset the family's medical bills by painting a mural in the hospital—a mural that captured the attention of a surgeon who was also the captain of a Mardi Gras krewe. Blaine began designing floats soon afterward and was eventually hired to fashion a complete parade. In 1947, he established Blaine Kern Artists (which eventually evolved into Kern Studios) in Algiers and, over time, became the Big Easy's leading parade creator, working with Rex, Zulu, Bacchus, and all the legendary krewes.

Following his travels to Italy, where he was impressed by the extravagant animation and prop concepts that distinguished the European style of float building, Blaine began to embrace the monumental scale and lavish ornamentation that mark contemporary Mardi Gras parades. Today, Kern Studios produces floats and props for more than 40 New Orleans parades, including Endymion and Orpheus, as well as pageants throughout the world. Kern props and sculptures also enhance themed environments in Walt Disney World, Universal Studios, and Japan's Toho Park.

Superdome (1500 Sugar Bowl Dr., 504/587-3822 or 800/756-7074, www.mbsuperdome.com) is home to the NFL's New Orleans Saints, college football's Allstate Sugar Bowl, as well as major concerts and some of the city's most popular annual events. The city commissioned construction of the dome in 1966; however, construction didn't begin until 1971, finishing four years later. The gargantuan arena is the largest domed stadium in the world, holding more than 76,000 football fans. The roof alone covers about 13 acres and rises to a height of about 273 feet (nearly as tall as a 30-story building).

In the immediate wake of Hurricane Katrina, the Superdome became infamous for its role as an evacuation center. In 2011, the Superdome underwent an $85 million renovation that completely modernized the facility, adding three elevators, more than 3,000 new seats, extra restrooms, and other amenities.

Garden District
Lafayette Cemetery No. 1
Established in 1833, **Lafayette Cemetery No. 1** (1400 Washington Ave., www.lafayettecemetery.org; 7am-2:30pm Mon.-Fri., 7am-noon Sat.; free) is one of only a few "cities of the dead" in New Orleans that are relatively safe to explore, at least during the day. Bordered by Prytania Street, Washington Avenue, Coliseum Street, and 6th Street in the Garden District, the cemetery is especially popular with fans of Anne Rice's *The Vampire Chronicles* trilogy and was featured in the movie *Interview with the Vampire* (1994). The Lafayette Cemetery was once part of a plantation owned by the Livaudais family. As a cemetery, it has always been nonsegregated and nondenominational;

you'll see the tombs of American merchants, African families, and German, Irish, Italian, English, Scottish, and Dutch immigrants, not to mention several Union and Confederate soldiers.

The office is at 1427 6th Street. Taking a properly vetted, guided tour is preferable, especially for history buffs. Tours are offered by various companies, most notably **Save Our Cemeteries** (SOC, 501 Basin St., #3C, 504/525-3377, www.saveourcemeteries.org; adults $15, free under 12), a nonprofit organization that preserves the city's burial grounds. The one-hour walks occur daily at 10:30am, which means that it's still possible to experience the cemetery on Sunday, when it's normally closed to the public. Please be respectful; this is an active cemetery that still welcomes mourners.

Southern Food & Beverage Museum

In a city that is celebrated around the world for its cuisine, it's surprising that the **Southern Food & Beverage Museum** (SoFaB, 1504 Oretha Castle Haley Blvd., 504/569-0405, http://natfab.org; 11am-5:30pm Wed.-Mon.; adults $10.50, seniors and students $5.25, free under 12) has only been open since 2008. It features the **Museum of the American Cocktail** as well, included in the price of admissions. Dedicated to the discovery and appreciation of the food, drinks, and related culture of the American South, the museum's temporary and permanent exhibits explore an assortment of tasty topics, including Southern barbecue and liquor, Gulf Coast seafood, and praline vendors. A visit will surely stimulate your appetite for the Big Easy's varied culinary offerings, if not those throughout the South.

Uptown
Audubon Zoo
Below Magazine Street lies 58-acre **Audubon Zoo** (6500 Magazine St., 504/861-2537 or 800/774-7394, www.auduboninstitute.org; 10am-5pm

Mon.-Fri., 10am-6pm Sat.-Sun.; adults $23, seniors $20, children 2-12 $18, free under 2), a significant part of the larger Audubon Park. Established in 1914, it contains historical buildings, notable sculptures, and nearly 2,000 animals from around the world. This relatively small zoo is a wonderful place to stroll, watch the animals' antics, and explore verdant gardens rife with nearly every species of flora known to Louisiana.

The award-winning **Louisiana Swamp** exhibit is the next best thing to taking a swamp tour and even better in one respect: You're guaranteed to see marsh wildlife up close and personal. The swamp exhibit is a recreation of a Depression-era Cajun swamp settlement, complete with old bayou shacks and a trapper's cottage. The albino alligators never cease to amaze and the ever-frisky river otters are endlessly amusing. Another highlight is the **Jaguar Jungle** exhibit, which recreates a Mayan rain forest and houses two jaguars, along with toucans, spider monkeys, and sloths.

If you're taking the St. Charles streetcar, disembark at the Audubon Park stop for both the park and the zoo. If you're coming by car, the zoo has plenty of free parking, though the lot and nearby grassy areas can fill up quickly during annual events like Soul Fest or Boo at the Zoo. From fall to spring, the zoo has shorter operating hours and is closed most Mondays.

St. Charles Streetcar
No one should leave New Orleans without taking a ride on one of the city's famous, oft-photographed streetcars. While there are five separate lines—the St. Charles, the Loyola-UPT, the Canal-Cemeteries, the Canal-City Park/Museum, and the Riverfront—the most famous by far and most beloved by residents and tourists alike is the **St. Charles line** (Canal St. and Carondelet St. to S. Carrollton Ave. and S. Claiborne Ave., 504/248-3900, www.norta.com; hours vary daily; $1.25

one-way), which dates back to 1835 and has been featured in numerous films over the years, including *Runaway Jury* (2003) and *The Skeleton Key* (2005). Because of the line's presence on the National Register of Historic Places, the olive-green Perley Thomas streetcars currently in use must be preserved as they looked in 1923, which makes for a historical riding experience. Complete with old-fashioned wooden seats, the St. Charles streetcar takes passengers from Canal Street, at the lower edge of the CBD; past the historic homes, restaurants, and attractions of oak-shaded St. Charles Avenue, including the Garden District, Loyola and Tulane Universities, and Audubon Park; to the restaurants, boutiques, and residential areas of South Carrollton Avenue. The line terminates at South Claiborne Avenue, a transfer point for the city's bus lines. A one-way ride on the St. Charles line, which runs 24 hours daily, lasts about 45 minutes and is well worth the time.

Tremé and Mid-City
★ City Park

Near the Lakeview and Mid-City neighborhoods, **City Park** (1 Palm Dr., 504/482-4888, http://neworleanscitypark.com; hours vary seasonally; free) is bordered by Robert E. Lee Boulevard, Marconi Drive, City Park Avenue, and Wisner Boulevard. Considerably larger than New York City's Central Park, this 1,300-acre spread sits on what was once a swampy oak forest. It still contains the nation's largest collection of mature live oaks, some believed to date to the 1400s or earlier. Stop by the **Timken Center,** housed in a 1913 Spanish Mission-style building, for sandwiches, ice cream, and refreshments before exploring the park.

City Park encompasses several worthwhile attractions. The **New Orleans Botanical Garden** (10am-5pm daily; adults $6, children $3) is filled with thematic gardens, making it a wonderful place for a relaxing stroll. Another

tranquil locale is the **Sydney and Walda Besthoff Sculpture Garden,** a free outdoor extension of the New Orleans Museum of Art.

Children are especially fond of the **Carousel Gardens Amusement Park** (11am-6pm Sat.-Sun. Mar.-May and early Aug.-mid-Nov., 10am-5pm Tues.-Thurs., 10am-10pm Fri., 11am-10pm Sat., 11am-6pm Sun. June-early Aug., 6pm-10pm Sun.-Thurs., 6pm-11pm Fri.-Sat. late Nov.-early Jan.; $4 admission, $4 per ride or $18 for unlimited rides, free for kids 36 inches and under), which features numerous rides and a mini train that tours the park. The historic carousel was established here in 1906 and eventually listed on the National Register of Historic Places; it's now the last antique wooden carousel in Louisiana.

If with kids, don't skip the year-round **Storyland** (10am-5pm daily; $4 pp, free for kids 36 inches and under). The property features 25 larger-than-life sculptures, each based on a different fairy tale, from Captain Hook's pirate ship to the Three Little Pigs. Paid admission to Storyland, the New Orleans Botanical Garden, or the Carousel Gardens Amusement Park allows you access to all three.

Families might also appreciate **City Putt** (10am-10pm Sun. and Tues.-Thurs., 10am-midnight Fri.-Sat.; adults $8, children 4-12 $6, free under 4), which encompasses two 18-hole minigolf courses.

New Orleans Museum of Art

The vast holdings of the fabulous **New Orleans Museum of Art** (NOMA, 1 Collins Diboll Circle, City Park, 504/658-4100, http://noma.org; 10am-6pm Tues.-Thurs., 10am-9pm Fri., 11am-5pm Sat.-Sun.; adults $12, seniors and students $10, children 7-17 $6, free under 7) total about 40,000 objects that span a variety of cultures and eras—from pre-Columbian, Native American, and Mayan artwork to French Impressionist paintings. The city's oldest fine arts institution is justly known for its excellent rotating exhibits, including everything from creative bookmarks to the 19th-century mass production of British decorative arts. The museum is also an architectural marvel, an imposing Beaux Arts-style building that dates to 1911. A cleverly appended modern addition was completed in 1971 and renovated in the 1990s.

The **Sydney and Walda Besthoff Sculpture Garden** (10am-6pm Mon.-Fri., 10am-5pm Sat.-Sun.) is an outdoor attraction that's free to visit. Peppered with magnolias, pines, and ancient, Spanish moss-draped live oaks, this peaceful, five-acre spread encompasses lagoons, pedestrian bridges, and more than 60 impressive sculptures. Noted works include sculptures by Pierre Auguste Renoir, Ida Kohlmeyer, and Claes Oldenburg. A free cell-phone tour is available.

NOMA offers ample free parking, but you can also reach the museum by bike, bus, or the Canal streetcar line. Each Wednesday, the museum is free to Louisiana residents. The last admittance to the museum and sculpture garden occurs 45 minutes before closing.

St. Louis Cemetery No. 1

Arguably the oldest and most famous of New Orleans's "cities of the dead," **St. Louis Cemetery No. 1** (425 Basin St., 504/482-5065, http://nolacatholiccemeteries.org; 9am-3:30pm Mon.-Sat., 9am-12:30pm Sun.; free) was established in 1789, following the Great Fire of 1788, and set outside what was then the city border. Since New Orleans sits below sea level and has a high water table, bodies were buried aboveground, as earlier attempts to bury the dead underground had resulted in caskets floating to the surface during floods.

Bordered by Basin, Conti, Tremé, and St. Louis Streets, the cemetery currently contains more than 700 tombs and has interred thousands of people. Most of these aboveground structures are owned by families and designed to hold multiple sets of remains. Though constructed of brick, the elaborate tombs are often covered in concrete or stucco; some of the oldest ones are little more than crumbled ruins and piles of brick dust. One curious element is the segregated Protestant section near the rear of the predominantly Catholic cemetery.

Famous residents here include Homer Plessy (of *Plessy v. Ferguson* fame) and the much-loved voodoo priestess **Marie Laveau,** whose supposed tomb is a frequent stop on daily tours. Movie star Nicolas Cage has staked his own perpetual claim in this crowded cemetery; just look for the incongruous white pyramid that many locals consider an eyesore.

As of March 2015, the Archdiocese of New Orleans requires all tourists (those unrelated to the deceased) to enter the premises with a licensed tour guide. While several organizations offer guided tours, one of the most well-respected is **Save Our Cemeteries** (504/525-3377, www.saveourcemeteries.org; 10am, 11:30am, and 1pm Mon.-Sat., 10am Sun.; adults $20, free under 12), which leads hour-long excursions through the cemetery. Tours depart from the lobby of the nearby Basin Street Station. View the full list of licensed guides on the website (http://nolacatholiccemeteries.org).

Backstreet Cultural Museum

If you're a fan of HBO's acclaimed show *Treme* or simply curious about the Big Easy's vibrant African American culture, you're in for a treat. Not far from Louis Armstrong Park—the original site of Congo Square—lies the fascinating **Backstreet Cultural Museum** (1116 Henriette Delille St., 504/657-6700, www.backstreetmuseum.org; 10am-4pm Tues.-Sat.; $10). The museum contains the world's most comprehensive collection of costumes, films, and photographs from jazz funerals and pleasure clubs, plus Carnival-related groups like the Mardi Gras Indians, Baby Dolls, and Skull and Bone Gang. Beyond the permanent exhibits, the museum presents public performances of traditional music and dance.

Greater New Orleans
Longue Vue House & Gardens

One of the city's most impressive attractions is often overlooked by visitors simply because it's slightly off the beaten path. Near the border between New Orleans and Old Metairie, the **Longue Vue House & Gardens** (7 Bamboo Rd., 504/488-5488, www.longuevue.com; 10am-5pm Mon.-Sat., 1pm-5pm Sun.; adults $12, seniors $10, students 11-17 $8, children 3-10 $5, free active military and child under 3) is a lush, exotic, eight-acre estate that once belonged to local community pillars Edgar and Edith Stern and their children. Designed and constructed between 1939 and 1942 by architects William and Geoffrey Platt and landscape architect Ellen Biddle Shipman, the tranquil property was intended to be one organic whole, uniting the house and gardens seamlessly. Ultimately, the designers did just that.

Today, this serene place represents one of the last Country Place Era homes built in America. It comprises a period-furnished Classical Revival-style manor house, several outbuildings, 14 spectacularly landscaped garden areas, and 22 ponds and fountains. Such large residential properties had their heyday between 1880 and 1940, when designers worked closely with their clients to create extravagant, European-influenced gardens. Guided house tours are offered every hour on the hour (the last one at 4pm). On such tours, you'll see not only well-appointed chambers like the dining room, library, ladies' reception room, and master bedroom, but also modern art exhibits and displays about the creation of Longue Vue.

Guided and Walking Tours

As you might have guessed, photogenic New Orleans boasts a slew of guided tour companies. One of the most authentic is **Historic New Orleans Tours** (various locations, 504/947-2120, www.tourneworleans.com; hours vary; adults $25, seniors and students $15, children 6-12 $7, free under 6). Walking tours focus on French Quarter history, voodoo culture, the city's jazz scene, the Garden District, and legendary hauntings. On the two-hour Garden District Tour, guides explain the history of the city's American Sector, point out notable buildings (including the former homes of Anne Rice and Peyton Manning), and discuss their colorful heritage; you'll also get the chance to explore the aboveground tombs within Lafayette Cemetery No. 1, which has made notable appearances in such films as *Interview with the Vampire* (1994) and *Double Jeopardy* (1999). This well-respected company also offers swamp and plantation tours, plus van excursions through the city's varied neighborhoods.

For an intimate tour of the French Quarter, take one of the two-hour, narrated strolls led by the nonprofit **Friends of the Cabildo** (701 Chartres St., 504/523-3939, www.friendsofthecabildo.org; 9:30am-4:30pm Mon.-Fri.; adults $20, seniors, students, and active military $15.60). Conducted by licensed guides, these well-respected tours highlight the history, folklore, and architecture of one of the country's oldest neighborhoods, known alternatively as the Vieux Carré. Tours depart from the **1850 House Museum Store** (523 St. Ann St., 504/524-9118; 10am-5pm Tues.-Sun.) and are offered daily at 10:30am and 1:30pm. All proceeds benefit the Friends of the Cabildo, a volunteer group that supports the Louisiana State Museum, which oversees such historic properties as the Cabildo and the Presbytère.

While strolling along Decatur Street in front of Jackson Square, you'll surely notice the mule-drawn carriages waiting beside the sidewalk. Whether you're a tourist or not, do yourself a favor and join one of these narrated excursions by

Royal Carriages (Jackson Square, 700 Decatur St., 504/943-8820, www.neworleanscarriages.com; 8:30am-midnight daily; cost varies) at least once. Whether you opt for a romantic ride in one of the smaller carriages or join one of the larger groups, you'll remember this unique tour of the Vieux Carré. After all, there's nothing quite like clip-clopping along these historic streets, relishing the architecture and curious characters through the eyes of a local guide.

Riverboat Tours

Launched by the **New Orleans Steamboat Company** (504/586-8777 or 800/365-2628, www.neworleanssteamboatcompany.com) in 1975, the **Steamboat Natchez** (Toulouse St. Wharf, 504/569-1401 or 800/233-2628, www.steamboatnatchez.com; hours and cost vary) is an authentic, steam-powered sternwheeler modeled after the *Virginia* and the *Hudson,* two sternwheelers of old. The *Natchez* offers two-hour **harbor cruises** (11am and 2pm Mon.-Sat.; adults $32, children 6-12 $13, free under 6), departing from the foot of Toulouse Street, just behind the Jax Brewery. While on board, you can visit the steam engine room, listen to live narration about the history of the port, enjoy a concert of the onboard, 32-note steam calliope, and opt for a Creole lunch (adults $44, children 6-12 $22, children 2-5 $9; price includes cruise). Alternatively, you can board a **dinner jazz cruise** (7pm daily; adults $48-81, children 6-12 $24-37, children under 6 free-$17.25), which features decent buffet-style dining, live jazz by the Dukes of Dixieland, and gorgeous views of the city. Although sightseeing on the deck is a highlight of any *Natchez* excursion, climate-controlled indoor seating is always available (and especially welcome on hot or rainy days).

For a memorable excursion along the Mississippi River, board the majestic **Creole Queen** (1 Poydras St., 504/529-4567 or 800/445-4109, www.creolequeen.com; hours and cost vary), an authentic paddlewheeler that, with its Victorian-style furniture and wrought-iron deck railings, harkens back to those of the mid-1800s. Operated by New Orleans Paddlewheels, Inc., the *Creole Queen* offers two daily historical river cruises (9:30am and 1:30pm; adults $34, children 6-12 $14, free under 6). You can also opt for the nightly three-hour **dinner jazz cruise** (6:30pm daily; adults $48-79, children 6-12 $24-36, children 3-5 free-$12), which includes a scenic river cruise, a Creole buffet, and live jazz music.

For all cruises, it's a good idea to make reservations; you should arrive 30 minutes before boarding time.

Entertainment and Events

Nightlife

New Orleans is famous for its nightlife. The city boasts a cornucopia of funky watering holes, festive gay bars, stylish hotel lounges, and legendary tourist magnets like Pat O'Brien's, famous for its knock-me-under-the-table hurricanes.

The Big Easy's reputation as a party town is well deserved, and the pulse of that party is often found on Bourbon Street in the French Quarter. Unabashed strip clubs, karaoke bars, daiquiri shops, pulsating dance spaces, and a few well respected jazz venues line the colorful strip. But it can also be a loud, sometimes obnoxious, often smelly thoroughfare that can become frighteningly crowded at Mardi Gras and Halloween. A drunken scene most nights, Bourbon is not for everyone, but it's worth a look.

It's the boisterous music scene that truly distinguishes New Orleans. This is one of the world's premier destinations for jazz, blues, rock, soul, zydeco, and Cajun music. The city's live music venues are equally varied, ranging from friendly neighborhood bars to capacious

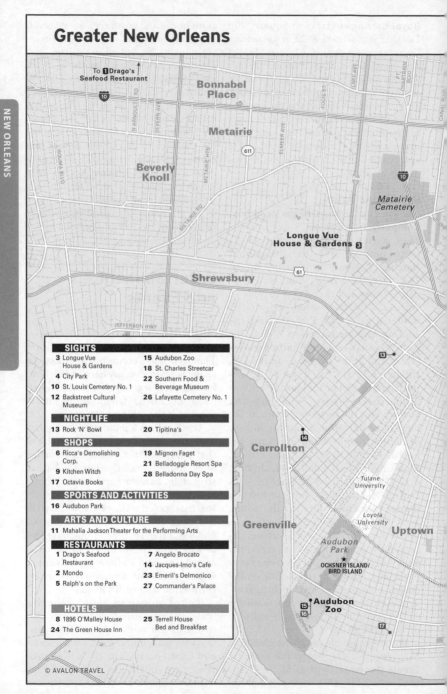

Greater New Orleans

To **1** Drago's
Seafood Restaurant

10

**Bonnabel
Place**

Metairie

611

**Beverly
Knoll**

10

*Matairie
Cemetery*

**Longue Vue
House & Gardens 3**

61

Shrewsbury

JEFFERSON HWY

13

SIGHTS

3 Longue Vue
House & Gardens
4 City Park
10 St. Louis Cemetery No. 1
12 Backstreet Cultural
Museum

15 Audubon Zoo
18 St. Charles Streetcar
22 Southern Food &
Beverage Museum
26 Lafayette Cemetery No. 1

NIGHTLIFE

13 Rock 'N' Bowl

20 Tipitina's

SHOPS

6 Ricca's Demolishing
Corp.
9 Kitchen Witch
17 Octavia Books

19 Mignon Faget
21 Belladoggie Resort Spa
28 Belladonna Day Spa

SPORTS AND ACTIVITIES

16 Audubon Park

ARTS AND CULTURE

11 Mahalia Jackson Theater for the Performing Arts

RESTAURANTS

1 Drago's Seafood
Restaurant
2 Mondo
5 Ralph's on the Park

7 Angelo Brocato
14 Jacques-Imo's Cafe
23 Emeril's Delmonico
27 Commander's Palace

HOTELS

8 1896 O'Malley House
24 The Green House Inn

25 Terrell House
Bed and Breakfast

14

Carrollton

*Tulane
University*

*Loyola
University*

Greenville

Uptown

*Audubon
Park*

★
OCHSNER ISLAND/
BIRD ISLAND

15
16
● **Audubon
Zoo**

17

© AVALON TRAVEL

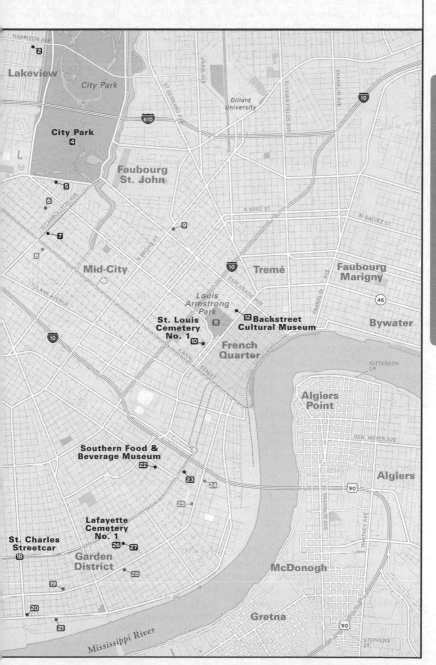

music halls. Beyond music, visitors might also appreciate the resurgence of burlesque that's taken place throughout the city—in joints like the AllWays Lounge & Theatre in the Marigny and One Eyed Jacks in the Quarter.

Many bars are cash-only, and restrooms are typically reserved for paying customers. On busy nights like New Year's Eve, many music venues will charge a nominal entrance fee. Given the prevalence of 24-hour bars and restaurants, New Orleans is a wonderful place for night owls.

Safety

The city's revelry can be disarming. This is a town with drive-through daiquiri shops, where you can walk down Bourbon with enormous "go-cups" of beer, and where residents tend to be a friendly bunch. Unfortunately, though, this is still a relatively dangerous city, where tourists have been known to wander off the beaten path and encounter aggressive muggers. This is particularly true in the French Quarter, where criminals expect to find tourists unaware, but it does happen throughout the city. The best advice is to travel in groups, have fun in moderation, be aware of your surroundings at all times, and make sure that someone is sober enough to find a safe path back to your hotel.

Bars and Lounges
French Quarter

While the elegant and upscale **Bombay Club** (830 Conti St., 504/577-2237, www.bombayclubneworleans.com; 4pm-10pm Sun.-Thurs., 4pm-11pm Fri.-Sat.), decorated in the style of an exclusive British gentlemen's club, offers sumptuous contemporary Creole cuisine, many patrons come for its reputation as a fashionable martini bar. It's well known for its leather-bound, velvet-lined cocktail menu, featuring designer martinis, such as the James Bond-influenced Vesper or the Sweet Heat Margarita. On most

weekends, you'll be treated to live jazz. Casual attire is permitted, though jackets are preferred for men.

Even if you're not staying at the legendary Hotel Monteleone, you can still enjoy a libation in the colorful **Carousel Bar & Lounge** (Hotel Monteleone, 214 Royal St., 504/523-3341, http://hotelmonteleone.com; 11am-close daily) on the first floor. The prime attraction—the kitschy, 1940s-style, 25-seat bar—is festooned with bright lights and garish decorations, but the real treat is that, as its name implies, the bar almost imperceptibly revolves around the center of the room. Stop by to savor the old-world ambience, watch passersby on Royal Street, listen to live music in the adjacent lounge, and drink in the literary company of Tennessee Williams and Truman Capote.

Contained within a building that dates back to the early 1800s, **Jean Lafitte's Old Absinthe House** (240 Bourbon St., 504/524-0113 or 504/523-3181, www.ruebourbon.com/oldabsinthehouse; 9am-3am daily) is popular among lawyers and other professionals. Furnished with antique chandeliers, a copper-topped bar, and the paraphernalia of famous football legends, this cozy tavern is an ideal spot to sip malt scotches and fancy concoctions like the Ramos Gin Fizz or Absinthe House Frappe. With friendly, well-trained bartenders, it can definitely get crowded at night, but this historic place is well worth a stop.

According to legend, pirate Jean Lafitte operated this spot as a blacksmith shop to serve as a front for other, less legitimate enterprises. Built before the city's devastating 18th-century fires, **Lafitte's Blacksmith Shop Bar** (941 Bourbon St., 504/593-9761, www.lafittesblacksmithshop.com; 10am-4am daily) is one of the few original French-style buildings left in the Quarter. A bar since the 1940s, when Tennessee Williams frequented it, this cozy, candlelit place is now one of the city's most popular hangouts. Tourists, locals, and celebrities alike flock here to listen to live piano music, commune with the on-site ghost, and watch the eccentric passersby.

If you find yourself wandering down Decatur in the wee hours, you'll discover relatively deserted sidewalks and many closed-up establishments, save for places like **Molly's at the Market** (1107 Decatur St., 504/525-5169, www.mollysatthemarket.net; 10am-6am daily), a boisterous dive bar that's often the savior of night owls. Founded in 1973, this often-loud hangout has a loyal local following. Patrons appreciate the fun-loving ambience and flock here for special events like the annual Halloween and St. Patrick's Day parades.

Fabled **Napoleon House** (500 Chartres St., 504/524-9752, www.napoleonhouse.com; 11am-10pm Sun.-Thurs., 11am-11pm Fri.-Sat.) was once proffered as a refuge for Napoleon during his exile. Built in 1797 and owned by the Impastato family since 1914, this world-famous landmark is a terrific place to park your feet, especially if you favor classical music and a casual atmosphere. Even the food is worth a stop; the menu features Italian and New Orleans cuisine, from bruschetta and spumoni to boudin and jambalaya.

Even if you shy away from pricey tourist traps, you should experience the world-famous **Pat O'Brien's** (718 St. Peter St., 504/525-4823 or 800/597-4823, www.patobriens.com; noon-close Mon. Thurs., 10am-close Fri.-Sun.) at least once. Here, you'll find several unique spaces, including the crowded main bar, the lively piano bar (show begins at 6pm Mon.-Thurs. and 2pm Fri.-Sun.), the courtyard restaurant (624 Bourbon St.; 11am-close daily), the intimate Bourbon Bar, and the spacious patio, which features a rather cool flaming fountain. The hurricanes and mint juleps can be strong.

Faubourg Marigny and Bywater
Nestled within a quiet residential area, **Mimi's in the Marigny** (2601 Royal St., 504/872-9868, http://mimismarigny.com; 3pm-4am Sun.-Thurs., 3pm-5am Fri.-Sat.; no cover) has long been a popular hot spot, particularly among locals. Downstairs, you'll find a neighborhood bar with couches, stools, and a pool table, while the upstairs space is often a live music venue, with a decent amount of room for dancing. At times, you can expect concerts and DJ-helmed dance parties, not to mention dance lessons. Try the tasty tapas on offer, from almond-stuffed dates to beef empanadas; the kitchen is typically open Sunday-Thursday 6pm-2am and Friday-Saturday 6pm-4am.

Central Business and Arts Districts
You have to admire the perseverance of the folks who run **Handsome Willy's Patio Bar & Lounge** (218 S. Robertson St., 504/525-0377, www.handsomewillys.com; 3pm-11pm Mon., 11am-11pm Tues.-Wed., 11am-1am Thurs., 11am-3am Fri., 4pm-3am Sat., 4pm-midnight Sun.). This rockin' music club and bar that opened on the site of a former brothel in 2005 was virtually destroyed by Hurricane Katrina and yet managed to reopen only a few months later. The club has developed a loyal following for booking great bands, from funk to hip-hop. Its proximity to the Superdome and Smoothie King Center also makes it popular among sports fans. Besides offering weekday happy hours (2pm-6pm), Willy's serves free food on Friday (5pm-9pm) and opens on Sunday during the Saints' home games.

Nestled within the Arts District, **Lucy's Retired Surfers Bar & Restaurant** (701 Tchoupitoulas St., 504/523-8995, www.lucysretiredsurfers.com; 11am-close Mon.-Fri., 10am-close Sat.-Sun.) feels like a frat-sorority party on most evenings, especially on weekends. It's one of the city's more popular pickup bars, and it's also a great place to slurp down a few margaritas. You can enjoy a delicious brunch on Saturday and Sunday mornings—the perfect cure for a hangover.

The shrimp and grits happens to be one of the tastiest versions in the city. There's also a Lucy's in Baton Rouge.

The elegant Windsor Court Hotel is home to the **Polo Club Lounge** (Windsor Court Hotel, 300 Gravier St., 504/522-1992 or 504/523-6000, www.grillroomneworleans.com or www.windsorcourthotel.com; 11:30am-midnight Sun.-Thurs., 11:30am-1am Fri.-Sat.), a classy space furnished with equestrian oil paintings, historical memorabilia, and leather furniture, all of which recall the ambience of a private British club. Adjacent to the Grill Room, this second-floor lounge presents live nightly jazz in addition to hard-to-find wines, champagnes, and specialty liquors, and a menu that includes caviar and truffle fries.

The Sazerac Bar (The Roosevelt New Orleans, 130 Roosevelt Way, 504/648-1200, www.therooseveltneworleans.com; 11am-close daily), at the CBD's grand Roosevelt New Orleans, is perhaps the most famous hotel lounge in the city. Named for the noted cocktail—a concoction of rye whiskey, Pernod, sugar, lemon oil, and the local Peychaud's bitters—the bar was once a favored haunt of Governor Huey P. Long, the infamous "Kingfish" of Louisiana.

Named for the Peruvian liquor made from grapes, **Pisco Bar** (Catahoula Hotel, 914 Union St., 504/603-2442, http://catahoulahotel.com, 7am-midnight daily) serves the classic Peruvian pisco sour, of course, plus more unusual beverages, such as the cinnamon-topped Chinguerito. The bar is packed early in the evening, as it is a popular post-work stop for locals before venturing out for the night. The bartenders are knowledgeable and friendly, making this a great place to try something new.

Dance Clubs
French Quarter
At a rather busy corner on Bourbon Street, the ever-popular, two-story karaoke bar **Cats Meow** (701 Bourbon St., 504/523-2788 or 504/523-2951, www.701bourbon.com; 4pm-3am Mon.-Thurs., 2pm-6am Fri.-Sun.) has a loyal following. Celebrities like "Weird Al" Yankovic and Tori Spelling have stopped by to entertain the masses. Visitors can dance to live and DJ-mixed swing, classic rock, disco, dance, pop, and hip-hop music, or opt for a bit of people-watching on the upper balcony.

A favorite dance spot in the Quarter, **One Eyed Jacks** (615 Toulouse St., 504/569-8361, www.oneeyedjacks.net; hours and cover vary) is a spacious, bordello-style venue, with red walls, curious paintings, and moody lighting. Beyond the intimate front bar, revelers will encounter a large showroom, which features a horseshoe-shaped bar, limited seating, an ample stage, and oodles of room for dancing. While live concerts are common here, regulars also come for thematic events, like 1980s-style dance parties, burlesque shows, and vaudeville nights, which often include comedy sketches, old-fashioned jazz performances, acrobatics, and sexy dance routines.

Faubourg Marigny and Bywater
One of the more spacious venues in the Marigny, the multilevel **Maison** (508 Frenchmen St., 504/371-5543, www.maisonfrenchman.com; 5pm-close Sun.-Thurs., 4pm-close Fri.-Sat.; no cover), a bar, restaurant, and live music venue, consists of three separate areas: a front dining and music room; a rear lounge and stage; and the upper Penthouse bar, which comprises a separate stage, a comfortable lounge, and plenty of room for dancing. The Maison is home to concerts and DJ-helmed dance parties, featuring jazz, funk, soul, Latin dance music, and even swing dance lessons.

As with many nighttime venues in New Orleans, **Siberia** (2227 St. Claude Ave., 504/265-8855, www.siberianola.com; 4pm-close daily; cover varies) defies categorization. Depending on the night it can be an eclectic live music venue, a DJ-spinning dance club, or a Slavic restaurant. At any given time, you might find yourself belting karaoke songs, grooving to local bands like Rory Danger and the Danger Dangers, or sputtering laughter on a comedy and burlesque night. Whatever you do, though, be sure to sample the food, which ranges from a surprisingly delicious beet and goat cheese salad to apple and asparagus blinis to traditional pierogi and kielbasa.

Central Business and Arts Districts

One block from the Ernest N. Morial Convention Center, you'll encounter the two-story, upscale **Metropolitan** (310 Andrew Higgins Dr., 504/568-1702, www.themetropolitannightclub.com; hours and cover vary), which, at more than 36,000 square feet, is often the host for major events, from tailgate parties to fashion shows. This warehouse-turned-club contains two main rooms, equipped with smoke machines, strobe lights, and video screens and featuring DJ-spun hip-hop, rock, house, techno, and other popular formats. In addition to a slew of bartender stations and VIP sections, the Metropolitan offers valet parking and VIP table service. Expect pricey drinks and high cover charges.

Gay and Lesbian Venues
French Quarter

One of the most popular gay dance clubs sits at the often-rowdy corner of Bourbon and St. Ann. The **Bourbon Pub & Parade** (801 Bourbon St., 504/529-2107, www.bourbonpub.com; 11am-3am Sun.-Thurs., 11am-5am Fri.-Sat.; cover varies) has a typically packed video bar on the ground level, a slick dance floor upstairs, and a long wraparound balcony on the second floor—a favorite perch from which to gaze at the throngs of revelers on Bourbon Street. Music lovers can expect to see plenty of retro music videos downstairs, while everything from drag and burlesque shows to hot guy contests to karaoke nights is happening upstairs.

Cafe Lafitte in Exile (901 Bourbon St., 504/522-8397, www.lafittes.com; 24 hours daily; no cover) has been serving the local gay community for roughly as long as any bar in town. It draws a 30- to 50-something crowd. You can watch music videos in the downstairs bar and observe curious passersby from the upstairs balcony, which can be particularly eye-opening during uninhibited, skin-baring events like Mardi Gras and Southern Decadence.

If you prefer a relaxed, off-Bourbon watering hole that's inviting to gay and heterosexual patrons alike, head to the **Golden Lantern Bar** (1239 Royal St., 504/529-2860; 24 hours daily; no cover), a small, dark locals' bar on a quiet, residential stretch of Royal that serves one of the best Bloody Marys in the city.

The mellow, longstanding **Good Friends Bar** (740 Dauphine St., 504/566-7191, www.goodfriendsbar.com; 1pm-5am Mon.-Thurs., 24 hours Fri.-Sun.; no cover) isn't too loud or flashy. It's just a casual, pet-friendly neighborhood watering hole, where you'll find a pool table, affordable beer and cocktails, a slightly fancier upstairs area, and attentive bartenders. Saints fans come here, as do low-key locals, and no matter your sexual orientation, you're welcome to join in the karaoke fun every Tuesday night (9pm-midnight).

Oz (800 Bourbon St., 504/593-9491, www.ozneworleans.com; 24 hours daily; cover varies) often seems to be far less crowded than other venues in the Quarter. Nevertheless, many locals consider it one of the city's top gay dance clubs, especially during special events like Mardi Gras and New Year's Eve. Opposite Bourbon Pub & Parade, Oz provides plenty of room for dancing on the ground floor and more lounge-like spaces upstairs.

Faubourg Marigny and Bywater

Definitely not for the faint-hearted, the rowdy **AllWays Lounge & Theatre**

(2240 St. Claude Ave., 504/218-5778, www.theallwayslounge.com; 6pm-close daily; cover varies) welcomes everybody, though it has a predominantly gay and lesbian following. Nudity, wacky sexual acts, and strange musical performances are common in the lounge. The theater features ever-changing productions, including bizarre concerts and counter-culture musicals like *The Rocky Horror Picture Show*. Shows generally start at 10pm.

Although **The Country Club** (634 Louisa St., 504/945-0742, www.thecountryclubneworleans.com; 10am-1am daily; no cover), set in a magnificent Bywater mansion, isn't technically a gay bar, it definitely embraces an anything goes vibe, with its clothing-optional pool, sauna, Jacuzzi, and on-site massage and spa services. You can sip cocktails in the indoor or outdoor bars, enjoy creative cuisine in the restaurant (Sun.-Thurs. 10am-9pm, Fri.-Sat. 10am-10pm), or watch movies, music videos, and sporting events on the 25-foot screen. If the crowd is really hoppin', the joint might not close until 2am or later. Expect to pay $8-15 to access the area that houses the pool.

Jazz

French Quarter

No matter the evening, it's difficult to cross the corner of Decatur Street and Esplanade Avenue without catching some of the fantastic tunes coming from the usually open doors of the funky **Balcony Music Club** (1331 Decatur St., 504/301-5912; 5pm-2am Mon.-Thurs., 3pm-4am Fri.-Sat.; cover varies), known colloquially as the BMC. Though you're most likely to hear brass, jazz, or funk, anything is possible. If you're still in the mood for fun after this place closes, just hop across Esplanade to **Igor's Check Point Charlie** (501 Esplanade Ave., 504/281-4847; 24 hours daily), a lively 24-hour bar, grill, music club, game room, and self-service laundry.

On the ground floor of the elegant Royal Sonesta hotel, in the heart of Bourbon Street's revelry, the stylish **Irvin Mayfield's Jazz Playhouse** (Royal Sonesta New Orleans, 300 Bourbon St., 504/553-2299 or 504/586-0300, www.irvinmayfield.com; showtimes vary, no cover) welcomes jazz aficionados and curious tourists every night of the week. Although the musicians rotate nightly, you're always guaranteed to hear some stellar performers. On Friday night, stick around until midnight to experience a classy burlesque show. You can purchase a limited number of reserved seats online for $20 (one-drink minimum), and the remainder of seating is for walk-ins.

One of the Big Easy's most famous and delightful live jazz venues is the **Palm Court Jazz Cafe** (1204 Decatur St., 504/525-0200, www.palmcourtjazzcafe.com; 7pm-11pm Wed.-Sun.; no cover), in a handsome, 19th-century building near the historic French Market. Besides Southern-style ceiling fans and an elegant mahogany bar, the restaurant features exposed-brick walls lined with photos of jazz greats, plus a kitchen producing tasty Creole fare. Because seating is arranged at tables over dinner, reservations are a must.

Since 1961, **Preservation Hall** (726 St. Peter St., 504/522-2841, www.preservationhall.com; 8pm-11pm Mon.-Wed., 6pm-11pm Thurs.-Sun.; cover $15-20) has been one of the city's top places to hear true New Orleans jazz. The band and the venue were formed expressly to keep the legacy of the city's distinctive style of jazz music alive for generations to come, and top musicians continue to perform in the surprisingly intimate concert hall. Housed within a weathered, 1750s-era house, it's a charming, laid-back place, with vintage wooden benches, folding chairs, and a good bit of standing room. After the all-too-brief concert (usually less than an hour), feel free to stroll along the carriageway, to the landscaped courtyard for a breath of fresh air. Get here early, as the line forms quickly for these nightly concerts (8pm, 9pm, and 10pm Mon.-Wed., 6pm, 8pm, 9pm, and 10pm Thurs.-Sun.). If you'd rather skip the line altogether, opt for the limited "Big Shot" seating ($35-50).

One of the newest jazz joints in the French Quarter, **21st Amendment at La Louisiane** (725 Iberville St., 504/378-7330, www.21stamendmentlalouisiane.com; 3pm-midnight Mon.-Thurs., 2pm-1am Fri.-Sat., 3pm-11pm Sun.) honors America's Prohibition era of the 1920s, when both the mafia and speakeasies thrived. Decorated with black-and-white images of the country's most notorious mobsters, including Capone himself, this cozy bar occupies part of a 19th-century building that was owned by local mobsters Diamond Jim Moran and Carlos Marcello from the 1950s to the 1980s. Today, you can savor a delicious cocktail, made from homemade syrups and infused spirits, while listening to live old-time jazz and blues music, which is offered nearly every afternoon and evening.

Faubourg Marigny and Bywater

Situated between the French Quarter and the Faubourg Marigny since 1939, **Buffa's Bar & Restaurant** (1001 Esplanade Ave., 504/949-0038, www.buffasbar.com; 24 hours daily; no cover) feels like a well-kept secret, despite its obvious location on Esplanade. A popular neighborhood hangout, Buffa's offers a variety of vittles and libations all day and night. The real treat is the back room (6pm-close Mon.-Tues., 11am-close Wed.-Sat., 10am-close Sun.), where patrons can listen to traditional jazz musicians. A favorite regular band is the Royal Rounders, whose eclectic, often chuckle-worthy shows might feature, in addition to jazz, everything from blues to pop to R&B.

At the aptly named **Snug Harbor Jazz Bistro** (626 Frenchmen St., 504/949-0696, www.snugjazz.com; 5pm-midnight Sun.-Thurs., 5pm-1am Fri.-Sat.; $15-35 pp), a cozy, classy, contemporary spot, you can sip cocktails in the downstairs bar or relish tasty regional cuisine in the adjacent dining room, before heading upstairs to catch some of the city's top jazz acts. Occupying a renovated, 19th-century storefront on Frenchmen, Snug Harbor has been showcasing top musicians, from Ellis Marsalis to Charmaine Neville, as well as nurturing young talent for more than three decades.

Practically across the street from Snug Harbor lies the **Spotted Cat Music Club** (623 Frenchmen St., www.spottedcat-musicclub.com; 4pm-2am Mon.-Fri., 2pm-2am Sat.-Sun.; no cover, one-drink minimum), a less famous, cash-only jazz club that qualifies as one of the coolest little music finds in the city. Often featured on HBO's *Treme* series, this happily cramped, dark, and sweaty dance hall offers a long happy hour, a nice selection of designer martinis, and terrific live bands. Although you'll occasionally hear rock, blues, bluegrass, salsa, and other dance-worthy musical styles, modern and traditional jazz are definitely the mainstays here. Local favorite Meschiya Lake and the Little Big Horns, known for their old-time jazz performances, often pack in the crowds and inspire old-fashioned dancing among the regulars.

On a historic street along the sketchy edge of the Faubourg Marigny, you'll find **Sweet Lorraine's Jazz Club** (1931 St. Claude Ave., 504/945-9654; 5pm-close Tues.-Sat., 7pm-close Sun.; cover varies), a local favorite for live jazz. While you listen to the ever-changing performers, be sure to sample Southern-style dishes like blackened catfish, cornbread-stuffed chicken breasts, and pecan pie with praline sauce. The club also features a selective wine and martini menu.

Featuring a snug dining area, a small bar, and an even smaller stage, **Three Muses** (536 Frenchmen St., 504/252-4801, www.3musesnola.com; 5pm-close Wed.-Mon.; no cover) is a terrific place to sample eclectic tapas-style dishes like Moroccan eggplant bruschetta, Gulf fish tacos, and cardamom panna cotta while listening to some of the finest blues, jazz, and swing musicians in town. Though reservations are necessary on the weekends, be prepared to relinquish your table after 90 minutes. Seemingly a harsh policy, it's actually quite reasonable given the enormous popularity of this cozy joint.

Central Business and Arts Districts
The **Little Gem Saloon** (445 S. Rampart St., 504/267-4863, www.littlegemsaloon.com; 5pm-10pm Tues.-Fri., 5pm-11pm Sat.; cover varies) is part bar, part restaurant, and part live music venue. While many patrons come for the tasty Cajun and soul food, which ranges from crawfish cheesecake to fried chicken, plenty of others flock here for the live music, whether during the weekday happy hour (5pm-7pm), on a weekend night, or during the Sunday jazz brunch. Regular performers include local favorites like the New Orleans Swinging Gypsies, The Messy Cookers Jazz Band, and Kermit Ruffins and the BBQ Swingers. Given the popularity of this venue, you must reserve a table to guarantee seating.

Blues and Rock
French Quarter
Part of the famous chain, the predictably popular tourist haunt **House of Blues** (225 Decatur St., 504/310-4999, www.houseofblues.com/neworleans; 11:30am-close daily; cover varies) has been enticing legions of music fans since its 1994 opening. Home to a large folk art collection, the funky, colorful concert venue features two music halls, which can accommodate about 370 and 840 guests, respectively. Various performers play here, from major rock bands to local jazz and blues musicians, and the on-site restaurant serves New Orleans favorites like shrimp po'boys and key lime pie. Especially popular is Sunday's Gospel Brunch, which combines world-class performances with a Southern-style buffet.

Faubourg Marigny and Bywater
Just steps from The Spotted Cat Music Club, in the heart of the Marigny's lively music scene, the intimate, somewhat dingy **Apple Barrel Bar** (609 Frenchmen St., 504/949-9399; 1pm-3am Sun.-Thurs., 1pm-5am Fri.-Sat.; no cover, one-drink minimum) lures an ever-revolving crowd of blues and jazz lovers nightly. Hip yet happily low-key, this is an ideal spot for sipping cocktails before heading out to the noisier music clubs along Frenchmen—though, be advised, it can still get pretty loud in here, depending on who's playing.

A Faubourg Marigny mainstay and a frequent sight on HBO's *Treme,* the spacious **Blue Nile** (532 Frenchmen St., 504/948-2583, http://bluenilelive.com; 7pm-2am Sun.-Thurs., 6pm-4am Fri.-Sat.; cover varies) presents a broad mix of cool music, from blues and jazz to reggae and garage rock. Frequent acts include the Honey Island Swamp Band and local fave Kermit Ruffins and the BBQ Swingers. Typically, there are two shows each night, with the first starting around 7 or 8pm and the second kicking off at 10 or 11pm. With its plush lounge seating and tile floors, it's a funky yet elegant place to socialize early in the evening.

Located in a building from the late 19th century, the dimly lit **d.b.a. New Orleans** (618 Frenchmen St., 504/942-3731, www.dbaneworleans.com; 5pm-close Mon.-Thurs., 4pm-close Fri.-Sun.; cover varies) is a good place to meet locals, hear live rock and blues bands, and, on occasion, catch performances from the likes of Jimmy Buffett and Stevie Wonder. The drink selection encompasses about a zillion beers (including plenty of imported options), plus many types of whiskey and tequila, and the crowd is young and laid-back but with a touch of style.

Central Business and Arts Districts
For the most part, you'll catch top blues and funk acts at the **Howlin' Wolf** (907

S. Peters St., 504/529-5844, www.the-howlinwolf.com; 11pm-2am daily; closing time and cover vary), a cavernous nightclub in the Arts District, not far from the city's convention center. This is one of the Big Easy's largest and most prominent live music venues, which has been known to host rock, alternative, pop, and R&B bands, too. Over the years, some of the more famous performers have included Allison Krauss, Harry Connick Jr., and the Foo Fighters.

In the downtown Arts District, **Republic New Orleans** (828 S. Peters St., 504/528-8282, www.republicnola.com; hours and cover vary) occupies a cavernous, historic space that was once a coffee warehouse and a set for Oliver Stone's film *JFK*. Now, this upscale music club and special-events facility is often the site of concerts, parties, and fashion shows.

Uptown

For catching rock (both hard-edged and down-home), jazz, zydeco, Cajun, and blues, there may be no club in the city more acclaimed or more festive than **Tipitina's** (501 Napoleon Ave., 504/895-8477, www.tipitinas.com; hours and cover vary depending on show), a longstanding venue in the heart of Uptown. Purists may tell you that Tip's has lost its edge and no longer presents the best—or at least most distinctive—local acts, but anybody looking for an introduction to the city's eclectic music scene should head here. Entertainment varies greatly, but no matter what's playing, you can probably dance to it.

Cajun and Zydeco

Central Business and Arts Districts

Mulate's (201 Julia St., 504/522-1492, www.mulates.com; 11am-10pm Sun.-Thurs., 11am-11pm Fri.-Sat.; no cover) features live bands, plenty of dancing space, and a menu filled with Louisiana favorites. In the Arts District, this downhome Cajun restaurant and dance hall occupies a large building. The music

is far superior to the food. In fact, you can expect live entertainment nightly (7pm-10pm).

Greater New Orleans

Rock 'n' Bowl (3000 S. Carrollton Ave., 504/861-1700, www.rocknbowl.com; 11:30am-midnight Mon.-Thurs., 11:30am-2am Fri.-Sat., hours vary Sun.; cover varies) is a music (and bowling) institution, luring couples and families alike. An offbeat place to catch live bands of all types, it's especially known for zydeco, jazz, blues, and swing, but anything is possible here, including performances by regional favorites like Tab Benoit and Amanda Shaw. Savvy locals often show up early for a few rounds of bowling, which, if you time it right, could enable you to catch the concert without paying a cover charge.

Wine Bars

French Quarter

The intimate **Orleans Grapevine Wine Bar & Bistro** (720 Orleans St., 504/523-1930, www.orleansgrapevine.com; 4pm-midnight daily) is one of the rare reasonably priced yet sophisticated bars in the French Quarter. Set inside a restored 1809 building, it's a classy yet casual bistro in the oft-overlooked block between the peaceful rear garden of the St. Louis Cathedral and the craziness of Bourbon Street. Besides featuring an extensive list of 450 bottled wines and 75 varietals by the glass, the Grapevine turns out an elegant and tasty menu, including revolving delicacies like baked brie and stuffed flounder. Expect meal service Sunday-Thursday 5pm-10:30pm and Friday-Saturday 5pm-11:30pm.

Faubourg Marigny and Bywater

Often spotted in HBO's acclaimed show *Treme,* **Bacchanal** (600 Poland Ave., 504/948-9111, www.bacchanalwine.com; 11am-midnight daily) is a wine bar and retail shop, a New York-style deli, an international bistro, and, when weather allows it in the exposed courtyard, a live music venue. This local favorite offers an ever-changing, culinary experience that you must embrace firsthand to understand. The kitchen usually closes around 11pm.

The Arts

A longtime haven for artists, writers, and musicians, New Orleans has a rich, multicultural tradition in the arts.

The city is home to numerous outstanding galleries, with particularly strong concentrations along Royal and Chartres Streets in the French Quarter, around Julia Street in the Arts District, and along funky Magazine Street in Uptown.

Galleries

French Quarter

Fine art lovers should head to **Callan Fine Art** (240 Chartres St., 504/524-0025, www.callanfineart.com; 10am-5pm Tues.-Sat. and by appt.), which focuses on European paintings from 1830 to 1950. You'll find representative works from the Academic, Pastoral, Neoclassic, Impressionist, and Post-Impressionist movements, with the artwork of French Barbizon painters a particular specialty. Curiously, local musician Tony Green displays quite a few of his own drawings and paintings here, most of which capture the vibrancy of jazz musicians, Mardi Gras, and the French Quarter.

The eye-catching **Craig Tracy's Fine-Art Bodypainting Gallery** (827 Royal St., 504/592-9886, http://craigtracy.com; 10am-6pm daily) presents the innovative creations of Craig Tracy, an internationally known artist who paints landscapes, storms, animal prints, and other patterns on naked human bodies, then photographs his living creations. Gorgeous and mesmerizing, his artwork typically requires intense concentration to discern the human form. At the gallery, you can often speak to the artist himself and watch videos that document his fascinating process.

As you stroll through the historic French Market, visit the **Dutch Alley Artist's Co-op** (912 N. Peters St., 504/412-9220, www.dutchalleyartistsco-op.com; 10am-6pm daily), founded in 2003 by artist Ric Rolston. Operated by the two dozen artists whose work is on display, the gallery features a wide array of creations, from John Fitzgerald's prints to Kimberly Parker's seafood collages to Linda Sampson's beaded accessories and mourning jewelry.

Although New Orleans boasts several art galleries that focus exclusively on photography, you'll find the largest assortment at the **Gallery for Fine Photography** (241 Chartres St., 504/568-1313, www.agallery.com; by appt. Tues.-Wed., 10:30am-5pm Thurs.-Mon.). Established in 1973, this prestigious emporium features the work of such titans as Ansel Adams, Walker Evans, and Diane Arbus, plus the visionary creations of newer artists. Be prepared for hefty price tags.

In the shadow of the St. Louis Cathedral, the **Jamie Hayes Gallery** (617 Chartres St., 504/596-2344, http://jamie-hayes.com; 9am-7pm daily) features the whimsical multicolored paintings, dolls, and jewelry of color-blind artist Jamie Hayes. Many New Orleanians favor his unique perspective of the city, which celebrates in a wacky, childlike way the unique music, traditions, and festive spirit of this one-of-a-kind place. Jamie's other gallery (8314 Oak St.) is in Uptown's Riverbend neighborhood.

If you favor offbeat contemporary art from local artists and artisans, then the **Kako Gallery** (536 Royal St., 504/565-5445, www.kakogallery.com; 10am-6pm daily) might be right up your alley. You'll find unique sculptures, paintings, and jewelry from artists like Don Picou, who frequently paints muted scenes of bayous and swamps, and Stan Fontaine and Diane Millsap, two visionaries whose kaleidoscopic paintings feature the city's most famous landmarks and neighborhoods, from the St. Louis Cathedral to Pirate's Alley.

World-famous **Martin-Lawrence Galleries** (433 Royal St., 504/299-9055, www.martinlawrence.com; 10am-6pm daily) has locations throughout the United States. It's no surprise then that New Orleans, a city favored among art lovers, would boast its own branch on venerable Royal Street. Founded in 1975, Martin-Lawrence Galleries specializes in sculptures, original paintings, and limited edition graphics by such astounding artists as Pablo Picasso, Marc Chagall, and Andy Warhol.

Owned by one of the most respected artists in Louisiana, the eponymous **Michalopoulos Gallery** (617 Bienville St., 504/558-0505, www.michalopoulos.com; 10am-6pm Mon.-Sat., 11am-6pm Sun.) carries dozens of James Michalopoulos's vibrant architectural renderings, with their trademark skewed angles and impressionistic brushwork. Many of his works feature Creole houses or classic French Quarter townhouses. Sharon Stone, Bruce Willis, and Bonnie Raitt are among his most notable collectors, and the New Orleans Jazz & Heritage Festival and Foundation often commissions him to create the official Jazz Fest poster. His studio is in the nearby Marigny (527 Elysian Fields Ave.).

Although the famous Cajun "Blue Dog" artist George Rodrigue passed away in 2013, you can still visit his **Rodrigue Studio New Orleans** (730 Royal St., 504/581-4244, http://georgerodrigue.com; 10am-6pm Mon.-Sat., noon-5pm Sun.) on Royal Street, in a warmly lighted space not far from the St. Louis Cathedral. Here, you can buy everything from inexpensive gifts to original oil paintings, depicting the "Blue Dog" amid swamps, cemeteries, and other picturesque places. The inspiration for these works was twofold: a Cajun legend about the *loup-garou* (werewolf) and the

owner's terrier, Tiffany, who had died several years before.

Enticing to many a passerby, the storefront of **Tanner Original Art** (830 Royal St., 504/524-8266, www.hauntingart.com; 10am-7pm Thurs.-Mon.) features the artist Tanner's spellbinding, often eerie paintings of stark forests shrouded in fog, illumined by sunshine or starlight, or enhanced by otherworldly hues. The scenes resembling photo negatives are especially haunting. You can purchase canvas and paper reproductions or, if you're lucky, the original paintings, but the prices aren't cheap. Even if you can't afford one of his paintings, you can still peer through the window of the adjacent **Tanner Open Studio** (832 Royal St.), where the artist may be working on his latest creation.

Faubourg Marigny and Bywater

The curious **Barrister's Gallery** (2331 St. Claude Ave., 504/710-4506, www.barristersgallery.com; 11am-5pm Tues.-Sat.) is located at the edge of the Faubourg Marigny, a funky neighborhood that seems to suit the variety of Asian, African, Haitian, and Oceanic folk and outsider art available at Barrister's. Its primary focus is on monthly contemporary exhibits that have an eclectic, unorthodox bent. Unfortunately, the gallery's location isn't the safest place in the city.

Central Business and Arts Districts

In the city's Arts District, posh New York-style galleries seem to prevail, so **LeMieux Galleries** (332 Julia St., 504/522-5988, www.lemieuxgalleries.com; 10am-5:30pm Mon.-Sat. and by appt.) offers an intriguing change of pace. LeMieux presents a wide assortment of visionary, contemporary artwork, including Bobby Wozniak's infrared photographs, Theresa Honeywell's knitted pieces, and John Donovan's small yet impactful sculptures, which invariably make political statements about America's military history.

At the 25,000-square-foot New Orleans School of **GlassWorks & Printmaking Studio** (727 Magazine St., 504/529-7279, http://neworleansglassworks.com; 10am-5pm Mon.-Sat.; free), you can observe highly skilled glassblowing, torchworking, printmaking, metalworking, and stained-glass artisans in action. Besides browsing their wares, you can also learn how to create your own glasswork, jewelry, and paper arts by taking one of the studio's exceptional classes, which range from two-hour courses on paper marbling to six-week workshops about Venetian glassblowing.

With its high ceilings, lofty windows, white brick walls, and uncluttered displays, the spacious **Søren Christensen Gallery** (400 Julia St., 504/569-9501, http://sorengallery.com; 10am-5:30pm Tues.-Fri., 11am-5pm Sat., and by appt.) resembles the kind of place you might find in New York City. A stroll through this elegant gallery gives art lovers a view of contemporary paintings, sculptures, and photography by nationally and internationally recognized artists.

Performing Arts

Founded in 1916 and relocated to its current spot near Jackson Square in 1922, **Le Petit Théâtre du Vieux Carré** (616 St. Peter St., 504/522-2081, www.lepetittheatre.com; hours and costs vary depending on show) is one of America's oldest community theaters. Following an extensive renovation, Le Petit houses both a highly regarded Louisiana Creole restaurant (Dickie Brennan's latest, Tableau) and a comfortable place for patrons to watch a wide range of dramas, comedies, musicals, and intimate concerts. Recent productions have included *Hair, Merrily We Roll Along, Death of a Salesman,* and musical performances by local legends Marcia Ball and Terence Blanchard.

Within walking distance of Lee Circle, the **Contemporary Arts Center** (CAC,

900 Camp St., 504/528-3800 or 504/528-3805, http://cacno.org; event and ticket prices vary) is a multipurpose venue that houses an innovative art gallery (11am-5pm Wed.-Mon.) as well as performing arts spaces. In addition to staging lectures, performances, and concerts, the CAC often serves as a main location for the New Orleans Film Festival and other annual events. Stop by the on-site café (9am-5pm Mon.-Fri., 11am-5pm Sat.-Sun.) for refreshments. Louisiana residents can enjoy the gallery for free on Sundays.

Within Louis Armstrong Park, the **Mahalia Jackson Theater for Performing Arts** (1419 Basin St., 504/287-0350, www.mahaliajacksontheater.com; hours and ticket prices vary depending on show) is a popular venue for live concerts, operas, musicals, comedy shows, dance performances, and festival events, especially since its complete restoration following Hurricane Katrina. Named for New Orleans-born gospel singer Mahalia Jackson, the theater hosts regular performances by the **New Orleans Opera Association** (504/529-2278 or 504/529-3000, www.neworleansopera.org), the **Louisiana Philharmonic Orchestra** (504/523-6530, www.lpomusic.com), and the **New Orleans Ballet Association** (504/522-0996, www.nobadance.com), which books some of the world's most important ballet companies. Parking is inside the gated park, accessible via the Orleans Avenue entrance. This can be an unsafe part of town, especially at night, so avoid coming to the theater alone, and be aware of your environs at all times.

Occupying a 3,800-square-foot performance hall in the rear of the 55,000-square-foot New Orleans Healing Center, **Café Istanbul** (2372 St. Claude Ave., 504/975-0286, http://cafeistanbul-nola.com; hours and ticket prices vary) does a lot to foster local performance art. In addition to presenting live concerts, dance and theatrical performances, and comedy shows, Café Istanbul offers poetry readings, film screenings, and an upper gallery dedicated to visual arts, particularly the paintings and photography of local artists.

The imposing structure that now houses the **Marigny Opera House** (725 St. Ferdinand St., 504/948-9998, www.marignyoperahouse.org; hours and ticket prices vary) once served as the Holy Trinity Catholic Church, which was founded in 1847 for German Catholics, built in 1853 by architect Theodore Giraud, and known for its excellent music. Perhaps it's fitting then that the Marigny Opera House considers itself a nondenominational, neighborhood "church of the arts." Home to the Marigny Opera Ballet, a professional contemporary ballet company founded in 2014, the Opera House hosts various musical concerts, spotlighting everything from classical to jazz, as well as other cultural events.

Festivals and Events

The Big Easy offers a cornucopia of festivals worth planning a trip around, especially in fall, winter, and spring. Well-known events like Mardi Gras and the New Orleans Jazz & Heritage Festival are just the tip of the iceberg. Most events revolve around food and music.

New Orleans also has its share of holiday-related events. You'll discover plenty of Christmas revelry during the month of December, when the St. Louis Cathedral offers free jazz concerts, restaurants offer special *réveillon* menus, and the trees and structures of City Park are illuminated during Celebration in the Oaks.

During popular events—especially Mardi Gras and Jazz Fest—the city can fill up quickly, so it's wise to book your trip well ahead.

★ Mardi Gras

Few festivals exemplify the joyous spirit of New Orleans more than **Mardi Gras** (various locations, www.mardigrasday.com; hours vary; free), a French term meaning "Fat Tuesday." If you're a fan of colorful, exciting festivals, there's no better time to visit New Orleans than during Mardi Gras season, which usually falls in February or early March and lasts 2-3 weeks prior to Lent (from Epiphany to Ash Wednesday). Festivities include everything from colorful street masks and costumes to gala balls and events. But Mardi Gras's most famous events are the free public parades sponsored by krewes and featuring colorful floats, marching bands, motorcycle squads, dancers, entertainers, and, sometimes, a royal court (the king, queen, maids, and dukes of a krewe). Participants often toss beaded necklaces, stuffed animals, commemorative doubloons, and other trinkets to spectators lining the route. For most krewes, each year brings a new theme, usually with a historical, mythical, or topical bent. Some of the most worthwhile parades include the krewes of Endymion, Bacchus, Orpheus, Zulu, and Rex. Dog lovers might appreciate the Mystic Krewe of Barkus in the French Quarter, while sci-fi and fantasy fans look forward to the Intergalactic Krewe of Chewbacchus.

Planning Checklist

Know when to go. Carnival season technically begins on January 6 (known as Twelfth Night, or the Feast of the Epiphany), but Mardi Gras Day shifts every season (February 13 in 2018, March 5 in 2019, and February 25 in 2020). Mardi Gras parades usually start about two weeks prior to Fat Tuesday, but most revelers venture to New Orleans for the weekend preceding the climactic day—from the Friday before Fat Tuesday through midnight on Mardi Gras.

Book a bed. Make reservations at least six months in advance. Note that many hotels require a minimum stay of three nights during Mardi Gras weekend, and costly special-event rates may apply. Although you'll find cheaper hotels near

Mardi Gras Lingo

- **ball:** a masquerade or lively extravaganza that usually occurs at the end of a parade

- **boeuf gras** (BUFF grah): the fatted bull or ox, the ancient symbol of the final meat eaten before the Lenten season of fasting

- **captain:** the leader of each krewe

- **doubloon:** large coins made from aluminum, plastic, or other materials and stamped with the insignia and theme of a krewe

- **favor:** a souvenir, given by krewe members to friends attending the ball and usually bearing the krewe's name, insignia, and year of issue

- **flambeaux** (FLAM-bohz): naphtha-fueled torches, once carried by white-robed black men as the only source of nighttime parade illumination, still used in many nighttime parades today

- **king cake:** an iced or sugared coffee cake, often shaped like a ring, served during the Mardi Gras season and containing a small plastic baby, the finder of which, according to tradition, must purchase the next king cake or throw the next party

- **krewe:** private Carnival organization

- **Lundi Gras** (LUN-dee grah): the day before Mardi Gras, also known as Fat Monday

- **Mardi Gras Indians:** groups of local black men who, led by separate Big Chiefs, chant, dance, and compete with one another in ceremonial processions along ever-changing routes through residential neighborhoods on Mardi Gras Day, all while wearing handmade beaded and feathered costumes as a tribute to American Indians, who often assisted escaping slaves

- **throw:** an inexpensive trinket, such as an aluminum doubloon or plastic medallion necklace, tossed by krewe members

the airport, staying there will require renting a pricey car and enduring long commutes to reach the main festivities. You'll save time by staying in a more convenient neighborhood, such as the French Quarter. For a good night's sleep, stay in the CBD or Faubourg Marigny, both of which lie within walking distance of the Quarter. As an alternative, you can stay in some of the quieter inns throughout the Garden District, Uptown, and Mid-City, most of which are accessible via the streetcar lines.

Use social media. Utilize Facebook, Twitter, and other social networks for last-minute hotel deals, ride-sharing possibilities, and other ways to save time and money during peak travel weeks. The New Orleans CVB routinely posts information about upcoming events.

Beware of scams. During Mardi Gras, many residents rent out rooms and cottages. While you may find a good deal this way, make arrangements as early as possible and be aware of unscrupulous landlords.

Pick your neighborhood. If you seek debauchery, the French Quarter will not let you down. However, celebrations elsewhere in the city—notably in Uptown along the St. Charles Avenue parade route or in Metairie along Veterans Memorial Boulevard—are much more family-oriented and tend to be dominated by locals, or at least Louisianians.

Plan your transportation. During Mardi Gras, the French Quarter is closed to non-essential vehicular traffic. Hailing a cab can be difficult, so many visitors prefer getting around town via bus,

Laissez les Bon Temps Rouler!

Only a few official **Mardi Gras parades** run through the French Quarter, including the raunchy Krewe du Vieux, the wine-themed Krewe of Cork, and the dog-filled Krewe of Barkus. Most of the other parades in and around the city (including Uptown, Mid-City, Metairie, and communities on the west bank and north shore) are surprisingly family-friendly. Some have special throws, such as the hand-decorated shoes offered by the Krewe of Muses, which usually rolls on the Thursday before Mardi Gras weekend. Parade routes are listed in the *New Orleans Times-Picayune* and online (www.nola.com, www.mardigras.com, www.mardigrasday.com, www.mardigrasneworleans.com). Here are the major parades.

Endymion

The Krewe of Endymion (www.endymion.org) is the city's largest parade, a "super-krewe" that features enormous floats, magnificent court costumes, and celebrity grand marshals.

When: 4:30pm on the Saturday prior to Mardi Gras.

Where: Starts near City Park and travels down Canal Street and St. Charles Avenue, culminating with its ball in the Mercedes-Benz Superdome.

Bacchus

The Krewe of Bacchus (www.kreweofbacchus.org) is a "super-krewe" that features incredible floats and celebrity kings, from Danny Kaye to Will Ferrell. Signature floats include the Bacchasaurus, Bacchagator, and Baby Kong.

When: 5pm on the Sunday prior to Mardi Gras.

Where: From Napoleon Avenue and Tchoupitoulas Street, it rolls through Uptown on Napoleon Avenue, along St. Charles Avenue, and down Canal Street, ending at the Ernest N. Morial Convention Center.

Orpheus

Co-founded by Harry Connick Jr., the Krewe of Orpheus (www.kreweoforpheus.com) has featured a slew of celebrity monarchs, from Stevie Wonder to Anne Rice.

When: 6pm on Lundi Gras.

Where: From the corner of Napoleon Avenue and Tchoupitoulas Street, it rolls through Uptown on Napoleon Avenue, then along St. Charles Avenue, down Canal and Tchoupitoulas Streets, to the Orpheuscapade, a black-tie event at the convention center.

Zulu

The Zulu Social Aid & Pleasure Club (www.kreweofzulu.com) presents one of the season's most anticipated parades, during which spectators vie for painted coconuts, the krewe's signature throw. Zulu also hosts the Lundi Gras Festival, a free music event on the day before Fat Tuesday.

When: 8am on Mardi Gras.

Where: From the corner of Jackson and South Claiborne Avenues in Uptown, it travels along Jackson Avenue, continues north on St. Charles Avenue, follows Canal and Basin Streets, and ends at Orleans Avenue and Broad Street.

Rex

Since 1872, the king of the Krewe of Rex (www.rexorganization.com) has reigned as the king of Mardi Gras. The parade features majestic floats, masked riders, and a royal court. Mardi Gras officially ends with the Rex Ball at the Sheraton New Orleans Hotel on Canal Street.

When: 10am on Mardi Gras.

Where: The parade travels down Napoleon Avenue from the intersection with South Claiborne Avenue in Uptown, then along St. Charles Avenue and down Canal Street toward the Mississippi River.

streetcar, or foot. Some even opt to rent a bicycle (or bring their own).

Prepare for mayhem. The French Quarter might be the rowdiest neighborhood, but the less wholesome aspects of Mardi Gras, such as public nudity, drunkenness, crowds, and opportunistic crime, can occur anywhere. Travel in groups, arrange regular meeting spots with friends, avoid quiet streets at night, conceal money and valuables, and exercise caution at all times. Float riders in the major parades, like Endymion and Bacchus, tend to hurl trinkets with unnecessary force, so look out.

Stake out seats. If you want to be close to the floats, it's often necessary to arrive several hours early. For major parades, such as Endymion, many people set up blankets, chairs, and ladders the day before. (It's illegal to leave such marked areas unattended.) It's best to choose a spot near a public restroom. Consider bringing snacks, beverages, and portable chairs. Given the influx of out-of-towners, it's advisable to make restaurant reservations or dine at off-peak times.

Wear a costume. On Mardi Gras Day, you'll see costumed revelers dressed as everything from pop culture icons to political statements. Do as the locals do and wear a costume (or at least purchase a mask, available in shops throughout the Quarter). Remember to prepare for the possibility of cold, rainy weather, which is common in February and March.

Eat king cake. King cake, essentially a large cinnamon roll, is the season's most famous treat. Grab a slice at a local coffeehouse or pick up an entire cake at places like Rouses Market, Gambino's Bakery, Haydel's Bakery, Maurice French Pastries, and the seasonal Manny Randazzo King Cakes.

★ New Orleans Jazz & Heritage Festival

Established in 1970, this musical extravaganza, which takes place at Mid-City's Fair Grounds Race Course, has grown to be nearly as popular as Mardi Gras. Held on two long weekends in late April and early May, the **New Orleans Jazz & Heritage Festival** (Fair Grounds Race Course & Slots, 1751 Gentilly Blvd., 504/410-4100, www.nojazzfest.com; hours vary; adults $70-80, children 2-10 $5, free under 2), also known as Jazz Fest, features music workshops, artisanal and culinary demonstrations, Native American powwow performances, arts-and-crafts vendors, an unbelievable array of food stalls, and numerous stages that buzz with jazz, blues, zydeco, rock, gospel, and folk musicians. Among the top acts who have performed at Jazz Fest are Fats Domino, Etta James, and various members of the Marsalis and Neville clans.

The **New Orleans Jazz & Heritage Foundation** (1205 N. Rampart St., 504/558-6100, www.jazzandheritage.org), the organization behind this popular festival, also sponsors smaller food-and-music events, all of which are free to attend. Two of these events occur in the Tremé's Louis Armstrong Park: the **Congo Square New World Rhythms Festival** (mid- to late Mar.) and the **Louisiana Cajun-Zydeco Festival** (late June). The other two take place in the CBD's Lafayette Square: the **Crescent City Blues and BBQ Festival** (mid-Oct.) and the **Tremé Creole Gumbo Festival** (mid-Nov.).

French Quarter Festival

Begun in 1984 to support local musicians, the four-day **French Quarter Festival** (various locations, 504/522-5730 or 800/673-5725, http://fqfi.org/french-quarterfest; hours vary; free), which typically occurs in early or mid-April, has since evolved into Louisiana's largest free music event. The roughly 20 outdoor stages—from the Old U.S. Mint to Jackson Square to Woldenberg Riverfront Park—host local and regional jazz, gospel, funk, zydeco, classical, bluegrass, folk, and blues acts, so you likely won't see mega-stars like Sting here. Besides live music, you'll also find plenty of food for sale, including jambalaya, boiled crawfish, and sno-balls.

Other Festivals
Spring
Since 1979, the **Crescent City Classic** (Mercedes-Benz Superdome to City Park, 504/861-8686, www.ccc10k.com; free to watch, $30-50 to enter race), one of the nation's largest 10K road races, has been held in New Orleans every March or April, usually on the Saturday of Easter weekend. Roughly 20,000 people from around the globe participate. From its start at the Mercedes-Benz Superdome, the course runs through the French Quarter, then heads up Esplanade Avenue to culminate in City Park. The rollicking post-race festival, a celebration of local music and cuisine, is free for participants; all other attendees must pay a fee ($10 pp). The pre-race, two-day health and fitness expo is free.

If you're a "mudbug" lover, do yourself a favor and head to Chalmette in late March for the **Louisiana Crawfish Festival** (Frederick J. Sigur Civic Center, 8245 W. Judge Perez Dr., Chalmette, 504/278-1506, http://louisianacrawfishfestival.com; hours and costs vary). Since 1975, this popular, family-friendly event has celebrated crawfish season with live music, arts and crafts, amusement games and rides, and, of course, regional cuisine. Besides shrimp and alligator dishes, sno-balls and king cakes, and classic all-American options, the samplings encompass almost every crawfish-related meal imaginable, including crawfish étouffée over fried green tomatoes.

Typically held in late March, the **New Orleans Spring Fiesta** (various locations, 504/581-1367 or 800/550-8450, www.springfiestanola.com; $25-30 pp for home tours, $15-20 pp for walking tours) grants you the unique opportunity to step inside nearly two dozen private homes, gardens, and courtyards in the French Quarter, Garden District, and Uptown neighborhoods—an unparalleled experience that is completely worth the seemingly steep cost. For eight decades, this one-of-a-kind event has honored the city's unique history and charm by offering such eye-opening tours, plus a delightful parade of horse-drawn carriages and the presentation of the Spring Fiesta Queen and her court at Jackson Square.

Devotees of the city's most famous literary luminary rush to the Big Easy in late March or early April to attend the **Tennessee Williams/New Orleans Literary Festival** (various locations, 504/581-1144 or 800/990-3378, www.tennesseewilliams.net; hours and costs vary). For three decades, this event has celebrated the playwright who gave us such iconographic works as *A Streetcar Named Desire* and *The Glass Menagerie*. The five-day gathering is replete with writing classes helmed by experts, celebrity interviews, panel discussions, stagings of Williams's plays, fiction and poetry readings, and the endlessly entertaining Stanley and Stella Shouting Contest.

Summer
In late June and/or early July, visitors typically descend upon New Orleans for the annual **Essence Festival** (various locations, www.essence.com/festival; hours and costs vary), a four-day celebration of African American music and culture. Besides DJ parties at the Sugar Mill, the main events of this much-anticipated festival consist of concerts and comedy shows at the Mercedes-Benz Superdome and empowerment presentations at the Ernest N. Morial Convention Center. Recent headliners have included Chance the Rapper, Mary J. Blige, and John Legend.

New Orleans celebrates the legacy of one of its most famous sons in early August with **Satchmo SummerFest** (Old U.S. Mint, 400 Esplanade Ave., 504/522-5730 or 800/673-5725, http://

fqfi.org/satchmosummerfest; adults $5/ day, free under 13), a popular, three-day event that's organized by the same folks behind the equally popular French Quarter Festival. This festival, which mainly takes place on the well-mani-cured grounds of the Old U.S. Mint, includes live music by brass, swing, and early jazz bands, plus free dance lessons and an assortment of local cuisine. At other locations throughout the Quarter, you can experience seminars and exhibits about Louis "Satchmo" Armstrong and his era. During the festival, make time for the special jazz Mass at the St. Augustine Church, followed by a traditional second-line parade.

Every Labor Day weekend, the French Quarter and the Faubourg Marigny are flooded with eager participants and on-lookers of **Southern Decadence** (various locations, www.southerndecadence.com; hours and costs vary), an annual Mardi Gras-like festival that's been celebrating the city's gay lifestyle, music, and culture since 1972. Held at various gay-friendly venues, from Rawhide 2010 to Bourbon Pub & Parade, the six-day event includes dance and pool parties, beefcake contests, singles' mixers, drag shows, and a leather-gear block party. It's one of the wildest and most popular LGBT celebrations in the country.

Fall

Though relatively new on the Big Easy's foodie scene, the **Oak Street Po-Boy Festival** (Oak St. and S. Carrollton Ave., www.poboyfest.com; free) has quickly become a much-anticipated event every fall. For one day in October or November, residents and out-of-towners converge at the intersection of Oak Street and South Carrollton Avenue in Uptown's Riverbend area for this mouthwater-ing event. Besides listening to a slew of live music, attendees can peruse arts and crafts, learn about the history of the po'boy, and, of course, sample a va-riety of local cuisine from more than

40 restaurants. You'll have the chance to purchase an assortment of po'boys, including a shrimp rémoulade po'boy, which is especially tasty if served with fried green tomatoes.

Winter

The Mercedes-Benz Superdome is the site of one of the most beloved college football games, the **Allstate Sugar Bowl** (Mercedes-Benz Superdome, 1500 Sugar Bowl Dr., 504/828-2440, www.allstate-sugarbowl.org; hours and costs vary). Typically, it's played in early January be-tween two of the nation's top collegiate teams. There's usually an Allstate Fan Fest, a free music event that takes place in the parking lot beside Jax Brewery; past performers have included Blues Traveler, the Gin Blossoms, and Trombone Shorty. It's nearly impossible to find a hotel room in New Orleans when this event comes to town, so plan well ahead.

From late November through early January, City Park comes alive for **Celebration in the Oaks** (City Park, 1 Palm Dr., http://neworleanscitypark.com; $9 pp, free under 3), a fabulous holiday light show that draws more than 165,000 visitors annually. Sights include a lighted tableau inspired by the beloved children's tale *Cajun Night Before Christmas,* a 20-foot-tall poinsettia Christmas tree in the botanical garden, and the fanci-fully illumined Storyland and Carousel Gardens. You can drive through the park, walk the two-mile route, or see it via a quaint train ride ($5 pp). This magical trip through the largest live-oak forest in the world is not to be missed during the holidays.

Introduced to New Orleans during the 19th century by its many Sicilian immi-grants, **St. Joseph's Day** (various loca-tions, www.mardigrasneworleans.com/ supersunday.html; hours vary; free) is still celebrated with great ardor in the city's Italian American community. The observance of this feast on March 19 traces back to the Middle Ages, when

Halloween in the Crescent City

New Orleans is a wildly popular place for All Hallows' Eve. People venture here to visit the many voodoo shops and cemeteries, take a haunted walking tour of the French Quarter, and mingle with hordes of costumed revelers along Bourbon and Frenchmen Streets. Locals and visitors alike flock to seasonal attractions like **The Mortuary Haunted House** (www.themortuary.net), set inside a former mortuary that's supposedly haunted.

Many horror aficionados also appreciate the city's longtime vampire connection. The principal setting for Anne Rice's famous novel *Interview with the Vampire,* New Orleans is home to two annual vampire balls: the **New Orleans Vampire Ball,** sponsored by Anne Rice's Vampire Lestat Fan Club (www.arvlfc.com), and the **Endless Night Vampire Ball** (www.endlessnight.com). Vampire tours, which are available through **Haunted History Tours** (www.hauntedhistorytours.com) and **Bloody Mary's New Orleans Tours** (www.bloodymarystours.com), are also popular.

For less bloodthirsty revelry, purchase a ticket to the **New Orleans Witches' Ball,** hosted by the **New Orleans Black Hat Society** (www.nobhs.org), or take a walking ghost tour through **Historic New Orleans Tours** (www.tourneworleans.com) or **Spirit Tours New Orleans** (www.spirittoursneworleans.com).

In a town known for gay-friendly bashes, it's no surprise that there's also a gay-friendly Halloween celebration. Simply known as **Halloween in New Orleans** (www.gayhalloween.com), this weekend-long bash has evolved from a small gathering in 1984 into one of the biggest gay-and-lesbian parties in the country. If you're looking for well-dressed drag queens, this is definitely the time to visit the Big Easy.

New Orleans also hosts family-friendly events like Audubon Zoo's **Boo at the Zoo** (http://audubonnatureinstitute.org/batz), which usually occurs during the last two weekends of October and features trick-or-treat fun, a ghost train, and a haunted house. On Halloween itself, Molly's at the Market presents **Jim Monaghan's Halloween Parade** (www.mollysatthemarket.net/halloween), a spirited procession through the French Quarter. Since 2007, the **Krewe of Boo!** (www.kreweofboo.com) has been the city's official Halloween parade, typically entailing a downtown procession of colorful, mildly scary floats created by Kern Studios.

New Orleans is predominantly Catholic, which means that **All Saints' Day** (Nov. 1) and **All Souls' Day** (Nov. 2) are important holidays—a time when many residents make a point of visiting their loved ones at cemeteries. Simultaneously, lots of locals celebrate the Mexican holiday of **Día de los Muertos** by dressing in black, painting skulls on their faces, and congregating in front of the St. Louis Cathedral—truly a sight to behold.

people built altars to St. Joseph, who they believed had answered their prayers and delivered them from famine. Modern participants continue to celebrate by constructing elaborate and riotously colorful altars in their homes and churches. Besides a public parade in the French Quarter, smaller celebrations take place in private homes; signs welcome friends and strangers alike to view family altars and enjoy cakes and breads. Oddly enough, the Italian holiday has also become significant for the city's Mardi Gras Indians, an African American troupe of Carnival revelers who usually host a vibrant parade on **Super Sunday,** the Sunday preceding or following St. Joseph's Day.

Shopping

In New Orleans, shopping opportunities embrace the most popular aspects of the city's heritage—its cuisine, music, art, literature, and historical preservation.

The most interesting shops and boutiques lie in the French Quarter, Arts District, and Uptown neighborhoods. The French Quarter is rife with praline shops, and visitors rarely leave without strolling through the varied food stalls of the historic French Market. Art and antiques hounds can browse the emporiums along Royal and Chartres Streets, which carry some of the most lavish and expensive furnishings in the South, while the Garden District stretch of Magazine Street is considered a less pricey yet still ample source of art, antiques, jewelry, and vintage clothing.

New Orleans is an easygoing town, with a flexible sense of time. When it comes to shops, that means that posted hours aren't always strictly enforced. Hours can also change from season to season; in the summer, when the weather is unbearable and tourism slows, shops tend to close earlier.

Shopping Districts

Known for upscale antiques and first-rate art galleries, **Royal Street** is the most exclusive address for shopping in the French Quarter, though parallel **Chartres Street** has similarly high-end emporiums. In the **Lower Quarter,** from Jackson Square to Esplanade Avenue, you'll find funkier, more youthful boutiques, such as mod clothiers and edgy galleries. **Decatur Street,** meanwhile, is a good place to find cheesy T-shirts, Tabasco sauce, crawfish-embroidered items, souvenir "go-cups," as well as gifts, toys, and novelties that emphasize the off-color humor and irreverent aspects of this festive town. Decatur is also sandwiched by two shopping malls: the **French Market,** which contains retail shops, food stalls, and a flea market, and **The Shops at Canal Place,** a more upscale offering beside Canal Street.

Magazine Street, which follows the curve of the Mississippi River for about six miles from the CBD to Audubon Park, offers an astonishing variety of shops and boutiques. Sassy secondhand clothiers, colorful oyster bars, jamming music clubs, convivial java joints, and historic homes line the way, but it's the lower stretch of Magazine—from about Canal Street to Jackson Avenue—that possesses the city's most fascinating antiques district. While you'll spot a few chain stores, the neighborhood maintains its independent, offbeat vibe. Uptown also boasts the **Riverbend** area, which features several curious shops around the intersection of St. Charles and Carrollton Avenues.

French Quarter
Antiques and Vintage

Established in 1898, **James H. Cohen & Sons, Inc.** (437 Royal St., 504/522-3305 or 800/535-1853, http://shop.cohenantiques.com; 9:30am-5pm Mon.-Sat.) is the oldest and largest coin store in the city. Known for its vast, rather expensive selection of ancient coins, Western-style rifles and revolvers, and other authentic artifacts, from poker chips to iron shackles, it's understandably a popular place to browse.

Since 1899, when it was established by Hermina Keil, **Keil's Antiques** (325 Royal St., 504/522-4552, www.keilsantiques.com; 9am-5pm Mon.-Sat.) has been specializing in 18th- and 19th-century antiques from France and England. The inventory includes everything from marble mantels to magnificent crystal chandeliers to garnet chokers. The Keil family operates two other well-respected stores in the Quarter, **Moss Antiques** (411 Royal St., 605/522-3981, www.mossantiques.com, 9am-5pm Mon.-Sat.) and **Royal Antiques** (309 Royal St., 504/524-7033, http://royalantiques.com, 9am-5pm Mon.-Sat.), but Keil's has the most enticing window displays, especially at Christmastime.

Occupying a 19th-century building near Jackson Square, charming **Lucullus** (610 Chartres St., 504/528-9620, http://lucullusantiques.com; 9am-5pm Mon.-Sat.) appeals to gourmet cooks, wine connoisseurs, and avid entertainers—not surprising given that it's run by Patrick Dunne, author of *The Epicurean Collector: Exploring the World of Culinary Antiques.* You'll find a wide assortment of culinary treasures, including bronze mortars, English basaltware teapots, and Italian lace tablecloths. The store also offers decorative items like candlesticks, chandeliers, and framed still lifes.

A family-owned, French Quarter landmark since Max Rau opened its doors in 1912, **M.S. Rau Antiques** (630 Royal St., 888/711-8084, www.rauantiques.com; 9am-5:15pm Mon.-Sat.) is one of the oldest antiques shops in New Orleans. Today, the 30,000-square-foot showroom houses a stupendous collection of 19th-century paintings and sculptures, exquisite clocks and music boxes, and striking bedroom and dining sets. If you're looking for a special piece of jewelry, you might find it here as well; precious items range from Colombian emerald rings to Cartier diamond necklaces and Tiffany & Co. bangle bracelets.

At **Vintage 329** (329 Royal St., 504/525-2262, www.vintage329.com; 10am-5:30pm daily), you might find signed Hemingway novels, an autographed Aerosmith guitar, or an oversized golf ball bearing the signatures of Rodney Dangerfield, Bill Murray, Chevy Chase, Ted Knight, and Michael O'Keefe—the principal cast members of *Caddyshack.* In addition to signed first editions, music memorabilia, and vintage movie posters, you'll spy old maps, swords, and sports-related items, including football helmets signed by entire NFL teams. Vintage 329 is truly an oasis for history buffs, especially those with deep pockets.

Arts and Crafts
Literally across the street from the French Market, the somewhat cluttered **Artist's Market & Bead Shop** (85 French Market Pl., 504/561-0046, www.artistsmarket-nola.com; 10am-6pm daily) is filled with paintings, photographs, pottery, textiles, woodwork, and hand-blown glass from more than 75 local and regional artists and artisans, plus curious gifts and decorative items, such as snow globes and red velvet Carnival masks. Beading enthusiasts will find a large selection of glass and sterling silver beads, semiprecious stones, and beading tools. Newbies can even take a jewelry-making class. The shop has two entrances; the second one is at 1228 Decatur Street.

A half block from Jackson Square, charming **Maskarade** (630 St. Ann St., 504/568-1018, www.themaskstore.com; 10am-5pm daily) presents a wide assortment of masks, crafted by artists from New Orleans and elsewhere around the country. You'll spy feathery Carnival masks, golden Venetian-style masks, and black leather masks, as well as masks that resemble creatures like ladybugs, leopards, and dragons. If, despite such a selection, you don't spot what you like, an artist can customize a mask for you—just in time for Mardi Gras, Halloween, or any other occasion.

The mission of **RHINO Contemporary Crafts Co.** (The Shops at Canal Place, 333 Canal St., 2nd fl., 504/523-7945, www.rhinocrafts.com; 10am-7pm Mon.-Sat., noon-6pm Sun.) is to promote and sell the handcrafted ceramics, jewelry, furniture, accessories, and decorative arts of local talents. RHINO stands for Right Here in New Orleans, which is where all the goods were created.

Books and Music
On the relatively quiet block behind the St. Louis Cathedral, **Arcadian Books & Art Prints** (714 Orleans St., 504/523-4138; 9:30am-5:30am daily) is the quintessential well-used bookstore, filled with cramped, musty pathways and stacks upon stacks of new and secondhand volumes, some stretching close to the high ceiling. Owned and operated by one of the friendliest, most helpful, and most knowledgeable proprietors in the French Quarter, this shop particularly appeals

to locals and visitors in search of French books as well as titles related to New Orleans and Louisiana. Vintage postcards and art prints are also available.

Crescent City Books (230 Chartres St., 504/524-4997 or 800/546-4013, www.crescentcitybooks.com; 10am-7pm Mon.-Sat., 10am-5pm Sun.) contains two floors of out-of-print and antiquarian titles, plus antique maps and prints. Open since 1992, it's always been an exceptional source for local history and literature, scholarly books, and hard-to-find titles on philosophy, ancient history, and literary criticism—a real book lover's bookstore.

Hidden in the alley between the Cabildo and the St. Louis Cathedral, the small **Faulkner House Books** (624 Pirate's Alley, 504/524-2940; http://faulknerhousebooks.com, 10am-6pm daily) occupies the same space that novelist William Faulkner inhabited in 1925, when he first arrived in New Orleans as a young poet. It was here, in fact, that he wrote *Soldiers' Pay*. Operated by a knowledgeable staff, frequented by writers and collectors alike, and closed only on Mardi Gras Day, this charming place sells new and used books, including rare first editions, titles about Southern Americana, and literature by Faulkner, Tennessee Williams, and Walker Percy.

Peaches Records (4318 Magazine St., 504/282-3322, www.peachesrecordsandtapes.com; 10am-7pm daily) features a slew of local tunes, from traditional jazz standards by Louis Armstrong and Jelly Roll Morton to modern funk by the Meters and the Neville Brothers—plus blues, rap, and zydeco. Ernie K-Doe, Rockin' Dopsie, and the Dukes of Dixieland are just some of the local performers represented. Beyond music, there's a small selection of local books, such as travel guides, historical nonfiction, and Cajun children's tales.

Clothing and Shoes
Although the local Trashy Diva chain

seems to have cornered the vintage-inspired clothing market for women, you can never have too many places to buy retro dresses, shoes, and accessories reminiscent of the early- to mid-20th century. Boasting two carefully decorated store windows that entice customers with their bold patterns, curvy bodices, and flared skirts, **Dollz & Dames** (216 Decatur St., 504/522-5472, http://dollzanddames.com; noon-6pm daily) has quickly become a welcome find for women of all shapes and sizes.

The striking window displays of the elegant **Fleur de Paris** (523 Royal St., 504/525-1899 or 800/229-1899, www.fdphats.comt; 10am-6pm daily) tempt visitors to linger for just a moment. Beyond the lovely, Parisian-style facade, this classic, well-renowned millinery, which opened in 1980, specializes in customized hats for various occasions, whether an afternoon tea or a Mardi Gras gala. Additionally, you'll find elegant evening gowns, antique jewelry, and, not surprisingly, classy lingerie.

Not far from historic Jackson Square, **Trashy Diva Clothing Boutique** (537 Royal St., 504/522-4233, www.trashydiva.com; 11am-7pm Sun.-Fri., 10am-7pm Sat.) specializes in vintage-style dresses that suit a wide array of female shapes and sizes. Stop by the sister stores, which offer more dresses (2048 Magazine St.) as well as corsets and lingerie (712 Royal St. and 2044 Magazine St.) and old-fashioned shoes (2050 Magazine St.)—all of which can make for a killer retro look, though not a bargain purchase.

Furniture and Home Decor
While strolling through the French Quarter, it's hard to miss the old-fashioned gas and electric lights posted along the sidewalks, hanging beneath the galleries, and mounted beside many doorways. If you're eager to possess this atmospheric aspect of New Orleans, then stop by **Bevolo Gas & Electric Lights** (318 Royal St., 504/522-9485, www.bevolo.

com; 9am-5:30pm Mon.-Wed., 9am-7pm Thurs.-Sat., 10am-4pm Sun.). Open since 1945, this spacious showroom features an eye-pleasing variety of copper light fixtures. Bevolo has an extensive collection of antiques and reproduction pieces, including alabaster mirrors, sugar kettles, and iron chandeliers. Handmade Christmas ornaments and copper office accessories are also available. Bevolo has a second, smaller location (521 Conti St., 504/522-9485, 8am-5pm Mon.-Fri., 9am-4pm Sat.).

The small, ever-fascinating **Java House Imports** (523 Dumaine St., 504/581-1288, www.javahouseimports.com; 10am-5pm daily) presents an intriguing collection of imported wares. The walls are covered with elongated African masks, the shelves are teeming with misshapen wooden bowls and Buddha figurines, and you'll see a wide array of colorful tunics from foreign lands. If you're looking for statues of Hindu deities, kites shaped as dragons, and intricately carved faces that might frighten small children at night, then Java House Imports is definitely the place for you.

Queork (838 Chartres St., 504/481-2585, www.queork.com, 10am-6pm daily) features all sorts of high-end accessories made from cork fabric: shoes, handbags, dog collars, glasses cases, wallets, hats, and more. The cork wears like leather (develops a patina over time), but it is stylish and vegan. Queork has two other stores—in New Mexico and Florida—but is headquartered in New Orleans, and many of the products are made locally.

Gifts and Souvenirs

If you need a late-night cigarette fix, you can always stop by Mary Jane's Emporium in the 1200 block of Decatur, but for something more distinctive, venture to the **Cigar Factory New Orleans** (415 Decatur St., 504/568-1003 or 800/550-0775, www.cigarfactoryneworleans.com; 10am-10pm Sun.-Thurs., 10am-11pm Fri.-Sat.), where you can actually watch cigars being rolled. Besides various tables for enjoying a smoking break, cigar lovers will appreciate the wide selection, walk-in humidor, and knowledgeable staff. There are two smaller Cigar Factory branches on Bourbon Street and Decatur Street.

On the first floor of one of the most photographed buildings in the entire French Quarter, gift shop **Forever New Orleans** (700 Royal St., 504/586-3536; 9am-10pm daily) gets quite a lot of foot traffic. It doesn't hurt that it's halfway between Jackson Square and Bourbon Street. You'll be lured inside by the plethora of fleur-de-lis souvenirs, from jewelry sets to stationery to glassware. The inventory seems to change often, so it's easy to find a new trinket that you never noticed before. Forever New Orleans is especially popular with tourists, so much so that there are now four other locations in the French Quarter.

Owned by a local named Ken Ford, the **Idea Factory** (924 Royal St., 800/524-4332, http://ideafactoryneworleans.com; 10am-6pm Mon. and Wed.-Sat., 10am-5pm Sun.) is a local favorite. This cozy place contains a treasure-trove of handcrafted wooden objects, including clocks, mechanical toys, and chessboards. This fascinating place sells marvelous gifts, from gorgeous clipboards and odd-looking back massagers to curious puzzle boxes and ingenious cooking utensils.

As the name indicates, the small, elegant **Papier Plume** (842 Royal St., 504/988-7265, www.papierplume.com; 10am-6pm daily) offers a plethora of high-end writing supplies and utensils, neatly arranged throughout the well-lit space. Amid the stylish pens, dipping feather quills, brass seals and wax sticks, and leather-bound journals, you might find something to appeal to that special writer in your life.

Unlike most tourist-focused shops, **Roux Royale** (600 Royal St., 504/565-5272 or 855/344-7700, http://shoprouxroyale.com; 9am-10pm daily) has a definitive purpose: to celebrate the unique cuisine of New Orleans. From colorful aprons and fleur-de-lis glassware to fabulous local cookbooks and Tabasco products, you'll find almost everything you need to bring the taste of the Big Easy home with you—even boxed pralines. If you can't find the right cookbook here, try **Kitchen Witch** (1452 N. Broad St., 504/528-8382, www.kwcookbooks.com), a bookstore that specializes in rare secondhand cookbooks, including those that pertain to Cajun, Creole, and Louisiana cuisine.

Gourmet Treats

For specialty food items, there's no place quite like the **Central Grocery** (923 Decatur St., 504/523-1620; 9am-5pm daily) on bustling Decatur. Famous for its oversized muffulettas—and the orderly, strictly enforced line that's required to purchase them—this often-crowded grocery stocks all manner of gourmet goodies and seasonings, from olive salad to Italian cookies to Zatarain's crawfish boil.

Not surprisingly, the French Market boasts more than one praline vendor. A few doors down from **Aunt Sally's Creole Pralines** (810 Decatur St., 800/642-7257, http://auntsallys.com; 8am-8pm daily), you'll encounter one of the city's oldest such stores. For more than a century, **Evans Creole Candy Factory** (848 Decatur St., 504/522-7111; 10am-6pm Mon.-Thurs., 10am-7pm Fri.-Sun.) has been crafting delicious pralines. Still today, you can watch the candy-makers working on a fresh batch of pralines through the big windows of this shop, which is also an excellent source for hand-dipped chocolates, dark-chocolate turtles (Creole pecans topped with caramel and dipped in chocolate), and chocolate-covered maraschino cherries.

Southern Candymakers (334 Decatur St., 504/523-5544, www.southerncandymakers.com; 9am-7pm daily) stands out among the French Quarter's longstanding praline shops. A couple blocks from Canal Street, this is a full retail shop with pralines, toffees, nut clusters, chocolate alligators, marzipan, peanut brittle, and fudge. If you find yourself closer to Esplanade, stop by the Quarter's other location in the French Market (1010 Decatur St., 504/525-6170, 9am-6pm daily).

Health and Beauty

For more than 160 years, the aromatic **Bourbon French Parfums** (805 Royal St., 504/522-4480, www.neworleansperfume.com; 10am-5pm daily) has been creating custom-blended fragrances. Schedule a one-hour private sitting with a specialist who will analyze your body chemistry, assess your personality, and record your preferred scents. Once your "secret" formula is created, you can order an entire set of toiletries, including perfume, lotion, and foaming bath gel. If you lack the time or patience, you can just as easily choose from the perfumes, musk oils, and voodoo potions available onsite. Also on display are elegant perfume bottles, decorated with everything from frogs to fleurs-de-lis.

Jewelry and Accessories

Whether you have a Halloween parade, Mardi Gras party, or special occasion in your future, outrageous **Fifi Mahony's** (934 Royal St., 504/525-4343; noon-6pm Sun.-Wed., 11am-7pm Thurs.-Sat.) is your one-stop salon and makeup counter if you're hoping to make a bold statement. Pop in and browse the wigs that come in every color of the rainbow, Tony and Tina cosmetics, and offbeat handbags.

A French Quarter fixture since 1938, **New Orleans Silversmiths** (600 Chartres St., 504/522-8333 or 800/219-8333, www.neworleanssilversmiths.com; 10am-5pm Mon.-Sat., 11am-4pm Sun.) specializes in modern gold jewelry, estate jewelry, and antique silver holloware. You'll also find decanters, candlesticks and candelabra, and handcrafted, sterling silver animal figurines. For a taste of New Orleans, the

Voodoo vs. Hoodoo

Given the Big Easy's historical ties to the voodoo religion, it surely comes as no surprise that the city is still home to several voodoo practitioners. So, whether you're seriously interested in the faith or just curious about this often misunderstood aspect of New Orleans's culture, you'll find several voodoo-related shops in town, most of which provide everything from gris-gris bags to potion oils to handmade African crafts, not to mention rituals and readings. In the French Quarter, such emporiums include **Voodoo Authentica, Reverend Zombie's House of Voodoo,** and **Marie Laveau's House of Voodoo.**

If you've seen *The Skeleton Key* (2005), you might be aware that some southern Louisianians also practice hoodoo. So, what, you might wonder, is the difference between voodoo and hoodoo? Well, depending on who you ask, that can be a rather complicated question.

The voodoo of New Orleans is similar to that of Haiti, Cuba, and other Caribbean islands, where the ancient West African religion of Vodoun has been heavily influenced by Catholicism. Hoodoo, by contrast, is not a religion, but a folk magic that blends the practices of various cultures, from African and Native American traditions to European grimoires. Often referring to magic spells, potions, and charms that include conjuration, witchcraft, rootwork, and Biblical recitation, hoodoo supposedly enables people to access supernatural forces in order to improve aspects of their daily lives, including love, luck, health, wealth, and employment. Naturally, some people also use hoodoo for more nefarious reasons, such as revenge on those who have "crossed" them. No matter what your intentions, though, as with other magico-religious traditions, hoodoo often involves the utilization of herbs, roots, minerals, animal bones, candles, bodily fluids, and an individual's possessions.

In truth, many modern-day voodoo followers integrate hoodoo folk magic into the practice of their religion. For more information about both traditions, consult Jim Haskins's *Voodoo & Hoodoo: Their Tradition and Craft as Revealed by Actual Practitioners* (New York: Original Publications, 1978), Stephanie Rose Bird's *Sticks, Stones, Roots & Bones: Hoodoo, Mojo & Conjuring with Herbs* (St. Paul: Llewellyn Publications, 2004), and Denise Alvarado's *The Voodoo Hoodoo Spellbook* (San Francisco: Red Wheel/Weiser, LLC, 2011).

shop even offers café au lait sets as well as fleur-de-lis jewelry and cuff links.

Occult and Voodoo

Besides offering more than 100 varieties of fine tea, the cozy **Bottom of the Cup Tea Room** (327 Chartres St., 800/729-7148, www.bottomofthecup.com; 10am-6pm daily) has been giving authentic psychic readings since 1929. In fact, the name of the store is derived from its early days, when the resident psychic would read the tea leaves left at the bottom of a customer's cup. This is also a good spot for tarot cards and metaphysical gifts like crystals, amulets, and wands.

In a city obsessed with vampire lore and Anne Rice's legacy, it's hard to believe that there aren't more vampire shops. The only one that comes to mind is **Boutique du Vampyre** (709 1/2 St. Ann St., 504/561-8267, www.feelthebite.com; 10am-9pm daily). In this cozy spot between Bourbon and Royal Streets, you'll find plenty of vampire accoutrements, from sexy capes and old-fashioned hats to customizable fangs and temporary bite tattoos. The proprietors, Marita and Steve, stock candles, books, soap, tarot cards, wine-related paraphernalia, and Gothic jewelry.

Amid the inebriated tourists on Bourbon Street lies **Marie Laveau's House of Voodoo** (739 Bourbon St.,

Farmers Markets

Farmers markets have been a part of life in New Orleans since the French and Spanish governments ruled the city in the 18th century, and they remain just as vibrant to this day. In fact, the recently renovated farmers market in the historic **French Market** is perhaps the most famous place in the city to procure gourmet edibles. Here, you'll find pralines and baked goods, fresh seafood and produce, Cajun spices and cooking kits, plus an array of freshly prepared foods, from gumbo and boudin to smoothies and sno-balls.

If you love browsing market-fresh food, also consider the **Crescent City Farmers Market** (504/861-4488, www.crescentcityfarmersmarket.org), held four times a week at different locations around town and featuring a phenomenal roster of vendors and chefs. Throughout the year, you'll spy pastries, Creole cream cheese, tamales, alligator sausage, Cornish hens, and freshly cut flowers. Depending on the month, you might also see fresh shrimp, soft-shell crabs, kumquats, and figs. It's held in Uptown on Tuesday (200 Broadway St.; 9am-1pm), in the French Market on Wednesday (1235 N. Peters St.; 2pm-6pm), in Mid-City on Thursday (3700 Orleans Ave.; 3pm-7pm), and in the Arts District on Saturday (750 Carondelet St. at Julia St.; 8am-11am). Vendors accept only cash and market tokens, a special currency that comes in $1 and $5 increments, never expires, and can be purchased in the Welcome Tent via credit card.

504/581-3751, http://voodooneworleans.com; 10am-11:30pm Sun.-Thurs., 10am-1:30am Fri.-Sat.), a small, often crowded space filled with incense, voodoo literature, symbolic pendants and figurines, locally crafted voodoo dolls, and souvenir posters and T-shirts. Opposite the register, you'll spy a cluttered, hands-off voodoo altar, while in the rear room, you can experience private tarot-card readings (noon-close daily). The folks behind Marie Laveau's also operate **Reverend Zombie's House of Voodoo** (723 St. Peter St., 504/486-6366, 10am-11:30pm Sun.-Thurs., 10am-1:30am Fri.-Sat.), which offers many of the same items and services, plus a wide array of cigars. Photos aren't allowed in either store.

Owned and operated by voodoo practitioners since 1996, **Voodoo Authentica** (612 Dumaine St., 504/522-2111, www.voodooshop.com; 11am-7pm daily) carries the typical French Quarter voodoo shop items: incense, potions, gris-gris bags, ritual kits, handmade voodoo dolls, Haitian crafts, helpful books and DVDs, and unusual jewelry, such as necklaces made of alligator claws and teeth. Besides offering spiritual consultations, this unique cultural center presents **Voodoofest,** a free annual festival that occurs on Halloween and celebrates the voodoo religion's influence on New Orleans traditions through educational presentations, book signings, and an ancestral healing ritual.

Shopping Centers and Malls

Not far from Jackson Square lies the **French Market** (Decatur St. and N. Peters St. btwn. St. Peter St. and Barracks St., 504/636-6400, www.frenchmarket.org; 10am-6pm daily, hours vary depending on the business), a picturesque, multi-block collection of shops, eateries, and stalls that partially date to 1813. Besides **Café Du Monde** (800 Decatur St., 504/525-4544, www.cafedumonde.com; 24 hours daily) and other eateries, the market houses retail shops that sell everything from toys, souvenirs, and candies to African oils, Latin American hammocks, and local artwork. One of the highlights is the open-air pavilion at the eastern end. It features a small **farmers market** offering bottled hot sauce, Cajun spices, homemade pralines, fresh seafood and produce, sandwiches, sno-balls, and other local vittles, plus a collection of locally made arts and crafts. There's also a daily **flea market,** which presents a wide array of jewelry, dresses, cookbooks, and African masks. Though it's rather crowded on the weekends, nothing here costs much.

Along the southwestern edge of the French Quarter, the massive **Shops at Canal Place** (333 Canal St., 504/522-9200, www.theshopsatcanalplace.com; 10am-7pm Mon.-Fri., 10am-8pm Sat., noon-6pm Sun.) is the fanciest full-scale mall in the immediate downtown area, with branches of such acclaimed emporia as Saks Fifth Avenue, Brooks Brothers, and Anthropologie. Other fine shops include Jeantherapy, known for upscale denim; local jeweler Mignon Faget; and Wehmeiers, purveyor of alligator boots and ostrich handbags. There's also a small food court, a Westin hotel that features amazing river views, and a movie theater that serves gourmet meals along with independent films and blockbusters.

Faubourg Marigny and Bywater
Arts and Crafts
Artists in need of supplies will surely find what they're looking for in the Bywater at the well-regarded **New Orleans Art Supply** (3041 N. Rampart St., 504/949-1525, http://nolabarkmarket.com; 9am-7pm Mon.-Fri., 9am-5pm Sat., 10am-5pm Sun.), part of the New Orleans Conservation Guild. In addition to art books and magazines, you'll find a sizable selection of high-quality supplies for glassblowers, printmakers, painters, ceramic artisans, and sketch artists.

Books and Music
Located at the corner of Chartres and Frenchmen Streets in the heart of the Marigny's famous music scene, the cramped, no-frills **Faubourg Marigny Art Books Music** (600 Frenchmen St.,

504/947-3700, www.fabonfrenchmen.com; noon-10pm daily) is often still open when the bands are starting to play. Somehow fitting with its authentic environs, this eclectic secondhand store is rife with curious choices, including New Orleans cookbooks, local short-story collections, and vintage gay adult publications.

The **Louisiana Music Factory** (Frenchmen St., 504/586-1094, www.louisianamusicfactory.com; 11am-8pm Sun.-Thurs., 11am-10pm Fri.-Sat.) isn't far from the famous music clubs of Frenchmen Street. This noted music shop offers a great selection of local and regional blues, jazz, funk, R&B, gospel, Cajun and zydeco, reggae, swamp pop, rock, and hip-hop. This is an especially great place if you're looking for Mardi Gras music, performers of which range from brass bands to Mardi Gras Indians to the Neville Brothers. You'll find both used and new CDs, plus vinyl records, books, DVDs, videos, and T-shirts.

Gifts and Souvenirs
Run by longtime voodoo practitioner Sallie Ann Glassman, the spiritual supply shop **Island of Salvation Botanica** (2372 St. Claude Ave., Ste. 100, 504/948-9961, http://islandofsalvationbotanica.com; 10am-5pm Tues.-Sat.) is a good place to find herbs, oils, specialty candles, Haitian artwork, decorated spirit boxes, and dashboard statues. You can even purchase custom-made gris-gris bags, made with various herbs, stones, and other materials—including a clipping of your own hair or nails. Housed within a ramshackle building along the edge of the Faubourg Marigny (admittedly, not the best part of town), the Island of Salvation Botanica also provides readings and healings.

Jewelry and Accessories
A top pick among locals, the popular **Electric Ladyland Tattoo** (610 Frenchmen St., 504/947-8286, http://

electricladylandtattoo.com; noon-midnight Mon.-Sat., noon-10pm Sun.) is nestled among some of the city's best live music joints in the Marigny. Besides state-certified tattoo artists, who are capable of inking everything from vampires to Celtic crosses to New Orleans-style fleurs-de-lis, you'll find a resident piercer on-site. Bear in mind that this is a cash-only shop.

Central Business and Arts Districts
Clothing and Shoes
If you need a men's jacket for your dinner at Galatoire's, consider **Rubensteins** (102 St. Charles Ave., 504/581-6666, http://rubensteinsneworleans.com; 10am-5:45pm Mon.-Thurs., 10am-6pm Fri.-Sat.), a classic, family-owned outfitter carrying such exclusive lines as Hugo Boss, Ralph Lauren, and Brioni. Situated in the CBD since 1924, this well-respected emporium is one of the finest men's specialty stores in the country, featuring suits, sweaters, jeans, and fine footwear. Special services include complimentary valet parking, expert alterations, and personal shoppers.

Health and Beauty
Quirky **Aidan Gill for Men** (550 Fulton St., 504/566-4903, http://aidangillformen.com; 10am-6pm Mon.-Wed. and Fri.-Sun., 10am-7pm Thurs.) entices its loyal male customers—as well as tentative first-timers—with old-fashioned shaving instruments, upscale bath products, and well-made neckties and cuff links. Many come to experience "The Shave at the End of the Galaxy," a luxurious hot-towel shave in the back room. There's also a location in Uptown (2026 Magazine St., 504/587-9090, 10am-6pm Mon.-Fri., 9am-5pm Sat., noon-6pm Sun.).

Jewelry and Accessories
Among New Orleans's many enticing jewelry shops, **Adler's** (722 Canal St., 504/523-5292 or 800/925-7912, www.

adlersjewelry.com; 10am-5:30pm Mon.-Sat.) has the most loyal following—it's been serving the Crescent City since 1898. Fine watches and bracelets, engagement rings and wedding bands, and crystal stemware are among the offerings. Adler's is also affiliated with the longstanding **Waldhorn & Adler** antiques shop (343 Royal St., 504/581-6379, www.waldhornadlers.com, 10am-5pm Tues.-Sat.).

Established by Sam H. Meyer in 1894 as Meyer's Hat Box, the family-run **Meyer the Hatter** (120 St. Charles Ave., 504/525-1048 or 800/882-4287, http://meyerthehatter.com; 10am-5:45pm Mon.-Sat.) boasts the South's largest collection of headwear, from stylish Stetsons and satin top hats to jazz band caps and black-and-gold Saints visors.

Markets
It's very fun—and very NOLA—to shop for art late at night. The **Frenchmen Art Market** (619 Frenchmen St., 504/941-1149, http://frenchmenartmarket.com; 7pm-1am Mon. and Thurs.-Sat., 6pm-midnight Sun.) is a hub of activity after the sun goes down, with local artists showing off jewelry, paintings, textiles, and more. Twinkling lights transform the empty lot into an outdoor gallery space. Remember to be aware of your surroundings as you walk back to the hotel with your purchases after midnight.

Shopping Centers and Malls
While **The Outlet Collection at Riverwalk** (500 Port of New Orleans Pl., 504/522-1555, www.riverwalkneworleans.com; 10am-9pm Mon.-Sat., noon-7pm Sun.) resembles many other midsize shopping malls, it's notable for its sweeping views of the adjacent Mississippi River. This lengthy, serpentine building has nearly 75 shops, some of which proffer local goods, souvenirs, and crafts, such as a Cajun-themed apparel store, a mask shop, and a hot sauce emporium. You'll also find a small food court, several

sit-down restaurants, and concierge desks for booking area tours.

Garden District
Health and Beauty

Hip celebs often call at **Belladonna Day Spa** (2900 Magazine St., 504/891-4393, http://belladonnadayspa.com; 9am-6pm Mon.-Tues. and Fri.-Sat., 9am-8pm Wed.-Thurs., noon-5pm Sun.), an airy, modern bath-and-body shop that's also a top-notch unisex spa. Set inside a Victorian house, the interior treatment rooms are soothing and minimalist, with a Japanese ambience. Detoxifying seaweed body treatments, therapeutic massages, and replenishing facials are among the most popular services, though you'll also have the option of various manicures, pedicures, and body buffs. This tranquil spa also offers an assortment of spa products and fine linens. And don't forget about the **Belladoggie Resort Spa** (815 Washington Ave., 504/309-9510, www.belladoggie.com; 7am-7pm Mon.-Sat., 10am-5pm Sun.), where your beloved pets can be pampered, too.

Uptown
Books and Music

Within easy driving distance of Audubon Park and Tulane University, and only a couple blocks south of Magazine Street, **Octavia Books** (513 Octavia St., 504/899-7323, www.octaviabooks.com; 10am-6pm Mon.-Sat., 10am-5pm Sun.) is especially popular among local residents and college students. Besides offering biographies, memoirs, and fiction, the store features plenty of local travel guides and cookbooks, as well as books about New Orleans's unique history, art, and celebrations.

Jewelry and Accessories

Mignon Faget (3801 Magazine St., 509/891-2005 or 800/375-7557, www.

Top to bottom: French Market; Octavia Books; Rouler.

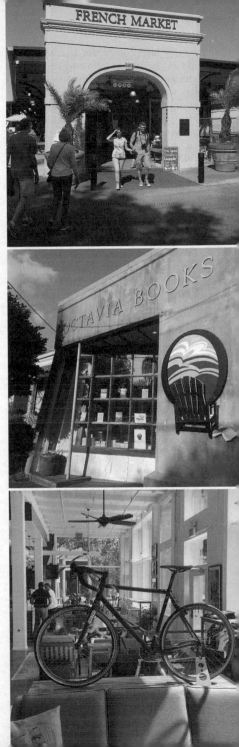

mignonfaget.com; 10am-6pm Mon.-Sat.) has an almost cult following among New Orleans's devotees of fine jewelry. Faget has won countless awards for her creations, many of which incorporate icons and images familiar to Louisianians, such as oyster earrings, red-bean charm necklaces, and fleur-de-lis cuff links. You'll find other locations inside The Shops at Canal Place and the Lakeside Shopping Center.

Tremé and Mid-City
Furniture and Home Decor

Just south of City Park, **Ricca's Demolishing Corp.** (511 N. Solomon St., 504/488-5524, http://riccasarchitectural. com; 9am-5pm Tues.-Fri., 9am-4pm Sat.) is one of several wrecking companies in New Orleans that have seen a huge boom in business as a result of Hurricane Katrina. Since Peter A. Ricca opened it in 1956, this 50,000-square-foot emporium has been a source of new and used building materials, including mahogany doors, fountains, and hitching posts, and all sorts of vintage brackets and hardware. Some materials have been salvaged from historic New Orleans homes. Ricca's provides custom woodwork fashioned from reclaimed cypress and pine.

Sports and Recreation

Parks and Plazas

South of Poydras Street lies the attractive **Lafayette Square** (St. Charles Ave. and Camp St., www.lafayette-square.org; 24 hours daily; free), which was laid out in the late 18th century as the American Quarter's version of the Place d'Armes (now Jackson Square). Bound by St. Charles Avenue, Camp Street, and North and South Maestri Places, it is named in honor of the Marquis de Lafayette, who visited the city in 1825. With its ample park-bench seating, the shaded, landscaped park—one of the CBD's few patches of greenery—continues to be a pleasant place to relax, read a newspaper, or listen to live music. In fact, you can catch free concerts by some of the city's top bands and musicians every Wednesday 5pm-8pm, from mid-March to late May. Known as the **YLC Wednesday at the Square** (504/585-1500, http://wednesdayatthesquare.com), this 12-week concert series has featured the likes of Tab Benoit, Marcia Ball, and The Iguanas. Local bars and restaurants sell food and drinks to benefit the Young Leadership Council. You can also purchase the work of local artisans in the Artist Village.

Not far from the American Italian Cultural Center, you'll encounter the picturesque **Piazza d'Italia** (377 Poydras St.; 24 hours daily; free), which is dedicated to the city's Italian American community and its indelible influence on New Orleans. Designed in 1978 by the renowned, postmodernist architect Charles Moore and partially restored in 2004, the plaza serves as a gathering place for residents, a relaxing spot for a lunch break, and site of St. Joseph's Day celebrations.

Between the Audubon Aquarium of the Americas and The Outlet Collection at Riverwalk, the pleasant **Spanish Plaza** (1 Poydras St.; 24 hours daily; free) is an ideal spot to gaze at the bustling Mississippi. The square was rededicated by Spain in 1976 to commemorate its influence on the Crescent City's history and to serve as an ongoing promise of fraternity. As a symbolic reminder, the seals of Spanish provinces encircle the central fountain. Spanish Plaza is a common gathering place for residents and tourists alike, as well as the site of free public concerts throughout the year.

One of New Orleanians' favorite places for strolling is verdant **Audubon Park** (6500 Magazine St., 504/861-2537, www. auduboninstitute.org; 5am-10pm daily; free), a 340-acre property that occupies the former estate of Etienne de Boré, the city's fist mayor, and extends from St. Charles Avenue to the Mississippi

River. Besides encompassing Audubon Zoo, this beloved park features a pleasant lagoon, moss-draped live oak trees, and lush lawns with picnic areas. Named after ornithologist John James Audubon, who once lived in southern Louisiana, Audubon Park offers a slew of athletic facilities, including tennis courts and soccer fields, three playgrounds, a golf course, a swimming pool, and a paved 1.8-mile path ideal for walking, jogging, and in-line skating. You can take horseback-riding lessons at **Cascade Stables** or view egrets, herons, and cormorants on **Ochsner Island,** which sits within the park's lagoon and is more commonly known as Bird Island.

Since **Crescent Park** (Mississippi riverfront btwn. Elysian Fields Ave. and Mazant St., 504/658-3200, www.nola.gov; 8am-6pm daily; free), an edgy Bywater sanctuary, opened in February 2014, the 1.4-mile-long, 20-acre strip has lured countless recreationists. Besides scenic views of the downtown New Orleans skyline, the Mississippi River, and Algiers Point, you'll find picnic areas, a fenced dog run, and a network of paths suitable for walking, jogging, and biking. A parking lot is situated near Piety and Chartres Streets, where you'll also spot the Piety Street Bridge, a rusted steel arch that safely delivers pedestrians over the active riverfront railroad tracks. Certain activities, such as cooking, swimming, and littering, are not allowed, as are skateboards, motorcycles, and bottles.

The 23,000-acre **Barataria Preserve** (6588 Barataria Blvd., Marrero, 504/689-3690, www.nps.gov/jela; 9am-5pm daily; free), a unit of Jean Lafitte National Historical Park and Preserve, is a popular **bird-watching** spot among locals and visitors. On the west bank of the Mississippi River, this enormous preserve comprises bayous, swamps, marshes, forests, and roughly nine miles of hiking trails (where pets, even leashed ones, aren't allowed). Don't miss the **Bayou Coquille Trail,** a half-mile, pavement-and-boardwalk path that's known for myriad sightings of snakes, alligators, nutrias, and some of the more than 300 bird species that dwell here. At the **visitor center** (9:30am-4:30pm Wed.-Sun.), you'll spot exhibits that highlight how the Mississippi River created Louisiana's wetlands, the national significance of this region, and the relationship between the land and its people. In the bookstore, you'll find music, field guides, and children's books. Free guided wetlands walks are available Wednesday-Sunday at 10am. The park, which is closed only on Mardi Gras Day, is also favored among canoeists, kayakers, boaters, and licensed anglers.

Biking

Despite potholes, narrow streets, and steady traffic, New Orleans lures its share of biking enthusiasts, particularly in the Quarter, the Marigny, and City Park. It helps that the city has relatively flat terrain and an increasing number of bike-friendly roadways. To tour the Big Easy at your own pace, head to the helpful **American Bicycle Rental Company** (325 Burgundy St., 504/324-8257, www.bikerentalneworleans.com; 9am-5pm daily; $10 hourly, $40 daily), which rents cruisers by the hour or by periods of 4, 8, or 24 hours. Each rental includes a lock, helmet, basket, and cycling map, plus lights for nighttime riding. You can also book an excursion with the on-site **Free Wheelin' Bike Tours** (504/522-4368, www.neworleansbiketour.com; $50).

Amid the live music clubs of Frenchmen Street stands laid-back, full-service **Bicycle Michael's** (622 Frenchmen St., 504/945-9505, www.bicyclemichaels.com; 10am-5pm Sun.-Tues., 10am-7pm Thurs.-Sat.; $35-110 daily, $140-320 weekly), which handles sales, provides rentals, and even offers repair services, perfect if you intend to bike the Trace from south to north and need a tune-up before you start. Choose among city hybrids, mountain bikes, off-road bikes, and tandems. Then, depending on how long

Who Dat!

If you're ever in town during the NFL football season, you'll notice "Who Dat" flags and banners hanging from many porches and balconies, and you might even hear someone shout "Who Dat!" at no one in particular. If you're wondering about the origins of such a funny-sounding call of solidarity, just know that you've arrived in the heart of the **Who Dat Nation** (www.whodatnation.com), a popular term used to describe the entire community of fiercely loyal Saints' fans.

Once a common dialogue exchange between performers and spectators at minstrel shows and vaudeville acts in southern Louisiana, the "Who Dat" chant was eventually adopted by the **New Orleans Saints** in the 1980s. Part of a longer chant—"Who dat say dey gonna beat dem Saints?"—that is often heard at Saints' games, "Who Dat" has now become a rallying cry of team support for New Orleanians everywhere. Not surprisingly, the cry resounded through the French Quarter when the Saints won their first Super Bowl in 2010.

you keep the rental (from a half day to a full week), you can explore the Faubourg Marigny, the nearby French Quarter, City Park, the Lake Pontchartrain shoreline, and other key areas in this relatively compact city. Although locks, biking advice, and local tips are free, there are nominal costs for helmets ($5 daily), baskets ($5), and maps ($6-8).

If you're a bicycle person (which you definitely are if you just pedaled 444 miles down the Natchez Trace), **Rouler** (601 Baronne St., 504/327-7655, http://roulercycling.com, 7am-9pm Mon.-Fri., 6am-9pm Sat., 7am-9pm Sun.; $7.50-8.50) is your kind of place. It's a bike shop with a café during the day and a bar at night. Grab a coffee or a beer and chat with like-minded folks about all things cycling. Lots of fun gear for sale, too, like a water bottle that looks like a hot sauce bottle. Rouler also offers repair services.

Spectator Sports

The NFL Super Bowl has been held in the iconic 73,000-seat **Mercedes-Benz Superdome** (1500 Sugar Bowl Dr., 504/587-3822, www.superdome.com) several times since 1978. It's home to the **New Orleans Saints** (504/731-1700, www.neworleanssaints.com). The Saints' unusual name derives from both the popular jazz anthem "When the Saints Go Marching In" and the fact that this predominantly Catholic city was awarded the NFL franchise on November 1, 1966 (All Saints' Day).

Adjacent to the Mercedes-Benz Superdome, the 18,000-seat **Smoothie King Center** (1501 Dave Dixon Dr., 504/587-3822, www.smoothiekingcenter.com) is the official home of the **New Orleans Pelicans** basketball team (504/525-4667, www.nba.com/pelicans).

Mid-City's **Fair Grounds Race Course & Slots** (1751 Gentilly Blvd., 504/944-5515 or 504/948-1111, www.fairgroundsracecourse.com; 9am-midnight daily; $10 pp for clubhouse, $0-5 pp for grandstand) offers live horse races from Thanksgiving through March. Events at the track include the Louisiana Derby and the Fair Grounds Oaks. It's also the longtime home of the annual **New Orleans Jazz & Heritage Festival** (www.nojazzfest.com).

Food

The city's reputation for culinary excellence is well deserved. This is the place that shaped famous chefs Paul Prudhomme, Emeril Lagasse, and John Besh—all of whom have embraced the Big Easy's Cajun and Creole roots, not to mention its abundance of fresh seafood.

While New Orleans certainly has its share of upscale restaurants celebrated

The City Is Your Oyster

While in town, oyster-lovers should sample some versions of the shellfish for which New Orleans is known:

* **Oysters Bienville:** Oysters that have been baked in their shells, along with shrimp, mushrooms, green onions, herbs, and seasonings in a white wine sauce. Since the dish was invented at **Arnaud's** (page 367), you should sample it there first.

* **Oysters Rockefeller:** Baked oysters

on the half-shell, topped with bread crumbs, butter, and a green sauce made of puréed herbs (such as parsley). **Antoine's Restaurant** (page 367), where it was invented, serves some of the city's finest (and keeps the recipe a closely guarded secret).

* **Oyster Pernod:** This dish consists of raw oysters served with a dipping sauce made with Pernod, an anise-flavored French aperitif. Try one of the best versions at **Adolfo's** (page 379).

for their impeccable service, creative fusion cuisine, ever-changing menus, and reliance on fresh, seasonal ingredients, it also boasts a wide array of old-time neighborhood haunts. Historic joints, such as Café Maspero in the French Quarter, are often known for classic local staples like roast beef po'boys, gumbo, and crawfish étouffée.

Restaurants can fill up quickly around holidays like Christmas and Mardi Gras, and during special events, such as Jazz Fest. At such times, reservations are highly recommended; for places where reservations aren't accepted, such as Mona Lisa Restaurant in the Quarter, it's best to go on weekdays, when it's generally less crowded. You'll often avoid crowds and save money by visiting at lunchtime.

French Quarter
Cajun and Creole

One of the true granddaddies of old-fashioned French-Creole cooking, **Antoine's Restaurant** (713 St. Louis St., 504/581-4422, www.antoines.com; 11:30am-2pm and 5:30pm-9pm Mon.-Sat., 11am-2pm Sun., $27-48) opened in 1840 and has served everyone from President Coolidge to Judy Garland. Several well-known dishes, from oysters Rockefeller to eggs Sardou, were invented at this elegant restaurant, and the solicitous waitstaff will

happily explain the endless menu of culinary options. Deciding what to eat is only half the challenge: You'll also have to choose from one of 14 dining rooms, including the Mardi Gras-themed Rex Room. Before dinner, have a cocktail in the on-site **Hermes Bar,** and during the day, enjoy a treat at **Antoine's Annex** (513 Royal St.), a small coffeehouse offering gelato and pastries.

The active corner of Bourbon and Bienville might seem an unlikely place for a fine-dining establishment, but **Arnaud's** (813 Bienville St., 504/523-5433, www.arnaudsrestaurant.com; 6pm-10pm Sun.-Thurs., 6pm-10:30pm Fri.-Sat., $27-37) is a terrific spot to sample traditional Creole cuisine and enjoy friendly, attentive service. Established by Arnaud Cazenave, a French wine salesman, in 1918, Arnaud's serves favorites like baked oysters, seafood gumbo, and speckled trout amandine. Dine in the elegant main dining room or the smaller jazz bistro. Before dinner, have a cocktail in **French 75,** the on-site bar, and check out the stunning costumes at the **Germaine Cazenave Wells Mardi Gras Museum** (free). For a more casual meal, head next door to Arnaud's other eatery, **Remoulade** (309 Bourbon St., 504/523-0377, www.remoulade.com; 11:30am-11pm daily).

It's hard to bypass **Brennan's** (417

Royal St., 504/525-9711, www.brennansneworleans.com; 9am-2pm and 6pm-10pm Mon.-Fri., 8am-2pm and 6pm-10pm Sat.-Sun.; $21-38), the legendary pink eatery that initiated the Brennan clan's rise as the Crescent City's first family of the restaurant business. Opened in 1946 by Owen Edward Brennan, the restaurant encompasses several dining areas, plus a lush courtyard. While the atmosphere can be loud, and visiting celebrities tend to get better service than regular folks, the food is definitely worth sampling. Two of the dishes invented onsite include eggs Hussarde (which combines poached eggs with Canadian bacon, hollandaise, and Marchand de Vin sauce) and bananas Foster.

The owner of **Coop's Place** (1109 Decatur St., 504/525-9053, www.coopsplace.net; 11am-close daily, $7-20) sought to create a space that's equally bar and restaurant, and this underrated hangout on raffish Decatur Street succeeds on both counts. Since 1983, this popular local joint has offered the convivial spirit of a neighborhood pub, complete with a pool table in the rear, as well as New Orleans cuisine that's consistently high caliber. Dark wooden tables and exposed brick walls give the place a warm feel, as does the welcoming staff. Reservations are not accepted, and, thanks to the presence of video poker machines, guests must be 21 and older.

The French Quarter boasts several historic restaurants, including the **Court of Two Sisters** (613 Royal St., 504/522-7261, www.courtoftwosisters.com; 9am-3pm and 5:30pm-10pm daily, $25-37), established in 1880 by two Creole sisters, Emma and Bertha Camors. It's now run by the Fein brothers. Though the old-fashioned interior can be an elegant yet casual spot for a romantic dinner, the real appeal is the lush, spacious courtyard, particularly during the daily jazz brunch buffet, which features a live jazz trio and made-to-order omelets, turtle soup, and shrimp rémoulade.

Among those few remaining New Orleans restaurants where men must wear a jacket in the evening (and all day Sunday)—and no patron may stroll in wearing shorts—is ★ **Galatoire's Restaurant** (209 Bourbon St., 504/525-2021, www.galatoires.com; 11:30am-10pm Tues.-Sat., noon-10pm Sun., $24-42), which opened in 1905 and has been run by the Galatoire family ever since. Galatoire's lures many loyal patrons, and true regulars have been coming here for generations, often taking their seat at the same table. Almost as much fun as dining here is watching the local politicos hobnob and broker deals, especially on Friday afternoons. The enormous French-Creole menu includes everything from lavish high-end dishes, such as filet béarnaise, to affordable chicken and seafood entrées. Sweet potato cheesecake and banana bread pudding stand out among the rich desserts. Though the lower dining room doesn't accept reservations, you can reserve a seat in the upstairs area.

Given its location near Jackson Square, the **Gumbo Shop** (630 St. Peter St., 504/525-1486, www.gumboshop.com; 11am-10pm Sun.-Thurs., 11am-11pm Fri.-Sat., $9-22) can be a touristy place and doesn't always live up to the hype. Many of the dishes are worth sampling, from shrimp Creole to crawfish étouffée. The complete Creole dinners are a steal, offering you the choice of an appetizer, vegetable, entrée, and dessert for around $25; the Creole creamed spinach and warm bread pudding are particularly good options.

It's not fair to describe **K-Paul's Louisiana Kitchen** (416 Chartres St., 504/596-2530 or 877/553-3401, www.kpauls.com; 5:30pm-10pm Mon., 11am-2pm and 5:30pm-10pm Tues.-Sat., $29-37) as traditional, since much of the food at Paul Prudhomme's famous restaurant is innovative. The celebrity chef was largely responsible for popularizing Cajun cooking outside Louisiana, and this is an excellent, though pricey, place to sample such fare. Situated within an 1834 building with a cozy courtyard, K-Paul's has an open kitchen on both the first and second floors, allowing diners the chance to watch their dishes being prepared.

Opposite the imposing Hotel Monteleone, **Mr. B's Bistro** (201 Royal St., 504/523-2078, www.mrbsbistro.com; 11:30am-9pm Mon.-Sat., 10:30am-9pm Sun., $28-38) is a popular place for business lunches. Given its fashionable bar, attentive service, and classy decor, it's easy to understand why. It also doesn't hurt that this bustling eatery—operated by Cindy Brennan, of the famous Brennan clan—serves delicious Creole cuisine. Though the ever-changing menu depends on seasonal ingredients, you can expect classic dishes like gumbo ya-ya, barbecue shrimp, and pasta jambalaya. Save some money by opting for weekday cocktail specials and two-course luncheons. Mr. B's also offers a wonderful jazz brunch on Sunday, and there's usually live piano music 7pm-10pm. Reservations are accepted but not required, and the dress code is upscale casual.

Muriel's Jackson Square (801 Chartres St., 504/568-1885, www.muriels.com; 11:30am-2:30pm and 5:30pm-10pm Mon.-Fri., 11:30am-2:30pm and 5pm-10pm Sat., 11am-2pm and 5pm-10pm Sun., $19-39) isn't actually on Jackson Square, but given its corner location at St. Ann and Chartres Streets, it definitely offers a picturesque view of this historic plaza. One of the more elegant restaurants in the Quarter, Muriel's appeals to a wide array of diners. The menu boasts delicious contemporary Creole cuisine. In addition to offering two-course lunch specials and three-course prix fixe dinners, Muriel's features a pre-theater menu.

Top to bottom: Brennan's; Court of Two Sisters; K-Paul's Louisiana Kitchen.

If you don't mind sassy service, make a beeline for **The Old Coffeepot Restaurant** (714 St. Peter St., 504/524-3500, www.theoldcoffeepot.com; 8am-9pm Sun.-Mon. and Thurs., 8am-2pm Tues.-Wed., 8am-11pm Fri.-Sat., $8-14), which was established in 1894 and now features one of the best breakfasts in the Quarter. One favorite morning dish is callas cakes, essentially spiced, deep-fried rice balls dusted with powdered sugar and served with creamy grits and maple syrup. Lunch and dinner, featuring Cajun and Creole dishes, are also available.

The **Palace Café** (605 Canal St., 504/523-1661, www.palacecafe.com; 8am-11am, 11:30am-2:30pm, 5:30pm-close Mon.-Fri., 10:30am-2:30pm and 5:30pm-close Sat.-Sun.; $22-36) ranks among the most cosmopolitan of the Brennan family restaurants in New Orleans. It can seem touristy, but don't let that dissuade you—the kitchen prepares some of the city's best and most exciting local fare, and the staff is highly personable and efficient. Signature dishes include andouille-crusted fish, an oyster pan roast, and a crabmeat cheesecake baked in a pecan crust. Every dish is tasty and presented with great flourish. Housed within the historic Werlein's building, this classy restaurant also serves an enjoyable Sunday jazz brunch.

Nestled inside the posh Royal Sonesta New Orleans since opening in June 2012, **Restaurant R'evolution** (777 Bienville St., 504/553-2277, www.revolutionnola.com; 6pm-10pm Mon.-Thurs., 11:30am-2:30pm and 5:30pm-10pm Fri., 5:30-10pm Sat., 10:30am-2pm and 5:30pm-10pm Sun.; $24-58) is the brainchild of award-winning chefs John Folse and Rick Tramonto. The menu consists of varied, reimagined versions of classic Cajun and Creole cuisine. The Sunday jazz brunch (10:30am-2pm) brings together local favorites like crab beignets, eggs Sardou, and strawberry pain perdu. Grab a drink in the on-site **Bar R'evolution** (5:30pm-11pm Mon.-Fri., 12:30pm-11pm Sat., 10:30am-11pm Sun.).

Described as a modern Creole saloon, **SoBou** (310 Chartres St., 504/552-4095, www.sobounola.com; 7am-10pm daily; $25-48) was created inside the W New Orleans—French Quarter by the culinary experts behind Café Adelaide and Commander's Palace. The menus, which feature signature cocktails and classy Louisiana street food, change throughout the day. You might have Louisiana strawberry pancakes for breakfast, sweet potato beignets for lunch, and, for dinner, egg and duck bacon on brioche with a foie gras ice cream float. Besides the main dining room—which is stylishly illuminated by shelves of glowing bottles—SoBou (short for "south of Bourbon") offers an on-site bar (11:30am-close daily), a beer garden, and semi-private dining areas, plus limited complimentary parking via the hotel.

Inside the same historic building that houses Le Petit Théâtre du Vieux Carré, Dickie Brennan's latest offering, **Tableau** (616 St. Peter St., 504/934-3463, www.tableaufrenchquarter.com; 11:30am-10pm Mon.-Thurs., 11:30am-11pm Fri.-Sat., 10am-10pm Sun.; $21-38), has earned rave reviews for its French Creole cuisine. Classic dishes include shrimp rémoulade, Creole court bouillon, and praline monkey bread pudding. Given its grand staircase, elegant decor, and modern, open kitchen, Tableau is a fine addition to the New Orleans dining scene. The dress code is upscale casual, and as with most Brennan-helmed establishments, reservations are recommended, especially on Le Petit's performance nights, when pre-theater menus are available. If possible, go for the Saturday and Sunday brass brunch (10am-2:30pm) or live music Thursday-Saturday.

Tujague's (823 Decatur St., 504/525-8676, www.tujaguesrestaurant.com; 11am-2:30pm and 5pm-10pm Mon.-Fri., 10am-3pm and 5pm-10pm Sat.-Sun.; $29-42) is an atmospheric corner tavern that's been around since 1856, making it the second-oldest continuously operated restaurant in New Orleans. It sits opposite the French Market and serves much of the local Louisiana produce and seafood sold there. The six-course Creole menu varies little from what diners might have eaten more than a century ago, including beef brisket in Creole sauce and shrimp rémoulade. In addition to the usual cocktails and wines, Tujague's serves its own microbrewed beer. Drinking here has quite a legacy—the cypress-wood bar is original, shipped from France the year that the restaurant opened, and it's played host to everyone from President Truman to Harrison Ford.

Trinity (1117 Decatur St., 504/325-5789, http://trinityrestaurantneworleans.com; 6pm-10pm Sun.-Thurs., 6pm-11pm Fri.-Sat.; $7-39) is a modern interpretation of a classic NOLA eatery, with a long marble bar that will make your jaw hit the ground. Chef Michael Isolani is a local favorite, and the menu has five different oysters as starters. Make your reservation for one of the few tables on the charming outdoor balcony.

Kingfish (337 Chartres St., 504/598-5005, http://kingfishneworleans.com; 11am-10pm Mon.-Thurs., 11am-11pm Fri.-Sat., 10am-10pm Sun.; $7-42) brings modern restaurant design to a vintage building and modern twists on traditional Creole menus and a killer cocktail list. An open kitchen allows diners to see the action.

American

Red-meat lovers swear by the hefty cuts served at **Dickie Brennan's Steakhouse** (716 Iberville St., 504/522-2467, www.dickiebrennanssteakhouse.com; 5:30pm-10pm Sat.-Thurs., 11:30am-2:30pm and 5:30pm-10pm Fri.; $26-42), which is known for its oyster-topped filet served with creamed spinach and roasted potatoes. Though a clubby, upscale space, the restaurant has a relaxed mood, and presentable casual attire is customary.

Johnny's Po-Boys (511 St. Louis St., 504/524-8129; 8am-4:30pm daily; $7-11) opened in 1950 as an unprepossessing, family-owned eatery with tables sheathed in red-checkered cloths and surrounded by bentwood chairs. Though it's only open until the afternoon, Johnny's fills up daily for breakfast and lunch. Not surprisingly, it's best known for its namesake sandwiches, but you can also order omelets, seafood platters, and ice cream treats.

Dark and divey **Port of Call** (838 Esplanade Ave., 504/523-0120, www.portofcallnola.com; 11am-midnight Sun.-Thurs., 11am-1am Fri.-Sat., $10-23) is so popular for its hefty burgers—made with freshly ground beef and piled high with mushrooms or melted cheddar—that there's often a line outside the door. Besides burgers, the simple menu also features traditional comfort foods. The nautical decor and strong cocktails make Port of Call a worthy stop.

In the elegant Omni Royal Orleans, the historic **Rib Room** (Omni Royal Orleans, 621 St. Louis St., 504/529-7046, http://ribroomneworleans.com; 6:30am-10:30am, 11:30am-2pm, and 6pm-9:30pm Mon.-Thurs., 6:30am-10:30am, 11:30am-2:30pm, and 6pm-10pm Fri., 6:30am-10:30am, 11:30am-2pm, and 6pm-10pm Sat., 6:30am-10:30am, 11:30am-2:30pm, and 6pm-9:30pm Sun.; $29-48) is one of the city's best steakhouses. The dining room is unabashedly retro, with its soaring ceilings, comfortable leather chairs, and huge arched windows overlooking Royal Street. The staff is deft and fun-loving—many employees have been here for several decades. Frequent patrons favor this hip dining venue for its delicious, sometimes innovative, dishes, ranging from well-prepared prime rib and seared tuna medallions to local favorites like Creole gumbo and turtle soup. Rib Room offers a delectable Sunday jazz brunch.

Inside Erin Rose Bar, **Killer Poboys** (811 Conti St., 504/252-6745, http://killerpoboys.com; noon-midnight Wed.-Mon.;

Round-the-Clock Eats

For night owls, the Big Easy really delivers. In addition to bars, pubs, and live music venues that stay open until the wee hours, you'll find a slew of 24-hour eateries, ideal for late-night or early-morning cravings.

Perhaps the most well known of these round-the-clock joints is **Café Du Monde,** which, except for a brief time around Christmas (6pm on Dec. 24 to 6am on Dec. 26), is open 24 hours daily. Stop in for late-night coffee and beignets.

If you have a yen for more than dessert in the French Quarter, head to the **Clover Grill** (900 Bourbon St., 504/598-1010, www.clovergrill.com; $4-7), a cozy diner where seating is often hard to snag and sassy waiters serve up hamburgers, sandwiches, and omelets.

A couple blocks down Bourbon, the **Quartermaster** (1100 Bourbon St., 504/529-1416, www.quartermasterdeli. net; $6-10) offers only a few seats alongside the front window, but plenty of culinary options at the deli counter in the rear of this often crowded, albeit dingy, store. After a night of tireless bar-hopping, the Quartermaster, also known as The Nellie Deli, is a popular place to stock up on junk food in addition to jambalaya, stuffed potatoes, and roast beef po'boys. Be aware; the employees here are rife with attitude.

Just a block east on nearby Royal, in the shadow of the supposedly haunted La-Laurie Mansion, stands another longtime, 24-hour market and deli. Popular with the late-night crowd, especially post-shift bartenders and servers, **Verti Marte** (1201 Royal St., 504/525-4767; $4-6) prepares a slew of options, from omelets to barbecue and seafood entrées to scrumptious desserts.

Patrons 21 years old and over might prefer the **Déjà Vu Bar & Grill** (400 Dauphine St., 504/523-1931, www.deja-vunola.com; $8-18), where you'll find a wide selection of beers, cocktails, and tasty vittles—from burgers and po'boys to seafood platters and breakfast specialties. The Quartermaster, Verti Marte, and Déjà Vu offer free delivery for all phone-in food orders.

If you find yourself near Frenchmen Street in the wee hours, you can always head to **Buffa's Bar & Restaurant** (1001 Esplanade Ave., www.buffasbar. com; $7-14), a 24-hour bar and music club that lies on the border between the French Quarter and the Faubourg Marigny. It also happens to serve some terrific American, Cajun, and Creole grub, such as shrimp Creole omelets, redfish po'boys, and bratwurst jambalaya, any time of the day.

$6-13) twists the po'boy on its ear. The menu includes many traditional sandwiches, like beef debris. But what people love here are the unusual takes, such as cheddar omelets and peanut butter po'boys. This location is 21 and older. **Big Killer Poboys** (219 Dauphine St., 504/462-2731) is open to all.

Asian

Though New Orleans isn't known for sushi, **Sekisui Samurai Sushi** (239 Decatur St., 504/525-9595; 11:30am-10pm Sun.-Thurs., 11:30am-10:30pm Fri.-Sat., $11-16) isn't a bad option if you're craving edamame, sashimi, and miso soup. Between the House of Blues and the Kerry Irish Pub, this cozy, often tranquil eatery offers a slew of freshly prepared *nigiri* and sushi rolls, plus tuna *tataki,* seafood udon, and shrimp tempura.

Coffee and Desserts

Beginning as a humble coffee stand to serve the customers and employees of the produce stalls in the French Market in 1862, **Café Du Monde** (800 Decatur St., 504/525-4544 or 800/772-2927, www.cafedumonde.com; 24 hours daily; $2-5) has grown into one of the most legendary food operations in the country. Part of its mystique and popularity is due to its round-the-clock hours (except for Christmas) and its small menu, conveniently plastered on the napkin dispensers. The mainstays are beignets and dark-roasted coffee laced with chicory and traditionally served *au lait*. The mostly open-air café has dozens of small marble tables beneath the green-and-white awning, the sides of which can be unfurled on chilly days, though you can also sit inside the small, fully enclosed dining area. Servers clad in white shirts with black bow ties and white-paper hats whisk about gracefully, delivering plates of beignets at almost breakneck speed. While no visit to New Orleans is complete without experiencing this original location, you may notice other branches throughout the city, including those in the Riverwalk (500 Port of New Orleans, Ste. 27; 8am-9pm Mon.-Sat., 8am-7pm Sun.) and Lakeside malls (3301 Veterans Blvd., Ste. 104; 7am-9pm Mon.-Fri., 8am-9pm Sat., 11am-6pm Sun.).

The Quarter has a branch of one of the city's most famous coffeehouse chains, **CC's Coffee House** (941 Royal St., 504/581-6996, www.ccscoffee.com; 6am-9pm Mon.-Fri., 7am-9pm Sat.-Sun.; $2-5), at the corner of Royal and Dumaine Streets, just opposite the neighborhood's only elementary school. It's a cozy spot, meaning that seating is limited, but it's also warmly lit and charmingly furnished, with several cushy armchairs. Besides tasty coffee drinks and delectable cookies, muffins, and scones, this café provides free wireless Internet access. Numerous other CC's coffeehouses can be found throughout New Orleans and southern Louisiana, from Metairie to Lafayette.

A source of delightful pastries, from napoleons to dark chocolate mousse, the **Croissant d'Or Patisserie** (617 Ursulines Ave., 504/524-4663, www.croissantdornola.com; 6am-3pm Wed.-Mon.; $2-6) is a classic French bakery that also serves delicious sandwiches, fresh salads, and yummy breakfasts. In the Lower Quarter, not far from the Old Ursuline Convent, this spacious café—with plenty of tables, local artwork, and a simply furnished courtyard—makes a nice break from exploring the neighborhood's rich architecture. Be prepared for long lines, especially in the morning.

A wonderful place to while away an afternoon, hang out with friends, and watch curious passersby, **En Vie Espresso Bar & Cafe** (1241 Decatur St., 504/524-3689; 7am-midnight Sun.-Thurs., 7am-1am Fri.-Sat.; $6-12) brews a strong coffee and serves plenty of interesting teas and pastries. This local favorite prepares decent salads and sandwiches, not to mention excellent breakfasts, including a prosciutto and asparagus omelet. Patrons will find lots of seating, free wireless Internet access, and open French doors that make this corner café even airier. There's another location at 308 Decatur Street (504/598-5374).

In the alley behind the Cabildo sits **La Divina Gelateria** (621 St. Peter St., 504/302-2692, http://ladivinagelateria.com; 11am-10pm Mon.-Wed., 8:30am-10pm Thurs. and Sun., 8:30am-11pm Fri.-Sat.; $7-10), a delightful café with limited outdoor seating, heavenly panini, and plenty of artisanal gelato. Though the gelato flavors change often, standards include dark chocolate and pineapple mint sorbetto. Some of the best flavors take advantage of local ingredients, such as bourbon pecan, sweet potato, and bananas Foster. For sandwiches, try the Muffalino, a reinvented New Orleans classic featuring mortadella, Italian ham, provolone cheese, and homemade olive salad. You'll find another location of La Divina in Baton Rouge (3535 Perkins Rd., Ste. 360, Acadian Village).

Cafe Beignet (311 Bourbon St., 504/525-2611, http://cafebeignet.com; 8am-midnight daily; $4-10) may not be as famous as Café Du Monde, but many locals think their beignets are just as good, if not better. The location, nestled next to Musical Legends Park, makes for a lovely alfresco dining experience.

Eclectic

A highly regarded restaurant on a quiet stretch of Dauphine, **Bayona** (430 Dauphine St., 504/525-4455, www.bayona.com; 6pm-9:30pm Mon.-Tues., 11:30am-1:30pm and 6pm-9:30pm Wed.-Thurs., 5:30pm-10pm Fri.-Sat., $28-34) fuses traditions, recipes, and ingredients from a handful of cultures, namely American, French, Italian, Mediterranean, Asian, and North African. Award-winning chef Susan Spicer dreams up such imaginative combos as peppered lamb loin with goat cheese-zinfandel sauce. Desserts are no mere afterthought, and there's a commendable wine list. The setting—an 18th-century Creole cottage filled with trompe l'oeil murals of the Mediterranean countryside, plus a lush courtyard—is the quintessence of romance, though the interior acoustics can make it rather loud on certain nights.

Opposite the oft-photographed Cornstalk Hotel, you'll encounter the enticing **Café Amelie** (912 Royal St., 504/412-8965, www.cafeamelie.com; 11am-3pm and 5pm-9pm Sun. and Wed.-Thurs., 11am-3pm and 5pm-10pm Fri.-Sat.; $16-29), a cute, warmly furnished spot that sits beyond a lush, intimate courtyard, which is favored for anniversaries and other romantic occasions. Locals and tourists alike often pause before the simple, ever-changing menu that's posted daily by the wrought-iron gates. The menu, while eclectic, embraces Louisiana-style cuisine, including such classics as citrus-drizzled crab cakes and jumbo shrimp and grits with corn maque choux.

Occupying the first two floors of a white-brick building on Decatur, the **Crescent City Brewhouse** (527 Decatur St., 504/522-0571 or 888/819-9330, www.crescentcitybrewhouse.com; 11:30am-10pm Sun.-Thurs., 11:30am-11pm Fri.-Sat.; $15-18) is considered by some locals a tourist magnet. As brewpubs go, it serves surprisingly decent and

Café du Monde is a must-visit for coffee and beignets.

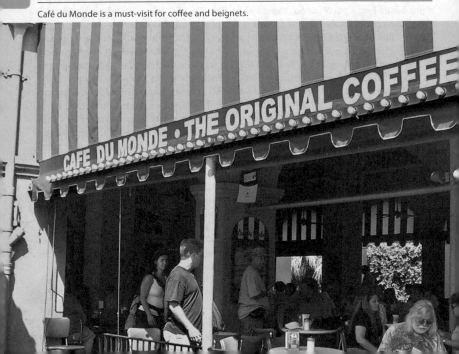

varied food. Offerings include baked brie, shucked oysters, and seafood cheesecake. Many diners come to sample the various microbrews, which are prepared Bavarian-style, with simple, natural ingredients. The light Weiss beer is a house favorite. This inviting space lures passersby with its exposed brick walls, shiny brewing equipment, and live music. If possible, opt for balcony or courtyard dining.

NOLA (534 St. Louis St., 504/522-6652; 6pm-10pm Tues.-Wed., 11:30am-2pm and 6pm-10pm Thurs.-Mon.; $22-40), Emeril Lagasse's restaurant in the French Quarter, delivers great cooking and a lively dining experience that nearly lives up to the hype. The menu changes often, but favorites include garlic-crusted drum, a stuffed chicken wings appetizer with homemade hoisin dipping sauce, and fried green tomatoes with shrimp rémoulade. There's also a selection of excellent desserts, such as king cake bread pudding with Creole cream cheese ice cream. It

can be hard to get a table, so book ahead and expect a wait even when you show up on time for your reservation.

Italian

In the quieter Lower Quarter, at the corner of Chartres and St. Philip Streets, stands a nondescript building that looks more like a warehouse than a fine-dining establishment. Nevertheless, the well-favored **Irene's Cuisine** (539 St. Philip St., 504/529-8811; 5:30pm-10pm Mon.-Sat.; $17-30) is popular among gourmands, especially for romantic dinners and special occasions. The service is attentive, and the Italian and French cuisine is often quite tasty, with highlights like bruschetta, soft-shell crab pasta, and crème brûlée. Given the restaurant's popularity, reservations are definitely recommended; be prepared for a crowd and charges on soda refills.

If you appreciate well-prepared Italian cuisine and would rather avoid the crazier end of the French Quarter, head to the more residential part of Royal Street, where you'll find a local favorite, the **Mona Lisa Restaurant** (1212 Royal St., 504/522-6746; 5pm-10pm Mon. and Wed.-Thurs., 11am-10pm Fri.-Sun.; $13-16). As ideal for romantic dinners as it is for family outings, this cozy eatery has at least three things going for it: friendly service; affordable yet delicious food; and warm, homey decor, including ceiling fans, red and-white checkered tablecloths, and walls that are covered with assorted *Mona Lisa* renditions, from copies of the classic da Vinci painting to a Picasso-style version. Recommended menu items include the Mediterranean pizza, chicken parmesan, and Mardi Gras pasta, which features shrimp and sausage with linguini and a creamy red sauce.

Mexican

A favorite late-night haunt for inexpensive and tasty tacos, burritos, and tamales is **Felipe's Taqueria** (301 N. Peters St., 504/267-4406, www.felipestaqueria.com;

11am-11pm Sun.-Tues., 11am-1am Wed., 11am-11pm Thurs., 11am-2am Fri.-Sat.; $4-8). The space is attractive and inviting, with high ceilings, solid wood tables, and a separate bar area, where the television is always tuned to sporting events. The menu is fairly simple, and all dishes are made right in front of you, which explains why everything tastes so fresh. Order the Felipe's Special, an appetizer consisting of corn chips, salsa, guacamole, and queso dip. There are also locations in Uptown (6215 S. Miro St.) and Mid-City (411-1 N. Carrolton Ave.).

Seafood

Since 1910, the **Acme Oyster House** (724 Iberville St., 504/522-5973, www.acmeoyster.com; 10:30am-10pm Sun.-Thurs., 10:30am-11pm Fri.-Sat.; $9-22) has been a reliable option for fresh bivalves. Decked out with red-checkered tablecloths and packed with tourists, this casual place is crazy at times, but for some, it's worth braving the frenzy for tasty soft-shell crab po'boys, shrimp platters, and a first-rate oyster Rockefeller bisque. While it might not be oyster nirvana, as some people claim, Acme's rich history and convenient location make it a decent choice. There are additional Acme Oyster Houses in Harrah's casino (8 Canal St.), Metairie (3000 Veterans Blvd.), Covington (1202 N. Hwy. 190), and Baton Rouge (3535 Perkins Rd.).

For more than four decades, **Café Maspero** (601 Decatur St., 504/523-6250, www.cafemaspero.com; 8am-10pm Sun.-Thurs., 8am-11pm Fri.-Sat.; $7-14) has been one of the Quarter's most popular eateries. Ideal for budget-conscious travelers, it features several local staples, including jambalaya and muffulettas. Despite the reasonable prices, portions are usually gigantic, and while there are occasional lulls, this spacious, admittedly dingy joint is typically hopping with full tables, bustling servers, and long lines of tourists and locals. The oft-open French doors invite refreshing breezes from the Mississippi River.

Across the street from Ralph Brennan's Red Fish Grill, you'll encounter **Bourbon House Seafood** (144 Bourbon St., 504/522-0111, www.bourbonhouse.com; 6:30am-10pm Sun.-Thurs., 6:30am-11pm Fri.-Sat.; $20-36), an often-crowded seafood eatery. Besides the enormous raw oysters, other favorite dishes include the grilled alligator, seafood gumbo, and shrimp po'boy. Aptly, this popular restaurant also houses an incredible assortment of bourbon; in fact, it's the official home of the New Orleans Bourbon Society. With its large glass windows, it offers entertaining views of the madness along Bourbon Street, but service can be slow, and the wait for a table can be long.

Just off crazy Bourbon Street, **Felix's Restaurant & Oyster Bar** (739 Iberville St., 504/522-4440, www.felixs.com; 11am-11pm Mon.-Thurs., 11am-1am Fri.-Sun.; $11-20) has been serving local seafood fanatics since the early 1900s. Though known for its oysters on the half shell, this casual joint prepares all of New Orleans's seafood favorites well, including the shrimp rémoulade, blackened alligator, and oysters Bienville. Unfortunately, the service can be spotty.

Although many local dishes are offered at **GW Fins** (808 Bienville St., 504/581-3467, www.gwfins.com; 5pm-10pm daily; $21-46), their kitchen serves fresh fish from all over the world, ranging from Canadian salmon to New Zealand John Dory. The setting, a converted warehouse with lofty ceilings, warm wood, and cushy booths, is contemporary and upbeat—seemingly more suitable for the CBD than the French Quarter. Worthy specialties include wood-grilled pompano, New Bedford sea scallops, and parmesan-crusted lemon sole. There's nothing overly convoluted or cutesy about the cooking—just fresh fish with modern ingredients, presented with flair—and the wine list is equally impressive.

Reservations are recommended, and the dress code is business casual.

The multilevel **Oceana Grill** (739 Conti St., 504/525-6002, www.oceanagrill.com; 8am-1am daily; $12-26) encompasses numerous, colorfully decorated rooms, plus a courtyard. It's not far from bustling Bourbon Street. This late-night, family-owned joint offers friendly service and specialty cocktails, not to mention dishes like crabmeat cakes, Cajun jambalaya pasta, and chocolate Kahlua mousse. The raw oysters are usually large, clean, and perfectly chilled.

Ralph Brennan's Red Fish Grill (115 Bourbon St., 504/598-1200, www.redfishgrill.com; 11am-10pm Sun.-Thurs., 11am-3pm and 5pm-11pm Fri.-Sat.; $23-34) on exuberant Bourbon Street is worth seeking out. Opened in 1996, the restaurant, just a block from Canal, helped to revive a block that once felt a bit dark and ominous at night. The cavernous main dining room reverberates with piped-in rock music, and huge redfish mobiles dangle overhead. The noisy, festive ambience makes it fun for singles, friends, and anybody hoping to experience Bourbon's nightlife. To one side lies a spacious oyster bar with huge oyster half-shell sculptures; you can order from the main menu in here, too. The barbecued oysters are a great starter, served with a tangy blue-cheese dipping sauce, and the kitchen also turns out a decadent chocolate bread pudding. Few dishes beat the hickory-grilled redfish topped with jumbo lump crabmeat.

Faubourg Marigny and Bywater
Cajun and Creole
Situated within a modest white-frame house by the levee, along the southern edge of the Bywater, easygoing **Elizabeth's Restaurant** (601 Gallier St., 504/944-9272, www.elizabethsrestaurantnola.com; 8am-2:30pm and 6pm-10pm Mon.-Sat., 8am-2:30pm Sun., $18-26) serves exceptional breakfast and lunch, though it does require a lengthy journey from the Quarter. Elizabeth's is operated by chef Bryon Peck, who maintains the beloved eatery's commitment to imaginative meals and friendly service. One popular choice is the salmon and brie grilled cheese on rye, topped with fried eggs and hash or grits, but be sure to order a side of praline-flavored bacon. Lunch favorites include smoked turkey sandwiches, fried shrimp po'boys, and fried green tomatoes with shrimp rémoulade.

For a sublime blend of soul and Creole cooking, drop by **The Praline Connection** (542 Frenchmen St., 504/943-3934, www.pralineconnection.com; 11am-10pm Mon.-Sat., 11am-9pm Sun., $13-24). Since it opened in 1990, it's been famous for both its crawfish étouffée and its bread pudding with praline sauce. In two simple dining rooms, the staff, clad in natty white shirts, black bow ties, and black fedoras, move about efficiently with hot platters of jambalaya, red beans and rice, and fried okra. Local beers and wines are sold here, and you can pick up the ingredients and seasonings to prepare your own versions of these foods back home.

American
The enormous, garishly colored **Dat Dog** (601 Frenchmen St., 504/309-3362, http://datdognola.com; 11am-midnight Sun.-Wed., 11am-1am Thurs., 11am-3am Fri.-Sat., $7-10), an outpost of a local chain, offers a variety of tasty hot dogs and sausages, from Polish kielbasas to Louisiana-style sausages made from crawfish or alligator meat. The very filling Guinness dog pairs well with the slightly sweet bun and toppings like mustard, bacon, and onion. Various condiments, fries, shakes, and cocktails round out the menu, but it's the dogs that draw the crowds, especially those with a case of the late-night munchies. A friendly, casual joint, Dat Dog has indoor and outdoor seating. You'll find two other Dat Dog restaurants in the Uptown area.

New Orleans might not be known for its barbecue, but that doesn't stop local meat lovers from heading to **The Joint** (701 Mazant St., 504/949-3232, www.al-wayssmokin.com; 11:30am-10pm Mon.-Sat., $8-12), a super-casual dive on the eastern end of the Bywater celebrated throughout the city for its "carnivore cuisine." Featured on Guy Fieri's popular Food Network show *Diners, Drive-Ins, and Dives,* this down-home, often crowded place offers delicious pork spareribs, beef brisket plates, and Cajun sausage. Even the sides are stellar, so save room for the macaroni and cheese, baked beans, and cole slaw. If you're really hungry, you won't go wrong with the desserts either, particularly the peanut butter pie.

Plenty of locals swear by the spacious, art-filled **Satsuma Dauphine** (3218 Dauphine St., 504/304-5962, www.satsumacafe.com; 7am-5pm daily, $6-10) despite its slow service. In addition to standard coffeehouse fare, such as espresso drinks and lemon-blueberry muffins, the cafe has a wide array of delectable, often healthy breakfast and lunch options. The freshly squeezed juices are worth sampling, especially the Popeye, which consists of spinach, lemon, kale, and apple. Some of the soups, sandwiches, and muffins are vegan.

Asian

For some of the best Thai food in the city, drop by **SukhoThai** (2200 Royal St., 504/948-9309, www.sukhothai-nola.com; 11:30am-2:30pm and 5:30pm-10pm Tues.-Fri., 11:30am-10pm Sat.-Sun., $20-30), a relatively quiet eatery. Here, the friendly service and local artwork help to create a hip yet informal vibe, and the menu is quite extensive, offering tasty soups, vegetarian dishes, and seafood specialties, including the glass noodle shrimp bake. In case you get hungry while antiques shopping, there's also a location in the Uptown area.

Near the edge of the Faubourg Marigny, just a few blocks up Frenchmen Street from the main cluster of bars and restaurants, sits the dark, cozy **Wasabi Sushi & Asian Grill** (900 Frenchmen St., 504/943-9433, www.wasabinola.com; 11:30am-2:30pm and 5pm-10pm Mon.-Thurs., 11:30am-2:30pm and 5pm-11pm Fri.-Sat., 5pm-10pm Sun., $16-23), at once a mellow neighborhood bar and a stellar Japanese restaurant. Besides excellent sushi and sashimi, Wasabi serves delightful dishes like crab asparagus soup, squid salad, and wasabi honey shrimp, plus daily specials.

Coffee and Desserts

Occupying a busy corner about four blocks east of Washington Square Park, the **Flora Gallery & Coffee Shop** (2600 Royal St., 504/947-8358; 6:30am-midnight daily) is a funky little place with sidewalk seating, worn-in furnishings, big portions of coffee elixirs, and homestyle cooking. While it's not a bad place to read a book, peruse groovy art, or chat with eccentric locals, it's admittedly not for everyone—particularly at night. After all, it's not far from the somewhat sketchy border between the Marigny and Bywater.

To satisfy your sweet tooth, venture to the homey **New Orleans Cake Cafe & Bakery** (2440 Chartres St., 504/943-0010, www.nolacakes.com; 7am-3pm daily), which prepares to-die-for treats, such as red velvet cake with cream cheese frosting, plus specialty cupcakes flavored with champagne, mimosa, and chocolate mousse. This well-regarded neighborhood eatery also serves delicious breakfast and lunch items, including spinach and goat cheese omelets, shrimp and grits, and roasted vegetable sandwiches. The service is friendly and easygoing, and the crowd is a comfortable mix of students, retirees, artists, and hipsters. Be prepared for long lines, especially during the weekend brunch.

Eclectic

Nestled deep within the funky Bywater

neighborhood lies the laid-back, ultra-creative **Booty's Street Food** (800 Louisa St., 504/266-2887, http://bootysnola.com; 9am-11pm Sun.-Thurs., 9am-midnight Fri.-Sat., $6-13). Inspired by the global explorations of owner and travel journalist Nick Vivion, Booty's Street Food celebrates the world's diverse cuisine with an assortment of easy-to-eat dishes, which, depending on the day, might include a Thai chicken salad, Vietnamese catfish tacos, and a zesty Cubano. Besides the affordable vittles, this airy café provides plenty of pastries, craft cocktails, homemade ice cream, and speedy Wi-Fi access.

Located in the same block as Frenchmen Street's most famous music clubs, the **Marigny Brasserie** (640 Frenchmen St., 504/945-4472, www.marignybrasserie.com; 11:30am-10pm Sun.-Thurs., 11:30am-11pm Fri.-Sat., $14-22) is a slick, modern space whose kitchen puts a unique spin on Louisiana, Southern, Italian, French, and Mexican ingredients and recipes. The BBQ shrimp with rosemary grits reflects the kitchen's simple approach to contemporary food. Besides tasty salads, tacos, and sandwiches, classic New Orleans dishes are available, including fried green tomatoes and shrimp rémoulade. The stylish bar is a pleasant place to sip creative cocktails and listen to live music before heading to one of the nearby clubs.

Press Street Station (5 Press St., 504/249-5622, http://pressstreetstation.com; 10am-9pm Tues.-Thurs., 10am-10pm Fri., 9am-10pm Sat., 9am-3pm Sun., $12-21) has a menu featuring dishes from the New Orleans Center for Creative Arts (NOCCA) culinary students. Helmed by chef Jonathan Schmidt, Press Street offers a medley of breakfast, lunch, and dinner dishes, which are served all day. You can sample an assortment of treats, from boudin-stuffed mirlitons to shrimp tamales. Profits from the restaurant support financial aid for NOCCA students and guest artists.

Perched on the edge of the St. Roch

neighborhood, sandwiched between the Faubourg Tremé and the Faubourg Marigny, stands the cavernous, high-ceilinged **St. Roch Market** (2381 St. Claude Ave., 504/609-3813, www.strochmarket.com; 9am-11pm daily), a refurbished gathering place for foodies and families alike. With its white, minimalist decor, plentiful indoor and outdoor seating, and assorted stalls, offering everything from cold-pressed juices and savory crepes to raw oysters and Korean-Creole dishes like the "Japchalaya," it's a welcome addition to the local food scene. It's also a decent place to pick up coffee, pastries, specialty meats, fresh produce, and wine.

Indian

Set inside a strikingly restored historic building, **Silk Road** (2483 Royal St., 504/944-6666, www.silkroadnola.com; 7:30am-10pm Tues.-Sat., 7:30am-3pm Sun.) is a full-service restaurant offering both highly praised Indian fare as well as classic New Orleans dishes. On any given day, you might sample BBQ shrimp and grits for breakfast, Louisiana crawfish eggrolls and masala shrimp wraps for lunch, and samosas, chicken and andouille gumbo, and lamb vindaloo for dinner. If you really love it here, you can even spend the night, as the family-owned Balcony Guesthouse (504/810-8667, www.balconyguesthouse.com) is located upstairs.

Italian

Large portions of traditional Italian and Creole fare are heaped onto the plates at **Adolfo's** (611 Frenchmen St., 504/948-3800; 5:30pm-10:30pm daily), a longtime neighborhood standby that's especially strong on seafood dishes, such as oysters Pernod and the "ocean sauce," which features shrimp, crawfish, and crab. Granted, it's a small hole-in-the-wall, where the service can be slow, reservations are typically not accepted, and no credit cards are allowed, but it's a good choice for dining before heading to one of Frenchmen's nearby music clubs. Downstairs, the **Apple Barrel Bar** (609 Frenchmen St., 504/949-9399) is a dark and cozy spot to nurse a cocktail before or after dinner.

Mediterranean

In addition to offering a richly stocked Lebanese and Greek grocery, **Mona's Café** (504 Frenchmen St., 504/949-4115, http:// monascafeanddeli.com; 11am-10pm Mon.-Thurs., 11am-11pm Fri.-Sat., noon-9pm Sun.) serves inexpensive Middle Eastern food, including appetizers like falafel, imported olives, and spinach pie. The extensive menu boasts savory entrées, such as chicken kabobs, gyros, and grape-leaf platters. The only drawback is the easily distracted waitstaff. Be sure to stop by Mona's other locations in Uptown and Mid-City.

Central Business and Arts Districts

Cajun and Creole

Housed within a building erected in the 1840s and featuring brick walls, wrought-iron chandeliers, and red-checkered tablecloths, the nostalgic, amiable **Bon Ton Cafe** (401 Magazine St., 504/524-3386, www.thebontoncafe.com; 11am-2pm and 5pm-9pm Mon.-Fri., $19-36) has been serving well-favored Cajun cuisine since 1953 (although other restaurants have been in this location since 1900). Dishes like the turtle soup, seafood gumbo, and bread pudding with whiskey sauce are legendary among the regulars. Given the challenging street-parking situation, arriving by foot, cab, or streetcar is recommended. Dinner reservations are strongly recommended; the wait is long without one.

Set inside the glamorous Loews New Orleans Hotel, **Café Adelaide** (Loews New Orleans Hotel, 300 Poydras St., 504/595-3305, www.cafeadelaide. com; 7am-10am, 11:30am-2pm, and 6pm-9pm Mon.-Thurs., 7am-10am, 11:30am-2:30pm, and 6pm-9:30pm Fri.,

7am-12:30pm and 6pm-9:30pm Sat., 7am-12:30pm and 6pm-9pm Sun.; $24-32) is a highly touted member of the Brennan family, offering delicious food for breakfast, lunch, and dinner. At dinner, begin with the shrimp and tasso corn dogs, then choose from notable main dishes like shrimp court bouillon, jumbo seared sea scallops with beluga lentils, and filet mignon with garlic-roasted artichokes. Lighter fare, as well as a long list of colorful cocktails, is available in the trendy **Swizzle Stick Bar.**

Noted chef Donald Link, of Herbsaint Bar and Restaurant, runs **Cochon** (930 Tchoupitoulas St., 504/588-2123, http:// cochonrestaurant.com; 11am-10pm Mon.-Thurs., 11am-11pm Fri.-Sat.; $9-32) in a rustic, renovated warehouse space. It serves a stellar blend of Cajun and contemporary American victuals, specializing in small, tapas-style portions. Highlighted entrées include rabbit and dumplings, smoked ham hocks with bitter greens, and smoked beef brisket with horseradish potato salad. Save room for the hummingbird cake, made with pecans, pineapples, bananas, and a cream cheese frosting.

The celeb photos lining the walls of **Mother's Restaurant** (401 Poydras St., 504/523-9656, www.mothersrestaurant. net; 7am-10pm daily; $12-18) attest to its longstanding popularity. Opened in 1938, this glorified cafeteria with brash lighting, Formica tables, and chatty servers draws a mix of downtown office workers, hungry tourists, and local politicos. The most famous dishes are the roast beef and baked ham po'boys, but you'll also find delicious jambalaya, seafood gumbo, and crawfish étouffée. It opens earlier than most CBD restaurants—a handy fact if you happen to be returning to your hotel with hunger pangs after a night of barhopping.

One of John Besh's more affordable restaurants, **Lüke** (333 St. Charles Ave., 504/378-2840, www.lukeneworleans. com; 7am-11pm daily; $13-35) keeps people coming back for more, thanks to crawfish beignets, shrimp and grits, and Bienville oysters. Don't skip the Brussels sprouts.

American
Named in honor of the CBD's former moniker, **The American Sector** (The National WWII Museum, 945 Magazine St., 504/528-1940, www.nationalww-2museum.org; 11am-9pm Sun.-Thurs., 11am-11pm Fri.-Sat.; $13-18) is a wonderful addition to The National WWII Museum. With decor that resembles an old-fashioned airport, this delightful eatery features creative versions of American staples, such as mini-cheeseburgers with bacon-onion marmalade, heirloom tomato soup with grilled ham and cheese, and bananas Foster shakes. The portions are generous. Try a vintage cocktail, such as the Last Waltz, which blends vodka, strawberries, mint, ginger, and champagne. Parking is free for patrons after 3pm.

Popular local chef John Besh struck gold with **Besh Steak** (Harrah's New Orleans, 8 Canal St., 504/533-6111, www.harrahsneworleans.com; 5pm-10pm Sun.-Thurs., 5pm-11pm Fri.-Sat.; $33-79) at Harrah's, a lavish restaurant that keeps gamers happy and gives the big spenders something to blow their cash on. This is a loud, fancy place, with brown leather seats, bold canvases of George Rodrigue's iconic "Blue Dog," and other contemporary touches. A Louisiana spin on a traditional steakhouse, Besh Steak offers large portions and tasty entrées, such as the New York strip steak (aged 30 days) with blue-cheese butter and Abita Amber-battered onion rings.

Just around the corner from the well-respected Cochon, the aptly named **Cochon Butcher** (930 Tchoupitoulas St., 504/588-7675, www.cochonbutcher.com; 10am-10pm Mon.-Thurs., 10am-11pm Fri.-Sat., 10am-4pm Sun.; $10-14) offers some of the city's most delectable sandwiches. Its small but eclectic menu ranges from classics like pastrami and sauerkraut on rye, to local twists like the Cajun pork dog on a pretzel bun, to more exotic fare such as the Moroccan spiced lamb with cucumbers, tzatziki, and chili oil on flatbread. Given the eatery's proximity to the convention center, it's a popular spot at lunchtime. It's cozy, with limited outdoor seating, so you might have to take your sandwich to go.

Eclectic
If you can reserve a table at **Emeril's New Orleans** (800 Tchoupitoulas St., 504/528-9393, www.emerils.com; 11:30am-2pm and 6pm-10pm Mon.-Fri., 6pm-10pm Sat.-Sun.; $29-50), go for it—Emeril didn't become famous for no reason. He's an excellent cook with a great kitchen staff, and the food here is more complex and imaginative than at NOLA, his French Quarter restaurant. The bigger and louder of Emeril Lagasse's acclaimed restaurants, Emeril's takes its hits from critics who complain about haughty service and high prices, but this is the domain of one of the world's most famous chefs, and it's always packed. The menu changes often, though you might be lucky enough to sample dishes like the innovative "mac 'n' cheese"—sautéed Gulf shrimp with *trofie* pasta, vermouth cream, *guanciale*, and brioche crumbs. Desserts might include classics like Black Forest Doberge with cherry compote or Dutch apple tart with maple ice cream. The space is airy, high-ceilinged, and dramatic, the quintessence of Arts District chic.

Root (200 Julia St., 504/252-9480, http://rootnola.com; 5pm-10pm Tues.-Thurs., 5pm-11pm Fri.-Sat.; $16-40) has been praised by all manner of publications, including *Bon Appétit*. Helmed by executive chef and co-owner Phillip L. Lopez, Root offers an incredibly varied menu, not to mention an extensive wine, beer, and cocktail list. Whether you come for lunch or dinner, expect to share an assortment of house-made charcuterie

Famous Big Easy Chefs

Brennan Family

The most well-known dynasty is the Brennan clan, who own and operate restaurants throughout New Orleans. In the French Quarter, sample eggs Hussarde and finish with bananas Foster at **Brennan's.** Opt for dinner at Dickie Brennan's Steakhouse, known for its steaks and desserts. For fresh seafood, dine at **Ralph Brennan's Red Fish Grill** or **Dickie Brennan's Bourbon House Seafood.** You can also savor New Orleans cuisine at **Palace Café,** a Sunday jazz brunch at **Mr. B's Bistro,** and a pre-theater meal at the **Tableau.**

Beyond the Quarter are Brennan-owned restaurants like **Café Adelaide** in the CBD, **Commander's Palace** in the Garden District, and **Ralph's on the Park** in Mid-City.

John Besh

John Besh (www.chefjohnbesh.com) celebrates his southern Louisiana roots in eight acclaimed restaurants, six of which lie within walking distance of one another in the CBD. These include **Besh Steak,** a modern steakhouse in Harrah's New Orleans; **Restaurant August,** a contemporary French restaurant; **Lüke** (333 St. Charles Ave.), an homage to Franco-German brasseries; **Domenica,** an inviting Italian eatery in the Roosevelt New Orleans; **Borgne,** a seafood restaurant in the Hyatt Regency New Orleans; and **Johnny Sánchez New Orleans** (930 Poydras St.), a lively taqueria. If you're headed to Uptown, you'll also find **Pizza Domenica** (4933 Magazine St.), a casual spinoff of Domenica.

Emeril Lagasse

Emeril Lagasse (www.emerils.com) has an affinity for New Orleans. He became a celebrity at the legendary Commander's Palace, where he served as the executive chef for more than seven years. In 1990, he established **Emeril's New Orleans,** a fine Louisiana-style restaurant in the

Arts District. In 1992, he opened **NOLA,** a French Quarter eatery that offers creative seafood dishes. Six years later, he established **Emeril's Delmonico,** featuring modern Creole cuisine in the historic Garden District. His newest is **Meril,** a casual spot in the Arts District.

Donald Link

Inspired by his grandparents' cooking styles, Louisiana native Donald Link (www.linkrestaurantgroup.com) infuses his restaurants with his Cajun and Southern roots. Such winners include the **Herbsaint Bar and Restaurant,** which features French-inspired Southern cuisine; **Cochon,** a rustic eatery serving traditional Cajun dishes; **Cochon Butcher,** where popular sandwiches include the muffuletta and the Cubano; and the newest offering, **Pêche Seafood Grill.** All four are in the Arts District.

Paul Prudhomme

Born and raised in Louisiana, Paul Prudhomme (www.chefpaul.com) developed a passion for cooking at his mother's side and, as an adult, learned to blend his native cuisine with other cultural influences. The results of such innovation are evident at his distinctive restaurant, **K-Paul's Louisiana Kitchen.** Today, the ever-changing menu includes such classic dishes as crawfish étouffée and blackened Louisiana drum.

Susan Spicer

In 1979, Susan Spicer began her cooking career in New Orleans as an apprentice to chef Daniel Bonnot at the award-winning Louis XVI Restaurant. Spicer established her own restaurant in 1990. **Bayona** presents an eclectic, ever-evolving menu that embraces a variety of cuisines, including American, French, Italian, Mediterranean, Asian, and North African. Most recently, Spicer opened **Mondo,** a casual, family-style restaurant in Lakeview, where she's lived for the past two decades.

and sausages with your dining mates and sample creatively presented dishes like smoked scallops, grilled cobia, and "sweet tea" country-fried chicken wings. The menu changes often, the decor (including exposed wooden rafters and vivid green chairs with branch-like designs) is modern and fresh, and reservations are recommended.

French

A boisterous power-lunch bistro that's also a hit with the dinner crowd, trendy **Herbsaint Bar and Restaurant** (701 St. Charles Ave., 504/524-4114, www.herbsaint.com; 11:30am-10pm Mon.-Fri., 5:30pm-10pm Sat.; $27-36) sits along a nondescript stretch of St. Charles, its setting brightened by tall windows, soft-yellow walls, and a youthful, good-looking staff. The menu blends Southern, French, and Italian influences. Main courses range from the fish du jour to grilled organic chicken with turnip mashed potatoes and roasted mushrooms. The wine selection is terrific, though you can also try a variety of cool cocktails.

Restaurant August (301 Tchoupitoulas St., 504/299-9777, www.restaurantaugust.com; 5pm-10pm Mon.-Thurs. and Sat.-Sun., 11am-2pm and 5pm-10pm Fri.; $34-47) is presided over by talented and charismatic chef John Besh, the Louisiana born-and-bred kitchen wizard who helms several acclaimed eateries in New Orleans. He opened this Arts District restaurant in 2001, inside a handsome 19th-century French-Creole building, and it's been tough to get a table here ever since. Besh presents uncomplicated yet richly nuanced contemporary French fare, with both local and Mediterranean ingredients. The menu here is ever-evolving, but main courses might include a prime filet of beef with porcini and oxtail marmalade or fried soft-shell crab amandine with a warm crab and haricots verts salad. Try to save room for the goatmilk cheesecake with almonds, honey ice cream, and balsamic caramel.

Italian

Inside the longstanding, extensively renovated Roosevelt hotel, chef John Besh's **Domenica** (The Roosevelt New Orleans, 123 Baronne St., 504/648-6020, www.domenicarestaurant.com; 11am-11pm daily; $13-30) is a warm yet contemporary space that features rustic Italian fare. Popular dishes include the fried eggplant panini, redfish with celery root purée, and spiced apple cake with buttermilk gelato. If possible, come for happy hour (2pm-5pm daily), when all pizzas, beers, well cocktails, and wines by the glass are offered at half price. Domenica boasts an amiable, knowledgeable staff and a classy ambience, punctuated by the high ceilings, unusual chandeliers, and dark wooden tables. For a more casual experience, stop by **Pizza Domenica** (4933 Magazine St., 504/301-4978; noon-9pm Sun.-Thurs., noon-10pm Fri.-Sat.), chef Alon Shaya's Uptown spinoff, which offers wood-fired pizzas as well as traditional Italian appetizers.

Tommy's Cuisine (746 Tchoupitoulas St., 504/581-1103, www.tommysneworleans.com; 5:30pm-10pm Sun.-Thurs., 5:30pm-11pm Fri.-Sat.; $22-28) is a reliable pick for creative, Creole-inspired Italian fare. Housed within a charming space in the Arts District, the warmly lit dining room—with its paneled walls, mirrors, and old-fashioned sconces—creates an appealing scene. Menu items include mussels marinara, oysters Tommy (baked in the shell with Romano cheese, pancetta, and roasted red pepper), or chicken roasted with white wine, olive oil, and rosemary-garlic jus. If you have room, try the pecan praline bread pudding with a bananas Foster sauce and vanilla ice cream—a glorious combination of the city's greatest desserts.

Seafood

Borgne (Hyatt Regency New Orleans, 601 Loyola Ave., 504/613-3860, www.borgnerestaurant.com; 11am-10pm Sun.-Thurs., 11am-11pm Fri.-Sat.; $22-32) is one of the newest of John Besh's varied restaurants in the CBD. On the ground floor of the Hyatt Regency New Orleans, the casual yet stylish eatery features local artwork, a lengthy concrete bar, and large columns of Louisiana oyster shells that anchor the spacious dining area. Helmed by chef Brian Landry and named in honor of nearby Lake Borgne, the restaurant focuses on coastal Louisiana cuisine, such as raw oysters, seared yellowfin tuna salad, and seafood paella. Weekday Southern-style lunch specials ($10 pp) include red beans and rice on Monday and fried chicken on Thursday, and there are always several sinful desserts on offer, from dark chocolate pâté to Ponchatoula strawberry shortcake.

The **Pêche Seafood Grill** (800 Magazine St., 504/522-1744, www.pecherestaurant.com; 11am-10pm Mon.-Thurs., 11am-11pm Fri.-Sat.; $16-27) is focused on regional seafood and owned by local culinary star Donald Link, the man behind other CBD favorites (Cochon, Cochon Butcher, and Herbsaint Bar and Restaurant). Save for the elegant bar area, Pêche exudes a chic rustic vibe, and the menu includes entrées as well as small plates and raw bar items. Whether you come for lunch or dinner, you'll likely relish dishes like the seafood salad, curried shrimp bisque, and smothered catfish. Wine, beer, specialty cocktails, and scrumptious desserts are also available, and reservations are recommended, especially on the weekend.

Desserts

What's not to love at **Bakery Bar** (1179 Annunciation St., 504/265-8884, http://bakery.bar, 11am-midnight Tues.-Fri., 10am-midnight Sat.-Sun., $6-13)? This spot is, as the name suggests, both a bakery and a bar. Sip on a Suffering Bastard and snack on a deep-friend chocolate chip cookie—then carry on with your revelry.

Garden District
Cajun and Creole

If you must put one place at the top of your restaurants list, make it ★ **Commander's Palace** (1403 Washington Ave., 504/899-8221, www.commanderspalace.com; 11:30am-1:30pm and 6:30pm-10pm Mon.-Fri., 11am-1pm and 6:30pm-10pm Sat., 10am-1:30pm and 6:30pm-10pm Sun.; $39-45), which was established in 1880 and became part of the famed Brennan family empire in 1974. Nestled within a blue-and-white Victorian mansion in the Garden District, this local landmark is a terrific place to try turtle soup, griddle-seared Gulf fish, and bread pudding soufflé. Lunch isn't too expensive, especially if you opt for the wonderful two-course Creole luncheon (about $35). The weekend jazz brunches are the stuff of legend, and advance reservations are a must for any meal.

Uptown
Cajun and Creole

On bustling Oak Street, funky ★ **Jacques-Imo's Cafe** (8324 Oak St., 504/861-0886, http://jacques-imos.com; 5pm-10pm Mon.-Thurs., 5pm-10:30pm Fri.-Sat.; $20-34) presents a mix of eclectic contemporary dishes and New Orleans standbys. Locals rave about the charismatic staff and the ever-changing list of specials, which has featured smothered rabbit with roasted-pepper grits and country-fried venison chop with wild mushrooms. Every meal comes with delicious butter-topped cornbread muffins, salad, and sides. Finish off your meal with energy-pumping coffee-bean crème brûlée. Reservations are available for large groups, and the place fills up quickly, so expect a wait on most nights. You can always pass the time at the charming bar. To reach the loud, rambling dining room, you have to walk through the oft-crowded bar and bustling kitchen, where you can take a peek at the dishes being prepared.

Sweet Treats

Beignets aren't the only dessert worth sampling in New Orleans. Here are some of the city's quintessential treats and where to try them:

- **Bananas Foster:** A rich dessert consisting of bananas, butter, brown sugar, cinnamon, and rum, invented by Paul Blangé at **Brennan's** (page 367) in 1951. It's often prepared as a flambé in a tableside performance, then promptly served over vanilla ice cream.

- **Bread pudding:** A traditional dessert made from soaked French bread and often served with rum or whiskey sauce. For the classic version, head to the CBD's **Bon Ton Cafe** (page 380).

- **Calas** (KAH-luhs): Creole rice fritters usually covered with cane syrup or powdered sugar. Similar to beignets, they're a popular breakfast dish at **The Old Coffeepot Restaurant** (page 370) in the French Quarter, though you'll see them as "callas cakes" on the menu.

Tremé and Mid-City
Coffee and Desserts

After a day of exploring City Park, head southwest on Carrollton, toward Canal Street, and take a snack-break detour at ★ **Angelo Brocato** (214 N. Carrollton Ave., 504/486-1465, www.angelobrocatoicecream.com; 10am-10pm Tues.-Thurs., 10am-10:30pm Fri.-Sat., 10am-9pm Sun.; $3-6), an old-world bakery and ice cream parlor that's famous not only for its superb Italian pastries, such as the classic cannoli, but for tantalizing house-made ice cream, Italian ice, and gelato in all kinds of tempting flavors, such as spumoni, chestnut, and amaretto. The most popular treat is the lemon ice, a simple yet expertly blended concoction of water, granulated sugar, and fresh lemons.

Eclectic

Within steps of leafy City Park, the aptly named ★ **Ralph's on the Park** (900 City Park Ave., 504/488-1000, www.ralphsonthepark.com; 5:30pm-9pm Mon., 11:30am 2pm and 5:30pm-9pm Tues.-Thurs., 11:30am-2pm and 5:30pm-9:30pm Fri., 5:30pm-9:30pm Sat., 11am-2pm and 5:30pm-9pm Sun.; $24-32) is one of only two Brennan family-helmed dining operations in Mid-City, and it's absolutely worth the trip. It's far from the crowds of the Quarter and CBD, making for a relaxed, convivial dining experience. It's also set inside a lovely historical building. Then there's the elegant, innovative food, such as flaky mushroom tarts, blue crab beignets, and rib-eye-wrapped scallops with foie gras, cauliflower purée, and port wine beef sauce. It's also one of the best brunch options in town, offering tasty dishes like turtle soup, crawfish Benedict, and Gulf shrimp and grits.

Greater New Orleans
Seafood

Try to make a reservation a few days in advance for ★ **Drago's Seafood Restaurant** (3232 N. Arnoult Rd., Metairie, 504/888-9254, www.dragosrestaurant.com; 11am-9pm Mon.-Sat.; $17-51), a riotously popular restaurant with limited seating and parking. As the name indicates, the emphasis is on seafood, much of it prepared with a Louisiana slant. The lobster dishes are particularly noteworthy; try the lobster Marco, a whole lobster stuffed with fresh sautéed shrimp and mushrooms in a light cream sauce over angel hair pasta. You can sit at the bar, which affords a clear view of the grill-cooked charbroiling oysters, or dine in one of the noisy but festive dining rooms. With the high volume of business, the waitstaff often seems harried. There's also a Drago's inside the CBD's Hilton New Orleans Riverside (2 Poydras St., 504/584-3911).

Accommodations

At once classic and Bohemian, New Orleans contains a wide array of unique lodging options. Historic hotels dot the French Quarter, like the literary Hotel Monteleone and the elegant Royal Sonesta New Orleans, not to mention smaller, more affordable guesthouses. Beyond high-end chain establishments, such as the pet-friendly Loews New Orleans Hotel, the Central Business District (CBD) houses boutique-style options like the International House New Orleans. The Garden District and Uptown areas feature elegant inns, such as the traditional Terrell House Bed and Breakfast. The Tremé and Mid-City areas encompass laid-back hostels and guesthouses, such as the 1896 O'Malley House.

You'll find plenty chain hotels here, especially in the CBD and near Louis Armstrong New Orleans International Airport. Besides standard amenities, these often spacious hotels typically offer swimming pools, business centers, meeting rooms, and off-street parking.

Where you choose to stay will greatly depend on whether you have a car. Fortunately, staying in the main neighborhoods of the French Quarter, the CBD, the Garden District, and Mid-City will ensure convenient access to public transportation, namely the streetcar lines. Not all hotels welcome pets and children. Accommodations are completely smoke-free. Most of the privately owned inns have minimum stay requirements, particularly during the peak winter and spring seasons. At such times—especially during events like New Year's Eve, the Sugar Bowl, Mardi Gras, French Quarter Fest, and Jazz Fest—expect higher rates as well as the need to book in advance. Even in the slower summer season, certain annual events—such as the Essence Festival and Southern Decadence—might necessitate a reservation.

Choosing a Hotel

There's no shortage of motels, hotels, inns, and cottages available in the Big Easy, and many websites and organizations can help narrow down the options. If you're looking for a bed-and-breakfast, consult the **Professional Innkeepers Association of New Orleans** (PIANO, www.bbnola.com) or the **Louisiana Bed & Breakfast Association** (LBBA, www. louisianabandb.com). You might also benefit from local reservation services like **New Orleans Bed & Breakfasts** (www. neworleansbandbs.com) and the **Inn the Quarter Reservation Service** (800/570-3085, www.innthequarter.com). For more specific accommodations, check out **Historic Hotels of America** (800/678-8946, www.historichotels.org) and **Bluegreen Resorts** (800/456-0009, www. bluegreenrentals.com).

French Quarter
$100-150

Essentially a complex of historic buildings that includes a former 1830s military hospital, the **Hôtel Provincial** (1024 Chartres St., 504/581-4995 or 800/535-7922, www.hotelprovincial. com, from $119) has been owned by the Dupepe family since 1961. The cheery guest rooms are decorated with Southern antiques and reproduction French period furnishings; some feature balconies, views of the river, or access to sunny, private courtyards. Amenities include a free continental breakfast, two swimming pools, an on-site bar, and secured valet parking ($30 daily). The staff is efficient and friendly, reason enough to stay at this upscale, family-run inn.

One of the Quarter's most popular mid-priced hotels, **Le Richelieu in the French Quarter** (1234 Chartres St., 504/529-2492 or 800/535-9653, www. lerichelieuhotel.com, from $115) books up quickly. Contained within two historic buildings, the 69 guest rooms are clean and simple, but with reproduction antiques, varying color schemes, and, in some cases, pleasant views. There are also 17 suites with spacious sitting areas. This European-style property lies along a quiet stretch in the Lower Quarter, not far from the French Market and the Marigny. An on-site café serves breakfast all day, and there's also a lounge, an unheated swimming pool, and 24-hour concierge services. The hotel offers satellite TV, laundry and babysitting services, and secured self-parking ($30 daily).

Housed within a regal three-story, 19th-century structure, the affordable **Prince Conti Hotel** (830 Conti St., 504/561-8951 or 800/366-2743, www.princecontihotel.com, from $110) offers 76 basic guest rooms and suites, which vary greatly in features. For instance, some rooms don't have windows! The Prince Conti provides 24-hour concierge services. Given its location near Bourbon Street, this can be a particularly loud place to spend the night, so select your room carefully. Perhaps the hotel's best features are the on-site **Café Conti,** open for breakfast, and **The Bombay Club** (504/577-2237, www.bombayclubneworleans.com), a sophisticated restaurant, martini bar, and live music venue.

$150-200

Featuring hand-painted murals and wrought-iron balconies, the intimate, renovated **Bienville House Hotel** (320 Decatur St., 504/529-2345 or 800/535-9603, www.bienvillehouse.com, from $143) sits along Decatur, close to the river as well as several good bars and eateries with a more mellow ambience than those on Bourbon. By French Quarter standards, the 83 rooms are large and airy with stylish furnishings, attractive bathrooms, and upscale amenities, such as luxurious robes, 300-thread-count linens, and designer toiletries. The best rooms have an inviting sun deck; there's also a heated saltwater pool with a surrounding courtyard.

Budget-conscious travelers favor the **Biscuit Palace Guest House** (730 Dumaine St., 504/525-9949, www.biscuitpalace.com, $125-175), a classic Creole mansion on a quiet stretch of Dumaine. Built in 1820, this no-frills inn features four mini-suites, three full suites, and one rooftop apartment, all individually decorated and equipped with tiny bathrooms. Curiously, most are named after key streets in the Vieux Carré, the city's oldest neighborhood. Though the staff is accommodating, be prepared for a funky, old-world building, in need of some renovations and safety updates.

The hospitable **Chateau LeMoyne—French Quarter** (301 Dauphine St., 504/581-1303 or 877/834-3613, www.chateaulemoynefrenchquarter.com, $130-170) occupies four mid-19th-century townhouses on Dauphine, one block from noisy Bourbon Street. Managed by Holiday Inn, the 171 nicely furnished rooms include period reproductions with the usual chain amenities. Some rooms are built in the classic Creole style, while others are richly architectural with cypress wood beams and exposed-brick walls. Depending on the room, balcony access may also be available. Facilities include a 24-hour business center, tree-shaded redbrick patios anchored by a heated pool, and the on-site **RF's** (504/586-0972, www.rfsnola.com), which offers classic Louisiana cuisine and live nightly music.

The lovely, pet-friendly **Courtyard New Orleans Downtown/Iberville** (910 Iberville St., 504/523-2400 or 877/703-7072, www.marriott.com, $146-169) features clean, spacious suites with separate sleeping and sitting areas, wet bars and refrigerators, and Bath & Body Works toiletries. It's ideal for families, business travelers, and small groups. Laundry service, pricey valet parking ($43 daily), and simple continental breakfasts are available. As a bonus, guests can access the pampering services offered by its elegant neighbor, The Ritz-Carlton New Orleans, whose spa (504/524-1331) features a fitness center, a resistance pool, a retail store, and an assortment of spa treatments.

Opened in 1969, the elegantly simple **Dauphine Orleans Hotel** (415 Dauphine St., 504/586-1800 or 800/521-7111, www.dauphineorleans.com, from $149) provides tranquility only a block from boisterous Bourbon. Inside the magnificent main building, you'll find 111 comfortable, contemporary guest rooms. The Dauphine Orleans also manages the 14-unit Hermann House, which features whirlpool tubs, and the 9-unit Carriage House, with period antiques and courtyard views. Other in-room amenities include bathrobes, free bottled water, and spa services. At the main property, guests can take a dip in the saltwater pool, enjoy the fitness room, and imbibe in **May Baily's Place** (4pm-midnight daily), the hotel bar. Concierge services, secured valet parking ($40 daily), and free continental breakfasts and afternoon teas are available.

Quirky, low-key, and affordable, the family-run **Olivier House Hotel** (828 Toulouse St., 504/525-8456, www.olivierhousehotel.com, from $149) isn't far from the hubbub of Bourbon Street. Set within a towering 1839 Greek Revival-style townhouse and other nearby buildings, the rooms and suites boast a mixture of antique and modern furnishings. Each space has a different layout, from small, single-bed rooms to two-bedroom suites with a kitchenette and courtyard access. Three specialty options include the Honeymoon Suite, with a four-poster bed, working fireplace, and stunning balcony; the Garden Suite, a split-level space with tropical decor; and Miss Anna's Creole Cottage, featuring brick floors, a convenient kitchen, and a private courtyard. Other amenities include a swimming pool, off-street valet parking

($25-38, and 24-hour concierge services. Children and pets are welcome.

Many out-of-towners choose the ★ **Royal Sonesta New Orleans** (300 Bourbon St., 504/586-0300 or 800/766-3782, www.sonesta.com/royalneworleans, from $151) for its prime location on Bourbon Street, especially if they're able to snag a balcony room. From this perspective, you can oversee and participate in the late-night revelry, as many partygoers expect you to toss down a Mardi Gras-bead necklace or two. An even better enticement is the on-site jazz club, not to mention the hotel's hospitable staff, stylish decor, and pet-friendly policy. The 483 well-appointed guest rooms and suites feature standard amenities plus king-size pillows. Guests also appreciate the fitness center, outdoor swimming pool, spa services, and on-site eateries **PJ's Coffee Café,** the **Desire Oyster Bar,** and **Restaurant R'evolution.**

Over $200

If money is no object, then stay at the charming 18th-century **Audubon Cottages** (509 Dauphine St., 504/561-5858 or 504/586-1516, www.auduboncottages.com, $349-700). Guests appreciate the seclusion of this aging property. The clean, comfortable one- and two-bedroom cottages offer features like private courtyards, antique furnishings, and whirlpool tubs. Besides a daily continental breakfast, guests have access to the on-site swimming pool plus the Dauphine Orleans Hotel's fitness center and secured valet parking.

The enormous **Bourbon Orleans Hotel** (717 Orleans St., 504/523-2222 or 866/513-9744, www.bourbonorleans.com, $295-509) occupies most of a block at Bourbon and Orleans Streets. It also lies within a heartbeat of Bourbon's all-night craziness, so if you plan to sleep, book a room facing one of the side streets. This historic, European-style hotel is one of the Quarter's finest properties. The rooms and suites are large and elegant,

Illegal Guesthouses

Some of the most charming rooms in the city are found in unlicensed, illegal B&Bs, guesthouses, or vacation rentals. Many of these "underground" establishments advertise heavily online, especially during major annual events, such as Mardi Gras and French Quarter Fest. Likely no harm will come to you for staying at one, and plenty of travelers do it, so why think twice before booking a room at such a property?

First, the city of New Orleans requires all short-term rentals to be licensed, and yet it seems to make little effort to enforce this rule. Consequently, upstanding innkeepers who have gotten the approval (and paid the various fees) to open an inn are at a competitive disadvantage compared to those who run properties illegally.

Second, by staying at an illegal B&B, you have little or no recourse for rem-

edying any disputes that arise, and you have no legal protection should you be injured. Illegal short-term rentals often fail to comply with fire and safety regulations, as nobody inspects them. They also rarely carry the proper commercial insurance that is required of licensed inns.

Finally, choosing to patronize only licensed, legal establishments actually helps the city of New Orleans. Illegal vacation rentals don't contribute taxes to the city.

The easiest way to ensure that the B&B in which you're interested is licensed, legal, and adhering to proper standards is to choose one of the more than 50 properties that are members of **PIANO, the Professional Innkeepers Association of New Orleans** (www.bbnola.com), an organization that's been going strong since 2000.

with tall windows, luxurious beds, and, in some cases, balconies. Amenities include concierge and in-room spa services, a heated outdoor pool, and valet parking. The on-site contemporary Creole restaurant, **Roux on Orleans** (504/571-4604), serves breakfast daily and dinner Tuesday-Saturday.

With its distinctive, cornstalk-inspired, cast-iron fence, the gorgeous, Victorian-style **Cornstalk Hotel** (915 Royal St., 504/523-1515, www.thecorn stalkhotel.com, $230-320) offers 14 sumptuous guest rooms, all of which feature high ceilings and antique furnishings. Besides the amicable staff, another advantage is the location, which offers an ideal spot for people-watching and easy access to art galleries, carriage tours, seafood restaurants, and late-night bars.

Occupying the site of the 19th-century French Opera House, the **Four Points by Sheraton French Quarter** (541 Bourbon St., 504/524-7611 or 866/716-8133, www. fourpointsfrenchquarter.com, $221-599) contains sumptuous rooms, many

of which offer views of active Bourbon Street, quieter Toulouse, or the picturesque courtyard. In-room amenities include impressive carved beds. Elsewhere in the hotel are a business center, fitness room, outdoor pool, and cocktail bar. Valet parking, laundry services, and a free continental breakfast are available, and the front desk is staffed 24 hours daily. Given the hotel's location on Bourbon, early birds may find it hard to sleep in certain rooms.

Topped by a large red neon sign, the marvelous ★ **Hotel Monteleone** (214 Royal St., 504/523-3341 or 888/647-2301, www.hotelmonteleone.com, $290-400) hosted Tennessee Williams many times, as well as Ernest Hemingway, Truman Capote, and Anne Rice. The enormous hotel offers 600 luxurious rooms and 55 suites, equipped with marble-and-granite bathrooms. The sumptuous suites feature Jacuzzi tubs and, in some cases, wet bars and sofa beds. On-site amenities include the stylish **Carousel Bar & Lounge,** the **Criollo Restaurant** (http://criollonola.

com), the **Spa Aria,** a modern fitness center, and a rooftop pool that's heated year-round. Its location on Royal Street is another bonus.

With a prime spot in the Quarter and a hospitable staff, the lavish, rambling ★ **Omni Royal Orleans** (621 St. Louis St., 504/529-5333 or 888/444-6664, www. omnihotels.com, from $199) contains 346 smartly furnished rooms with 19th-century decor and marble bathrooms. Premier rooms and certain suites feature balconies, and just about all options afford an impressive view of the Quarter. On the roof, you'll find a state-of-the-art fitness center, a heated pool, and a year-round observation deck. Other on-site amenities include a beauty salon, a full-service barber shop, a 24-hour business center, concierge and babysitting services, the cozy **Touché Bar,** and the hallowed **Rib Room** restaurant. Pricey valet parking ($47.50 daily) is available.

The **Place d'Armes Hotel** (625 St. Ann St., 504/524-4531 or 888/626-5917, www. placedarmes.com, $169-269) stands only a few steps from Jackson Square and just a short walk from Café Du Monde. This charming hotel consists of eight restored 18th- and 19th-century townhouses, containing 84 snazzy rooms and surrounding a delightful courtyard shaded by crape myrtle and magnolia trees and filled with lush plants and old-fashioned fountains. Some rooms have balconies, and all have exquisite furnishings. Other amenities include a daily continental breakfast, 24-hour concierge services, and a lovely swimming pool.

This is the perfect choice for the ultimate pampering vacation: **The Ritz-Carlton New Orleans** (921 Canal St., 504/524-1331 or 800/542-8680, www. ritzcarlton.com, from $289) has a state-of-the-art day spa and fitness center; the **Davenport Lounge,** which presents live jazz and afternoon tea service; and **Bistro,** serving fresh, local cuisine. The well-trained staff tends to guests' every need, from valet parking to babysitting services

to a free overnight shoeshine. Richly furnished rooms feature 400-thread-count sheets, goose-down pillows, and Italian marble baths. For extra-special attention, stay at the hotel's club-level **Maison Orleans** (904 Iberville St.).

The **W New Orleans—French Quarter** (316 Chartres St., 504/581-1200 or 888/627-8260, www.wfrenchquarter.com, from $285) combines the alluring pizzazz and old-world charm of the French Quarter with the modern elegance and high-tech sophistication associated with this pet-friendly chain. The 98 rooms, which include two deluxe suites and four carriage houses, are decorated in cool earth tones with pillow-top mattresses, 350-thread-count linens, wireless high-speed Internet access ($15 daily for in-room; free in lobby), and Bliss bath products. Sip cocktails in the W Living Room or take a dip in the courtyard pool. The helpful staff will make your stay memorable.

Faubourg Marigny and Bywater
$100-150

Situated above the **Silk Road Restaurant** (504/944-6666, www.silkroadnola. com)—a popular hangout for artists, musicians, and other Bohemian types—the airy **Balcony Guesthouse** (2483 Royal St., 504/810-8667, www.balconyguesthouse. com) offers four guest rooms and one suite, all of which have hardwood floors, simple furnishings, microwaves, and mini-fridges. Two of the rooms also feature French doors and direct balcony access. The guesthouse lies only four blocks from Washington Square Park and the music clubs along Frenchmen Street. Be prepared for tight bathrooms and the possibility of noisy revelers on the sidewalk below.

Nestled within the residential Faubourg Marigny, the whimsical, red-white-and-blue cottage of **The Burgundy Bed and Breakfast** (2513 Burgundy St., 504/261-9477, www.theburgundy.com)

epitomizes the 19th-century, Eastlake-style shotgun doubles prevalent throughout New Orleans. Boasting original hardwood floors, 12-foot ceilings, and louvered shutters, this lovingly restored inn houses four cozy guest rooms, each of which has distinctive decor. Guests can utilize the communal kitchen, relax in the parlor, and enjoy the clothing-optional spa and sunbathing area. Smoking is allowed on the back porch or in the courtyard.

Those seeking an authentic New Orleans ambience—and a bit more peace and quiet than most French Quarter hotels—will appreciate the accommodating **Lions Inn Bed & Breakfast** (2517 Chartres St., 504/945-2339 or 800/485-6846, www.lionsinn.com) in the heart of the Faubourg Marigny. The two-story home contains 10 simply furnished rooms, and on-site amenities include a daily continental breakfast, a wine-and-cheese gathering each afternoon, and a fabulous pool and hot tub in a garden setting. Unfortunately, you'll have to rely on street parking, but once parked, you're welcome to use the available bikes to tour the city. The Lions Inn also manages a few off-site properties, including a Marigny cottage and a French Quarter condo.

The charming **Old Historic Creole Inn** (2471 Dauphine St., 504/941-0243, www. creoleinn.com) lies just a few blocks downriver from Washington Square Park and about eight blocks from the Quarter. A mix of single and two-bedroom suites, the inn features high ceilings, hardwood floors, and antique beds. Guests can relax on the outdoor patio, use the computer station in the parlor, and take advantage of amenities like free parking. This friendly, easygoing guesthouse is indeed one of the better values within walking distance of the Quarter.

$150-200

To experience life in one of New Orleans's most charming and historic neighborhoods, stay at the romantic **B & W Courtyards Bed and Breakfast** (2425 Chartres St., 504/322-0474 or 800/585-5731, www.bandwcourtyards.com) set inside three mid-19th-century Creole cottages with connecting courtyards. This peaceful hideaway is a favorite with guests seeking privacy, and consequently is not suitable for children. The four rooms and two suites are decorated with fine antiques and linens; most rooms open onto one of the courtyards. In the rear patio, you can soak in a whirlpool tub under the stars. Other amenities include a small business center, unlimited local calls, and a continental breakfast.

The Frenchmen (417 Frenchmen St., 504/945-5453, www.frenchmenhotel. com) is an ideal lodging option for those hoping to explore the Marigny and the Quarter, as it's literally steps from the border between these two distinctive neighborhoods. This hospitable, though somewhat aging, hotel offers cozy guest rooms and spacious suites, some of which contain canopy beds, decorative fireplaces, and private balconies. Additional amenities include a free continental breakfast, affordable on-site parking, and a romantic brick courtyard with lush plants, wrought-iron tables, and a small pool and Jacuzzi. You're also close to the popular clubs of Frenchmen Street, so music can be heard into the wee hours.

The **Hotel de la Monnaie** (405 Esplanade Ave., 504/947-0009, http:// hoteldelamonnaie.com) promises convenience for travelers hoping to explore the Faubourg Marigny, the French Quarter, and the Mississippi riverfront. It's also a good place for families and small groups of friends, since it only offers clean, affordable suites with one or two bedrooms, dining and living areas, and kitchenettes. Built in 1984, the year that the World's Fair came to New Orleans, this spacious hotel blends traditional elements, such as balustrades, period furnishings, and outdoor courtyards, with modern amenities, such as whirlpool tubs. Other on-site features include a fitness center, a wading pool, and free parking.

Located on the Marigny side of Esplanade Avenue, the elegant yet unpretentious **Maison DuBois** (1419 Dauphine St., 866/948-1619, www.maisondubois.net) provides easy access to jazz clubs, funky eateries, and major French Quarter attractions. The five clean, comfortable suites can accommodate up to 16 guests, making the inn ideal for reunions. All of the suites have antique furnishings. On-site amenities include a palm-shaded saltwater pool and hot tub, a well-appointed parlor and dining room, and a free continental breakfast served daily in the kitchen or sun room. The charming hosts do their best to accommodate special requests.

Near the northern edge of this funky neighborhood, the **Marigny Manor House** (2125 N. Rampart St., 504/943-7826, www.marignymanorhouse.com) sits along a quiet stretch that offers a wonderful sampling of vintage 19th-century residential architecture typical of New Orleans. Built in 1848, this lovingly restored Greek Revival-style house presents four color-themed, high-ceiling rooms, neatly furnished with designer fabrics, antique furnishings, and, in some cases, crystal chandeliers, four-poster beds, and Oriental rugs over hardwood floors. One room has a balcony overlooking the brick fern-and-flower-bedecked courtyard. Amenities include delicious Southern breakfasts. The offbeat bars and restaurants of Frenchmen Street are only a short walk away.

Just a few blocks east of Washington Square Park, the moderately priced **Royal Street Courtyard Bed & Breakfast** (2438 Royal St., 504/943-6818 or 888/846-4004, www.royalstcourtyard.com) with five cozy guest rooms occupies a rambling 1850s Greek Revival-style home with a wrought-iron balcony and towering 14-foot ceilings. The tropical courtyard is punctuated with fishponds, blooming flower gardens, and a secluded hot tub.

A free continental breakfast is served. Children are not allowed.

If you're adventurous and don't mind noisy places, then you'll likely love the **Royal Street Inn** (1431 Royal St., 504/948-7499, www.royalstreetinn.com), a funky guesthouse situated above a popular neighborhood bar. You'll find five unique, unpretentious suites, from the cozy Marigny to the spacious Royal. All feature queen-size beds and couches; three suites offer balcony access. This so-called bed-and-beverage even divvies out drink tickets to its overnight guests in an attempt to entice you downstairs, where the boisterous R Bar has a pool table, a decent jukebox, and endless opportunities to mingle with eccentric locals and wide-eyed fellow travelers.

Over $200

Conveniently situated on tree-lined Esplanade Avenue, the **Lanaux Mansion** (547 Esplanade Ave., 504/330-2826, www.lanauxmansion.com, $199-275) lies within easy walking distance of laid-back eateries, famous jazz clubs, and the French Market. Built in 1879 by prominent attorney Charles Andrew Johnson, and featured in the film *The Curious Case of Benjamin Button,* this exquisite Victorian hideaway offers four gracious lodging options: two spacious rooms in the former kitchen and servants' quarters, a suite in the main house, and a private cottage with its own patio. All possess sitting areas, antique furniture, and hardwood floors. Other possible amenities include kitchenettes and shared balcony access. You can relax in the enchanting garden, enjoy a daily continental breakfast in privacy, and consult the hospitable owner about the city's highlights.

Central Business and Arts Districts
$100-150

Constructed in 1907, the world-renowned **Le Pavillon Hotel** (833 Poydras

St., 504/581-3111 or 800/535-9095, www.
lepavillon.com, from $112) offers some
of the most elegant rooms and suites in
the CBD. Besides tall ceilings, mahogany
armoires, and handmade drapes, you can
expect terry-cloth robes, designer bath
products, and minibars. There are also
seven exquisite suites; each has a unique
theme, from art deco to presidential.
Relax in the stunning lobby or take a dip
in the heated rooftop pool, which affords
incredible views. Also on-site is the well-
regarded **Crystal Room**.

Just blocks from the French Quarter,
Old No. 77 Hotel & Chandlery (535
Tchoupitoulas St., 504/527-5271, http://
old77hotel.com, from $120) is a funky
and fun, yet affordable hotel, that also
functions as an art gallery. The Where
Y'Art annex is a gallery just off the lobby.
Work from students of the New Orleans
Center for the Creative Arts, the city's tu-
ition-free arts high school, adorns the hotel's 167 trooms. The hotel is pet friendly,
too.

$150-200

For a clean, comfortable room at a relatively affordable price, the **Country Inn &
Suites by Carlson—New Orleans French
Quarter** (315 Magazine St., 504/324-5400
or 800/830-5222, www.countryinns.com,
from $149) promises quiet accommoda-
tions within easy walking distance of
Harrah's New Orleans, the riverfront
aquarium, and French Quarter diversions. Encompassing seven 19th-century
buildings, this historic hotel combines
old-world charm with modern amenities, such as an outdoor pool, a 24-hour
fitness center, a lending library, concierge
services, and valet parking, plus free hot
breakfasts.

The Midwest-based **Drury Inn &
Suites—New Orleans** (820 Poydras St.,
504/529-7800 or 800/378-7946, www.
druryhotels.com, from $169) offers one of

Top to bottom: Hotel Monteleone; Catahoula
Hotel's bar; The Columns Hotel.

the best values in the CBD. Occupying a handsome eight-story building, this 156-unit, pet-friendly hotel lies five blocks from both the French Quarter and the Superdome. The standard rooms and suites feature contemporary—if generic—furnishings. Many of the building's original details, such as the ornamental lobby staircase and Waterford crystal chandeliers, have been carefully preserved. Other amenities include a rooftop pool and hot tub, 24-hour fitness and business centers, off-site valet parking ($30 daily), a hot continental breakfast, and evening refreshments.

The **Hampton Inn & Suites New Orleans Convention Center** (1201 Convention Center Blvd., 504/566-9990 or 800/292-0653, www.neworleanshamptoninns.com, $115-246) differs a bit from the usual modern chain properties—it's set inside a five-story, redbrick, early-20th-century building where burlap sacks were once manufactured. Though completely renovated, the 288-unit hotel still contains original hardwood floors, exposed brick walls, tall windows, and high ceilings. Airy, spacious guest rooms, studios, and suites—some with kitchens—are available. An outdoor pool, business and fitness centers, a lobby bar, concierge services, and a free hot breakfast round out the amenities. The National WWII Museum, the Arts District, the Riverwalk shops, and Harrah's New Orleans all lie within walking distance.

Stay at the ★ **ACE Hotel** (600 Carondelet St., 504/900-1180, http://ace-hotel.com/neworleans, $150-250) to see and be seen. The art deco building is a modern oasis with a rooftop pool and bar that attracts beautiful people for drinks and merrymaking. The 234 guest rooms are sleek and modern. Local touches include work by New Orleans artists and suites with turntables and Martin guitars. Dark hallways, a live music venue, and a Stumptown Coffee outlet cement its ultra-hip reputation. Full-service

restaurant Josephine Estelle rounds out the offerings.

Part of the widespread Loews hotel chain, the towering downtown **Loews New Orleans Hotel** (300 Poydras St., 504/595-3300 or 866/211-6411, www.loewshotels.com, from $179) contains 285 spacious rooms and suites, featuring 300-thread-count linens, all-natural bath products, luxurious robes, Keurig coffeemakers, and, in some cases, spectacular views. Other draws include the on-site **Café Adelaide and Swizzle Stick Bar,** the indoor swimming pool, and the popular **Balance Spa.** Guests may also appreciate the babysitting and laundry services, complimentary shoeshine, valet parking ($42 daily), and live weekend entertainment in the lobby lounge. Pets ($25 daily, $100 nonrefundable fee) are both welcome and pampered here.

Intimate and nearly hidden away on a narrow CBD street, classy **Omni Royal Crescent Hotel** (535 Gravier St., 504/527-0006 or 888/444-6664, www.omnihotels.com, from $143) offers low-key, boutique-style ambience. The 97 renovated rooms and suites of this eight-story property are decorated in earthy tones with custom-made mattresses, imported bath amenities, plush robes, and honor bars; some of the suites have whirlpool tubs, and many rooms boast floor-to-ceiling windows. The pet-friendly Omni Royal Crescent also features a rooftop sun deck and hot tub, a 24-hour fitness center, and a gourmet burger restaurant. Guests can take advantage of daily continental breakfasts, business and laundry services, and currency exchange.

Part of the Marriott chain, the **Renaissance New Orleans Pere Marquette Hotel** (817 Common St., 504/525-1111 or 800/372-0482, www.marriott.com, from $146) rises 18 stories over the CBD, with 272 spacious, smartly furnished rooms and suites. Each room features the work of local photographers, and every floor commemorates a jazz luminary. Amenities include deluxe bedding and stereos. The huge bathrooms are done in sleek marble and equipped with lighted makeup mirrors. This hotel offers an outdoor heated pool, a fitness center, high-speed Internet access ($11 daily), and valet parking ($43 daily).

Over $200

The stunning ★ **International House New Orleans** (221 Camp St., 504/553-9550 or 800/633-5770, www.ihhotel. com, $125-319) occupies a 1906 Beaux-Arts building that once served as a bank and is now one of the coolest addresses in town. The 117 rooms, suites, and penthouses are decorated in stylish, muted tones with stereo systems, down comforters, and Aveda bath products. A 24-hour concierge and pricey valet parking are available. There's no pool, but you can work out in the fitness center and relax in the top-notch spa afterward. Given the fashionable clientele it courts, it's no surprise that the hotel's **Loa** bar is a favorite spot for the well-heeled to rub elbows. Several times each year, the ornate lobby is reborn to celebrate a particular festival or holiday that's dear to New Orleanians, from All Saints' Day in early November to the voodoo-based St. John's Eve in late June.

Contemporary yet urbane, the pet-friendly **Le Méridien New Orleans** (333 Poydras St., 504/525-9444, www.lemeridienneworleanshotel.com, $311-594), which recently underwent a $29 million renovation, occupies a 23 story downtown skyscraper, not far from the aquarium, Harrah's New Orleans, the Riverwalk shops, and the galleries of the Arts District. Rooms on the upper floors have exceptional river and city views. Large LED televisions, 350-thread-count sheets, and monochromatic color schemes complete the oh-so-cool look and feel of the varied rooms and suites. The hotel's coffee-shop-and-cocktail-bar **Hub,** sleek **LMNO** restaurant (www.lmnonola.com), on-site business and fitness centers, and rooftop pool make this a favorite spot for young business execs.

The **Catahoula Hotel** (914 Union St., 504/603-2442, http://catahoulahotel. com, $249-350) feels straight out of a Wes Anderson movie, with 35 minimalist rooms on a small side street, around a signature NOLA courtyard. Amenities include luxury bath products, Wi-Fi, and more. Showers don't have doors, better for couples than just friends, but the Bunk Room is ideal for a group of four who just want a place to crash. The on-site Pisco Bar, rooftop deck, and coffee shop are perfect places to sit and stay for awhile. The pet-friendly hotel is named after the state dog of Louisiana.

The upscale **Renaissance New Orleans Arts Hotel** (700 Tchoupitoulas St., 504/613-2330 or 800/431-8634, www. marriott.com, from $175), a Marriott property, occupies a five-story former warehouse dating from 1910. Its boutique-like ambience is distinctly urban—the 210 rooms and seven suites are modern, airy, and spacious with tall windows, luxurious bedding, marble bathrooms, and Aveda bath products. Guests can also enjoy the heated rooftop pool, an on-site fitness center, and the in-house restaurant, **Legacy Kitchen,** a neighborhood favorite for its creative American cuisine. Pricey amenities include high-speed Internet access ($11 daily) and valet parking ($45 daily).

Operated by the Waldorf Astoria hotel chain, the magnificent **Roosevelt New Orleans** (130 Roosevelt Way, 504/648-1200 or 800/925-3673, www.therooseveltneworleans.com, from $243) has exuded old-world charm since 1893. Fringing the French Quarter, this landmark features 369 stunning guest rooms and 135 sumptuous suites with 300-thread-count sheets, down-filled comforters, and Ferragamo bath products. This pet-friendly hotel also offers pricey extras like high-speed Internet access ($135 daily) and valet parking ($46 daily). **The Sazerac Bar** is a highlight of

Welcome, Pets!

In New Orleans, surprisingly few hotels allow pets. If you're traveling with your animal companion, consider one of these pet-friendly options.

Royal Sonesta New Orleans (page 388), in the French Quarter, allows pets under 25 pounds for a nonrefundable fee of $75 per animal.

W New Orleans—French Quarter (page 390) provides comfy pet beds, pet treats, and dog-walking services. The hotel allows only one pet per room and charges a daily cleaning fee of $25 as well as a nonrefundable deposit of $100.

ACE Hotel (page 394) welcomes pets with a $25 fee and the signing of a pet waiver. Pets must be crated when left alone in the room.

Loews New Orleans Hotel (page 394), in the CBD, offers rooms specifically intended for pets, a pet-centric room service menu, pet-walking and pet-sitting services, and gifts such as placemats, water bowls, and special treats, plus maps of local dog-walking routes. Loews limits the number of pets to two per room and charges both a $100 nonrefundable cleaning deposit and a daily $25 pet fee.

Catahoula Hotel (page 395), a CBD hotel named after the state dog of Louisiana, welcomes pets with a $75 fee.

---

this property, as is **Teddy's Café,** a coffee lounge and sweets shop. The well-regarded **Domenica** restaurant, a rooftop pool, and the **Waldorf Astoria Spa** round out the amenities. Pets up to 25 pounds are allowed with a $175 fee.

Established in 1984 and recently refurbished, the art-filled **Windsor Court Hotel** (300 Gravier St., 504/523-6000 or 800/928-7898, www.windsorcourthotel. com, $252-480) has been ranked among the top hotels in the world. The large rooms, most of them full suites, contain elegant furnishings and Italian-marble baths, giving them the air of a posh English country home. Amenities include valet parking, 24-hour concierge services, in-room spa sessions, and afternoon teas. Guests can take advantage of the 24-hour business center, the pool and health club, a stylish boutique, the upscale **Polo Club Lounge,** and **The Grill Room**. Pets are welcome (two up to 40 pounds each) for a $150 fee.

Garden District
Over $200

The unusual ★ **Green House Inn** (1212 Magazine St., 504/525-1333, www. thegreenhouseinn.com, $159-289), set in the Lower Garden District, offers a pleasant change of pace from many of New Orleans's richly urbane B&Bs. Constructed in 1840, the Greek Revival-style townhouse has a tropical, whimsical vibe, from the palm tree-shaped, clothing-optional pool to the verdant landscaping. The flower-named rooms are well outfitted with the kind of amenities you'd expect at a much pricier hotel: king-size beds, deluxe sheets and towels, all-natural bath products, and guest robes. Additionally, the pet-friendly inn offers gated off-street parking, an oversized hot tub near the pool, and easy access to area attractions like Coliseum Square and The National WWII Museum.

Set amid the historic homes of Uptown's Lower Garden District, the hospitable ★ **Terrell House Bed and Breakfast** (1441 Magazine St., 504/247-0560 or 866/261-9687, www.terrell-house.com, $175-250) is a magnificent, Italianate-style mansion. Built in the mid-19th century, it offers luxurious accommodations, plus delicious Southern-style breakfasts. Only a block from restful Coliseum Square, this beloved B&B ensures convenient access to the shops and eateries along Magazine Street, plus the St. Charles streetcar line. Two-night minimums may apply.

RV Resources

New Orleans is a challenging destination for RV travelers. Besides the pothole-riddled streets, tight corners, and numerous blind spots, there aren't many RV parks in the Greater New Orleans area. These campgrounds offer cable television, Internet access, 50-amp electrical service, full hookups, and a swimming pool. Weekly and monthly rates are often available.

• **French Quarter RV Resort** (500 N. Claiborne Ave., 504/586-3000, www. fqrv.com; $105-250): Though in a sketchy part of town, between I-10 and Louis Armstrong Park, this gated, pet-friendly resort is the most convenient choice for those interested in exploring the nearby French Quarter. Besides the 52 paved sites, amenities include showers, a hot tub, a recreation room, fitness and laundry facilities, and 24-hour on-site management and security.

• **Jude Travel Park of New Orleans** (7400 Chef Menteur Hwy., 504/241-0632 or 800/523-2196, www.judetravelparkofneworleans.com; $30): Situated in New Orleans East, this gated, pet-friendly park is relatively far from the city's major attractions. Take advantage of the laundry area, hot tub, heated showers, and shuttle service.

• **Mardi Gras RV Park & Campground** (6050 Chef Menteur Hwy., 504/243-0433 or 800/290-0085, www.mardigrasrvparkandmotel. com; $20-25): In New Orleans East, this gated, pet-friendly campground lies within easy driving distance of the French Quarter. Offering 100 grassy and paved lots (including tent and pull-through sites), the park also provides a convenience store, meeting and exercise rooms, laundry and dining areas, gas and dump stations, barbecue facilities, phone access, and 24-hour surveillance and patrol.

• **Pontchartrain Landing** (6001 France Rd., 504/286-8157 or 877/376-7850, www.pontchartrainlanding.com; $57-153): This waterfront campground offers easy access to Lake Pontchartrain. This well-lit, gated community offers 125 sites (some pull-through), 24-hour camera surveillance, 24-hour laundry access, a convenience store, a bar and seafood restaurant, a playground, a boat launch ramp, a dumping station, showers, propane gas, shuttle service to the French Quarter, furnished villas and campers, and proximity to a full-service marina.

Yet another spot that feels straight out of a movie set, rather than real life, **The Columns Hotel** (3811 St. Charles Ave., 504/899-9308, http://thecolumns.com, $180-250) is a quirky inn inside an 1883 Italianate home. Its outdoor patio bar is popular among locals. There are 20 rooms, including some suites, with fireplaces, clawfoot tubs, four-poster beds, and antique furniture. The location is ideal.

Tremé and Mid-City
$150-200

Not far from the busy intersection of Canal Street and North Carrollton Avenue, the **1896 O'Malley House** (120 S. Pierce St., 504/488-5896 or 866/226-1896, www.1896omalleyhouse.com, $155-200) is one of the more hidden, less-touristy inns in the city. This gracious, Colonial Revival-style mansion features original cypress-wood mantels, pocket doors, and other artful details. The eight sumptuous suites are filled with exceptional antiques, handsome Oriental rugs, plush four-poster beds, and elegant tables. Most rooms have whirlpool tubs. Run by exceedingly hospitable hosts, the house lies within walking distance of several restaurants and just steps from the Canal streetcar line, which links City Park to the French Quarter. A bounteous continental breakfast is included.

Information and Services

Visitor Information

New Orleans Welcome Center (529 St. Ann St., 504/568-5661, www.crt.state. la.us, 8:30am-5pm daily) is the place to grab Louisiana highway maps, as well as literature about New Orleans attractions and free coffee.

Emergency Services

Dial 911 for police, fire, or ambulance in an emergency. For non-emergency, but still urgent service, call the **New Orleans Police Department** (715 S. Broad St., 504/821-2222) or the **New Orleans Fire Department** (317 Decatur St., 504/658-4700).

If your emergency is medical in nature, you have a lot of options. **New Orleans Emergency Medical Services** (2929 Earhart Blvd.) is open 24 hours. **Tulane Medical Center** (1415 Tulane Ave., 504/988-5263) is a world-class facility. Other choices, depending on where you are in town, include: **Children's Hospital New Orleans** (200 Henry Clay Ave., 504/899-9511), **New Orleans East Hospital** (5620 Read Blvd., 504/592-6600), and **University Medical Center New Orleans** (2000 Canal St., 504/702-3000).

Bicycle Rental and Repair

A bike is a great way to get around the Crescent City. **Arts District Bike Rental** (1121 Margaret Pl., 504/521-6390; 7am-9pm Mon. and Wed.-Thurs., 7am-11:30pm Tues. and Fri.-Sun.; rentals $20 for up to 24 hours) is one block from The National WWII Museum. Stop here for rentals that include a lock, lights, and helmet. Some bikes also have cup holders and baskets. **New Orleans Bike & Board Shop** (8136 Oak St., 504/866-4439; 10am-6pm Tues.-Fri., 10am-3pm Sat.) offers bike sales and rentals, plus parts and repairs, and also carries

skateboards. **Mike the Bike Guy** (4411 Magazine St., 504/899-1344; 10am-6pm Mon.-Fri., 10am-5pm Sat.; $30-40 daily) has rentals that include a helmet, lock, and light. At **Rouler** (601 Baronne St., 504/327-7655, http://roulercycling. com; 7am-9pm Mon.-Fri., 6am-9pm Sat., 7am-9pm Sun.), you can get a beer or a cup of joe while you get your bike repaired.

Motorcycle Rental and Repair

EagleRider Motorcycle Rentals & Tours (2830 Canal St., 504/821-9575, www.eaglerider.com, 9am-5pm daily, rentals from $99 per day) rents brands including BMW, Honda, Harley-Davidson, Indian, and Triumph. **Redbeard Cycles** (8022 Orpheus Ct., 504/483-3232, 9am-5pm Mon.-Fri., 9am-noon Sat.) is a local motorcycle repair shop. **FX Motorsports** (3248 Chippewa St., 504/267-4517, 9am-5pm Mon.-Fri.) offers weekday-only sales and repairs for mopeds, scooters, and motorbikes. **New Orleans Harley-Davidson** (6015 Airline Dr., Metairie, 504/208-1909, 10am-7pm Mon.-Fri., 9am-5pm Sat., 11am-4pm Sun.) is a full-service dealership with a parts and service department.

Baton Rouge

Ever since Hurricane Katrina, when many evacuees of New Orleans relocated to Baton Rouge, the city has witnessed a population increase, as evidenced by the number of new restaurants, shops, and hotels—not to mention the increased traffic.

Racial unrest, rioting, and flooding in 2016 taxed Baton Rouge's good spirits and resources. In spite of all of that, Baton Rouge thrives. Sprawling in virtually every direction with charming residential neighborhoods, Baton Rouge feels clean and prosperous. At once the state capital and home to Louisiana State

⚑ Detour to Abita Springs

Once a Choctaw village named after the nearby springs, today Abita Springs is a sweet town of just 2,300 people. But it's known to beer-drinkers worldwide: **Abita Brewing Co.** was founded here in 1986, making beer from the namesake medicinal springs. If you love your ale, a visit here is worth a detour.

Obviously, you have to visit the **Abita Tap Room** (166 Barbee Rd., 985/893-3143, http://abita.com; 11am-7pm Sun.-Thurs., 10am-8pm Fri.-Sat.). Sit inside the taproom or outside in the beer garden and have a pint; they also do growler fills. The only food is chips and pretzels, but food trucks can usually be found on Saturday. Guided tours (2pm-3pm Wed.-Thurs., 1pm-3pm Fri., 10:30am-3pm Sat., 2pm-3pm Sun.) leave every half hour, but you can also take a self-guided tour (10am-2pm Mon.-Tues., 10am-2pm Wed.-Thurs., 11am-1pm Sun.).

When you're hungry, head to **Abita Brew Pub** (72011 Holly St., 985/892-5837, www.abitabrewpub.com; 11am-9pm Tues.-Thurs., 11am-10pm Fri.-Sat., 11am-9pm Sun.; $9-17), a restaurant housed in Abita Brewery's original brewery and bot-tling facility. You can buy growlers and six-packs to take home, too.

Right next to the pub is **Abita Springs Trailhead & Park** (22049 Main St.; dawn-dusk daily; free, donations accepted), which has a lovely pagoda, walking trails, and the **Abita Springs Trailhead Museum** (22049 Main St., 985/871-5327; 10am-5pm Mon.-Fri., 10am-5pm Sat., noon-5pm Sun.), a small art and history museum.

Getting There

To get to Abita Springs from New Orleans, take I-10 West to the Lake Pontchartrain Causeway. (Make sure someone has a camera ready for the beautiful views as you cross the lake.) The causeway continues for about 24 miles. Once you're on the north side of the lake, merge onto I-12 East, then exit at LA-59 toward Abita Springs, about five miles north. You could take I-10 around the east side of the lake, but skipping the bridge is far less scenic and doesn't necessarily save you time. Abita Springs is a 45-mile, one-hour drive from New Orleans.

University, Baton Rouge is the sort of town where government and education have formed its personality.

For the most part businesses have bounced back since the 2016 flood, but it never hurts to call ahead.

Getting There

Baton Rouge is an 81-mile, 1.5-hour drive northwest from New Orleans. Take I-10 west out of the city for 80 miles. At the junction with I-110, keep right to merge onto I-110 North. After a mile, take exit 10 to the left to get to downtown Baton Rouge.

To get to Baton Rouge from Natchez, it's a 90-mile drive south along US 61. After 80 miles, take the exit for I-110 South. Continue on I-110 for eight miles, then take exit 1E for Capitol Access Road/Capitol Park to get into downtown Baton Rouge. This drive will take just under two hours.

Stopping in Darrow

The most direct drive from Baton Rouge to New Orleans is along I-10. You can make a stop to tour **Houmas House Plantation and Gardens** (40136 LA-942, Darrow, 225/473-9380, http://houmashouse.com; 9am-8pm daily; mansion and garden tours $24, garden/grounds tours $15). Named after the native Houma people of Louisiana, this former sugar plantation was started in the 1700s. You can make it a quick trip to see the gardens and the home, which was built in 1840, or you can stay overnight at the **inn** ($350-425) and dine in the restaurant.

Taking the Great River Road

If you really want to get a feel for the region, you can skip the interstate and take the **Great River Road** to Baton Rouge from New Orleans. This road runs for about 70 miles on both sides of the Mississippi and is nicknamed Plantation Alley. Along this route you'll witness a juxtaposition of grand plantation home and trees dripping with Spanish moss against small working-class towns and petrochemical plants. If you choose to take the Great River Road, you'll have the opportunity to stop at several plantations.

San Francisco Plantation House (2646 LA-44, Garyville, 888/322-1756, http://sanfranciscoplantation.org; 9:30am-4:40pm daily Apr.-Oct., 9:30am-4pm daily Nov.-Mar.; $10-17) will be unlike anything you've seen, even if you looked at all the homes in Natchez. This restored home, finished in 1855, is an opulent steamboat Gothic style, with 14 rooms and quirky grounds.

Other popular plantations on the way include **Oak Alley Plantation** (3645 LA-18, Vacherie, 225/265-2151, www.oakalleyplantation.com; $22) and **Laura Plantation** (2247 LA-18, Vacherie, 225/265-7690, http://lauraplantation.com; $20).

The Great River Road route would take about three hours from New Orleans to Baton Rouge without stops. But if you're not going to stop and look around, there's little reason to go this way.

Sights

Downtown has a particularly rich public art collection. Make time to stroll on foot to enjoy the many interesting sculptures, particularly by the library and near the riverfront. You'll find several of Louisiana's most engaging attractions here.

Louisiana State Capitol

The **Louisiana State Capitol** (State Capitol Dr. and N. 3rd St., 225/342-7317, www.crt.state.la.us; 8am-4:30pm daily; free) was completed in March 1932. A nifty 34-story art deco wonder, it took 14 months to build with a resulting price tag of about $5 million. It is, at 450 feet, the tallest U.S. capitol building and unlike any other you've seen. One of the highlights of a visit here is touring the 27 acres of spectacularly landscaped gardens. In addition, you can look around the grand entrance and Memorial Hall; peek inside the chambers (when the state legislature is not in session); ride the elevator to the 27th-floor observation deck, which affords spectacular views of the city; and see exactly where flamboyant governor Huey P. Long was assassinated.

Louisiana's Old State Capitol

Louisiana's Old State Capitol (100 North Blvd., 225/342-0500, http://louisianaoldstatecapitol.org; 10am-4pm Tues.-Fri., 9am-3pm Sat.; free) is different from the Louisiana State Capitol. Built in 1847, this national landmark has been carefully restored and now houses the city's political history museum. Come here for artifacts and memorabilia about the state and for temporary exhibitions, such as one about the first ladies of Louisiana. Don't miss the lovely garden of established live oak trees around the building.

Old Louisiana Governor's Mansion

First resident (and 40th governor of the state) Huey Long wanted this building to look like the White House. And that it does. The **Old Louisiana Governor's Mansion** (502 North Blvd., 225/387-2464; tours 10am-3pm Tues.-Fri., adults $10, seniors $9, students $8, free for children under 5 and military) is a stucco Georgian edifice, built in 1930.

Louisiana State University

Don't miss the opportunity to check out the beautiful magnolia-lined campus of **Louisiana State University** (225/578-3202, www.lsu.edu), including its stadium and the LSU Lakes (2883 E. Lakeshore Dr.), where you can stand-up paddleboard with **Muddy Water Paddle Co.** (4355 Perkins Rd., 225/800-6848, http://muddywaterpaddleco.com, 10am-4pm Wed.-Fri., 10am-2pm Sat. and by appointment; rentals $25/hour; lessons $45/hour).

The school, established in 1860, has more than 31,000 students (graduates and undergraduates). The campus has some 250 buildings and covers about 2,000 acres just south of downtown Baton Rouge. One of the campus highlights, across from Tiger Stadium, is **Tiger Walk,** a 15,000-square-foot sanctuary and home to Mike the Tiger (www.lsu.edu/miketheetiger), the school's live tiger mascot. The sanctuary allows visitors to see Mike and learn about worldwide tiger conservation.

LSU Rural Life Museum

Only a short drive southeast of downtown, the **LSU Rural Life Museum** (4560 Essen Ln., 225/765-2437, http://rurallife.lsu.edu; 8am-5pm daily; adults $10, seniors $9, children 6-11 $8, free for children under 5) is a living-history museum situated on the 450-acre **Burden Research Plantation.** Dedicated to preserving and interpreting the lifestyles and cultures of preindustrial Louisiana, the museum comprises numerous buildings and exhibits, which show different aspects of early Louisiana living. The plantation quarters constitute a complex of authentically furnished 19th-century structures, including a kitchen, a schoolhouse, and slave cabins. Inside a large barn, you can examine tools and vehicles spanning more than 300 years. You'll also spy several historical houses that reveal Louisiana's rich tradition of folk architecture, from a country church to an Acadian house to a shotgun home. You can also tour ($3) the extensive Windrush Gardens, a 25-acre plot of semiformal gardens abundant with winding paths,

ponds, and flora typically found in 19th-century plantation gardens.

USS *Kidd* Veterans Museum

The **USS *Kidd*** (305 S. River Rd., 225/342-1942, www.usskidd.com; 9am-5pm daily; adults $10, seniors $7 senior, children 5-12 $6, free for children under 5) is the only ship of its kind that's still in its wartime camouflage paint. This World War II-era Fletcher-class destroyer was awarded 12 battle stars for serving during World War II and the Korean War; it was struck by a Japanese kamikaze plane during the World War II Battle of Okinawa, an attack that killed 38 members of the *Kidd*'s crew. It has been carefully restored and can now be toured, along with the nearby Veterans Memorial Museum, which features a nuclear-powered submarine, a World War II-era fighter plane and a Vietnam-era bomber, and the South's largest model ship collection.

Spanish Town

Established in 1805, **Spanish Town** (bounded by State Capitol Dr., 5th St., North Ave., and 9th St., http://spanishtownbr.org) is Baton Rouge's oldest neighborhood. Just west of downtown, the neighborhood is characterized by bright, colorful homes and an offbeat character. It is listed on the National Register of Historic Places. It's best to visit Spanish Town during daylight hours.

Entertainment and Events
Nightlife

Between bars, music clubs, and casinos, Baton Rouge provides a decent share of nightlife options. The low-key **Phil Brady's Bar & Grill** (4848 Government St., 225/927-3786; 11am-2am Mon.-Fri., 5pm-2am Sat.) is a fun place to drink with pals, play a round of pool, or enjoy some live music, particularly the well-attended Thursday night blues jams. College students and other music fans have been packing into **The Cadillac** (5454

Bluebonnet Blvd., 225/296-0288, www. cadillaccafe.net; 4pm-11pm Mon., 4pm-2am Tues.-Fri., 7pm-2am Sat.) since 1989 for hard-driving rock and blues. Karaoke and DJ dance parties are also big draws at this cutting-edge joint.

The city's favorite gay and lesbian dance club is **Splash Nightclub** (2183 Highland Rd., 225/242-9491, www. splashbr.com; 9pm-2am Thurs.-Sat.), situated in a slightly dodgy neighborhood near LSU's campus. Featuring multiple rooms and several bars, Splash presents a variety of music, from country to techno, plus one of Baton Rouge's best drag shows.

If you're in more of a gambling mood, head to the **Belle of Baton Rouge Casino** (103 France St., 225/242-2600 or 800/676-4847, www.belleofbatonrouge.com; 24 hours daily), which is housed inside a three-deck riverboat that's docked permanently on the Mississippi River. There are restaurants and bars in the casino, including Shucks on the Levee.

Ask an LSU alum where you should go when in town and you'll get just one answer: **The Chimes** (3357 Highland Rd., 225/383-1754, www.thechimes.com, 11am-2am Mon.-Sat., 11am-11:30pm Sun.). You'll find lots of local craft beers on tap, Southern-inspired, if average, bar food, and live music. There's also a second Baton Rouge location, **The Chimes East** (10870 Coursey Blvd., 225/296-4981, 11am-2am Mon.-Sat., 11am-11:30pm Sun.).

The Arts

For a bit of culture, head to the **Theatre Baton Rouge** (7155 Florida Blvd., 225/924-6496, www.brlt.org), which has been presenting live theater since the late 1940s. Each season's lineup typically includes several well-known plays and musicals, such as *A Streetcar Named Desire* and *Hairspray*. Another cultural option is the **Varsity Theatre** (3353 Highland Rd., 225/383-7018, www.varsitytheatre.com), a legendary concert venue that features

Louisiana State University

salsa, alternative rock, and everything in between.

Festivals and Events

From balloon festivals to Fourth of July fireworks displays, Baton Rouge presents a slew of crowd-pleasing events throughout the year. One of the most popular is the **Baton Rouge Blues Festival** (www. batonrougebluesfestival.org), a free, one-day event that usually takes place in mid-April in the city's Town Square. Founded in 1980, it's one of America's oldest blues festivals, featuring a lineup of well-respected blues guitarists, pianists, and bands.

In late October, literary fans will appreciate the **Louisiana Book Festival** (www.louisianabookfestival.org), a free, one-day event that typically occurs at various locations in downtown Baton Rouge, such as the Louisiana State Capitol and the State Library of Louisiana. Activities include readings, workshops, and a book discussion group.

Food

Where there are politicians, there are almost always good restaurants, and Baton Rouge confirms this rule with its wide variety of well-favored eateries. It's also a student town, which means you can find lots of decent, relatively affordable joints around LSU's campus.

Perhaps the most stylish restaurant in Baton Rouge is **Juban's** (3739 Perkins Rd., 225/346-8422, www.jubans.com; 5:30pm-10pm Mon. and Sat., 11am-10pm Tues.-Fri., 10:30am-3pm Sun.; $10-60). Juban's has been serving innovative Louisiana-influenced fare since the early 1980s, when owner-chef John Mariani's temple of fine cuisine was named one of America's "Best New Restaurants" in *Esquire*. The restaurant is known for such signature dishes as Louisiana crawfish pasta with shiitake mushrooms and white truffle Madeira cream, seafood-stuffed soft-shell crab topped with Creolaise sauce, and a pork rib chop with honey-bourbon glaze.

For local flavors that won't blow your budget, head to **Jasmines on the Bayou** (6010 Jones Creek Rd., 225/753-3668, www.jasminesonthebayou.com; 10:30am-8:30pm Mon.-Thurs., 10:30am-9:30pm Fri., 11am-9:30pm Sat.; $11-17). Essentially a Cajun seafood restaurant, Jasmines offers such tasty regional fare as corn and crab bisque, grilled shrimp rémoulade, and pasta jambalaya. Start with an order of rocket shrimp, which are lightly battered and tossed in a spicy chili aioli sauce.

Southern-inspired small plates such as boudin balls, fried green tomatoes with crabmeat, and truffled fried oysters are on the menu at **Beausoleil Restaurant and Bar** (7731 Jefferson Hwy., 225/926-1172, www.beausoleilrestaurantandbar.com; 11am-9pm Tues.-Thurs., 11am-10pm Fri.-Sat., 11am-3pm Sun., $17-38). Like many restaurants in Baton Rouge, it is a great place to hear live music while eating local seafood.

City Pork Deli & Charcuterie (2363

Hollydale Ave., 225/300-4550, http://citypork.com, 11am-9pm Mon.-Fri., 9am-9pm Sat., 9am-3pm Sun., $9-14) is boutique deli with meat-heavy sandwiches, cheese and charcuterie, local beers, and craft cocktails. Sibling spots include **City Pork Brasserie & Bar** (7327 Jefferson Hwy., 225/615-8880, 11am-9pm Mon.-Thurs., 11am-10pm Fri.-Sat., 11am-8pm Sun.) and **City Pork Kitchen & Pig** (6721 Exchequer Dr., 225/248-6453, 6am-2pm Mon.-Fri.).

Louie's Café (3322 Lake St., 225/346-8221, www.louiescafe.org, 24 hours daily, $4-15) is popular with college kids because it is cheap and open 24 hours a day. But this classic 1940s diner appeals to everyone with its red vinyl stools, checkered floors, and buttermilk biscuits.

Accommodations

Most of the city's lodging options comprise major chain hotels and motels, primarily set just off I-12 and I-10, on the southeast side of town. Perhaps Baton Rouge's most impressive property is the **Hilton Baton Rouge Capitol Center** (201 Lafayette St., 225/344-5866 or 877/862-9800, www.hiltoncapitol-center.com; $149-199), which opened in 2006 in the historical buildings that once housed the Heidelberg and Capitol House Hotels. Developers spent about $70 million creating this elegant property with 290 smartly furnished rooms, a full-service spa and fitness center, a pool deck overlooking the Mississippi River, and a lavish restaurant, Kingfish. Other amenities include complimentary newspapers and 24-hour room service.

Wyndham Garden Baton Rouge (5600 Bluebonnet Blvd., 225/293-1199, $95-119), while technically a motel, has rooms with microfridges and microwaves, plus amenities such as a hotel bar, business center, and fitness center. The **Renaissance Baton Rouge** (7000 Bluebonnet Blvd., 225/215-7000, www.marriott.com, $199-239) is a very contemporary, clean, and

The USS *Kidd* is docked near downtown Baton Rouge.

sleek hotel with eclectic lobby decor and a decidedly big-city feel. Some rooms have a view of Jimmy Swaggart's mammoth bible college.

If you're coming to town to visit the LSU campus, stay at the **Cook Hotel and Conference Center at LSU** (3848 W. Lakeshore Dr., 225/383-2665, http://the-cookhotel.com, $119-179).

The **Stockade Bed & Breakfast** (8860 Highland Rd., 225/769-7358, http://

thestockade.com, $150-215) has four regular guest rooms, plus one two-bedroom suite. Leave time to walk the nature trails on the grounds.

Information and Services

For more information about the state's charming capital city, consult **Visit Baton Rouge** (359 3rd St., 225/383-1825 or 800/527-6843, www.visitbatonrouge. com; 8am-5pm Mon.-Fri.).

Essentials

Getting There

Getting to Nashville

Thanks to a friendly, accessible airport, easy access to several interstates, reliable bus services, and a plethora of rental cars, getting to Music City shouldn't be a hassle (although no guarantees about the rush-hour traffic once you arrive).

Many visitors to Nashville drive their own cars. In fact, the city is said to be within a day's drive of one-half of the U.S. population. The highways are good, distances are manageable, and many, if not most, destinations in the city and surrounding area are not accessible by public transportation.

Air

The **Nashville International Airport** (BNA, http://flynashville.com) brings back some of the pleasure to air travel. Despite shuttling 12 million passengers annually, it is easy to navigate, affordable to park at, and only overwhelmingly crowded during big events like CMA Music Festival. BNA offers email updates that tell travelers when to expect congestion, so they can plan accordingly. BNA is about nine miles east of downtown, a 20-minute drive in average traffic.

The terminal is filled with local art and live music and comfortable waiting areas for those picking up in-bound passengers. There's even a health clinic for routine medical care. Exchange currency at **SunTrust Bank** near A/B concourse or at the **Business Service Center** (Wright Travel, 615/275-2658) near C/D concourse.

Airport Transportation

Many of the major hotels offer shuttles from the airport; a kiosk on the lower level of the terminal can help you find the right one.

BNA was the first airport in the United States to include "transportation network companies," such as Lyft and Uber, in their plans. A designated ride sharing area is on the ground floor where hotel shuttles wait, past the taxi stand.

Taxis are also a feasible option for ground transport from BNA. Rates start at $7 plus $2.10 per mile. To downtown or Opryland, the flat rate is $25.

Bus

Greyhound (709 5th Ave. S., 615/255-3556, www.greyhound.com) fully serves Music City, with daily routes that crisscross the state in nearly every direction. In 2012 the city opened a LEED-certified depot. The environmentally friendly building has parking for picking up passengers, a restaurant, a vending area, and ample space for buses coming and going. Service goes to major cities in most directions, including Atlanta, Chattanooga, Memphis, and Louisville.

Budget-friendly **Megabus** (http://us.megabus.com) leaves from the same station. Megabus boasts free Wi-Fi on board.

Getting to New Orleans

New Orleans's airport is well served by most major airlines and has direct flights to many of the nation's largest cities. The city also has direct Amtrak train service and Greyhound bus service from many big cities, but these modes of transport are often quite time-consuming and, especially in the case of trains, not always less expensive than flying.

Air

Louis Armstrong New Orleans International Airport (MSY, 900 Airline Dr., Kenner, 504/303-7500, www.flymsy.com), 15 miles west of downtown New Orleans via I-10, is a massive facility with service on several airlines. It's easy to find direct flights from most major U.S. cities. British Airways flies direct from London four times per week. A new $807 million terminal at Louis Armstrong will include 30 new gates, 2,000 more parking spaces, and a new access road. It's slated to open in October 2018.

Commercial air service is also available to Baton Rouge, Lafayette, and Lake Charles. Situated roughly eight miles north of downtown Baton Rouge via I-110, **Baton Rouge Metropolitan Airport** (9430 Jackie Cochran Dr., 225/355-0333, www.flybtr.com) is served by American Airlines, Delta, and United, with frequent direct flights to and from Atlanta, Dallas, Houston, and Memphis. **Lafayette Regional Airport** (200 Terminal Dr., 337/266-4400, www.lftairport.com) is three miles southeast of downtown Lafayette via US-90. It is served by Delta, American Airlines, and United, with direct flights to and from Atlanta, Dallas, Houston, and Memphis. **Lake Charles Regional Airport** (500 Airport Blvd., 337/477-6051, www.flylakecharles.com) is nine miles south of downtown Lake Charles via LA-385. You can take direct flights to and from Houston, courtesy of United, and Dallas, courtesy of American Airlines. If you choose to fly into one of these three regional airports, you'll have to rent a car to reach New Orleans. Avis, Budget, Hertz, National, and Enterprise serve all three locales.

Airport Transportation

Depending on traffic, the 15-mile trip from the airport to the French Quarter can take 25-35 minutes by car. A **taxi** from the airport to the Central Business District (CBD) usually costs $33 for one or two passengers and $14 per person for three or more passengers. Pickup occurs on the airport's lower level, just outside the baggage claim area. Extra baggage might require an additional charge; credit cards are typically accepted.

Using a ride-sharing service like Lyft or Uber costs about $33, plus a $4 airport surcharge. There's a designated meeting place on the ground level for these services.

If you'd prefer to travel in style, consider **Airport Limousine** (504/305-2450 or 866/739-5466, www.airportlimousineneworleans.com), the airport's official limo service, which has handy kiosks in the baggage claim area. The number of passengers will determine the type of vehicle selected: sedans for up to three passengers, SUVs for up to five, and limos for six or more. For one-way trips to the French Quarter and CBD, rates start at $58 for one or two passengers; a nominal fuel charge is generally applied to all rides.

To save a little money, opt for the **Airport Shuttle** (504/522-3500 or 866/596-2699, www.airportshuttleneworleans.com; $24 adult one-way, $44 adult round-trip, children under 6 free), which offers shared-ride service to hotels in the French Quarter, the CBD, and Uptown. From the upper level of the airport outside Door 7, you can also hop aboard the **E2 Airport Bus** (504/818-1077 or 504/364-3450, www.jeffersontransit.org, $2 pp). On weekdays, the bus takes about 35 minutes to reach the CBD; on weekends, it only travels to Mid-City and you'll have to rely on an RTA bus route to reach destinations in uptown or downtown New Orleans.

If you're headed north of New Orleans, there are two helpful services at the airport. **Airport Express** (985/386-3861) offers shuttle service to and from Slidell, Covington, Hammond, and other north shore communities. Advance reservations are required. The **Tiger Airport Shuttle** (225/333-8167, www.tigerairportshuttle.com) provides transportation to and from Baton Rouge.

Train

Amtrak (800/872-7245, www.amtrak.com) operates three rail routes across southern Louisiana, all of which include stops at the **New Orleans Union Passenger Terminal** (1001 Loyola Ave., 5am-10pm daily). There are rental car agencies at Amtrak stations in most big cities.

These rail routes serve New Orleans:

- **City of New Orleans** runs daily from Chicago to New Orleans, with major stops in Memphis, Jackson, and Hammond (19 hours).

- **Crescent** runs daily between New York City and New Orleans, with major stops in Philadelphia, Baltimore, Washington, D.C., Charlotte, Atlanta, Birmingham, and Slidell (30 hours).

- **Sunset Limited,** an east-west train, runs from Los Angeles to New Orleans three times weekly, with major stops in Tucson, El Paso, San Antonio, Houston, Lake Charles, and Lafayette (48 hours).

Bus

Greyhound (800/231-2222, www.greyhound.com) is the definitive bus provider for New Orleans, with frequent and flexible service throughout the country. Buses depart daily from the **New Orleans Greyhound Station** (1001 Loyola Ave., 504/525-6075, 5:15am-9:30pm daily) with multiple stops throughout Louisiana to many neighboring states. Travel times can be significantly longer than by train, but fares are generally much cheaper.

Road Rules

Car and RV Rental

If you don't bring your own car, a dozen major rental agencies have fleets of cars, trucks, and SUVs at Nashville's airport. Agencies include **National** (615/340-6546, www.nationalcar.com), **Avis** (615/361-1212, www.avis.com), and **Hertz** (615/361-3131, www.hertz.com).

U.S. car rental companies charge a

significant fee if you want to drop off your rental at a different location than where you picked it up. Depending on the time of year and the return location, this fee can be $200 or more. However, if you want to drive the length of the Natchez Trace Parkway one way, this may be the best method.

Driving along the Natchez Trace Parkway in an RV is one of the most popular ways to see its 400-plus miles. But there are some limitations. According to the National Park Service, RVs must be less than 40,000 pounds and fewer than 55 feet long (including a tow vehicle, if you have one). Almost all parkway stops are RV-accessible. If not, they are well-marked with "no circular drive" signage at the entrance. These include: Devil's Backbone (milepost 394), Old Trace Drive (mileposts 375.8 and 401.4), Twentymile Bottom Overlook (milepost 278.4), Grindstone Ford/Mangum Mound (milepost 45.7), and the southern trailhead of the Potkopinu section (milepost 17).

One of the largest RV rental companies is **Cruise America** (www.cruiseamerica.com), which has locations in Nashville (B&C Rentals, 201 Donelson Pike, 615/885-4281), Memphis (A Aaron Moving, 10230 US 70, Lakeland, 901/867-0039), and Birmingham (Cooley RV, 23307 Diesel Dr., McCalla, 205/477-4780; Adair Tire, 2253 Decatur Hwy., Gardendale, 205/631-0042). Because Cruise America does not have a New Orleans location, you may have to adjust your route if you want to do a one-way drive with a rented RV. Otherwise, inquire with regional RV rental companies in Nashville or New Orleans. Renters should be 25 years or older. Rental rates vary depending on the size of the vehicle and other factors. They also charge for mileage, and you can buy kits that include sheets, towels, dishes, and other basic necessities. Cruise America rents RVs of standard (five-person) and large (seven-person) sizes.

Driver's Licenses

Alabama, Mississippi, Louisiana, and Tennessee recognize other U.S. driver's licenses and learner's permits. The legal driving age in all four states is 16. Most driving regulations are similar to those in other states.

Traffic Regulations

Speed limits in this region vary. Along the Trace, the speed limit is never more than 50 miles per hour, and it's as low as 40 mph in some sections. The charm of the Trace is its scenic, slow pace.

It is required by law that all drivers and passengers in a moving vehicle wear their **seatbelts.** In all four states covered in this guide, infants less than one year old must be restrained in a rear-facing car seat; children 1-3 years must be restrained in a front-facing car seat. A child of 4-8 years who is less than four feet, nine inches tall must have a booster seat. When in doubt, check the applicable state's Department of Transportation website for specific regulations.

Drunk driving is dangerous and against the law. It is illegal to drive with a blood alcohol concentration of 0.08 percent or higher in Alabama, Mississippi, Louisiana, and Tennessee.

If a police car or other authorized vehicle is on the right shoulder, and you can safely do so, you should pull into the left lane.

Texting while driving is illegal in all four states included in this guide, with Louisiana imposing the heftiest fines ($175) on offenders. Having Bluetooth or other technology that allows you to use your phone hands-free is your best option.

Fuel Availability

There are no gas stations along the Natchez Trace Parkway, so you'll need to plan accordingly to fuel up at locations off of the Trace. Each chapter of this guide has details on where to exit

Slow Down

The Natchez Trace Parkway is meant to be enjoyed at a slower pace. The speed limit is no more than 50 mph (and in some places, 40 mph). You should adhere to it not only to avoid a pricey speeding ticket, but also because at a faster pace you'll miss the many breathtaking sights and wildlife. In addition, the Natchez Trace is a popular cycling route, so drivers need to be alert and watch out for two-wheeled tourists. Bicyclists are permitted to ride in the road, and signage directs cars to drive in the opposite lane (when possible to do so safely) to pass. Driving the route prescribed in this guide (north to south) means that the Trace's milepost markers will appear in descending order. Markers will be on the left side of the parkway as you drive south and generally have the number printed on both sides of the post.

The parkway is open to RVs, although some sections of the Old Trace—the original (sunken) road that intersects the parkway in many places—are not. The same is true of trailers and other large vehicles. The parkway is off-limits to commercial vehicles, with exceptions for those that have secured a permit (800/305-7417) in advance.

the Trace to reach a gas station. Options may be limited in rural areas, particularly if your car requires premium gasoline.

Roadside Assistance

Despite the rural nature of the Trace and the Mississippi Blues Trail, you're never too far from help. However, there are no gas stations or service stations on the Trace. Fuel up in advance to avoid issues on the parkway.

Breaking down on the road doesn't have to be a vacation killer. A few preventive measures (including a full tank of gas, flares, and a spare tire) can help. Even when you're on what feels like the most remote section of the Natchez Trace, you're never that far from cell service, park rangers who patrol the parkway with some regularity, or even a good Samaritan.

Need help while on the interstate in Tennessee? Text *847 while on state highways and a HELP Program emergency responder will reply. HELP trucks patrol the area to help motorists in trouble. For non-emergency incidents in Nashville, dial 615/862-8600 to report a traffic incident or request roadside assistance. In Memphis, the local non-emergency number is 901/545-2677.

For AAA Roadside Assistance in Tennessee, Alabama, Mississippi, or Louisiana, call 800/222-4357.

The **HONK app** (www.honkforhelp.com) can be useful for roadside assistance, provided you are somewhere with strong enough cell service to run the app.

Because so many people bicycle the Trace, there are bike repair shops in most nearby cities.

Road Conditions

The weather from Nashville to New Orleans is generally mild. It's rare that significant snowfall accumulates on any portion of the Natchez Trace or surrounding roadways. However, because snow, sleet, and hail aren't common in these parts, few municipalities have equipment for significant snow removal. If it comes down, prepare for roads to be slick, with little salt or sand; local drivers will be unfamiliar with how to best drive on those roads.

Park rangers have good information on road conditions and frequently communicate with rangers elsewhere on the Trace. Start by calling the **Natchez Trace Parkway Headquarters and Visitor Center** (milepost 266, 800/305-7417) in Tupelo or check under "Current Conditions" on the Trace website (www.

nps.gov/natr/planyourvisit/conditions. htm). Depending on where you are along the Trace, the rangers at the **Parkway Information Cabin** (milepost 102.4) in Ridgeland or the **Mount Locust Historic House** (milepost 15.5) near Natchez may also be helpful. They can call ahead to ranger stations along your route to get you the current weather conditions of your destination.

Other than snow or hail in **winter,** heavy rain and wind can make driving difficult in this area. These can happen any time of the year, but spring is when tornadoes are most likely to whip through the area. Tornadoes aren't a common occurrence, but heed weather warnings that suggest you take shelter in a windstorm.

Early **summer** is thunderstorm season in the South. Pull over in a strong rainstorm if you are having any visibility issues. Southern rainstorms can be intense, but they're over quickly. If you are considering taking any of the unpaved sections described in this guide, check for significant rainfall to avoid getting stuck in the mud. Summer can be hot and humid in the South. Bring water; don't leave pets in parked cars. Heatstroke is a real risk.

In **fall,** you may be slowed down by leaf-peepers, but you aren't likely to run into weather complications. The end of summer through fall is hurricane season in New Orleans (Hurricane Katrina took place August 23-31, 2005), however, so listen to weather reports and heed any warnings to head inland.

As always, adjust driving speeds in inclement weather. When driving in rural areas, it's wise to keep an emergency kit in the trunk of your car.

Maps

Rand McNally publishes good state, regional, and city maps of this region. You can buy Rand McNally maps from bookstores and through online sales outlets. Rand McNally also sells downloadable PDF maps that you can view on your computer or print out.

Most states also create good maps of their cities and towns. Check for free downloads from each state's department of transportation website.

The Trace by Motorcycle

The absence of commercial traffic, stop signs, and stoplights and the abundance of scenic views make the Trace a popular route for motorcycle travel. Motorcyclists must abide by speed limits and other road regulations. Many of the inns, B&Bs, and restaurants nearby cater to motorcyclists.

Tennessee, Alabama, Mississippi, and Louisiana all require both drivers and passengers on a motorcycle to wear a helmet. In addition, you'll want to have eye protection, a protective jacket, long pants, boots, gloves, and a tool kit for basic repairs. Consider wearing bright colors to ensure that you're easily visible to other vehicles on the road. Check the applicable state's Department of Transportation website for specific regulations as they pertain to motorcyclists.

The Trace by Bicycle

There are no designated bicycle lanes on the Natchez Trace, in part because the National Park Service has designated the Trace in its entirety as a bicycle route. Bicyclists share the road with recreational vehicles. This means that when it's safe, drivers should move into the left lane to give cyclists more room.

If you'd like to cycle a portion of the Trace, it's possible to leave your car parked for an extended period in one of several parking lots, provided you complete a vehicle contact form (www.nps. gov/natr/planyourvisit/extended-vehi-cle-parking.htm). A few of the lots recommended by the park service are at Garrison Creek (milepost 427.6), Gordon House and Ferry Site (milepost 407.7), Natchez Trace Parkway Headquarters and Visitor Center (milepost 266), and the Parkway Information Cabin

Motorcycle Repair Shops

Franklin, Tennessee

* **Harley-Davidson Cool Springs**
  (7128 S. Springs Dr., Franklin, 615/425-3494, http://hdcoolsprings.com)

Memphis, Tennessee

* **Bumpus Harley Davidson** (2160
  Whitten Rd., 901/372-1121, http://bumpushdmemphis.com)

Florence, Alabama

* **T&M Cycles and ATVs** (3922 Cloverdale Rd., 256/ 768-3011)

Jackson, Mississippi

* **Cycle Service Plus** (2607 US 80 E.,
  Pearl, 601/939-5077, www.cycleserviceplus.net)

New Orleans, Louisiana

* **EagleRider Motorcycle Rentals &
  Tours** (2830 Canal St., 504/821-9575,
  www.eaglerider.com/neworleans)

* **Redbeard Cycles** (8022 Orpheus Ct.,
  504/483-3232)

* **New Orleans Harley-Davidson**
  (6015 Airline Dr., Metairie, 504/208-1909)

(milepost 102.4). See the NPS website for more recommended lots.

Because so many people bike the Trace, most hotels and bed-and-breakfasts offer secure places for guests to lock bicycles. Park bikes, cars, and motorcycles in well-lit parking lots. Use locking bike racks if traveling with bicycles on your car.

There are five bike-only campgrounds on the parkway:

* junction with TN-50 (milepost 408)

* Colbert's Ferry Site (milepost 327)

* Witch Dance (milepost 234)

* Natchez Trace Parkway Headquarters and Visitor Center (milepost 266)

* town of Kosciusko (milepost 159)

To get your bicycle to the start of this epic adventure, you'll want to ship it ahead. **Bike Flights** (541/705-2453, www.bikeflights.com) is a concierge service that will help you pack and ship your bike—and get it back home when you're done. They offer several shipping speeds

and methods. Prices vary based on shipment origin but start at around $60 each way.

Bike Tours and Shuttles

If you don't want to do it alone, there are tour companies and shuttles to help you out. **Lizard Head Cycling Guides** (970/728-5891, http://lizardheadcyclingguides.com, $2,740 pp) has both spring and fall guided trips, on which you can bring your bike or rent one. The cost of the seven-day trek includes meals, lodging, shuttles, and mechanical support. These trips begin in Natchez and head north to Nashville.

VBT (800/245-3868, www.vbt.com, from $2,145 pp) offers a six-day tour of the Mississippi section of the Trace, including lodging, meals, tours of Vicksburg National Military Park, and more.

Black Bear Adventures (888/339-8687, http://blackbearadventures.com, $3,100 pp) takes nine days to tour the Trace on bicycle, with options in both spring and fall.

Downtown Karla Brown (907/540-0001, www.downtownkarlabrown.com,

$500), based in Natchez, offers a shuttle service. Leave your car in Natchez, let Karla drive you and your bikes to the northern terminus, then bike south. Karla also offers a three-day, 100-mile bike tour of the Trace ($600 pp).

The Trace on Horseback

Horseback riding is a popular way to see portions of the Natchez Trace, along horse trails that run adjacent to the parkway in Tennessee and Mississippi. They include:

- Natchez Trace National Scenic Trail, Leiper's Fork Segment (milepost 408-428)

- Natchez Trace National Scenic Trail, Tupelo Segment (milepost 260)

- Witch Dance Horse Trail, Tombigbee National Forest (milepost 233)

- Natchez Trace National Scenic Trail, Ridgeland Segment (milepost 115)

- Natchez Trace National Scenic Trail, Rocky Springs Segment (milepost 59)

Horses aren't allowed in the campgrounds or picnic areas along the Trace, but there are hitching posts on the trails. Plenty of private campgrounds near the parkway allow horses, and many have horse stalls and private trails.

Note that if you are bringing a horse trailer, the Park Service has regulations:

- Bring proof of an official negative test for equine infectious anemia (EIA) dated within the last year.

- Horse trailers combined with their tow vehicle must be no longer than 55 feet.

- Load and unload horse trailers only at designated horse staging areas (marked on parkway maps).

- Only one rider per horse is allowed.

History of the Natchez Trace

In 2016 the Natchez Trace Parkway was the ninth most visited national park site in the country, with 5.8 million people driving, cycling, and walking its winding way. This was possible thanks to people who saw the Trace's historical and recreational value. Originally, each section of the Trace was maintained (or, in many cases, neglected) by local municipalities. Getting them to work together was a challenge.

But a handful of women, members of the Daughters of the American Revolution (DAR), made it happen. In 1892, Elizabeth Jones was the first DAR member from the state of Mississippi when she began advocating for a group to preserve what she called "the once famous military road." She was followed later by Lucille Mayfield, another DAR member who became the first president of the Natchez Trace Military Highway Association (later renamed the Natchez Trace Association). Mayfield and others had commemorative markers erected at important sites, often traversing the woods in the long dresses of the time to do the work themselves. They lobbied in Washington DC, to have the road paved and made part of the National Park Service.

Marketing materials from 1934 called it "the Road to Yesterday; the Pathway to Tomorrow." Nearly six million people annually can thank these women for their perseverance and foresight.

Travel Tips

Visas and Officialdom
Passports and Visas

Most citizens of a foreign country require a visa to enter the United States. There are many types of visas, issued according to the purpose of your visit. Business and

Bike Repair Shops

Nashville, Tennessee

- **Cumberland Transit** (2807 West End Ave., 615/321-4069, http://cumberland-transit.com)

- **Trace Bikes** (8400 TN-100, 615/646-2485, http://tracebikes.com)

- **EastSide Cycles** (103 S. 11th St., 615/469-1079, www.eastside-cycles.com)

- **Halcyon Bike Shop** (2802 12th Ave. S., 615/730-9344, http://halcyonbike.com)

Memphis, Tennessee

- **Peddler Bike Shop** (3548 Walker Ave., 901/327-4833, http://peddler-bikeshop.com; four other locations in greater Memphis)

- **Bikes Plus** (7007 Stage Rd., 901/385-8788, www.bikesplus.net))

Florence, Alabama

- **Spinning Spoke Cycle Hub** (221N S. Seminary St., 256/349-5302, www.spin-ningspoke.com)

Tupelo, Mississippi

- **Trails and Treads** (549B Coley Rd., 662/690-6620)

- **Bicycle Pacelines** (2120 W. Jackson St., 662/844-8660, www.bicyclepace-lines.net)

- **Tupelo Performance Cycles** (3402 Main St., 662/840-4488, www.tupelo-performancecycles.com)

Starkville, Mississippi

- **Boardtown Bikes** (200 S. Montgom-ery St., Ste. C, 662/324-1200, www.boardtownbikes.com)

Jackson, Mississippi

- **The Bike Rack** (2282 Lakeland Dr., Flowood, 601/936-2100, http://thebik-erackms.com)

- **Indian Cycle Fitness and Outdoor** (677 S. Pear Orchard Dr., 601/956-8383, http://indiancyclefitness.com)

- **The Bike Crossing** (115 West Jackson St., 601/856-0049, http://thebikecross-ing.com).

Natchez, Mississippi

- **Trippe's Western Auto** (180 Sgt. S. Prentiss Dr., 601/445-4186)

Baton Rouge, Louisiana

- **The Bicycle Shop South** (3347 High-land Rd., 225/757-5471)

- **Pedal Play Bicycles** (13726 Perkins Rd., Ste. E, 225/761-9286)

New Orleans, Louisiana

- **New Orleans Bike & Board Shop** (8136 Oak St., 504/866-4439)

- **Rouler** (601 Baronne St., 504/327-7655, http://roulercycling.com)

pleasure travelers apply for **B-1** and **B-2 visas,** respectively. When you apply for your visa, you will be required to prove that the purpose of your trip is business, pleasure, or for medical treatment; that you plan to remain in the United States for a limited period; and that you have a place of residence outside the United States. Apply for your visa at the nearest U.S. embassy. For more information, contact the **U.S. Citizenship and Immigration Service** (www.uscis.gov).

Nationals of 38 countries may be able to use the **Visa Waiver Program,** operated

A Timeline of the Trace

The Natchez Trace has been used for thousands of years, with each set of users demonstrating how important the Trace was for their era.

- According to researchers, some **10,000 years ago,** herds of bison likely made their way along what's now the Natchez Trace from the mighty Mississippi water source to salt licks in Tennessee.

- **Several thousand years ago,** Native Americans also walked this way, perhaps in search of the migrating bison—perhaps, too, in search of resources like salt and water. Throughout the route there are places to stop and see Indian burial mounds and sites of former villages. Tribes that lived in this region include (from north to south) Cherokee, Shawnee, Chickasaw, Choctaw, and Natchez.

- European explorers probably first reached the Mississippi Valley in the **1500s,** when Spaniard Hernando de Soto and his army traveled west from what is now Florida. By the **1700s,** white settlers battled with Native Americans over land and resources along the Trace.

- By the **end of the 1700s,** Nashville was a thriving region. So-called "Kaintucks," boatmen who may or may not have been from Kentucky, would travel on boats down to the Mississippi to sell their wares in Natchez and New Orleans. Then they'd head home on foot, along the Trace.

- As early as **1801** the postmaster-general of the United States suggested making the Trace easier to navigate to improve mail service. By **1803** about 264 miles had been widened and smoothed. These improvements led to more use, and many inns and stands opened to accommodate weary travelers.

- When General Andrew Jackson needed to move his troops to New Orleans during the War of **1812,** the Trace was a natural choice for a route.

- In **1837,** the U.S. government forced Native Americans from their land and homes in the southeast region westward to Oklahoma. Portions of the Trail of Tears intersect with the Trace.

- Before and after the **Civil War,** iron ore mining near the northern sections of the Trace kept local economies humming. Several decades passed, with the Trace being passed over in favor of other modes of transportation. Steamboats could travel upstream, unlike the Kaintucks' self-propelled boats. New roadways bypassed the Trace. Railroads made other routes faster, too. The Trace fell into disrepair.

- In the **early 1900s** the Daughters of the American Revolution (DAR) began to advocate for restoration and preservation of the Trace.

- In **1934** Congress approved a survey of the "Old Indian Trail" with the idea of making the national Natchez Trace Parkway. Construction began in **1938.**

- The Old Trace was added to the National Register of Historic Places in **1976,** which helped raise funds for finishing construction of the roadway.

- The Double Arch Bridge, near the northern terminus, was finished in **1993,** just in time for the Tennessee Bicentennial in **1996.**

- The final sections of the parkway (in Jackson and Natchez) were completed in **2005.**

by Customs and Border Protection. Presently, these 38 countries are: Andorra, Australia, Austria, Belgium, Brunei, Chile, Czech Republic, Denmark (including Greenland and Faroe Islands), Estonia, Finland, France, Germany, Greece, Hungary, Iceland, Ireland, Italy, Japan, Latvia, Liechtenstein, Lithuania, Luxembourg, Malta, Monaco, the Netherlands (including Aruba, Bonaire, Curaçao, Saba, and Sint Maarten), New Zealand, Norway, Portugal (including Azores and Madeira), San Marino, Singapore, Slovakia, Slovenia, South Korea, Spain, Sweden, Switzerland, Taiwan, and the United Kingdom.

Take note that in recent years the United States has begun to require visa-waiver participants to have upgraded passports with digital photographs and machine-readable information. They have also introduced requirements that even visa-waiver citizens register in advance before arriving in the United States. For more information about the Visa Waiver Program, contact the **Customs and Border Protection Agency** (www.travel.state.gov).

All foreign travelers are required to participate in **U.S. Visit,** a program operated by the Department of Homeland Security. Under the program, your fingerprints and photograph are taken—digitally and without ink—as you are being screened by an immigration officer. The visa requirements and screening process are subject to change. If you're traveling from overseas, check current visa requirements before setting out.

Embassies and Consulates

Many consulates have offices in Chicago and Houston, which are significantly far from the Natchez Trace Parkway. The exception is the **Consulate-General of Japan** (1801 West End Ave. #900, Nashville, 615/340-4300) in midtown Nashville. Your best bet is to check with the appropriate agencies before your departure.

Customs

Upon entering the United States, international travelers must declare any dollar amount over $10,000 as well as the value of any articles that will remain in the country, including gifts. A duty will be assessed for all imported goods, though visitors are usually granted a $100 exemption. Illegal drugs, Cuban cigars, obscene items, toxic substances, and prescription drugs (without an accompanying prescription) are generally prohibited. In order to protect American agriculture, customs officials will also confiscate certain produce, plants, seeds, nuts, meat, and other potentially dangerous biological products. For more information, consult **U.S. Customs and Border Protection** (703/526-4200, www.cbp.gov).

Visitor Information

Many cities have their own tourist organizations. In some rural areas, counties have teamed up to develop visitor information for the region. Other organizations, such as the National Park Service, Army Corps of Engineers, and state parks, publish visitor information for certain attractions. Specific listings for visitor information are found throughout this book.

Tennessee

The **Tennessee Department of Tourism Development** (615/741-2159, www.tnvacation.com) is a source of visitor information about Tennessee. It publishes an annual guide that contains hotel and attraction listings. The website has lots of links to local attractions and chambers of commerce.

Several regional tourism organizations provide useful information and publications: Middle Tennessee has the **Middle Tennessee Tourism Council** (www.middletennesseetourism.com), which covers the counties around Nashville; the **Upper Cumberland Tourism Association** (www.uppercumberland.org), which promotes the region surrounding the Cumberland River and the northern plateau; and the **South Central Tennessee Tourism Association** (www.sctta.net).

Alabama

For information on the tiny corner of the Yellowhammer State through which the Trace cuts, there are several tourism organizations with good information and Southern hospitality. Start with the **Shoals Chamber of Commerce** (20 Hightower Pl., 256/764-4661, www.shoalschamber.com) and **Visit Florence** (200 Jim Spain Dr., 256/740-4141, www.visitflorenceal.com), which serves the city of Florence in the Quad Cities area. **Colbert County Tourism** (719 US 72 W., 256/383-2080, www.colbertcountytourism.org) covers Muscle Shoals, Tuscumbia, Florence, and Sheffield and operates a **visitors center** (8:30am-5pm Mon.-Fri.).

Mississippi

If you take the Natchez Trace Parkway or the Mississippi Blues Trail, you'll be covering much of the Magnolia State. **Visit Mississippi** (501 N. West St., Ste. 500, 601/359-3297, www.visitmississippi.org) fields general inquiries and provides travel guides.

Visit Vicksburg (52 Old Hwy. 27, Vicksburg, 800/221-3536, http://visitvicksburg.com) offers a free guide for visitors and is particularly well-versed in information for veterans and others interested in military history.

The **Greater Starkville Development Partnership** (662/323-3322, www.starkville.org/visit) has a prime downtown location in Starkville and lots of information on the college town. **Visit Oxford Visitor's Center** (1013 Jackson Ave. E., Oxford, 662/232-2477, http://visitoxfordms.com, 8am-5pm Mon.-Fri., 10am-4pm Sat., 1pm-4pm Sun.) is well located in the town of Oxford and chockfull of maps, information, and Southern charm.

Louisiana

For general information about traveling in southeastern Louisiana, your best resource is the state-run **Louisiana Office of Tourism** (800/994-8626, www.louisianatravel.com), which offers a tour guidebook, interactive maps, travel tips, and oodles of information about the state's accommodations, restaurants, attractions, events, live entertainment, and outdoor activities, plus live operators willing to assist with your tourism needs.

Visitors to the Big Easy should consult the **New Orleans Convention & Visitors Bureau** (2020 St. Charles Ave., 504/566-5011 or 800/672-6124, www.neworleanscvb.com, 8:30am-5pm Mon.-Fri.) or the **New Orleans Tourism Marketing Corporation** (2020 St. Charles Ave., 504/524-4784, www.neworleansonline.com), both of which provide a slew of information about the city's myriad lodging, dining, and activity options. The **New Orleans Welcome Center** (529 St. Ann St., 504/568-5661, www.crt.state.la.us, 8:30am-5pm daily) also provides maps and brochures and arranges tours.

For information about the Greater New Orleans area, consult the **Jefferson Convention & Visitors Bureau** (1221 Elmwood Park Blvd., Ste. 411, 504/731-7083 or 877/572-7474, www.experiencejefferson.com).

Visit Baton Rouge (359 3rd St., Baton Rouge, 225/383-1825, www.visitbatonrouge.com) is the official travel resource for visitors to Louisiana's capital city.

Access for Travelers with Disabilities

Several national organizations offer information and advice about traveling with disabilities. The **Society for Accessible Travel and Hospitality** (www.sath.org) publishes links to major airlines' accessibility policies and publishes travel tips for people with all types of disabilities, including blindness, deafness, mobility disorders, diabetes, kidney disease, and arthritis. The society publishes *Open World,* an online magazine about accessible travel.

Wheelchair Getaways (800/642-2042, www.wheelchairgetaways.com) is a national chain specializing in renting vans that are wheelchair accessible or otherwise designed for drivers and travelers with disabilities. Wheelchair Getaways has locations in Memphis, Tennessee (901/795-6533 or 866/762-1656) and Jackson, Mississippi (901/795-6533 or 866-762-1656), and it will deliver to other locations.

Rental car company Avis offers **Avis Access,** a program for travelers with disabilities. Call the dedicated 24-hour toll-free number (888/879-4273) for help renting a car with features such as transfer boards, hand controls, spinner knobs, and swivel seats.

Some of New Orleans's older hotels, cobblestone streets, and other charms can make accessible travel a challenge. Within new hotels, some large restaurants, and most major attractions, you can expect to find wheelchair-accessible restrooms, entrance ramps, and other helpful fixtures; RTA buses are wheelchair-accessible. But New Orleans has many hole-in-the-wall cafés, tiny B&Bs, historical houses with narrow staircases or uneven thresholds, and other buildings that are not easily accessible to people using wheelchairs. Unfortunately, the city's historic streetcars are also not wheelchair-accessible. If you're traveling with a guide animal, be sure to contact every hotel or restaurant in question to confirm access and accommodation. Some of these issues also apply in older cities in this region, such as Vicksburg and Natchez.

Traveling with Children

Although New Orleans tends to be geared more toward adults than children, there are nevertheless some outstanding attractions for kids, such as the Audubon Aquarium of the Americas, the Audubon Butterfly Garden and Insectarium, Blaine Kern's Mardi Gras World, the Audubon Zoo, Storyland at City Park, and the Louisiana Children's Museum, right in the CBD. Many of the excursions offered throughout the city, such as swamp tours, riverboat rides, and haunted strolls, are a big hit with kids, especially teenagers. For more ideas, consult **New Orleans Kids** (www.neworleanskids.com), which offers a slew of tips regarding family-friendly hotels, restaurants, attractions, and activities.

While plenty of inns and hotels welcome children—such as the French Quarter's Ritz-Carlton New Orleans and the CBD's Loews New Orleans Hotel, both of which offer babysitting services—some lodging options are adults-only establishments.

Senior Travelers

Both the Natchez Trace Parkway and the Mississippi Blues Trail are popular trips for seniors. Want some help getting started? **Road Scholar** (800/454-5768, www.roadscholar.org), formerly called Elderhostel, organizes educational tours in Memphis, Nashville, Baton Rouge, and New Orleans for people over 55.

For discounts and help with trip planning, try the **AARP** (800/687-2277, www.aarp.org), which offers a full-service travel agency, trip insurance, a motor club, and the AARP Passport program, which provides seniors with discounts for hotels, car rentals, and other things.

Travelers over 55 should always check for a senior discount. Most attractions and some hotels and restaurants have special pricing for senior citizens. In general, the concept of Southern hospitality is put into action daily: People are exceptionally helpful, so senior travelers should have little trouble finding assistance here.

Although the wild nightlife scene around the French Quarter can be off-putting to some, New Orleans appeals to senior travelers, particularly those who appreciate historical architecture and one-of-a-kind attractions, such as The National WWII Museum. For those who'd prefer a quieter place to sleep, consider staying in the Garden District or Uptown, especially at one of the hotels and inns along St. Charles Avenue.

LGBT Travelers

Lesbian, gay, bisexual, and transgender people are presented with a mixed bag when visiting the South. In 2013, Tennessee lawmakers introduced a bill, often referred to as the "Don't Say Gay" bill, that would have banned teachers from even saying the word *gay* in the classroom. (It failed to make it through the legislative process.) Mississippi state law does not address discrimination on basis of sexual orientation—although some cities in the Magnolia State, including Oxford and Jackson, have such laws. Similar laws exist in Alabama; some officials there have been outspoken about their opposition to same-sex marriage. In 2016, the British Foreign Office issued a warning to British LGBT travelers to be aware of a Mississippi law that permits businesses to refuse service to someone based on sexual orientation.

On the other hand, there has been no better time to be gay in the South. More and more social, civic, and political organizations are engaging the gay community, and there are vibrant gay scenes in several of the region's larger cities.

For gay travelers, this means that the experience on the road can vary tremendously. You can find gay nightlife and gay-friendly lodging in many cities, but you may experience chilly treatment in the countryside. Memphis is progressive and welcoming, but rural areas along the Mississippi Blues Trail may be more conservative.

New Orleans is a bastion of gay-friendliness, with gay newspapers, numerous gay and lesbian organizations and gay-owned businesses, and several gay-dominated bars and nightclubs, many of which are in the midst of the nightlife district in the French Quarter. The Quarter, the Faubourg Marigny, and Uptown tend to have the highest lesbian and gay populations.

Three annual events—Mardi Gras in the late winter, the Southern Decadence celebration over Labor Day weekend, and Halloween in the fall—draw the greatest numbers of gay and lesbian visitors to New Orleans, but the city is always popular with gay and lesbian travelers. Many inns and B&Bs, especially in the Faubourg Marigny, are gay-owned.

Resources for LGBT Travelers

Several guidebooks and websites give helpful listings of gay-friendly hotels, restaurants, and bars. The **Damron LGBT Travel Guides** (www.damron.com) offer Tennessee listings; the **International Gay and Lesbian Travel Association** (IGLTA, www.iglta.org) is a trade organization with listings of gay-friendly hotels, tour operators, and much more. San Francisco-based **Now, Voyager** (www.nowvoyager.com) is a gay-owned and gay-operated travel agency that specializes in gay tours, vacation packages, and cruises.

Out and About (www.outandaboutnewspaper.com) is a free monthly newsmagazine for the gay, lesbian, bisexual, and transgender community in Nashville. **OUT Memphis** (892 S. Cooper St., Memphis, 901/278-6422, www.outmemphis.org) is a clearinghouse of information for the gay and lesbian community. They offer a directory of gay-friendly businesses, host social events, and promote tolerance and equality.

Mid-South Pride (www.midsouthpride.org) organizes Memphis Pride in June.

Unity Mississippi (http://unityms.org) is the state's LGBT business and social network.

For more information about gay and

lesbian activities in New Orleans, consult the free bimonthly *Ambush Mag* (www. ambushmag.com). The same publication also has a website just for gay goings-on during Mardi Gras (www.gaymardigras. com). Another helpful website is www. gayneworleans.com.

Traveling without Reservations

Part of the serendipity of a road trip is traveling without reservations and staying where the spirit moves you. Unless you are traveling during a special event (like CMA Music Festival in Nashville, Pilgrimage in Natchez, or Mardi Gras in New Orleans), traveling without booking reservations ahead of time is generally possible.

However, many of the inns and bed-and-breakfasts listed in this guide have just a handful of rooms, so they may be sold out by the time you arrive. In cities such as Florence, Tupelo, and Jackson, you'll be able to find a decent hotel without trouble. If you have special requests or needs, you're best off booking in advance.

Communications and Media
Area Codes

Tennessee has seven different area codes. Of those, Memphis and vicinity use 901; Nashville and the counties immediately north of the city are in 615 and 629.

In the Shoals area of Alabama area codes are 256 and 938.

Mississippi has four area codes. Southern Mississippi is covered by 769 and 601, and northern Mississippi uses 662.

In Louisiana, Baton Rouge uses 225 and New Orleans uses 504.

Cell Phones

Cell phone signals are powerful and reliable in cities and along the interstates. On rural sections of the Natchez Trace and less populated sections of the Mississippi Blues Trail, you should not count on your cell phone having service.

Money

Bank debit cards and major credit cards are accepted throughout the southeastern region, particularly in major cities. However, it's not unusual for gas stations, markets, roadside stands, and other shops in rural areas to be cash-only. Don't rely solely on credit cards on this road trip, particularly along the Natchez Trace Parkway and the Mississippi Blues Trail.

Banks and ATMs

In Tennessee, the most prevalent banks are **SunTrust** (800/786-8787, www.suntrust.com), **First Tennessee** (800/382-5465, www.firsttennessee.com), and **Regions** (800/734-4667, www.regions.com). Alabama is also **Regions** territory, and you may find plenty of **Compass Bank** (800/266-7277, www.bbvacompass.com) locations. In Mississippi **Regions** and **BancCorpSouth** (800/844-2723, www.banccorpsouth.com) are reliable choices. In Louisiana, try **Chase** (800/935-9935, www.chase.com), **Iberia Bank** (800/682-3231, www.iberiabank.com), **First NBC Bank** (866/441-5552, www.firstnbcbank.com), **First Bank and Trust** (888/287-9621, www.fbtonline.com), and **Bank of Louisiana** (800/288-9811, www.bankoflouisiana.com).

Automated teller machines (ATMs) are prevalent throughout the region, and most banks provide access to ATMs inside and/or outside their branches. Be prepared to pay $2-3 per transaction if the machine isn't operated by your bank.

Currency Exchange

For up-to-date exchange rates, consult www.xe.com. In Nashville, the **Wright Travel Business Center** has a currency exchange location on the departures level of Nashville International Airport (http://flynashville.com), between Southwest and Delta Airlines.

In New Orleans, foreign currency can be exchanged at **Whitney Bank** (900

Airline Dr., Kenner, 504/838-6491 or 800/844-4450, www.whitneybank.com; 9am-5pm Mon.-Fri.) in the ticket lobby of the Louis Armstrong New Orleans International Airport; cash advances and travelers checks are also available.

Sales Tax
Tennessee
In Tennessee, sales tax is charged on all goods, including food and groceries. Sales tax is split between the state and local governments. Tennessee's sales tax is 5 percent on food and groceries and 7 percent on all other goods. Cities and towns add an additional "local use tax" of 1.5-2.75 percent, making the tax as high as 9.25 percent in Nashville and Memphis.

Alabama
Alabama's sales tax is 4 percent, but in some cities the combined rate reaches 11 percent. The combined rate in Florence is 8.5 percent.

Mississippi
Mississippi's statewide sales tax is 7 percent.

Louisiana
The combined state and city sales tax in New Orleans is 10 percent, making it one of the highest in the nation. Baton Rouge doesn't have a city sales tax, so you'll just pay the state sales tax of 5 percent.

Hotel Tax
Tennessee
There is no statewide tax on hotel rooms, but 45 different cities have established their own hotel tax, ranging 5-7 percent.

Alabama
A statewide hotel tax of 4 percent applies everywhere except the Alabama Mountain Lakes Region in North Alabama, which includes the part of Alabama through which the Natchez Trace runs.

Mississippi
There's a 2 percent tax on hotel rooms (but not food or entertainment) in Jackson County.

Louisiana
There is no statewide tax on hotel rooms, but Jefferson and Orleans parishes have a 4 percent room tax.

Tipping
Tipping is standard in this region. You should tip servers 15-20 percent in a sit-down restaurant. It's acceptable to tip 5-10 percent in a cafeteria-style or counter-service restaurant.

Tip bellhops or bag handlers $1 per bag—more if they went out of their way to help you.

Health and Safety

Medical Services
Dial 911 for police, fire, or ambulance in an emergency. Most medical and dental facilities will require insurance or a partial payment before admitting patients for treatment or dispensing medication.

Tennessee
Health care is a big industry in Nashville, so there are a lot of hospitals. Should you need emergency medical care, the majority of the hospitals are clustered in midtown, near Vanderbilt. **The Monroe Carell Jr. Children's Hospital** (2200 Children's Way, 615/936-1000, www.childrenshospital.vanderbilt.org) at Vanderbilt is among the best in the country. **TriStar Skyline Medical Center** (3441 Dickerson Pike, 615/769-2000, http://tristarskyline.com) is the closest hospital to Music Valley and parts of east Nashville.

Nashville's local number for "urgency without emergency" is 615/862-8600.

Midtown Memphis is referred to as Medical Center for the number of hospitals and medical facilities there. Among them are **Regional One Health** (877

Jefferson Ave., 901/545-7100, www.regionalonehealth.org) and the **Methodist University Hospital** (1265 Union Ave., 901/516-7000, www.methodisthealth.org).

In east Memphis, **Baptist Memorial Hospital** (6019 Walnut Grove Rd., 901/226-5000, www.baptistonline.org/memphis) is the cornerstone of the huge Baptist Memorial Health Care System.

Mississippi

In Oxford, **Baptist Memorial Hospital** (2301 S. Lamar Blvd., 662/232-8100, www.baptistonline.org) is a full service hospital.

Starkville's **OCH Regional Medical Center** (400 Hospital Rd., 662/323-4320, www.och.org) has a 24/7 emergency room and other services.

In Natchez, **Merit Health Natchez** (54 Seargent Prentiss Dr., 601/443-2100, www.merithealthnatchez.com) is the hospital closest to the southern terminus of the parkway.

Louisiana

Baton Rouge locals call it Mid City or The General. The official name is **Baton Rouge General Medical Center** (3600 Florida Blvd., 225/387-7000), and it's the place to go in a medical emergency. It is open 24 hours.

There are several well-regarded hospitals and clinics in New Orleans and its environs, including the **Tulane Medical Center** (1415 Tulane Ave., 504/988-5263, www.tulanehealthcare.com), the closest general hospital to the French Quarter and the CBD; the **Interim LSU Public Hospital** (2021 Perdido St., 504/903-3000, www.mclno.org), the active part of a major medical center still in progress; and the **Ochsner Baptist Medical Center** (2700 Napoleon Ave., 504/899-9311, www.ochsner.org), an Uptown hospital with a 24-hour emergency room.

If you're in need of emergency dental care, consider the **Louisiana Dental Center** (4232 St. Claude Ave., New Orleans, 504/947-2958, www.ladentalcenter.com, 7:30am-4pm Mon.-Thurs., 7:30am-3pm Fri., 9am-3pm Sat.), which offers several locations in southeastern Louisiana, from Metairie to Gonzales.

In the event of a hurricane or other natural disaster, contact the **New Orleans Office of Homeland Security and Emergency Preparedness** (504/658-8700) for instructions and evacuation assistance.

Wilderness Safety
West Nile Virus

West Nile virus was first recorded in humans in the United States in the early 2000s, and by 2007 nearly every state, including Tennessee, Alabama, Mississippi, and Louisiana, had reported confirmed cases of the disease. West Nile is spread by mosquitoes.

Summer is mosquito season in the southeast. You can prevent mosquito bites by wearing an insect repellent containing 30-50 percent DEET. An alternative to DEET, picaridin, is available in 7 and 15 percent concentrations and would need to be applied more frequently. Wearing long-sleeved pants and shirts and not being outdoors during dusk and dawn are also ways to avoid exposure to mosquitoes.

Fever, chills, weakness, drowsiness, and fatigue are some of the symptoms of West Nile virus.

Lyme Disease

Lyme disease is a bacterial infection spread by deer ticks. The first indication you might have Lyme disease is the appearance of a red rash where you have been bitten by a tick. Following that, symptoms are flu-like. During late-stage Lyme disease, neurological effects are reported.

Ticks are external parasites that attach themselves to warm-blooded creatures like dogs, deer, and humans. Ticks suck blood from their host.

Tick bites are unpleasant enough, even

if there is no infection of Lyme disease. After coming in from the woods, especially if you were walking off-trail, carefully inspect your body for ticks. If one has attached itself to you, remove it by carefully "unscrewing" it from your body with tweezers.

You can avoid ticks by wearing long sleeves and pants, tucking in your shirt, and wearing a hat. You can minimize your exposure to ticks by staying on trails and walking paths where you don't brush up against trees and branches.

White-Nose Syndrome

In 2006 in upstate New York, a caver noticed a substance on the noses of hibernating bats, as well as a few dead bats. The next year, more of both were found. Now bats dying of a fungus called white-nose syndrome have been found across the country.

Researchers are still trying to find out what causes the deadly (to bats, not people) fungus. Until then, certain caves may be closed to prevent the disease from spreading. Check individual cave listings before heading out.

Poison Ivy

If there is one plant that you should learn to identify, it is poison ivy. This woody vine grows in woods all around the southeast. Touching it can leave you with a painful and terribly uncomfortable reaction.

Poison ivy is green, and the leaves grow in clusters of three. There are no thorns. Its berries are a gray-white color, and if the vine is climbing, you will notice root "hairs" on the vine. The following mnemonic might help: "Leaves of three, let it be; berries white, danger in sight."

An estimated 15-35 percent of people are not allergic to poison ivy. But after repeated exposure this protection is worn down. People who are allergic will experience more and more severe reactions with each episode of exposure.

Poison ivy is easily spread over your body by your hands or from person to person through skin-to-skin contact. Never touch your eyes or face if you think you may have touched poison ivy, and always wash yourself with hot soapy water if you think you may have come into contact with the vine.

Treat poison ivy rashes with over-the-counter itch creams. In severe cases, you may need to go to the doctor.

Heatstroke

Hot, sunny days are common in the southeast, and it's crucial to prepare for them. Apply sunscreen frequently and liberally. Prolonged sun exposure, high temperatures, and little water consumption can cause dehydration, which can lead to heat exhaustion—a harmful condition whereby your internal cooling system begins to shut down. Symptoms may include clammy skin, weakness, vomiting, and abnormal body temperature. In such instances, you must lie down in the shade, remove restrictive clothing, and drink some water.

If you do not treat heat exhaustion promptly, your condition can worsen quickly, leading to heatstroke (or sunstroke), a dangerous condition whereby your internal body temperature starts to rise to a potentially fatal level. Symptoms can include dizziness, vomiting, diarrhea, abnormal breathing and blood pressure, cessation of sweating, headache, and confusion. If any of these occur, head to a hospital as soon as possible.

Wildlife
Venomous Snakes

The vast majority of snakes in Tennessee are nonvenomous. Only four species of venomous snakes exist there. Copperheads (northern and southern) live throughout the state, along with the timber rattlesnake.

In both Alabama and Mississippi, there are six species of venomous snakes, five of them related to pit vipers. Rattlesnakes, cottonmouths, and copperheads are among the seven species of venomous snakes in Louisiana.

Crime

Wherever you are, to minimize any threat to your safety and your belongings, follow these commonsense precautions:

- Never leave valuables in plain view on a car seat; secure them in the trunk where they can't be seen.

- In case of an accident on the highway, do not abandon your vehicle.

- Don't display money, valuables, or jewelry conspicuously.

- Keep your money, credit cards, identification, and other important items hidden on your person; purses and backpacks are much easier to steal.

- Leave all but the most necessary items at home or at your hotel.

- Store laptop computers, cameras, jewelry, or any other expensive or irreplaceable items in the hotel safe.

- Secure your bike whenever it's left unattended.

- Lock your hotel and car doors at all times.

- Pay attention to your surroundings and walk along well-lit, well-traveled streets.

- Avoid dark and mostly residential areas.

- Never go into cemeteries after dark.

- Travel in groups of at least two whenever possible.

- Take cabs to parts of town with which you're unfamiliar.

- If you're traveling via RV, do not boondock alone in an isolated place; try to stay in an RV park, a campground, or, at the very least, a well-lit parking lot.

Tennessee

Areas that cater to tourists in Nashville are popular with pickpockets. Call **Nashville Crime Stoppers** (615/742-7463, www.nashvillecrimestoppers.com) if you see suspicious activity.

Memphis's crime rates are a topic of discussion, and certain neighborhoods can shift from generally safe to not-as-safe fairly quickly. Single travelers, especially women, should take special care to stay in well-lit and highly populated areas, especially at night. It's a good idea to avoid walking alone down Beale Street at night, although security cameras have made the area safer in the last few years. Downtown and Midtown are considered the safest neighborhoods. Though Graceland is a heavily touristed area during the day, it's not a good idea to wander the area at night, when it's quieter and more isolated.

Mississippi

Jackson has a varied reputation when it comes to crime. Parts of the capital are picture-perfect for a stroll; others see their share of crime. Farish Street and downtown in particular have a different vibe at night than they do during the day. If you're traveling alone, consider staying in Ridgeland, which is close enough to visit Jackson during the day but sleepier at night.

Louisiana

New Orleans has a reputation for crime—partially deserved, partially exaggerated. While crime is prevalent in neighborhoods like the Tremé and Bywater, a lot of crime is also centered in or near tourist areas, and muggings or carjackings, while infrequent, do occur.

The most frequent targets of crime in New Orleans are inebriated tourists, and these, unfortunately, are easy to find in the French Quarter late at night. If you're planning a night of revelry, keep the name and address of your hotel written down someplace safe—but never write your hotel room number down somewhere that a thief or pickpocket could get it. Also be sure to carry the name and number of at least one or two cab companies, and keep your cell phone handy.

If you require assistance while in downtown New Orleans, contact **SafeWalk** (504/415-1730, 10am-10pm daily), a free service provided in the CBD and Arts District. With at least 20 minutes' advance notice, Public Safety Rangers will escort residents and visitors to their cars or other areas within the designated zone. If you do find yourself in trouble, whether in the CBD or another area of New Orleans, don't hesitate to find a phone and dial **911.**

If you witness a crime of any kind while in New Orleans, contact the **Greater New Orleans Crimestoppers** (504/822-1111 or 877/903-7867, www. crimestoppersgno.org) to offer an anonymous tip. Likewise, you can consult the **Orleans Parish Sheriff's Office** (504/822-8000 or 504/826-7045, www.opcso.org).

Suggested Reading

Travel Guides

Bachleda, F. Lynne. *Guide to the Natchez Trace Parkway.* Birmingham, AL: Menasha Ridge Press, 2011. A survey of the Trace's merits and history, plus a Top 20 list of sights to stop at during your trip along the Trace.

Cheseborough, Steve. *Blues Traveling: The Holy Sites of Delta Blues.* Jackson, MS: University Press of Mississippi, 2009. Check out maps, photos, and descriptions of relevant sights and sounds for blues fans chasing musical history through Mississippi.

Martone, Laura. *Moon New Orleans.* Berkeley, CA: Avalon Travel, 2016.

Steed, Bud. *The Haunted Natchez Trace.* Charleston, SC: Haunted America/ History Press, 2012. Paranormal tales along the Trace are detailed in this book, written in a conversational tone.

Summerlin, Cathy and Vernon. *Traveling the Trace: A Complete Tour Guide to the Historic Natchez Trace from Nashville to Natchez.* Nashville: Rutledge Hill Press, A Thomas Nelson Company, 1995. This guide features a narrative retelling of sights and points of interest in communities within 30 miles of the Natchez Trace Parkway, with a slant toward visitors traveling by bicycle.

Timme, S. Lee, and Caleb C. K. Timme. *Wildflowers of the Natchez Trace.* Jackson, MS: University Press of Mississippi, 2000. More of a field guide, this volume is full of photos to help you identify what you see.

Wanner, Glen and Ann Richards. *Bicycling the Natchez Trace: A Guide to the Natchez Trace Parkway and Nearby Scenic Routes.* Nashville: Pennywell Press, 2005. Written by two musicians in the Nashville Symphony who are also avid outdoorspeople, this guide focuses on traversing the Trace on two wheels.

Music

Berry, Jason, Jonathan Foose, and Tad Jones. *Up from the Cradle of Jazz: New Orleans Music Since World War II.* Lafayette, LA: University of Louisiana at Lafayette Press, 2009. A terrific survey tracing the history of music in the Big Easy, from the 1940s to the post-Katrina era.

Escott, Colin. *Hank Williams The Biography.* New York: Back Bay Books, 2004. No country star had a bigger impact on Nashville's evolution to Music City than Hank Williams. This detailed history shares his failings, downfall, and remarkable legacy.

Gioia, Ted. *Delta Blues: The Life and Times of the Mississippi Masters Who Revolutionized American Music.* New

York: W. W. Norton & Company, 2009. A music critic, historian, and musician himself, Gioia walks through blues history with the help of archival research, interviews, and narrative accounts.

Havighurst, Craig. *Air Castle of the South: WSM and the Making of Music City*. Champaign, IL: University of Illinois Press, 2007. Havighurst is known as the preeminent Nashville music historian and this tome delves deep into an important piece in Nashville's musical hierarchy.

Kingsbury, Paul, ed. *Will the Circle Be Unbroken: Country Music in America*. London: DK Adult, 2006. An illustrated collection of articles by 43 writers, including several performing artists, this book is a useful reference on the genre's development from 1920 until the present.

Kossner, Michael. *How Nashville Became Music City: 50 Years of Music Row*. Milwaukee, WI: Hal Leonard, 2006. This profile of country music focuses on the people you've never heard of: the executives, songwriters, and behind-the-scenes technicians who really make the music happen. An interesting read for fans who don't mind seeing how the sausage is made; a good introduction for people aspiring to be a part of it.

Lomax, Alan. *Mister Jelly Roll: The Fortunes of Jelly Roll Morton, New Orleans Creole and "Inventor of Jazz."* Los Angeles: University of California Press, 2001. Originally published in 1950, this fascinating examination of a New Orleans jazz luminary also explores the development of the city's music scene.

Murphy, Michael. *Hear Dat New Orleans: A Guide to the Rich Musical Heritage & Lively Current Scene*. New York: Countryman Press, 2016. Take an indepth look at music venues in New Orleans in this guide also featuring photos from photographer Marc Pagani.

Palmer, Robert. *Deep Blues: A Musical and Cultural History of the Mississippi Delta*. New York: Penguin Books, 1982. An oldie but a goodie, this tome chronicles blues from its early beginnings through its heyday, touching on key figures such as Muddy Waters, B. B. King, and Robert Johnson.

Internet and Digital Resources

Music

Americana Music Triangle
http://americanamusictriangle.com
The roads between Nashville, Memphis, and New Orleans are paved with gold records. Explore this website full of photos and suggested itineraries.

Mississippi Blues Trail
http://msbluestrail.org
There are nearly 200 landmarks along this trail. Use this website to plot a trip or just immerse yourself in armchair travel.

The Roots of American Music Trail
http://musictrail.una.edu
Documents where to explore music of the 20th and 21st century, including hits from the 1960s, 1970s, and 1980s, in Northern Alabama.

Mississippi

Visit Jackson
http://visitjackson.com
Get a free travel guide to "the City with Soul."

Visit Natchez
http://visitnatchez.org
Immerse yourself in the history of this 300-year-old city on the Mississippi at this website.

Visit Oxford, Mississippi
http://visitoxfordms.com
Explore the cultural and literary gem

from the comfort of your phone at this mobile-friendly website.

Natchez Trace Parkway
Nashville's Trace
www.tnvacation.com/
tntrailsandbyways/trail/
nashvilles-trace-trail
This free, downloadable or printed 16-page brochure from the State of Tennessee Trails and Byways is a self-guided tour of the section of the Trace near Music City.

National Park Planner
http://npplan.com
An unofficial website comprised of one photographer's impressions of each stop along the Natchez Trace Parkway, as well as other national parks.

Scenic Trace
www.scenictrace.com
A comprehensive website by the Natchez Trace Compact suggests places to do and things to do along the way.

New Orleans
New Orleans Convention & Visitors Bureau
www.neworleanscvb.com
This comprehensive website offers a ton of resources for travelers to the Big Easy, including maps, current temperatures, and information about the city's music, dining, shopping, lodging, nightlife, tours, festivals, attractions, and outdoor recreation.

Tennessee
Tennessee Encyclopedia of History and Culture
www.tennesseeencyclopedia.net
The online edition of an excellent reference book, this website is a great starting point on all topics Tennessee. Articles about people, places, and events are written by hundreds of different experts.

Visit Music City
www.visitmusiccity.com
The official tourism website for Nashville, this site offers concert listings, hotel booking services, and useful visitor information. Listen to the Highway 65 Nashville-centric music stream as you browse. There's also a free app to help you on the road.

Index

WXYZ

LIST OF MAPS

PHOTO CREDITS

ACKNOWLEDGMENTS

Every book I've ever written requires a long list of "thank yous." This list feels like it should go on for 444 miles.

First and foremost are the rangers and employees of the National Park Service, particularly Jane Farmer, who care for this land and the people who use it. To the men and women who had the foresight to protect the tales these roads tell, I hope my encouraging others to visit and appreciate them are "thank you" enough.

Since my first guidebook (*The Dog Lover's Companion to Chicago*) was published by Avalon Travel, I've been aware that I work with the most supportive publishers around. This was even more evident on this book, which at times overwhelmed me with its 10,000 years of history, and miles (and miles) of must-sees. All of the crew was top-notch, including Darren Alessi, Kat Bennett, Elizabeth Hollis Hansen, Nikki Ioakimedes, Kevin McLain, and Deana Shields. My editor Leah Gordon went above and beyond in bringing this guide out of the woods, both literally and figuratively.

The hard-working Lisa Arnett kept track of my random unintelligible notes about an amazing doughnut shop or park we just *had* to add at the last minute, checking facts and seeking photo permissions.

Moon's New Orleans expert Laura Martone shared her years of expertise (and photos) of a complicated city with much to explore.

Georgia Carter Turner was the first person, many years ago, to encourage me to drive the Natchez Trace. It was a pleasure to have her assistance making this book look good with photos and secret tips. She's no longer with the Florence/Lauderdale Convention and Visitors Bureau, but her colleagues absolutely fill her big shoes.

Others who came through with great photos to illustrate this guide include: Amanda Hargrove of Visit Natchez; Stephen Martin of Visit Meridian; Sarah Mynatt and Heather Middleton of Nashville Convention & Visitors Bureau; Chrissy Garner of Tunica Convention & Visitors Bureau; Christy Chachere of Visit Baton Rouge; Jennie Bradford Curlee of Visit Tupelo; Dennis Sherer of Colbert County Tourism; and Peggy Collins of Alabama Tourism Department. Vickie Jackson of the GRAMMY Museum Mississippi showed me not only the institution, but the depth of music history in her town. Yolanda Clay-Moore of Visit Jackson not only provided photos, but fed me and showed me all her favorite spots in her adopted home town. Kinney Ferris introduced me to the amazing Jack Mayfield and we uncovered Oxford's many charms.

Having an excuse to reconnect with my old friend Cynthia Joyce in her new home of Oxford was one of the unexpected pleasures of this research.

Scott Foreman and the rest of the Cultivor Labs team allowed me to play tour guide while they worked; seeing the Trace through their eyes was a rewarding end to a year of solo road trips. I hope reading this book and seeing their photos inspires everyone to explore a piece of American magic.

ALSO AVAILABLE

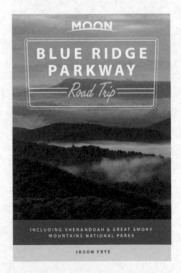

MAP SYMBOLS

≡≡≡	Expressway	○	City/Town	✈	Airport	⚑ Golf Course
	Primary Road	◉	State Capital	✈	Airfield	🅿 Parking Area
	Secondary Road	⊛	National Capital	▲	Mountain	≜ Archaeological Site
------	Unpaved Road	★	Point of Interest	✛	Unique Natural Feature	⌖ Church
———	Feature Trail	•	Accommodation			🛢 Gas Station
- - - -	Other Trail	▾	Restaurant/Bar	🌿	Waterfall	〰 Glacier
··········	Ferry	■	Other Location	▲	Park	Mangrove
	Pedestrian Walkway	Λ	Campground	🚩	Trailhead	Reef
▮▮▮▮	Stairs			⛷	Skiing Area	Swamp

CONVERSION TABLES

°C = (°F - 32) / 1.8
°F = (°C x 1.8) + 32
1 inch = 2.54 centimeters (cm)
1 foot = 0.304 meters (m)
1 yard = 0.914 meters
1 mile = 1.6093 kilometers (km)
1 km = 0.6214 miles
1 fathom = 1.8288 m
1 chain = 20.1168 m
1 furlong – 201.168 m
1 acre = 0.4047 hectares
1 sq km – 100 hectares
1 sq mile = 2.59 square km
1 ounce = 28.35 grams
1 pound = 0.4536 kilograms
1 short ton = 0.90718 metric ton
1 short ton = 2,000 pounds
1 long ton = 1.016 metric tons
1 long ton = 2,240 pounds
1 metric ton = 1,000 kilograms
1 quart = 0.94635 liters
1 US gallon = 3.7854 liters
1 Imperial gallon = 4.5459 liters
1 nautical mile = 1.852 km

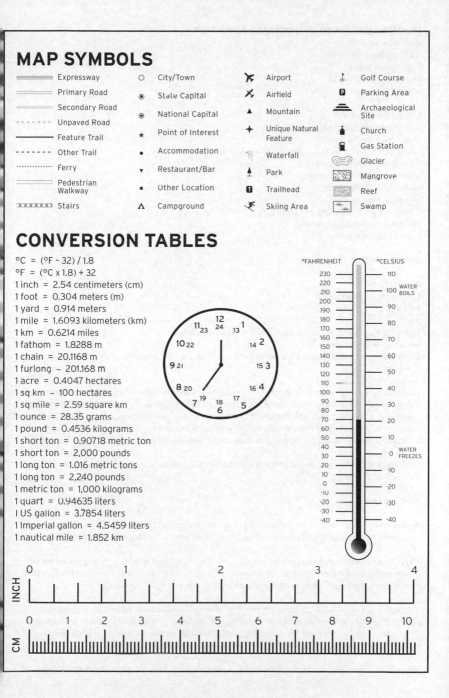

MOON NASHVILLE TO NEW ORLEANS ROAD TRIP
Avalon Travel
Hachette Book Group
1700 Fourth Street
Berkeley, CA 94710, USA
www.moon.com

Editor: Leah Gordon
Series Manager: Sabrina Young
Copy Editor: Deana Shields
Production and Graphics Coordinator: Darren Alessi
Cover Design: Erin Seaward-Hiatt
Interior Design: Darren Alessi
Moon Logo: Tim McGrath
Map Editor: Kat Bennett
Cartographers: Brian Shotwell, Larissa Gatt
Proofreader: Rosemarie Leenerts
Indexer: Rachel Kuhn

ISBN-13: 9781631215780

Printing History
1st Edition — January 2018
5 4 3 2 1